D0458149

CARL BLUMAY
WITH
HENRY EDWARDS

———

SIMON & SCHUSTER

NEW YORK   LONDON

TORONTO   SYDNEY

TOKYO   SINGAPORE

THE
DARK SIDE
OF POWER

—

THE REAL

ARMAND
HAMMER

SIMON & SCHUSTER
Simon & Schuster Building
Rockefeller Center
1230 Avenue of the Americas
New York, New York 10020

Designed by Barbara M. Bachman

Manufactured in the United States of America

10 9 8 7 6 5 4 3 2 1

Library of Congress Cataloging-in-Publication Data
Blumay, Carl.
    The dark side of power : the real Armand Hammer /
Carl Blumay with Henry Edwards.
        p. cm.
    Includes index.
    1. Hammer, Armand, 1897–   . 2. Businessmen—
United States—Biography. 3. Capitalists and financiers
—United States—Biography. 4. Statesmen—United
States—Biography. 5. United States—Relations—Soviet
Union. 6. Soviet Union—Relations—United States.
I. Edwards, Henry. II. Title.
HC102.5.H35B58 1992
338'.092—dc20
[B]   92-29845
                                                CIP

ISBN 0-671-70053-7

TO

MY BELOVED WIFE VIRGINIA, WHO MADE MANY PERSONAL SACRIFICES AND SUPPORTED AND HELPED ME IMMEASURABLY DURING THE PREPARATION OF THIS BOOK, THE MEMBERS OF OUR FAMILY, AND TO OUR FRIENDS, WHO ADDED THEIR ENCOURAGEMENT. I AM THANKFUL AND INDEBTED TO THEM ALL.

CARL BLUMAY

TO

CYNTHIA MERMAN AND ANSELL HAWKINS. I COULD NOT HAVE GONE FORWARD IF NOT FOR YOUR LOVE AND SUPPORT.

HENRY EDWARDS

CONTENTS

1. "RETIREMENT IS BORING"   13

2. "THE BOLDER I AM, THE MORE MONEY
   I MAKE"   24

3. A CLASSIC INFLUENCE OPERATION   34

4. "SCREW THEM BEFORE THEY SCREW YOU"   52

5. JFK CALLING   63

6. FIRST LENIN; THEN KHRUSHCHEV   72

7. AGENT OF INFLUENCE   83

8. "THERE CAN BE NO BUSINESS
   WITHOUT EXAGGERATION"   95

9. "MY SWEETENERS DID THE TRICK!"   109

10. THE MULTIMILLION-DOLLAR OVERRIDE   121

11. ON THE MERGER TRAIL   131

12. "THIS COMPANY IS NOT MANAGED,
    IT'S UNMANAGED"   145

13. SAVING LIBYA FOR EVERYONE   157

14. "I LIKE CONSENT DECREES"   176

15. "MAKE THIS MESS LOOK GOOD"   185

16. THE NIXON ONE HUNDRED THOUSAND
    DOLLARS CLUB   197

17. THE BIGGEST DEAL IN HISTORY   213

18. "DON'T PUT ANY OF THIS JUNK INTO
     THE BOOK"   223

19. THE NEW "DIRECTOR OF CORPORATE ART"   232

20. BREZHNEV DISAPPEARS FROM VIEW   249

21. THE PERIL OF DEATH   269

22. MIRACULOUS RECOVERY   282

23. UNOFFICIAL REPRESENTATIVE   301

24. MAN OF CONSCIENCE   316

25. IN PURSUIT OF THE NOBEL PRIZE   329

26. DR. HAMMER'S DOG AND PONY SHOW   351

27. PIMP OF THE POLITBURO   365

28. THE REAGAN REPUBLICAN   375

29. "THE DOCTOR ISN'T GIVING UP"   392

30. DESCENDED FROM THE MACCABEES   409

31. FAMILY LOYALTY   419

32. DEFIANCE OF DEATH   435

33. "HE'S LIVED TWO YEARS TOO LONG"   453

34. EMPTY STAGE   462

     INDEX   474

PREFACE

On December 10, 1990, southern California's 11 P.M. news programs all headlined the same story. Dr. Armand Hammer, chairman and chief executive of Occidental Petroleum Company, was dead at the age of ninety-two. In disbelief, I flipped from channel to channel to confirm the news, thinking to myself how often Armand had told me that he was immortal, that he would never die. I went to bed that night troubled by many other thoughts about Armand's words and deeds.

From 1955 to 1980 I had first been Armand's personal public relations director and then Occidental's director of public relations and advertising. Although ten years had passed since I had left the company, there were some reporters who were always going to view me as Armand's official spokesperson and my phone began to ring off the hook before I was barely awake the next morning. Did I know the real cause of Armand's death? What preparations had Occidental taken to fend off potential takeovers? Was Occidental planning to write off the multibillion-dollar debt that had accumulated during the last year's of Hammer's turbulent management? I referred these calls to Occidental's PR department and pretended that I knew nothing. But friends and former colleagues had been telling me for months that Occidental was on a death-watch. There was even speculation that home remedies had been used to hasten his demise.

I had spent twenty-five years selling Armand to the world as a man of true greatness and trying to position his problem-plagued company as a reliable and stable organization. I had always submerged or left unsaid anything that contradicted those illusions. But the man I had worked for was a master salesman in his own right, and by careful design, day in and day out, year in and year out, he sold the myth of his heroism and benevolence. If his were errors of commission, mine were errors of omission. In order to know what to leave out, I had to know what was really going on behind the scenes not only at Occidental but in Armand's personal life. Even after ten years it was not the kind of knowledge I could easily forget.

Armand read and studied every word written about him and his company to make sure it supported his image of himself, and when I read his four-page obituary in the *Los Angeles Times* on the morning after his death, I automatically scoured it to see if it contained anything that might have provoked the explosion of rage from Armand that inevitably followed any bit of unfavorable publicity. The headline read ARMAND HAMMER DIES; BILLIONAIRE, ART PATRON. It was the headline of his dreams. Armand had never come close to being that rich, but whenever he was introduced to someone of importance, within the first few minutes of their conversation, he never failed to proclaim that he was a billionaire. As for his patronage of the arts, that, too, had been the target of severe criticism. Still, his fortune and his art collections were among his chief claims to fame, and it was perhaps inevitable that he exaggerated their size and importance. For him, exaggeration was the truth.

Armand would have been pleased to find himself portrayed as a man of "keen intelligence," "bold strategies," and "flamboyance" who "retained access to the [Soviet Union's] leaders that was remarkable for a private U.S. citizen." That was all true. But he also possessed, in the words of his obituary, "questionable ethics" and "an unquenchable thirst for publicity and self-promotion," and was thought of by the energy industry as a "betrayer," "a man who could not be trusted," and the reason for the "end of cheap oil." Furthermore, Occidental was considered a company that was under constant scrutiny by the Securities and Exchange Commission and had "failed to win the approval of the Wall Street investment community." Armand himself was "the P. T. Barnum of the oil business." Also true, but he would have been appalled.

"I don't think I've ever failed," Armand was quoted as saying. But even as I read those words that morning, Occidental was initiating a secret contingency plan to erase from memory Hammer's thirty-two-year tenure as its leader. Yet he was the man who had single-handedly transformed a tiny corporate shell into the sixteenth-largest industrial company in America. He was the man who, even before investing in Occidental as a tax shelter, had earned fortunes as, among other things, a concoctor of patent medicines, a manufacturer of pencils, a dealer in art, a distiller of whiskey, and a breeder of cattle. He was the man who, by hook or by crook, had hovered near the centers of power in both the Soviet and American governments—from Lenin to Gorbachev, from Roosevelt to Bush. He courted kings and princes, and counted among his "dear friends" the rich, the powerful, and the celebrated all over the world. And he gave away millions and millions of dollars in great public displays. What was true during Armand's life remained equally true upon his death. He had never done anything ordinary. He had performed in a nonstop series of larger-than-life dramas consisting only of planned or unplanned, often improbable main events. Occidental's determination to deconstruct the image he had labored so hard to create was merely the last act in this fantastical chain.

How, I wondered, would Armand Hammer be remembered? By and large the public perceived him as a caring, compassionate, and wise man. But I knew he had been ruled by a dark side hidden from the public's view. I was among the very few who had seen this side of Armand's journey through life. This is an eyewitness account of the many turbulent events that occurred along the way. These are my memories of Armand Hammer.

1.

"RETIREMENT IS BORING"

I met Armand Hammer for the first time in 1955 after Los Angeles Municipal Art Department director Ken Ross told me that Armand, whom Ross called "Dr. Hammer," and his brother, Victor, were planning to exhibit their art collection at a municipal gallery. Hammer wanted to hire a local public relations man, and Ross had recommended me.

A week later the Hammer brothers turned up at my office. Armand, fifty-seven years old, was an owlish man, just five foot six, with a large square head, big expressive eyes, a prominent nose, and a pugnacious jaw. He wore a shabby, unpressed suit. Victor was four years younger, a little taller and considerably thinner. His face was dominated by the largest pair of ears I had ever seen, and he was dressed in a red-and-yellow sport jacket with a red carnation on his lapel, a dark blue shirt, checked blue slacks, and a bright red-and-blue bow tie. He looked like a dapper clown.

Armand didn't say hello, introduce himself, or attempt to shake my hand. He threw Victor a steely look, and Victor opened a big satchel-type briefcase. Armand reached in, withdrew some papers, and handed them to me. "Here are some notes about my collection. Study them," he said brusquely. The Armand Hammer Collection is a multimillion-dollar assortment of Dutch and Flemish Old Masters. After I exhibit in L.A. I want to tour the West Coast. In order to interest gallery owners and museum directors on this side of the country, I'm going to need lots of publicity here. That's where you come in."

He raised his eyebrows and stared at me.

I had already given some thought to a publicity stunt that would give the paintings a send-off. "How do you plan to transport your collection from New York?" I began.

"The normal way. I'll fly them into LAX and truck them to the gallery."

"I suggest stationing a corps of armed guards on the airstrip, rifles at the ready, to protect the paintings as they're taken off the plane. Then we'll load them into a fleet of armored vehicles. This extraordinary level of security is bound to generate a lot of TV and newspaper coverage about the priceless value of your collection and make gallery and museum directors eager to exhibit it."

I had no way of knowing and Armand chose not to tell me that three years before in San Antonio, Texas, Victor had tipped reporters that a police escort was going to meet him at the plane because he was arriving with a $250,000 diamond necklace. Armand had concocted the promotion and it had worked splendidly. Continuing to stare at me, he asked, "How will you maintain the credibility of the paintings in the face of all the manufactured hoopla?"

"Your natural authority as you discuss your collection will convince the reporters that the paintings are as valuable as we say they are."

"How can you be sure that I'll be interviewed?"

"I'll call in a few favors. Once I get one journalist to say yes, the others will fall into place."

"If you can get me interviewed, the job is yours."

He took a piece of paper from his pocket. It was folded into three columns. He found his place in the middle of the second column, jotted some notes on it, and put the paper back into his pocket.

"How long have you been collectors?" I asked.

"Victor and I began collecting art during the 1920s. In 1930 we decided to become dealers and formed a partnership with our half brother, Harry. Five years later we opened the Hammer Galleries on the most fashionable section of Fifth Avenue. We deal fine art to some of the richest and most important people in the world. We were the sole representatives of King Farouk of Egypt until his abdication."

"Do you enjoy being an art dealer?"

Armand was not modest. "I've been very successful," he said. "I branched into whiskey distilling in 1943. Two years ago I sold that business and its inventory to Schenley's for six and a half million dollars cash and my industrial and medical alcohol business to Publicker Alcohol and Chemical for a million. I'm a millionaire many times over. When you're as rich as I am, you might as well retire. That's what I did."

I asked if he was enjoying his retirement.

"I was glad to have made a lot of money in the hootch business and glad to get out of it. But retirement is boring. That's why I've taken on some art projects."

The meeting was over. Armand signaled to his brother. Victor bent down and picked up Armand's briefcase. Armand turned on his heel, and, with Victor trailing in his wake, they were on their way.

Over the next few days, Victor paid me a number of unannounced visits. It wasn't hard to figure out that they were spy missions designed to find out exactly what I did. Unlike his brother, Victor was a nonstop talker and responded to questions by telling me far more than I asked for. He also enjoyed playing the clown and traveled with a leather-bound looseleaf notebook that contained his collection of dirty jokes.

"Did you always want to be in the art business?" I asked.

"No. I wanted to be a comedian or an actor."

"Why didn't you become one?"

"Armand thought show business was too risky. He persuaded me to work with him, and that's how I've spent my life."

There was an unmistakable hint of sadness in Victor Hammer's eyes.

A few weeks later I was amazed to read in the newspapers that Armand's only child, his twenty-six-year-old son, Julian, had been arrested for shooting to death his former college roommate, Bruce Whitlock. The slaying had occurred in Julian's home in Los Angeles after a night-long birthday celebration where there had been heavy drinking. I thought about calling Hammer and volunteering to help him with the press, but he was so cold and self-contained, I refrained.

A month later I heard from him. Armand's plan to exhibit his art collection in Los Angeles seemed to have evaporated. Another art project now preoccupied him. "As soon as I heard that Utrillo had died," he told me, "I rushed off to Paris to have first pick of his estate and bought myself a plum. I'm storing it at the Pasadena Museum of Art. Be there Thursday at 10 A.M."

This time Victor wasn't with Armand; in his place was a woman named Frances Tolman. She was in her early fifties and had the slightly equine face of Eleanor Roosevelt. Frances wasn't pretty, but she was so gracious and well mannered one hardly noticed.

As we looked at the painting Armand said, "It's one of Utrillo's familiar Montmartre street scenes, but much larger than the typical Utrillo. Go to work on it immediately and publicize this unusual characteristic. If you make it sound like something special, I'll be able to exhibit it all over the country."

Again our meeting ended abruptly. Hammer's Rolls was parked a few blocks away from the museum, and I walked with him and Frances to the parking lot. When we passed a pay phone, he came to an abrupt halt.

"Do you have any change?" he asked.

I reached into my pocket and handed him a coin. A block later he encountered another pay phone and begged another coin. Just before we reached the parking lot, he spotted a third phone and asked for one more coin. As I got to know him better, I learned that although he was willing to spend vast sums to impress other people, he was miserly by nature and hated spending a cent of his own money on himself. There was a glint of pleasure in his eyes every time he got someone else to plunk down the change to pay for his calls, candy bars, and newspapers.

While he was on the phone, Frances remarked, "A telephone is to Armand what a fireplug is to a dog. He can't pass one without using it. The only difference is, he raises the receiver instead of his leg."

A few days later, when Victor delivered a fact sheet about the Utrillo, I mentioned that I had felt uneasy discussing Julian Hammer's unfortunate accident with his father. "It was a terrible experience, but it had a happy ending," Victor said. "The judge at the arraignment didn't believe Julian. Armand called Jimmy Roosevelt, who recommended a lawyer named Arthur Groman. Senator Styles Bridges also gave him some good advice. Luckily for us, the autopsy showed a large amount of alcohol in Whitlock's blood, and Julian's wife, Sue, was the only witness. She corroborated Julian's claim that he acted in self-defense, and Groman was able to get the case dismissed."

I was curious that Armand's friends included Jimmy Roosevelt, a liberal Democratic congressman from California, and Styles Bridges, the conservative, anti-Communist Republican senator from New Hampshire. But Victor explained that party affiliations and political philosophy didn't mean anything to Armand. "He just wants to make sure there's someone powerful around when he needs a favor."

According to Victor, Armand had met Jimmy Roosevelt, the eldest of FDR's four sons, through another Roosevelt son, Elliott, a client of the Hammer Galleries, and had been a heavy contributor to Jimmy Roosevelt's congressional campaign the previous year. Then he told me that Armand and Styles Bridges had known each other for twelve years.

"Armand went into the distillery business because someone told him that straight whiskey could be stretched five times by combining it with 80 percent of cheap neutral spirits, and his second wife, Angela Zevely, knew how to extract alcohol from potatoes. He decided to buy a distillery, buy a lot of rotting potatoes, and use Angela's method to make a killing. The building he was after was in New Hampshire and was owned by the federal government. So Armand went to Washington to enlist Senator Bridges's support. Bridges has been helping him—and he's been finding ways to make money for Bridges—ever since.

"Armand's line of Gold Coin blended whiskey was immensely profitable," Victor continued. "The spirits industry hated him for it because they didn't know the first thing about how to manufacture alcohol from potatoes, but he was an outsider who was raking it in. My brother's a maverick genius. He always upsets the status quo, and he always makes a mint doing it."

Again I was astonished at Victor's willingness to talk so openly about his brother. A few months later Armand returned to Los Angeles, and I landed him a radio interview on a local news program. Both Frances and Victor came with him to the station, and while Armand was on the air, Frances casually remarked that her wedding had been so hectic she was feeling a little tired. It was the first I had heard about the marriage.

"How did you two meet?" I asked.

"I met Armand for the first time twenty years ago. His half brother, Harry, and my husband, Elmer, had some business dealings, and the three of us used to vacation together. Harry introduced me to Armand and I think it was love at first sight, but I was a married woman and I didn't consider becoming involved with him. Elmer was thirty years older than I was and in poor health, and I was devoted to him. Armand and I wrote to each other, but life marched on and we fell out of touch.

"Then two years ago I was in the beauty parlor and I picked up one of those tabloids and came across an article about Armand. He was in the midst of the most lurid divorce imaginable! I sent him a telegram offering my help and comfort if he needed me." Looking slightly embarrassed, she added, "I also told him that I had become a widow. Armand took the next plane to Los Angeles and turned up on my doorstep. It was a whirlwind courtship. Armand creates excitement wherever he goes."

I asked Victor later that day why Armand had kept his marriage a secret.

"Armand believes that being single hurts business because it suggests instability and insecurity. That's why he married Angela three weeks after he divorced his first wife, Olga. His divorce from Angela became official on January nineteenth; he married Frances six days later in a quick ceremony Arthur Groman arranged for him. Because Armand views marriage as a business tool and he's always secretive about anything that deals with business, he rarely says a word about his marriages."

"Frances told me she had read about Armand's divorce in the scandal sheets."

"When a wealthy socialite like Angela sues the owner of a prestigious New York art gallery for what she believes is half his worth —ten million dollars—it's bound to make news. Angela was interested in breeding Aberdeen Angus cattle, and Armand persuaded her to start a cattle-breeding operation and make him a fifty percent partner. Eventually, he turned her eleven-acre farm in Red Bank, New Jersey, into a four-hundred-fifty-acre, multimillion-dollar cattle-breeding operation."

"What's wrong with that?"

"He used company money to buy himself a plane and a yacht and to purchase paintings for the Hammer Galleries," Victor replied with his usual candor. "Then customers began accusing him of selling them calves with fraudulent pedigrees and injecting them with water to make them look fatter and healthier. One man even accused him of selling him a bull whose belly had been painted to make it look like a prizewinner. When the American Aberdeen Angus Breeders' Association threatened to throw him out, Armand realized that his customers would have the grounds to sue him for millions of dollars. His only option was to pay them off in order to shut them up and keep them out of court.

"Then Angela walked out. Angela is beautiful, smart, a terrific businesswoman, and a drunk. Armand and she were married in my apartment, and Angela filled her perfume bottles with booze so that she could tank up during the ceremony. Once she got so drunk she chased my family around with a broom.

"Angela accused Armand of infidelity with Frances. He claimed that he awoke one night and found her standing over him threatening to burn his eyes out with a lit cigarette. She said that he threatened to beat her brains out with a metal pipe. Armand accused her of calling him 'a dirty Jew.' She said he was cold, calculating, hard, cruel, unfeeling, and manipulated or bought off everybody he ever dealt with. Everyone who saw them together was convinced they were going to kill each other.

"Armand always hires the best lawyers and he hired Louis Nizer to defend him, but he's his own expert in legal technicalities, which he believes are safety zones from the law. He knows how to find the loophole in every contract and every statute. No one who takes him to court ever wins. He sold off the farm assets for a million dollars, had the divorce case tried in New Jersey instead of New York because the New Jersey laws would favor him, and set out to prove that Angela was a crazy drunk. She asked for ten million dollars and wound up with twelve thousand a year. It's not that much, but Armand hates paying it, especially because he's still paying forty-five hundred yearly to his first wife, Olga.

"Armand's also been fighting the IRS for ten years. They claim that two of his distilling company's tax returns are fraudulent and that he owes five hundred thousand dollars," the voluble Victor continued. "Armand was so afraid that the IRS and Angela were going to get their claws into his money, he buried all of it in Swiss bank accounts. These days Armand's a rich man without a liquid nickel. But he's always had terrific luck. He told me the only solution was to marry a rich widow. Frances turned up exactly when he needed her."

Victor explained that Frances Hammer's father had been a successful Chicago businessman and her late husband had been the son of a prominent Chicago banker. "Elmer Tolman was also an alcoholic," Victor said. "That's why Frances managed his money and she did brilliantly. After Elmer died, she inherited property in L.A. and Chicago and millions more in cash and other assets, all on top of a vast amount of her own family money. She's a lot richer than Armand. So he flew to L.A., rented a house near hers, and began to hold her hand. That's how she wound up being named corespondent in his divorce.

"When Julian was arrested, Armand didn't have a cent he could get his hands on. He was in no mood to call his Swiss bankers, so he got Frances to put up the fifty thousand dollars' bail. Wait and see. He's already figuring out ways to use her money to put himself back into business."

Victor's prediction was right on the mark. Six months later, during the summer of 1956, Hammer called again. I expected him to tell me about a new painting, but he talked about a tax shelter plan that had caught his fancy. "I persuaded Frances to lend fifty thousand dollars to a local oil company, Occidental Petroleum Corporation," he told me. "The money is going to be used to drill two oil wells, and Frances and I are going to retain a fifty percent working interest."

At that time in California, oil-drilling investments were popular tax avoidance schemes because all of the costs of drilling and developing an oil well could be deducted during the first year of the investment instead of being capitalized and depreciated over the productive life of the well. This deduction was often far greater than the size of the actual investment.

"What happens if you strike oil?" I asked.

"Occidental isn't much more than a shell that's been struggling to survive for thirty-seven years," Armand replied. "Its six hundred thousand outstanding shares are worth a hundred and eight thousand dollars, its true worth is thirty-four thousand dollars, and its stock sells for eighteen cents a share. Last year it declared an interest earning of $232.01. Does that sound like the kind of company that's going to find oil?"

Joking, I said, "If by any chance the wells come in anyway, I'll be glad to turn on the publicity machine for you."

The possibility of publicity seemed to be exactly what Armand wanted to hear and probably the reason why he'd called in the first place. "I'll keep you posted," he said.

The next time he called it was to report that, contrary to all expectations, the drilling had been successful. "One well came in as a producer, the other as a discovery well," he told me. A producer is a well drilled on an already-established field. A discovery well usually establishes a brand-new oil field.

Three months later Armand delivered another news bulletin. "Occidental had the opportunity to purchase nine producing oil wells and several undrilled locations in Dominguez, a suburb of L.A. It was short of money and offered Frances a fifty percent participation. We each lent $112,500, against a purchase price of $1.75 million. I oversaw the purchase from the owner, J. F. G. Wadley. We did the deal so quickly that my lawyer, Arthur Groman, wrote out the contract in longhand on hotel stationery. Wadley's a rugged wildcatter in a Stetson hat and cowboy boots. He's spent his entire life drilling in untried, unproven locations. He plays his hunches until he gets the bonanza other people are afraid to go for. Wadley reminds me of me."

Over the next nine months Armand called periodically with up-
dates about the tiny oil company. Frances had sold off half of her
interest in the Dominguez oil field and taken an option to convert
the remainder of her investment into Occidental stock and Armand had decided to exercise the option. "We could have bought
the stock originally at eighteen cents a share, but then it was overpriced," he told me. "Now Occidental's two successful wells and its
part ownership of the nine others drove the price up to a dollar
fifty. At eighteen cents a share it was overpriced; at one-fifty it was
a good deal."

Armand Hammer was off and running in the oil business, and
in July 1957 he became president of Occidental. "The board of
directors asked me to replace Dave Harris, who's been here just
seventeen months," he reported. "Unfortunately, he's still on the
board and still hanging around. Once I get rid of him and his
cronies, I'm going to hire you."

At the same time that Armand was taking over Occidental,
Frieda Hennock, a friend who was a member of the Federal Trade
Commission, gave him a tip that a syndicate headed by radio station manager Paul Roberts, was attempting to buy the Mutual
Broadcasting System. The coast-to-coast radio network served
hundreds of stations, and its flagship station was WOR in New
York. After using Frances' money to put him into the oil business,
Armand moved quickly to persuade Occidental's board of directors to expand and diversify the impoverished oil company's interests by investing $100,000 in the syndicate, and he and Frances
each acquired a minority interest for $53,000. On July 25 the syn-
dicate purchased the broadcasting company for $650,000. Thus,
Armand Hammer became the new chairman of the Mutual Broadcasting System and Paul Roberts, its new president. "Mutual's in a
lot of financial trouble, but it's still a dirt-cheap price for a national
radio network with five-hundred affiliates," he explained to me.
"It's cost Frances and me only $106,000 to make me the new Bill
Paley."

Even though Armand was simultaneously running a broadcasting company in New York and an oil company in Los Angeles, he
had not forgotten his art collection as a generator of the publicity
he seemed to crave so much. In December he told me that he had
finally made the time to exhibit his collection at Barnsdall Park
Municipal Gallery and that he was ready to fly it to Los Angeles
and exhibit it at the beginning of the New Year. According to the
plan I had outlined on the day we had met for the first time three

years before, a slew of reporters and TV news crews were on hand to witness the impressive-looking line of armed guards that I had stationed on the airstrip to protect the "priceless" collection and the armored cars waiting off at the side. I hovered in the background, prepared to jump in if Armand encountered any difficulty while he was being interviewed. It wasn't necessary. In public Armand affected a disarming grandfatherly persona that was irresistible. He was a master salesman, and his feigned ingenuousness that day had the press eating out of his hands.

That night he made all the local TV news programs, and by the end of the week, articles about him had appeared in all of the local publications. When I took them to him, he was fascinated and pleased by this small flurry of attention and seemed to be committing every word to memory as he slowly read the articles. From that moment on he would demand that press clippings be delivered to him on a daily basis.

"This publicity should help you sell the paintings for quite a tidy profit," I remarked.

"I'm not going to sell them," he said. "If I donate them to a museum or a school, the tax law enables me to base my deduction on the appreciated value, not the purchase price. The more I inflate their value, the more I'll be able to write off. When the time comes, these clippings will help me back up my claim."

In February 1958, seven months after Armand took over the Mutual Broadcasting System, he called a secret meeting of the board of directors that excluded Paul Roberts. Armand accused Roberts of taking kickbacks from advertisers and presented as purported evidence documents that had been retrieved from Roberts's desk after he had ordered a search. At Armand's insistence, the board voted to remove Roberts, and when Roberts and his investors threatened to sue, Armand offered to buy their stock options. As a result, Roberts was gone, Armand had complete control, and Mutual's publicity department began issuing one triumphant news release after another, repeatedly reinforcing the theme that under Hammer's management Mutual's profits were beginning to soar. One day when Victor dropped in to say hello, he confided that, despite the hype, the radio network remained in financial trouble. Five months later Armand unexpectedly sold the radio network to Hal Roach Studios for $2 million, achieving more than a 100 percent profit on their one-year investment for Frances and himself.

Deciding to devote all of his energies to Occidental Petroleum, he told me that he had been impressed by the amount of publicity I had generated for him and his art collection at the beginning of the year and asked me to come to Occidental's corporate headquarters "to discuss my future." "Corporate headquarters" turned out to be four cramped rooms filled with cheap rented furniture on the second floor of 8255 Beverly Boulevard, a shabby two-story building in a rundown section of West Los Angeles that Occidental was renting on a monthly basis. The minute Armand saw me he pushed some Polaroid photographs of pumping oil wells across the desk top for me to look at.

"The day after I closed the deal to buy the oil wells at Dominguez, I drove to the field," he told me. "When I looked at the pumping jacks rocking up and down, it seemed to me that they were getting ready to pump money. Carl, how would you like to get into the oil business?"

We talked for an hour. I explained that I had a standing rule with each of my PR clients that I did business only with the man in charge and had access to him at all times. He agreed to the rule and to all of my other conditions, and I agreed to add Occidental to my client list.

A few minutes later the man whom Hammer had replaced at Occidental, Dave Harris, came into the room and Armand told him that I'd just become Occidental's PR man.

"How many years have you been in the oil business?" Harris asked me.

"None."

"You've got to know the business inside and out before you even can think about handling Occidental's PR."

Armand jumped to his feet and glared at Harris. "Before I got into the oil business I'd never seen a derrick and I wouldn't have known a barrel of oil if I had fallen into one. Carl and I are going to roll up our sleeves and take this small, insignificant, unsuccessful company and put it on the map. Nothing or nobody is going to stop us!"

Soon after I signed on with Armand, it was alleged that Alexander Guaterma, owner of Hal Roach Studios, to whom Armand had sold the Mutual Broadcasting System, had bought the network on behalf of Dominican Republic dictator Rafael Trujillo so that Trujillo could use it as a propaganda outlet. Subsequently, Guaterma went to jail for stock fraud and the Mutual Broadcasting System was placed in bankruptcy. "Guaterma was a nice man. I never would have believed he was a crook," Armand told me with what appeared to be genuine surprise. "Anyway, he's the one that got in trouble, and I'm the one who made a tidy profit. That's always the only thing that counts."

2.

"THE BOLDER I AM, THE MORE MONEY I MAKE"

To the sounds of his favorite music, orchestral arrangements of chestnuts like "Home on the Range" and the latest hits of Nat King Cole, Armand began each day with a half-hour swim in his indoor pool. After breakfast, if he didn't have to go to the office, he worked at home in his bathrobe until lunchtime. Then he napped. In midafternoon, just as everyone else was running down, he arrived at Occidental raring to go and demanding the same response from everyone else.

This schedule required me to make frequent morning visits to the Hammers' surprisingly dowdy two-story house at 10431 Wyton Drive in the Holmby Hills section of West Los Angeles, which Frances and Elmer Tolman had purchased from actress Gene Tierney and her husband, fashion designer Oleg Cassini, in 1946. Armand worked either in a small library situated between the entry hall and the swimming pool or in his bedroom on the second floor. The bedroom was off limits, so I always met him in the library. A mediocre collection of books was stacked in the floor-to-ceiling bookshelves. Once as I was thumbing through them, Armand remarked, "A businessman cannot spend his life educating himself. If he does, he'll always be poor."

Occidental's tiny offices were so crowded I had to work at a beat-up desk in the common hallway. From my vantage points in the Hammers' library and behind that desk, I watched Armand work at a relentless pace from dawn until late at night every day of the workweek and often over the weekend. The intensity of his concentration amazed me.

Occidental was so poor it had no funds for capital development and so small it lacked an oil and gas division. Therefore, there were no oil drillers on its staff and no drilling equipment in its inventory. Armand's immediate goal was to drill wells on three oil fields controlled by Occidental, which meant that he had to face the daunting challenge of persuading bankers to grant loans and individuals to make small investments in a company that could barely function.

He lived on the phone and thought nothing of tracking people down all over the world and calling them repeatedly to get them to invest. Before he tackled a banker or a potential investor, he made a quick study of the man's interests so that he would appear to have knowledgeable opinions about a wide range of topics and could make engaging small talk. By alternately soft-soaping, flattering, and bullying everyone with whom he spoke and by hounding people until they became exhausted by his unrelenting pursuit, he persuaded them to say yes, if only to get him off the phone. Genuinely impressed, even worshipful of those who were rich, famous, or important, whenever he met such people, he showered them with gifts and praise until they fell under his spell and eventually handed over money. Armand also loved beautiful women and went out of his way to flirt with them and make them feel desirable. That ability enabled him to secure even more money for Occidental.

Armand demanded total devotion to his cause and he called me repeatedly at home at dawn while I was still asleep, late at night after I had gone to bed, and throughout the weekend in order to go over each and every detail. If my wife, Virginia, or one of our three children answered, he didn't engage in any small talk. The children, Nancy, Steve, and John, sometimes tried to penetrate his iciness by enticing him into conversation, but they never received a response. In my twenty-five years with him, Armand never asked about my children or asked to meet them.

A peculiar combination of the impassive and the irascible, he ignored insults, coldness, and rudeness and always maintained a neutral expression during his encounters with people outside the company. If I saw him rubbing the thumb of his left hand back and forth against the side of his index finger during these meet-ings, I knew that he was seething despite the fact that he seemed in total control.

Within the confines of Occidental, however, Armand never sup-pressed his fierce temper, and he utilized threats, insinuations, and tantrums to get whatever he wanted the minute he wanted it. In order to ward off his rage everyone worked at a frenzied pace. The more they produced, the more he demanded. When I suggested that everyone was working so hard they deserved to be paid a compliment, he replied, "I'm the one who's getting them to work so hard. *I'm* the one who deserves the compliment."

Armand could shout longer and louder than anyone I had ever known. I made a promise to myself that he would never shout at me. The first time he tried it, I yelled back. His response was stunned silence. Later he approached me and said, "Dammit, Carl, I'm beginning to like you. You're one of the few people I've met who doesn't scare easily." Embarrassed by this rare admission of feeling, he then beat a hasty retreat.

My job was to find a way to use the news media to send word to banks, stockbrokerages, financial analysts, venture capitalists, and the investing public in general that Occidental was a going concern. I couldn't publicize the company because it was so obscure. No one knew who Hammer was either. Invariably, after I mentioned his name, reporters asked, "Does he have something to do with the Arm & Hammer baking soda company?"

One reporter insisted that Armand had once been a Mafia king-pin and gave me the phone number of an old-time crime reporter with a reputation for having a razor-sharp memory about the his-tory of the Mob. It was this man's recollection that Hammer had gone into the beer barrel business when Prohibition came to an end in 1933. "The breweries were Mob controlled, and the feds were convinced Hammer was in bed with the Mob," the reporter told me. "He was such a slick operator and he was so good at making payoffs, the feds were never able to trace his connections."

No matter what Armand had been up to in 1934, there was nothing newsworthy about him in the late 1950s. This was the age of advertising spokespeople like Ronald Reagan, whose ability to project sincerity and likability had become an intrinsic part of Gen-eral Electric's corporate image. It seemed to me that if I could make Armand a public figure and position him as Occidental's spokesman, I would be able to call attention to the company he represented. I knew that he was an art dealer and collector and had also been in the liquor-distilling and cattle businesses, but I needed a stronger angle. What I had to do was get him to find the time to sit down and talk freely about his life in order to supply me with colorful details and anecdotes that I could use to tantalize the press. But he was too busy.

I proposed this plan a number of times and was always ignored. Finally, I struck the right chord: "I want to make you famous, Armand. If you're famous, I can make Occidental famous. It's that simple."

The word "famous" ringing in his ears, Armand agreed to go to lunch and discuss his life. He began by telling me that his parents were named Julius and Rose and that everyone called his mother Mama Rose. Julius had died of a stroke in 1948 at the age of seventy-four; Rose was still alive and lived in Scarsdale, New York. He added that Julius had been born in Russia and brought to the United States by his parents, Victoria and Jacob, in 1874, when he was just a year old. The family had settled near New Haven, Connecticut. "Times were tough," Armand said. "Pop was a burly kid. He went to work as a laborer, and he worked like a dog. I got the ability to work without stopping from him."

When Julius was nineteen, he convinced his parents that moving to the Lower East Side of Manhattan would give the family an opportunity to earn a better living and a chance for him to obtain a better education. Four years later he met Rose Lipshitz at a picnic. She was Russian born also, two years older, widowed, and the mother of a three-year-old son, Harry. Julius and Rose were married a year later. Armand was born a year after that, in 1898, and Victor was born in 1902. Armand characterized his younger brother as "the baby in the family. I was put in charge of him. I still am."

After Julius arrived in New York City, he got a job in a drugstore and became a registered pharmacist. He saved enough money to buy out the owner, launched a wholesale pharmaceuticals business, and opened a small chain of drugstores. Subsequently, Julius decided to become a doctor and enrolled in the Columbia College of Physicians and Surgeons. "My dream was to go into practice with him," Armand said. "That's why I went to Columbia, too, and earned a medical degree. I graduated in June 1921."

"Did you ever practice medicine?" I asked.

"I renew my medical license regularly, but I don't even know how to lance a boil. There was going to be a six-month wait before there was an opening and I could begin my internship at Bellevue

Hospital. It was just four years after the Russian Revolution. When I read a newspaper story about the thousands of people in the Urals who were dying as a result of famine, I had trouble sleeping nights and I decided to help. I bought a portable army surplus hospital at a cost of a hundred thousand dollars, an ambulance for another fifteen thousand dollars, gathered up sixty thousand dollars' worth of instruments, medicines, and medical supplies from my father's business, and set out to work as a doctor in the famine area."

It was amazing to venture into Bolshevik Russia during those turbulent days, and equally amazing that an unemployed college graduate was capable of investing that much money in the trip. Armand explained that his father's business had been facing insolvency and that after he had taken charge, he had discovered that he was the real businessman in his family. "I made enough money to rent a small carriage house in Greenwich Village and move away from home. By the time I was twenty-one, I had earned a million dollars on the side."

Before I could digest that startling piece of information, he plunged into a description of his trip to Russia. "I was alone in a depressing, run-down country, and I couldn't speak Russian and couldn't get enough to eat. I was going to leave, but I remembered that before Pop went to work in the drugstore, he was told he had to be able to speak Italian and he learned it in two weeks. I spent my time teaching myself a hundred Russian words a day from a Russian-English dictionary."

Two weeks after his arrival, Armand said, he encountered a group of Soviet engineers and observers by chance and was invited to join them on a trip to the Ural Mountains to conduct an industrial survey. "Our train stopped for twenty-four hours in the famine area. Starving children banged against the windows and begged for a piece of bread. There were piles of bodies everywhere waiting to be buried in mass graves. I heard stories of mothers who slaughtered their weakest child to keep the others alive. I'll never forget what I saw. It haunts me to this day.

"I went to the Soviet officials and asked how much grain they would need to feed all of these people until the next harvest. The reply came back: one million bushels. I told them I had a million dollars and that there was a grain glut in the U.S. and wheat was selling for only a dollar a bushel. Then I proposed a barter deal: I would have my company lease some ships and load them with grain if they, in turn, would fill those ships with Russian products, things like furs, hides, semiprecious gems, lumber, and caviar, that I could sell in America. The next thing that happened was the most momentous event of my life. Lenin sent for me, and I was taken to his office in the Kremlin.

"Lenin smiled sweetly at me," Armand continued. "As he thanked me for my efforts to save Russia's starving and dying children, his eyes filled with tears. But there were other things on his mind. He asked if I would like to become the first foreign businessman to obtain a Soviet concession. It was his suggestion that I could take over an abandoned czarist asbestos mine and turn it into a profitable business operation. To this day I find it astonishing that I met Lenin and became close to him. There are those who have said that he was cruel and ruthless, but I knew him personally, and I have never met a gentler, more compassionate man."

According to Armand, his grain deal saved many lives. "Overnight I became a hero in Russia. The following year I was rewarded for my efforts when I received permission to serve as the Soviet agent for U.S. machinery and farm equipment. The first thing I did was go to Detroit and bag the Ford Motor Company."

Henry Ford, although a great American folk hero, was a well-known anticommunist and anti-Semite with a firm belief in "the Jewish conspiracy." "How did you persuade Henry Ford to go along?" I asked.

"I told him that the Bolsheviks had control of the country and were destined to stay in power and that if he wanted to make money in Russia he would have to deal with them. I also appealed to his vanity by telling him that the Russian people thought he and Thomas A. Edison were the most wonderful men in America. That's what really did it."

Taking their lead from Ford, thirty-eight other American companies, including Ingersoll-Rand, Parker Pen, Underwood Typewriter, and U.S. Rubber chose Armand to represent them in the Soviet Union, and he received permission to conduct business independently of Russia's trade monopoly. Subsequently, the Soviets put up $250,000 so that he could purchase a majority interest in the Harju Bank in Reval (now Tallinn), Estonia. And in 1925 he was given a concession to manufacture pencils and established the A. Hammer Pencil Company.

"The Bolsheviks were determined to wipe out illiteracy among the peasants," Armand said. "They instituted thousands of adult education classes, and they needed lots of pencils. A pencil that cost a nickel here cost fifty cents there, and all of the pencils were imported. They banned imports, gave me the pencil monopoly, and I wound up making millions."

In 1930, Armand left the USSR after making a profitable deal to sell his businesses to the Soviet government. "Lenin died in 1924," he said, "and things weren't the same. Lenin hated capitalism, but he knew that he would have to deal with capitalists. Stalin hated capitalism *and* capitalists and I couldn't do business with him. By then I was a millionaire many times over, so I came home."

Armand expressed his need to maintain the upper hand in dozens of symbolic little ways. When our lunch was over, he stood up and threw me the look he used to signal Victor to pick up his briefcase. When I refused to budge, he picked it up himself and sped from the restaurant, moving so quickly I could hardly keep up with him.

It had been five years since the Senate had voted to condemn Senator Joseph McCarthy, which marked the beginning of the end of the McCarthy era, but words like "Bolshevik," "Communist," and "Soviet" still resounded negatively in the American psyche. By having had a personal relationship with Lenin, living in Bolshevik Russia for nine years, and utilizing his energies to build the Soviet economy, Armand had to have known how easy it would be to label him "un-American," and I understood why he was so reticent about discussing his past. Yet it was not his nature to reveal his "Russian connection" unless he expected me to find a way to make it palatable to the press and the public.

The story of a young self-made millionaire who puts aside political considerations to feed the starving people of Russia and becomes the young American capitalist to whom Lenin turns in an effort to rescue the Bolshevik economy was a PR man's dream. My job was to create a foolproof context for the aspects of this biographical material that conservatives might find offensive. Therefore, Armand had to be established as a patriotic capitalist. To counter the speculation and rumor that was always to accompany Hammer's insistence on secrecy, it was also essential that his public persona appear to be the epitome of openness.

Armand always insisted on being addressed as "Dr. Hammer." In the mid-fifties, Americans loved and trusted their doctors, and doctors often endorsed health and food products. But as far as I know Armand was the first M.D. to run an oil company, and this undeniable novelty seemed to me to be the angle that would enable me to position Armand as a man with the admirable and trustworthy qualities of a beloved family doctor.

Back at the office I picked up a pencil, started toying around with slogans for an "oil company M.D.," and came up with two: "Dr. Hammer: a physician who practices business" and "Dr. Hammer: a physican who gives the right injections to sick businesses and restores them to robust health." After I established the loving, trusting, capitalistic Dr. Hammer image, I believed I would be able to promote his "Russian connection" without unpleasant side effects.

Armand spoke in platitudes and clichés and his conversation sounded like B-movie dialogue, but he really believed what he said. If business was his god, these homilies were the commandments of his faith. I thought the platitudes that peppered his speech could be included in my news releases as examples of the good Dr. Hammer's business "prescriptions" and I jotted down a few:

"I never let wishes take the place of work."

"When an idea bursts in my mind, I give it all I've got, which is plenty."

"I dare to be bold. The bolder I am, the more money I make."

The first Occidental news release I wrote concluded with the words "it was announced by Dr. Armand Hammer, president." Drops of water wear down stones, and when "Dr. Armand Hammer" and "Occidental Petroleum" began to pop up in print, I knew I had made a beginning. To pave the way for larger stories, once or twice a week I visited the newspaper and wire service editorial rooms, going from desk to desk to talk up "the doctor" and Occidental. I was making friends and making progress, but "Dr. Hammer" had a long way to go before he became a household name.

Armand never resisted an opportunity to brag, and one day in his office he couldn't wait to tell me that he had won his thirteen-year battle against the IRS's attempt to collect $500,000 in back taxes based on claims that his distilling companies had filed fraudulent tax returns. "My dear friend Eleanor Roosevelt agreed to be called as a character witness on my behalf," he said. "Her brilliant testimony was packed with praiseworthy things about me. It did the trick, and I won the day."

"How did you meet Mrs. Roosevelt?" I asked.

"I always try to become friendly with influential and powerful people. I do whatever it takes to please them. That's the way I won over Herbert Hoover, Harry Truman, and Dwight Eisenhower. But FDR was my personal hero."

As Armand spoke, I realized that he attempted to model the

speaking style he used in public after the intimate but formal style of Roosevelt's fireside chats. However, Roosevelt had avoided clichés, which Armand relied on.

"FDR and I met for the first time in 1933, when he invited me to stand by his side as he announced that the U.S. was resuming diplomatic relations with the Soviet Union. In 1940 I became his personal adviser. Subsequently, I gave him the idea for Lend-Lease. FDR and I had a lot in common. He was a born leader, so am I. He would have made an excellent corporate president or chairman of the board. I'd make a great president!

"I became really close to Eleanor after I bought Campobello in 1952," Armand continued. He was referring to the Roosevelt family's summer home, a thirty-four-room Dutch colonial house situated on twenty acres on Campobello Island in Canadian waters off the Maine coast. "Eleanor appreciated the fact that I spent hundreds of thousands of dollars to refurbish it so that it would look the same as when the Roosevelts used it regularly."

Besides bragging about his friendship with the Roosevelts, when Armand was sure everyone was in hearing range, he liked to boom commands like "Get me Congressman Roosevelt on the phone" or "I want to talk to Senator Bridges." Phone calls like these went on all day long.

"You certainly do have lots of friends in high places," I kidded him after a call to Roosevelt.

"Not in high places. In my hip pocket."

One day Armand approached me with a plan to use my PR company to launder a monthly bribe to a member of the California state legislature. "I study the voting records of everybody in the local and state governments so that I can cultivate politicians who can help us," he told me. "This guy is willing to tip us about the activities of the state legislature and the Public Utilities Commission."

He outlined his plan, which would put him at a safe distance from the bribe. First he would increase my monthly retainer by $1,500; then my bookkeeper would issue a $1,500 monthly check for "business expenses" to a corporation whose name Hammer would give me. That corporation would pay the legislator the money as a fee.

"It sounds illegal," I said nervously.

"I would never ask you to do anything illegal. Many others have done this. They've never gotten into trouble."

I refused to budge, and Armand turned on the charm. When that didn't work, he began to bring up the matter three or four times a day until, weary of it, I let it happen. Every month when check-writing time rolled around, I was uncomfortable and prayed that the representative would be voted out of office at the next election.

Around the same time I was asked by a *Wall Street Journal* editor to supply some background material about an Occidental project. I wrote a detailed statement, which I automatically sent to Armand for his approval. "I don't like it. It's too factual. I don't want the public to know exactly what we're up to," he complained. "Make up some good lies and send them in."

I explained that Occidental was in no position to jeopardize its credibility, and neither was I.

His rage boiled over, and he shouted at the top of his voice, "Those who always insist on telling the truth never have any future! Sometimes the only way to build the future is to build it on lies!"

I finally persuaded him to let me have my way. But I was reminded of a lesson I had learned as a child. My father was a minister, and one conviction he had instilled in me was the belief that once someone tells you one lie, you can never trust anything else he says. I've always believed my father was right. From the moment Armand told me he was a firm believer in lying, I found myself forced to question the credibility of everything he told me.

3.

A CLASSIC INFLUENCE OPERATION

In August 1959, when I persuaded Associated Press reporter Jack Leffler to interview "the doctor," it was the biggest publicity opportunity thus far. Armand really believed it when he told Leffler, "The oil business is romantic. It gets into your blood. I like it better than anything else I have ever been in." The only time I winced was when he bragged that Occidental's value had grown from $120,000 to $12 million during his two-year presidency. In actuality, the company was headed toward a $684,000 loss at the end of the fiscal year.

Leffler's long, glowing article appeared under the headline of my dreams: DOCTOR OF MEDICINE PRACTICES BUSINESS and it enabled me to get a number of other reporters to interview "the business M.D." During a popular radio call-in program, the host asked Armand to explain why he had chosen to become a businessman upon completion of his medical studies. Armand repeated almost verbatim the story he had told me about going to the Soviet Union. The interviewer attempted to move on, but Armand continued to dwell on his years in Russia and to gush about the Russian people and their leadership.

The host took a call. "Lenin was a Communist. He believed in the overthrow of our government," said a listener. "Didn't it bother you to go and sit in his office?"

The caller was not going to be pleased by Armand's reply. "Lenin was a fine, warmhearted man, a humanitarian, and one of the greatest leaders of history and destiny."

The host asked Hammer to describe his experiences with Henry Ford.

"Ford was just like Lenin. Both were determined to help large numbers of people. Both were mocked as dreamers. Both were great achievers with the strength of character to make their dreams come true."

Another caller asked, "What do you think of Nikita Khrushchev?"

"Khrushchev is just like Lenin," Armand replied, "another caring, compassionate man striving to do everything he can to give the Russian people a better life." He then reeled off what was considered at that time the official Communist propaganda line: "There is no unemployment in the Soviet Union. Every Russian citizen has a job, good clothing, and food and is provided a nice home and total guaranteed health care by the government. The Russian people are very happy and contented living under the benevolent rule of their Communist leaders."

After a year's hard work I could not understand why Armand seemed determined to inflame the public and potential investors, especially when Occidental was in such bad financial shape. My only option was to lay my cards on the table and try to convince him that the only practical thing to do was to stick to the script of all-American business doctor. I dreaded doing it because Armand found opposition intolerable. He refused to lose arguments and his mastery of logical fallacies made him a formidable debater. He also changed the subject if he didn't feel like discussing it and delivered wearying monologues in order to deflect probing questions. Or he simply ignored whatever he didn't want to hear.

The next morning I pulled a chair up to his desk. "This is L.A., not New York, Armand," I began. "Conspiracy theories of the right as well as the left flourish here. That's why you might be able to get away with showering Russia with praise in New York, but you've got to be careful in L.A. People can't think you're a Communist. I don't want a reporter to write an article that accuses you of spreading Communist propaganda."

"Relations between our country and Russia are lousy," he countered. "I'm determined to do something to ease international tensions."

"You're a businessman, not a diplomat."

"I don't need diplomatic recognition. I know and understand the Russians. That gives me plenty of leverage. We're facing the probability of nuclear war. The Americans and the Russians have got to stop shaking fists at each other and learn to live together or we're going to blow each other up. Benjamin Franklin said that trading partners usually don't make war, and I agree with him. When countries trade, they put aside their differences because they profit from each other. That's why I'm determined to do everything I can to promote trade between our country and Russia."

I reminded him that Germany had gone to war against its trading partners in both world wars. His eyes slid past me as if I weren't there. "Carl, take it from me: trading partners do *not* go to war." Like a skilled propagandist who takes a slogan, an unqualified assertion, or a sweeping generalization and repeats it over and over again until his listeners accept it as truth, from that moment on, Armand would repeat his lie about trading partners at every opportunity.

When I returned to my office, I called Victor in New York and asked him how to temper his brother's Soviet ardor. His response was a burst of hearty laughter. "Armand has always looked to the Kremlin with the same kind of reverential regard a deeply devoted Moslem pays to Mecca," Victor said. "I'll explain it to you when I see you."

The following morning I received a call from a man who identified himself as a member of the Catholic War Veterans. He proceeded to tell me that Armand's father, Julius Hammer, had been one of the founding members of the American Communist Party and that Armand had really traveled to Russia as Julius's representative. I replied that I could discuss these accusations with Dr. Hammer only after I had seen proof.

A few days later I received an envelope containing an excerpt from a Scotland Yard report, filed in 1919, and a copy of a transcript of testimony delivered before the House Committee on Un-American Activities in 1956.

The report read: "In Julius Hammer, Martens [Ludwig C. A. K. Martens, a Russian-born Communist who lived in the United States and was appointed "ambassador" to the United States by Lenin in 1919] has a real Bolshevik and ardent Left Wing adherent who came from Russia. He was one of the organizers of the Left Wing movement in New York and speaks at meetings on the same platform with such Left Wing leaders as Reed, Hourwich, Lore and Larkin." The transcript consisted of testimony of an "expert witness under oath" and included the statements that "Victor Hammer was the son of one of the founding members of the Communist Party of the United States of America" and that Ireene

Wicker Hammer, Victor's wife, had "married into what had been the aristocracy of the communist movement."

When I handed Armand these documents, he stared at me as if I had caused the problem. "All you have to say about my father," he told me, "is that he was a principled man who worked hard his whole life to provide a good home for our family, but that he was also naïve and let emotion rather than reason rule his behavior. All you have to say about me is that I was a young capitalist entrepreneur who made large profits in the heart of a drab, anticapitalist country."

It came to me that Armand, who had a motive for everything, had been testing the waters by going public with his pro-Soviet assertions and had learned that the only repercussion was a single letter with odds and ends of allegations. I filed the documents and drafted a neutral statement to read to the anti-Communist watchdog if he called again. I never heard from him.

During the next few interviews Armand controlled his tendency to praise Lenin but did comment at length about his business relationship with Henry Ford. Subsequently, the chief librarian of the Henry Ford Library in Dearborn, Michigan, sent me a letter stating that information in the library archives confirmed that Ford had become involved with the post-revolution Soviet government in 1919, three years before he had met Armand, had participated in a single, short meeting with him, had refused Julius Hammer's overtures to build an automotive plant in the USSR, had never wanted to do business directly with the Hammer family, and had dealt with them only because they were the only representatives available in the USSR at that time.

I passed on this letter to Armand.

"Henry Ford was a very simpleminded man," he snapped and tossed the letter back to me.

The following week Victor turned up in Los Angeles. From our first meetings through the many years that we knew each other, I always took Victor seriously, never treated him as a clown or gofer, and made it clear I would never betray him to Armand. We did a lot of talking, and in bits and pieces, I was able to piece together an accurate family history of the Hammer brothers. According to Victor, their father, Julius Hammer, had joined the Socialist Labor Party in 1890, when he was seventeen years old. Their mother, Rose, had also been a socialist, and she had met her future husband at a Socialist Labor Party function. Contradicting Armand, Victor told me that Rose had not been a widow but was married at the time and had left her husband for Julius.

Victor also revealed that his brother had not been truthful about the origin of his name. "Even though Armand says he was named after the hero in *Camille*," Victor told me, "he was named after the symbol of the Socialist Labor Party, a working man's arm and hammer. I was named Victor because it meant victor over capitalism."

Victor described his parents' relationship as stormy. "Pop had swept a married woman off her feet, and after they were married, he never hesitated to sweep other women off their feet the same way. Mama Rose has always been an enormously powerful woman and the ultimate Jewish mother, but she couldn't control Pop. The fact that she was a suffragette who fought for the emancipation of women, and yet was trapped at home with a man who was always playing around, drove her crazy. Their fights were brutal."

In our discussions Victor never mentioned Rose's son by her first husband, his older half brother, Harry, who worked at the Hammer Galleries in a supervisory capacity and never came to Los Angeles. I only met Harry once in New York and found him taciturn and colorless.

Victor agreed. "He's never smiled once!"

Julius and Rose were so busy they had handed their three sons over to a live-in nanny, Marie Doll, a teenage Polish immigrant who could hardly speak English. "The only thing Marie had no difficulty saying was 'I'm much better than your parents because they're *Russians*, and I'm not.'"

Julius Hammer came from a Jewish background, but Victor described his father as "violently anti-Semitic." "Pop's parents were merchants who prospered under the czar and denied being Jewish. When they came to this country, my grandfather Jacob chose the name Hammer because he thought it sounded Swedish.

"When Pop became a doctor, every time he delivered a baby, if Jewish parents gave their children what he considered a Jewish-sounding first name, he changed the name on the birth certificate. He beat it into us that being Jewish was a hindrance. To this day, Armand refuses to admit that he comes from a Jewish background."

The turning point in Julius Hammer's life came in 1907, when he was twenty-two years old and traveled to Stuttgart, Germany, to attend a nine-hundred-delegate international socialist congress. "I remember him telling us as little children that he had met Lenin, how smart and brave Lenin was, and how he'd finally come in contact with a leader who knew how to speak to the people."

That was not the only thing that was unusual about the Hammer brothers' childhoods. In 1903 when Harry was twelve, Armand five, and Victor one, the Hammer family moved from a tenement on the Lower East Side to a large house in the Bronx. Julius had just graduated from the College of Physicians and Surgeons of Columbia University and launched his medical practice in a room in his new home. At the same time he was busy selling off his drugstores and burying his assets before filing for bankruptcy. "The bankruptcy proceedings were particularly ugly," said Victor, "and dragged on for years. Every member of our family lied under oath. Telling the truth was not the important thing. Dad was determined that all of our money stay with us. Our family's job was to fight to make sure that no one was going to be able to touch a cent of it." At the age of ten, Armand was sent to live for five years in Connecticut with the family of one of Julius's socialist friends. Victor lived in upstate New York with Daniel De Leon and his family. De Leon, a professor of international law, was the acknowledged father of the American Marxist movement and the leader of the Socialist Labor Party. Harry lived with a rabbi's family in Waterbury, Connecticut. According to Victor, Armand joined the Socialist Labor Party in 1916 when he was eighteen, but he had himself declined, mainly because he had no interest in politics.

While Armand and Victor were away, their father grew even more committed to the socialist cause. "Pop even gave dynamite to a young radical," Victor said. As he told it, his father was determined to destroy the privileged bureaucracy and create a world where every poor person could participate in the government and where there was a fair distribution of income. But he was also a first-generation American who craved success and money. "Pop never understood the irony of his position," Victor remarked. "Armand's desire to be a doctor, help the Russians, serve Lenin, and become rich—all of it came from the contradictions that were a part of Pop's nature. Pop lent the Soviets $110,000 to buy oil machinery, then he charged them $50,000 in interest. He taught Armand to behave the same way at the same time that Mama Rose taught him how to control everybody and everything."

At the beginning of 1917, Leon Trotsky arrived in New York to seek financial support for the cash-hungry Bolshevik movement, and Julius went to the ship to meet him. Trotsky had carried with him negotiable securities that Julius converted to cash. Victor said he was thirteen when he met Trotsky. He recalled the Bolshevik leader as "a real intellectual and idealist. He also had a huge ego, and you couldn't argue with him. I think Trotsky craved power and didn't like sharing center stage with Lenin. What he really liked was to suffer. Lenin gave him plenty of opportunity."

After the February 1917 revolution, which saw the abdication of Czar Nicholas II and the end of the three-hundred-year rule of the Romanoffs, Trotsky hurried back to Russia, traveling on a Canadian passport arranged by Julius Hammer. The galvanizing event for the Hammer family was the Bolshevik Revolution, which began on November 7, 1917. Armand was nineteen at the time; Victor, fifteen.

"It was a dream come true!" Victor said. "A mere eleven thousand men had seized control of one-sixth of the world! We saw the Bolsheviks as freedom fighters and Lenin and Trotsky as gods. Everything about Russia seemed to be touched by genius. There wasn't a socialist alive who didn't want to go there."

Infused with revolutionary zeal, Julius Hammer left the Socialist Labor Party to join the more radical Left Wing, which believed in the inevitability of violent revolution. In 1919 he was elected to a steering committee to convert the Left Wing into an official American Communist Party. It was headquartered in a building on the Lower East Side that Julius rented and then donated. Later he made a contribution to purchase another building that would house an unofficial U.S.-Bolshevik embassy, the Soviet Bureau. This was where Ludwig Martens set up offices, functioned as Soviet trade representative to the United States, and organized shipments of supplies to the USSR. Julius, whose title was "commercial attaché," served as director of the financial department.

"Ludwig was supposed to be the direct link between Lenin and the American Communists," Victor said. "He was blunt, practical, and really not that bright. His job supposedly was to build party cells inside the labor movement and the armed forces, but his bottom line was that unless Russia caught up technologically to the West, it could not lead an international socialist revolution. So Pop and Ludwig set out to find ways to beat the U.S. trade embargo against the USSR."

The American government freeze of Soviet currency reserves and gold led Julius to witness financial transactions between Martens and the National City Bank of New York. With the aid of Martens, Julius established a pharmaceutical supplies company, Allied Drug and Chemical Corporation, in a secret partnership with the Bolshevik government. Subsequently, he was described in State Department documents as "one of the first to establish one of the 'front' corporations and purchasing agencies" that were controlled by "Soviet Jewish elements under the direction of the Soviet Government of Russia."

Victor told me that *The New York Times* had written that, after his father went to work for the Bolsheviks, the Hammer family had moved into an expensive apartment in Manhattan and purchased several cars. "Helping the Bolsheviks was a money-maker. Soviet couriers smuggled czarist gems into the country, and Pop turned the jewels into cash and took a commission off the top. The money was supposed to be used to establish and maintain contact with radicals across the country.

"Boris Reinstein, an old friend of Pop's from the days when they both met Lenin in Stuttgart, ran the Bolshevik Department of International Propaganda. He told me that immediately after the Revolution, the Bolsheviks announced that they were putting up two million rubles to finance international revolutionary movements. Some of this money had to have passed through Pop's hands, because our life-style really improved."

In 1919, U.S. Attorney General A. Mitchell Palmer launched twenty-five-year-old J. Edgar Hoover's career by appointing him chief of the Justice Department's brand-new General Intelligence Division. Hoover staged the Palmer Raids, a series of large-scale roundups of radicals and aliens, and compiled a list of 400,000 radicals that included all of the members of the Hammer family.

"After twenty-five Communist Party members were arrested and charged with criminal anarchy," Victor said, "Pop bailed them out with two hundred fifty thousand dollars' worth of Liberty Bonds. Everyone said that persecution and repression encourage revolution and that the arrests had made them even more like Bolsheviks."

"Where did your father get two hundred fifty thousand dollars?" I asked.

"Pop and his friends all knew how to turn a buck and put their savings into Liberty Bonds, just like everybody else. Armand also had a lot of money. Prohibition was in effect, and there was a medical product, a mixture of carbonated water and tincture of ginger, which contained a great deal of alcohol and was the equivalent of a pretty stiff highball. Armand had a stroke of genius and he hired agents to buy up all the ginger on the world market. He always says he made his first million running Pop's business. He really was a very shrewd bootlegger.

"I don't know if he really did make a million," Victor continued, "but it was a lot of money. Armand had proved that he was the smart one in our family. He kept reminding Pop and Mama Rose that he was rich and that if they knew what was good for them, they would listen to him. He said the word 'millionaire' so many times Mama Rose started to get scared and she lost control over him. It taught Armand the lesson of his life. The more money he earned, the more control *he* could have. It became his life's work."

On November 8, 1919, 249 aliens and radicals, including Ludwig Martens, were deported to Russia on an Army transport ship that became known as the "Soviet Ark." Julius Hammer was arrested also, not for revolutionary activities but for performing an illegal abortion on Marie Oganescoff, the wife of a czarist diplomat, who subsequently died. Julias was convicted of first-degree manslaughter, and received a three-and-one-half-to-fifteen-year sentence, which he began serving in Sing Sing Prison on September 18, 1920.

Another man might have said that the sentencing was a miscarriage of justice or an an excuse to jail a man because he was Jewish, an alien, and a Communist, but Victor and Armand shared a lack of compassion and empathy that extended even to their families, and Victor dismissed the sentencing as if it was just another of life's trivial occurrences. "Armand was the one who really took it personally," he said. "He thought *his* life was ruined because he was going to be considered the son of a jailbird. Armand can be very childish. He's always told me that he won't settle for anything less than a perfect report card.

"His cause wasn't helped when the FBI staked out our family because they believed our business was a cover for smuggling czarist gems into the country. And they've never stopped watching us. As recently as nine years ago, they got Senator Bridges to back off when he was helping Armand lease that former Army plant in New Hampshire for his distilling company. When Armand was turned down for a passport in 1952 because he was a 'suspected Communist,' it was also the FBI's doing."

"Armand's convinced the FBI won't rest until it finds a way to put him in jail. At the same time I've always believed that he's determined to prove he's smarter than the people in charge. Armand has a great appetite for revenge. No matter how long it takes, he always gets even. He's spent the last forty years waiting to have the last laugh on the U.S. for daring to threaten his respectability, and he's not going to stop until he gets it."

At the time of his arrest, Julius Hammer had been planning to go to the USSR in order to collect some of the $150,000 the Bolsheviks owed him and to establish new business relationships with the Russians and help them solve their monetary problems. "Britain closely monitored Soviet foreign policy, but Scotland Yard rarely stopped doctors en route to Moscow," Victor told me. "Therefore, Armand was the ideal replacement for Pop. He took sixty thousand dollars' worth of medical supplies and surgical instruments with him as a cover and pretended he was going as a volunteer M.D. Pop also gave him a letter of introduction to deliver to Lenin."

Armand was traveling on a passport that said he planned to visit five European countries for "commercial business and pleasure" and did not mention the Soviet Union as his destination. On July 18, 1921, the U.S. embassy in London received an MI5 report that he "was carrying messages." When the S.S. *Aquitania* tied up in Southampton before setting sail for Hamburg, from which Armand planned to take a train to Moscow, Scotland Yard came on board, confiscated a reel of film that he was supposed to deliver to Ludwig Martens, refused to allow him to enter the country, and kept him in quarantine until the ship departed for Germany.

"What was on the film?" I asked Victor.

"Armand said it was a harmless home movie of the departure of the Soviet Ark. But Martens had been in charge of industrial espionage and was supposed to document U.S. industrial processes for the Soviets. Over the years the British secret service has suggested that the film contained footage of the manufacture of material that could have been put to military use."

Armand had told me that he had known no one in Moscow. Victor said that from the moment of his arrival he was surrounded by old family friends, among them Ludwig Martens, whom Lenin had appointed to head the Soviet mining industry after his deportation from the United States; Boris Reinstein, whose functions as Soviet propaganda minister included serving as guide to visiting Americans; Julius Hammer's partner, Abe Heller, whom the State Department categorized as "a notorious Bolshevik; and the Hammer family's European representative, Boris Mishell, whose first assignment was to locate a Mercedes Benz for Armand. According to Victor, Armand had traveled to the Urals at the suggestion of Boris Reinstein, and during that trip, contrary to Armand's version of the story, the Bolshevik propaganda chief had proposed the grain deal to him and had also told him about the potential profits that could be obtained from asbestos mining. Armand had not only agreed to Reinstein's proposal but had also urged Reinstein to allow him to obtain a mining concession. Reinstein had conveyed this information to Lenin and persuaded Lenin to meet with Armand.

I asked Victor why Lenin would want to meet his brother, and he said, "Lenin perceived Armand as the son of a very important man—Julius Hammer, Russian born, a Communist leader, a millionaire who was willing and eager to use his money to support the revolution, and a political prisoner of the American capitalist system. Still Lenin didn't want to do business with Armand because he was looking for a much bigger capitalist firm to take over the first concession. So Armand pressured Reinstein, who, in turn, pressured Lenin."

Lenin had launched his New Economic Policy (NEP), a modified form of capitalism that was going to allow foreign firms to obtain Soviet concessions. It was his belief that the involvement of these firms would not only stimulate the moribund Soviet economy but also convince other Western capitalists that the Bolsheviks were not going to confiscate their property and that they could receive competition-free monopolies that would produce substantial profits. Lenin's goal was to publicize this practice and use it as propaganda to attract other Western investors. Thus, the asbestos concession took the form of the classic Soviet espionage activity known as an influence operation, an action designed to cause a targeted country to take a beneficial action on behalf of the USSR. In this instance, the West had been targeted to provide investment capital and trade credits that would strengthen the USSR, ultimately furthering the revolutionary cause.

Victor explained that Armand was determined to prove he could make a profit and that he had extracted a promise from Lenin to give him his full support. "The only way to get anything done was to have the Cheka, the Soviet secret police, on your side. Two Cheka officers were assigned to Armand on the spot. Armand's always bragged about this. Nobody's ever realized that this wouldn't have happened unless he was taking orders from the Bolshevik government."

Armand claimed that Lenin had summoned him to the Kremlin to thank him for his million-dollar grain deal to feed Russia's hungry, and when I threw up my hands in disbelief at his bold-faced, oft-repeated lies about his altruistic intentions, Victor remarked that his brother had told his story about Lenin so many times, he had come to believe it himself. "How many twenty-three-year-olds ever get the chance to talk with someone who's changed the course of history? Everyone I met who knew Lenin described him as intense, austere, and spellbinding, and Armand was bowled over," Victor said. "Pop had gotten his orders from Ludwig Martens. But Armand's orders came directly from the mouth of Lenin. Lenin himself—not Ludwig Martens—appointed Armand the first foreigner to obtain a Soviet concession. Lenin never signed autographs for 'capitalist imperialists,' but he autographed a photograph for Armand because Armand was his 'comrade.' Armand's connection to Lenin made him feel special then and just as special now. After all, it was *he* and not Pop who was dealing with the man on top. It was as if Armand had decided that Lenin had chosen him to be his *son* and he was determined to prove that Lenin had made the right choice. I've always believed that Armand began to harbor the notion that someday he could be just as powerful and important as Lenin. The only difference is that Armand wanted to be a lot richer."

Victor added that as part of his deal with Lenin to obtain the asbestos concession Armand agreed to serve as a courier for the communists and carry thousands of dollars from Moscow to New York to fund the American Communist Party.

To combat rampant inflation, the Russians began issuing a gold-backed currency, the *chervonetz*. In order to obtain the mining concession for Armand, Julius agreed from Sing Sing to put up $50,000 in gold as collateral, which was to be used to help underwrite the new currency. "It was deposited in the Soviet State Bank," Victor said, "which made us the first depositers in the world's first Bolshevik bank." He also explained the real purpose of Armand's grain deal: "The grain really wasn't going to be used to feed starving Russians but to feed our mine workers. Therefore, what we really were doing was shipping grain to our own overseas business, and we took only a five percent commission on either end."

My flabbergasted expression made Victor laugh so hard there were tears in his eyes.

Toward the end of 1921, Armand returned to New York, traveling on the freighter bearing the goods the Russians had traded the Hammer family for the grain. He formed a Delaware corporation, Ural-American Refining and Trading Company, whose chairman was Julius Hammer. Its name was eventually changed to Allied American Corporation, Alamerico.

"Unlike any of the other U.S. companies doing business in Russia," Victor said, "ours was financed by the Soviets, which enabled them to take a healthy percentage of our profits. In return, they gave us a monopoly over all Russian exports to the U.S. and allowed us to take a percentage of every item that left the country. Two of the directors were Soviets and they were really the ones who were in control. Alamerico maintained its bank account at the Midland Bank in London, where it was supervised by Bolshevik representatives. Inevitably, some of the profits were funneled to the American Communist Party."

At a later meeting with Victor, I was curious to know how he had become involved with his brother's business operations. "When did you go to Russia for the first time?" I asked.

"On November 7, 1922, the fifth anniversary of the Revolution," he replied. "I had gone to Colgate University and then to Princeton because I wanted to join the Triangle Club and appear in their theatricals. Princeton was all about fraternities, eating clubs, and teams. Jews were excluded from all of them, and the policies of the Triangle Club were no exception, which meant that I didn't have a shot. So Armand convinced me to leave Princeton and go to Russia to study theater. He also insisted that I go to secretarial school and learn typing and shorthand so I could work as his secretary if I wasn't able to make a living as an actor. When I got to Russia, he kept me so busy I never had a chance to study acting. He even put me to work in our asbestos mine. He planned it that way because he was dead set against me becoming an actor."

By this time Armand had already had his sole meeting with Henry Ford. The introduction had been arranged by a man Victor called Uncle Sasha. He was Alexander Gomberg, the brother-in-law of Victor and Armand's paternal grandmother and the leading American trade representative in Bolshevik Russia. Before the Revolution, Gomberg had sold Ford cars in Russia and had maintained a relationship with Henry Ford and other key Ford executives. "Uncle Sasha was a truly committed radical," said Victor. "He'd been deported from Norway after he was accused of being a Bolshevik agitator, had been involved in an international scandal after he passed forged documents that were sold to the U.S. government, and was among those who smuggled czarist gems into the United States to help the revolutionary cause.

"Despite his affection for Uncle Sasha, Henry Ford was already in business in the Soviet Union and he gave Armand the back of his hand," Victor said. "But Armand contacted companies across the U.S., saying that he was Ford's representative and describing the Soviet concession system in glowing terms. He was such a good salesman he signed up thirty-eight important firms. Part of Armand's job was to set up an exchange program and get Soviet engineers into the U.S. to study American industry. Most were spies who were trained to steal industrial secrets, and he even got them into the Ford tractor factories. He also was supposed to talk up U.S.-Soviet trade in the press. Even though the goods the Russians had traded us for the grain were of low quality and not worth all that much, he told reporters that we'd made a two hundred fifty percent profit and that doing business with Russia could make you rich."

Armand had previously given an interview to *The New York Times* extolling the virtues of trade with the Soviets: "I told them I was a capitalist; that I was out to make money. . . They said in effect, 'We understand you do not come here for love. As long as you do not mix in our politics, we will give you our help.' "

In January 1923 Julius Hammer was paroled and released from prison even though there were thirteen months left to his sentence. Victor explained that Armand had made generous contributions to local Democratic representatives and had pressured influential people to petition New York Governor Alfred E. Smith. Julius had also applied pressure to the Jewish Board of Guardians. Because he was a naturalized citizen and had not received a pardon, U.S. immigration law required that he leave the country and reapply for citizenship at a later date. At the end of April, Julius and Rose traveled to Moscow and Julius took official charge of the Hammer family trading company, Alamerico, but when the Soviets formed the state-owned trading company, Amtorg, the following year, the Hammers had no choice but to dissolve Alamerico. Next Julius paid the Bolshevik government $250,000 in return for a majority interest in the Harju Bank in Reval, Estonia. "Money was passed through Harju Bank to the Comintern to foster world revolution," Victor said. "Essentially, though, it was used to do secret deals for party leaders who wanted to turn their money into marks and dollars. They knew better than anybody how useless their own currency was. The bank also provided us with an opportunity to transfer our profits to America." The Harju Bank was dissolved within a year, with employee thievery and embezzlement given as the official reasons.

On January 21, 1924, Lenin died after a series of strokes. Armand visited his body while it lay in state in the House of Columns, watched as workmen toiled around the clock to erect a mausoleum, and joined the funeral procession and parade of workers as Lenin's body was carried through Red Square to its final resting place.

Victor's response to Lenin's death was purely pragmatic. "Lenin believed that the means justified the end, no matter what," he said. "We took him at his word, thought about the glorious future, and looked the other way. Almost every Westerner in Moscow was so enamored of the revolution that he refused to acknowledge—or even bothered to learn—that twelve million people had died during Lenin's six years in power."

In 1925 the Soviets gave the Hammers a concession to manufacture pencils in Moscow. The Hammers' new business, the A. Hammer Pencil Company, was incorporated in New York City, with Julius Hammer listed as president. "Once again the Bolsheviks were our secret partners," Victor said, "which is why they granted us another monopoly. To drum up propaganda for our new business and encourage other Western investment, Armand cultivated *New York Times* Moscow correspondent Walter Duranty. Duranty reported regularly to the OGPU [the foreign arm of the Soviet Secret Police and a predecessor of the KGB], so it wasn't hard to get him to print that we made a million dollars a year. It was blatant propaganda. All our enterprises together grossed about half that.

In the struggle for power that arose between Stalin and Trotsky after Lenin's death, Walter Duranty convinced Armand that Stalin was going to emerge the victor. "Each time there's a new leader, you've got to prove your loyalty all over again and our family began to cultivate Stalin with a vengeance," Victor said. By then the Hammer pencil factory was turning out 72 million pencils and 95 million pens yearly for domestic consumption and export to Europe and the Middle and Far East, and the Hammers were living better than ever. After e. e. cummings spent a few weeks as their house guest in Moscow, he parodied the experience in a novel, *Eimi*, characterizing Julius Hammer as "O my yes, very rich indeed."

In 1929 American Communist Party leaders Benjamin Gitlow and Jay Lovestone visited Moscow and discovered that Julius Hammer had learned directly from Stalin before they were notified that they were to be replaced and that Stalin had chosen Armand to convey the news to Walter Duranty so that it could be printed in the *Times*. "They were convinced," Victor said, "that Pop had sided with Stalin against them because he was more interested in doing business with Stalin than reaffirming his commitment to socialist goals. When they got home, Stalin added to their embarrassment by claiming that they had pocketed seven years' worth of American Communist Party dues, which they had collected from Pop while they were in Moscow."

During their Moscow stay Armand and Victor each took a Russian wife, and each became the father of a son. Victor married twenty-two-year-old Vavara (Vava) Sumski in 1925. Their son, Armand Victorvich, or Armasha, born in 1927, was named after Armand at Armand's insistence. The same year Armand married Baroness Olga von Root, a well-known Moscow cabaret singer whose stage name was Olga Vadina. Their son, Julian, was born in 1929.

Determined to rid the Soviet Union of any hint of capitalism, Stalin eventually established a competitive state-owned pencil factory and then made it clear that he planned to nationalize the Hammers' pencil business. "Armand convinced the Soviets that once he left Moscow he was going to remain loyal to them. That's why they allowed him to *sell* them our pencil factory," Victor explained to me.

When the Soviets took over the pencil factory in 1929, the Hammer family decided to send Victor home. "My marriage ended abruptly after I caught Vava in bed with my best friend," he told me ruefully. "My two-year-old son had an American passport, registered in Berlin, but the Soviets demanded that he stay behind with his Russian mother."

Armand departed in 1930, and Julius and Rose left the next year. Arriving in England, they were refused entry because of the subversive activities of another member of their family. In 1927 Scotland Yard had raided the offices of the Soviet-U.K. trading company Arcos Ltd., and subsequently British intelligence had supplied New York police with the tip to raid Moness Chemical Company, a cover for a large-scale Soviet espionage operation led by Comintern agents. The police discovered papers stuffed in a stove in Moness's offices, which revealed that Harry Hammer, who had refused to live in Moscow and was operating out of London on behalf of the Hammer family at the time, had made substantial loans to the company. British intelligence concluded that he was laundering Soviet funds through his family's businesses to Moness in order to foster world revolution.

Julius and Rose next traveled to Germany, where Julius was arrested and charged with the nonpayment of $106,000 to German creditors for pencil-manufacturing equipment. When he insisted that he did not have to pay because the debt had been incurred by Alamerico, a defunct corporation, he was jailed for swindling. Armand hired Henry French Hollis, a distinguished attorney and former senator from New Hampshire with close ties to FDR, to defend his father and to ensure that his U.S. citizenship would be restored. The case was resolved out of court, enabling Rose and Julius Hammer to return to the United States.

Despite the fact that the United States was in the midst of the Great Depression, on their return Rose and Julius attempted to buy a home in an exclusive neighborhood in Westchester, New York, that was restricted for Jews. When they failed, they bought a home nearby. They traveled back and forth to Moscow on a number of other occasions, but Rose essentially returned to her causes and Julius had a succession of love affairs and continued to be active in leftist organizations. When Armand returned to America, he lived for a time in the tiny carriage house in Greenwich Village where he had stayed during his student days at Columbia University, and Victor rented an apartment on fashionable upper Fifth Avenue.

The decade of the 1930s would see the Hammer brothers devoted to building their art business, with Armand making occasional excursions into other business ventures as well. Victor, still single, remained at his brother's beck and call. Then, in 1941, Victor remarried. His second wife, Ireene Wicker, who was also divorced, wrote, produced, and performed a children's radio show and was known as "The Singing Lady." At the time of their marriage she had spent three years as the most popular children's entertainer in the country. Ireene was the mother of a teenaged daughter, Nancy, and a son, Walter Jr., who was in the Royal Canadian Air Force and would serve as a fighter pilot during World War II. He was killed in action in 1942.

After being named in a newsletter as a pro-Communist member of the broadcasting industry, Ireene's twenty years of radio stardom came to an abrupt end in 1950. The primary accusation was that her loyalty had been tainted because of her marriage into the Hammer family. Along with Wicker, actors Fredric March and Florence Eldridge were also named, and they asked Ireene to join them in a libel suit, but she refused. After the Marches sued, the newsletter settled out of court and withdrew its allegation. Exonerated, the Marches resumed their careers.

Armand did not lift a finger to help his brother's wife. In fact, he was behind the refusal to file suit. "The last thing Armand wanted was to be interrogated by the House Un-American Activities Committee about his background with the Soviet Communists and his business ties with them. He was afraid of bad publicity, a fall-off in business revenues, and especially a jail sentence," Victor said. "The House Un-American Activities Committee was primarily concerned with movie stars, union leaders, teachers, scientists, people like that, and Ireene certainly was a star, which meant more publicity for them. They had no interest in an art dealer who also owned a liquor-distilling business, and Armand wanted to keep it that way. He also had Senator Styles Bridges in his hip pocket, which helped a lot. Besides, he always makes sure to bribe all of the little people who handle the information that can eventually get him into trouble. So he ordered Ireene not to fight or do anything else that would call attention to our family history."

Nor did Armand, with all all his powerful connections in both the American and Soviet governments, help Victor obtain his son Armasha's release from Russia. In 1956 Victor returned to the Soviet Union and saw his son for the first time in twenty-two years. "Armasha was a grown man with a little girl of his own," he told me. "The following year, Eleanor Roosevelt introduced me to Khrushchev at Hyde Park and asked him to intervene on Armasha's behalf, and Armasha received permission to visit.

"Armasha had a mouth full of steel teeth that were just horrible," Victor said. "I took him to the dentist and spent thousands getting him new teeth. But there were problems. He went for a drive. When the car broke down, he said he could start the engine by heating the motor with a match. He was so arrogant and so convinced he was an expert, he had to be thrown to the ground before he blew up the car. Then he and Armand had a big fight when Armand insisted on taking him out on a Sunday rather than a weekday because you could buy two subway fares for the price of one. Armand was very angry and told me that he thought Armasha had turned out terribly."

Victor told me halfheartedly that he wished Armasha would obtain a permanent exit visa and move to the United States, but it was clear that he didn't mean it. He was too afraid of Armand's displeasure and of any relationship that made demands on him.

Summing up his brother's equivocal relationship with the two most powerful governments in the world, Victor said, "Underneath it all, Armand's always had a screw-you attitude about the U.S. and Russia. If he does have a preference, it's Russia and he's always wanted to get back into business with the Russians. I think he's opened up to you so that you can publicize the story of his days in Russia in a way that puts him in a favorable light here *and* there. He's using you to help pave the way."

4.

"SCREW THEM BEFORE THEY SCREW YOU"

During 1959 Armand transformed Occidental into a functioning oil company by acquiring a full-fledged oil and gas division through a merger with Gene Reid Drilling of Bakersfield, California. The idea had been suggested by board member Nico van Wingen, a professor of petroleum engineering at the University of Southern California.

"Reid's a top-notch driller," Armand told me. "Companies send for him when they're experiencing drilling difficulties their own people can't solve. But he's been having a bad run and the recession hasn't helped. He's even had to sell off some of his rigs. Because of him lots of men became millionaires, but he told me that he couldn't say the same for himself. That was all I needed to hear. I traded him a hundred sixty thousand shares of capital stock [around $320,000] for all of his outstanding stock. Now, if he comes through and finds oil for Oxy, he's going to be a millionaire many times over. The money he's going to make will exceed his wildest dreams."

Reid was a colorful, straight-shooting, rough-hewn oilman. In the tradition of wildcatters, he was also incurably optimistic. He had assembled a crackerjack team of young men that I dubbed the "oil and gas boys." They included his son Bud (exploration manager), two of Bud's former classmates at Stanford University, Dick Vaughan (chief geologist) and Bob Teitsworth (geologist), Charley Horace (chief engineer) who had attended U.S.C., and a few others. Each was versed in all aspects of oil and gas exploration and production and equipped with a complete understanding of the latest technology, and they shared a conservative pro-America, probusiness, passionately anti-Communist point of view. This ideology differed considerably from Armand's, but his passion for risk taking enabled them to view him as a kindred spirit. He also gave them generous stock options, which meant they, too, would make fortunes if oil was struck. So they looked the other way during his frequent tributes to Lenin and never questioned his determination to find a way to make trading partners of Occidental and the Soviet Union.

Gene Reid Drilling controlled a natural-gas field in San Juan Basin, New Mexico. Two factors, a state law that allowed drilling only a few days a week and the extremely low price of natural gas at that time, had led Bud Reid to recommend the abandonment of the field. The SEC requires an energy company to register the number of recoverable reserves on a property before it publishes that figure in fund-raising prospectuses. Not only did Armand insist on going forward, he was also determined to claim huge recoverable reserves and use the inflated figures to ensnare investors for this and other Occidental projects.

Reid argued that it was going to take Occidental thirteen years to recover its investment and that the impracticality of the venture demanded that the company not jeopardize its credibility with the SEC. In response, Armand roared that he was the boss and that his was the only judgment that counted. He then hired an outside engineering firm to perform a reserves study, and its figures miraculously confirmed his own. Reid was ordered to file the new "information" with the SEC.

Reid confided to me that during SEC director Tel White's inspection of the filing documents, he had told White that if it were up to him, he would have cut the reserves numbers in half. White trusted Reid, and he halved the estimate on the spot. Subsequently the SEC rebuffed Armand's protest. To the day Hammer died, he never knew that his new explorations manager had become a whistle-blower almost immediately after he took the job.

Toward the end of 1959, a few months after Gene Reid came aboard, the state legislator my PR company was paying under the table tipped Armand that the Public Utilities Commission was attempting to sneak through a bill that would give it unlimited authority to take full control of California's natural-gas industry. Declaring that speed was of the essence, Armand chartered a private plane and sent two oil and gas boys and me on a four-day statewide expedition to newspaper offices, radio and TV stations, county boards of supervisors, city councils, business organizations, chambers of commerce, and offices and homes of local labor leaders. Our job was to spread the message that the passage of the bill would inevitably lead to unemployment and would depress the state's economy. Before any other gas producer could even begin to launch a strategy, we roused a hornets' nest of opposition and forced the Public Utilities Commission to schedule a public hearing.

On the morning of the hearing, Armand and I arrived in Sacramento and went directly to the hotel where the gas industry delegates were caucusing. A group of energy executives was clustered in the corner of the large suite. They didn't know who I was, and I heard them describe Armand as "untrustworthy," "a loner," and "only out for himself." They were jealous because he had shown them up, but it was more than that. Armand was an outsider who did not belong to this good-old-boys club. If that wasn't bad enough, his aloofness indicated that he viewed not belonging as a badge of honor.

On the flight back to Los Angeles I told Armand about the comments I had overheard. "I'm never curious about those who don't think as I do," he replied. "Unless it affects business, I ignore them. If it does affect business, I screw them before they screw me."

He buried himself in the pile of papers on his lap and did not say a word for the remainder of the flight. Later that day, responding to the furious opposition at the hearing, the Public Utilities Commission voted to table the bill, and it was never mentioned again.

It had taken several days, but I had gotten an international wire service to use one of my news releases after it appeared that it was not going to be printed. When Armand asked how I had accomplished it, I explained that I had asked a friend, a newspaper editor, to call the wire service and ask to have the story released on its system, so that his newspaper could take it off the wire and print it. As I spoke Armand made notes on his yellow sheet of paper. A few weeks later a *New York Times* editor inadvertently revealed that Armand was repeating my strategy, using his brothers, Victor and Harry, as shills. Confessing annoyance, the editor told me that every time I issued a news release, the *Times* received calls from two men, each named Mr. Hammer, insisting that the *Times* call the wire services and tell them it was interested in printing the story.

I looked Armand straight in the eye and ordered him to cut it out. His response was one of his "prescriptions": "Opportunities are all around. It's my nature to reach out, grab every single one of them by the forelock, and turn it into a profit. Then you'll find that one good thing will lead to another."

His ability to turn anything into an opportunity for profit was just one of the many things that Armand liked to boast about. Another was his colossal energy. At night, when he was not phoning all over the world, he practiced deep-relaxation exercises, believing that this trancelike state would relax him for the next day's business. Convinced that the ability to project an image of superhuman strength was a negotiating ploy that would enable him to maintain the upper hand, he had trained himself to nap anywhere for a specific length of time. If he became tired during a meeting, he excused himself, went into another room, slept for a few minutes, and returned invigorated. Every employee who spent any time with him was amazed that the minute he concluded a business transaction, he often put himself to sleep and awoke exactly when he wanted to, without any concern about where he was or whom he was with. He explained this ability by declaring that his body was just like a corporation. "I'm the chief executive. Each of my systems is a subsidiary. Every division is under my complete control."

I don't know who was more surprised, he or I, when that corporation rebelled a few weeks later. During a lunchtime interview with *Wall Street Journal* Los Angeles bureau chief Mitch Gordon, Armand became nauseated and complained of severe pain. When I called his doctor, Jack Magit, he advised me to call an ambulance and get Armand to the hospital. Even though he could hardly walk, Armand insisted on driving himself to the hospital—in his Rolls-Royce convertible with the top down. Afraid that he might lose consciousness, I followed closely. At the hospital he learned that he had suffered a gallbladder attack but refused to undergo surgery, declaring that he was going to "tough it out."

Over the next eight years Armand would suffer a series of attacks, including one so severe that he banged his head hard on the wall as he collapsed unconscious onto the floor. Finally, he conceded that one of his "systems" had stopped taking orders from its "chief executive" and grudgingly checked into the hospital.

A few days after his first gallbladder attack, I found Armand sitting quietly at his desk. I thought he might be in pain, but there was something else on his mind. "My son Julian has been arrested on a misdemeanor charge," he told me. "They say he was drunk and threatened his wife and a neighbor with a gun. I've already called the lawyers. They'll have the charges dismissed for lack of evidence. What I don't understand is why Julian is always armed. Why does he feel in danger?"

It was one of Armand's rare moments of reflection, and he began to talk about his first wife, Olga. "She lives out here someplace, but I never see her," he said. "She sang gypsy folk songs professionally, and when I met her in 1925, she was one of Moscow's great cabaret stars. I had never seen anyone so beautiful. She was married, and she divorced her husband to marry me.

"Unfortunately, she was a White Russian, the daughter of a czarist general and Russian to the core. When I brought her to America, she couldn't speak English and refused to adjust. That discouraged me, and we drifted apart. She moved to Hollywood and resumed her singing career and raised Julian out here. I've had nothing but grief and trouble from him from that day on."

In a later conversation with Victor, he confirmed that Olga's father had been a czarist general, adding that Olga had been a Bolshevik and had convinced her father to join the Bolshevik Party in order to save his life. "Olga was trained as an agent of the OGPU and was one of a number of strikingly beautiful White Russian women assigned to have affairs with Westerners and to spy on them. The goal of these Kremlin ladies was to marry Westerners and be taken to the West so they could recruit other Soviet émigrés and spy on those who might be plotting counterrevolutionary activities.

"By nature the Russians are highly conspiratorial. So is Armand. Nine years in Russia taught him to be as harsh and merciless as the most highly placed Soviet intelligence agent. Armand married Olga because he knew it would be good for business. Then he decided to divorce her. But the Soviets wanted to get Olga into the United States and they insisted that he stay married to her until he brought her home with him. That's how Olga wound up alone and stuck with a kid in a strange country, without much money and absolutely no skills."

Armand hated Richard Nixon. When the vice president was nominated for president by acclamation at the Republican National

Convention on July 27, 1960, he went into a frenzy. "I wouldn't vote for that bastard for dogcatcher! I'm going to do whatever it takes to help Jack Kennedy beat him into the ground."

Hammer didn't deal in issues and didn't explain why he loathed Nixon, but it seemed safe to assume that he considered any violently anticommunist politician an enemy. Therefore, he was relieved when John F. Kennedy achieved his slim victory on November 8. Armand had stayed in the cattle business after his divorce from Angela Zevely in 1954, and his partner remained Senator Albert Gore, Sr. of Tennessee, a loyal friend, who had defended Armand against accusations of attempted bribery on the floor of the U.S. Senate. The next day he placed calls to Gore and Jimmy Roosevelt, asking them to get President Kennedy's official approval for him to travel to the USSR and have a face-to-face meeting with Nikita Khrushchev.

Another thing that was on his mind that day was Samuel Yorty's Los Angeles mayoral victory. Armand remained expressionless as I reminded him that during Yorty's tenure as a California state assemblyman, he had been one of the sponsors of the resolution that had created the California Assembly's Un-American Activities Committee and had led the fight to cleanse the State Relief Administration of Communists. Hammer made a number of phone calls, which enabled him to compile a list of Yorty's attributes. Yorty swam and played paddle tennis, was a reader of biographies, and held conservative political views but also supported some liberal causes. Armand had printed in block letters at the bottom of the list: MOTHER IS A DEVOUT IRISH CATHOLIC YORTY WANTS TO BE GOVERNOR. Clearly, Armand intended to court Yorty and had figured out a strategy. Next, he set his sights on city administrative officer C. Erwin Piper, and when Piper and he became friends, he had Piper introduce him to the mayor.

A week or so after President Kennedy's inauguration, Senator Gore told Armand that the new secretary of commerce, Luther Hodges, had expressed interest in Armand's proposed trip to the USSR, but the only security clearance he was going to receive was one that allowed him to travel as a private citizen. Therefore, he could not stack the cards in his favor with Khrushchev by saying he was traveling under the aegis of the American government.

Although Armand had never met Kennedy, he kept repeating that the president had asked him personally to see what he could do to establish better trade relations with Russia. Khrushchev had refused to meet with almost all Westerners over the twenty months since the Soviets had shot down a U.S. U-2 spy plane but had welcomed Kennedy to office by freeing the plane's crew, and Armand was convinced that he was going to have access.

"When Khrushchev deposed Malenkov six years ago, he declared himself Lenin's disciple and successor," he told me. "Then he discredited Stalin at the Twentieth Party Congress and restored even more glory to Lenin. But Khrushchev never met Lenin, and I have. Lenin was my friend, not his. I went to Lenin's funeral; he didn't. I've got letters from Lenin to prove we were friends, and I'm going to take them along. Lenin is the Soviets' only universal and durable ideal, and I knew the man, not the symbol. Khrushchev is going to be thrilled to meet me."

Victor was equally convinced. "Armand was very jealous when Eleanor Roosevelt was one of the first Westerners to go to Russia to meet Khrushchev," he said. "Then Eleanor refused to invite Armand to Hyde Park when Khrushchev repaid her visit in 1959. The fact that I was there and he wasn't drove Armand crazy." He added that he had sneaked a call from Hyde Park to *New York Post* gossip columnist Leonard Lyons and asked him to print a column item about the meeting. "Armand got even more upset when he read about Khrushchev and me in the gossip columns," Victor said.

"During the 1920s," he continued, "we did a lot of business with Khrushchev's deputy prime minister, Anastas Mikoyan, when he was just the local party secretary. Mikoyan will know in a minute that Armand is determined to relive his youth in the Soviet Union, relive his Lenin fantasy with Khrushchev, and make another fortune while he's at it. Mikoyan is going to march him into Khrushchev's office, Armand is going to start proving to Khrushchev that he'll do anything he wants, and we're going to be back in business."

Armand went to Russia, and, as Victor had predicted, on February 17, two days after his reunion with Mikoyan, Khrushchev sent for him. Armand was jubilant. He told me that during their "long" meeting in Khrushchev's office in the Kremlin, which they conducted in Russian, he and the general secretary had discussed a number of high-level economic and political issues. According to Armand, the Soviet leader also had given him a personal message for the White House.

He picked up a gold automatic pencil topped by a ruby in the shape of a star. "Khrushchev gave this to me because I established the first pencil factory in Russia," he said. "Khrushchev learned to write using a pencil marked HAMMER. Everybody in Russia did. That's one reason why everyone in Moscow knows who I am."

He couldn't wait to start talking to the press about his trip. But Armand's tendency to mouth Communist propaganda led me to suggest that I position him as an unofficial diplomat. I hoped this approach would help me smooth over any negative reactions to the things he might say.

At that time newspapers were wary about printing anything that might contradict official government positions, and I expected resistance to interviewing Hammer because he had traveled to the USSR as a private citizen. But the foreign affairs editor at the *Los Angeles Examiner* was fascinated by the idea of interviewing someone who had actually been inside the Kremlin and had met the Soviet leader. After I obtained a promise that the story would be in print the following morning, which would not allow the paper to do too much checking and dig up any information about the Hammer family's background, I told him to send over a reporter.

Just before the interview I looked Armand in the eye. "Khrushchev isn't Albert Schweitzer, Armand," I said. "Don't praise him to the skies. Only discuss the issues that came up at the meeting."

He did splendidly. Still, there was a difficult moment when the reporter asked in all seriousness, "Did you ever think of suggesting that the solution to the Soviet Union's economic problems might be the initiation of some form of free enterprise?"

Armand bristled. "Khrushchev is a dedicated Communist. He'll never change, and neither will his people. The capitalists and the Communists have got to learn to get along so that we can all live in peace. I've always been a man of peace, and that's the real reason why I went to Russia."

The next morning a large photograph of Hammer holding his giant-sized Russian pencil souvenir, accompanied by a lengthy interview, appeared on the front page of the *Examiner*. This story enabled me to get the wire services to conduct interviews. A week or two later *The New York Times* concluded that Armand's trip was newsworthy and printed its own version. Thus the groundwork was laid to begin establishing Hammer as the only private citizen in the entire world to whom the Russian leadership spoke freely.

Even though Armand said he had a message from Khrushchev for President Kennedy, it appeared that the president was in no rush to receive it. After six months of overtures and a telegram or two, Jimmy Roosevelt escorted Armand to the White House, but Armand was not invited into the Oval Office and instead delivered his message at a "brief unscheduled meeting." Victor told me that Armand had caught JFK by surprise in a hallway.

The next day Armand said to me, "Jack Kennedy just appointed me his unofficial roving economics envoy."

I did not announce the "appointment" to the press.

A few days after his return from Moscow, Armand and I fell into a discussion about Occidental's future, and I told him that no matter how much publicity I generated, I could go only so far. "Oxy's growth is going to remain limited as long as its production is exclusively domestic."

"Exactly," Armand agreed. "Oxy has got to be a growth company, and I want that growth to be dramatic. I've got to obtain some overseas oil fields for us."

Whereas I had been merely theorizing, Armand was never one for daydreams, and he confided that he had already launched a plan to take Occidental into Libya.

In 1959 a major oil discovery had occurred in the Jebel Zelten area of the desert country. Subsequently, the Seven Sisters, the World's seven largest international oil companies—Gulf, Mobil, Socal, Texaco, British Petroleum, Royal Dutch/Shell, and Standard Oil Company of New Jersey (which would become Exxon in 1972) —had won drilling rights, and each had made a successful strike. The Seven Sisters controlled 80 percent of all international oil production outside the Communist Bloc countries and ensured high profits for themselves by setting prices and by working in tandem to determine the growth rate of the international oil supply. These gigantic companies were classified as "international majors," while companies like Occidental were classified as either "domestics" or "international independents." The majors were determined to discourage the independents because the smaller companies, with their far lower overhead, were capable of selling oil at cut-rate prices.

"While I was overseas," Armand told me, "I went to Libya to case the oil situation, learn as much as I could about the country and its people, and get a sense of how they operate. I've already established an Oxy subsidiary, OXYLIBYA, to keep me informed. In that way I'll be able to take charge quickly and start operations immediately if—and when—Oxy acquires drilling rights."

A few days later Armand introduced me to a strange little man he described as his "Arabist consultant" and an "OXYLIBYA operative." The man spoke Arabic and understood Arabic customs, and Armand was flying him back and forth to Libya "to obtain the latest information."

"You've got to hand it to the doctor," Gene Reid conceded. "Oxy's having a modest domestic success, but the doctor's convinced it's ready to compete against Big Oil. Some people put the cart before the horse. He's put the cart on the moon."

Occidental's merger with Reid was eighteen months old, and Reid was yet to deliver anything of major importance. But Armand remained optimistic, recalling that Reid had drilled forty dry holes in a row before he had merged with Occidental, and had never given up. In fact, major strikes were just around the corner. After Occidental acquired a 50 percent working interest in the Arbuckle Extension gas field in Colusa County, California, Reid and his oil and gas boys drilled seven successful gas wells. The next day Armand laid plans to initiate a public offering and to move Occidental from the Pacific Coast Stock Exchange to the American Stock Exchange.

At the end of September 1961, Texaco drilled a test well on the Lathrop field, a 5,600-acre property in San Joaquin County, California, which came up dry. Texaco abandoned the site, but oil and gas boy Bob Teitsworth insisted that his geological studies demonstrated that Texaco had neither drilled in the right place nor drilled deeply enough. Armand unhesitatingly trusted the passion of a knowledgeable young man attempting to buck conventional wisdom and ordered the Oil and Gas Division to lease the field and drill a test well.

"If big Texaco failed," I asked, "why should little Oxy have any better luck?"

Armand replied, "If we haven't got the courage to take calculated risks, we'll never get anywhere."

On October 3, the oil and gas boys not only struck gas but also discovered that they had located the second-largest natural-gas field in California, Occidental had hit the jackpot.

Early the next morning, while I was at *The Wall Street Journal* supervising the release of the story about the Lathrop discovery, Armand called. "I just wanted to make sure you're where you're supposed to be," he said. "This is very big news, and there can't be a second's delay. Wait until you see what this does to our stock price. Our little company finally has an exciting future!"

"The story is already on the Dow Jones ticker," I replied with some annoyance. "I'd appreciate it if you never check up on me again."

He hung up.

The next day I presented Armand with a set of the news stories generated by my release and remarked casually that Bob Teitsworth deserved a lot of credit for the discovery. He stared angrily at me. "Teitsworth's guess was exactly on target. But *I'm* the one who took the chance, produced the risk money, and gave the go-ahead. *I'm* the one who deserves the credit."

From that moment on, it became company policy that no matter what anyone else did, Armand received *all* of the credit. He also ordered the staff to refrain from discussing with one another any achievements that might be credited to someone else.

At the end of fiscal 1961, Occidental climbed out of the loss column for the first time and reported a net income of $947,769 on sales of $5.3 million. Armand was euphoric. "Our profits are going to continue to grow and grow. We'll be able to launch more drilling projects, make more acquisitions, and consider the possibility of paying dividends. And the people who took the risk of privately investing in the Lathrop field program are going to become rich—or richer! In order to succeed, a businessman has to have a love affair with money. That's why I'm such a brilliant businessman. Money is my first, last, and only love."

5.

J.F.K. CALLING

I was with Armand on November 7, 1962, when he got the news that Eleanor Roosevelt had died. The first thing he did was to pick up the phone and begin the search for potential buyers for the Roosevelt family home on Campobello.

Later that week, my wife, Virginia, and I joined Ireene and Victor for dinner, and the conversation inevitably turned to Campobello and Armand's long relationship with the Roosevelt family. Victor commenced the tale by explaining that after FDR's death, the five Roosevelt children had gotten into a huge squabble about their father's possessions. "There were more than six thousand items involved—china, silver, glassware, jewelry, ship models, paintings, photographs, things like that. Eleanor resolved the problem of FDR's inheritance by keeping the china and glass as her fair share and dividing the rest equally.

"Among the items was an authentic Fabergé music box worth five thousand dollars that Armand had given FDR in 1933 on the day the U.S. announced that it was resuming diplomatic relationships with the Soviets. Walter Duranty had been Armand's houseguest before going to Washington to cover the announcement for *The New York Times* and he'd already met FDR. Armand knew that Walter's weakness was young girls, and he supplied him with a steady stream. No wonder Walter couldn't say no when Armand begged to tag along and decided to give the music box to FDR. In 1951, when Elliott Roosevelt came to the Hammer Galleries because he needed money and wanted to sell his part of the inheritance, he sold the Fabergé music box back to us for twenty grand. I hadn't even wanted Armand to give it away in the first place."

Ireene picked up the story and told us that after Armand had made the decision to promote the sale of Elliott's inheritance as an offering from "The Private Collection of Franklin and Eleanor

Roosevelt," there was an uproar in the press because reporters objected to the commercialization of the memory of a beloved leader. "Eleanor was used to being reviled in the press and ignored the fuss," Ireene said, "but she was concerned about Elliott. She continued to support the Left, but her experience as a U.N. delegate had convinced her that the Soviets were standing in the way of disarmament and that they were bullies. Then FDR Jr. told her that Elliott had fallen under the influence of the Communist propaganda apparatus. Eleanor believed that Armand had used the fact that he and Elliott both admired Russia to manipulate him in order to take advantage of him and grossly underpay him. She was quite upset."

In order to defuse the criticism, Armand then decided to turn over a part of the proceeds from the sale to Mrs. Roosevelt's pet charity, the Infantile Paralysis Fund, and invited her to attend the invitational preview. It was a ploy he had tried unsuccessfully once before, in 1940, when he had attempted to convince Mrs. Roosevelt to attend an exhibit of czarist treasures at the Hammer Galleries. "Eleanor never believed Armand was a genuine philanthropist," Ireene said. "She viewed him as a publicity hound who wanted to use her to call attention to himself and beef up his claims about his friendship with FDR."

Virginia and I had never met Ireene before, but we instantly recognized her soothing speaking voice from her days as a radio star. What surprised us was her brassy light-brown hair color and heavily applied makeup. Twelve years had passed since she had been blacklisted, and Victor's interest had waned as her fame diminished. But it had not stopped him from frittering away and making bad investments with Ireene's $1.5 million earnings until the formerly wealthy ex–radio star had become dependent on her husband and reduced to performing his favorite gypsy folk songs at his dinner parties. Ireene didn't say much during dinner, but she had a great deal to drink.

Victor told us next that Mrs. Roosevelt had wanted to convert Campobello into a family club with the family members dividing the costs of its upkeep. But eventually she sold the estate to Elliott for $12,000, with the proviso that it remain in the family. In 1952, a year after the Hammer Galleries' sale of the Roosevelt family's artifacts, Elliott, again in desperate need of cash, sold Campobello to the Hammer brothers for $5,000. "Armand always says that FDR left Campobello to Elliott," Victor said. "He doesn't want people to know that he got it for $7,000 less than Elliott paid his mother. Eleanor was livid, but Armand convinced Elliott he was going to turn the house into a shrine to FDR, which is what Elliott told Eleanor in order to calm her down."

Despite Armand's promise to maintain the property, Victor related that over the years Armand had tried to sell it but had been dissuaded by the threat of criticism in the press. "He says he spent hundreds of thousands of dollars restoring the house," Victor said, "but the actual cost was sixty thousand, which Harry and I shared with him. Armand agreed to the improvements only because it would help get him a better price."

Mrs. Roosevelt traveled to Campobello in 1957 to inspect the restoration on the condition that Armand not be present while she was there. Her reaction was dismay. Admission was being charged; all of the family's personal possessions were tagged and on sale; a line of cheap commemorative souvenirs was also available.

Her anger was compounded by Armand's treatment of Dr. David Gurewitsch, her close friend and frequent traveling companion since 1947. Gurewitsch had accompanied Mrs. Roosevelt to Moscow when she went to see Khrushchev and had taped their discussion. Subsequently, he had placed his own spoken English translation over Khrushchev's voice. "Armand owned the Mutual Broadcasting System at the time," Victor said, "and he offered David five hundred dollars to play the tape over the air. He also promised to pay for the time it took David to make his voice sound clear on the tape. The job took hours and hours. Then Armand refused to pay the overtime. When Eleanor complained, he volunteered to cough up another hundred dollars. She became so upset she could hardly talk."

In August 1962, three months before her death, stipulating again that Armand was not to visit her, Mrs. Roosevelt returned to Campobello to dedicate a bridge named after FDR. Armand turned up anyway and convinced her to write to President Kennedy to ask that the U.S. government buy Campobello from the Hammer brothers. In her letter, Mrs. Roosevelt suggested the conversion of the grounds into an FDR memorial park and the house into a conference center bearing the late president's name.

It was Victor's hunch that Armand was going to continue to pressure the government into buying Campobello. Otherwise, he would have to weigh the size of the tax deduction he could claim if he donated the estate to the government against the profits he would receive from selling it to a private party. "Armand told Khrushchev that JFK was his good friend and that JFK was going to help him help the Soviet Union," Victor said. "You can bet that Armand's going to find a way to use the estate to get the president on his side."

Over the next few days I had a chance to observe Armand in action with Victor and Ireene, and he was never less than cordial to both of them. But in private he confided his dislike of his sister-in-law. "She believes in numerology, which is a lot of bunk, and spells her first name with an extra 'e' because her numerologist told her that it would bring her good luck, good health, prosperity, or some crap like that. One time, she and her pet poodle left Victor and traipsed off to Paris so that she could study French. She couldn't speak French when she left. She couldn't speak it when she came home a year later." Some time later I learned that Armand, in fact, had ordered Victor to get Ireene to leave the country for six weeks because he was using Victor as a go-between in his negotiations with the Mutual Broadcasting System and was determined to operate in secrecy.

"I've never liked Ireene," he continued. "She has a daughter, Nancy, whom I don't consider a part of the family. I don't like her either. Victor's first wife, Vava, cheated on him and it was a terrible shock for Victor. I never liked Vava or their son, Armasha. He grew up in the Soviet Union, but he's so spoiled, amoral, and materialistic that you'd never know it."

In 1960 Armand had traded a large donation for a membership on the board of trustees of the Eleanor Roosevelt Cancer Foundation. After the U.S. government founded the Eleanor Roosevelt Memorial Foundation, he sent word to the White House staff that he was willing to make another large donation in return for a membership on the board of governors, and he received a presidential appointment to serve a term. I was ordered to tell the press that President Kennedy had personally requested his services.

Armand bought these honorary posts not only for their publicity value but also to network the other trustees and board members. Through the Eleanor Roosevelt Memorial Foundation, he became close to another member of the board, Myer Feldman, a well-connected Washington lawyer. Feldman was a member of President Kennedy's White House staff, a Kennedy speechwriter, and an adviser to columnists Drew Pearson and Jack Anderson. When he began to suggest ways that Armand might wear down Kennedy's resistance, Armand invited him to join Occidental's army of outside attorneys. His persistence was formidable, and I knew that somehow, some way, he would eventually get to the president.

• • •

The profits from the Lathrop field discovery enabled Occidental to move from its cramped, shabby offices on Beverly Boulevard to a small six-office suite in the Kirkeby Center Building in Westwood. They also triggered a series of offers to sell Armand other companies. But he categorically rejected any that were not energy providers, explaining that his goal was to effect a series of vertical mergers, a combination by common ownership of firms producing the same or similar products.

The acquisition of all of the outstanding capital stock of Signet Oil and Gas Company in 1961 had given Occidental interests in twelve producing oil wells in California and other oil and gas properties in Colorado and Nebraska. Armand moved quickly, acquiring either alone or with partners eight more properties, and drilled eighteen new successful gas wells and three new oil wells. Everywhere he went, he trumpeted each new success, concentrating on the brokers who flogged Occidental stock at the major brokerage houses. He didn't let up until the brokers swore they would start selling large blocks.

After test drilling produced a dry hole, Bud Reid advised Armand against the development of the Kettleman Hills South Dome prospect in Kings County, California, in a joint venture with a group of outside investors. Armand was in the midst of conducting merger talks with another company and feared that the failure of the Kettleman Hills South Dome project would make Occidental less attractive to the company he was wooing. Therefore, even though he had been told by his experts that the result was bound to be another dry hole, he ordered Bud Reid to drill a second well anyway. Reid was shocked by Armand's desire to deceive his investors and to waste their money and told him so, but Armand scoffed at what he considered Reid's excessive virtuousness. "They're all in the fifty percent bracket or higher, and they're going to be able to write off their losses with a smile," he said. "And what they don't know won't hurt them." Reid was left with no choice but to drill the well, which, as predicted, was unsuccessful.

A gas or oil well discovery is legitimate news; the commencement of drilling, which is called "spudding in," isn't. Oil companies spud in all the time, and the result is often failure. Because Occidental was so small and insignificant, I had to fight for every inch of column space. Therefore, whenever Occidental spudded in, I issued a dramatic news release packed with quotes from Hammer and loaded with geological terms to give it authenticity. These releases were often printed verbatim by those editors who did not understand the unnewsworthiness of a lowly spud. But they eventually led business page readers to perceive Armand as an intrepid explorer and someone to root for. I invented a slogan, "Go with Hammer!" that "fans" could use to cheer him on.

Bit by bit a cult was forming, and Armand began to receive letters from shareholders and strangers addressing him as if they knew him personally. There were also phone calls, and the staff members who responded on Armand's behalf invariably concluded their conversations by conveying warm regards from "the doctor." This cult hungered for a business hero who satisfied the requirements of the Faust legend: a capitalist with the fame and charisma of a movie star and a thirst for power and wealth that made him willing even to sell his soul to achieve his dreams, and that's how I decided to sell him.

An occasional Occidental executive objected to Armand's Faustian streak. Behind closed board room doors, the company's new chief counsel, former deputy attorney general of California Robert Rose, accused him of substantially bloating the size of Occidental's oil and gas reserves, announced that he could not be a party to defrauding the public, and enraged Armand when he produced accurate figures to substantiate his claims. After Oil and Gas Division Land Manager Noeth Gillette left the company, Armand moved to rescind Gillette's stock options, but Rose stopped him cold and bluntly told him that his proposal was illegal and grossly immoral.

Armand repaid these objections by subjecting Rose to a series of loyalty tests. When the attorney's four-year-old daughter was rushed to the hospital, Armand became so furious that Rose had dared to leave the office to be with his child that he refused to speak to him. Subsequently, when Rose became ill and was hospitalized, Armand called him, and ordered him to remove the intravenous needle from his arm and report back to work. Rose was vactioning with his family in Palm Springs when Armand insisted that he return to the office and then ignored him once he got there. "He couldn't bear seeing me in a resort that caters to celebrities and rich people," Rose told me. "He thinks that only he should be allowed to go to places like that."

From the first days of Hammer's regime, Occidental had financed its drilling through Armand's fund-raising abilities. Now his plans demanded far larger sums. When the company announced that it was going to begin selling natural gas based on its future production for large sums that were to be paid in full up front, Mutual Life Insurance Company of New York paid $15 million for an eighteen-year supply. At the same time a $3.9 million offering of fifteen-year subordinated convertible debentures was oversubscribed by more than $1 million. Armand's determination and ability to wheel and deal were clearly going to make him and his colleagues very rich, and the first to sense this were the Occidental shareholders, who clamored for a dividend. Armand advised them that the money would be better spent on acquisitions and development. This indication of future growth and even greater profits contented the shareholders and allowed Armand to continue to use all of the money as he saw fit.

At the end of fiscal 1962, Occidental reported net income of $6 million (a staggering increase over the previous year's $947,000) on sales of $13.9 million and declared its first dividend after twenty-eight years, 25 cents cash and 4 percent stock. Although the dividend was small, Armand was convinced that it would be perceived as an indication of bigger and better things to come and would inspire another rise in the stock price—which is exactly what happened.

Armand demanded total loyalty from his staff at Occidental. Corporate treasurer Gladys Loudenslager and Armand's secretary, Dorothy Prell, shared a small office. Dorothy arrived at nine A.M. and often worked by Armand's side until eight or nine at night. Every day she took Hammer's notes and typed up the comments he'd written down in three columns on each side, cross-indexing them by person and subject. In this way he never lost an "opportunity."

Not too long after I joined Occidental, Dorothy told me that she had broken up with her boyfriend because she had no time for him. Although she had the rare ability to placate Armand during his foul moods and was extremely protective of him, he repeatedly tested her devotion by making her endlessly retype correspondence that he declared "was never quite right." As for Gladys, she never placated Armand and he surprisingly allowed her to have her say, even though he referred to her behind her back as "a stubborn old witch."

After toughing out several years together, Dorothy, Gladys, Paul Hebner, the corporate secretary, and I considered ourselves "family." There was never the slightest fear that one of us would discuss the other with Armand. If Armand could count on our compliance and discretion, he took stronger measures to keep his board of directors in line. One day Gladys showed me a series of undated letters of resignation to be signed by all nominees to the board. If Armand wished to oust a director, all he had to do was date the presigned letter. It was an indication that Armand was planning to make a number of major acquisitions and offer places on the board as part of the bait. Therefore, men from outside the company and from his circle of business acquaintances, whom he did not know well or did not know at all and who had not proven their trustworthiness, were going to sit on the board. In order to make sure that these new members would not disagree with him and engage in troublesome deliberations, Hammer had devised this devilish and previously unheard-of measure. Meanwhile, a large corporate expansion was indeed waiting in the wings.

Early in May 1963, Armand offered to donate Campobello to the American and Canadian governments. A few weeks later, he called me at home at seven on a Saturday morning. "Jack Kennedy is going to phone me in exactly two hours to discuss my offer," he said with great excitement. "It's not every day the president gives you a call, and I want to tape-record it. Can you get a sound technician over here who can do it?"

I called a friend who was a recording buff, Bruce Angwin. Amused by the idea of bugging a call from the president, he agreed to head over to the Hammer household. Later Angwin told me the real reason for the call. Canadian Prime Minister Lester Pearson had gone to Hyannis Port the day before to visit the president, and Kennedy had told him about Hammer's gift of Campobello. The two men decided to accept the gift and to make a joint announcement of the donation on Saturday afternoon. They asked Jimmy Roosevelt to get Armand to send them a telegram confirming the gift, and when the telegram did not arrive, Hammer received word by telephone early that morning that he would have to confirm the gift by telephone directly to the president.

With Angwin's recording equipment in place, at nine sharp the call came through and the president immediately brought up the matter of confirmation. Armand volunteered to read him a copy of the telegram while a secretary on the president's end took it down in shorthand. Leaving the president dangling, he dropped the receiver and raced upstairs to search for a copy in his bedroom. After what seemed an eternity, Frances headed upstairs after him.

Finally Armand, empty-handed, came downstairs, picked up the phone, and improvised the contents. Kennedy asked if there were any stipulations. Armand replied that he might occasionally like to use one wing of the house during summers. Kennedy agreed and said that he wanted to accept the donation publicly in honor of the memory of Mrs. Roosevelt and his mother, because they had been good friends.

Armand's chutzpah knew no bounds. He told Kennedy that he knew the president was going to be in Los Angeles on June 7 and invited him to swim in the Hammers' heated indoor swimming pool. Kennedy thanked him, but said he hoped it would be warm enough to swim outside and handed the phone to his press secretary, Pierre Salinger.

As soon as the call was completed, Armand insisted on listening to a playback. Angwin told me everyone looked uncomfortable during the long stretch of dead air at the beginning, but Armand had described it as "a historic pause." On Monday he corraled his key aides at the office and made them listen to the tape. And for days afterward, every time someone visited his home or office, he insisted on playing the tape for them, too. Occasionally, when he was alone, I found him listening to it for his own pleasure. Eventually he put it away, but he never stopped talking about it. Given to wild exaggeration, he embellished the story each time he told it. The last time he related it, just before I left Occidental, he said that he had ordered loudspeakers set up in his house and gathered together a large group to hear the conversation.

Shortly after the president's announcement, I heard from a *Washington Post* reporter who said she had always believed that Mrs. Roosevelt had disliked Hammer and wanted a direct quote from him about the nature of their relationship.

Armand had a foolproof reply. "If Eleanor disliked me, why did she appear as a character witness in my tax fraud case in 1959?"

It was a good question, and the next time I spoke to Victor I asked him about it. He said that Mrs. Roosevelt believed her appearance at the trial was going to be mere window dressing and was convinced that if the government had a case against Hammer, their evidence would prevail. "So Eleanor decided to teach Armand a lesson," Victor said. "She agreed to testify only if he paid David Gurewitsch a fair price for the overtime he owed for work on the Khrushchev tape and apologized to David for being dishonorable and a cheat. After the trial, she told me, 'Your brother got away with not paying the government five hundred thousand dollars, but I'm the first person who forced him to behave with some degree of decency and respect for other human beings. I've had the last laugh.' "

6.

FIRST LENIN;
THEN
KHRUSHCHEV

Armand scheduled Occidental's annual meeting for May 24,
1963, three days after his sixty-fifth birthday. The meeting was to
take place at Maison Jaussaud, a small French restaurant near
Gene Reid's office in Bakersfield. The day before, he handed me a
scrap of paper with an address on it. "Meet me at this motel an
hour before the meeting," he said. "I'll be with the president of the
company Oxy has just acquired. You can take down the details of
this big merger and write your news release on the spot. This is
top secret until I announce the news at the meeting, so don't say
anything to anybody."

When I got to the motel, I found Armand with Lowell Berry,
founder and president of Best Fertilizers Company, a large independent agrichemicals firm based in California and Texas. As I
made notes, Armand told me that Occidental had paid a little more
than $10 million in stock for Best and Berry was to continue on as
president and take a place on Occidental's board. Best had reported sales of $22 million in 1962; Occidental had reported sales
of $14 million. It was indeed "a big merger" for Occidental.

Berry was a slim, conservatively dressed man in his early fifties,
given to understatement and wholly dedicated to his products and
reputation. He had begun his business by mixing chemical fertilizers in his garage, then bagging them and delivering them personally to neighboring farmers. A trained agronomist, he was often
asked for advice about crops, pest control, and soil productivity.

His company's name reflected his pride in his and Best's accomplishments.

Armand was especially intrigued by a Best research project involving atmospheric control devices to preserve perishable goods during transportation. Berry explained that the utilization of nitrogen allowed Best's process to place produce into "a state of suspended animation. A bushel of California strawberries refrigerated this way can be transported cross-country and 'awakened' a week later, looking and tasting as if it had just been picked."

"It sounds like a real money-maker to me," Armand chimed in.

Later, as we waited for the shareholders' meeting to be called to order, I asked Armand if negotiating the acquisition had been difficult. "I gave Berry a lot of stock," he replied. "He's worth a lot more today than he was yesterday, and he knows that sticking with me will make him even richer. He's not going to bat an eye when he finds out I've decided to name his research project the OXY-TROL system."

After Armand announced the acquisition to the eighty-two shareholders in attendance, he explained that he had rejected a number of offers that involved diversification. Then he reeled off his reasons for changing his mind: the Occidental-Best merger was bound to trigger a substantial rise in the stock price and provide funding for even larger acquisitions; it would enable Occidental to use Best's Texas facilities to launch an expansion into Texas's natural-gas fields; and now Occidental could sell large amounts of natural gas from its Lathrop field to a neighboring Best ammonia plant. "One hand is going to wash the other, and both hands are going to make lots of money," he said.

After the applause died down, Armand added that he had seen an enormous amount of hunger on his recent overseas trip and that he and Berry were going to dedicate themselves to doing something about it. It was hard to read Berry's look, but it seemed to be somewhere between skepticism and discomfort.

As Armand had anticipated, many of the shareholders remained behind to wish him a happy birthday. "Go with Hammer!" they cheered as they shook his hand. Lowell Berry was standing next to Armand, and he watched but said nothing. Finally Armand left the room and Berry trailed behind him. From a distance he could have been mistaken for Victor Hammer.

It was the beginning of the era of corporate mergers and acquisitions, and this shortcut to instant expansion was an ideal way for Armand to convert Occidental into a growth company. He relished the prestige, power, and excitement of negotiating. At this time the varied financing tactics and flexible accounting procedures that accompanied merger deals enabled the acquiring companies at least temporarily to declare dramatic increases in earnings after the deals had been concluded.

Armand's new goal became the acquisition of companies that would give Occidental a large, self-sufficient, highly profitable agrichemicals division. As he shopped for agrichemicals companies, streams of industrial lawyers poured in and out of his office. "You look like you've just met with the entire roster of the American Bar Association," I kidded.

"Lawyers are full of crap," he replied. "They're the most negative people in the world. The reason that so many companies run themselves into the ground is because they pay attention to them. Lawyers expect to get paid for saying something can't be done. I make my lawyers tell me how it *can* be done. When you take the risks I do, you're bound to have trouble. Most lawyers say, 'I told you so.' My lawyers say, 'Don't worry. I know how to get you off the hook.' "

Before Armand hired a legal firm, he checked its client list and tended to hire those whose clients he wanted to meet. He also paid large retainers and generous fees, which established his worth as a "good" client and made it even harder for his lawyers to refuse to meet his demands.

Armand made these legal armies an intrinsic part of his negotiation strategy. This process was always launched with a heady dose of personal diplomacy, and the wooing went on for a very long time until he was convinced that he was seen as trustworthy and generous. But when contracts reached the final stage, he would inevitably say that the agreement did not reflect his offer and blame his lawyers, who must have "misunderstood" him. The new contracts would reveal that he was claiming a bigger bite than before. Another round of negotiations would commence, and invariably Armand would obtain more concessions. When the next set of contract revisions appeared, he would again claim that his lawyers had misunderstood him and relaunch the process. This would go on as many times as he could get away with it.

The moment his opponent dug in his heels and refused to budge, Armand would threaten to withdraw. By then his opponent was in so deep, so exhausted by the process, and so distressed by the size of his legal fees, he usually made even more concessions. Thus Hammer invariably achieved his hidden agenda.

In October, Occidental paid $5 million in stock to acquire Jefferson Lake Sulphur Company, the third-largest domestic sulfur producer. A few weeks later, Occidental paid $2.8 million in stock to acquire International Ore & Fertilizer Corporation (INTERORE), a New York–based firm that was the largest marketer of fertilizers in the world. INTERORE had outlets in fifty-nine countries. When Armand networked a young mining engineer, George Brooks, who told him that even though phosphate experts disagreed, there were 30 million tons of high-grade unmined phosphate ore in the Hamilton County section of Florida, Armand concluded on the spot that Brooks was another Bob Teitsworth.

On Brook's recommendation, Occidental acquired a 3,500-acre tract on the Suwannee River. The production of certain phosphate fertilizers depends on combining ground rock phosphate with sulfuric acid to produce a highly concentrated compound, superphosphoric acid (SPA). Armand was so determined to make Occidental a major producer of SPA that he ordered the construction of a huge phosphate-fertilizer complex at the mine site. As soon as the project was announced he sent a telegram to President Kennedy: "I believe our organization will be able to furnish American know-how to help hungry people throughout the world to raise their standard of living which is the best answer to Communism and other oppressive systems endangering peace."

The message had been designed purely to grab the president's attention. "The Communists are always going to be Communists, and the Americans will always be capitalists," he said. "It's not up to us to decide which system is better. That decision belongs to the historians."

The White House did not respond.

Even though he didn't know a great deal about the agrichemicals business, Armand set out to take control of Occidental's trio of agrichemicals acquisitions. He identified the key players in each firm and arranged secret meetings with them. After this genial, grandfatherly old man tempted them with large sums of money, stock options, and other promises for their futures, he was able to establish a mole or two in each company. Whenever Armand was tipped that something had gone wrong, he staged a dramatic confrontation with the offenders. Efficiency was not the issue because the acquired companies were already successful and well run. These episodes were engineered solely as demonstrations that Armand was the only boss.

Nevertheless, some of the employees at the acquired companies were always going to owe their allegiance to their original bosses.

Operating through intermediaries, Armand began approaching experts in the field whose names had been supplied to him by his high-powered attorneys. After he compiled a list of outsiders who would be willing to abandon their jobs and go to work for Occidental or for him personally on a free-lance basis when and if he summoned them, he began to replace those executives he felt would never be loyal to him directly. The result was a systematic undermining of the old managements, but Armand was not fazed by the danger of running these companies into the ground. The only thing that mattered was that he obtained control.

Armand usually maintained his habit of arriving at the office in the middle of the afternoon, but there were days when he stayed at home and ordered his secretary, Dorothy Prell, to tell his callers he was in meetings or out of town. After Dorothy compiled a list of each of INTERORE's twenty-eight foreign offices, along with the name of the head of state in which the office was located, Armand launched a series of overseas excursions, rarely telling anyone where he was going or what he was trying to accomplish.

One of these journeys took him back to Libya so that he could deliver a letter of introduction from Senator Albert Gore to the American ambassador, instructing him to arrange an audience for Armand with Libya's seventy-three-year-old patriarch, King Idris I. Before the meeting Armand met with his OXYLIBYA operatives and learned that King Idris's ancestors were buried in Kufra, an oasis in the central Sahara that lacked the drilling facilities to tap its underground water supply. At their meeting Armand promised King Idris that if Occidental received a grant of concessions in the next oil properties auction, it would drill for water in Kufra and turn the sacred burial ground into bountiful farmland as an enduring memorial to the king's ancestors who lay at rest there.

Before Armand left Libya, his operatives also supplied him with another significant tip. The Libyan Council of Ministers was eager to build an ammonia plant and had sent word that if Occidental committed to such a venture, it stood a good chance of winning concession grants.

One day back in the office, Armand presented me with a photograph of him and a young, good-looking man dressed in an expensive, well-tailored business suit. The man was King Hassan of Morocco, and Armand had just returned from visiting him. "King Hassan is a young man—only thirty-three," he said. "That's why he dresses like an affluent American businessman and why he thinks like one."

These banalities were Armand's way of hiding the true nature of his travels. Morocco's largest industry was the mining of phosphate rock, and he was secretly concluding an agreement with King Hassan that would allow Occidental to construct the world's first high-analysis SPA plant on Moroccan soil. Once the deal was finalized, Armand pointed out that it was Occidental's entry into international fertilizer production and ordered me to publicize it to the hilt. Then he seemed to forget all about it.

Subsequently he reported to the board that he had traveled to Saudi Arabia and had struck an agreement to construct an ammonia plant in the port city of Dammam. The total capital investment was going to be supplied by the Saudis, and Occidental would receive 10 percent of the net profits and INTERORE 5 percent of the gross as marketing agent. The deal called for Occidental to sell the entire output or purchase what could not be sold at the prevailing world price. Citing the decline in international fertilizer prices, Bob Rose questioned the wisdom of placing Occidental in the position of having to buy huge amounts of ammonia, which he believed was going to lead to substantial losses.

Armand flew into a fury, shouted that he was in charge, and announced that he was going to obtain another opinion from an outside consultant. Rose realized there was no use arguing. No outside consultant ever contradicted Hammer. Nor did Rose have any way of knowing that Armand had no desire to build an SPA plant in Morocco and already knew that the deal in Saudi Arabia was going to be unprofitable. Both projects were really PR stunts calculated to convince the Libyans that Occidental had the capability to launch agrichemicals projects in the Arab world.

The year was drawing to a conclusion, and I began to gather information for the next annual report and for the corporate summaries that would soon appear on the nation's financial pages and in business magazines. The year before, I had been forced to make Occidental's meaningless spudding-in activities seem exciting. This year, Occidental's string of acquisitions had more than doubled the company's size, and there was genuine news to report. I was at my desk working on these projects when John F. Kennedy was assassinated on November 22. Armand didn't mention a word about the assassination, and on his yellow pad that day the initials LBJ were printed so big I could read them upside down. Underneath was a list of names, everyone he could think of who could help him make contact with the new president.

A few weeks after Kennedy's death, Hammer began to bombard the Johnson White House with letters. The return mail brought exactly the same form letters any citizen receives when he or she writes to the president. Armand declared that he and the president were carrying on "an important correspondence" and that LBJ wanted him to become an adviser.

Early in January, press secretary George Reedy issued an invitation to all three Hammer brothers to attend a luncheon at the White House to celebrate their donation of Campobello. Armand announced that he had received a personal invitation from the president, adding that he was going to take Mrs. Johnson a gift. He spread a collection of jade earrings, pins, and rings across his desk and asked me to help him choose the most attractive. As I looked them over he told me that he had entered the jade business in 1954 and co-owned Imperial Jade, a mining and merchandising business, and that the jade we were looking at came from one of Imperial's mines in Wyoming. I began to question him further, but he cut me off.

Later I found out that an Imperial Jade director, Joseph Imhoff, was suing him for fraud and that the litigation had been going on for years. There were also speculations that Armand had attempted to use the Russian-speaking employees at the mine to pass messages back and forth between him and the Stalin government.

Armand returned from the White House with a personally inscribed photograph of President Johnson. Although he acted as if he had met with the president in the Oval Office, Victor told me he hadn't.

The New York Stock Exchange grants listings on the Big Board based on the size of a company's earning power and net tangible assets and the value and number of its publicly held shares. Convinced that Occidental met these qualifications, Armand's next decision was to apply for a listing, and the news of Occidental's acceptance made him so excited that he dashed up and down the halls, shouting, "We've made it! We've made it!" It had taken him just seven years to build a three-man corporate shell into a firm that had moved from the Pacific Coast Stock Exchange to the American Stock Exchange and, finally, to the Big Board itself.

On March 3, 1964, I accompanied Frances and Armand and a group of directors and executives to New York City for the listing ceremony, which traditionally allows key members of a corporation to stand on the trading floor, place the first order of their company's stock, and watch the company's symbol appear for the first time on the ticker that runs across the Big Board after the trade is completed. As Armand led us onto the trading floor, a guard refused to allow Frances to join us. Female employees of the exchange were allowed to enter, but there was an unwritten rule that other women, unless they were company directors or executives, had to stand in a balcony overlooking the floor. When Occidental's name appeared on the ticker, we let out a collective cheer, turned as a group, looked up, and waved to Frances. She was cheering, too.

Even by the less stringent standards of 1964, Frances could in no way be described as liberated. Whatever arrangement existed between Armand and her, it seemed to serve them both. Her pleasures consisted of cooking, keeping house, and looking after Armand. Everyone described her as an ideal wife, a gracious hostess, and a thoughtful traveling companion. Even though she and Armand slept in separate bedrooms and there seemed to be no warmth or intimacy in their marriage, their relationship was never less than friendly.

Armand demanded to be the center of attention, and he instructed me never to supply the press with photographs of him with Frances or of Frances alone. If a photographer approached them, he usually stepped away so that she was not in the picture. She was also not to be told if a journalist asked to interview her, nor was such an interview ever to take place. Frances was aware of this, but her manners were impeccable and her concern was directed toward me. Repeatedly she told me that she disliked publicity and asked me to make sure she didn't get any. It was her way of making sure that I was not upset by her husband's selfishness.

That evening Frances and I stood together at a party in New York to celebrate Occidental's Big Board listing. As we watched Armand work the room, she remarked, "My husband has a profound instinct for knowing who's influential, wealthy, powerful, or famous. If you're none of those, he doesn't waste a second on you." There was neither bitterness nor sadness in her tone; on the contrary, she was rather amused and accepting.

Back in Los Angeles I continued work on the annual report, which was going to be larger and more elaborate than previous ones and contain a large photograph of Hammer along with a lengthy report on his accomplishments and adventures. One of Armand's strictest rules was that he see everything before it was made public. When the page proofs arrived I drove to Occidental to give him the first set, but his office door was closed and I put the proofs down on a ledge. A half hour later, I noticed that his door was open and I picked up the proofs and went inside.

Armand was in a rage. "Get this straight!" he shouted. "This is *my* company! I see the proofs—and everything else—first! I thought I could trust you, but I was wrong. I'd rather trust a rattlesnake!" He got up and headed toward me, and for a moment it seemed as if he might strike me. "Nobody gets away with anything around here, and you've been caught red-handed. You handed out proofs to everyone before you gave me mine."

I held the proof set in my hand. "This is the first set I've given anybody," I said. "It's for you."

"You're a double-crosser! I hate double-crossers!" He went to his desk, picked up a proof set, and waved it at me. "Someone gave this to me before you set foot through the door. You passed these proofs out behind my back. Now you've got the nerve to lie to me about it. You make me sick!"

He grabbed me by the arm, shoved me out of his office, tossed the proof set after me, and slammed the door.

It took Gladys Loudenslager only a few minutes to find out what had happened. Another executive had stumbled onto the proofs I had put on the ledge, picked up a set, and given it to Armand. I was so unnerved that Gladys asked me to join her after work for a cup of coffee in order to calm down.

"Everybody's gotten the same treatment from Armand at one time or another," she told me. "On the one hand, he's capable of making the riskiest decisions and toughing anything out. On the other hand, he'll chop off your head over the slightest infraction, even get rid of you, rather than wait until you're in a position to challenge his authority. Don't worry about it. I know where a lot of the skeletons are buried. In fact, I've helped him bury a few."

I had recently found Armand in his office having a conference with an "outside PR firm on special assignment." I never saw these men again and never found out what they had done for him. I don't even know if they were really public relations professionals. It didn't surprise me. Strangers were constantly coming and going and were always "on special assignment." That evening Gladys explained that these men were Armand's personal operatives who carried out secret assignments. They were paid from something she called "the doctor's secret payroll," her catchall phrase for cash stashed in safety deposit boxes in a number of banks and company funds that Armand had transferred into Panamanian, Swiss, and Bahamian bank accounts and placed in paper corporations in Liechtenstein and other countries with similar easy banking laws.

"I'll take care of it," Gladys assured me, referring to Armand's blowup over the proofs.

I had learned that she could.

The following day, when I went to see Armand, I felt a little awkward. He greeted me as if the incident had never happened, picked up the page proofs, and quickly went through them with me in a businesslike fashion. When he was finished, he said, "I'm working on the biggest deal in history: a one-billion-dollar fertilizer agreement with the Russians."

"Have the terms been set?" I asked, remembering the Moroccan SPA plant that had never been built.

He had roughed out the basic terms on a yellow legal pad. Occidental was to build as many as ten fertilizer plants in the USSR, each costing $100 million to construct. It would also sell agrichemicals to the Soviets and drill for natural gas in Kamchatka Peninsula in Siberia.

"How are you going to raise the billion dollars?" I asked.

"I'm going to go to the Export-Import Bank."

The Export-Import Bank provides financing for U.S. trade overseas by granting easy credit to American companies doing business abroad and to the purchasing nations. However, the Soviets were barred from participating in the lending program, and exceptions required presidential approval. In the context of the Cold War, the funding of a one-billion-dollar deal with the Soviets did not seem like the sort of project President Johnson would choose to endorse, especially in an election year.

Armand remained optimistic. "My friend Albert Gore is the head of the Senate Foreign Relations Committee. He's going to bear down on LBJ. But history is on my side. The NATO countries have an agreement that the Russians can't obtain trade credits for a period longer than five years, but nobody wants to lose out on a business opportunity. Over the past year France, Italy, and England have extended credits for longer terms. Now there's a lot of pressure from the U.S. business community to open up the market. My friends in Congress tell me they're working on a study that will recommend the lifting of all restrictions on U.S. credits and exports to the Russians. I'm one of the first to know about this liberalization movement. I want to be the first to benefit from it."

"How do you think the shareholders will respond?" I asked.

"As the developer, Oxy is entitled to take a piece off the top and get a percentage of the profits. We'll also make money selling fertilizer to the Russians. I've even sent a team to Siberia to make sure we can get the natural gas out of the ground. Opening up this vast, unexplored market is going to be immensely profitable for Oxy.

The shareholders don't care where their dividends come from as long as they're hefty ones. They're going to be thrilled."

When Victor and I talked about Armand's plans, he told me that after Armand had reminded Khrushchev at their 1961 meeting that he had fed the Russian people with $1 million worth of grain in 1921, Khrushchev had asked him to feed them again by building the fertilizer plants. "Let's face it," Victor said with a laugh. "Armand's merely listening to orders. He kept insisting that he was against diversification. Then he saw Khrushchev and he plunged Oxy into the agrichemicals business, and began telling everyone that his sole motive was diversification. Why do you think he was so determined to meet with JFK and now with LBJ? He made a promise to Khrushchev, and now he's got to find a way to get Occidental to keep it.

The real reasons for the speed with which Armand had built an agrichemicals division now became clear to me. He *was* attempting to repeat history by reenacting what he perceived were charitable acts on the behalf of the Russian people. He wanted to impress Khrushchev the way he believed he had impressed Lenin. He was convinced that he would make even more money doing business with the Russians during the economic boom of the 1960s than he had made during the 1920s. Those actions reflected his global vision—and his monumental selfishness.

7.

AGENT OF INFLUENCE

During his next trip to Moscow Armand presented his plan to the Soviet leadership and reported that Khrushchev had responded favorably. "He's manipulating me so that he can crack open trade credit restrictions against the Russians," he said. "And I'm manipulating him so that I can corner a large piece of the unexplored world market for Oxy."

Armand's strategy was to use the press to plant the idea that the Occidental-Soviet fertilizer deal was a fait accompli, which he hoped would discourage the kind of acrimonious public debate that would eliminate any hope of presidential approval. So he told reporters that he had gone to Moscow to meet with Soviet Minister of Culture Yekaterina Furtseva, the first woman ever to be a member of the Politboro. As a result of Khrushchev's policy of détente and peaceful coexistence, he had received permission from Furtseva to launch the first U.S.-Soviet art exchange in history. The Hammer Galleries represented Grandma Moses, and after the Pushkin Museum mounted an exhibition of her paintings, the Hammer Galleries would respond by offering an exhibition of paintings by septuagenarian Russian painter Pavel Korin.

According to Armand, Furtseva had become so excited by the prospect that she had taken him to Khrushchev, and he and Khrushchev had found themselves agreeing to the fertilizer deal as another act of altruism with a little business on the side. He did not mention that *he* had been the one to suggest the art exchange to Furtseva after she had complained that the State Department had refused to allow the Red Army Chorus to go to the United States because it believed that past visits had included KGB agents, and that Furtseva had agreed with Armand that the art exchange could be the first step toward changing the State Department's mind.

One thing Armand did not tell me, but Victor did, was that his brother had become romantically involved with Furtseva, whom he described as "a tough cookie." "Our mother was a strong, domineering woman and she had a real influence on Armand. He's always been attracted to 'tough mommas,' " he said. "Furtseva's almost as tough as Mama Rose."

In July 1964, Barry Goldwater received the Republican presidential nomination. His conservative rhetoric and fervent anticommunism irritated Armand at the best of times. Now he realized that President Johnson was going to have to move farther to the right to counter the inevitable Republican campaign charges of being soft on communism, and the more to the right he moved, the harder it would be to obtain presidential approval for the fertilizer project.

Armand launched a series of phone calls to send the word to the president that he planned to be a major campaign supporter, speaking to, among others, Texas oilman and Johnson supporter John Mecom, whom Armand had put into the cattle business in the early 1950s, and Washington attorney Myer Feldman, who was directing Johnson's "anticampaign," designed to provoke and humiliate Barry Goldwater.

Around this time I was sitting with Armand in his office when a tall, slender, handsome man stepped into the room, put his arms around him, and kissed him on the lips in the style of a Russian son greeting his father. This was my first glimpse of thirty-five-year-old Julian Hammer. Unlike his perpetually rumpled father, Julian was immaculately groomed and dressed and a large "Goldwater for President" button was pinned on his lapel.

Armand's reaction was predictable. "What's the matter with you? Take that stupid button off!"

"I think Goldwater's a good man," Julian said.

I stepped outside.

From that day on Julian began to appear at the office on a regular basis. He always wore his Goldwater button and frequently brought Goldwater campaign literature with him, and his car was festooned with colorful Goldwater bumper stickers. These visits took the form of a ritual. Armand and Julian always kissed in a display of genuine affection, Hammer then berated his son about his Goldwater paraphernalia, and Julian seemed to enjoy every minute of it.

By nature the oil business is politically conservative, and many Occidental staffers secretly supported Goldwater. But Julian's politics had less to do with a deep commitment than with a belated adolescent desire to separate himself from his father by disagreeing with him on an issue Armand held dear. Although he was pleasant and polite, Julian was also remote and somewhat melancholy and seemed to me to be a textbook example of the rudderless son of an overwhelming father.

Julian had been married for ten years to Glenna Sue Ervin, and they had two children, a nine-year-old son, Michael Armand, and a seven-year-old daughter, Casey. Julian had also adopted Ervin's young daughter by a prior marriage. Her name was Sue, and while I often found Michael and Casey playing at Armand's house under the supervision of Frances, I never saw Sue there because Armand did not consider the child a legitimate member of the Hammer family.

In order to instill at least some sense of responsibility in Julian, who was accountable for the welfare of three children, Armand decided to hire him as a part-time art director. My agency handled Occidental's advertising activities, and I was involved with the projects Armand threw to his son. My work load was so great that I often met with Julian at his home at night, and he usually had a drink in his hand. One night, when my car was in the shop, he volunteered to drive me home. En route he opened the glove compartment, and I spotted a gun. Julian told me matter-of-factly that he was always armed.

As we began to spend time together, Julian became forthcoming about his life. He described himself as having been raised by "two exceptionally neurotic women," his natural mother, Olga, and his paternal grandmother, Mama Rose, and one "nonexistent" father, Armand. "Mother is an aristocratic White Russian and never lets anyone forget it," he said. "She has a dark and moody Russian temperament and a tendency to become depressed." Olga had found life in the United States difficult, Julian told me. She clung to her foreign ways and resisted becoming Americanized.

Caterpillar Tractors was among the American companies Armand had represented in the USSR, and soon after his return to the United States in 1932, he had discovered that Caterpillar was attempting to salvage its Soviet business, which had been jeopardized by Stalin's plans for nationalization. After persuading Caterpillar to hire him as a consultant, Armand had moved Olga and Julian to Peoria, Illinois—Caterpillar headquarters—for a year and a half, deposited them in a house paid for by Caterpillar, and then busied himself with other activities. "Eventually, Caterpillar suspected that the Soviets were trying to steal their methods, and Armand's consultancy came to an end. He moved the family to New York, but Olga and Julian were stuck up in the country or down in Palm Beach, and Armand was almost never around.

"I was thirteen when my parents divorced," Julian said. "Mother's alimony was three hundred dollars a month. Another woman in her situation would have received a great deal more. She's always been very talented, and we headed to Hollywood, where she sang in Russian cabarets and worked in the movies playing gypsies. She hasn't had a happy or easy life. She's not going to have an easy death, either. She has cancer."

Armand hadn't wanted the responsibility of raising Julian, but he enjoyed making Olga unhappy by demanding that Julian be shipped back and forth between her and Mama Rose in Scarsdale, New York. Julian's reaction to his grandmother was no different from anyone else's: Mama Rose's determination to control his every move left him exhausted.

"The only things I remember about Dad from those days were the times he'd invite me out," he said. "The day would come, I'd be all excited, but he never remembered. He'd say, 'I haven't got time' or 'Something came up.' Dad likes making you hang by your fingernails while you wait to see if the other shoe is going to drop. I was no exception.

"He's always wanted me to a big business success like him. When I was about to enter Marshall College in West Virginia, he said to me, 'When I was a college student, I made a million dollars on the side. I expect you to do the same.' How would you have felt if that kind of pressure had been put on you? It's never let up."

One Saturday night Armand called and told me some unsettling news. Julian had scheduled a meeting with a free-lance graphic designer at the office that morning and had held the artist captive at gunpoint for hours.

"Julian said that the phones were bugged and took them apart one by one," Armand recounted. "Then he said that the office was bugged and ripped it apart. He even tore down sections of the ceiling. Finally, he let the man go."

The artist was not going to press charges, but Armand was concerned that the press might get hold of the story, and he wanted me to have a statement ready.

On Monday morning, the artist was still shaking. "I really didn't know whether or not he'd pull the trigger. I just sat there trembling for hours not knowing if I was going to live or die." When I relayed this conversation to Armand, he seemed almost not to hear it. "Julian needs psychiatric care," he murmured offhandedly. Then he turned to other matters.

At the end of July, a strike by Best workers shut down Occidental's ammonia plant in Lathrop, California. Afraid that the Soviets were going to think that he couldn't control his business, Armand ordered Lowell Berry to settle the strike at any cost and get the men back to work. Rather than set a precedent that could create greater problems during future contract negotiations, Berry urged Armand to wait out the strike until the workers ran out of money and the union had no choice but to settle.

Armand had no interest in this long-range approach and threatened to take matters into his own hands unless the strike was quickly brought to a halt. I sat beside Berry a few days later on a return flight from Bakersfield. Reticent by nature, he was so upset he spoke openly about the tactics Armand had used to acquire Best.

"The doctor poured on the charm," he told me. "He called me everywhere and kept telling me how much he wanted to go into business with me. He even told me that I was the son he never had. I didn't know then that he already had a son. Then he dangled an amazing deal in front of me that was impossible to turn down. As soon as he had me, he lost interest in me and began mucking up everything I'd accomplished over my lifetime. I've always prided myself on my integrity. I've done plenty to solve the problem of world hunger by making good products, but I don't brag about it. The doctor's an egomaniacal money man who plays a dirty game and then keeps sending out bulletins that he's a saint."

True to his word, Armand met with the strikers, worked out the broad outlines of a settlement, then told Berry to conclude the negotiations. True to his word, Berry refused. At the time Bob Rose was working in Occidental's New York office. Armand ordered him to fly back to Los Angeles, fire Berry, and then return to New York. It was Rose's impression that Armand couldn't do it himself because even he was aware of how miserably he had treated Berry. After Berry was fired, he filed a $12 million suit against Occidental, claiming that this sum was owed him in future salary and stock options. Armand, who was always willing to buy someone off to save trouble, offered a $2.5 million settlement. But Berry was an angry man, and he made a number of other demands.

Armand turned them down categorically. "My lawyers drew up ironclad agreements, and I had Berry sign them," he told me. "I'm going to go to court, and I'm going to win this." He did. Although morality might have been on Berry's side, the law was on Occidental's. Berry even had to pay Occidental's $90,000 legal fees and wound up with only a few additional fringe benefits. He lost his future salary and the stock options that would have accompanied those earnings, but in the long run, as the price of the stock he already owned rose, Berry kept on earning substantial dividends. His fourteen-month experience with Hammer left him disenchanted and disenfranchised, but not poor.

Armand always seemed to be battling someone in court. During the Best strike, an agrichemicals company, Armour Agricultural Chemical, attempted to obtain a preliminary injunction to halt the construction of the massive chemical-recovery complex Occidental was about to build as part of its phosphate rock–mining operation at White Springs, Florida. The gist of this action alleged that Occidental had wrongfully obtained trade secrets and confidential information about the manufacture of superphosphoric acid (SPA) from Armour by employing ten former employees (including George Brooks, who had originally suggested the phosphate-mining operation to Armand). An injunction is a stringent remedy that the courts are hesitant to grant, and the judge ruled that Armour had not proved that it would be permanently damaged by the building of the plant, even though there might be limited damage when it was functioning.

Armand was pleased with the court's ruling. "It will take years before the case goes to trial," he said. "When it does, my lawyers will run rings around them!"

Whenever Victor came to Los Angeles, he read through my news releases to get an overview of what was going on. The one about the Armour suit made him laugh. "When the Soviets gave us the concession to open a pencil factory in 1925, Armand didn't know the first thing about making pencils. He went to Nuremberg, where the Faber Pencil Company was located, and got a former Faber engineer to come back to Russia and to work for us. That's how he obtained Faber's trade secrets. In order to obtain the German technology itself, Armand also bought an entire pencil factory in Nuremberg, disassembled it, shipped it to Berlin, and shipped it to Moscow piece by piece. Those techniques worked then; why shouldn't they work now?"

Although there were many other projects on his plate, Armand continued to court the Johnson White House. He was delighted to learn that Lady Bird Johnson was going to Campobello Island on August 20 to represent the White House at the ceremony marking the opening day of Roosevelt Campobello International Park. "My sources tell me that Lady Bird is going to enjoy meeting me," he said with typical self-confidence. "It seems she's impressed by men who are unlike her husband and have an interest in the arts and culture."

Even though Armand smothered the First Lady with charm, he did not receive the presidential invitation he hoped for. And the problem of networking President Johnson was exacerbated when Armand's Washington sources tipped him that fourteen other American companies, some with far better links to the Johnson administration than Occidental's, had filed applications to build fertilizer plants in the USSR. But suddenly, in mid-September, it seemed that he had found a way to finance the project. Armand had convinced the British government to underwrite the entire $1 billion cost of the venture over the next ten years.

"Oxy is going to build two fertilizer plants in central Siberia and may even build as many as eight more," he explained to me. "This is only the second time the British have extended credit to the Soviets for a period longer than five years. They agreed because Oxy is going to use British materials and workmanship exclusively and the project will provide a lot of British workers with jobs."

Armand had spent a great deal of time cultivating Lord Roy Thomson, the Canadian-born financier and publisher who owned a large newspaper enterprise that published *The Times* of London, *The Sunday Times*, and two other British Sunday papers, and Thomson's newspapers gave Hammer's coup a big play. Britain was in the midst of its first general election in eight years, and Harold Wilson's Labour Party was determined to end the thirteen-year monopoly held by Prime Minister Sir Alec Douglas-Home and the Conservatives, but unemployment was at a low ebb and was not one of the prime campaign issues. Yet the Conservatives chose to deflect criticism of their involvement in the fertilizer deal and what seemed to be overly generous terms to the Soviets by repeating Armand's argument that the deal would produce additional jobs created for British workers.

One key campaign issue was the belief that Britain's considerable balance-of-payments deficit and sharp fall in sterling reserves were going to require a devaluation of the pound. Sentiment was on the side of Labour, which made the Douglas-Home government determined not to devalue the pound. Therefore, it was essential that the government maintain its ability to borrow from the banks if need be to raise money to stabilize prices, gold and foreign currency exchange rates, and the pound.

A rumor swept through British business circles that Hammer had persuaded a powerful London-based international banker to link the British-Soviet loan to assurances that nothing would interfere with the Conservative government's ability to borrow from his banks. Gladys Loudenslager confirmed the rumor and added another piece of information. "The doctor insists that because he brokered the deal between the British and the Soviets, he's entitled to commission on both ends of the loan."

Hammer stared blankly at me when I brought up the matter. "Tell the reporters that an international consortium of bankers did help me to put the deal together. They cooperated because they agreed that it was going to be profitable for all of the parties involved. Don't say a word more."

In the closest race in fourteen years, the Conservatives lost the election. A short time later, in order to stop a serious run on the pound, the new government borrowed $1 billion from the International Monetary Fund and received another $3 billion from the banks. When reporters called to ask if Armand had helped arrange these loans, too, he told me to tell them that Britain's problems were "simply a case of bad management. I could run that little country with my eyes shut."

Armand was delighted when *The New York Times*'s coverage of the Occidental-Soviet-British deal compared his business activities with Khrushchev to his former dealings with Lenin. When I asked for more information about his background to pass on to the press, he went farther than ever with stories about his early days in Russia. "When Lenin saw what I could do for him, he made sure all my needs were taken care of," he told me during one of our meetings. "The average Russian had little more than slop to eat, but I could buy the finest foods in special stores. I had an automobile, one of the few in Russia then, and I also rode in a chauffeur-driven limousine. At first I lived like a prince in a mansion across from the Kremlin, the Sugar King's Palace, which had been owned by a wealthy beet-sugar merchant before the Revolution. My private suite had a bathroom with hot and cold water, and I slept in a large bed with beautiful linens. There were a large living room, a dining room, and a kitchen. My domestic staff included a butler and a chef. The food was always excellent, and the wine cellar was stocked with the finest vintages.

"Later, when I married, I moved to a thirty-four-room mansion, the Brown House. I threw brilliant parties there. American congressional delegations and Western journalists came to visit. John Dewey, Averell Harriman, Douglas Fairbanks and Mary Pickford, Will Rogers, Gene Tunney, and H. G. Wells were among those who signed my guest book."

Victor explained the reasons for this opulence. Lenin wanted his Western guests to carry favorable reports back to their governments, which is why the Bolsheviks made sure the Hammers lived in luxury and enjoyed a life-style that almost matched their lives at home. "If you were a party official, a member of the Cheka [the Soviet secret police], an artist, or a visiting capitalist, socialism really had created a paradise," Victor said. "For us, Moscow was a Bohemian wonderland, 1920s Berlin and Paris as well as Sodom and Gomorrah rolled into one. Lenin believed in free love, and we followed his lead. There were orgies, prostitutes, and private gambling clubs. Prohibition was in effect, but we could get all the alcohol we wanted. There was even experimentation with opium."

The fact that Julius Hammer was an important American Communist encouraged the Bolsheviks to make sure the Hammer family wanted for nothing. "Once when a railroad train carrying food to our asbestos mine was detained," Victor told me, "Armand complained, and the Cheka shot and killed the official who caused the delay. After another official hinted that he wanted a payoff, Armand reported him also and the Cheka arrested the man. Before they had a chance to shoot him, he committed suicide."

Victor said that the Brown House had been designed as a showplace for foreign visitors. "We were PR spokesmen for the Bolshevik government. In return the Soviets allowed us to make a lot of money and have one hell of a good time. We all knew that our household staff informed to the OGPU. So Armand always made sure to say things in front of them that he knew they would carry back. In that way he made himself look even more valuable."

The czar's political police force, the Okhrana, had supervised one kind of operative known as an *agent vliyana*, or agent of influence. At that time an *agent vliyana* was usually a Western journalist who took bribes in return for exerting influence in his own country by writing articles that would encourage his government to grant loans to the czarist government and to convince businessmen not to worry about the safety of their investments in Russia. Within a month after the Bolshevik coup, Lenin renewed the policy of finding Westerners who would take directions and conduct influence operations. Armand insisted that the life he enjoyed in Moscow was a reward for his good deeds, and he was determined that this assertion should go unchallenged. But when Victor said that his family had served as "PR spokesmen for the Bolshevik government," I knew it was another way of saying that they had been agents of influence.

A few days after the fertilizer deal was announced, a British reporter called to say that he had seen confidential documents that revealed that the fertilizers that were going to be manufactured by the Occidental-Soviet plants would not be used domestically but would be exported for hard currency. If the reporter's story was true, Armand's pronouncements about building the plants in order to feed the Soviets were a pack of lies, just like his stories about how he had fed the Russians in the 1920s when he was really feeding his own asbestos workers. The reporter asked, "Why is Dr. Hammer putting the Soviets into business with no guarantees that their profits would not be diverted for military purposes, including outfitting the Vietcong?"

Circumstances intervened before I had a chance to tell Armand that he was about to be accused of portraying a complex maneuver intended to help a hostile and dangerous government as an act of corporate altruism. On October 15 Nikita Khrushchev was suddenly removed from office and replaced by Leonid Brezhnev as first party secretary and Aleksei Kosygin as premier.

A month later, Armand returned to Moscow to supervise the exhibition of paintings by Grandma Moses at the Pushkin Museum. He also joined ninety-one American businessmen at a trade conference sponsored by Business International, cochaired a lunch for Anastas Mikoyan, and held meetings with Aleksei Kosygin and Soviet foreign minister Andrei Gromyko. Kosygin indicated that Khrushchev's hope for a stronger détente with the West and his desire to spend less money on the military and more on modernization and the production of consumer goods had been among the reasons for his ouster. The priority of the new administration was beefing up the military. So the deal folded, and Armand's desire to use Occidental "to feed the Soviet people," and possibly even Armand's access to the top Soviet leadership, had come to an end—for the moment at least.

"Don't worry," Victor told me. "Michael Bruk will look after Armand."

The name was familiar to me. The previous spring Armand had flashed a copy of *Soviet Life,* a glossy propaganda magazine aimed at Western readers. It contained an article about him under Michael Bruk's byline. Victor explained that Bruk and Victor's son, Armasha, had met when they were both attending the Institute of Foreign Languages in Moscow and that Armasha had recommended Bruk to Hammer as a translator. "Mikhail was a brilliant language student and learned to speak English perfectly. That's why the KGB picked him up and used him to prepare Soviet diplomats to attend international conferences."

Subsequently, Bruk became a correspondent for Novosti, the Soviet news service and an acknowledged arm of the KGB. Victor added that Novosti staffers often worked as translators, guides, and chauffeurs for important foreign visitors in order to spy on them. At the same time Novosti's connection to the KGB allowed Westerners to use its reporters to gain access to the most important members of the Soviet bureaucracy. "Mikhail is Armand's caseworker," said Victor. "Armand can send messages to the leadership through him, and the KGB can send messages to Armand through Mikhail to tell him what needs to be done."

A week or two after Armand returned from Moscow, a *Wall Street Journal* reporter called. The Soviet Union was not on his mind, but Libya was. A source had told him that Armand, while he was in London working on the British financing of the Soviet fertilizer deal, had met in Claridge's with Herbert Allen, a partner with his brother Charles in the Wall Street investment banking firm Allen & Co. Also at the meeting were three other men who claimed to be intimates of the Libyan ministry: Pegulu de Rovin, a French general; Ferdinand Galic, a Paris-based Czech businessman with a reputation as a playboy; and Taher Ogbi, the Libyan labor minister. The reporter had been told that Hammer had paid Galic $200,000 to use his influence with his friend and business partner Fuad Kabazi, oil minister of Libya. He had also paid de Rovin $100,000 because he had brought Ogbi to the meeting, and he assumed Ogbi was going to use his influence on King Idris's adviser, Omar Shalhi, minister of the Libyan court. Because Allen & Co. had introduced Hammer to Galic, who had assembled the rest of the group, it was going to receive a 25 percent interest in any Libyan oil concessions obtained by Occidental as a result of the efforts of the three men.

The reporter wanted Armand to confirm or deny the story and I told him I'd call him back. When I asked Armand about the meeting, he said, "This is my comment: 'There's nothing to it.' No. Tell the reporter that *you* don't know anything about it. That's what I want you to say: *You* don't know anything about it."

The reporter's information was so detailed that it could have come only from someone in the upper echelon of Allen & Co, and by asking Armand to confirm or deny the story, the reporter had let him know there was a leak. It would be plugged by the time I left the building.

After I called the *Journal* and said exactly what Hammer had told me to say, I returned to his office and said I had made the call.

He ignored me. But when I turned to go, he called out, "Carl, my ideas are beyond the comprehension of ordinary mortals. The brilliance of my mind can only be described as dazzling. Even I'm impressed by it!"

I left him there, knowing this was one of many days when he would remain at the office late into the night. He always said he had to work late. But over the years I heard reports from executives and other employees that there were nights when a limousine would deliver some of the most beautiful women in Los Angeles. If Armand was alone, they would stay in his office with him. When he was entertaining political figures, business associates, or foreign officials, they would go to what my sources mysteriously described as the "House in Benedict Canyon." It was merely another expense incurred by a man who was determined to do whatever it took to turn a small domestic oil company into an international giant.

8.

"THERE CAN BE NO BUSINESS WITHOUT EXAGGERATION"

Armand portrayed Occidental's attempt to obtain Libyan oil concessions as a battle to the death against the Seven Sisters. But in fact, the Libyans were as wary of Big Oil as he was. It was their fear that if the majors gained a monopoly over the Libyan oil supply, they would limit production rather than allow massive amounts of oil to go to market, which would force the majors to lower the oil prices of their rich Persian Gulf concessions. Determined to extract the maximum amount of money from their oil supply in the shortest time possible, the Libyans had decided to limit the influence of the Seven Sisters by alternating the awards of the concession sites between majors and independents at the next oil properties auction.

In order to convince everyone that victory would depend solely on his genius, Armand neglected to share this information with anyone at Occidental. He also kept secret the fact that the Libyan Council of Ministers had presented prospective bidders with a list of fourteen demands (which they called "preferences") and had asked them to respond with a list of the things they were prepared to do for Libya in order to obtain oil concessions. This procedure was meant to rectify the fact that none of the oil companies in operation in Libya had plowed a cent of its profits back into the country.

High on the Libyans' list was a stipulation that concession owners finance and build petrochemical plants, conserve the large quantities of natural gas that are usually burned off during the oil recovery process, and utilize the natural gas to manufacture ammonia fertilizer. Although this preference confirmed Armand's information that Occidental would stand a good chance of receiving concessions if it committed to building a Libyan ammonia plant, he had only one thing to say: that Occidental was the underdog of underdogs but that *he* would save the day.

Four years of intelligence-gathering efforts enabled Armand to know exactly what to do when he got word that the Council of Ministers was prepared to accept bids on July 29, 1965. "I'm going to send four nice sweeteners along with our bid—things the majors will never think of," he said. "They're going to do the trick."

It was no surprise that one preference consisted of a pledge to conduct a feasibility study for an ammonia plant that Occidental would build jointly with the Libyan government. After outside geologists confirmed that Kufra had a plentiful underground water supply, he elected as his second preference a commitment to drill for water at the site of King Idris' ancestral burial ground. The third preference was a promise to give the Libyans use of the OXYTROL food transportation and preservation system.

At that time oil producers paid oil-exporting countries a standard 12.5 percent royalty and a taxation payment consisting of 50 percent of the profits, both of which were computed on the "posted," or official, per-barrel oil price set by the Seven Sisters and not the actual market price of the crude. Armand's fourth preference was a self-imposed tax of an additional 5 percent of pretax net profits, to be paid to the Libyan government for "agricultural development." "Don't think for a second that I'm planning to upset the traditional taxation formula for Oxy's benefit," he commented to me. "Lack of rainfall makes it virtually impossible for the Libyans to sustain any form of agriculture. Most survive at subsistence level. I was in Russia during the Great Famine of 1921 and saw the horrors with my own eyes. That's why I'm so committed to doing something to feed the Libyans."

Armand's consultations with his Arabist also figured in his presentation. "Unlike the other companies, Oxy is going to present its bid in the traditional Arab way—on sheepskin parchments rolled up and tied with black and green ribbons, the colors of the Libyan flag. This little demonstration of respect for Arab culture is also going to help. But my sweeteners are the real key to our success or failure, and I've thought them up all by myself."

A few days after Armand announced his intention to bid for the Libyan concessions, I ran into Victor as he was heading for his brother's office. "Armand may not accept the fact that he was born Jewish," he told me, "but that's not going to matter to the Libyans. He could be kidnapped or murdered while he's in Libya. Like it or not, he's got to watch his step."

After a conversation with Victor, Armand sent for Bob Rose and executive assistant Tom Wachtell. "The Libyans have funny ideas about Jews, and I don't want them to think that I'm Jewish. I think I should join a church. Name some religions."

"Methodist . . . Roman Catholic . . . Presbyterian . . . Baptist . . . Unitarian . . ."

"What's a Unitarian?"

Neither knew.

"Look it up."

After Armand learned that Unitarianism emphasized humanistic concepts and not religious dogma and that its services were not of a religious nature, as quietly as possible he joined the Unitarian Community Church of Santa Monica and obtained a letter from its minister stating that he was a Unitarian in good standing who attended church regularly and made frequent contributions. When his Libyan informants tipped him that the Libyan ministers were planning to hand over the worst plots to those independents that were unable to declare exactly the concessions they wished to obtain, he slipped the letter to a delegation of oil and gas boys and sent them off to Libya to hunt down the best concession sites. If and when a Libyan asked if Hammer was a Jew, they were to present the document. The oil and gas boys scouted the sites, and on their return they reported that occasionally they had had to use the letter, but that after reading it the Libyans had usually responded with a shrug. Meanwhile Armand maintained his Unitarianism by making a modest donation to his new house of worship each and every Christmas.

From his Libyan operatives, Armand learned that the Libyans were nervous about Occidental because it was "an unknown California independent." In the past such companies either had been forced to abandon their concessions because they had no means of transporting, refining, and marketing their oil discoveries or had used up their funds drilling dry holes. Armand approached Signal Oil and Gas Company, a refining and marketing firm trusted by the Libyans, and made a deal to have Signal refine and market any crude Occidental discovered in Libya. A financial statement from Chase Manhattan Bank, placing Occidental's net worth at $48 million, which Hammer believed would demonstrate that Occidental had the capacity to finance an extended drilling program, was also forwarded to the Libyans.

Armand had convinced Ferdinand Galic that he and Oil Minister Kabazi would make a fortune if Occidental won, and he also sent word to Galic to have Kabazi tell the other ministers that Occidental did not anticipate money problems in Libya because it had access to the considerable financial resources of its secret partners Allen & Co. Armand was so concerned about secrecy that he instructed Kabazi and Galic to use the alias "Braset Marteau," French for "arm and hammer," whenever they discussed him. When Galic and Kabazi accidentally ran into each other on a plane, they were so afraid of Armand's spy network, they did not speak.

It took almost to the last minute to prepare the documentation to prove to the Libyans that Occidental could implement its preferences. A half hour before the deadline for the submission of bids on July 29, Occidental presented the Libyan Council of Ministers with a four-inch-thick leather-bound appendix to its offer. The following morning representatives of 120 oil companies from all over the world gathered in the mountain city of Beida to participate in the day-long ritual of opening the bids. "Exactly as I thought," Armand reported later. "All of the other oil companies turned in puny loose-leaf notebooks. When our sweeteners were read out loud, our competitors gasped. Oxy flabbergasted the ministers. They proclaimed us the hit of the day."

There was nothing to do but wait until February 20, 1966, when the names of the winners would be announced. Meanwhile, Armand busied himself with other ventures. Among the sweeteners he had offered to the Libyans was the use of the OXYTROL nitrogen food preservation process. After OXYTROL underwent a series of successful tests, Armand set a date to present the innovation to the New York Society of Security Analysts. These presentations allow the financial community to form opinions about the potential growth of a company, and a positive response has a direct and swift influence on stock prices. Armand himself described the agricultural revolution that Occidental was about to launch, and ended his speech by saying, "I have a little gift for each of you, a bag of beautiful tomatoes. They were picked in California and came cross-country 'fresh-r-ized' by OXYTROL. You'll think they've just been picked." The night before Victor had been dispatched to a wholesale food supplier to buy the best tomatoes available and have them attractively packaged.

Shortly after Armand returned from New York, we were riding together in his limousine when we spotted a housing development that was under construction. Armand asked his driver to pull over, and we chatted for a minute or two about the home-building boom that was occurring throughout Los Angeles. After purchasing his Greenwich Village carriage house outright three years before, Armand had formed a real estate partnership to speculate on other Greenwich Village properties and had begun to turn a small profit. Spurred on by those profits and the potential for even greater profits in southern California, before the week was over Armand authorized Occidental to acquire a real estate development company, S. V. Hunsaker Sons, for stock valued at $5.6 million, followed by the purchase of Deane Brothers, another home-building firm, for stock valued at $4 million. Subsequently Occidental acquired two land development companies, Family Realty Corporation and William Development Corporation, for stock valued at $5.3 million and another real estate firm, Monarch Investment Company, for stock valued at $2.6 million.

William Development had been owned by William Weinberg. A week after Occidental purchased Family Realty and William Development, Occidental sold some of the land holdings owned by Family Realty and William Development to William Weinberg's brother, Lawrence Weinberg, and entered a $2.9 million profit on the books. A week after Occidental acquired Monarch Investment, in another speedy maneuver, it sold off some of Monarch's holdings for $2 million. All Armand would say about these dealings was that his knowledge of which companies to acquire was allowing him "to beef up Oxy's bottom line. Oxy is going to construct a large tract-home development and make a killing. That's the thing that counts."

In the midst of these activities, the oil and gas boys reported the possibility of large oil reserves in the West Pico section of Los Angeles, Occidental filed with the city zoning administrator for permission to drill a core hole and obtain a test sample. The results indicated that the modest middle-class neighborhood was perched on top of a 1,600-acre oil field with a production capacity of 100 million barrels valued at $50 million.

An application for a permit to establish a drilling district was filed immediately with the city oil administrator. It received a quick approval and was passed to the City Planning Commission, where it received another speedy endorsement. Next a date was set for a public hearing. This obligatory step made Hammer nervous because a number of residents were complaining that derricks hovering over their backyards were going to lower property values. Much of the opposition would fade when the homeowners discovered that they would be paid a monthly royalty in return for leasing the mineral rights to their properties, but Armand wanted to make doubly sure there would be no objections. "They're afraid that we're going to lower property values," he told me, "so we've got to throw them something that *raises* them. It's an ugly neighborhood. We ought to show them that we're going to leave them something pretty to look at."

This thought inspired a decision to do something that had never been tried before—encase the 161-foot drilling rig in a soundproof blue-gray steel shell, which would transform it into an object that resembled a sleek, modern ten-story office building. After the drilling was completed, additional plans called for the landscaping of the drill site and the construction of a twelve-foot-high flagstone wall. The cost was $1 million. Armand considered it a bargain, and he was right. The public hearing went off without a hitch.

Subsequently, Occidental's drilling application sailed through the offices of the planning examiner, the director of the planning department, and the City Planning Commission. After a second public hearing, it was finally sent to the City Council. This vote was crucial, which was why Armand had spent so much time cultivating council members. The council voted in favor, leaving one last step, an endorsement from Mayor Yorty, which proved not to be a problem. The company had wended its way through this Byzantine bureaucratic process in a mere four months.

"I can't figure out whom the doctor bribed," Gladys Loudenslager commented on the day drilling began. "It could be anybody; it could be everybody."

When Armand was informed that the test well had been drilled, he ordered the choke opened as far as it would go. The resulting artificial rush of oil would produce at the rate of two hundred extra barrels per day. The oil and gas boys protested that it was a violation of standard petroleum practices.

"There can be no business without exaggeration," Armand declared. "Open the choke now."

I generated an enormous amount of publicity for "the skyscraper derrick." Finally I contacted the Los Angeles Chamber of Commerce and suggested that Hammer receive a Los Angeles Beautiful Award, which is given annually to the citizen who has done the most to beautify the city. The Chamber of Commerce readily complied, and flanked by Mayor Yorty and his good friend Occidental director Benjamin Gimbel, Armand was hailed for his understanding that industrialization and beauty can be complementary. I trumpeted him to the media as "the Beautify Los Angeles industrialist," and that's how commentators referred to him on the evening TV newscasts.

Another civic-minded matter was preoccupying the Beautify Los Angeles industrialist. Seven years had passed since he had told me that he did not plan to donate his collection of forty-nine Flemish and Dutch Old Masters to a museum or university until its value had increased sufficiently for him to claim a large tax deduction for the donation. That moment had arrived. "The value of my collection has amortized to a million dollars," he told me, "so I've decided to donate it to the University of Southern California. I want an enormous amount of PR to accompany this good deed."

Armand and Victor owned a collection of paintings and sculptures by Charles Russell, the American realist painter who had specialized in dramatic depictions of the Old West, and I asked if he also planned to donate the Russells. "No," he said. "I'm going to donate them individually to the politicians we need to help us. They love Russell's stuff because it reeks of Americana."

It was USC's plan to place Hammer's collection on permanent exhibition in its on-campus Fisher Gallery, and it scheduled a formal reception for the second week of March. Armand was delighted. "USC is a rich, privately held school, and the board of directors will all be there," he said. "They've all got a lot of money. I'm looking forward to meeting them in a social setting."

"Why did you choose USC?" I asked.

"I've always wanted to receive an honorary degree. I expect USC to show its appreciation by giving one to me."

I suggested that he and USC President Dr. Norman Topping announce the donation at a press conference, which would be followed by a press preview the day before the reception to generate articles dealing with Armand as art dealer, collector, and benefactor. The crowning event would be the transformation of the reception into a major society event.

"We'll get out a batch of celebrities, corporate heads, political figures, artists, and local society leaders," I told Armand, "and plaster the society pages with photographs of you and them." It was exactly what he wanted to hear, and he demanded a daily report on my progress.

The first thing on my agenda was the preparation of a detailed set of press materials tracing Armand's thirty-three-year career in the art world. I asked him to tell me the story. Once again I sat back and listened while he took a core of truth and spun another web of self-serving myths around it.

"When I took Victor back to Russia with me in 1922," he began, "he discovered that priceless things were being sold dirt cheap on the streets and spent the next six years scooping them up. In 1928 I met an American art dealer, Emery Sakho. He wanted to export art from Russia but couldn't get anywhere with the bureaucracy. I felt bad for him, so I invited him to the Brown House for dinner. His mouth fell open when he looked over our collection. After all, the mansion overflowed with icons, tapestries, brocades, eighteenth-century furniture, Russian Old Masters, services of Meissen and Sèvres porcelain, and vestments woven with threads of pure gold and silver, which had been worn by Russian Orthodox priests. Sakho told me that if I found a way to ship home these treasures, he'd be able to sell them at a handsome profit. He had the expertise and I had the merchandise, so we became partners.

"It took me quite some time, but I finally persuaded the authorities to allow me to take the artworks out of the country in return for a 15 percent export tax on their estimated worth. My collection filled three huge warehouses and the tax was large, but it was nothing compared to the value of what was in those crates. But when I returned to New York, the country was in the midst of the Depression and Sakho had been wiped out. I was a millionaire before I went to Russia, and I returned a millionaire many times over. I was able to buy him out at a very good price.

"Even during the Depression, women loved to shop," Armand continued, "especially in department stores, and they were fascinated by the romance of royalty. I made up my mind to revolutionize the way fine art was sold and sell it the same way cosmetics, handbags, and fancy soap are sold. So I wrote to a number of leading department stores to request the use of an entire floor on which to exhibit and sell my treasures, and I gave them a rich no-risk deal: forty percent of the selling price and a piece of my profits."

"Were you asked how you got those objects?"

"I simply told the truth. The instability of the ruble had forced me to convert my Russian earnings into something tangible that I could sell when I got home."

One department store, Scruggs-Vandervoort-Barney in St. Louis, responded to Hammer's offer. "I promoted the hell out of the sale by giving it a healthy dose of snob appeal," Armand said. "I ordered the printing of fancy price tags embossed with the Imperial Romanoff two-headed eagle crest and prepared an elaborate catalog that paid tribute to the 'skilled artisans devoted to the glory of the czar.' I even wrote a book that detailed my adventures in the Soviet Union and described the value of my collection. It was called *The Quest of the Romanoff Treasure.* My good friend Walter Duranty wrote the introduction. It was also for sale."

Duranty had received international recognition when he became the first Western journalist to interview Stalin, and his introduction gave enormous credibility to Hammer's book, essentially an artfully contrived manual designed to encourage Westerners to invest in Soviet enterprises.

According to Armand, buyers turned out in droves. "Our success in St. Louis led to sales in eight other stores, culminating in a huge sale at Lord and Taylor in New York at the beginning of 1933. I trotted out my Fabergé collection and sold thirteen diamond-studded Fabergé eggs at prices ranging from fifty to a hundred thousand dollars. In those days that was an *enormous* amount of money!"

These sales created spectacular attention and enabled Armand to cultivate every important newspaper publisher in New York City. The Hammer Galleries went into business with Lord & Taylor and opened a branch in the Waldorf-Astoria. In 1934 another branch was opened in Palm Beach, Florida. When the Hammer brothers ended their association with Lord & Taylor the following year, they moved to a new location at 682 Fifth Avenue. "Because of my great success selling the Romanoff treasures, the Hearst organization approached me to stage a sale of William Randolph Hearst's twenty-thousand-item art collection," Armand continued. "It took almost two years to put together. We held it at the Gimbel brothers' department store and Saks Fifth Avenue on January 20, 1941, and it made the front page of *The New York Times.* Over the next nine months, we grossed five million dollars. Hearst's publishing empire was crumbling, and then I came along. The sale and the way I promoted it saved him from extinction."

I sent reporters and art critics a summary of this colorful information well in advance of the press conference at which Armand would announce his donation to USC. By now I knew there were going to be curve balls. Two or three critics with expertise in Russian art had voiced the same harsh conclusion: that the Soviets would never have allowed any American to amass a vast amount of art and that the objects that filled the Brown House were owned by the Soviet government, not Hammer. The Soviets were desperate for hard currency and had looked to Dr. Hammer to get it for them. "He wasn't selling his art, but theirs," said one critic. Another labeled him "Stalin's U.S. field representative."

Others blasted the "Romanoff treasures" as "slipshod goods," described the department store sales as "con jobs designed to defraud naïve purchasers," and objected to Hammer's mass-market sales approach. "He's a honky-tonk peddler who had terrible taste then and has terrible taste now."

I had no choice but to review Armand's story point by point with my best source, Victor. "Did the objects in the Brown House belong to you or to the Soviet government?" I began.

"I didn't know the first thing about collectibles," Victor replied, "but I loved to go shopping, and a lot of the things I bought turned out to be pretty valuable. But almost all of the priceless items in the Brown House belonged to the Soviets and were placed there to impress Western vistors. A commissar and team of assistants made regular inspections to take an inventory and make sure we didn't steal anything."

"Who was Emery Sakho?"

"Sakho and a theatrical impresario, Morris Gest, were partners with Armand in the beginning. But Anastas Mikoyan was unwittingly the real source of the idea to sell Soviet art in the West. After Lenin's death, Mikoyan threw his weight behind Stalin and rose to a very high Central Committee post, people's commissar for external and internal trade. In 1928 he told us that he wanted to raise a large amount of hard currency quickly and offered us a ten percent commission to sell forty masterpieces from the Hermitage. We came back with an offer of five million dollars, but the paintings were worth a lot more than that, and everybody knew it.

"Eventually Mikoyan realized that no one in the West was going to turn down the opportunity to buy a masterpiece, even if he had to buy it from a Communist, and he sold them himself. Andrew

Mellon paid $1.6 million for just one painting in the group, Raphael's *Alba Madonna*. Armand and I always call that 'the deal that got away.'

"Armand had earned a million rubles manufacturing pencils. But our pencil factory was going to be nationalized. Losing the Hermitage deal *and* the factory was too much for him to swallow, and he talked Mikoyan into allowing us to take our art holdings out of Russia and to pay for our concessions with art objects—the Soviets had no hard currency and were glad to do it. Our pencil concession agreement ran until 1935, and Armand also persuaded Mikoyan to allow us to sell Soviet objects on consignment until 1935 at the same time that we sold ours."

While these negotiations were going on, Victor joined his half brother, Harry, in New York City and began preparations with Morris Gest to open L'Ermitage Art Gallery and then the Hammer Galleries, both in New York and both to be fed by a continuing stream of art objects from Moscow.

Meanwhile Armand was in Paris where he came up with another ingenious scheme to make money. The lack of hard currency forced the Soviets to pay foreign businessmen with three-year government notes. Calling himself Braset Marteau for the first time, Armand opened his own bank. He knew that the Soviets would honor their financial obligations because they were determined to establish their legitimacy, but he used his experience in Moscow to convince French businessmen that they planned to default. Eventually 'M. Marteau' was able to buy up the notes at enormous discounts, as much as seventy-two percent, and Armand cleaned up when he cashed them in at face value.

The first shipment of art from Moscow, a collection of Hammer family- and Soviet-owned merchandise, arrived in New York while Armand was still in Paris. Harry and Victor held an auction. "Romanoff family members tried to close us down, charging that we were dealing in stolen goods," Victor said. "Although they obtained a temporary injunction, the real problem was the Depression, and the bidding was very low. We wired Armand, told him we were in trouble, and asked him to come home."

A thirty-thousand-dollar deduction against the Hammers' old trading company Alamerico had been disallowed, and the first thing waiting for Armand when he returned to New York was a lawsuit from the IRS. "That was a lot of money in those days, and Armand resisted paying it. He found some loopholes, went to court, and won," Victor continued. "After a friend of his, a dress manufacturer, told him that he was making money holding cut-rate dress sales in department stores, Armand decided to try the same tactic with the Soviet art objects."

I asked Victor about the quality of those objects.

"They were genuine in the sense that they were made of real gold and real silver. But these were not the carefully wrought works that were the classics of the period. A lot of it was ordinary, if you can call a gold cigarette case ordinary. We hired Prince Mikhail Gounduroff, a big Russian guy with a huge nose who insisted that he was a legitimate Romanoff and might have been telling the truth. He was just as arrogant and rude as the rest of them, and they were all hemophiliacs, and so was he. Before an auction Prince Mikhail worked the crowd and pointed out the priceless things that had been stolen from his family. That convinced the women that the objects really had once belonged to nobility and encouraged them to pay ridiculous prices."

I asked Victor about the large number of Fabergé objects that had passed through their hands. "Our Moscow office was located in Fabergé's old shop and workrooms," he said, "which Armand rented for the equivalent of twelve American dollars a month. Each piece of Fabergé jewelry was signed with a Fabergé hallmark, but the hallmarks had disappeared after the Revolution. Before Armand left for Paris, the Bolsheviks gave him a set of these punches. In Paris Armand hunted down a craftsman who had trained with the same masters who had taught Fabergé and was capable of knocking off new objects in the Fabergé style. Of course, he did not have access to the precious stones from the Urals and could not duplicate Fabergé's complicated enameling process. But he certainly could knock off the second-rate pieces, which could only be authenticated by the hallmarking. And, luckily, we had the hallmarks. Therefore, these objects were worth a lot of money to us despite the fact that many were really quite mediocre. Side by side with the Soviet-owned Fabergé, we sold our own perfectly hallmarked Fabergé pieces and kicked back commissions on both to Mikoyan. In 1938 we had a very big Fabergé sale and sold so many real pieces and so many counterfeits we grossed millions."

I should have been shocked, but the scheme was so brazen, I laughed in spite of myself.

When I asked Victor if Armand had converted any of his rubles into art, he replied that he had functioned as his brother's money changer. "I converted every ruble he earned into *valuta*—hard currency—on the Russian black market. By the time Armand left

Moscow, he'd transferred a million dollars out of the country. In the U.S., when we had to send the Soviets their profits and commissions, Armand always got someone to wire the money into Swiss bank accounts. That someone never knew that the money was converted instantly into French francs and transferred to Paris, where the French took a commission and then sent the money on to Moscow. Armand said the risk was theirs, not his. He always makes sure that he's not the one who gets caught.

"Armand has lived an exceedingly dangerous life," Victor added. "Even during the days of the McCarthy hearings, we continued to sell Soviet art and kick money back to the Stalin government. We didn't call it quits until the Hammer Galleries moved to its present location on West Fifty-seventh Street in 1956. Armand honestly believes that it's a simple fact of nature that he's never going to get caught."

The same could not be said of Victor. He said his brother had made him wear a floor-length overcoat with false pockets so that he could smuggle pornographic art objects and books into Egypt for King Farouk. In 1948 Victor repeated the stunt en route from Moscow and was charged with smuggling Soviet-owned paintings into the United States. It was also reported that proceeds from these sales had been returned to the Soviet Union. "I told you Armand was never the one who got caught," he said somewhat ruefully.

Fortified by Victor's information, I handed Armand a list of the accusations made by the art press. His response was his standard party line: "I was a young capitalist entrepreneur who made large profits in the heart of a drab, anticapitalist country. My story is unique, the only story there is and the only story you've got to tell."

It was Armand's belief that a few cranky art critics didn't stand a chance of diminishing the glory that was going to accompany his USC donation. Again he was right. Everything he said at the press conference went unchallenged, and no embarrassing questions were asked.

On the night of the USC reception, Virginia and I watched him go from person to person. In between conversations, he scribbled quick notes so that new contacts could be added to his files. During the course of the evening he came face to face with an attractive middle-aged woman who was a member of a nationally known family and was married to a successful businessman. She stared angrily at him for a second, then turned away, and he looked somewhat taken aback.

"What's that all about?" Virginia asked.

I did not have an answer.

Later Armand stopped to study a lovely Flemish painting, *Rest on the Flight into Egypt* by Hans Rottenhammer and Paul Bril. It depicted Mary tenderly holding the Christ child with Joseph by their side as they paused in the midst of their long journey.

Virginia and I approached him.

"Why did they go to Egypt?" he asked.

Virginia was surprised, but she explained that King Herod had ordered all children two years old and under to be killed and that God had instructed the Holy Family to flee to Egypt in order to save the life of the Christ child.

Armand, who never missed anything, had caught her look of surprise. He knew she must be wondering why he collected art he knew nothing about. "The thing I enjoy most about collecting is the hunt," he said, "outbidding everyone at an auction and getting a work away from someone who wants it badly. My father was a stamp collector, and I was too. I collect art the way I collected stamps. Once you get a stamp and mount it in your album, you don't spend your time looking at it. You're too busy hunting for the next one. Once you get a painting, you don't waste your time looking at it either. You resume the hunt."

9.

"MY SWEETENERS DID THE TRICK!"

After Armand met Lady Bird Johnson at Campobello, he placed her at the top of his VIP mailing list and bombarded her with his press clippings accompanied by personal notes. She did not respond. When he sent jade jewelry to Luci and Lynda, for the first time he received personally dictated thank-you notes, not form letters, and he showed them around proudly. Then he decided that he wanted Mrs. Johnson to attend the invitational opening of the exhibition of paintings by Pavel Korin at the Hammer Galleries on April 5, 1965.

"Get the White House press people on the phone," he ordered me. "Make sure they know that this event is the second half of the first U.S.-Soviet art exchange and that Soviet Minister of Culture Furtseva is going to be there. Convince them that Lady Bird's appearance will be a big step toward improving Soviet-American relations."

Under Brezhnev and Kosygin, the USSR had embarked on a rapid buildup of intercontinental ballistic missiles and had hinted that it planned to step up aid to Hanoi. Therefore, I did not expect the White House to cooperate with Armand, and I was proved right when White House press secretary Liz Carpenter's assistant told me right off the bat that Mrs. Johnson was probably going to decline the invitation.

When Armand urged me to keep pressing for an acceptance, I called a Washington-based journalist with major White House contacts and asked his advice. He checked with his White House sources and called me back to tell me that the Johnson administration viewed cultural exchanges with the Soviets mainly as propaganda exercises that enabled the Soviets to make a favorable impression with Americans. "They think Dr. Hammer and the Russians are using these art shows to break down resistance to further exchanges and that Hammer's trying to use Mrs. Johnson on behalf of the scheme. They're worried about his loyalty."

When I consulted Victor, he agreed that Armand wanted to use the First Lady to impress Leonid Brezhnev with his importance and "to get to LBJ to talk him into making Armand an unofficial trade envoy to the Soviet Union." A few days later Armand received Mrs. Johnson's official declination in the mail. He did not show it around.

When the White House scheduled a state dinner for King Faisal of Saudi Arabia, Armand requested an invitation, using the fact that Occidental and the Saudi government were business partners as a pretext. He was turned down. Undaunted, he called Riyadh and spoke to King Faisal's brother, Prince Abdul Ahmed Azias. By the time the conversation was over, he had scheduled an appointment with King Faisal in Washington and persuaded Azias to call the White House on his behalf. The White House found it impossible to refuse the prince's request to issue Armand an invitation and he marched around the office declaring that LBJ had personally invited him to dinner. On his return from Washington, he categorized his encounter with President Johnson as "friendly."

As usual, when Armand set his sights on a target, in this case meeting with President Johnson, he found a way to do it.

"Who introduced you?" I asked him.

"My good friend Marvin Watson."

W. Marvin Watson was LBJ's executive assistant and appointments secretary. Subsequently Victor explained that Armand's Washington lawyers had tipped him that after the 1964 presidential election the Democratic National Committee had suffered a deficit of $4 million, the biggest campaign deficit in history, and that the FBI and seven other agencies were conducting investigations into the way contributions had been handled. "LBJ doesn't want a word of this leaked," Victor said. "He trusts Marvin Watson, so he turned over control of the Democratic National Committee to him. Watson's supposed to find the money to balance the books, replace the money that seems to have gone astray, and put together a huge campaign fund for 1968. Armand made a special point of telling Watson how much he admired the president and his policies, and hinted that he wanted to make a *large* contribution. By the time their meeting was over, things were beginning to warm up."

On February 20, 1966, Armand called at three in the morning to report that Occidental had been successful in the Libyan oil auction and he was so excited he could hardly talk. "Esso-Libya offered more money than we did, and we won anyway!" he crowed. "My sweeteners did the trick. We beat the hell out of the 119 other companies fighting it out for Concession 102, and we also won Concession 103."

When I arrived at Occidental that morning just after dawn, Armand was already at his desk. "Watch me crack the whip," he said. "Watch me get everybody hopping. Watch me get that Libyan oil out of the ground and to the market in record time!"

Later that day I learned that only seventeen bidders had competed for Concession 102, and two of the Seven Sisters had not bid at all (the other five had received only modest plots). But I forgave Armand his hyperbole. He had spent five years working for this success and had scored a well-deserved personal triumph. I couldn't wait to start sending out the news. Referring casually to Armand as "Hammer of Libya," I related the unlikely tale of a sixty-seven-year-old adventurer who had gone into the desert and, against all odds, emerged a victor. The news coverage reflected this approach and business pages across the country carried the story of Occidental's victory in the oil auction under such headlines as "Dr. Hammer's Desert Triumph."

Armand's next task was to put together a staff with experience in desert drilling. Through intermediaries, he sent out feelers to Seven Sisters employees. While unable to offer substantial salary increases, he could dangle generous stock option programs that would "make them rich" and a cleverly designed package of perks, including the previously unheard-of use of a company car paid for and maintained by Occidental, and a steady stream of Seven Sisters defectors began banging on Occidental's door. In response, the Los Angeles division of one Seven Sisters company established a policy of firing an employee on the spot if he was seen speaking to anyone with a connection to Hammer or Occidental.

In order to avoid wasting the $1 million cost of drilling a dry hole and the devastating blow to morale that would accompany the failure, at the beginning of April Armand authorized $2 million worth of seismic testing before the commencement of drilling. When the drill bit finally hit the sand at the beginning of the summer, he exuded his usual enormous confidence. But the drilling produced a dry hole, followed by a second, and a third. Armand remained optimistic but everybody else was panic-stricken.

During Armand's twelve-year reign at Occidental, he had trained his staff never to challenge him. This time it was different. Corporate headquarters resounded with the message that "Hammer's folly" had to be terminated before "Hammer of Libya" led his company into bankruptcy. The criticism rolled off Armand's back. "The board wants to terminate the drilling program," he told me. "They say that a company with a net income of twenty-one million dollars should never have thrown away five million in the Libyan desert. But *I'm* running Oxy, and we're going to do it my way, and my way is to keep drilling."

In response, the directors declared that Gene Reid alone would make the decision about whether to terminate the Libyan activities and ordered Reid to go to Libya on a fact-finding mission. In defiance Armand declared that he was about to authorize Occidental to begin the Kufra irrigation project and dispatched Occidental's geologists to the desert oasis to determine exactly how much water existed underground.

While this drama was ripping Occidental apart, Victor confided that a new drama was already under way. Armand had been deathly ill with food poisoning for a few days. "Armand got sick in Venezuela," Victor explained. "He'd received a tip that Venezuela was planning to make new oil properties available, and he decided that he wanted to case the scene. The Hammer Galleries represents a group of paintings by Venezuelan artists. As a cover we made a secret trip to Caracas and pretended we wanted to sell them to the government."

Victor went on to tell me that while they were in Caracas, an American expatriate, John Askew, with twenty years of experience in the Venezuelan oil industry, had approached Armand. He and Askew had cut a deal. Armand was going to supply Askew with $3 million. In return Askew would monitor the activities of the national oil company, Corporación Venezolana del Petróleo (CVP), the administration of President Raúl Leoni, and the other oil companies operating out of Venezuela. As soon as Askew learned the date of the next oil properties auction he was to do whatever was necessary to secure Occidental's victory in the bidding.

. . .

The financial difficulties caused by the Libyan drilling failures were compounded by the fact that not too long after Occidental constructed a huge local tract-home development, a housing slump swept across the United States. Four hundred homes remained unsold, and many that had been sold were repossessed. Convinced that Occidental had to write off its $15 million real estate investment and place its financial resources elsewhere, Finance Vice President Dorman Commons made a thorough presentation to Armand.

"Dorman's facts and figures prove conclusively that real estate is the wrong bet for Oxy, especially in light of our ongoing Libyan losses," Armand reported. But before I had a chance to agree, he added that he had just opened negotiations and was attempting to acquire another large home-building company. "No one can tell me what to do. When I say that we're going to have a large, successful real estate division, I know what I'm talking about."

Armand rarely admitted mistakes, but he often addressed them elliptically. A few days later he told me that investing in art was always more sensible than investing in real estate, especially during a recession. It signaled that he had already decided to take another plunge into art investment. Before the week was over, he was receiving calls from art collectors and dealers offering him "odd lots," large, undistinguished collections at discount rates. "I'm going to build a new collection that's bigger and better than my last one, has greater investment value, and will get me even more publicity," he told me. "*Better* art at *lower* prices is what I'm looking for this time around."

For Armand people were also commodities to be collected and then disposed of. Following the pattern he had established with Lowell Berry, whenever he set out to acquire a company, he convinced its president that he would be his "son" and would inevitably become Occidental's next chief executive. When Occidental acquired Permian Corporation, a Midland, Texas, crude-oil marketing and transportation firm, its corpulent president, Walter Davis, became a senior vice president of Occidental and Armand raved about Davis to everyone in earshot and declared him his heir apparent.

It wasn't long before Davis and Hammer, both strong-willed personalities, were at each other's throats. Armand began the process of getting rid of someone by complaining about the man. These complaints became increasingly more intense until Armand terminated the executive in a fit of righteous indignation. One day

Hammer said to me, "Walter Davis makes me nervous. I'm going to have him checked out."

I knew the process of eliminating Davis had begun.

Meanwhile, as the debate surrounding Libya continued to mount, Armand attempted to deflect it with a stunning piece of news. Occidental's newly formed minerals division had just made a series of "sensational" new discoveries. Armand dictated the exact comment I was to make about Occidental's mine on the Walker River Indian Reservation in Nevada: "It appears we may have one of the largest iron-ore deposits in the western part of the United States."

On the day the financial press printed this news, Occidental's stock price shot up a couple of points. Before the day was over Armand also received a call from the SEC. Dorman Commons was flabbergasted. "The SEC knows the doctor's full of bull and that the release was a phony," he told me. "We've got to put out an immediate retraction."

Two days later Occidental, guided by a phalanx of attorneys, issued a masterpiece of jargon climaxed by the blunt statement that "work done thus far on the property has not established the existence of a commercially mineable ore body." It did not diminish Commons' concern. "The SEC is watching this company's every move. They don't trust the doctor, and therefore they don't trust Oxy."

A few days later the federal regulators dispatched a team to see Hammer and order him to reform Occidental's accounting procedures. It was decided that he and I were to stop writing news releases on our own and from that moment on, all company information that was going to be released to the press and public had to receive clearances from the accounting and legal departments and Occidental's outside auditor, Arthur Andersen & Co., the biggest of the Big Eight accounting firms. The new procedure was followed, but after fighting Armand for the next two years, the Arthur Andersen account executive assigned to Occidental threw up his hands in despair, walked out the door, and never returned.

The situation in Libya left Gene Reid exhausted and upset. Reid talked and acted as though he had never left the oil patch, and he was typically blunt when he urged the board to get Occidental out of Libya before the company was destroyed. "I told them that we're laying a big egg there," he said to me soon after he returned from his fact-finding mission. "Oxy doesn't belong in a desert country.

This is one for the big boys. I've been in the oil business all my life, and I've taken a million risks. But I had only myself to worry about. I told the same thing to the old doc, but it fell on deaf ears because he wants to keep on drilling. I respect his determination, but he's dead wrong and he's taking the company down the drain!"

Reid's observations were more than sufficient to convince the board to order Armand to throw in the towel.

Armand remained defiant. "Gene Reid forgets that he was broke when our companies merged," he told me. "He's gone along with my ideas and become a millionaire many times over. Now he's afraid he'll lose his millions if we wind up going broke in Libya. He overlooks the fact that if we succeed, he'll be even richer than he is now. We've been drilling for only six months. It's taken a lot of oil companies much longer than that to find oil, and they didn't have the oil and gas boys we do. This is a calculated risk, and we've got to take it."

At its next meeting, the board moved to vote on whether Occidental should leave Libya and Armand stormed out of the boardroom. "There are some spineless bastards around here!" he roared at the top of his voice. "To hell with those weak sisters. I'm the one who's running this company. Like it or not, we're going to keep right on drilling, and we're not going to stop until we either discover oil or we all go down with the ship!"

He summoned each director to his office and made it clear that he was willing to use anything in his arsenal, including his signed but undated letter of resignation, in order to get his way. The objections instantly came to a halt.

Armand's persistence and strong-arm tactics paid off. In November the oil and gas boys drilled a discovery well on Concession 102. There was a roar, the ground began to shake and a huge pillar of black-and-orange smoke and flame rose from beneath the earth. Then the high-gravity crude oil with a low sulfur content known as "sweet oil" began to flow. The well tested at a rate of 14,860 barrels per day and was classified a significant discovery.

Armand was triumphant, and later that day I took a small group of business reporters to his office to discuss the discovery.

"When did you go to Libya for the first time?" one asked.

He smiled modestly. "In 1961. It was part of my mission. You see, Jack Kennedy had appointed me his personal trade envoy."

The cost of discovering oil in Libya had nearly capsized Occidental. The $30 million cost of building an export pipeline across the

Libyan desert to transport the oil to market also held the danger of destroying the company's financial health. Undeterred, Armand was determined to move quickly and couldn't wait to take advantage of the Libyan law that allowed a company to deduct *all* of its expenses, including the cost of dry holes, in the first year it went to market.

Among its other stipulations, the Libyan petroleum law ordered an oil producer's excess pipeline capacity to be made available to other producers in return for a fee. British Petroleum and Mobil Oil each owned an underutilized pipeline close to Occidental's concessions, but no independent was going to have an easy time making a pipeline deal with a major. When Armand sensed that negotiations with the two companies were going nowhere, he called them to a halt.

A few days later he told me that Esso had approached him and wanted to make a deal. It was surprising news because Esso-Libya had a reputation for stomping on independents and refusing to share its pipeline with them. For information on this situation I turned to a financial editor who specialized in the internal operations of Standard Oil Company of New Jersey, the parent company of Esso-Libya. "Jersey views Dr. Hammer as a small, agile, rich competitor who plays a very tough game," he told me. "Every oil company involved in the Libyan auction bribed the ministry, but Jersey was amazed at the astonishing amount of money that Dr. Hammer threw around."

The editor went on to confirm my suspicion that the Jersey management feared that its profits and power were about to be threatened by Occidental's ability to flood the world with cheap Libyan oil. They also loathed the fact that Hammer had used tricks and cunning to force his way into the world of Big Oil and raid the staffs of the Seven Sisters whenever he needed particular expertise.

I also learned that Jersey had historic objections to dealing with Armand. In 1920, after a flood of Russian oil on the European market had lowered prices, Jersey had set out to stabilize world prices in its favor by acquiring a 50 percent ownership of the largest foreign-owned oil fields in the USSR and organizing all of the international oil companies operating there to prevent the Bolsheviks from nationalizing their concessions. Two years later, while Jersey was doing its best to create a united front against the Bolsheviks, Armand had attempted to secure Soviet oil concessions on behalf of a large German oil group. That Hammer would represent Germany, a hated enemy in World War I, a mere four years after its defeat and was also on intimate terms with the Bolshevik leadership had earned him a permanent place in the Jersey history books as a mercenary and spoiler.

"Then why does Jersey want to go into business with him?" I asked the editor.

"As I understand it," he replied, "Dr. Hammer sent word through his Libyan field managers that *he* wanted to see *them.*"

The irony was inescapable. Occidental had been awarded these concession grants in order to prevent the growth of Esso-Libya. Yet Armand couldn't wait to approach the Esso management in order to make a deal.

Hammer's meeting with Esso President Hugh Wynne put him into good spirits. "The head guys of the big oil companies have been looking down their noses at me ever since I entered the petroleum business. But that was before we hit the big time. There I was standing eyeball to eyeball with those snobs. The fun was seeing how much they resented it!"

Four oil and gas boys had accompanied Armand to the meeting. They confided that Armand had attempted to put Wynne on the defensive by demanding to know why Wynne had summoned him. After Wynne had set the record straight, Armand had then pretended that he was unprepared because he really had believed that Wynne had called the meeting. He had walked out of the meeting, presumably to figure out the terms of a deal, and had left Wynne cooling his heels for a half hour. After concluding that Wynne would now be more vulnerable to an offer that had in fact been prepared days in advance, he had returned to the negotiation.

In return for half of Occidental's Libyan operation, Armand asked Esso to pay Occidental $100 million, with Esso marketing Occidental's crude through its pipeline, refinery, transportation, and sales systems, and Wynne had seemed favorably disposed.

Armand explained that he made the offer because it exceeded Occidental's net worth, and that he and Wynne had both agreed that their respective boards of directors would approve it automatically. Occidental's board voted a quick acceptance. But to Armand's surprise the Jersey board voted it down. Behind the scenes, Jersey Chairman Kenneth Jamieson had indicated that he thought Occidental had neither the experience nor the transportation facilities to work its concessions effectively, and was convinced that Occidental was doomed to abandon its entire Libyan acquisition, at which time Esso would have the chance to scoop it up for far less than Hammer's asking price. When his offer was refused, Armand kept his surface calm, but once again fear began to surface at Occidental that unless something happened quickly, Jamieson was going to be proven right.

In March 1967 Corporate Counsel Bob Rose became the eighth senior executive to decide suddenly to resign. Rose had objected frequently and publicly to Hammer's methods; in return Armand had made Rose's life miserable. When he learned that Rose was planning to spend St. Patrick's Day with his former employer, California Governor Pat Brown, and Cardinal James Francis McIntyre, head of the Catholic diocese of Los Angles, he ordered Rose to stay over in New York City and not return to Los Angeles until St. Patrick's Day had passed. Armand also summoned Rose from the Palm Desert Classic Pro-Am Golf Tournament for a meaningless half-hour meeting, just before the match began.

Before he left Oxy, Rose told me the story of his "resignation." "After meeting with Hammer daily, he suddenly turned over all of my work to independent attorneys and law firms. Then he told the other executives not to talk to me or they'd be in trouble. After he isolated me, he let me cool my heels doing nothing for a year. The first time I met with him was just before the last board meeting. We exchanged pleasantries. Then he handed me a letter of resignation and asked me to sign it. He had spent a year softening me up for this moment. I was glad to go, and I signed the letter."

Utilizing their digital seismic drilling equipment, the oil and gas boys began to inspect Libyan Concession 103. Probing far deeper than the drilling level previously established by Mobil, which had failed at the location and had abandoned it, they concluded that they had found oil. During March a very deep discovery well was drilled, which produced an astonishing 44,000 barrels a day. Occidental had discovered a reef, a concentration of oil so bountiful that it flows indefinitely without the use of pumps, indicating the presence of vast oil reserves. After arranging to be King Idris's house guest at the royal palace, Armand rushed to Libya to see the miracle with his own eyes.

"Do you know how Oxy really got those concessions?" Victor asked rhetorically during his brother's absence. "When Armand first began to travel to Libya, he usually arrived by chartered plane, and King Idris asked him about it. Armand looked the king in the eye and said that it was his private plane. Then he said, 'Take it, it's yours,' and handed over the plane on the spot."

"Why did King Idris want the plane?"

"He didn't. He's so rich his wife flies around in her own personal jet. Armand forced the plane on him because he knew that once the ministers heard about it, they'd know that he'd be willing to give them *anything* to get into Libya."

On his return Armand pretended that he had just met the seventy-seven-year-old Libyan monarch for the first time. "King Idris wears a full-length robe and headdress. He has a long beard and carries a wooden shepherd's staff. He reminds me of an Old Testament prophet. He's a simple, devout holy man who lives modestly and cares deeply about his people and their welfare."

"Reporters tell me," I said, "that his regime is one of the most corrupt in the world."

"King Idris is too nice and too naïve, which allows some of his ministers and aides to take advantage of him," Armand replied. "They're the ones who give this fine, honest man a bad reputation. What's important is that he likes me and appreciates what Oxy and I are doing for his country. He looked at me with love in his eyes and said, 'Allah sent you to Libya!' This is what I want you to incorporate into the text of the upcoming annual report: 'His Majesty King Idris I graciously permitted the new oil field to be named *Idris* in his honor.'"

I said I didn't think that Moslems allowed oil fields to be named after them.

"You're right," he replied, "but in this instance King Idris will be too modest to object. I'm even thinking of getting him to change the name of Kufra, the sacred birthplace of kings, to Hammer."

I said I was sure that no Moslem was going to give a Jewish family name to a sacred shrine.

"Hammer is a *Swedish* family name!" he barked.

Jersey responded to the substantial size of Occidental's new discovery by ordering cutbacks in Kuwaiti and Saudi production, and Armand believed the moment had come to initiate another secret overture. The terms he proposed were the same, with one significant exception. "Six months ago I asked Esso for a hundred million dollars," he said. "But our new discovery enabled me to double the ante: two hundred million or nothing."

Eager to gain control over Occidental's Libyan production, the Jersey executives agreed quickly, but once again the offer was rejected by the Jersey board. Armand thought he knew why. "They want me to believe I'll never be able to go to market without them and make me so desperate I'll beg for mercy and accept whatever cheap terms they dictate. That miserable stuffed-shirt bunch of Big Oil clowns disgusts me, and I'm never going to give in."

During interviews Armand invariably plugged two things, Occidental and himself, and kept stressing that his efforts alone were personally responsible for the increased dividends being earned by Occidental's shareholders. The numerous Occidental publications mailed to shareholders also stressed the same theme. On May 9 Occidental held its annual meeting, and hundreds packed the room to see the chief executive who had successfully led the Libyan expedition that was going to prove so profitable. When Armand stepped before them, he was given a prolonged ovation. Later he said to me, "The shareholders love me because I'm going to make them rich."

He had come a long way, I thought. When I had first become involved with Hammer, nobody knew who he was and he was inevitably confused with Arm & Hammer baking soda. Eleven years later everybody knew his name, due in part to my hard work and in part to his genius for self-promotion. Once it had taken a multitude of phone calls to get media attention for him. Now, reporters called me to obtain the latest information about his activities.

"Armand, you're famous!" I announced one day after fielding a battery of such calls.

He stared at me from behind his horn-rimmed glasses. "I'm famous because I knew Lenin," he said. "I don't need you to make me famous. Your job is to make me immortal."

10.

THE MULTI-
MILLION-
DOLLAR
OVERRIDE

The third Arab-Israeli War, the Six-Day War, broke out on June
5, 1967 and Egypt closed the Suez Canal, Iraq and Saudi Arabia
shut down their pipelines, and Libya joined four other Arab nations in an oil embargo against all countries friendly to Israel.
When angry mobs of Libyans began to storm foreign oil company
offices and attack Western oil workers, evacuations were ordered,
and planes filled with fleeing Westerners began to leave every half
hour.

There was general agreement that Libya's behavior would have
a very detrimental effect on Occidental's ability to secure additional
investment capital, especially when the company still had no way to
transport its oil across the desert. Armand disagreed. "Our oil
doesn't have to pass through the Suez Canal in order to go to
market. It's more valuable today than it was yesterday. Besides, the
Libyans are eventually going to calm down. Ultimately they care
more about money than they care about Arab unity. Once they feel
the pinch of losing all those oil revenues without seeing anything
for it except the bill for footing the war, they'll change their tune.
There's never been a better moment to build a pipeline and port
facilities in Libya."

Bechtel Corporation, a multimillion-dollar international construction and engineering firm, had built the first Libyan pipeline for Esso-Libya in 1961, which had earned it a reputation for knowing how to get things done in Libya. "I'm going to ask Steve Bechtel to build the pipeline," Armand continued. "I'm going to ask for credit, and I'm going to let him know how much money he'll make if he goes along with me."

When Armand returned from Bechtel's corporate headquarters in San Francisco, he related that he had been received triumphantly by Bechtel and other members of the senior staff. Subsequently, Bechtel Corporation agreed to grant Occidental a letter of credit for $150 million, which Occidental could use to borrow another $150 million from the banks. Armand attributed his success to his powers of persuasion over Stephen Bechtel and did not mention that he had been asked to produce the SEC registration of the number of recoverable reserves in the Libyan reef before Bechtel Corporation approved the plan.

Occidental's petroleum-engineering consultants, DeGolyer and MacNaughton, had enormous credibility with the SEC, which enabled them to accomplish the unheard-of feat of obtaining registration of 1 billion barrels on the basis of a *sole* discovery well. This official declaration established Occidental as a foolproof credit risk with the banks. "The SEC says we have *three* billion barrels of oil waiting for us," Armand told everyone as he flogged Occidental's stock during an endless round of phone calls.

Bechtel Corporation's fee was $43 million. It also charged as much as 18 percent of a company's profits in return for the use of its capital and its ability to use efficient payoff systems to smooth over any problems with the Libyans. The fact that Bechtel Corporation had provided Occidental with the means to obtain loans of $300 million obliterated any concerns Occidental might have had when Bechtel Corporation's fees began to rise and did not stop until they reached $147 million.

When the Libyan Council of Ministers demanded that Occidental hire Libyan crews to build the pipeline, Hammer and Bechtel Corporation vetoed the idea. Bechtel Corporation solved the problem by awarding lucrative "subcontracts" to a number of Libyan companies. Occidental also placed Libyan officials on the payroll and itemized their salaries as business expenses that would be deducted before Occidental made its initial taxation payment under the Libyan Petroleum Law. Thus the officials were being bribed with tax revenues that normally would have been paid to their government. Armand also supplied a further demonstration of goodwill when he handed over another aircraft, this time to Minister Kabazi.

Building terminal facilities and a pipeline from the heart of the Sahara Desert to the Mediterranean coast was a three-year job, but Armand didn't have three years. Bechtel Corporation hired two large construction crews to work on double shifts. The first began work at the concession sites and the second in the port city of Zueitina, where the pipeline would end. When the crews met somewhere in the middle of the desert, the 40-inch, 135-mile pipeline capable of moving a million barrels of crude oil per day would be complete. Simultaneously, other crews began to construct a loading terminal at Zueitina, which would contain thirteen huge storage tanks with a 7-million-barrel capacity and monobuoy sea berths for the huge tankers that would load and transport Occidental's oil to world markets.

Construction started in August. The workers received larger salaries than they had ever earned before and were invigorated by the enormity of the project and the breathless speed of the construction. No complaints filtered back despite the severe heat, constant sandstorms, flies, sand fleas, and scorpions. It was a great adventure, and I commissioned a script and camera crews for a promotional film to be shown at the next shareholders' meeting. Naturally, its star was Armand. In the film, for dramatic purposes, he becomes alarmed when he learns that the pipeline is falling behind schedule. Dressed in his rumpled business suit, he sets off to Libya and is seen in the desert, giving a stirring oration to his "troops" and ordering them to work around the clock. They instantly make up the lag and complete the project in record time. I offered the film at no charge to television stations across the country, and they began airing it at all hours, which provided another dose of national attention. It was the first of ten promotional films that became free TV commercials for Occidental and the myth of Armand Hammer.

Each of the Seven Sisters is an "integrated" company, engaged in all stages of the oil business: crude production, refining, and marketing. Occidental's inability to refine and market the oil it produced had required that it hire Signal Oil and Gas to do those jobs; unlike Occidental, Signal possessed almost no oil discoveries and bought the oil it marketed from the Seven Sisters. Occidental obtained an option to acquire Signal and when it exercised the option, Armand remarked, "I'd like to be a fly on the wall at the next Standard Oil board meeting. Just imagine them discussing how they turned down my two offers and allowed Oxy to grow and grow until it's become their small but dangerous eighth sister."

He did not discuss the fact that both Jersey and Gulf Oil had entered into negotiations to buy crude from Occidental and that after he had made the deal with Signal, he had abruptly halted the negotiations with them. The senior staff was convinced he was paying them for the way they had treated him when he had tried to make deals with them, and he probably was.

Emboldened by the progress of the Libyan venture, Armand became even more determined to meet with President Johnson. He made a series of large donations to the Democratic National Committee, and the president responded by renewing his appointment to the board of governors of the Eleanor Roosevelt Memorial Foundation. Occidental and Holiday Inns were coventuring construction of four hotels in Morocco, and Armand had no difficulty receiving an invitation to a state dinner for King Hassan in Washington. But the turning point in his relationship with the Johnson administration occurred at a state dinner for the shah of Iran.

"Mike Mansfield tipped me that LBJ was all excited because some rich publisher had just donated a Frederic Remington sculpture to the White House," Armand told me when he returned from the dinner. "So I told Lady Bird that I was planning to donate Charles Russell's *Meat for Wild Men* to the White House, and her eyes lit up. She told me she knew that LBJ would love having a Russell sculpture in the LBJ library. I smiled at her and said, 'May I donate two, one to the White House and one to the library?' She nearly fainted when she heard that. Mark my words. I'm in now!"

The conversation with Mrs. Johnson was pure fabrication. Actually Armand had written to Mansfield to suggest a donation of artworks and Mrs. Johnson had conveyed through Mansfield that she would be delighted to receive two Russell sculptures, one for the White House and one for the Lyndon Johnson Library.

Armand planned to celebrate the completion of the construction of the Libyan pipeline with a "one-million-dollar dedication ceremony that will put Esso's dedication ceremony in 1961 to shame. When I get up to speak, I want to read a personal message from LBJ."

President Johnson had spent his entire career fighting for the interests of Texas gas and oil, and I commented that I didn't think he was going to want to offend his contributors by praising a California independent.

"I'm a contributor, a *big* contributor," Armand shot back. "What makes you think he's going to want to offend me?"

The next day Armand had Russell's *Meat for Wild Men* crated and shipped to the White House. Mrs. Johnson responded with a traditional formality extended to donors, an invitation to a small tea party in Hammer's honor. But when Armand asked Marvin Watson to submit a request to LBJ for a statement that he could read at the dedication ceremony, Watson reported back that the president had turned him down.

In early fall, Armand asked me to come to his home on a Sunday morning. He took this occasion to announce that he wanted me to work for Occidental full time out of corporate headquarters. Before I made the move, it was essential that I list my demands and obtain his agreement on each and every one of them. I told him that I wanted complete autonomy over my department, adequate office space, a sufficient budget, the proper number of salaried assistants, and renewed confirmation of our original agreement that I report only to him and have access to him at all times.

He quickly agreed, got up, walked to the window, and stared out at the day, while I was left to wonder what was really behind this sudden move. Armand's capacity to use drama to get what he wanted included a startling ability to cry on cue. When he turned around, tears were streaming down his face. "I'm concerned about my son, Julian," he said. "He's always in trouble. He constantly messes up his life, and I always have to bail him out. I don't know how to put a stop to it or where it's going to end."

Armand never asked for help directly because he considered such requests a display of weakness and vulnerability. So I was going to have to ask him what he wanted, and I did.

"I want Julian to work for you," he replied. "He respects you. You can be his model while you keep an eye on him."

Julian was so locked into the mechanics of not giving his father anything he wanted, I knew that any professional relationship with him was doomed. "What makes you think he'll listen to me?" I asked.

"I'll make it clear that you're the boss. I'll be on *your* side, not his."

"What happens if I want to fire him?"

"Let's cross that bridge when we come to it. It's my hope he'll apply himself and that won't be necessary."

"If I don't succeed, how will you feel about me?"

"All I'm asking is that you give it a try and do your best. If it doesn't work out, I'll understand."

It was the only time I ever saw Armand display anything ap-

proaching genuine feeling for another human being. Despite the
fact that he was doing his best to manipulate me with his finely
honed acting skills, I think he did care about Julian. He also hated
defeat, and the fact that Julian was winning the war between them
was making him feel awful.

"I'll give Julian a two- or three-week trial period," I said quietly.

"Fair enough." Armand looked exhausted. "I wanted so much
for Julian to follow in my footsteps. I guess it just wasn't meant to
be."

I decided to keep a detailed log of Julian's performance, which
I would submit to Armand if it became necessary for me to complain about his misbehavior. Julian's first week began with several
days of no-shows followed by his turning up drunk. Then he
stayed away again, and I called his home and spoke to his wife. He
replied with a telegram advising me that he was "booked solid" and
to check with his secretary.

His second week was a repetition of the first. One excuse for his
absence followed another until he told me that his mother had
died, something that Armand never mentioned. I sensed that he
was using her death as an excuse. Finally, he sent me a perplexing
memo:

> In light of what appears to be a persistent misunderstanding on
> your part of both the nature and extent of your "official" cognizance
> over the subject task, I have taken the initiative and called a private
> meeting with Dr. Hammer on the same subject for this evening. I
> feel that any meeting between us prior to reclarification by Dr.
> Hammer would not only be pointless, but detrimental to the com-
> pany's interest.
>
> I do not discount the possibility that it is I, and not you, who is
> under a misapprehension, but if that is the case, Dr. Hammer will
> have to refute his own words which I have on record with both
> fidelity and forthrightness.

I stapled the memo into the log and went to Armand. As he
flipped through the pages, a look of weariness and discouragement
spread across his face. "You certainly are the bearer of bad news,"
he said.

"The bottom line is that Julian has severe emotional problems
and a drinking problem. He needs professional help."

Armand didn't react.

"What are you going to do?"

"Terminate him. You can forget about him. Thanks for trying."

Julian was fired later that day.

Several days later Armand placed a photograph of Lenin on the table behind his desk. Then he sent for me so I could look at it. The photograph was inscribed in English, "To Comrade Armand Hammer from V. I. Ilyanov (Lenin), 10.XI.21."

I was very busy and in no mood to listen when he launched into his monologue about his "dear, sweet friend." "How did you develop this amazing relationship with Lenin when you were only with him for an hour?" I asked sharply.

He bristled. "Don't believe anybody who tries to tell you that I didn't have a warm and close relationship with Lenin. I've got proof."

Hammer reached into a desk drawer, withdrew three pieces of Lenin's correspondence, and handed them to me. They included a short, cordial note welcoming him to the Soviet Union in 1921, a letter of introduction to a Soviet official, and a brief explanation of Hammer's business plans that was addressed to "Comrade Stalin." "That should convince you that Lenin was my very good friend," Armand said, taking the letters from me and putting them back into the drawer.

A few days later Armand showed me a photograph of him and Dwight Eisenhower. Standing between them were two men I did not recognize. "Get rid of the other two," he said.

An expert airbrusher blotted out the unwanted figures and moved Hammer's image next to Ike's. The retouched photograph was placed on a table just a few inches away from the photo of Lenin. It was the start of what would become a huge and impressive collection of vanity photographs consisting either of autographed portraits of heads of state or photographs of Hammer posing with other heads of state, every one a "very good friend."

As 1967 neared an end, Concession 102 yielded eight development wells that pumped a total of 97,000 barrels a day. An additional seven wells were drilled on the Idris field, formerly Concession 103. One tested at close to 74,000 barrels per day, the largest flow rate ever recorded in Libya and one of the largest in the world. Suddenly, little Oxy's stock became the most hotly traded issue on the New York Stock Exchange, and its price reached an all-time high of $122 a share.

"People keep insisting we're lucky in Libya and they're right," Armand told me. "Let me tell you how to spell luck: g-o-o-d g-e-o-l-o-g-i-s-t-s."

It was at this moment that Armand received some bad news.

"Allen & Co. has just filed a hundred-million-dollar suit against Oxy," he confided. "They claim they provided the third party that enabled us to get our concessions and that I agreed to a joint venture if the third party helped us succeed. Even though they didn't spend a cent on exploration and development they want twenty-five percent of our profits.

I remembered the call from a *Wall Street Journal* reporter, who had described the 1964 meeting at Claridge's during which Hammer had reportedly paid Ferdinand Galic $200,000 to use his influence with Oil Minister Kabazi in behalf of Occidental.

"You lied to me," I said.

"I did hold that meeting, and I didn't lie to you," he countered. "I told you to say that *you* didn't know anything about the meeting. That was the truth."

But Hammer looked uncomfortable. "I'll tell you exactly why I didn't want you or anyone else to know about that meeting," he said. "Herbert Allen brought along a General de Rovin, a Ferdinand Galic, and a Libyan, Taher Ogbi. Galic said that his partner was Oil Minister Kabazi, and de Rovin said that he and Minister of Court Omar Shalhi were partners. So I decided to take a chance. I made them all big promises about how much money they would get if things worked out, and I gave Galic two hundred thousand dollars. Then I worked out additional financial arrangements with the other guys.

"When I had them checked out, I discovered those dirty bastards had put one over on me. De Rovin was an imposter. He wasn't really a general and had been a Nazi collaborator. He was also a swindler with a long history of passing bad checks. The others mispresented their influence over the Libyan ministers. Galic had walked away with two hundred thousand dollars and de Rovin, one hundred thousand, so I terminated them and that ended my agreement with the Allen brothers. If they hadn't filed that lawsuit, no one would ever have known that I was taken for a ride."

The actual scenario was somewhat different. It was Allen & Co. that had made the discovery that de Rovin, whose real name was François Fortune Louis Pegulu, had lied about his past, and had supplied Armand with this information early in 1965. Two weeks before the bidding on July 29, 1965, Occidental had notified Allen & Co., de Rovin, and Galic that their agreements had been canceled. Allen took the position that Armand had waited until he was convinced that the efforts of Galic and Kabazi had paid off and that Occidental was going to win the bidding before it used the information about de Rovin's background as a convenient excuse to cut the investment banking firm out of the deal.

Armand made an official declaration that he had severed all connections with anyone who was named in the suit. But I issued almost no releases about the legal action. To my relief, it did not receive much play in the press, an indication that the aura of hero-ism and nobility around Armand was becoming hard to penetrate.

As Armand prepared to give a deposition in the case, I learned from some of the oil and gas boys on their return from Libya that one of the parties in the suit, Labor Minister Ogbi, was continuing to receive secret payments from Occidental and that a horde of Ogbi associates and family members remained on the Occidental payroll. No matter what he said in public, Armand was not going to jeopardize the flow of oil from Libya by firing Ogbi or anybody else.

One day I was sitting in his office waiting for him to finish a call. "Okay," he said to the party at the other end of the line, "so the Libyan bastards want to get their palms greased. They're going to keep giving us trouble until they get some bribe money from us. What the hell. Pay them off and get the job done. That's what the Libyan overrides are for! Go ahead and use them!"

In addition to the basic 12.5 percent royalty on their profits that oil companies paid producing countries, they were also allowed to pay overriding royalties or ongoing commissions for any number of reasons to either individuals or corporations that have played a part in the development or maintenance of an oil property. Ham-mer's negotiation with Esso and then with Jersey included the de-mand that they assume payment of a 3 percent Libyan override. This was the money that was being transferred to Swiss bank ac-counts under a variety of names and being used to make payoffs to Kabazi, Ogbi, Shalhi, and the other key Libyan ministers who had maneuvered behind the scenes to help Occidental, as well as to other highly placed officials. Under Armand's direct supervi-sion, millions were reportedly being channeled into these secret bank accounts.

Even though offers were made on a number of occasions over the next six years to settle the Allen & Co. suit out of court, Ar-mand believed that the law was on his side and insisted on going to trial. As the trial date finally neared, he told me he had discovered that Herbert and Charles Allen had made "a dumb mistake." After Armand had terminated its services in the Libyan venture, Allen & Co. had been the underwriter of an Occidental debenture offering.

"When they filled out the SEC questionnaire, they foolishly wrote down that they didn't have a financial or economic involvement with Oxy," said Armand. "In that way they gave us the evidence in their own writing to prove they're not entitled to claim they are our Libyan partners. It's these little technical details that always enable me to win."

But the Allens believed they held a trump card. Armand became apoplectic when they submitted to the court a letter from Libyan Oil Minister Kabazi to Ferdinand Galic that acknowledged that Galic and he were partners and that Occidental's partnership with Allen & Co. had encouraged Kabazi to convince the Libyan ministry to award two concessions to Occidental. But Occidental's lawyers were able to demonstrate under cross-examination that Kabazi had probably backdated the letter and that it was a forgery.

Then Armand's intelligence network informed him that General de Rovin had fallen out with Galic. "Galic is supposed to get ten percent of anything the Allens get," he told me. "When de Rovin asked Galic for a piece of his share, Galic turned him down. De Rovin got mad and turned over evidence to us that will enable us to put Galic on the stand and destroy him bit by bit."

That was exactly what happened.

At the conclusion of the three-week trial, even though the judge viewed some of Hammer's testimony with great skepticism, he ruled in favor of Occidental. Armand was thrilled. "We beat the pants off the Allens!" he crowed. "So what if it took eight years? We beat them. That's what counts. If we had lost, it would have cost Occidental as much as two hundred fifty million dollars. But then, how could we have lost? After all the public record clearly demonstrates that I've *never* given a bribe to anybody."

11.

ON THE
MERGER TRAIL

When oil flowed through Occidental's Libyan pipeline for the first time on February 5, 1968, a mere eight months after the commencement of its construction, everybody agreed that it was a modern industrial miracle. Accompanied by Senator Albert Gore and two company directors, Armand and Frances set out for Zuei-tina. The highlight of Jersey's pipeline dedication ceremony in 1961 had been the participation of King Idris. Over lunch after the Hammers' return, Frances and I listened as Armand related how the king had outdone himself on behalf of Occidental.

"He arrived in a shiny black chauffeur-driven Mercedes with the Libyan flag flapping above the radiator and a caravan of ministers, other government officials, foreign diplomats, and local chieftains following behind him. The route was lined by shepherds and each had a sacrificial lamb on a leash. As King Idris rode by, they slit the lambs' throats in his honor."

Frances grimaced. "It's one of their traditional customs to show respect. Those lambs were going to be cooked for our dinner, but watching them get slaughtered was horrible."

"I had a red carpet spread out across the sand for King Idris to walk on after he stepped out of his car," Armand continued. "First he posed for a picture with me beside his Mercedes. Then he stepped inside. I followed right behind him and I also walked on the royal carpet."

"Only men were permitted in the assembly hall," Frances said. "I had to sit in the harem with the wives of the Libyan officials."

"How did you feel about being in a harem?" I asked.

"It's the custom, and I had no choice. And the women were very nice to me. At least I didn't have to cover my face with a veil like they did when they joined their husbands at the end of the ceremony."

While Frances was in the harem, Armand was seated on the platform with King Idris. "I was by his side almost the entire day. I even sat beside him during the feast."

Frances made another face. "One thousand people were packed into two huge tents. Many of them were tribesmen who had traveled great distances. I knew they were going to eat with their hands, and I was ready for them to reach across the table with their right hands and dip them into the communal bowl. But they did a lot more than dip. They grabbed and gulped and grabbed some more. They'd never heard of Emily Post."

"The bottom line is King Idris kept paying me compliments about the wonderful things I've done for his country. We're in terrific shape in Libya," Armand concluded proudly.

A sharp drop in world fertilizer prices and his desire to avoid incurring $15 million in building costs had led Armand to send word to the Libyan Council of Ministers that Occidental would not proceed with the construction of the promised ammonia plant unless it proved capable of earning back its $30 million investment over three years. Armand didn't mention that the Libyans had begun to perceive him as a liar and had responded by barring Occidental's participation in any future oil properties auctions. To pacify them, Occidental had started to drill for water at Kufra, but not before Armand had received permission to deduct the $13 million development costs of the oasis from Occidental's oil royalty payments, and to reverse the royal tax decree and compute Occidental's tax royalty on the per-barrel market price of oil rather than on the higher posted price. Thus, Armand had persuaded the Libyans to become the underwriters of one of the four preferences Occidental had used to obtain the oil concessions in the first place.

When Occidental's engineers struck the water at Kufra that Armand had known about for years, he declared the discovery "an amazing surprise! We've discovered the equivalent of two hundred years' discharge of the Nile on the site of a sacred shrine! That's got to be more points for us!" And by the time the Kufra project was completed, Occidental was pumping 600,000 barrels of Libyan crude a day and was that nation's largest oil producer.

"The Libyans have to be even more thrilled with us," Armand insisted. "Think of the enormous oil royalties and taxes they're earning from our production. And we've proved that we're agricultural good Samaritans by converting Kufra from a parched desert wasteland into a rich farming area."

Armand's determination that *his* "rich farming area" turn a quick profit outraged Libya's farming community. Under only the loose control of King Idris, the Libyan press inflamed the situation by declaring the oasis a vanity project initiated solely to flatter the king and reported that it was not only being subsidized by potential tax revenues but also loomed as unfair competition to the nation's other food producers. Additional questions were raised about why $13 million had been spent to irrigate a small desert outpost when so many more populous areas of Libya were desperately in need of water.

A secret Occidental engineering study had concluded that Kufra's underground water supplies were too limited to support large-scale farming, were being severely taxed by Occidental's high-tech drilling program and would take centuries to replenish. Determined to have the oasis transformed into profit-making farmland and to have its name changed to "Hammer," Armand buried the report as soon as he had read it.

Now the Libyans demanded that Occidental fulfill its promise to build an ammonia plant and Hammer ordered a study. It confirmed that the low price of ammonia on the world market would make the venture impractical. A subsequent Libyan study contradicted Occidental's statistics. Armand responded with another study which, in turn, repudiated the Libyan figures. Finally, he played his trump card. Occidental's concessions agreement had established a six-hundred-ton-per-day quota for the plant and stated that the Libyans were responsible for supplying the natural gas needed in the ammonia-manufacturing process. The Libyans did not have access to such a large amount of gas and Armand knew it. Therefore, he insisted that he was not bound to proceed until they found a way to supply it.

Occidental's Arabist consultant confided to me that the Libyans had a number of other grievances with Hammer and Occidental. They believed that Occidental was shipping large amounts of unmetered oil out of the country in order to avoid paying taxes on it; that massive overproduction on Occidental's oil fields was depleting them so quickly they would inevitably be destroyed; that an Arab worker had died in an accident as a result of faulty safety systems; and that when John McGuire, a Bechtel engineer, complained about bad working conditions, his life had been threatened. "The Libyans are convinced that the death threat was authorized by Dr. Hammer," the consultant told me. "They were so concerned about McGuire's safety they personally escorted him out of the country."

A short time later it became public knowledge that overproduction had caused a substantial drop in pressure in one of Occidental's fields and that the oil wells were being flooded with water in order to maintain the high flow rate artificially. Armand instructed me to announce the pressure drop as a "supposed decline."

Meanwhile, business reporters had observed that Occidental had placed itself in the dangerous position of being dependent on one country for its oil output, and Armand agreed with them. "If there's trouble, we're going to be in a hell of a fix. That's why I'm looking very hard at Venezuela. Their oil ministry is putting five new blocks on South Lake Maracaibo up for auction, and Oxy's going to enter the bidding."

Gene Reid had no idea that Armand had devoted four years to plotting Occidental's entry into Venezuela and had allocated $3 million to ensure a victory for Occidental in the auction. "Winning this one is going to be very tough," he told me. "Venezuela isn't Libya. Only five drilling blocks are being put up for bid, and dozens of companies are vying for them. I wouldn't say the odds are on our side."

In March 1968, CVP, the Venezuelan national oil company, announced that it was accepting sealed bids and would declare the winners on December 1, 1970. CVP officials also announced that the traditional concession agreements were going to be replaced with partnership arrangements called service contracts, requiring the producers to limit the length of their exploration period to three years, assume all financial responsibility for exploration investments, and turn over 10 percent of the produced oil to the national oil company in addition to paying the standard 12.5 percent royalty and 50 percent tax. "It's another battle to the death with the Seven Sisters," Armand declared. "We beat them in Libya; we can beat them again!" In reality, the severe terms set forth in the service contracts were going to limit the number of participants in the bidding competition drastically and Armand was guilty of his usual exaggeration.

On March 31, a couple of weeks after Occidental submitted its bids, President Johnson announced that he was not going to seek or accept reelection. The lame-duck president had nothing to lose by being nice to Armand, and he allowed Marvin Watson to set a

June date for a long-sought-after Oval Office meeting. Armand was going to use the occasion as an opportunity to present a proposal for ending the Vietnam War. I asked him to describe his peace plan, but he changed the subject.

Victor was more forthcoming. "Armand's going to tell LBJ that he can get Brezhnev and Kosygin to use their influence on Hanoi to end the war by tempting them with a commitment to build fertilizer plants in Russia. Then he's going to ask LBJ to appoint him his personal peace emissary to the Soviet Union so that he can put his plan into action."

President Johnson passed on the opportunity to make this particular appointment, but he did appoint Armand to a presidential trade policy committee. Hammer told reporters that he had become LBJ's personal consultant on trade policy, but he did not make much of a fuss about it because the president had only five months left in office.

Occidental's acquisition of Permian Corporation in 1966 was followed by the acquisition of another oil transportation company, McWood Corporation, and an industrial research firm, Garrett Research and Development Company. During 1968 Occidental made two major acquisitions. In January, it paid $150 million in stock to acquire Island Creek Coal Company, the third-largest U.S. coal producer. On July 24, in one of the largest mergers in history, Occidental paid $800 million in stock for Hooker Chemical Corporation, which was among the ten largest U.S. chemical firms. As a result Occidental jumped from number 102 on the *Fortune* 500 list of the largest U.S. corporations to number 48.

That was not all. According to Armand, the merger provided Occidental with an official heir apparent. "Hooker's president, Tom Willers, has given a stellar performance for years," he said. "Tell reporters that I've decided that Willers is going to be Oxy's next chief executive." I took that with a grain of salt. Armand had remarked on any number of occasions that he was eager to appoint a successor, but his hunger for power and complete control remained insatiable and it was virtually impossible to believe that he was serious about the possibility of eventual retirement. More likely he was simply trying to appease demands that a seventy-year-old chief executive have a competent replacement.

The senior management wondered if "heir apparent" Tom Willers would be a Hammer clone, quick-witted, fearless, unscrupulous, manipulative, and a workaholic. Was he perhaps the son

Armand wished he had had, an energetic, unorthodox, innovative entrepreneur? Was he a traditional corporate type who had convinced Armand to allow him to bring a stable element to his chaotic, secretive methods of operation? Or was he merely someone Hammer had seduced with the promise of becoming chief executive so that Occidental could acquire Hooker?

Willers, cherubic, middle-aged, and cautious, turned out to be an executive with a deep commitment to a team approach. One day Armand, who made every major decision on his own, complained that "a light bulb just burned out at Hooker and I can't get anybody on the phone. Tom Willers is holding an executive conference."

After Willers came to Occidental, I got a call from a business editor asking to interview him. Armand agreed to the interview, but then he was furious when he saw it in print. "What's Tom trying to do," he said, "give the impression that he's running Oxy?"

"You okayed the interview," I remarked.

"The hell I did."

"You okayed it to me."

"It doesn't matter. What matters is that Tom's trying to give the impression that he's the boss. Nobody runs this company but me. He'd better get that into his head fast or there's going to be big trouble."

Armand was equally displeased when Richard Nixon achieved the Republican presidential nomination a few days later on August 8. "The nation doesn't want Nixon," he said with disbelief. "Everyone knows he's no good. The thought that he could be president makes me sick." Three weeks later Vice President Hubert Humphrey became the Democratic candidate, and Armand moved quickly to let Humphrey know that he and Occidental planned to be major campaign contributors.

Politics aside, Armand was always on the lookout for opportunities to increase Occidental's bottom line. After John Buckley, a former editor of *Petroleum Intelligence Weekly*, tipped him that Jack Evans, the director of Independent Fuel Oil Marketers of America, was eager to build the first oil refinery in New England, Armand did some calculations and discovered that if Occidental built the refinery and used it to refine its Libyan crude, after recouping its investment it would earn a $75 million profit yearly. Armand contacted Evans, turned on the charm, and obtained a 25 percent partnership.

Evans had already approached Maine's governor, Kenneth Curtis, and one of Maine's senators, Democratic vice presidential candidate Edmund Muskie, and had worked with them to choose as the refinery site the coastal town of Machiasport. In order to protect domestic production against foreign imports, an import duty was attached to every foreign barrel brought into the United States. The removal of the duty was going to increase Evans's profits substantially, so he evolved a plan to convert Machiasport's neighbor, Portland, into a foreign trade zone, which would make it the equivalent of a duty-free port with Machiasport as a subzone.

Governor Curtis agreed with the strategy and authorized the State of Maine to file a trade-zone application with the Department of Commerce Foreign Trade Zones Board. And since the domestic oil industry was protected by mandatory quotas on oil imports, Evans's company, Business Development Fund, also filed an application with the Department of the Interior to obtain a 20,000-barrel-per-day import quota for the refinery. Thus, if the Foreign Trade Zone Board approved Maine's trade zone application and Interior approved the quota application, the Evans-Occidental refinery would achieve a projected $19 million yearly savings on its oil imports, enabling it to undersell every other company's petroleum products in the New England region by 10 percent.

Armand was determined to speed things along. After Senator Thomas McIntyre of New Hampshire was persuaded to hold a series of Senate subcommittee hearings on Secretary of Commerce and Chairman of the Foreign Trade Zone Board C. R. Smith's refusal to act on Maine's trade-zone application, Walter Corey of Governor Curtis's office stated his belief that his phone as well as McIntyre's was bugged. Armand recommended a surveillance expert who subsequently found a bug in Corey's office phone. But members of Curtis's staff told Governor Curtis that they were convinced the bug had been planted there in order to have Curtis go before the subcommittee and create sympathy for his cause with the news that his opponents had resorted to electronic eavesdropping to get their way. Curtis took their word over that of Armand's expert, and Armand began to search for other ways to get the New England Democrats to do what he wanted.

He knew Fred Vahlsing from his days as a cattle breeder and was under the impression that Vahlsing's son, Fred Jr., had the ability to exert a great deal of influence over Maine's Democratic hierarchy. One day, when I was working with Armand at his home, Fred Jr. turned up and greeted Armand by kissing him on the lips, an indication that he had become Armand's newest surrogate son. Subsequently, Armand and Fred Jr. cemented their bond with a business deal, and Occidental acquired a 33 percent equity interest in one Vahlsing company, Vahlsing Inc., and a 25 percent equity interest in another, Vahlco Corporation, in exchange for its interest in OXYTROL. But the environmental problems surrounding Vahlsing Inc.'s potato processing plant in Maine made Fred Jr. more of a liability than an asset, and he proved incapable of helping Armand bend Governor Curtis and Senator Muskie to his wishes.

Finally, all of the machinery to secure trade-zone status and an import quota did fall into place, and Armand demanded that Evans allow Occidental to buy him out or Occidental was going to withdraw from the project. Evans agreed to a $3.9 million settlement, payable on the condition that Occidental receive all of the necessary permissions to build the refinery, and he departed. At the end of July Interior revealed that Occidental had taken over Business Development Fund, was going to be the sole owner of the refinery, and had raised its quota request from 20,000 barrels per day to a number that would represent New England's fair share of the overall U.S. oil import quotas: 100,000. As a result Occidental would be able to offer *wholesale* heating oil 10 percent below the prices of all other competitors.

Not only Big Oil but also all of the domestic independents were aghast at Hammer's plan to construct a refinery with a 300,000-barrel-per-day capacity and import 100,000 barrels a day of duty-free crude, thereby flooding the Northeast with cheap oil, underselling all competitors, and becoming the Northeast's prime fuel supplier. Joining forces, the entire domestic oil industry declared war on what was perceived as a bold and dangerous attempt by Hammer to destroy the U.S. oil import quota program solely for Occidental's financial gain.

Two rounds of hearings were scheduled on Maine's trade-zone application, the first before the Foreign Trade Zones Board in Portland on October 12, the second in Washington one week later. By the time the twelfth rolled around, Occidental was in the middle of what the petroleum press labeled "the most controversial refinery project in history."

Governor Curtis told the Foreign Trade Zones Board that New England did not have a single refinery and New Englanders were penalized with the highest energy costs in the United States. The Big Oil lobby had always been able to initiate passage of restrictive legislation on the basis of "national security," but Curtis also claimed that the refinery would reduce the oil costs to the Department of Defense by $6 million annually and provide another significant storage capacity for defense purposes.

Lining up behind Curtis and Hammer were the six New England governors and thirty-seven congressmen. Their passionate presentation of the issue encouraged fifty-three other congressmen to press for an investigation into fuel price rises across the country. Opposing them were every U.S. oil company with the exception of Occidental, every petroleum trade organization, the petroleum press, and every elected official who received large campaign contributions from the energy industry.

The key spokesman for Big Oil was Louisiana Congressman Hale Boggs, the House majority whip. Boggs testified against the Portland refinery, returned to Washington, and called a press conference. He charged that Occidental had offered to contribute to his reelection campaign but that his acceptance would have been a tacit agreement not to testify against the refinery. Boggs added that one of Hooker Chemical's many plants was located in St. Charles Parish in his home state and alleged that he had been told that the prospective campaign contribution to him could be made through "Duck" Sellers, tax assessor for St. Charles Parish. For that reason he declared that he was planning to ask the SEC to determine if Occidental's relationship with Sellers had enabled it to violate insider trading rules during its acquisition of Hooker Chemical. And as if making those charges weren't enough, Boggs inserted a fifteen-page discussion of the alleged bribery attempt in the *Congressional Record.*

Armand issued an immediate denial, but he loathed the fact that Bogg's allegations had become a part of history and had sullied his public image. "That slimy bastard's been lining his pockets with Big Oil money for years!" he thundered. "Oxy's offer to contribute was perfectly legal, and he knew it. Why did he see us if he wasn't interested? Why did he have a photographer there? Why did he ask us a lot of questions and keep going until we said exactly what he wanted to hear? That son of a bitch set us up. Big Oil has him in their hip pocket! To top it off, he's a drunk."

Boggs demanded and got an FBI investigation, but Occidental warned *The New York Times* and *The Washington Post* that they would be sued for libel if they printed Boggs's scurrilous accusations. The investigation proved inconclusive and the coverage was light, which led Boggs to complain publicly that it did not get the attention it deserved.

Years later an author researching Armand and his family's

brushes with the federal government found that entries about Occidental and Armand in the governmental indexes in federal libraries and computer systems had been shuffled, making it harder to locate any unfavorable references that could be used to mar Armand's "perfect" report card.

A week after Boggs's press conference vice presidential candidate Spiro Agnew was the guest of honor at an oil industry fundraiser in Midland, Texas. Texas Campaign Finance Chairman John Hurd told the oil executives that Agnew had assured him that "Occidental's effort at Machiasport is dead. If he and Nixon are successful, there will be no refinery. I sure hope there are no Occidental people here."

Walter Davis stood up. "There sure are."

Armand scowled when he heard the story. "I've always hated Richard Nixon. Now I hate him more than ever. And he's going to know it when this story turns up in the political columns."

I was working with Armand on election eve. Despite the polls predicting Nixon's victory, Hubert Humphrey took an early lead and Armand shook with glee, refusing even to consider the possibility that Nixon might win. The next day Richard Nixon was the thirty-seventh president of the United States.

Even though Armand knew President Johnson would not receive a warm welcome when he returned to Texas if he sided with Occidental, he decided that his only option was to make a stab at obtaining Johnson's approval for the refinery project before he left office. On November 11, less than a week after Nixon's election victory, he wrote to Johnson, including an eighteen-page memorandum attacking Boggs with his letter. But Johnson and Boggs were old friends, and the lame-duck president tabled the problem, saying that it was a matter for the next president to decide. Armand's only remaining option was to find ways to pressure the president-elect, whom he despised.

He chose a rather oblique route. The ten-year rule of the majority party, Acción Democrática, had just come to an end in Venezuela with the election of a new president, Christian Democrat (COPEI) Rafael Caldera. One of Caldera's priorities was to wage war on the U.S. import quota system so that Venezuela could vastly increase its oil imports to the United States. The results of the Venezuelan oil auction were almost two years away, but Armand sent word to Caldera that if Occidental obtained service contracts it would announce that it planned to mix large supplies of oil imported from Venezuela with the Libyan oil it would process in its prospective refinery. Armand knew this information could be used by Caldera to pressure the Nixon administration to reduce quotas on Venezuelan oil and would at the same time prove a first step toward making Caldera a new "best friend." It would also become one of many grievances the Nixon White House soon came to harbor against Armand Hammer.

On December 4, Alaska Governor Walter Hickel ordered his state attorney general to file suit to enjoin the Foreign Trade Zones Board from proceeding with Maine's application. Five days later President-elect Nixon appointed Hickel secretary of the interior. The message was inescapable: Hickel had known about his appointment at the time the suit was filed and had been acting on orders from the new administration. It became even more important that Armand find a way to win over Nixon—quickly. It had previously been reported that Nixon's choice for secretary of the interior was the Republican lame-duck governor of Montana, Tim Babcock, and an elaborate plan was set into motion so that Armand could quiz Babcock about why Nixon had passed him over for Hickel.

"You saw the positive effect my Charles Russell sculpture had on LBJ," said Armand. "Russell lived in Great Falls, so I'm going to donate one of his paintings to the State Historical Society. Then I'll fly to the state capitol in Helena and present the painting to Babcock so that he can hand it over. Meanwhile, I'll look him over and decide whether I want to offer him a job."

Later Armand discovered he couldn't go, so I was sent in his place. Babcock had rugged good looks, a lot of poise, and a winning manner, and there was nothing of the professional politician about him. He dealt frankly with my questions, explaining that he had lost the election because of a powerful, heavily financed public power lobby. "They didn't like a Republican governor who was always going to support the private sector," he said. "They dislike big ranchers, businessmen, and the private power companies."

I remarked that I had expected him to be appointed secretary of the interior. "The Alaskan oil interests made large contributions to the Nixon campaign, and they wanted their own cabinet member," he explained. "To make matters worse, some well-meaning friends mounted a campaign for me without my knowledge. You just don't campaign for the cabinet."

As our conversation was drawing to a close, a surprising coincidence occurred when Babcock's secretary put through a call from the president. He and Nixon talked for several minutes, asking about each other's wives and children, discussing political issues and sports, and trying to find a time to get together.

When I returned to my hotel, I called Armand, gave him a favorable impression of Babcock, and mentioned the phone call from the president.

"Did he really call Nixon 'Dick'?" Armand asked, clearly impressed.

"Yes."

"Are you *sure* he said 'Dick'?"

"Yes."

I knew then that Tim Babcock would be coming to work for Occidental.

Meanwhile, Armand busied himself with attempts to discredit Hickel. Just before Hickel's mid-January confirmation hearings, Washington columnist Drew Pearson printed a devastating series of columns accusing Hickel of being a "careless bungler" and Nixon of appointing a cabinet that represented "lower ethical standards." The Nixon administration traced the source of the columns first to Pearson's legal consultant, Myer Feldman, and then to Hammer. Later, when word was leaked to Pearson that Republican Texas Campaign Finance Chairman John Hurd had stood beside Republican Vice-Presidential candidate Spiro Agnew during a campaign oil-industry fund-raiser and had stated that he was authorized to say there would be no refinery at Machiasport, Occidental executive Walter Davis was named in print as the source. Now Armand looked even more like a troublemaker to the new administration.

In March 1969, in another attempt to penetrate the Washington power elite, Armand announced the formation of Occidental International Corporation, a new subsidiary headquartered in the capital. Its ostensible purpose was to "coordinate Occidental's worldwide operations." President Johnson's former top aide and later his postmaster general, W. Marvin Watson, the man who had collected Armand's campaign contributions and had served as the intermediary between Armand and President Johnson, was appointed president and CEO of the embryo subsidiary, and Tim Babcock was appointed executive vice president. "Never refer to Occidental International as a lobbying organization. Its job is to fight world hunger," Armand cautioned.

Whenever he launched a new project, I was at his side from the beginning and supplied advice about how to position the project to

the news media. But one day, out of nowhere he told me to announce that Watson and Babcock were about to leave for India,
where Occidental had entered into a preliminary agreement to
construct a $150 million fertilizer plant as Occidental Internation-
al's first step in its war against hunger. The preliminary agreement
was announced with great fanfare. Thereafter nothing more was
said about it and if questions were asked about it, Armand gave
the questioner the runaround. The following year the project was
dismissed in the company's annual report as being "held in abey-
ance." It was the first in a string of dubious projects for the mysterious subsidiary.

Around the same time that Armand formed Occidental International, he acquired a Grumman Gulfstream II. The jet flew at
the same speed as a commercial airliner and contained extra fuel
tanks. Its stateroom slept two, and four of the five passenger seats
in the main cabin could be converted into beds. Perpetually restless, Armand began to use the Gulfstream to roam the world,
spending as much as half the year away from the office. On board
he always sat against the front bulkhead with his back to the cockpit
and rode backward so that he could monitor every activity in the
cabin.

"Where's Armand?" I asked Dorman Commons one day.

"Overseas," he replied matter-of-factly, "scouting new opportunities, flattering foreign leaders, and making secret contributions
to foreign political campaigns."

Sometimes Armand made a sudden decision to travel in the
middle of the night, and his aides were always kept on red alert.
Frances usually traveled with him, but Armand loved an entou-
rage, and Tim Babcock and Marvin Watson accompanied him, too.
Shunting his wife to the side, he liked to disembark flanked by his
glamorous trophies. "I'm the only chief executive in history," he
boasted, "who travels with a Democratic ex–postmaster general
and a Republican ex-governor in tow!"

One day Armand called Babcock and Watson and told them to
get ready to leave for Peru. On October 3, Major General Juan
Velasco Alvarado had engineered a military coup and become
president. Subsequently, the military junta had expropriated all of
the interests of Jersey's Peruvian subsidiary, IPC. Now, the Seven
Sisters were wary of becoming involved in the Peruvian oil industry, and Armand believed their fear provided Occidental with the
opportunity to replace them.

After the group arrived in Lima, Armand picked up the phone

in his hotel room and asked the operator to get General Alvarado on the line. Although it took over an hour and a number of calls back and forth before contact was made, he remained convinced that Alvarado would be thrilled to meet him, and he was right. Armand, Babcock, and Watson were invited to come immediately to the presidential palace. Acting the part of an unofficial head of state on a diplomatic mission, Armand listened sympathetically as Alvarado launched into a discussion about how the recent nationalization had hurt his country's oil industry. When he bemoaned the fact that his country desperately needed technical assistance, Armand expressed what appeared to be genuine concern. He explained that he understood and cared about Peru's problems and volunteered to send some Occidental oil personnel to Peru to help Alvarado. Of course, there were no strings attached—it was simply a humanitarian gesture. Alvarado seemed relieved to have encountered one American oilman who understood his country's difficulties. By the time the hour-long meeting was over, Armand had made a new "best friend," and he and Alvarado embraced warmly before they parted. "It's the beginning of my campaign to get Alvarado in my hip pocket," Armand told me on his return. "I'm not going to let up until I have him under my thumb."

Back in Los Angeles, I could only marvel at Armand's energy and the number of balls he kept in the air. To some who followed his travels to Venezuela, Peru, or wherever else he suddenly decided to go, he seemed peripatetic or merely restless. To those who really knew him, however, it was apparent that he was driven by two predominant motives: greater profits for Occidental and greater glory for Armand Hammer.

12.

"THIS COMPANY IS NOT MANAGED, IT'S UNMANAGED"

In 1954 Cyrus Eaton, an elderly Cleveland industrialist with a multimillion-dollar railroad and steel empire, had set out to sell steel to the Soviets. Subsequently he became so close to Nikita Khrushchev that he was awarded the Lenin Peace Prize. Spotting a photograph of Eaton and Khrushchev on the front page of *The New York Times*, Armand had declared, "Eaton's nothing but a Johnny-come-lately. I did it all before him."

Like Hammer, Eaton had no difficulty mouthing the official Communist Party line, and after Khrushchev was deposed in 1965, Kosygin and Brezhnev maintained a relationship with Eaton, who continued to tell his fellow Americans about the Russian paradise, its happy, thriving citizens, and peace-loving, trustworthy leaders. Then, in 1968, Eaton had set out to win the Nobel Peace Prize by flying to Moscow to meet with Brezhnev in an attempt to single-handedly broker an end to the Vietnam War. It was the kind of personal diplomacy Armand believed only he was entitled to practice, and he became even more irritated.

An Eaton-owned company, Tower International, was actively involved in trade and construction projects with the USSR and its satellites, and served as a front for American companies that did not want the public to know they were doing business with the Soviets. "It's another version of Alamerico, my 1920s U.S.-Soviet trading company. Eaton is eighty-five years old. I did it when I was a young man," Armand said dismissively. Nevertheless, he was still intrigued by Eaton's activities, especially because the Tower executives, who included a Romanian-born president, had the expertise to negotiate trade deals with the East bloc nations.

Eaton had seven children. A son, forty-one-year-old Cyrus Jr., served as chairman of Tower. After Armand learned that the company was losing money and needed financing, he announced that he was headed to Cleveland to meet with the younger Eaton, claiming that the purpose of the visit was the acquisition of another Eaton-owned company, West Kentucky Coal.

On his return, I asked, "Did you get the coal company?"

The acquisition was the one thing that had not been discussed. "I told Cyrus all about my early days in Moscow and my friendship with Lenin, and he was very impressed," Armand said. "One thing led to another. Before you knew it, he told me that it made sense to put my long experience with the Soviet Union together with his father's current Soviet activities. He wants to get into business with me."

Tower's projects were a tightly guarded secret, but Armand had managed to pry open Cyrus Jr.'s lips. "The Eatons plan to build a Soviet trade center and market Siberian natural gas," he related. "I presented the natural-gas idea to Khrushchev four years ago. I had no idea they were going ahead with it."

Armand also learned that the Eatons had developed a relationship with Dzherman Gvishiani, Deputy Chairman of the Soviet State Committee for Science and Technology. Gvishiani, a trade expert, was Premier Aleksei Kosygin's son-in-law, one of the few relatives of a Soviet leader allowed to achieve positions of power in the Communist Party hierarchy and someone with a great deal of influence over his father-in-law.

By casting Cyrus Jr. as an indispensable surrogate son, Armand gradually earned his trust. Then he let it drop that Occidental was involved in a joint venture with Holiday Inns and that hotel openings were scheduled in the Moroccan cities of Casablanca, Fez, Marrakech, and Tangier in 1971 and in Monte Carlo in 1972. Armand added that he thought he could persuade Holiday Inns to enter into another joint venture with Occidental and the Eatons to build hotels in the USSR and the Communist nations. A decision was made to construct hotels and industrial plants together under the umbrella of an Eaton subsidiary, Cleyton International.

Over the next year Armand and Cyrus Jr. became so close that Cyrus felt comfortable enough to ask Armand's financial help to further their joint Soviet projects. Hammer authorized Occidental to guarantee a loan to Cyrus from LaSalle National Bank of Chicago. As security, the younger Eaton gave Occidental the mortgages on a number of Eaton-family cold-storage plants in Montreal and Toronto and the mortgage on his home, a three-hundred-acre farm in the Cleveland suburbs. Occidental also received an option to acquire a 55 percent interest in Cleyton International.

"Why didn't Cyrus's father put up the money?" I asked Armand.

"Maybe Cyrus has taken to thinking of me as his father," he replied.

Under the auspices of Cleyton International, Armand launched occasional trips to the USSR. Before each one, my assistants would shop for inexpensive stationery and kitchen gadgets. The Soviets were starved for consumer items, and like a capitalist Santa Claus, whenever someone proved helpful, Armand would hand over a bottle opener or a pen set. Soviet law required that a two-man Soviet escort crew join him in London and navigate his Gulfstream into and over Soviet territory and Hammer was determined to find a way to convince the Brezhnev-Kosygin government that he was so important and trustworthy that the use of the Soviet crew was not necessary.

During these trips Armand and Frances stayed in the Lenin Suite at the National Hotel, which faced Red Square and was almost directly across the street from the Kremlin. "The honor of staying in the Lenin Suite is given to only a select few," Armand bragged.

Frances had a different opinion of their accommodations. "It's a down and dirty dump," she said with a wry expression. "You'd think they'd clean it every now and then. The first thing I do after we check in is scrub it down. But Armand likes it. You know how he feels about Lenin."

Like most Moscow hotel accommodations, the Lenin Suite was bugged and its phone was tapped. Armand insisted that no conversation of consequence be conducted until the radio was turned up loud. Even then he made the participants whisper into one another's ears. One night when Tim Babcock couldn't sleep, he took a stroll around St. Basil's basilica. KGB tails instantly fell into step behind him. Armand was also followed whenever he left the hotel, but he claimed that his tails were there to protect him and not to spy on him.

Armand's new round of activities in the USSR duplicated his initial entry into Libya. He recruited an outside staff who did the legwork and reported directly to him, and the Occidental staff was told nothing. Although Armand's deal with Cyrus Jr. involved hotel construction, from the beginning he enlisted the Eatons' Tower International executives to make the opening moves that could lead to the realization of his dream of a new Occidental-Soviet fertilizer agreement. When he learned that Sargent Shriver had a relationship with Dzherman Gvishiani, he hired Shriver as his Soviet legal consultant and ordered him to move the fertilizer deal along. Through Shriver, Armand met David Karr, a friend of Deputy Soviet Foreign Trade Minister Vladimir Alkhimov, who was in the process of using his relationship with Alkhimov to make a number of his own deals. In the same way that Armand convinced the younger Eaton to join forces with him, he persuaded Karr to become a "consultant."

I met Karr when he began to travel back and forth between Occidental's L.A. headquarters and his home in Paris. As a young man he had worked as a reporter for the official American Communist Party newspaper, the *Daily Worker*, and had been named as a Communist before the Senate Judiciary Subcommittee by a former colleague. Subsequently the former radical had transformed himself into an energetic, restless, wealthy entrepreneur who had owned his own PR agency, produced a Broadway play and two movies, and worked as columnist Drew Pearson's legman. A friend who had known Karr during those days remarked, "David thought nothing of rifling through a stranger's desk drawers and files. Restraint was not a part of his vocabulary."

Karr had just left Fairbanks Whitney Corporation (now Colt's Manufacturing) and Armand explained that his specialty was proxy raiding and the takeover of vulnerable companies. "The chairman of Fairbanks Whitney hired him to help defeat a proxy raid, and David did splendidly," Armand told me. "Then he turned the tables, led a successful raid against the chairman, and became the new chief executive. Eventually someone else went after Karr and he got thrown out. Now, I'm going to use him to fight off any takeover attempts."

I sensed that Armand was not going to keep someone with those particular skills around any longer than he had to.

Novosti reporter Mikhail Bruk was another member of Armand's team. The first time I met Bruk, he extended his hand and said politely, "How do you do. "I'm *Michael* Bruk," with an emphasis on the English pronunciation of his first name. Bruk had never left the Soviet Union before, but he sounded exactly like an upper-class Britisher.

"Soviet children who learn English are taught by someone with either an American or an English accent," he explained. "My teacher had an English accent, and so do I."

Talkative and friendly, if anything Bruk seemed the epitome of a prosperous international businessman. He grilled me pointedly about my family, career, and personal and political beliefs, listening carefully to my answers and studying me at the same time. When I described the experience to Victor, he burst into laughter. "Mikhail *is* the 'Manchurian candidate.' "

Victor went on to tell me that Bruk's ability to mimic any language perfectly as soon as he heard it had inspired a rumor that he had received special training in an English village built by the KGB outside of Moscow where agents were taught to pass as Englishmen. "The village never existed," Victor said, "but the fact that Mikhail can pass as English has helped him build a successful life. He's Jewish, so he can never become a KGB officer. But he does have permission to work as a KGB liaison and for Armand at the same time. Both sides pay him, which enables him to live in great comfort in a country where Jews have a hard time."

As the days went on, Victor and I watched Armand pull together his secret Soviet operation. "Armand's paving the way to launch Occidental of Moscow," Victor commented. "It's just like the good old days. He's in his glory, running around Moscow telling everybody about his love affair with Lenin, bribing everyone in sight, and convincing them that he'll do whatever they ask."

Shortly thereafter Victor and Ireene traveled to Moscow to see Victor's son Armasha. During their trip, Victor met with his first wife, Vava, whom he had not seen in almost forty years. Ireene's friends reported that she had found it "strange" to have been included in this reunion. To them it was another example of Victor's insensitivity to his current mate.

Meanwhile, at Occidental's Los Angeles office, when Armand expressed his willingness to accept the "resignation" of Walter Davis, his first so-called heir apparent, Davis replied that he had no desire to walk away from Permian Corporation, a company he had built from the ground up. Not too long after that, whenever I picked up the phone, I heard a change in the dial tone, and during conversations I often heard a click. Other executives reported the same experience, and it became policy whenever confidential material was about to be discussed to advise the person on the other end of the line that the phone was being tapped and to suggest that he weigh his comments carefully, put them into writing, or make a personal appearance. "Davis is tapping the phones," Armand told me. "He's looking for the evidence to help him get me kicked out."

Each year a tape recording was made of the annual meeting, and when Armand got the news that the tape of the 1969 meeting had mysteriously disappeared, he was convinced that Davis had put someone up to stealing it. Armand put up a good front, but he was frightened. This rare crack in his self-control was inspired by a belief that Davis had gone or was planning to go to the SEC with the evidence necessary to convince the federal regulators to investigate Occidental's financial practices. "People do get caught. They do get punished," he murmured.

I was with Armand a few days later when he learned that his mother had died. I offered a few solicitous words, but he cut me off. "Victor made the incredibly foolish mistake of giving Mama Rose a big eighty-fifth birthday party," he said. "The excitement was too much for her. When she woke up the next morning, her speech was slurred. She'd had a stroke, but Victor insisted that she was just sleepy. Finally, he had no choice but to put her in the hospital, and she never came out."

Hospitals reminded Armand of his own mortality which is why he never paid hospital visits and had not visited his mother during her hospitalization. "It's all Victor's fault," he said. "My brother betrayed me."

Every Labor Day, Virginia, our children, and I threw a pool party followed by a barbecue at our hillside home in Studio City. Labor Day 1969 was also on the minds of twelve young members of the Libyan army. Knowing that their elderly king had gone to Turkey for medical treatment and that the West would be distracted by its holiday, they decided it was the perfect time to put their plans into action. I was trimming the steaks when a *Wall Street Journal* reporter called to tell me that rebel officers had captured their army base and then the radio stations without anyone offering the slightest bit of resistance and that Libya had erupted in celebration after the officers broadcast the news that King Idris had been overthrown in what they described as a pro-Arab, anti-West, anti-

Zionist, bloodless coup. The reporter said that the new leader was named Muammar el-Qaddafi and asked if I could find out something about him.

I called Armand, and he was just as surprised as I was. I would learn later that it was common knowledge that King Idris wanted to abdicate or retire and that a revolution of one sort or another had long been simmering. Armand had always dismissed this information as unrealistic when it had been presented to him by his intelligence network, because he didn't want to believe that anything could interfere with his successful relationship with King Idris.

Armand and I agreed that our public stance would be one of confidence in order to minimize the certain negative effect on the price of Occidental stock. Then I issued the first of a long series of calming statements: in assessing the effects of the coup, Occidental "sees no reason to change any of the Libyan investment plans"; all company operations are proceeding as usual"; Occidental "has shipped the 300 millionth barrel of crude oil from its fields in Libya"; Occidental has achieved "all-time record earnings and revenues." Meanwhile Armand stopped payment on the overrides to the Swiss bank accounts of members of the Idris regime and ordered his Libyan intermediaries to find a way to let Qaddafi know that he was willing to pay these monies to him.

Fearing that Qaddafi would begin his rule by nationalizing foreign oil company assets, Armand set out to find out as much as he could about the twenty-seven-year-old colonel. He learned that Qaddafi had appointed himself chairman of the new governing body, the Revolutionary Command Council (RCC), and that the first official act of the RCC had been the imprisonment of a thousand administrators and politicians in the Idris regime. Armand, one of the prime bribe payers to Idris's ministry and a man who had given the name "Idris field" to one of Occidental's concessions, had reason to be worried. "When Qaddafi took advanced military training in England, he insisted on wearing Libyan tribal dress," Armand said nervously. "He's a fundamentalist Moslem *and* a fanatic nationalist. I smell real trouble."

In short order the RCC declared that all future businesses were going to be 100 percent Libyan owned and oil revenues were going to be distributed more equitably to the people. It was the type of pronouncement that usually precedes nationalization, but the RCC went to considerable lengths to assure foreign banks and oil companies that nationalization was not on the agenda.

Armand remained wary. "I've got to go to Libya and put some sense into Qaddafi just like I did with General Alvarado in Peru. He's got to stop acting like a crazy loon and running around like a chicken with its head cut off." But neither the American Embassy in Libya nor the State Department was in any rush to have Hammer pay the RCC a visit. American citizens are not allowed to travel to countries where the governments are in a state of flux.

Then in December, three months after the coup, the RCC issued its first major political position paper, the Constitutional Declaration. It renamed Libya the Libyan Arab Republic, described the change in government as a socialist revolution, and promised an end to economic exploitation through a redistribution of wealth and the elimination of class differences. "There's nothing wrong with that," Armand said. "Look at all the good things socialism has done for the Russian people."

I replied that having ideals was one thing, but that losing the income from Occidental's Libyan reserves would be quite another.

Armand looked stricken. Had he known at that time that the RCC had appointed as petroleum consultants oil dealer Dr. Nicholas Sarkisan and former Saudi Arabian minister of petroleum resources Abdullah Tariki, he would have been even more upset. The first thing Sarkisan and Tariki would reveal to Qaddafi and the army officers was that according to the formula used by the international oil industry, the per-barrel posted price of Libyan crude was far lower than the posted price set for the Persian Gulf nations. Thus the stage was set for Qaddafi to demand a large per-barrel price increase that would make Libya's oil price equal to that of the Persian Gulf, exactly the thing the Seven Sisters were determined never to see happen.

Hammer's concern about Occidental's future in Libya encouraged Walter Davis to choose this moment to zero in on the outside directors, who had independent sources of income and did not depend on Occidental for their livelihoods, in an attempt to convince them to stage their own coup. Davis hoped that the momentum of his activities would entice some of the inside directors to join in until a majority coalesced and Armand was fired. It was a bold maneuver. Like Colonel Qaddafi's coup, it was a quiet one, conducted mainly in whispers. The staff knew that Davis was making inroads, but his secretiveness made it impossible to judge his effectiveness.

With the threat of nationalization in Libya hanging over Occidental's head, Armand became even more determined to find alternative sources of oil for Occidental. British Petroleum had discovered an enormous oil field in the North Sea, and Armand leaped at the opportunity to form a consortium with J. Paul Getty, Lord Roy Thomson, and Allied Chemical Corporation and to set out to obtain drilling rights. The oil and gas boys were dispatched to the North Sea to conduct seismic testing in order to establish a basis for a bid and, when the testing proved successful, the consortium, which became known as "the Group," applied for a drilling license. Armand told me that he had lunched with fellow Group members Getty and Thomson in a plush London restaurant to celebrate the filing and that when the check was presented, it was discovered that none of the three multimillionaires was carrying any cash or had a credit card and each had expected one of the others to pick up the check. "Luckily, I spotted a man I knew at the other end of the dining room and borrowed his credit card," said Armand. The twinkle in his eye told me that he did not plan to pay back the Good Samaritan who had lent him the money.

Even with three multimillionaires at its helm, the Group experienced great difficulty dealing with the British government. A colleague of mine in the London office told me that Armand came up with a typically ingenious solution, one that was apparently inspired by John Profumo. He summoned a selection of London's most attractive women to his suite at Claridge's and conducted a very businesslike job interview with each concerning her special skills. The women were then "introduced" by Hammer to a number of British officials he believed could help the Group's quest. When Occidental's English staffers caught wind of these activities, they took to breaking each other up by posing the rhetorical question "Doesn't Armand already own a company named Hooker?"

Money was the lubricant in Armand's search for oil in the Middle East. After Texas oilman John Mecom tipped him about the possibility of acquiring offshore drilling rights in Umm al-Qaywayn, one of the Trucial States, seven tiny sheikdoms on the Persian Gulf that had been British protectorates since the end of the nineteenth century, Armand returned to Claridge's for a meeting with Sheikh Sultan al-Mu'alla, the crown prince and petroleum minister of Umm al-Qaywayn. Armand agreed to pay a $1 million "bonus"—$556,000 to the royal family and $444,000 to other government officials—in return for drilling rights and made a $217,000 cash down payment on the spot, in addition to picking up the prince's $13,000 hotel bill. When the prince asked for an additional $200,000, the funds were laundered through a dummy corporation in Liechtenstein and delivered in cash to Umm al-Qaywayn by a neutral party assigned by Hammer. More payoffs, amounting to several hundred thousand dollars, were made at the same time to other members of the royal family and the ministry.

In November, ten weeks after the Libyan coup, the British Foreign Office quickly approved an offshore concessions agreement between Occidental and Umm al-Qaywayn and Armand announced the news in London and received a lot of favorable play from Lord Thomson's English newspapers. But other British journalists set out to discover if there was any truth to the rumor that in order to gain approval from the British Foreign Office, Hammer had influenced Sir John Foster, Britain's legal adviser to Umm al-Qaywayn. The claim was based on the presumption that Foster had not consulted either the British Foreign Office or the government of the British protectorate before signing the consent agreement.

Armand dismissed such suspicions. "Sir John is a brilliant lawyer, a former member of Parliament, and a fellow of All Souls. How can anyone think that such a fine man would take a bribe?" Subsequently the staid, humpbacked English barrister began representing Occidental on a number of other projects and eventually became a member of the board.

Relieved to have secured a possible alternative oil source to Occidental's Libyan supply, Armand decided to obtain the offshore drilling rights of Ajman, another Trucial State. He dispatched Occidental's president, Tom Willers, to make the deal. "Tom is so steeped in chemicals," he told me, "it will be good for him to rub his nose in some oil."

Willers succeeded, which delighted Armand. But when the opportunity arose to obtain the drilling rights in a third Trucial State, Sharjah, he passed, explaining that he didn't want Occidental to overextend itself in that part of the world. Those rights went instead to a small California company, Buttes Gas and Oil.

In 1969 Armand had hired Everett Thierfelder, who had spent fifteen years with Jersey as a financial executive and international negotiator, and dispatched him to Lagos, Nigeria, "to keep me posted on future oil activities." Thierfelder had arrived in Nigeria during the second year of the bloody civil war between the federal government and the breakaway state of Biafra. A week or two later I had asked Armand if Thierfelder had returned. "No. He's going to live in Lagos until the civil war is over," he had replied. "Then the government will be able to turn its attention back to its oil industry, and we'll be ready to make our move. He could be there for a couple of years."

On January 10, 1970, the surrender of the Biafrans marked the end of the Nigerian civil war. By then, Thierfelder had been in Lagos for fifteen months. As Armand had predicted, the Nigerian government turned to rebuilding its economy and placed 1.6 million acres in the waters off the coast of the Niger River delta on the auction block. Subsequently, thirty oil companies submitted bids for what was considered a highly desirable property.

As usual, Armand greased the skids with large sums of money. Occidental gave expensive gifts to Nigerian leader Major General Yakubu Gowon and his family, picked up a number of family expenses, and made a payoff to one of Gowon's younger brothers. A payment of $300,000 was also made to Joseph Tanko Yusuf, the Nigerian counsel in Hamburg, West Germany, and Occidental paid the tuition bills for Yusuf's children in California and England. In return, Yusuf reported back about internal political developments in Nigeria and the activities of rival oil companies and introduced Occidental executives to other Nigerian officials. Portions of the money paid to Yusuf were laundered through banks in Liechtenstein.

One of the oil and gas boys told me that when Armand learned that some of the Nigerians were homosexual, he introduced them to attractive young men. No matter what it took, he remained determined to use any means available to find a backup to the threatened Libyan oil supply.

One day I dropped into Tom Willers's office to check some information about Hooker Chemicals for the annual report. The normally calm executive looked upset. "I've just had the argument to end all arguments with the doctor," he said. "It's inconceivable to me that Occidental has no established company policy, strategic planning, or budgetary controls. How can I run this company efficiently when its chief executive discourages any attempt to compile and distribute significant data about company activities and refuses to hold executive meetings?

"This company is not managed, it's unmanaged," Willers went on. "You can get away with it when you're just starting out, but Oxy isn't a small company and people's lives and livelihoods are at stake. You've got to have structure. But everything that happens here is a secret that suddenly becomes a surprise. Things are always going off in a million directions with absolutely no contingency planning. No one would believe how capricious and disorganized things really are."

There was another problem that Willers did not mention. Armand was determined to sell the Soviets Hooker-manufactured fire-retardant and lightweight plastics as well as Hooker's precious-metals technology, which had been an intrinsic part of the *Apollo 2* moon landing and was slated for use in other U.S. space projects. But Hooker's conservative board insisted that these products were dual purpose with direct military applications and that it was against the law to sell them to a hostile government.

A day or two later Armand complained to me that Willers lacked "the flexibility I need in a president. He's too damned structured. He doesn't have a diversity of interests like I do. I need a president who can adapt quickly to new things." That "lack of flexibility" included Willers's inability to understand Armand's desire to supply the Soviets with Hooker products.

At the beginning of 1970 Armand removed Willers from the presidency of Occidental, stripped him of his power by giving him an essentially meaningless title, vice chairman of the board, and appointed Island Creek Coal's Bill Bellano president, chief operating officer, and a company director. "Bill's tough, straightforward, and clear-thinking. I'm convinced he's going to make a great president. Things have never looked better," he proclaimed.

After Albert Gore, Sr., lost his re-election bid in November 1970 and his thirty-two years as a congressman and senator from Tennessee came to an end, Armand would reward him for his friendship by appointing him to the presidency of Island Creek Coal and by making him a vice president of Occidental. But his Panglossian outlook for Occidental flew in the face of the truth. At any second the Libyan oil supply, which accounted for 90 percent of Occidental's income, could be cut off, a secret SEC investigation triggered by Walter Davis might already be under way, and the sudden and inexplicable change in operating officers had made daily operations even more confusing and difficult.

1 3.

SAVING LIBYA
FOR *EVERYONE*

On January 29, 1970, Muammar Qaddafi declared himself the new Libyan prime minister. He summoned the representatives of the twenty-one foreign oil companies operating in his country and told them that either Libya was going to be granted an immediate 20 percent increase, forty-three cents per barrel on the posted price, or all oil supplies would be cut off and the Libyans would spend their next few years training their own workers to take control of the oil industry. The majors viewed his demand as an intolerable attempt to wrest control of the oil wealth from them and an incentive for every other sheikh and emir to do the same. The independents in Libya objected because they earned their profits by underselling the majors and any price increase would eliminate their competitive edge.

Reeling from a drop in the per-barrel posted price of Gulf oil from $1.60 to $1.30 as a result of the flood of cheap Libyan oil onto the international market, the majors took as their main objectives ending the competitive price-cutting tactics by the independents, especially Occidental, reexerting control over an unruly market, and reestablishing higher prices. Aware that their larger Persian Gulf oil interests would enable them to make up the difference effortlessly if Qaddafi stopped the flow of Libyan oil, they offered him a token five-cent raise and hoped his anger would be directed at their less fortunate independent competitors.

Qaddafi countered by dispatching the new head of the Libyan Oil Commission, Izz al-Din al-Mabrouk, to Moscow. The message was clear: if the Seven Sisters refused to cooperate, they would be supplanted by the Soviets. Mabrouk had no difficulty receiving a

Soviet commitment to help the revolutionary government "develop" its oil industry.

Armand's trips to Moscow coincided with these activities, and shortly after Mabrouk's visit, a rumor circulated that he had prevailed on his Kremlin connections to use their newfound influence with Qaddafi to protect Occidental's interests. It came straight from the PR departments of the Seven Sisters and reflected their paranoia about Hammer's ties to the Soviets and their hatred of the way he operated in Libya. If their aim was to upset him, they succeeded beyond their expectations. He ordered me to deny the rumor whenever any reporter asked. Even after it died down, he continued to express his concern. Much later he admitted that he *had* asked the KGB's help but didn't want anyone to know it. "The fact that Qaddafi wears full military dress in the morning and tribal Arab dress in the afternoon confused the KGB," he told me. "They said he was eccentric, naïve, cunning, vain, and politically sophisticated, all at the same time, and they didn't know how to deal with him." Nor did the majors. Over the next nine weeks Esso-Libya's offer would climb to twenty-three cents and when that offer was rejected, negotiations would grind to a halt.

Meanwhile Armand devised another way to get to Qaddafi. Obsessed with pan-Arabism, Qaddafi viewed Egyptian President Gamal Abdel Nasser as his mentor and shared Nasser's belief that the Arab world had to be liberated from Western domination through a union that included the liberation of Palestine. Qaddafi and Nasser had traded visits, and Libya's new one-party political structure replicated Nasser's Egyptian model.

Armand was still banned from travel to Libya, but nothing could stop him from going to Cairo. "My good friend Lord Thomson knows Nasser and he's paved the way" he told me. "The profits from our Libyan operations are helping to pay for Egypt's military equipment and supplies and Nasser's not going to want to see those profits interrupted. That's why I'm confident that he'll intercede with Qaddafi on our behalf."

An encounter between Nasser, the champion of nonalignment, anticolonialism, and pan-Arabism, and Hammer, a Western oil company president with a Jewish background, was an unlikely one. But Armand had no interest in the fate of Israel and therefore no qualms about meeting the man who had set out to liquidate Israel in the Six-Day War. Hammer also set a clever ruse into motion. The costs of the Six-Day War and Nasser's ongoing expenditure of 20 percent of Egypt's gross national product on the military had left his country almost bankrupt. But its petroleum industry had just begun to recover from the loss of the Sinai to the Israelis, and the Egyptians believed that the rich Libyan oil fields extended into Egyptian territory. Before he left for Cairo, Armand sent word to Nasser that Occidental was anxious to become involved in oil production in Egypt.

Inevitably, all the heads of state that Armand encountered were "kind" and "warmhearted," and Nasser was no exception—or so Armand reported on his return from Cairo. "We hit it off right away. I'm happy to say Nasser contacted Qaddafi and did a sell job for Oxy. My diplomacy did the trick."

Armand did not report that he had convinced Nasser that Occidental was interested in developing the Morgan field in the Red Sea and initiating oil exploration in the Western Desert. The possibility that his needy country could become the recipient of the same vast above- and under-the-table monies that Occidental had already poured into Libya seemed to have bought Nasser's cooperation. A team of negotiators was dispatched to Cairo so that Armand could maintain the illusion of Occidental's interest in Egypt's oil reserves, which he believed would enable him to continue to prevail on Nasser to prevail on Qaddafi, if and when he needed him to.

To Armand's great relief, it appeared that Occidental had located a backup source to its Libyan oil supply when seismic testing revealed oil off the coast of Abu Musa island in the territorial waters of Umm al-Qaywayn. Looking forward to obtaining a speedy return on the $1 million "bonus" he had paid to obtain the drilling rights and the $1 million or so Occidental had spent on preliminary testing, Armand gave the order to begin drilling. But to his dismay, Buttes Gas and Oil stepped forward and announced that its agreement with the neighboring Trucial State of Sharjah gave it the right to drill in exactly the same place. Buttes based its claim on the fact that it had formalized its agreement with Sharjah two months after Sharjah had issued a formal decree extending its territorial waters to include the waters surrounding Abu Musa island and two months before Occidental had formalized its agreement with Umm al-Qaywayn. Armand was convinced that the claim had been cooked up by Buttes and Sharjah after Occidental's tests had located oil and equally convinced that Occidental's grant of approval from the British Foreign Office gave him the legal right to drill.

At the end of 1971 Britain was planning to withdraw its military presence from the Persian Gulf, at which time the Trucial States would become members of the newly formed United Arab Emirates. Iran had a long-standing claim of sovereignty over the Trucial States, which would be rendered meaningless once they became part of the new federation. Therefore, Reza Pahlavi, shah of Iran, made a formal declaration that the territorial waters really belonged to Iran. But Armand dug in his heels. "I made a deal. An insignificant oil company and a half-assed sheikh made another deal to screw me. Then the shah comes along and decides to screw up the process of federation by stealing my oil field. I'm going to drill. Nothing's going to stop me."

When the British Foreign Office issued a proclamation that no drilling was to occur until Sharjah settled its dispute with Umm al-Qaywayn, Armand became even more determined to go ahead. "All the British government is doing is saying 'Where's your manners?'" he told me. "I don't care if there's an international incident. I won't be stopped!"

Searching for support for his position, Armand launched a furious round of calls, including one to Henry Kissinger and another to Lyndon Johnson. "Kissinger knows how much I hate Nixon," he reported to me. "He really enjoyed telling me that he couldn't do a thing. On the other hand, LBJ was a lot more helpful."

The former president had told Hammer that the shah was eager to purchase several million dollars' worth of fighter planes from McDonnell Douglas, the nation's largest weapons manufacturer, but wanted to pay in Iranian currency. When McDonnell had insisted on American dollars, the shah had offered to pay with Iranian oil. It was Johnson's idea to put Armand together with McDonnell's chief executive, James McDonnell, who was searching for an oil company to purchase the oil that would be paid to him by the shah.

Armand later maintained that Lyndon and Lady Bird Johnson had invited him to spend the weekend at their ranch and that, by coincidence, James McDonnell had also been a guest. But in fact he held a number of brainstorming sessions before he left for Texas, which produced a plan to have Occidental buy 200,000 barrels a day from the National Iranian Oil Company (NIOC) at 30 percent of the posted price and use the other 70 percent to buy planes from McDonnell Douglas. Then Occidental would give the planes to the shah. Subsequently Armand pretended that he had made up the "fighters-for-oil" deal on the spot at the Johnson ranch and that everyone had been thrilled by his ingenuity.

On June 1, just as preliminary discussions were launched with the Iranian government to pave the way for a meeting between Hammer and the shah, something happened that Armand had never expected. After repeated warnings from the British government to stop drilling at Abu Musa island, the Royal Navy boarded and impounded Occidental's drilling platform and rig while Royal Air Force warplanes flew overhead.

Armand was flabbergasted, but that did not stop him from devising another ingenious scheme, this one about Libya. "Our Libyan production is up thirty-one percent over last year. We're producing eight hundred thousand barrels a day," he told me. "Get this dramatic news out immediately." When executives challenged the figure, he shouted, "I'm the only one who needs to know what's going on in this company, and I'm the only one who does!" The statistics appeared in print according to Armand's exact specifications.

On June 12 the Libyan Oil Commission charged Occidental with overproduction and ordered a whopping daily production cutback from 800,000 to 500,000 barrels. He had been aware that a cutback was in the works and had sneaked an inflated figure to the public in order to help the stock price before trouble set in. Luckily, this action went unchallenged by the SEC.

Hammer admitted privately that the Libyans deserved a large price increase and that he had a sneaking admiration for Qaddafi's toughness and shrewdness. Although it was his nature never to pay anything to anybody without a fight, he decided to proceed cautiously, and his first move was to bombard his Libyan operatives with a new set of sweeteners to offer the Qaddafi regime. It didn't work. Next, he sent word that he was willing to increase Occidental's payoffs substantially. Still he got nowhere. "The Libyans are determined to divide and conquer the foreign oil companies," he explained, "and have targeted Oxy in particular because it depends almost entirely on Libyan oil for its petroleum production. By forcing us to accept their terms, they're convinced they can force all of the other companies to fall into line."

They also knew that Hammer was going to continue paying bribes, no matter what, and Armand's only option was to press harder for access to Iranian oil and he was sure the shah would cooperate. A consortium consisting almost exclusively of Seven Sisters companies paid taxes and royalties to the NIOC in return for permission to produce and market Iran's oil. The previous year, while the shah was renegotiating Iran's deal with the consortium,

Armand had paid a secret visit to him and offered to have Occidental market Iran's oil *at any cost*. The shah had been impressed by Armand's willingness to sabotage the Seven Sisters for the potential benefit of Occidental and grateful that Armand had provided him with a significant bargaining chip to extract more money from the consortium. After he had come to terms, one of the first to visit him was Armand, who had consoled him for deserving a better deal than the one he had received and concluded that he had convinced the shah that he sypathized with the fact that Iran was being victimized and that he was a new "best friend." Therefore, Armand was optimistic about his trip to Tehran.

He reported that the encounter had been successful. "Thankfully, the shah agreed to the terms of the 'fighters-for-oil' deal," he told me. "If he continues to sell us oil after the deal is completed, we'll have an ongoing backup supply that will help us during this mess with the Libyans. The shah is a majestic leader with a regal bearing and tremendous arrogance. He's also shrewd and sophisticated. He was so grateful to me for playing the middleman between him and McDonnell Douglas that he promised to prevail upon the Sharjah government to settle its dispute with Umm al-Qaywayn in Oxy's favor."

A few days later a reporter called to follow up a rumor that Armand had approached the CIA and offered a vast sum of money to help finance a Libyan countercoup to topple Qaddafi and that the payment was going to be funneled through two Bechtel employees operating out of Libya and supposedly CIA agents. The rumor spread like wildfire. Once again Armand and I suspected Big Oil. "They're trying to hurt us by encouraging the Libyans to think that I'm trying to kill their leader," he fumed. "Tell the press the CIA doesn't need my money and deny the rumor categorically."

On July 4, the Libyans celebrated U.S. Independence Day by nationalizing the marketing operation of Esso-Libya. With no oil forthcoming from either Umm al-Qaywayn or Iran and with the Libyan cutbacks eating away at profits, Armand realized that only one alternative remained. "I'd rather choke first than beg for help, but I've got no choice," he told me. "I've got to go to the other oil companies and get them to sell me oil at cost."

It was virtually impossible to believe that the Seven Sisters would lift a finger to help Occidental after Armand's activities in Libya, Iran and Machiasport, Maine, but he forged ahead and scheduled a meeting with Jersey Chairman Kenneth Jamieson on July 10. I called the financial editor whose area of interest was the Jersey management. He confided that Jersey had already decided that if Occidental agreed to the demands of the Libyan Oil Commission and Esso-Libya was subsequently forced to agree to the same price increase, it would simply pass the increase on to its consumers. Therefore, it was unlikely that Jamieson was going to lift a finger to help Hammer stave off Qaddafi.

When Armand got off the elevator on the fifty-first floor of the Esso Building in New York City, he was told to take a seat, and Jamieson made him cool his heels. Finally, Armand was escorted into Jamieson's office, and the short, wily, rumpled, seventy-two-year-old Hammer shook hands with Jamieson, a tall, reserved, central casting version of a big-business CEO.

Hammer explained what Jersey had already gone over in its boardroom: if Occidental capitulated to Qaddafi's demands, all of the other companies in Libya, including Esso, would be forced to follow suit and there would be a dramatic shift in the balance of power between the producing nations and the oil companies. He added that almost all of Occidental's oil came from Libya, and in order to hold the line against the Libyans it was essential that Occidental be able to buy oil from Jersey at cost or at a slight markup, perhaps 10 percent.

When he returned to Los Angeles, Armand reported that "Jamieson listened coldly and in silence, using his arrogance, good breeding, and classy manners as a mask. Finally he said that he couldn't give me an immediate answer. I have no idea whether I succeeded. I hate to think it, but it's possible that the Seven Sisters would rather take it out on the consumer than help me."

Jamieson kept Hammer waiting two weeks. Finally, he called to say that if he sold oil at cost to Occidental, he would be obligated to do the same for all of his other customers. Therefore, the only offer he could make was to charge Occidental the going market price. "No one else has ever told me to drop dead in such a well-mannered way," Armand commented.

Mulling over the Libyan situation, Hammer suddenly decided to take another of his "calculated" risks and he plunged Occidental into the oil transportation business. It was his belief that this new enterprise would offset the losses from the Libyan cutbacks and give Occidental an alternative source of income if there were a complete Libyan shutdown.

Grabbing ships left and right, many on unbreakable long-term charters at fixed rates, in no time at all Armand transformed Occidental's fledgling fleet of oceangoing tankers into a fifty-three-ship armada, which included a number of huge supertankers and even larger VLCCs (Very Large Crude Carriers). One supertanker was christened *Armand Hammer,* and its sister ship was named *Frances Hammer.*

Every time Armand proclaimed that Oxy had achieved one of the biggest oil tanker fleets on the high seas and that it had happened "overnight," the senior executives shuddered about the commitment of hundreds of millions of dollars to a tanker fleet at the same time that almost all of the company's oil supply faced the danger of being cut off by the Libyans. "World shipping rates are especially volatile," explained Dorman Commons. "Even if the Libyans leave us alone, if those rates suddenly bottom out, our losses are going to be *enormous.* The doctor's tanker binge holds the potential of taking the company down the drain."

"The financial guys better get something straight. *I'm* Oxy. Nobody makes the decisions but me!" Armand countered.

In the midst of this frantic ship-buying binge, Armand left for Athens to sign the final "fighters-for-oil" agreement with representatives of INOC. On his return, he told a preposterous story. He said he had gone to the bathroom after he had signed the agreement and had expected the Iranians to countersign it during his absence. But the Iranians had convinced his aides that it was necessary for the shah to reread the contract one last time and had taken the document with his signature on it and left. Armand had been accompanied by Bill Bellano, Claude Geismar, the head of Occidental's foreign oil refining and marketing division, and Hammer's London-based consultant, John Tigrett. After a lifetime in the coal business, Bellano was not the kind of man to let the Iranians put one over on him. Nor was Armand the kind of man who went to the bathroom before he had a fully executed contract in his possession. "Contracts are always signed by both parties at the same time," I observed. "It's just like a treaty. There's no time to go to the bathroom."

"I go to the bathroom when I have to," Armand retorted. "Besides, my bathroom habits weren't the problem. It's the dummies who work for me. They should never have let the Iranians get out the door." Obviously, Armand had been out maneuvered and, typically, he blamed his aides.

No one dared contradict the "official" version of this incident, so I didn't know what really happened. But it became clear that Armand had been set up by the shah when NIOC executives showed the document with his signature to the Seven Sisters consortium that operated Iran's oil industry. Ever fearful that Hammer and his maverick ways would get a toehold in Iran, the consortium topped Occidental's price and made a deal to purchase the oil earmarked for Occidental. Armand had suggested to the shah that he would be willing to help him defeat the Seven Sisters. Now the shah had used him as bait so that he could obtain even greater oil revenues for himself.

"The Seven Sisters will do anything to destroy us, but I'll get even!" Armand roared. As for the formerly "majestic" shah? "He's treacherous, tricky, and a cheat. When you're not watching, he'll eat your lunch. You better keep your hand on your wallet when you're doing business with that unscrupulous son of a bitch!"

Denied any alternative source of oil and fearing even greater pressure from the Libyans, Armand knew he had no choice but to reach a settlement with them. Occidental offered a twenty-cent increase (three cents lower than the last offer made by the Seven Sisters). Smelling blood, the Libyan Oil Commission ordered another 60,000-barrel per day cutback. Then Armand's Libyan intelligence network tipped him that the commission was planning to nationalize Occidental's concessions on Labor Day, the first anniversary of the coup. No one knew whether this was true or merely propaganda designed to increase Armand's panic, but the deadline was a hairbreadth away. "The travel ban has been lifted, and I'll go to Libya myself," he declared. "I'll be the first oil company CEO to visit the leaders of the new regime. That's got to work in my favor."

OXYLIBYA executives and State Department officials insisted that Qaddafi's government was made up of virulently anti-Semitic radical Arabs and warned Armand that no matter what he said, he would be considered not only a Jew but also a Jew who had a close relationship with King Idris. It was their opinion that by traveling to Libya he was putting himself in danger and might be held hostage. But Armand refused to be dissuaded. He decided to fly to Paris in secrecy, use the Ritz Hotel as a base, and commute to Tripoli daily to minimize the chance of kidnapping.

To the astonishment of one and all, after five days of fifteen-hour negotiation sessions, Armand returned to Los Angeles with a deal and a collection of wonderful new friends. "The negotiations were conducted by Oil Minister Mabrouk and Deputy Minister Jalloud," he reported. "I got along famously with both of them. Major Jalloud greeted me warmly and said, 'Hammer, you are the first and only chairman of an oil company operating in our country who ever paid me a personal visit. I am honored. Libya welcomes you.' How can you dislike a guy like that?

"With all his charm, Jalloud's very tough," Armand continued. "He tried to bluff me by flying into a rage and ordering me to leave the country. I got up, walked around his chair, put my arms around his shoulders, and calmed him down. Jalloud demanded a forty-cent-per-barrel increase and implied that if I didn't give it to him, Oxy would have to leave Libya. But I wouldn't give it to him, and we settled for thirty. We're going to stay, and we're not in danger anymore. I saved us singlehandedly!"

Taught a lesson by the shah of Iran in the art of signing agreements, Armand had demanded that Mabrouk's written authorization from the RCC to conduct the negotiations be attached to the agreement. When it was not produced, he authorized his representatives to sign the contract only when it was completed properly. "Then I dashed from the room," he said. "I feared arrest because I had not signed. Besides, I didn't want them to think I had been jerking them around. I rushed to the airport, jumped into the Gulfstream, and ordered a takeoff without obtaining clearance from the tower."

"They could have shot down the plane," I said.

"I knew I could die," Armand said. "Dying in a plane crash seemed easier than facing a Libyan firing squad."

A few days later, on September 1, Occidental representatives officially caved in to Libyan demands and signed a fully executed agreement, An escalation clause raised the posted per-barrel price from $2.23 to $2.53 (seven cents more than the Seven Sisters were willing to pay) and guaranteed further escalations of two cents per barrel a year for the next five years. The large price increase was accompanied by a boost in the tax rate from 50 to 58 percent and was the first rupture in the fifty-fifty profit-sharing agreements that were standard oil industry practices. "It's the beginning of the end of cheap energy," Gene Reid prophesied succinctly.

Meanwhile, complaints of overproduction evaporated and Occidental was allowed to start operating at its former capacity. A week later, Oasis, another independent, faced with the choice of leaving Libya or matching the new terms, capitulated. By the end of October all twenty-one oil companies operating out of Libya had accepted the raise, and the other oil-producing countries began making similar demands.

There was almost nothing I could do to counter the vitriolic international criticism that was leveled at Hammer over the next several months. Financial writers and political columnists joined together to blame him for causing the worldwide escalation in oil prices, the devastating economic consequences of the settlement, and the burden that was going to be placed on the oil consumer. Armand was repeatedly accused of putting Occidental's profits before the good of the Western world and of caving in so that he could punish the Seven Sisters for refusing to honor his request for cheap oil. Many took the position that had he toughed it out and not broken rank, the Libyans eventually would have backed down.

Armand's initial response was to try to blame his representatives because they, and not he, had signed the agreement. I told him it wasn't going to work and that I had to get out the story that he had done everything possible to find an alternative to making the deal and that only when all else failed had he come to terms with the Libyans. So he took another tack that seemed closer to the truth. "If I had allowed the Libyans to kick us out, Oxy would have gone down the drain," he told the press. "My responsibility is to the shareholders and the people who earn their living by working for this company. My job is to save Oxy, and that's what I did. If I hadn't settled, the Libyans would have nationalized all of the oil companies. I saved Libya for everyone. I ought to be praised and thanked instead of criticized and ridiculed. I was a hero. Everybody is too stupid to understand that."

Beyond that bit of self-congratulation, Armand took every opportunity to blame Kenneth Jamieson for the price explosion. Jamieson countered that the price increase had been inevitable, even if Jersey had sold Occidental oil at cost.

During November, the SEC informed Armand that it had launched a formal investigation of Occidental to determine whether company practices had interfered with the truthful disclosure of information to the shareholders and the public. Determined to stop anyone from providing the federal investigators with damaging information, Armand held closed-door meetings with those executives he suspected were going to be called to testify. Each was greeted with a handshake and a genuine smile of pleasure. Speaking softly, Armand created the impression that the man being interviewed was entering his private world and was dealing with the real Armand Hammer—open, vulnerable, friendly, sincere.

What followed was an exhausting monologue that contained a

three-pronged attack: an overwhelming dose of flattery; a stunning act of contrition in which Armand portrayed himself as an innocent who was about to go to the gallows through no fault of his own; and, finally, a plea for help that was so impassioned it reduced one executive to tears.

These men had every reason to suspect that Hammer was guilty of any charge leveled against him. But they were so dazed by their encounter with him that they came to believe he really was the target of an SEC vendetta and that Occidental's survival depended on the caginess of their replies. I don't know what was said during those SEC interrogations, but Real Estate Vice President Lawrence Kagan, ostensibly called to testify about Occidental's acquisition of the Kagan-owned Monarch Investment Company in 1966 and the windfall $2 million profit that Occidental acquired from this acquisition just days after the deal was made, must have said something damaging, because he never returned to his desk. Armand didn't mention his disappearance, and no one dared ask him about it. Finally, word spread throughout the company that Kagan had become the first executive not to "resign," but to evaporate.

Armand also kept track of the outside witnesses who were being summoned by the SEC, especially those Occidental had reason to believe would be hostile. Occidental's lawyers bombarded the investigators with information they hoped would discredit them and did their best to convince the SEC to suspend its investigation rather than listen to accusations from "disgruntled former employees."

As Armand had expected, Walter Davis had talked to the federal regulators. Davis was capable of doing real harm, so a team of private investigators was hired to dig up something to discredit him, and a laundry list of accusations about Davis's professional and personal life was supplied to the SEC.

As the SEC investigation continued, Armand showed no inclination to alter his no-holds-barred executive style. On November 11, his older half brother, Harry, died of heart trouble at the age of seventy-seven. "I did everything I could to save him," said Armand. "That's why I sent him to Methodist Hospital in Houston and had him treated by Dr. Michael De Bakey."

Victor told me that the doctors had given Harry up for lost until Armand had arrived. After a private meeting with Harry's doctors, Armand announced that Harry was going to be saved. "He had talked them into performing a 'miracle,'" Victor said. "Armand hates death so much he forced them to give Harry a hopeless pacemaker implant. That's why Harry lay in intensive care for four months before he finally passed away."

Armand gave strict orders that no executive was to attend Harry's funeral in New Jersey. Victor explained that Harry was being buried in a Jewish ceremony and that Armand did not want anyone to know. Later he told me that Harry, his late wife, Bette Barber Hammer, and Bette's half-sister Frances Colmery were in agreement that "Barber Harbor," a Barber family home in Vicksburg, Mississippi, should always remain in the family. With that understanding the Barber parents had given the home to Harry and Bette in return for a monthly income. But when Harry became ill, Armand had declared the agreement was null and void, and Frances Colmery took over the home and rented it in order to raise money to maintain the property and pay taxes. After Harry's death, Armand ignored Harry and Bette's wish that the house remain in the Barber family, and offered to sell it to Colmery for $40,000. When she said she couldn't afford it, he sold it for $22,000 and pocketed the money. "Armand views death as a profit-making activity," Victor joked. "Besides, he never considered Bette or Frances a part of the family."

It was another example of Armand's habit not only to eliminate but also deeply wound those he considered his inferiors, rather than risk being perceived as one of them. But making money was always the essential element, and Armand remained convinced that the accumulation of money more than anything else would help him maintain the illusion that he was larger than life and beyond anyone's control.

On December 1 the Venezuelan national oil company, CVP, announced that three of the five blocks put up for auction as oil concessions, an expanse of 375,000 acres, had been awarded to Occidental. Two majors, Royal Dutch/Shell and Mobil Oil, had received the other two. Armand called me from New York to boast of his victory. "How do you like that? We got three away from the big boys. I bet they can't guess how we did it."

I had a hunch they could.

The same day Armand ordered two key oil executives, Bud Reid and Dick Vaughan, to fly to New York that night on the red-eye. Reid had just returned from an inspection tour in Venezuela, and he assumed Armand wanted to hear his report before he met with the Venezuelan general counsel to discuss whether Occidental was going to accept the blocks. Bleary-eyed, the men arrived in New

York at six in the morning and headed straight for Hammer's Greenwich Village carriage house. They found that Hammer had been up for hours. "I've already met with the general counsel and given my go-ahead," he told them. "Go back to Bakersfield."

Armand turned next to a project that had been on his mind for five years. After Occidental had discovered reserves of 60 million barrels in the Pacific Palisades section of Los Angeles in 1965, three years had been devoted to obtaining a drilling site. Finally it believed it had achieved its goal in 1968 when it traded a 10.5-acre parcel in the Palisades for two nearby acres of city-owned, oil-rich beachfront property and $175,000 cash. But a grass-roots environmental group, No Oil Incorporated, had set out to prevent Occidental from obtaining permission to drill a core hole on these two acres and to find out who had approved the unconventional land swap in the first place. A team of private investigators had been hired to look into the matter.

Subsequently, No Oil Incorporated learned that Armand had donated $10,000 to restore a shrine in the birthplace of Mayor Sam Yorty's mother in Ireland and had traveled with Yorty to Ireland in Occidental's Gulfstream to attend the unveiling of the statue. It was also revealed that Yorty was using the Gulfstream to travel around California and elsewhere. Armand was undaunted by the disclosures. "I've invested too much time in this project, and nothing's going to stop me. I'm not going to die until I drill in the Palisades!"

His determination encouraged No Oil Incorporated to urge its investigators to dig deeper. In retaliation, when Armand discovered that the Center for Law in the Public Interest, which represented the environmental group, was funded by the Ford Foundation, he ordered his most trusted lawyer Arthur Groman to call several of the center's trustees and tell someone that he had a "dossier" on the activities of the center's attorneys that provided grounds to sue to remove the foundation's tax-exempt status. When Groman was asked to produce the dossier, he declined to do so. In response, the Center obtained an advisory opinion from the Los Angeles County Bar Association that such conduct by lawyers was "unethical." Armand shrugged it off. "My reputation as a civic-minded member of the community is going to mean more than anything No Oil digs up."

The primary vehicle that he planned to use to enhance that reputation was the newly formed Armand Hammer Foundation, a tax-exempt entity that was going to be funded largely through charitable contributions from Occidental and himself. Armand would also be able to claim tax deductions for the travel and entertainment expenses he incurred as he conducted "foundation business" all over the world and for the costs of any other self-promotional activities that would refine his image and, therefore, the image of his foundation. The appointment of family members and long-term advisers as trustees guaranteed that there would be no objections to the donations he chose to make, and by donating Occidental's funds through his foundation, he had found a foolproof way to create the illusion that *all* of the donations were his alone and that money, the only thing he really cared about, meant nothing to him unless he could use it to improve the quality of life. Thus, he provided me with an endless stream of opportunities to position him in the press as one of America's most selfless philanthropists.

Enormous local publicity accompanied the Armand Hammer Foundation's establishment of the Frances and Armand Hammer Million Dollar Purchase Fund at the Los Angeles County Museum of Art. Subsequently Armand used the $1 million to buy a Renoir, a Sargent, and a Modigliani and received another round of publicity when he "donated" them to the museum. He then made another $2 million donation, which was earmarked for architectural renovations. When he hinted that he would like a museum wing to bear his name, the County Museum instantly changed the name of the Special Exhibits Gallery to the Frances and Armand Hammer Wing.

As for the new art collection he had recently amassed—*"better art at lower prices"*—Armand ordered me to refer to it as the third Armand Hammer Collection, to describe it as "ninety-six Old Masters worth $25 million," and to say that it was the third major collection he had amassed. (The first two were the collection he had "exported" from the Soviet Union in 1930 and the collection he had donated to USC in 1965.) The first major exhibition of the new collection was scheduled for March 24, 1970, at the Smithsonian Institution of National History. Serious collectors were not inclined to display their paintings in the Smithsonian's old and harshly lit galleries, but Hammer explained that the curators had been so eager to show the collection that he couldn't turn them down. In reality, Armand had asked County Museum director Kenneth Donahue to find a major venue for the exhibition, and Donahue, who considered the new Armand Hammer Collection a mediocre assortment, had confided to me that he had spared himself the embarrassment of attempting to place it in a major museum by introducing Hammer to the directors of the Smithsonian.

Determined to take Washington by storm, Armand spared no expense as he planned a preexhibition black-tie dinner in the Hall of Gems and invited every important political and society figure in Washington. For days he seemed to spend all his time yelling into the phone, "How many Supreme Court justices are coming? How many ambassadors? How many senators? Make sure they know they're going to dine under the glow of the Hope Diamond, and let them know that I'm going to give their wives a large, expensive piece of jade from my mine as a gift."

In the days before the opening a handful of parties were given in Armand's honor by prominent members of the Los Angeles art and business communities. At one of them I noticed that he again came face to face with the woman who had snubbed him at the USC reception five years before. Her reaction was just as sharp. A few days later we ran into her again, and she abruptly turned her back on him.

An intimate of the Hammer family told me later that this woman's uncle and Armand had been business associates in the late 1930s and around that time Armand had attended a dinner party for her mother when she came to New York on a visit. According to my source Armand had made a pass at the mother, had been rejected, and had smoothed things over by volunteering to drive her to the airport the following day. Instead Armand had taken her to his Greenwich Village carriage house and had forced himself upon her because he "never took no for an answer." Then he had warned her that if she ever discussed the event with anyone, he would insist that she was the initiator, which would ruin her marriage. Years afterward she had confided the story to her daughter.

I was too shocked to pursue the matter further.

Shortly before the Armand Hammer Collection was placed on exhibition at the Smithsonian Institution, Armand decided to have it evaluated by an art expert. He asked me to accompany him to the County Museum, where we watched in silence as the expert, an intense academic type, slowly surveyed the canvases, which were lined up against the walls of a large, empty storage room. Occasionally he stopped and questioned Armand sharply about where and from whom he had purchased a canvas.

Finally, he expressed his opinion. "This collection consists of the mediocre and an occasional dash of the merely average," he said. "The authenticity of quite a few also deserves to be challenged. The theme of this collection is quantity. I suggest you make the theme quality. You should rebuild it so that each painting represents the best example of a particular artist's work, and not merely an uninteresting example of it."

Armand was fuming, but he held his peace until we were on the way out of the museum. "That dumb bastard doesn't know what the hell he's talking about," he roared. "He's nothing but a lousy cubist. He's also a fairy. A lot of these art world guys are fags. Fags always prefer modern art. What he just handed me was a hefty dose of art world fag judgment."

Nevertheless, the collection was sent to Washington as scheduled, and a few days after the opening at the Smithsonian, a long review appeared in *The Washington Post* under the headline "An Exhibition of Losers by Major Masters." Paul Richard wrote, "Three women, all in evening gowns, stood between the Rubens portrait and the Rembrandt, scornfully condemning the pictures on display. Their derisive comments, and those of other guests, sent hints of fraud and forgery drifting through the room. . . . Never have so many major masters been represented in this city by canvases so poor." The critic continued that even though the authenticity of the paintings in "almost every case" had been established, "yet the poisonous rumors will not fade. There is reason for their persistence." Richard also speculated that the entire event was an attempt by Hammer to inflate the value of the collection so that he could claim a fat tax deduction.

Outraged, Armand drafted a five-thousand-word reply also published in the *Post* that took the critic to task point by point. At the same time he decided to turn to John Walker, who had just retired as director of the National Gallery of Art. Armand knew Walker only casually from their encounters as trustees at the County Museum, so he dispatched Sir John Foster, a friend of Walker's, to Washington to persuade him to assess the collection and to improve it.

Walker refused, saying that he had spent thirty years trying to avoid criticizing private collections and collectors. But Foster convinced Walker to go with him to the Smithsonian to look at the paintings. Walker could see immediately that Hammer had terrible taste, but, as a favor to Foster, agreed to hold a meeting with him. Oozing with charm, Armand pleaded with Walker until the distinguished art expert succumbed. After determining which paintings were copies and mediocre works, he convinced Armand to discard half of the collection. When he said that Armand was a bargain hunter and that bargain hunting was the best way to amass an unsuccessful collection, Armand told Walker that he wanted to assemble a brilliant collection in record time and agreed to purchase any painting Walker recommended without regard to cost.

A huge spending spree followed, and in less than a year's time, Armand's collection of Barbizon painters, Impressionists, and post-Impressionists was enhanced by a number of Old Master drawings and paintings by prominent American artists and nearly doubled in size. It became, even in the eyes of formerly hostile critics, a respectable collection. At the same time that Walker continued the upgrading process, Armand made a list of galleries and museums across the country, tracked down a particular area of concern for each, and offered to make a contribution. In return he received an "invitation" to exhibit there. Within a few months, the new, improved Armand Hammer Collection was being shuttled from city to city and Armand was sponsoring promotional galas in his own honor in Columbus, Kansas City, Little Rock, Memphis, New Orleans, Oklahoma City, San Diego, and elsewhere.

Shortly after the debacle at the Smithsonian, Armand saw a TV interview with Dr. Jonas Salk. Eager to find a way to counteract the bad publicity that surrounded his collection, he speculated that if he funded a cure for cancer, he'd be "a hero for all time." A week later, he told me that we were about to leave for the Salk Institute for Biological Studies in La Jolla, California. "I'm giving them five million dollars. Dr. Salk is waiting for us."

Salk showed us the facilities, then took us to meet with the directors of the institute. He looked uncomfortable when Armand announced that "Dr. Salk discovered a way to prevent polio. I'm going to help him do the same thing with cancer."

"Polio is caused by three viruses that can be cultured and developed into a vaccine," Salk tried to explain, "but cancer exists in many forms. When you talk about finding a 'cure' for cancer, you're making an impossible supposition."

Armand ignored him. There had to be a cancer vaccine, and Salk had to discover it. Not only that, Salk had to discover it quickly so that the seventy-two-year-old Hammer could claim credit. In return for his donation, Armand was named a trustee of the institute and chairman of its executive committee, and his gift was used to establish an on-campus research facility, the Armand Hammer Center for Cancer Biology.

Armand wanted enormous publicity for his new crusade, and his role as a cancer fighter was a wonderful new angle for me to promote. In interviews he began to predict that such a cure would be found under his sponsorship. And when he saw the stack of news clippings I generated about his cancer fight, he knew he was onto a good thing. "I'm planning to fund annual cancer symposia at my institute and bring together medical researchers from all over the world," he told me. "Once they're all in the same room, maybe they'll get Salk to hurry up and invent the goddamned vaccine."

Convinced that his immortality rested on the imminent discovery of this "vaccine," Armand continued to put unrelenting pressure on the administration and staff of the center that bore his name. After all, once *he* decided to do something, it was all but accomplished. And he expected them to do the same.

14.

"I LIKE CONSENT DECREES"

Armand's gut instinct told him that there was going to be more trouble in Libya. He arranged a secret meeting with Shell Oil Chairman Sir David Barran and told him that any company that found itself the victim of another Libyan cutback or suspension had to be able to buy crude from the other companies at cost. Unlike Jersey Chairman Kenneth Jamieson, Barran agreed. A round of secret meetings between Armand's English consultant, John Tigrett, and representatives of Shell was set into motion to formulate a strategy that would join majors and independents in a united front against any new demands made by Libya or the ten-year-old Organization of Petroleum Exporting Countries (OPEC), which until this moment had been unable to exert that much power.

Armand's suspicions proved correct when Iraq cited Occidental's settlement with Libya as the pretext for demanding a twenty-cent-per-barrel increase. Iran followed with a sixteen-cent increase and added a 5 percent tax increase, which OPEC declared to be automatically in effect in all member nations. The day after this resolution, Deputy Prime Minister Abdel Salaam Ahmed Jalloud announced that Libya planned to reopen negotiations in Tripoli after the New Year.

A couple of days later, Armand buckled over in pain during a meeting. He was terrified of hospitals, but when it was discovered that he was suffering from kidney stones, he had no choice but to submit to surgery. Finding himself alive and kicking after the operation, he automatically incorporated the thing he feared most into his dramatic retelling of his life. Feigning great surprise, he announced that *just* as he was coming out of anesthesia "the phone in my room rang. Of all people, it was David Barran. He was calling to discuss my views about a united front."

Ego alone demanded that he make it look as if a Seven Sisters chief had come to him. But there was another reason. "The Seven Sisters hate my guts, so I'm letting them think the united front is Barran's plan," he told me. "They'd never be able to deal with the fact that I've just become their consultant."

On December 12, oil prices took another dramatic leap when the Venezuelan National Congress passed what became known as the Caracas Resolution. It raised the tax rate to 60 percent, and OPEC immediately called for a new round of negotiations for the Persian Gulf states. Now there were going to be two negotiations: one in Tehran, the other in Tripoli. Armand was furious. "We've got to join together and insist on only one negotiation. Otherwise, they'll have us whipsawing back and forth."

True to their word, on January 3, 1971, the Libyans announced that they were going to raise their taxes to 60 percent unless the United States changed its favorable policy toward Israel. Six days later, when this ploy had failed and there had been no response, they again resorted to their "divide-and-conquer" strategy. They called representatives from Occidental and another American independent, Bunker Hunt, and delivered the ultimatum that the companies had a week to agree to the tax increase, a sixty-cent increase in the posted price, and a twenty-five-cent-per-barrel reinvestment tax—or else. It was as if Armand's four-month-old negotiation had never happened. He was incredulous. "That lunatic Qaddah and his gang of ignoramuses ought to take some time off, go to business college, and learn about profit and loss. They don't understand that when you set your prices too high, you kill sales."

With the threat of Libyan nationalization once again hanging over their heads, a contingent of oil company leaders met in New York on January 11 to finalize details of the united front. Two results emerged. The first was the secret understanding that Armand had called for, which came to be known as the Safety Net Agreement, a joint protection plan that guaranteed compensatory amounts of oil at cost in response to any Libyan action that threatened a company's oil supply. The other result was a joint communiqué to OPEC, which became known as the Libyan Producers

Mutual Production Pact. Its purpose was to prevent the Libyans from either isolating any one company or staging a separate negotiation. Thus, the pact called for collective bargaining among representatives of the oil companies and representatives of OPEC rather than a series of individual negotiations with delegates from the oil ministries of each nation.

The oil and gas boys who attended the meeting reported that the majors had conveniently forgotten that Hammer had approached them before making a deal with Qaddafi and held him personally responsible for the newfound power of OPEC and the fact that they had been forced to help their most hated competitors, the independents. They also loathed the fact that he was in charge and that they had to treat him as an equal and give him whatever he wanted in order to prevent him from cutting another deal with Qaddafi that would cause even more trouble.

The Libyan Producers Mutual Production Pact was delivered to OPEC on January 16. OPEC responded instantly with a new set of demands and the threat of an entire oil industry shutdown unless those demands were accepted unconditionally within twenty-four hours. Determined to maintain the united front, a team of oil company negotiators left immediately for Tehran. In short order, to their consternation, they learned from State Department officials that the shah of Iran supported separate negotiations. To their even greater embarrassment, when they sat down with the Iranian negotiators, they discovered that the State Department was backing the shah and had withdrawn its support of the united front. Between the shah and the State Department, the Libyan Producers Mutual Production Pact had been thwarted a mere eight days after its enactment.

The oil companies' team was left with two choices: dissolve the united front and participate in separate negotiations in Tehran and Tripoli or else get ready for a shutdown by OPEC, which might lead to nationalization in every oil-producing state.

The U.S. position was a direct reflection of the Nixon-Kissinger view, which had coalesced into the so-called Nixon Doctrine of 1969. The theory was that the Vietnam War had shown that the United States could no longer serve as the world's policeman but could serve as the world's arms supplier. Those arms would go to Third World countries willing to assume the roles of surrogate policemen. The departure of the U.K. Persian Gulf security force at the end of 1971 dictated that the United States appoint someone to play policeman in a strategic region that contained 75 percent of the non-Communist world's oil reserves. The shah had proved the ideal choice because he was more than willing to step into the vacuum and fend off any Soviet aggression and radical Arab activity and he had the money to buy large quantities of American arms.

The news sickened Hammer. "The higher the oil prices, the more money the shah is going to make, and the more American weapons he's going to buy," he said. "That's why Kissinger is letting him seize control of OPEC. Then he and Nixon can write off the increased revenues from the weapons sales against the huge costs of importing foreign oil. They've decided to rob Peter to pay Paul at the same time that they screw every American oil consumer. Besides, selling that jerk of a shah billions of dollars worth of weapons that someday could be turned against us is one of the dumbest things anyone can do. They ought to tie Kissinger's hands and throw him into the Potomac! The bottom line is we've lost control of the price of oil. Nobody has a clue about the horrible consequences that are going to occur when prices go through the roof."

Unwilling to concede the collapse of their strategy, the oil company negotiators continued to try to convince the State Department that unless there was a showdown with OPEC, any semblance of price controls would be doomed. It was not to be. The shah stated that unless there were separate negotiations in Tehran and Tripoli, all oil industries would be nationalized after the expiration of the existing concession agreements. In the face of this declaration from the self-proclaimed leader of OPEC, the oil team had no alternative but to agree to separate negotiations, and a $3 billion package was put onto the table in Tehran. Eventually, on February 14, OPEC and the oil producers reached a $10 billion settlement, the so-called Tehran Oil Price Agreement.

As tough as the Tehran negotiations were, the negotiations in Tripoli would be even tougher. When they commenced on February 23, no one was surprised to hear the Libyans announce that the Tehran agreement was going to be used as the starting point. After a negotiation that dragged on for forty-four days, the Tripoli Agreement, which raised prices another twenty cents per barrel, was announced on April 2. Armand was resigned but apprehensive about the future. "The shah was the hero in Tehran," he told me. "He consolidated his power, controlled the whole show, and got a big raise for the Gulf states. But the oil companies lost respect in the Arab world, where prestige is very important, because we didn't have the guts to face down OPEC. Then the Libyans wound up with an even better deal. Now it's the shah's turn to save face. You can bet that snake is already plotting to get another raise for the Gulf states. It's not over yet."

Meanwhile, Armand had had to face up to a challenge to his own prestige. Just after the Libyan negotiations got under way, he told me some disturbing news. "The SEC is charging Oxy with fraud," he said. "The lawyers say I've got to sign a consent decree in order to stop them from going farther. But I don't want to sign it. I want to fight. I always fight, and I always win."

If sufficient information is uncovered to convince the SEC that further legal action is warranted, the agency seeks an injunction to restrain a corporation from committing any more acts in violation of the various federal securities acts. The particular injunction sought by the SEC, not only against Occidental but also against Hammer personally, accused them of three things: inflating Occidental's 1969 and 1970 net income totals by $13.8 million; failing to disclose the origin of certain profits so that accounting procedures could be used to make it appear that those profits had been earned in 1969 when they had really been earned in prior years; and releasing misleading information about the volume of Occidental's crude-oil production, projected coal production, and projected 1970 earnings as well as failing to announce that Occidental's oil output had been sharply curtailed by the Libyan government.

By digging deeply into the activities of Occidental Petroleum Land and Development Corporation, the umbrella for all of Occidental's real estate companies, the SEC was able to include in its charges the accusation that the real-estate subsidiary had engaged in two transactions that had generated a $4.2 million profit and had been disguised on the books as land sales.

Armand was indignant. "Oxy had record earnings of $174.8 million in 1969. It broke its own record by earning $175.2 million in 1970. That comes to $350 million. What's the big deal about misstating our net income by four percent for those two years? If that four percent drove us from loss to profit, then it certainly could be considered fraudulent. In our case it's merely bookkeeping carelessness. We're not going to revise our financial reports.

"Furthermore," he added, "the actions of the Libyan government were printed on the front pages of every newspaper in the world. Our shareholders know how to read. Those SEC bastards are out to get me."

The income figures cited by the SEC had appeared in news releases that I had written and in the quarterly and annual reports that had been produced under my supervision. I had obtained these figures from the financial and accounting staff, Financial Vice President Dorman Commons, Treasurer Charles Lee, and Controller Jim Murdy, and Armand had also approved them, as had Occidental's outside auditor for the past ten years, Arthur Andersen & Co. Despite his promise to the SEC in 1966 to curb his tendency to issue inflated statements, it was clear that Armand was continuing to find new ways to perform end runs around the checks and balances that had been instituted to bring him under control.

Instead of going through long, expensive court procedures, corporations are often given the option of signing a consent decree. This judgment waives all previous irregularities, and at the same time that a corporation does not admit that it has done anything wrong, it signs a contract promising never to do it again. During its four-month investigation, the SEC had learned a great deal about Occidental, and it probably could have learned more if it had gone on. The financial executives agreed and expressed concern that a protracted trial and public discussion of Hammer's financial practices would create reverberations in the financial community and inspire large institutional investors to lose confidence in Occidental stock. Therefore, signing a consent decree seemed the only reasonable option.

The adult Hammer knew that he would eventually have to sign, but the child in him acted up for a week and involved his closest aides in endless arguments about why he did not want to capitulate. Finally, he faced the inevitable. "The SEC is announcing its accusations tomorrow," he told me, "and I'm going to sign the consent decree. I'm doing it because the lawyers put the screws to me. That's the *only* reason. You know I never do anything wrong."

His paranoia about secrecy suddenly rose to the surface. "Executives are going to call you at home trying to find out things after they read the morning papers," he warned me. "Don't waste your time with them. If they give you any trouble, tell them to call me and hang up on them."

I did get calls, but there was nothing I could have told them that they did not already know or were not going to read in the newspapers.

After I told Armand that the press was not to be allowed near him and that the matter should be handled with one news release briefly acknowledging the accusations and defending Hammer and Occidental against the charges and a second announcing the signing of the consent decree, he and the attorneys spent the rest of the day honing each word of the latter release. Their purpose was to make sure that it was clear that neither Occidental nor Hammer admitted wrongdoing or liability and that the consent decree had been signed solely "to save the time of our executives in vindicating our position by formal legal proceedings."

The next morning the *Los Angeles Times* headline read S.E.C. AC-CUSES OXY OF FRAUD. Armand read everything that was printed about him or his company, and if he believed that an article was going to cause a drop in the stock price or suggest that he was unpredictable or untrustworthy, his temper flared and he ordered me to "take care of it." It meant one thing: the launching of a large-scale PR counteroffensive that portrayed Occidental as a happy and productive company and, more significantly, reinforced his image as a hero who deserved nothing less than unqualified glorification.

These latest clippings did not upset him in the least in spite of their decidedly unflattering tone. "I've decided that I like consent decrees," he said. "They're a real challenge. They make you want to see if you're smart enough to beat the bastards the next time around."

As part of the settlement with the SEC, Occidental was put into the embarrassing position of having to issue a revised set of profit figures for 1969 and 1970. Armand's signing of the consent decree also triggered the filing of twenty class-action suits by company shareholders charging that the company had created an artificially inflated market for its stock by issuing fraudulent reports.

Armand pretended to brush aside the lawsuits. "It's a racket, just a bunch of greedy ambulance-chasing lawyers goading unscrupulous people into trying to capitalize on our misfortunes in order to earn big legal fees. The shareholders should be happy that I usually do so well for them, and they should let me run the company my way—which is always the best way!"

Eventually the suits would be settled out of court at a cost of $11 million, while Occidental's outside auditor, Arthur Andersen, paid $1 million. But the SEC settlement triggered another company policy designed to rein in Hammer. After he approved the draft of any news release, it would be circulated internally to the senior executives whose names appeared on a distribution list. Their job would be to check it for errors and suggest improvements before the news was issued to the press and public.

Predictably, Armand immediately tried to circumvent the policy. One day, after approving a release, he handed it back to me and said, "I don't want Tom Wachtell to know about any of this until he reads it in the newspapers. Even though he's on the list, don't send him one."

I pointed out that by circulating the release to the others, Wachtell was bound to hear about it.

"Do it my way," he insisted.

That evening my phone rang at home. It was Armand, and he was so enraged he was almost incoherent. Wachtell had seen the release and had confronted him about it, and Armand had come to the erroneous conclusion that I had defied his order and given Wachtell a copy. "You disobeyed me and deliberately double-crossed me!" he shouted. "I'd like to see you put before a firing squad without a blindfold! And I want to be there when they pull the trigger!"

"I didn't give Tom a copy," I said evenly.

My answer surprised him. "How did he get it?"

"I don't know."

"Guess!"

Turning the tables, I asked, "Can't you guess?"

"Of course *I* can guess. I want you to guess."

"*You* tell me."

"Dorman gave it to him," Armand replied. "They have adjoining offices. I see them talking to each other all the time."

"I bet you're right."

It dawned on Armand that he had made a mistake by calling me. Now he needed another reason for having done so. "Why is Dorman being copied?" he demanded to know. "Are you giving Dorman advance copies of the press releases? What's wrong with you?"

"Dorman is on the distribution list."

"I don't want him to see any of the news releases. Why did you put him on the list?"

"I didn't."

"Then who the hell told you to put him on it?"

"You did!"

"The hell I did!"

"I'll show you your memo."

There was a pause. "Are you sure?"

"Yes."

"I remember now."

He slammed down the phone.

The signing of the consent decree removed the major obstacle inhibiting Occidental from selling new securities, and shortly after Hammer resolved his problems with the SEC, an offering of $125 million worth of convertible debentures was announced, to be followed by a new issue of 1,550,000 shares of common stock. The financial staff looked grim. No one was talking, but the feeling was that Occidental was losing a great deal of money and needed a large infusion of cash.

Armand always told me in advance when he was planning to fire someone, so that I would not be surprised if I got a call from a reporter who had caught wind of his decision. During the summer there was a shake-up in the executive ranks of the company, and I announced that Occidental Vice Chairman of the Board Tom Willers had "resigned." He tersely told business reporters that he admired Hammer's business genius but was disenchanted with the way Occidental was being run. Later, during a Senate investigation of Occidental business practices, Willers would admit under oath that he had received a severance pay of $160,000 a year for three years. It was standard procedure. Armand hated being known as a chief executive who was hard to work with, and executives hated seeing in print the fact that they had been fired. Therefore, in addition to the undated letter of resignation Armand usually asked an executive who was going to join the board to sign before he came to work for Occidental, he asked him to sign a confidentiality agreement known as the "privileged information document" upon his departure. This corporate equivalent of a gag order was tied to the employee's severance package and designed to prevent him from making public disclosures about Hammer's business practices after he left the company.

In return Hammer bestowed large secret settlements. The amounts usually depended on how much the employee had seen and were granted not only to important executives but also to many lower-ranking employees. Armand found it essential to buy off *anyone* who might say *anything* damaging about him that contradicted his heroic image.

15.

"MAKE THIS MESS LOOK GOOD"

The fear that the Libyans might eventually cut off Occidental's oil supply led Armand to obtain lease positions and partnership arrangements in the offshore waters of Ghana, Honduras, Jamaica, Nicaragua, Sierra Leone, Tobago, and Trinidad. Seismic tests and exploration were under way in all of those locations, but Armand maintained that the company's best bets remained its entry into the oil transportation business and the possibility of discovering oil in Venezuela.

Yet negotiations with the Venezuelan national oil company had dragged on for months. Oil and gas executive Dick Vaughan blamed the delay on nationalistic fervor and explained that the Venezuelan government and its oil industry were determined to eliminate all foreign ownership. Every Occidental employee who returned from Libya had complained that local contractors, customs officials, and deliverymen had expected payoffs. Insisting that Venezuela was even worse, Vaughan told Armand that all of Occidental's energies should be focused on North Sea exploration, or Occidental would find itself overwhelmed by the corruption in Venezuela and would also have to contend with the inevitability of nationalization.

Armand was a political animal. Venezuela was facing a year-end presidential election, and President Rafael Caldera was being heavily criticized for the lengthy negotiations that were preventing Venezuela from reaping any oil income from South Lake Maracaibo.

Hammer believed that the minority Caldera regime was about to realize that it had only another year left in office to line its pockets, which would ensure its cooperation. He had also supplied a $5,000 "tip" to every Venezuelan legislator in return for a promise that the negotiations would be concluded before the end of the current congressional session.

When the oil and gas boys grew more insistent about abandoning the negotiations, Armand pacified them by calling a special meeting of the board. Vaughan and his colleagues stated their case for leaving Venezuela. The case for continuing was presented by Charles Hatfield, the head of Occidental's Venezuelan operation, and a Venezuelan attorney whom Hatfield had brought with him. At the end of the meeting, Armand announced that Occidental was staying put in Venezuela *and* going to continue its efforts in the North Sea. The next day he removed Vaughan from the Venezuelan project, which eliminated internal opposition.

A formal agreement was reached with the Venezuelans on July 29, 1971, seven months after the award of the service contracts. The Venezuelan national oil company had estimated that there were recoverable reserves of 3.3 billion barrels in South Lake Maracaibo. Occidental purchased the official seismic surveys and conducted its own seismic work, which produced promising results. Two large offshore platform rigs were erected, and a full-scale drilling program was put into motion. One dry hole was followed by a second, and over the next two years Occidental and the two other auction winners, Royal Dutch/Shell and Mobil, would drill a combined total of eighteen dry holes. It had taken five years of scheming, negotiation, and bribery to obtain the service contracts, only to discover that a commercial accumulation of oil might not exist. As usual, Armand was undaunted. "I don't care what it costs. I don't care how many dry holes we drill. We're not going to stop."

Around the same time that Occidental finalized its agreement with Venezuela, it became the first foreign company to secure petroleum rights in Peru since the military coup in 1968. The production agreement provided for a fifty-fifty split between Occidental and the Peruvian national oil company (Petroperu) and relieved the state from collecting taxes and royalties. Occidental acquired for exploration 2.3 million acres in the Amazon jungle along the Peru-Ecuador border, and once again Bechtel Corporation was hired for another mammoth project, the construction of a 550-mile main pipeline that would traverse the Andes to transport Peruvian oil to the Pacific coast and a 161-mile pipeline to connect the oil fields to the main pipeline. The combined exploration and construction costs were estimated to be $500 million.

Armand explained that the deal was the result of the three years he had spent wooing the Peruvian military junta. "My good friend General Alvarado has grown to trust me," he gloated. "He believes me when I tell him about all the good things I'm going to do for his country." His next move was to attempt to convince Petroperu to pay for building the pipelines.

Because of the problems in both Libya and Venezuela, Armand was desperate to find oil in Peru. Bud Reid hired a reputable engineering firm to begin preparations for seismic testing. Following the standard procedure for a jungle terrain, the firm dispatched men to carve a narrow path through the dense jungle terrain. Small holes would be drilled along this path and dynamite exploded in them, and a seismograph would record the waves that bounced off the underground rock interfaces, allowing the engineers to plot the shapes and depths of the structures in order to determine if oil might be present.

A week into the project Reid received a call from Tom Wachtell asking for a progress report. Wachtell called back a few hours later and asked whether it was essential that the seismic work be conducted in a straight line. He explained that Armand had just completed a merger with a Texas road-contracting firm and the owner had told him that using a band of machete-wielding men was obsolete and that Hammer should use a Le Tourneau Tree Crusher. This huge, tractorlike machine clears forests and jungles in record time by rolling over the trees—and everything else—and grinding them into the ground.

Reid was disgusted. He told Wachtell there was no need to destroy a jungle to carve a tiny path. Besides the cost of using a Le Tourneau was ridiculously high and a Texas road contractor was the last person to listen to about seismic work in a tropical jungle. Armand thought otherwise. Calling Reid back in a rage, he screamed into the phone that he had the legal grounds to break the deal with the engineering firm because Reid had been authorized to sign contracts up to $500,000 but had contracted the firm for $2 million.

After Armand fired the engineering firm, Le Tourneau Tree Crushers were rented "to clear jungle land for cattle grazing." For Reid it was the last straw. Eleven years after Armand had inflated the size of Occidental's natural-gas reserves and Reid had confided the truth to the SEC, he had once again come face to face with the

Hammer who had upset him so much at that time: a man who thought nothing of destroying a jungle to carve a little path and didn't care how much money he wasted in the process. Before the year was over Reid left the company.

Soon after work commenced in Peru, Occidental learned that it was one of five companies to achieve victory in the Nigerian oil auction. Occidental had received the biggest award: 710,000 acres. Armand went to Lagos for the final negotiations and closed the deal effortlessly a full month before the other four winners. The deal was a thirty-five-year joint venture, with the Nigerian National Oil Company obtaining its biggest demand, more than 50 percent control. "*I* offered them 51 percent," Armand insisted contrary to the facts. "It was my way of letting them know I really was their friend."

Only four Occidental employees were on staff in Nigeria at the time: Managing Director of Operations Everett Thierfelder, an operations manager, an accountant, and a materials expediter. Armand urged them to go straight to work and pressured them unrelentingly. At the end of five weeks the preliminary seismic data work was completed and a huge semisubmersible drilling rig had been altered so that it could perform continuous drilling in deep water during rough conditions. Therefore, drilling was able to begin only five months after Occidental formalized its agreement.

On September 26, after four months of calm, there was another ominous rumble in Libya when the Libyan Oil Commission demanded an increase in payments to offset the decline of the U.S. dollar and asked that all oil taxes be paid in dinars. As a payment period arrived, the Libyans arbitrarily devalued the dinar in order to increase the amount they would receive. When Esso-Libya insisted on paying at the old dinar-dollar rate of exchange and demanded a fixed rate of exchange for future payments, the Libyans deducted $900,000 from Esso-Libya's Libyan bank accounts. "It means more trouble in the future," Armand remarked stoically.

That trouble came from another sector in the Middle East. On November 30, according to schedule, the British left the Persian Gulf and the Trucial States of Sharjah and Umm al-Qaywayn became part of the United Arab Emirates. Even though the shah had assured Armand that after the departure of the British he planned to give up his claim to Abu Musa island, he ordered Iranian troops to invade Sharjah. Within hours Sharjah turned over the disputed island to Iran.

Then the shah claimed two other islands, the Greater and Lesser

Tumbs, obtaining complete control of the entry to the Persian Gulf. It was believed that the shah's actions were the result of a secret deal between Iran and Britain with the tacit approval of the United States, so that he could replace Britain as the West's Persian Gulf policeman.

In response, Iraq, which claimed Abu Musa island under an ancient decree, broke off diplomatic relations with Iran, and Libya issued a denunciation of Britain, accusing it of plotting with a non-Arab "puppet government." A week later, the dreaded process of Libyan nationalization had finally begun when Libya struck back at Britain by nationalizing British Petroleum, which was 48 percent British owned. To make matters worse, utilizing Occidental's confiscated seismic data, Iran subsequently discovered a large oil field off the coast of Abu Musa.

Armand was speechless with anger.

At the beginning of 1971, Occidental International's senior staff tipped Armand that Henry Kissinger was involved in secret negotiations with both the Chinese and the Soviets. The U.S.-Chinese talks were an attempt to find a way to normalize relations between the two countries; the U.S.-Soviet talks were an attempt to stimulate trade. Both reflected Kissinger's assumption that China and the USSR were so afraid of each other that they would be threatened by the thought that the United States would form an alliance with one against the other. Therefore, each could be manipulated by shrewd diplomacy to use its power in Hanoi to help bring about a cease-fire and hasten the end of the Vietnam War.

Armand's inability to secure presidential approval for trade credits had been one of the great stumbling blocks to the 1964 Occidental-Soviet fertilizer deal. Now, with the distinct possibility of increased U.S.-Soviet trade, he urged Tim Babcock to lean on his friendship with President Nixon to set up a meeting. Babcock got nowhere, but Armand ordered him to keep at it. Finally, the White House let it be known that Hammer was a gadfly and troublemaker. The list of his transgressions was long: after Occidental's entry into Libya, he had disrupted the balance of power in the international oil industry; he had capitulated to Muammar Qaddafi *and* had been the architect of the oil company united front; he had attempted to destroy the U.S. oil imports quota system when he had set out to build an oil refinery at Machiasport, Maine, and announced the use of Venezuelan oil in the proposed refinery, which had put Nixon on the spot with the Venezuelans; and he had leaked negative items about Vice President Agnew and Secretary of the Interior Hickel to the press. Nixon also had full knowledge of the contents of the FBI files about the Hammer family.

Armand responded by urging Babcock not to let up.

On October 12, Washington and Moscow announced jointly that Nixon would become the first American president to visit Moscow for a summit meeting. Toward the end of November, an American delegation led by Secretary of Commerce Maurice Stans traveled to Moscow and met with Premier Kosygin. On November 27, the corporate trade group Business International held its first Moscow meeting in six years and set out to open legitimate trade channels between U.S. companies and the USSR. The delegates included the leaders of one hundred multinational corporations, with Tim Babcock representing Occidental. By this time Armand and his emissaries had secretly invested almost two years of legwork to give Occidental the competitive edge.

Although Armand was in business with Cyrus Eaton Jr., he'd never met Eaton Sr. A couple of weeks after the Moscow summit he and the elder Eaton were both in London, and Armand extended a dinner invitation. "We talked for hours, and I told him all about my friendship with Lenin," he reported to me. "We liked each other a lot, and he's really grateful for all the good things I'm doing for his son."

Never one to let an old dream die, Armand had persuaded Eaton to use his influence with Soviet Premier Kosygin and his son-in-law, Dzherman Gvishiani, to allow him to fly his Gulfstream into Moscow without Soviet assistance. As soon as he received official permission, he instructed me to release the news to the press. "It will send a signal to my American competitors that I've got special privileges they don't have," he said complacently. "I'll do everything necessary to make them back off."

The new and improved Armand Hammer Collection was scheduled to make its Los Angeles debut at the County Museum on December 20, before setting off for London's Royal Academy of Fine Arts and the National Gallery of Dublin on the first leg of a worldwide tour that Armand would sustain for the next fifteen years. In order to convert the County Museum preview gala into a major media event, Armand decided to bequeath the paintings in his collection to the museum and announce the donation at the gala. At John Walker's request, however, the drawings in the collection were to be bequeathed to his former employer, the National Gallery of Art in Washington, D.C., which would be a major coup for Walker's handpicked successor, J. Carter Brown, an aggressive pursuer of artworks and collections.

When *Los Angeles Times* Art Editor Henry Seldis called to say that he'd received a tip about the donation and wanted to speak to Hammer, Armand phoned Franklin Murphy, president of the County Museum board of trustees and chairman of the *Los Angeles Times,* to say that he was going to grant Seldis the interview but would ask him to hold publication until the day of the announcement so that the news would break simultaneously around the world. He instructed Murphy to make sure that Seldis obeyed instructions, implying that unless there was a publicity blitz he was inclined to cancel the donation. "Of course," Armand reported, "Murphy pledged his support. Powerful and important people are the only friends worth having."

Soviet Minister of Culture Yekaterina Furtseva was planning to visit the United States in mid-December, and Armand urged her to join him in Los Angeles and accompany him to the County Museum to view his collection. As Furtseva's visit neared, Armand's behavior underwent a noticeable change. By nature he was a relentless flirt, and he loved to impress women. But this was different: he seemed genuinely to care for Furtseva. Such feelings were so unusual for him and he was so unprepared for them that he became distracted and started acting like a lovesick teenager. I often found him staring into space or doodling Furtseva's name on his yellow pad.

Whenever I asked anyone who had met Furtseva to tell me about her, she was invariably described as "dour," "hard drinking," "rude," and "a tough cookie." The day she arrived, I was expecting a sour monster and was surprised to see a severely but smartly dressed woman in her early fifties with dark brown hair pulled into a tight chignon. The minute Furtseva saw Armand, her large, sparkling eyes latched onto him and never left. She did not speak English, so after a quick round of introductions, Armand spirited her into his office and closed the door. Later that day he asked me along when he took Furtseva to the County Museum. They chatted in Russian, and Furtseva continued to look affectionately at him and only occasionally at the art.

The next time I saw Victor I remarked that Furtseva didn't seem to be the monster she had been made out to be. "Don't be fooled," he replied. "Furtseva's been on the take for years. She's even been known to award state art prizes in exchange for cash. She'll do *anything* for money, including fooling around with Armand."

A few days later Armand reported that after seeing the Goya in his collection, Furtseva had said "that it broke her heart" that the Soviet government did not own a Goya. "It was a hint," he said. "I'm going to track down a Goya and give it to her."

He found the Goya in a rather roundabout way. When Victor told Armand the news that M. Knoedler and Company of New York, the oldest art gallery in the United States, was for sale, Armand formed a partnership that included Victor, Hammer's long-term financial adviser, Maury Leibovitz, and Bernard Danenberg, an art dealer, and set out to make the acquisition.

"It's a great deal," he proclaimed. "After ten years the paintings that haven't been sold have been written off the books. The inventory is worth millions, far more than the asking price." He would later discover, however, that the inventory contained a number of paintings of dubious value.

The partnership purchased Knoedler for $2.5 million, and Armand appointed himself chairman of the board. Victor explained that his brother's new duties included "ignoring the distinguished artists on the Knoedler roster, cultivating all of Knoedler's exceptionally rich patrons, and exhibiting the very latest in state-approved socialist art."

The Knoedler inventory included Goya's portrait of Dona Antonia Zarate. This mediocre example of the artist's work was estimated to be worth $150,000. Declaring that the painting carried a value of $1 million, Armand decided to fulfill his promise to Furtseva by donating it to the Pushkin Museum. A condition was attached to the gift. Furtseva was to arrange an exhibition of the Armand Hammer Collection at the Pushkin with the Goya as its showpiece, making Armand one of the first—if not *the* first—foreigner to have a private collection placed on exhibition in a Soviet museum. In order to transform this exhibition into an international media event, Armand planned to invite the press to a formal presentation ceremony at the opening-night reception.

His motives, as usual, were self-serving. And so, I discovered, were Furtseva's. Victor confided that Furtseva had really asked Armand to make the donation in order to justify the amount of time she was spending with Hammer to the KGB, if it ever came to that.

On January 20, 1972, after two years as Armand's second official heir apparent, Occidental President Bill Bellano was deposed and took "early retirement," one of the standard euphemisms corporations use when an employee has signed a muzzle clause. Armand reappointed himself president, appointed Occidental International President Marvin Watson executive vice president for corporate affairs and moved him to corporate headquarters, and hired Robert Caverly as executive vice president for operations. Caverly had been a consultant to the Howard Hughes organization in charge of reorganizing the Hughes enterprises in Las Vegas. Aware of the rumor that Hughes had been a major contributor to almost all of President's Nixon's political campaigns and that Nixon was "Hughes's man," Armand was determined to learn as much as he could from Caverly in his campaign to get closer to Nixon.

It was Armand's idea that Occidental would be managed by a troika consisting of Caverly, Watson, and himself. This led to the inevitable question: Was Watson, Caverly, or neither the new heir apparent? Hammer thrived on the confusion and answered all questions about his successor by smiling and saying softly, "I like it just the way it is." And it wasn't long before he subtly turned Caverly and Watson against each other, which would keep their minds off finding ways to get rid of him.

The peculiar change in management accompanied by Occidental's ongoing problems in Libya made the company's volatile stock price rise and fall sharply within a short period of time, and Armand urged me to "take care of it." That was going to be harder than usual because the SEC had just informed Hammer that its observation of Occidental's activities over the ten months since he had signed the consent decree mandated a reopening of its investigation. "If it gets out that the minute they finished one investigation they started another, the damage to Oxy's stock price is going to be incredible," he told me. "If anyone asks you about it, deny it with your life."

He didn't mention the investigation again and gave no clue about the methods he was using to deal with it. But I learned later that the SEC was conducting a fact-finding mission involving the informal testimony of a large group of people both inside and outside the company.

There was bad news in the wind. A week or two after Hammer established the tripartite management, I was summoned to his office, which was packed with financial executives.

Armand took the floor. "World shipping rates are plummeting with no end in sight, and Oxy's tanker fleet is sailing in a sea of red ink," he said. "Our only option is to write off eighty-eight million dollars against Oxy's 1971 operating income and set up a reserve of sixty-five million dollars against any other fleet losses in the future."

I was going to have to write a news release announcing that

Occidental had experienced a staggering $67 million earnings loss in 1971, even though it had reported a record-breaking net operating income of $175 million the year before. Drawing me aside, Armand said, "It's terrible news, Carl. Your job is to try to make it look good."

As had been suspected, the purpose of the two large stock offerings in June and July 1971 was to help offset Occidental's huge losses from the tanker debacle. But at the time those offerings were made, Armand had not authorized the disclosures that Occidental was experiencing significant losses and that if it chose to write off those losses it would not show a profit at the end of 1971. The few staff members who did know the truth had been sworn to secrecy. Therefore, even though everyone was aware that there were losses, no one knew how large they were. The ink on the consent decree that Hammer had signed in March 1971 was not even dry before he was in trouble again with the SEC.

The public perceived Armand as a successful industrialist, a multimillionaire, a philanthropist, and a celebrity. But there was no way I could make Occidental's enormous losses look good. Wall Street was shocked by Armand's misguided entry into the shipping business, which amplified the financial community's concerns about the first SEC investigation, the removal of Tom Willers and Bill Bellano, and the fact that Occidental was being managed by a troika. Those concerns, along with Hammer's untrustworthy management, led many of Occidental's large institutional investors to sell out and the stock price tumbled to $10 a share. Armand brushed it off. "They'll be sorry. They'll come running back begging for mercy. You watch and see."

With the plunge in the price of its stock, Occidental had become a prime target for a takeover, and soon the rumor spread that it *was* going to be taken over. By treating Occidental as a proprietorship and not a public corporation, Armand had made Occidental one of the few companies that was strongly identified with only one man. Therefore, a presentation was scheduled before the New York Society of Security Analysts in order to counteract the takeover rumor and to persuade the financial community that the company wasn't really an erratic one-man show but a trustworthy operation whose stock deserved their recommendation. I suggested that Armand make only a few introductory remarks and then turn the program over to the department and division heads who would tell about the accomplishments that were occurring under their supervision. A question-and-answer period would follow, climaxed by the screening of a film produced by my department that documented Occidental's worldwide activities.

Hammer agreed. But at the lectern he rambled on and on. During the executive presentations, the analysts began to get up and leave, and by the time the screening was over, the only people left were Occidental executives. Despite the problems the company was having, Armand resisted every effort to change his egocentric ways, and in the process he had sabotaged the presentation.

Over a two-week period Occidental's financial executives secretly evolved a step-by-step blueprint designed to eliminate debt and restore financial solvency. When the time came to present the plan, however, intimidated by Armand's temper and fearing that they might be asked to "retire," no one dared approach him.

Armand had his own debt reduction plan. Buried toward the end of the financial statements in the 1971 annual report was the information that Occidental owed $407 million in charter rentals. The long-term fleet contracts and charters were leased to a subsidiary, Occidental Worldwide Investment Corporation, essentially a corporate shell, and were unbreakable. Armand explained his strategy to me. "We'll sail the tankers back to their home ports and renegotiate the contracts for half their fees. If the charter companies don't play ball, we'll tell them that we plan to bankrupt Occidental Worldwide and then they won't get a cent."

Many of the shipping companies with which Occidental had contracted were based in England. The legal department pointed out that in the event suits were brought against the company for nonpayment, the U.K. Commercial Court might consider the threat of bankruptcy "commercial blackmail." Armand ignored the warning, and the ships were ordered to return to their home ports.

Armand had an even more difficult assignment for me. After looking enviously at the 1971 Man of the Year issue of *Time* magazine with Richard Nixon on the cover, he told me, "If *I* was *Time*'s Man of the Year, it would make it easier for me to win the Nobel Peace Prize."

For the next eight years he repeatedly reminded me about the *Time* cover. It would prove to be one of the few things I was not able to do for him. But I did convince a *Time* reporter to interview him for a feature article.

A short man, Armand refused to allow anyone to appear taller than he was in photographs, so I sometimes posed him sitting on two telephone books. He also hated the left side of his face because it "looks like a fried egg" and wouldn't allow himself to be photographed from that angle. During one photo session with the board of directors, Armand had refused to face the board because the left side of his face would be exposed to the camera and instead faced forward with his back to the directors. He looked like a bus driver; they looked like sixteen unhappy dark-suited passengers sitting behind him wondering if he was going to drive them over a cliff.

During his *Time* interview, Armand sat at his desk facing the reporter while a photographer, following my instructions, shot pictures of his right side. But then the photographer started moving to Armand's left, and with every step Armand gradually swiveled his chair in the opposite direction so that only the right side of his face would be exposed to the camera. The photographer continued his pursuit until finally Armand was facing the wall with his back to the reporter. Watching this scene with considerable amusement, I speculated that if and when Armand ever made the cover of *Time,* he would probably insist that not only his photograph, but also the text, show only his "good" side.

16.

THE NIXON
ONE HUNDRED
THOUSAND
DOLLARS CLUB

On January 26, 1972, Congress replaced the Federal Corrupt Practices Act of 1925 with a new law that required the disclosure of all federal political gifts of $100 and over and prohibited making federal campaign donations in another person's name. The old law was going to expire on March 10, and the new legislation would take effect on April 7. On March 11, President Nixon appointed Maurice Stans finance chairman of the Committee for the Re-Election of the President (CREEP) and named Peter Peterson to replace Stans as secretary of commerce. Under Stans's unrelenting pounding between the day of his appointment and April 7, a record $60 million would pour into the CREEP coffers. Only the president's secretary, Rose Mary Woods, knew the names of these contributors, which she recorded on a list that came to be known as "Rose Mary's Baby."

Armand had formed an international consortium to obtain exploration and development rights in the natural-gas fields of Siberia. Subsequently Occidental International's senior staff tipped him that Maurice Stans was aware that a second consortium, North Star, also wanted the drilling rights and that North Star's lawyer was former governor of Texas John Connally, head of Democrats for Nixon and one of the president's most trusted friends. Stans expected both North Star and the Hammer consortium to make large campaign contributions before the president decided which to favor. Presidential approval carried with it the implicit guarantee that Nixon would approve the trade credits necessary to finance the venture. Therefore, the consortium that received this approval would inevitably be the one chosen by the Soviets.

Once again Tim Babcock was dispatched to try to set up a meeting between Nixon and Armand. Nixon was not ready to meet with Hammer, but Maurice Stans sent word that he was eager to meet with Hammer. Armand was trapped, and he knew it. After pillorying Richard Nixon throughout his four years in office, the time had come for a startling transformation. "I thought that as a dedicated anti-Communist Dick Nixon would do everything in his power to wreck our relations with the Russians," he told me, "but he's finally figured out what I've known all along, that trading partners do not go to war. Nixon is going to go down in history as one of the great presidents. I've *got* to help him win."

During the first two weeks of March, while I was working with Armand at his home, he and Stans traded a number of calls. "Maurice is an expert arm-twister, and he's determined to raise every dollar he can," Armand said. "But he's acting like a madman. He wants me to contribute *two hundred fifty thousand dollars!*" Armand often said that he "gave to get." He was willing to spend *any* amount of money, including $250,000, to get what he wanted, but he hated spending a cent when he wasn't sure he would get something in return. And he feared that even after he made his contribution, Nixon might prove uncooperative and favor his competitors.

On March 15, the British government awarded a petroleum production license to the Group, the Occidental–Getty–Thomson–Allied Chemical consortium formed to search for oil in the North Sea. The only comment Armand made was "This new success is going to encourage Stans to want an even larger donation." He and Stans continued to haggle for another two weeks, with Armand insisting that $50,000 was his limit. Eventually a compromise was reached. "Maurice urged me to join the Nixon One Hundred Thousand Dollars Club. He made it clear that each member will receive some major goodies."

On March 30, Armand flew to Washington, carrying with him a suitcase containing $50,000 in cash, a $46,000 down payment, and $4,000 earmarked for tickets to a fund-raising banquet. That day he and Babcock met with Stans but did not go to CREEP's headquarters because Stans was involved in a solicitation and the law required that solicitation meetings be held away from the office. The next day Babcock walked the half block from his office to CREEP and handed over the $46,000 in cash to Stans.

Armand often contributed to both candidates in a political race. Therefore, he always kept his political contributions a secret and, in this instance, was especially determined to maintain the policy. He continued to harbor the fear that Nixon was not going to help him and, in that eventuality, he did not want anyone to know that he had wasted his money. Nor did he wish to offend his Soviet helpmates Sargent Shriver, rumored to be George McGovern's first choice as vice presidential running mate if McGovern received the Democratic presidential nomination, and David Karr, who had strong ties to the Kennedy family and was also a committed Democrat. Furthermore, Cyrus Eaton, Sr., had publicly declared that he despised Nixon and had thrown his considerable financial support behind McGovern.

Although a multimillionaire, Armand was so frugal that he often borrowed my automatic pencils, which he then slipped into his coat pocket and never returned. Therefore, handing over the remaining $54,000 of his pledge without proof that he was going to get something for his money was incredibly difficult for him and he let the April 7 deadline for making anonymous contributions pass without making further payment.

I was busy preparing the press materials for the 1972 shareholders' meeting when I learned that Victor had suffered a small stroke and was hospitalized in New York City. I tried to discuss his condition with Armand, but he ignored me. His fear of illness and death was so intense that he refused even to acknowledge that his brother was sick, which enabled him to insist that there was no reason for him to visit Victor in the hospital.

Armand's concern about his mortality was confirmed by the spectacular battle he continued to wage against the aging process. At the age of seventy-four, he seemed, if anything, to have even more energy than when I had met him seventeen years earlier. He was also more capricious and volatile, and his behavior was sometimes so erratic it bordered on the irrational.

Each year I invited the press to the annual meeting and set up a pressroom with typewriters, phones, and a plentiful supply of food and coffee. The reporters received a news release I had written that summarized the announcements that were going to be made at the meeting. The financial data in this release were checked and rechecked by the legal, financial, and tax staffs, corporate managers, other key executives, and, of course, Hammer.

This year's meeting was scheduled to take place at the Beverly Hilton Hotel at 10:30 A.M. At nine that morning, just as I was about to leave home, Armand called. "I want to make some changes in the release, and then I want you to print a new set. Get over here."

I called my staff and told them to be ready to run off a new release in less than an hour's time. Then I hurried to Armand's house. He was busy revising the financial statistics and some of the legal and accounting language, and he seemed to be making up the changes as he went along.

"What *are* you up to?" I asked.

"I haven't got time to explain," replied. "I've got to get to the meeting. Don't tell a soul about any of this. Just make a new release with my changes and give it to the reporters. If anybody from Oxy asks for a copy, either tell him you can't spare one or slip him the old one."

About fifteen minutes after the start of the meeting, I arrived at the hotel and distributed the new releases. After the meeting, the senior staff surrounded me. "We spent hours checking over this release and agreed last night there would be no changes," one senior staffer said angrily. "We could get into more trouble with the SEC. Why did you change it?

"You'll have to ask Armand," I replied.

There was a sinking feeling among the group. The men picked up their copies of the release and began to study the revisions. Everyone's response was the same: confusion. Was Hammer pulling rank, attempting to hide something, or was it something else? "Did he tell you why he was making these changes?" one staffer asked.

"He wouldn't tell me a thing."

Later that afternoon, Armand called. "I understand the boys grabbed you after the meeting. What did they say? Tell me every detail. Describe the expressions on each of their faces. Go slowly. I want to hear every word that each of them said, one by one."

As I gave him the details he asked for, I had the feeling he was making notes. Suddenly he began to laugh. "You're really enjoying the commotion you caused," I said.

He laughed even harder.

"Why did you make those changes?" I asked.

"Not now!" He abruptly hung up.

No one was ever able to figure out what Armand had been up to, and his behavior reinforced the suspicion that he was having bouts of irrationality. As time went on, I detected a pattern to his madness. Every executive who had dared to question his motives at that session after the meeting eventually "resigned" or "retired." By refusing unconditionally to accept his actions, they had failed his bizarre version of a loyalty test.

Although Armand and his Soviet operatives were hard at work attempting to negotiate a fertilizer deal with the Soviet State Committee for Science and Technology, Leonid Brezhnev seemed determined to resist Armand's overtures. When Armand found himself and Brezhnev at a reception, he relentlessly stalked the Soviet leader, but as he closed in, KGB agents stepped between him and Brezhnev. Armand lost his temper and began to yell. It did no good. Armand had told the Soviets that he knew Nixon and that Nixon had assured him that he would grant trade credits for Hammer's Soviet deals. But the Soviets knew he was lying. They respected power, and Armand still did not have it.

On July 8, Washington announced that the May 22–27 Nixon-Brezhnev Moscow summit had led to the largest grain transaction in history between any two countries. Over a three-year period the United States would sell the Soviets 19 million tons of American corn, grain, and wheat at a cost of $750 million. The only way the Soviets were going to be able to pay for the grain was by obtaining U.S. trade credits, and the granting of those credits would depend on their cooperation in helping to bring the Vietnam War to an end.

Immediately after the announcement of the grain deal, Armand told me that he was leaving for Moscow and to be prepared for a barrage of phone calls from reporters once he got there.

"What are you going to announce?" I asked.

"I can't tell anybody. Not even you."

In Moscow, Armand threw himself into a series of intense negotiations with eighteen Soviet senior ministers. Two years of legwork and enormous amounts of under-the-table monies enabled him to cut through the Soviet bureaucracy and finalize the terms of a trade protocol in just five days. It was a legitimate first step toward achieving a final deal with the Soviets, and Armand signed it without showing it to anyone, including Occidental's board and legal and senior staffs.

On July 18, in London, the British press corps was advised that he was about to make a historic announcement. The choreo-graphed media event began when Occidental's English represen-tatives leaked the news that Occidental and the Soviets had just signed the first agreement between a U.S. corporation and the USSR under the Nixon-Brezhnev détente. On Hammer's instruc-tion the executives implied that it was not only a solid deal but also "the biggest deal in history" and hinted that its value was an aston-ishing $3 billion.

Finally, Armand walked to the lecturn and told the British press that Occidental and the Soviet State Committee for Science and Technology had signed a historic five-year agreement that called for scientific and technical cooperation in a number of areas, in-cluding agricultural fertilizers and chemicals, metal treating and plating, exploration and production of oil and gas, utilization of solid wastes, and design and construction of an international trade center and hotel in Moscow.

London had been chosen as the site of this announcement pri-marily because both Armand and the Soviets feared having him face the hardened Moscow foreign press corps, which disdained the American businessmen who were streaming into Moscow to make deals and refused to acknowledge the abuses of Soviet soci-ety. On the other hand, in London, Armand could count on the unquestioning support of Lord Thomson's newspapers and a group of reporters who were not as knowledgeable about the tech-nicalities of East-West trade. But reporters did ask if the deal really amounted to $3 billion. All Hammer said was that the Soviets had asked him not to discuss figures. But by not denying the figure he tacitly confirmed it, and the reporters leapt to the conclusion that he really had achieved "the largest deal in the history of U.S.-Soviet trade."

Armand had forwarned me to expect a deluge of phone calls, and he was right. Reporters called me from all over the world, but I had nothing to tell them because I knew as little as they did. Meanwhile, as the news circled the globe, Occidental's sluggish stock became one of the most heavily traded issues in the history of the New York Stock Exchange. But how, I wondered, had Ar-mand pulled it off? Victor explained that his brother had played his trump card and had reminded the Soviets that Lenin had orig-inally granted him the asbestos-mining concession because he wanted Hammer to publicize it in the West in order to attract Western investment. "Armand pointed out that unlike other cor-porate heads he was famous," Victor said, "which gave him the ability to turn his announcement into an international publicity stunt that could work to their mutual advantage."

Egyptian president Anwar Sadat had chosen July 18 to announce that he was ordering the withdrawal of the sixteen thousand Soviet military advisers, soldiers, and pilots who were based in Egypt. The Soviets concluded that the announcement of a $3 billion trade deal with a U.S. corporation on the same day would not only promote U.S.-Soviet trade in the West but would also dilute the effect of the bad news coming out of Cairo. They—and Hammer—also knew that the announcement was going to provide Occidental, its shareholders, and its chief executive with substantial financial benefits, thus encouraging other companies to get involved with Soviet trade.

Armand's impressive commercial for U.S.-Soviet trade demonstrated that he could operate behind the back of the Nixon administration and achieve secret agreements with the Soviets. By suggesting that Occidental and, therefore, other U.S. corporations had the ability to secure private financing for these deals, Armand had challenged the Nixon-Kissinger insistence that American companies were not to circumvent their dependence on the presidential approval of trade credits in order to make deals with the Soviets. Eager to discover the administration's response to his maverick demonstration, as soon as the press conference was over, Armand flew to Morocco, where Secretary of Commerce Peter Peterson was visiting before leaving the following day for Moscow to negotiate MFN status with the Soviets.

From the air Armand phoned the commerce secretary and arranged a meeting. He briefed Peterson, who inspected the document Armand had signed and thanked him for coming to see him. Back in the air, Armand called Tim Babcock and asked him to try again to set up a meeting with Nixon. This time the president was more than willing, and an appointment was scheduled for July 20, just three days after Armand had made his announcement to the British press. Returning to Los Angeles, Armand boasted that "the president sent for me. He wants me to brief him about my deal." That, of course, was not entirely true. But after almost four years, Armand had finally wormed his way into the White House.

In what seemed to be a rehearsal for his encounter with Nixon, he settled back and recounted his version of how he had achieved the agreement. As he explained it, he had accepted an invitation from Dzherman Gvishiani to go to Moscow to meet the Soviet planners. Of course, Armand had told them about his friendship with Lenin, which had inevitably brought tears to their eyes. Then he had told them that if they had gone ahead with his fertilizer deal in 1964, they wouldn't now be in the position of having to buy a billion dollars' worth of grain from the United States. "They shook their heads knowingly," Armand said. "I was right—and they knew it." Thereafter, he said, he had received a call from the minister of the chemical industry, who had told him the Soviets were ready to do business. "That's how I made history in only five days."

There were those, however, who suspected the Soviet deal was more histrionic than historic. A day or two after Armand's return, the SEC, which was in the fourth month of its unofficial reinvestigation of Occidental and Hammer, requested a copy of Occidental's news release about the transaction and a transcript of the London press conference. When Secretary Peterson met with the Moscow foreign press corps, the first question posed to him concerned his reaction to the Occidental-Soviet deal. Peterson told the truth and dismissed it as merely an agreement to continue to negotiate and not a hard contract. After his remarks hit the news wires, Occidental's stock price dropped 3⅝ points.

Armand was livid. He had no reason to expect Peterson to lie for him, but he had hoped that, if the occasion arose, Peterson would take a more positive and diplomatic tone. The commerce secretary's remarks reinforced his gut feeling that the administration saw no reason to do favors for him. When he asked his Occidental International staff to find out why Peterson had been so uncooperative, they reported that Peterson hadn't known that his comments were going to hurt the stock price. After all, when Hammer and he had met, Hammer had failed to tell him that he had announced the protocol to the press and Peterson was so busy traveling he hadn't seen any of the news stories.

It was an acceptable explanation—*if* one was willing to believe that the Nixon administration had not communicated with its commerce secretary about a $3 billion trade deal between a U.S. corporation and the Soviet government at the moment when the secretary was about to launch strategic discussions with the Soviets about MFN trade status. Armand had blown up the balloon to an enormous size. And of all people, Richard Nixon had been the one to explode it.

Armand met Nixon as scheduled on July 20. After Marvin Watson had confided to him that LBJ had installed a secret taping system in the White House, Armand had installed similar systems in his office at Occidental and at his home. But he had no way of knowing that the president was using his secret recording system to tape their conversation. Nonetheless, he was smart enough to speak mainly in generalities. On his return to Los Angeles, he told me he had briefed Nixon about the protocol, thanked him for taking the initiatives that made it possible, and described how Occidental's stock price had run wild and how Secretary Peterson's remarks had caused it to plunge. "But I didn't dwell on it," Armand said. "I've hated Nixon's guts for years. I still don't like him. But he's dumped his anti-Communist hysteria, and he's opened the door to détente. He needs people like me to prove that U.S.-Soviet trade can work, and I need him to grant credits. So we had a nice talk."

Before he left the meeting, Armand said he had reminded Nixon that he had become "a bona fide member of the Nixon One Hundred Thousand Dollars Club" and assured him that he planned to credit him whenever he spoke to the press about his Soviet ventures. He pulled back the sleeves of his suit jacket. "Look at the presidential cuff links he gave me," he said with pride. "And he gave Frances a presidential pin."

When Armand sent word to the White House through Occidental International that he was grateful for the opportunity to meet the president and was not going to announce any more "$3 billion Soviet deals" without permission, word came back that Nixon was inclined to support the Occidental-Soviet fertilizer deal and to endorse Hammer's Siberian oil consortium over its competitor. It confirmed Armand's hunch that Nixon did in fact need him and that members of the Nixon One Hundred Thousand Dollars Club were going to receive tangible rewards. Armand, who had considered himself FDR's unofficial "Lend-Lease consultant" and JFK's unofficial "trade envoy," now believed he had opened the door that would lead to his becoming one of Richard Nixon's closest unofficial advisers on the USSR.

Occidental's Moscow branch office opened for business in July 1972 on the top floor of the National Hotel and was the subject of an official announcement by Soviet Premier Kosygin on September 13. As word traveled through Moscow that Mikhail Bruk was nominally in charge, a foreign correspondent called me to ask why the overseas division of a U.S. company was being headed by someone who was affiliated with the KGB. When I asked Armand, he threw me an exasperated look. "I have a KGB guy working for me because the KGB has got the power to get things done," he said. "If not for Michael, there are days when I wouldn't be able to make a long-distance call. Besides, the KGB protects me."

Things seemed to be going so well for Armand in Moscow that he should have been happy. But he wasn't. When he complained that the Eatons were spreading the rumor that Tower International had actually handled the negotiations for the Occidental-Soviet fertilizer protocol, I knew that the process of terminating Cyrus Jr. had begun. A few days later Armand confided his suspicion that the younger Eaton had been supplying his father with information about Occidental's Siberian natural-gas deal. "I was set up from the beginning. They're using me, but they're not going to get away with it."

Over the next weeks one complaint followed another until Armand sent for Cyrus Jr. Flanked by lawyers, he hurled a series of accusations at him and fired him. The next day, whether or not the accusations were true, he was perfectly calm. And when he learned that Cyrus Jr. was having difficulty meeting the payments on the loan that he had arranged, Armand authorized Occidental to purchase the note from the bank. Then he ordered his lawyers to begin foreclosure proceedings so that Occidental could seize the Eatons' cold-storage plants in Montreal and Toronto and Cyrus Jr.'s home and farm outside Cleveland. The proceedings were brought to a halt when the younger Eaton located the money and repaid the loan.

Armand then turned to another piece of unfinished business. He still owed CREEP $54,000, and although the new federal disclosure law made it illegal to make anonymous political contributions, he remained determined to keep this donation a secret. He instructed one of his Washington lawyers to approach Tim Babcock and feel him out about whether Babcock would make the contribution in his name. After Babcock indicated his willingness, Armand met with him on September 6 and explained that he had waited until then to satisfy the remainder of his pledge because he wanted to make sure that Nixon was going to win. It was a feeble explanation; polls taken at the end of July had already shown Nixon enjoying a huge lead.

Armand handed Babcock a big stack of bills totaling $15,000. Babcock began to pocket the cash, but Armand insisted that it be counted. Babcock followed instructions, only to discover that Armand was testing his honesty by inserting an extra fifty dollars in the pile. Furious, Babcock tossed the bill onto the desk.

Armand's plan was to have Babcock be the "contributor" of the entire $54,000. But after borrowing $350,000 from the Small Business Administration to finance a motel and convention center venture in Montana that was not working out, Babcock had fallen behind in his loan payments, and his shaky financial situation made it virtually impossible to believe that he was capable of making such a contribution. So, to avert suspicion, Armand asked Babcock to recruit some friends who would allow their names to be used as additional but fictitious contributors. Thereafter, Babcock enlisted four colleagues from Montana, his former gubernatorial campaign manager, Jerome Anderson; an attorney, Bill Holter; a dentist, Dr. Gordon Doering; and the owner of a trucking firm, Elmer Balsam. On September 15, he delivered $15,000 of the $54,000 to CREEP and said the money had not come from Hammer, but from some other contributors, and handed over a list of names.

Then Babcock waited for Armand to decide to part with the remaining $39,000. But Armand had other things on his mind. He had received word that after a nine-month preliminary examination, the SEC had decided to make its investigation of Occidental official. Armand masked his fear with outrage. "Those SEC bastards are digging a lot deeper than they dug the last time and sticking their noses where they don't belong," he told me. "They're out to get me. I have no doubt of that. I thought it'd shut them up when I signed the consent decree, but it didn't. This time I'm going to fight and they're not going to know what hit them. I'm going to bash them into the ground."

Trouble was brewing for Armand in another sector. From 1968 to 1972, the number of Soviet Jewish emigrés had grown from 400 to 35,000, and because the Soviets believed that this increase reflected badly on their idealized image of a classless society, they had imposed a large "education" tax on Jews who were attempting to leave, supposedly a repayment for the costs of the superior Soviet education they had received. In retaliation, Senator Henry "Scoop" Jackson had introduced a resolution that would deny trade concessions, including MFN status or government-guaranteed trade credits, to the USSR unless it rescinded the tax.

Armand saw a grave threat to his dealings with the Soviets and took the offensive. "It's a damn lie that Jews are being oppressed in the Soviet Union," he told anyone who would listen. "Nobody's buying that stupid fable. Furthermore, the Russian leaders have assured me that there is no anti-Semitism in the Soviet Union. That dirty bastard Scoop Jackson is trying to drum up a lot of favorable publicity and a lot of Jewish money so that he can run for president. Dig up some information about Jackson. I'm going to ruin him."

When reporters began to question Armand about Soviet anti-Semitism, he minimized it, termed it a wild exaggeration, brushed it off, or said that it wasn't true. Or he told bold-faced lies about his secret activities to assist certain Soviet Jews. A stream of prominent Americans and a number of American and foreign diplomats began to issue requests that he intercede with the Kremlin on behalf of the Soviet Jews. His responses:

"I'll think about it." . . . "Thank you for calling it to my attention." . . . "I'm working on it." . . . "I'm doing all I can under the circumstances." . . . "I'll give you information when I get it."

Armand had no desire to say or do anything that would interfere with his ability to make deals in the USSR, but greed was not his only motive. Naïve, childlike, and occasionally irrational when it came to anything that contradicted his romantic vision of the USSR, he believed and repeated verbatim whatever the Soviet leadership said to him, and his authority, success, and wealth gave credence to those lies. Thus, he was an ideal propagandist.

By and large Jewish voters disliked Nixon, and the president moved quickly to defuse the issue of the exit tax. Through back channels, he persuaded Leonid Brezhnev to grant exemption from the tax until after the election. In return, Nixon and Soviet Foreign Minister Andrei Gromyko signed a comprehensive trade agreement on October 18, which became known as the Trade Reform Act of 1973. Among its other provisions the agreement extended Export-Import Bank credits so that the Soviets could borrow the money to pay for the American grain they had previously contracted to buy. But the agreement was not sent to Congress because Nixon feared the attachment of Senator Jackson's resolution. "When it gets there, I'll have Jackson's idiocy smashed into the ground," Armand told me before moving on to another Soviet deal.

On October 29, El Paso Natural Gas announced that it had formed a consortium with Tokyo Gas Company and Occidental to develop the Siberian natural-gas fields and that Bank of America was going to supply the financing. The news meant only one thing to Cyrus Eaton: Bank of America had received firm assurances that Nixon was going to approve trade credits. Eaton surmised that Hammer must have made a huge campaign contribution to

CREEP in order to secure that approval and that his contribution had to have been made during the blackout period of March 10 to April 7 because there was no public record of it. Still smarting over the way Hammer had treated his son, Eaton confided to an important Washington journalist that Hammer had made an enormous, potentially illegal secret contribution. The journalist wrote down every word Eaton said but didn't print it because Eaton had no proof.

On November 3, one of Tim Babcock's associates delivered another $25,000 of Armand's contribution to CREEP, explaining that the name and addresses of the "contributors" would be supplied later. The last $14,000 was delivered on January 15, 1973, more than two months after Nixon scored his stunning reelection victory. Because this contribution arrived after the election, Maurice Stans gave Babcock the option of allowing CREEP to assign it along with the contribution of November 3, 1972, to an independent fund that was being used to update voter records. Stans explained that because the money was going to be spent on a nonelection purpose, CREEP did not require the names of the contributors, and Babcock agreed that it was a wonderful idea. Eventually $22,000 of the $39,000 would be turned over to a White House aide at the request of Counsel to the President John Dean to replenish money spent out of a secret $350,000 fund held by Nixon officials. Some of it would also be used to pay for Dean's honeymoon. Thus, the stage was set for a drama that would test Armand Hammer's self-proclaimed invincibility.

Armand had at last achieved a working relationship with Nixon, but he still hadn't met Leonid Brezhnev, whom he referred to as "the chairman of the board." From the moment of his return to Moscow in 1969, he began collecting information about the Soviet general secretary and bombarding him with letters, only to receive polite replies. But the one thing Hammer craved, an invitation to confer privately with Brezhnev in his office in the Kremlin, was not forthcoming. He recalled that when President Johnson had resisted his overtures, he had finally broken the ice by donating two sculptures. So when an art dealer offered him two letters written by Lenin, he decided to repeat the gesture and give them to Brezhnev.

The Soviet leader was hard at work developing a cult of personality around himself. Every Soviet leader manipulated the symbol of Lenin to his own advantage. Therefore, the gift of two letters written by Lenin from a great American capitalist *and* a man who had known Lenin personally would provide Brezhnev with a potent PR opportunity to reinforce his image as Lenin's rightful heir, something that Armand clearly understood when he decided to make this particular gift.

Meanwhile, as the opening of the Armand Hammer Collection at the Pushkin Museum on October 22 came closer, Armand convinced Soviet Minister of Culture Furtseva to send the exhibition to Kiev, Minsk, Odessa, Riga, and the Hermitage museum in Leningrad.

I don't think Frances knew anything about her husband's relationship with Furtseva. A day or two before they attended the opening at the Pushkin Museum, she and Armand were traveling through Moscow by limousine, accompanied by two Occidental executives. While Armand napped, the executives filled her in on the latest Moscow gossip and told her about the vice president of a large corporation who had been secretly filmed having sex in a Soviet hotel with an attractive young Soviet woman. The woman had turned out to be a KGB agent, and the Soviet government was using the film to blackmail the executive in an attempt to obtain a better deal. It was the same hoary story that was always being told about the KGB, but Frances enjoyed it. Poking Armand in the ribs, she urged him to start being careful. He opened one eye slightly and told her not to worry because he was so old, he could "barely pee out of it anymore."

On October 22, Armand stood proudly before the Armand Hammer Collection in the Pushkin Museum and presented the Goya to Furtseva. A number of high-ranking Soviet officials attended the ceremony, and the state-controlled press was also there —proof that the Soviet leadership was coming to the conclusion that Armand was to be taken seriously and deserved to be publicized.

During the reception Armand seized upon an idea that had the potential to make him the ringmaster of a legitimately major international media event. The collections of the Hermitage and Pushkin museums contained a number of important Impressionist and post-Impressionist paintings that had been owned before the 1917 Revolution by two of czarist Russia's richest merchants, Ivan Morozov and Sergei Shchukin, and had never been seen in the West. Explaining that art could be used to counteract the strong anti-Soviet feelings in the United States and make Americans more receptive to the concept of U.S.-Soviet trade, Armand obtained Furtseva's permission to import a selection from the Morozov-

Shchukin collection and promote the exhibition as a goodwill gesture and a prime example of Nixon-Brezhnev détente.

Then, on October 25, Armand addressed a letter to "The Honorable Leonid Ilyich Brezhnev, General Secretary, Central Committee of the Communist Party, Moscow, U.S.S.R." He wrote, "This offer of Vladimir Ilyich Lenin's personal writings, Mr. General Secretary, is intended to express my good will to the leaders of the people of the Soviet Union and my appreciation of a friendship that will always remain sacred to me. Respectfully yours, Armand Hammer."

Now all he had to do was sit tight and wait.

On his return to Los Angeles, Armand told me that one unpleasant thing had happened during his trip. His nephew, Victor's son Armasha, had turned up uninvited at the reception at the Pushkin. "Armasha is forty-four years old, but he refuses to get a job and continues to accept a monthly allowance from Victor," he complained to me. "He asked Victor for hundreds of LPs, and Victor gave them to him. Armasha didn't even say thank you. He was too busy selling them on the black market. He's always getting married, divorced, and remarried. Now Victor's got two grandchildren to worry about. Whenever I'm in Moscow, he trails after me, and I can't stand it. Armasha makes me sick."

Victor was upset about something else that had occurred during his brother's Moscow stay. "Armand had to slip that greedy bitch Yekaterina Furtseva *a hundred thousand dollars* in order to get her permission to take the Morozov-Shchukin collection out of the country," he told me. "Her balls may be even bigger than Brezhnev's!"

True to their word, the Soviets reinstituted the controversial exit tax at the end of January 1973, thus triggering a vigorous congressional debate about whether to link the granting of MFN trade status and the extension of trade credits to the Soviets to a repeal of the tax. As the debate heated up, Armand received word that Brezhnev would see him, and on February 15, he spent two hours with the general secretary in Brezhnev's Kremlin office. Once again, his persistence and determination had paid off.

"All I saw were the good traits," Armand reported on his return to Los Angeles. "Mr. Brezhnev is a brilliant man and an excellent leader. He's intelligent, personable, and sophisticated. Like Lenin, he's a warmhearted, caring man with deep emotions. When I said something that stirred him, his eyes filled with tears. The only troublesome thing I observed is that he tends to act impulsively."

Armand dangled a gold pocket watch I had never seen before. "When our meeting was over, Mr. Brezhnev gave me this finely made Soviet watch," he told me. "It was totally unexpected."

"Did you happen to give him a gift first?" I asked.

He frowned. "I did give him reproductions of the two Lenin letters to hang in his office. He was flustered and embarrassed that he didn't have a gift to give me in return. After fumbling around for a while, he reached into his vest pocket and gave me his watch. Recovering from this admission, he added, "It keeps perfect time."

From that moment on, Armand would take every possible opportunity to praise Brezhnev in public and use his authority to convince the American public that the Soviet leader was a trustworthy man. According to Victor, Brezhnev had loved receiving the Lenin letters, but he hadn't loved them as much as Armand's promises to promote him internationally as the reincarnation of Lenin, to provide his son, Yuri, with a well-paid job with Occidental of Moscow, and to give him gifts of a yacht and a custom Rolls-Royce.

Because the state had a monopoly over all of its industries, the Soviets automatically maintained a superior bargaining position in any deal with the West. They also extracted concessions based on their demands for "goodwill" concessions and their power to provide dirt-cheap or slave labor. In return for Brezhnev's endorsement of the Occidental-Soviet fertilizer protocol, Armand went even further, and during his encounter with Brezhnev, he promised that the price Occidental would set for the fertilizers it sold to the Soviets would be barely above cost. The established purpose of U.S.-Soviet trade was to create mutually advantageous deals, but Armand's concessions meant that Occidental would see almost no profits no matter how well Occidental did. It was a gesture that established the prevailing pattern in all of Occidental's future business transactions with the Soviets.

Soon after his meeting with Hammer, Brezhnev informed the White House that he had given his personal approval to the fertilizer venture and that he expected Nixon to grant trade credits for it. On March 15, Senator Jackson reintroduced his resolution, which held the potential to jeopardize the ability of every U.S. corporation to do business with the Soviet Union. Armand again went on the offensive. "I owe it to all Americans and all Soviets to fight this resolution to the grave," he declared. "Nothing can be allowed to hurt our Soviet deals. They're great for peace. They're even better for Oxy's bottom line! Wait until you see how much money we're going to make in the Soviet Union!"

17.

THE BIGGEST DEAL IN HISTORY

Toward the end of March 1973, the USSR shipped forty-one paintings from the Morozov-Shchukin collection to the National Gallery of Art in Washington, D.C. Included were works by Cézanne, Gauguin, Matisse, Monet, Picasso, Pissarro, Renoir, Rousseau, and van Gogh. Concerned that the paintings might be defaced as Michelangelo's *Pietà* had been in 1964, Armand insured them for $25 million and insisted that they be supplied with sturdier frames, exhibited behind bulletproof glass, and kept under surveillance by armed guards around the clock.

At the formal reception on April 1, Yekaterina Furtseva and Hammer accepted congratulations from Secretary of State William Rogers, Chief Justice Warren Burger, and other dignitaries, while Frances hovered in the background. A seemingly endless round of interviews accompanied Armand's international art coup. The Soviet propaganda machine was pursuing détente with single-minded determination. Armand followed suit. He repeatedly told reporters that the exhibition's "détente catalog" contained statements from Nixon and Brezhnev, predicted that the Nixon-Brezhnev détente was going to lead to even greater accomplishments, heaped praise on both leaders, and declared that his mission was "*exactly* the same as theirs." Furtseva also ran true to form. Just before she returned to the USSR, she had commented that "it broke her heart" that the Soviets owned only one painting by Raoul Dufy. Armand dutifully promised her that they were soon going to own two.

During Armand's Washington stay, Occidental International's senior staff tipped him that, after a seven-month wait, President Nixon was finally going to send the U.S.-USSR comprehensive trade agreement (now known as the Trade Reform Act of 1973) to Congress on April 10 and that Senator Jackson was going to respond by introducing his restrictive amendment formally on the Senate floor. Armand was on his way to Moscow and told me to expect another major announcement once he got there.

"About what?" I asked.

"We'll cross that bridge when we come to it."

On April 12, the Soviets summoned the foreign press corps to witness "a historic development." The presence of a number of high-ranking ministers and the state-controlled television network reinforced this description. Armand stood beside Soviet minister Nikolai Komarov while Komarov announced that Occidental and the Soviets were about to sign a twenty-year chemical-fertilizer barter agreement. He characterized the deal as "the largest U.S.–USSR trade agreement in history" and "the largest agreement ever made between a U.S. corporation and the government of a foreign country."

Hammer and Komarov signed the contract, posed for photographs, and ignored the salvo of questions concerning the financing of the deal and whether the United States was going to grant trade credits. Occidental's Soviet staff was of no help either because they had been given no information and had been instructed to tell reporters that they were not permitted to respond to questions. The correspondents later discovered that these same aides had briefed the Soviet press, enabling *Pravda* to report that the $8 billion pact entitled the Soviets to purchase "several hundred million dollars" worth of fertilizer-manufacturing equipment on "long-term credit" and that for twenty years, beginning in 1978, to exchange Soviet ammonia, urea, and potash for an equivalent amount, up to one million metric tons, of SPA (superphosphoric acid) from Occidental's phosphate fertilizer complex in White Springs, Florida. James Reston of *The New York Times* reported that it was the first time in history that the CEO of a U.S. corporation had supplied the details of an agreement made by that corporation to a state-controlled press but had refused to divulge the same information to the free press.

After Armand announced the Occidental-Soviet protocol from London, the British press printed the news, no questions asked. The Moscow foreign press corps knew that the Kremlin viewed the

1972 Soviet trade deficit of $1 billion as an indication that the so-called careful planning of the state-run economy under Leonid Brezhnev was failing, which fueled Brezhnev's desire to cultivate U.S.-Soviet trade. Therefore, it was their conclusion that Hammer and the Soviets had staged another commercial for U.S.-Soviet trade in an effort to show Congress that passing the Jackson amendment would be meaningless because U.S. companies were going to do business with the Soviets anyway, and to provide a demonstration of the kind of deals Brezhnev hoped to make during his forthcoming visit to the United States in June.

Izvestia confirmed these suspicions when it printed that the announcement had been timed to influence the U.S. Congress and quoted Brezhnev saying that he was going to the United States to make "multimillion-dollar deals like the Occidental deal." The skepticism of the Moscow press corps was echoed on Wall Street. Occidental's stock price actually *dropped* a few points after the announcement. But I persisted, and Occidental subsequently released a flimsy set of details.

I was barraged by reporters, and I told Armand that Occidental's credibility depended on the release of a statement clarifying at least some of the basic questions, but he brushed aside my concerns. He feared that any statement would lead to the revelation that what he had really signed was a letter of intent and not a final contract, that Occidental did not have the resources to finance the venture, and that he had agreed to obtain a $180 million Export-Import Bank loan for the Soviets in return for a final agreement, a promise he had put in writing without knowing whether he had the ability to fulfill the commitment.

Bank of America president A. W. Clausen had just received permission to open a Bank of America Moscow branch office, but he responded cautiously when Armand approached him to lend the Soviets $400 million to finance the deal. Clausen needed proof that the Soviets were creditworthy. Clearly eager to obtain the financing that Hammer could not supply, Soviet Deputy Minister of Trade Vladimir Alkhimov arrived in Washington on May 2 and met with Secretary of Commerce Frederick Dent and Export-Import Bank president Henry Kearns. Alkimhov took the position that his government insisted that Commerce supply him with a "formal endorsement" of the Occidental-Soviet letter of intent "to prevent any future embarrassment to the Soviets." That fear was not the real issue, and everyone knew it. A "formal endorsement" would be a clear indication that President Nixon was eventually going to approve trade credits and could be used as a letter of credit to secure a loan from the Bank of America, which the U.S. government would eventually use those trade credits to underwrite.

The same day, Armand wrote to Nixon and urged him to inform Commerce of his approval. But before the day was over the news broke that as a part of the Watergate scandal, Maurice Stans and CREEP Chairman John Mitchell had been indicted on charges of conspiracy to defraud the government and to obstruct justice. Armand was stunned. Declaring that "they're out to get Maurice Stans because they're jealous of his success," he tore into a monologue about how "stupid" and "unnecessary" laws stopped people like Stans from doing their jobs. He raged on until it became evident that he was really talking about what he thought could also happen to him.

The Senate Watergate Commission hearings were scheduled to begin on May 18, and the administration's preoccupation with Watergate was undoubtedly going to delay Nixon's response to Alkhimhov. When Armand was tipped that Leonid Brezhnev had confirmed his visit to the United States for the end of June, he secretly pressured *New York Times* publisher Arthur Ochs Sulzberger to assign a reporter to write a major feature story about his Soviet business wheelings and dealings. Then he gave the reporter the scoop that the Soviets needed written proof from the U.S. government before they would complete the Occidental-Soviet deal. Eight months had elapsed since Nixon had promised the Soviets a trade agreement, and Nixon had been unable to keep his word and it was Armand's hope that on the eve of Brezhnev's visit, when Nixon saw this statement in the *Times,* he would seize the opportunity to give Brezhnev something tangible: his formal endorsement of the Occidental-Soviet fertilizer deal.

On May 12, Secretary of State Henry Kissinger announced the impending visit. On May 20, Armand responded by delivering another commercial for U.S.-Soviet trade, an announcement that Occidental was "negotiating" a "massive" natural-gas pipeline with the Soviets. The following day, the feature story solicited by Hammer appeared on the front page of the business section of *The New York Times* under the headline HAMMER'S KREMLIN CONNECTION. It characterized Armand as a "curious amalgam of Yankee trader, circus barker, big-time entrepreneur and cultured devotee of the arts"; placed his personal worth at $125 million or more"; and described Occidental as a "$2.6 billion conglomerate with a debt of

$1 billion" and, therefore, incapable of financing Hammer's Soviet deals. Hammer's string of announcements about Occidental's Soviet deals was characterized as a conceivable "Soviet propaganda ploy" aimed at paving the way for Brezhnev's visit and an indication that Soviet propagandists might be using their special relationship with him to motivate other U.S. business leaders to work with the USSR, demonstrate to Congress the futility of attempting to stop the progress of U.S.-Soviet trade, and boost Leonid Brezhnev against those Soviet detractors who questioned the wisdom of détente.

Armand was flabbergasted. Fearing that the banks might conclude that Occidental's dealings with the Soviets were nothing more than pro-Soviet propaganda, he suddenly demanded that I prepare a position paper defending these deals and get it into the newspapers the following morning. Then he called Arthur Ochs Sulzberger and wouldn't get off the phone until Sulzberger promised to have him reinterviewed *and* print an analysis of the Occidental-Soviet business transactions. By the time the week was over, the *Times* had printed four stories about Armand and Occidental —two feature stories, one negative and one positive, both by the same reporter, a "think piece" supporting Hammer's Soviet activities, and a news story about Occidental's Siberian natural-gas negotiations.

On June 2, Nixon ordered Commerce to comply with Alkhimov's request, and Dent and Alkhimov signed letters endorsing the Occidental-Soviet letter of intent. The contents of these letters were kept secret, but news leaked out about how the construction of the fertilizer complex in the Soviet Union, a major component of the pact, would be financed. Occidental would put up no money except for necessary capital expenditures for the required fertilizer facilities in the United States. The Soviets would supply 10 percent of the capital and the remaining 90 percent would be financed by American credit with the approval of Nixon, an initial $180 million loan from the Export-Import Bank, at an interest rate of just 6 percent, and matching funds that would be lent to the Soviets by private Western banks. Therefore, Occidental would suffer little in the way of major losses if the fertilizer deal didn't pan out. Armand ignored the accusations and instructed me, in dealing with the press, to stop referring to the pact as an $8-billion deal and up the ante to $20 billion.

The next day Brezhnev announced that his objective during the forthcoming summit would be encourage U.S.-Soviet trade. On

June 8, Armand announced from Moscow that he had achieved an "agreement of intent" for a $4 billion Occidental-Soviet natural-gas venture. The Moscow foreign press corps was not surprised by his vagueness about the details and the financing and took the announcement as more propaganda geared toward helping Brezhnev achieve his stated objective when he arrived in the United States.

Brezhnev's itinerary included a state dinner on June 18 and a reception for representatives of the American business community at Blair House four days later. Armand attended both events and was pleased when the executives praised the Soviet general secretary's warmth, humor, and sincerity. During his visit, a Soviet newsreel journalist called and told me in halting English that Brezhnev had ordered him to interview Hammer.

I set a time for the reporter to go to Armand's home, and when he spotted my Cadillac parked outside, he asked if it was a government car. I replied that I owned it and had paid for it out of my salary. He was so amazed he decided that he wanted to film Armand standing in front of the car so that the Soviets could see the beauty of an American automobile and how well American workers were paid. I told him that he might be better off talking to Armand in his backyard. The interview was conducted in Russian. Armand later told me that he had been asked "to tell the Russian people about the miraculous nature of the October 1917 Revolution, describe the greatness of Lenin, and enumerate the wonders of the Communist system. And I did."

In August Armand's name was again in the newspapers when the Morozov-Shchukin collection arrived at the County Museum's Frances and Armand Hammer Wing after its exhibition at the Hammer brothers' Knoedler Gallery in New York. People ringed the museum for hours then had to cross picket lines set up by the Jewish Defense League and other protest groups that supported Soviet Jews. When two peculiar-looking packages were discovered inside, the museum was evacuated and the bomb squad was called. Armand learned later that the packages had been planted by the JDL and had contained railroad flares.

During Armand's next trip to Moscow, he staged another donation ceremony at the Pushkin Museum and presented Yekaterina Furtseva with the painting by Dufy he had promised her. On his return, he sent for Knoedler Gallery Vice President John Richardson and explained that the time had come for Furtseva to give him something in return. The art expert suggested a painting by Kasimir Malevich, the father of the Suprematist movement. Armand had never heard of Malevich, which surprised Richardson because Malevich and Hammer had both lived in Moscow during the 1920s.

Armand loathed modern art, but Richardson explained that the Soviets had hidden away Malevich's paintings because they were not reflective of approved state socialist art. Their removal from the market had made their value increase substantially and a noteworthy Malevich was worth $1 million. Armand sent word to Furtseva that day that he had to own a Malevich.

During Richardson's visit to Armand's house in West Los Angeles, he noticed a painting hanging on a living room wall. It was a copy of *Woman of the People* by Modigliani. Armand insisted that it was the original, and Richardson let him have his little joke. Finally Armand admitted that Frances had painted the copy. She had also copied other paintings in the Armand Hammer Collection. The next day, during lunch with Frances and Armand at their house, Armand told me the story. He was amused, but Frances looked embarrassed. "I was so upset I couldn't sleep," she said. "I don't like fooling people like that. In the middle of the night I went downstairs and painted my initials on the painting."

Armand threw her a look of exasperation.

She smiled sweetly. "Armand, I'm your wife—not your forger."

After Hammer received his Malevich, he tracked down an authority to determine its authenticity. Then he placed a $1 million price tag on it, put it up for sale, and hunted down a prospective buyer. When the buyer dropped out, Armand discovered that he had consulted the same authority and had been advised that the painting was in poor condition. Hammer decided to sue the expert into the ground. It was not until he sold his gift to another buyer for $750,000 that he called off the lawyers.

In early September, after a five-month wait, the House Ways and Means Committee was nearing a vote on the Jackson amendment. Tipped by the Occidental International senior staff that Henry Kissinger was planning to appear before the committee to argue the administration's case, Armand sped to Washington. He called each of the committee members, announced that he was on his way over, marched into the legislator's office, and delivered an impassioned monologue that stressed the need for peace and an end to world hunger, followed by a plea to vote against the amendment.

On September 17, Kissinger's visit was put off and the vote was postponed. It was too late for Armand to cancel a joint press conference with representatives of the Soviet Chamber of Commerce and Industry that had been scheduled to precede the vote. In another pitch for Soviet trade, he announced that Occidental and the Soviets were going to construct a $110 million international trade center in Moscow, and during the question-and-answer period, he told a *Tass* reporter that any congressman who voted against the Trade Reform Act was an "enemy of détente" and predicted that the Jackson amendment would be defeated. His comments were reported at length by the U.S. press.

Henry Kissinger testified on September 26. Directly afterward, the Ways and Means Committee voted to attach the Jackson amendment to the Trade Reform Act.

The following week David Karr was in my office when Armand called twice. "How do you stand it?" he asked.

I laughed. "It goes with the job."

"Armand's not happy unless he's dialing someone," Karr said. "We agree, then he changes his mind and calls me back. Then he changes it again and calls again. On and on it goes. He runs this company like a drunken driver. I think he's crazy."

No one dared criticize Armand publicly unless he had reached the breaking point. A few days later Hammer complained that Karr was hanging onto his coattails and "trying to use the advantages he's gotten from knowing me to make his own deals in the Soviet Union." Over the next couple of weeks he provided a litany of other objections. But what was really bothering him was the fact that he felt threatened because Karr's exceptional social and deal-making skills were enabling him to win over the Soviet leadership. Suddenly Armand performed his usual surgery and Karr was gone. Everyone who had participated in the initial legwork in the Soviet Union had now been eliminated, leaving Armand exactly what he wanted to be—the sole surviving member of the initiating group.

Not too long after the Watergate break-in on June 18, 1972, the lobbying group Common Cause filed suit in federal court to force the CREEP Finance Committee to disclose all federal contributions made between March 10 and April 7, 1972. After Nixon's stunning victory on November 7, 1972, CREEP had assumed the public interest group would drop its suit, but Common Cause refused to let up.

The more CREEP fought the suit in the courts, the more it appeared that it had something to hide—especially as the Watergate scandal led to the convictions of G. Gordon Liddy and James McCord and the resignations of Acting FBI Director L. Patrick Gray, Attorney General Richard Kleindienst, White House staff members H. R. Haldeman, John Ehrlichman, and John Dean, as well as the indictments of John Mitchell and Maurice Stans. CREEP, although not legally obligated to reveal the names, opted to clear the air by making a full disclosure of all of its contributors including the names of any previously unreported contributors whose contributions had been made after April 7, 1972. Subsequently Tim Babcock received notification that CREEP intended to reveal that he had contributed $15,000 after the April 7 deadline. Although the names of contributors of the $39,000 for a "nonelection purpose" did not have to be made public, CREEP insisted on releasing those names also and asked Babcock to turn them over.

On May 22, one week after the Senate Watergate Committee was convened, while President Nixon was making the public admission that "unethical as well as illegal acts" had occurred during the 1972 campaign, Babcock delivered a letter to CREEP stating that he had contributed $15,000; his friend Jerome Anderson, $15,000; Bill Holter, $10,000; Dr. Gordon Doering, $10,000; and Elmer Balsam, $4,000.

On June 10, following standard procedure, CREEP filed this information with the clerk of the House of Representatives. Cyrus Eaton had already told a prominent Washington journalist that Hammer had made a large, illegal campaign contribution, and that journalist had tipped the Senate Watergate Committee to be on the lookout for Hammer. CREEP's filing made the Watergate investigators wonder why it had taken CREEP nine months to report the donations and why Babcock, one of Armand Hammer's right-hand men, had made them in cash. Toward the end of the month Armand learned that the FBI was planning to investigate.

Concerned that Babcock's friends might prove unwilling to lie to the FBI or on the witness stand under oath, Armand decided to create a new scenario that would make it impossible to trace the money to him. His goal was to establish that Babcock's friends had *borrowed* the money from Babcock, the "real" contributor. But if it was unlikely that Tim Babcock was financially capable of making a $54,000 campaign contribution in the first place, it was also unlikely that he had lent $39,000 to his friends. Therefore, someone had to be willing to say that he had "lent" Babcock the $54,000 in the first place.

As John Dean was testifying before the Senate Watergate Committee about his role in the cover-up, Armand put his own cover-up plan into motion. It involved three men who were known only by the code names "the lender," "the consultant," and "the courier." "The lender" was Babcock because he was going to say that he had lent $39,000 to his friends. The "consultant" was Armand's London-based consultant, John Tigrett, who would be described as the source of a $54,000 loan to Babcock. Executive Vice President Marvin Watson was the "courier" because he was going to fly to London to deliver a fake promissory note from Babcock to Tigrett, which Armand believed could be offered as proof that Babcock had borrowed $54,000 from Tigrett before "lending" $39,000 to his friends. On July 2, Babcock, "the lender," drafted the promissory note and gave it to "the courier," Watson, and Watson set off to deliver the note to Tigrett, "the consultant."

Not long after, Armand and I were working at his home when he became agitated because he couldn't find some papers he wanted me to have. He left the library, went upstairs, and asked me to come with him. This was the first time in the eighteen years I had known him that I had been inside his bedroom. Stacks of magazines, files, reports, and correspondence were everywhere. It was like stepping into a maze, and it probably reflected the inner workings of Armand's mind.

He handed some pages to me and stepped outside. I remained behind and looked at them, wondering if they had any significance. "Carl, what are you doing up there? Come out!" he shouted at the top of his voice.

I stepped outside. "What's the matter?"

His face was contorted into rage and he could barely control himself. "I thought you were right behind me. I don't want you or anyone else in my bedroom unless I'm there. I don't even allow Frances in my bedroom by herself."

A few days later Victor told me that the FBI was in the process of interrogating Armand about the Babcock contribution. The day I went to Armand's house, the FBI had just left, which explained why he was so upset. "Armand's convinced he's going to go to jail," said Victor.

18.

"DON'T PUT ANY OF THIS JUNK INTO THE BOOK"

After investing seven years and millions of dollars in Venezuela, Occidental discovered oil on Block A of its South Lake Maracaibo service contract in May 1973. Armand greeted the news with relief because the Libyans had resumed their accusations that the oil companies were cheating them and overproducing their concessions and were threatening to demand even larger increases in their oil income.

Occidental's Libyan communications facilities were maintained by Northrop Communications. The firm was paid $840,000, which included a $110,000 payment to a Libyan agent. Concerned by the new developments in Libya, Armand "advised" Northrop to retain a second Libyan agent of Occidental's choosing and pay it $110,000 also. This kickback enabled him to install his own operative whose sole job was to provide intelligence about Muammar Qaddafi to him. This intermediary firm was known only by the incomprehensible code name Z-Comm Establishment.

The move was of no help, however, and on August 11, Libya nationalized 51 percent of Occidental's holdings. The staff gathered around Armand and started to give him the sympathetic, concerned reaction they thought he wanted, but he wasn't the least upset. "Their cutbacks were hurting our profits at the same time that Oxy's debt was growing," he said. "We're still going to operate the entire concession and market all of the oil, so we'll make a good profit. And they're paying Oxy compensation of $136 million in cash, not oil, for our nationalized properties. We'll use this beautiful bonus to pay the taxes and royalties on our forty-nine percent share and to purchase crude from the Libyans' share, and we'll make even more money. It could have been a lot worse."

Whenever there was trouble far away in Libya, there always seemed to be more trouble at the same time in Occidental's backyard concerning Armand's determination to drill for oil in Pacific Palisades. Around the time of the Libyan nationalization the grass-roots environmental group No Oil Incorporated announced that it had completed its investigation and was turning over its findings to the City of Los Angeles. Subsequently, a City Council committee was formed to look into No Oil's allegations that Occidental had bribed city officials to allow it to engage in the Pacific Palisades land swap in 1968 that had provided it with two acres of city-owned, oil-rich, beachfront property and that former mayor Sam Yorty's friendship with Hammer was the reason Yorty had struck down a council resolution to ban drilling within one-quarter mile of the coastline.

On October 29, Ray Morani, a stockbroker, told ABC News an amazing story. He said the former mayor's secretary, Dorothy Moore, had introduced him to Yorty at the same time that Occidental and the city were working out the land swap and that he and Yorty had discussed stock transactions involving Occidental stock during several evening meetings in Yorty's office. Then he and Dorothy Moore had flown to Jamaica, where he had opened a Jamaican bank account in the name of Moore's former husband, who was a Canadian. Morani had deposited $250,000 in cash and wired the money to the former husband's bank account in Toronto, where it had been used to buy Occidental stock on the Toronto exchange, and the stock had been placed in stock accounts bearing the names of Dorothy Moore and Elizabeth Hensel, Mrs. Yorty's maiden name.

Morani added that he was also a "friend" of Nina Anderton, from whom Occidental had purchased the property in Pacific Palisades that it subsequently swapped with the city. The stockbroker concluded by admitting that in the past week he had been involved in the purchase by various city officials of more than $1.5 million worth of Occidental stock under false names.

Directly after the broadcast, the U.S. Attorney's office called

ABC for a transcript of Morani's interview and submitted it to a federal grand jury that was investigating illegal stock transactions. The grand jury served Morani with a subpoena a few hours later.

Armand ordered me to deny the charges and accused Morani of being a stooge for No Oil. The Yortys also issued a statement that they did not know Morani and had never owned a single share of Occidental stock. By the end of the week, Morani's story had undergone substantial revision and he stated that he had never been involved in any stock transactions with the Yortys. When asked about his incriminating remarks on TV, he explained that he had assumed that his comments were going to remain "confidential." Dorothy Moore could not confirm or deny the story; she "was out of the state" and "could not be reached."

When the grand jury subpoenaed Morani's stock records, he insisted that they had been stolen from his car. At the same time the City Council committee called for the stock records of Hammer, the Yortys, four former city officials, and Nina Anderton, but it did not have the legal authority to enforce its request. Yorty declined an invitation to testify, which placed the committee in the awkward position of having to ask the City Council for subpoena power if they wanted to force the former mayor to appear.

Armand insisted that in time it would all fade away. His attention was focused on Venezuela, where Occidental had just discovered oil on Block E of its service contract. Occidental's agreement with the Venezuelan national oil company contained a clause that allowed Occidental to receive a reimbursement of its exploration and drilling costs if it discovered a "commercial" amount of oil. But Occidental's application for a $74 million reimbursement for its discoveries on Blocks A and E had been rejected on the grounds that its statement of recoverable reserves did not satisfy the definition of "commerciality," and Armand was furious. "They're a lousy bunch of robbers, and they're trying to take us to the cleaners," he told me. "I'm not going to let them get away with it."

The imminent Venezuelan election was inevitably going to produce a victory for the majority Acción Democrática party, but Occidental's Venezuelan general manger, Charles Hatfield, was deeply involved with leaders of the Christian Democratic Party (COPEI), so Armand replaced him with a Spanish-speaking lawyer named John Ryan. It was Ryan's task to make friends with high-level Acción Democrática officials to pave the way for a resubmission of Occidental's "commercialty" application.

Acción Democrática presidential candidate Carlos Andrés Pérez had hired a high-priced U.S. PR firm to plot his campaign. Although the fifty-two-year-old politician had once attempted to purge his country of leftist guerrillas, he was now being cast as a reformer who was going to use the tools of democracy to confront the evils inflicted on his country by foreign capitalism. "We'll do better than ever once Pérez takes over," Armand kept insisting to convince himself as much as his team of oil and gas boys, who had warned him not to get involved in Venezuela in the first place.

On November 4, the Los Angeles City Council committee convened its public hearing on the Pacific Palisades matter. OILGATE HEARINGS TO BEGIN screamed the headlines on the front pages of the local newspapers, but Armand remained convinced that he was going to emerge unscathed from Oilgate. Watergate, however, was another matter. The Senate Watergate Committee was about to begin the final phase of its investigation, the subject of campaign financing. Armand looked stricken, but he put up a brave front. "They won't find anything because there's nothing for them to find. They'll just be going up a dead-end street. Watergate prosecutor Leon Jaworski will do anything to get his name in the papers."

If there was trouble waiting for him, Armand wanted to initiate a long-range PR campaign that would reinforce his heroic image and help him overcome any unpleasant revelations that might become public. His plan was to commission a biography by a respected journalist and circulate the finished product as an objective account of his life. Armand's representatives approached Harper & Row and explained that Armand was prepared to spend the money to turn a prospective biography into an international bestseller and would also purchase thousands of copies for PR purposes. A publishing contract was signed, and syndicated columnist Bob Considine was hired to research and write the book for a $75,000 fee.

Considine was the author of twenty-five books, including *The Red Plot Against America*, an account of Communist infiltration of the United States. It did not take him long to discover that just about everything Armand said about his family history and his initial entry into the USSR was a lie. He and I spent a lot of time together going through the clippings files and corporate scrapbooks. While we worked, he confided that he had gathered enough data to prove that the Hammer family had performed influence operations for the Soviet Union during the 1920s in return for economic rewards.

When he summarized this information and handed it to Hammer, Armand exploded. "None of this is true. Don't put any of this junk into the book. You'll write exactly what I tell you to write and nothing else."

Considine pointed out to me that this information was not that hard to track down, but Armand insisted that the public record reflect only his version of his life. "He doesn't want anything in print suggesting that he or anyone else in his family took directions from Soviet intelligence because it might encourage speculations that he could be doing it again," I told Considine in strictest confidence. "Armand loves money too much to be a Communist, but he worships the Soviet leaders because they have the kind of power he craves."

"Ultimately, the Soviets view détente and peaceful coexistence as ways of weakening the resolve of the West until they eventually achieve global military supremacy," Considine replied. "They need someone like Armand to spread the propaganda that they're really nice guys.

I agreed. "Wait and see. He's bound to start telling America that Leonid Brezhnev is the best thing since Mom and apple pie."

After a number of arguments with Armand, Considine attempted to return his advance payment and quit, but Armand persuaded him to stay. "He really knows how to make a man change his mind," admitted the journalist.

I refrained from asking the size of his bonus.

Considine described his project with Armand to his neighbor, TV news producer Lucy Jarvis. As Jarvis told it, she approached NBC and received the go-ahead to produce a prime-time documentary about Armand's involvement with the Kremlin, to be called *The Russian Connection.*

For Armand, it appeared to be another opportunity for self-promotion and he flew Jarvis and her crew on a round trip from London to Paris and another round trip from London to Moscow. Jarvis marveled at the seventy-five-year-old man, who slept in sixteen-minute catnaps, never tired, and ran a multibillion-dollar corporation almost single-handedly by telephone, while his wife doted over him every second of the day. She filmed Hammer with Henry Ford II in Detroit at a party "suggested" by Hammer when Ford asked him to allow the Morozov-Shchukin exhibition to be shown at the Detroit Institute of Art; in England at J. Paul Getty's estate; and in Paris at a lavish party Armand threw at Rasputin, a czarist Russian nightclub, where he discussed the acquisition of oil rights with an Arab delegation and the formation of a partnership with the powerful agent Marvin Josephson to represent the international television rights to the 1980 Summer Olympic Games in Moscow.

The filming in the Kremlin was timed to coincide with a ceremony that found Armand center stage celebrating the fortieth anniversary of Soviet-American diplomatic relations. En route, Jarvis discovered that Armand did not know how to obtain permission to film inside the Kremlin, so she secured permission from her own Kremlin connection. Not to be outdone, Armand made his own inquiries and Leonid Brezhnev agreed to an on-camera appearance, but only if an all-Soviet crew was used to film him. At the last minute Jarvis declared that she was a qualified sound technician and joined the Soviet crew so that she could watch Brezhnev and Hammer in action. This sequence found Hammer being received by Brezhnev for a "special meeting" and joined by newsman Edwin Newman. Determined to court American business, the general secretary was charming and amenable. "I help Dr. Hammer, and he helps me," he told Newman, while Armand stood there beaming.

Before the session was over Brezhnev suddenly announced that he had a message for the American people. He stared into the camera and spoke at length in Russian. Later it was discovered that Jarvis had failed to record his remarks audibly. Bilingual Russians were located so that they could lip-read Brezhnev's comments in order to have them translated for the American viewing audience. But the attempt failed, and Brezhnev's message was irretrievably lost.

After the filming Premier Kosygin escorted Armand to Lenin's office. On Lenin's desk there was a small bronze sculpture of a monkey seated on a pile of books contemplating a human skull, which was meant to symbolize Darwin's theory of evolution. Subsequently *Time* reported that Armand had claimed that he had given the sculpture to Lenin in 1921, that it was the only object Lenin had kept on his desk, and that Lenin had died at his desk staring at it. *Time* added that Lenin had died in bed at his home in Gorky and that his desk was cluttered with all kinds of objects.

"That fabrication isn't going to help Armand get on the magazine's cover," I told Victor.

He replied that the gift had, in fact, come from Julius Hammer and that Armand had merely delivered it.

Meanwhile, I learned that the extraordinary amount of time and money NBC lavished on producing *The Russian Connection* had convinced the production executives that it was not merely another news documentary, but that NBC had been ordered, probably by the Nixon administration, to create a positive commercial for dé-tente, and to hold out until Hammer delivered a final deal with the Soviets that would form the triumphant climax of the show.

While Armand was away, I received a call from Robert Trent Jones Jr., the well-known golf-course architect. He told me that Armand had asked him to brief me about a golf course he was going to design and build as an adjunct to the international trade center in Moscow. On his return from Moscow, Armand confirmed the story. "I gave Brezhnev a golf club and a box of new golf balls in honor of the project. He didn't know which end of the club to hold, and neither did I. The Soviets deserve to have their first golf course, and I'm also going to throw in a swimming pool."

He was scheduled to address the Petroleum Club of Los Angeles the next day, and his plan was to plug U.S.-Soviet trade, announce the construction of the golf course and the swimming pool, and enumerate a list of qualities he had observed about Leonid Brezhnev, including his integrity, compassion, willingness to go to any length to help achieve harmony among nations, and determination to eliminate war.

Arab anger over U.S. support of Israel during the Israeli-Egyptian October War had led to an oil embargo on the U.S. by the Arab nations. So Armand also planned to portray Occidental's proposal to drill for oil in Pacific Palisades as a "patriotic act" and part of a war against "the greatest crisis in the history of the republic."

The following day, as Armand was telling the Petroleum Club about the positive effects Brezhnev was having on Soviet life, which included a rise in per capita income and a marked increase in automobile production, the large double doors at the back of the ballroom burst open and a group of protestors stormed in carrying signs that read: HAMMER, SAVE SOVIET JEWS! Chanting, "Stop helping Russia! Save Soviet Jews!" they headed down the aisle. But before they reached Armand, security guards surrounded them and managed to hustle them out.

Armand looked shaken, but he pulled himself together and finished his speech. Back at headquarters, he was still upset. "I'm glad they didn't hit me or shoot me."

I pointed out that he was encouraging these demonstrations by insisting that there was no anti-Semitism in the Soviet Union and that Soviet Jews were not being denied permission to emigrate. "You've got to say publicly that you're working behind the scenes to try to alleviate the plight of the Soviet Jews," I said firmly. "You can't pretend these problems don't exist."

He changed the subject and during later interviews he began to insist that Leonid Brezhnev had told him personally that there was no anti-Semitism in the Soviet Union. In response, two JDL members dressed in ski masks splattered red paint all over the lobby walls of corporate headquarters and protest groups sneaked past the security guards and staged anti-Hammer skits in front of the doorway that led to the executive offices. Other protestors marched and picketed in front of the Hammers' home.

Armand didn't seem to see or hear any of it.

On November 7, President Nixon addressed the energy crisis that had been precipitated by the Arab embargo and called for Project Independence, a program that would free the United States from its dependence on foreign oil. The most theoretical and visionary response to a fuel shortage was to build a synthetic-fuels industry and Occidental's research subsidiary, Garrett Research and Development Company in La Verne, California, initiated a pilot project involving a new Occidental research process that converted garbage into oil.

Envisioning Occidental's speedy entrance into synthetic fuels, especially the extraction of shale oil from rock, Armand ordered Garrett to create a shale-oil extraction process that could be patented. When he was informed that shale oil could be produced at a mere three dollars a barrel, he was ecstatic. "I'm a maverick, and so is Oxy," he told me. "We're going to be shale-oil pioneers. I don't care how many hundreds of millions this project costs to get off the ground, it's going to be a winner."

As the process was being developed on Occidental's tract in the Colorado Rockies, Armand left a trail of exaggerated claims about it. He told President Nixon's energy czar, William Simon, that Occidental could produce oil from shale at $1.18 per barrel. However, that figure represented only the operating costs pertaining to the recovery procedures and did not include any provision for recovering the investment in the facilities and other costs. When criticized, he changed his tune, saying Occidental could produce shale oil for $3 a barrel, then $4 a barrel, then $15 to $20 a barrel.

Apparently, however, the SEC objected to these maverick ways and Armand was served with a subpoena in connection with its latest investigation of Occidental's business practices. A few days after he testified, he was subpoenaed again. Armand wouldn't say a word about what was going on, but I knew he was concerned that further testimony could be damaging.

Armand's difficulties were compounded when Sam and Elizabeth Yorty were also subpoenaed. The Yortys maintained that they had never owned Occidental stock; yet the SEC announced that it planned to question them about profits earned from their Occidental stock during "periods of great stock activity."

Under SEC rules, insiders are required to make regular disclosures of their transactions. The possibility that Hammer, an insider, had used his position to supply information about Occidental stock to the former mayor and his wife, a number of city officials, and a property owner with whom Occidental was doing business was a potential bombshell.

On December 11, while Armand was confronting this dilemma, the House of Representatives passed the Trade Reform Act of 1973 with the Jackson amendment appended to it. It was a setback for Armand's grandiose trade deals with the Soviets, but he seemed unconcerned. "Don't worry," he said. "It's not going to stop me." He seemed to be right when on December 20 a Soviet trade deputy leaked the information that the Export-Import Bank had approved a loan to build the Occidental-Soviet Moscow international trade center. "How did you accomplish that?" I asked.

Armand smiled. "Watergate is smothering the White House, and Nixon's lost control of foreign policy. He knows that Brezhnev is aware that he's in trouble, but the Russians can't figure out why a little break-in, some spying, and some tax cheating is such a big deal. Nixon needs me to keep Brezhnev believing that he's still got power. Watergate has made me Nixon's unofficial ambassador to the Soviet Union."

Armand might have done better to improve his relations with the SEC, which had concluded its investigation and had offered him the option of signing another consent decree limiting the charges to one issue, Occidental's and Hammer's failure to disclose "certain important facts" concerning the losses incurred by the Occidental emergency tanker fleet during 1971. Signing the consent decree would put the matter to rest but Armand was dead set against it. Finally, at the very last moment, he gave in.

On December 27, the SEC filed a civil complaint detailing the charges against Occidental and Hammer. The same day, Armand signed a consent decree. It triggered another round of class-action and individual suits, which would eventually be settled out of court in 1978, but once again Armand seemed to be home free as the City Council, federal grand jury, and SEC investigations faded away. Only the Senate Watergate Committee investigation remained.

19.

THE NEW "DIRECTOR OF CORPORATE ART"

In January 1973, after ten months of effort in the North Sea and the drilling of two dry holes, Occidental brought in its first successful well. A second well two miles north of the original discovery followed in March. The underwater oil patch was named Piper field, and it was estimated that it contained recoverable reserves of 642 million barrels.

"At the end of fiscal 1971, there were devastating losses," said Armand. "By the end of fiscal 1972, Oxy had climbed out of the hole and there were operating profits of $10.4 million. At the end of this fiscal year, I'm told, we're going to see profits of $79 million. Wait until you see what the North Sea discovery does for this company. Carl, I'm a genius!"

Despite Armand's "genius," Occidental had become precariously leveraged, with a $1 billion debt, credit lines stretched as far as they would go, and a reputation so untrustworthy domestic banks refused to grant further loans. Armand's only option was to secure term loans with shorter maturity dates and higher interest rates from European banks. Even then he received a number of turndowns.

One London-based banker who was not put off by Occidental's lack of creditworthiness was thirty-nine-year-old Joseph Baird, the managing director and chief executive of an international banking consortium, Western American Bank (Europe) Ltd. Convinced that Baird had the skills to restore Occidental's fiscal credibility, Armand took his usual approach and set out to convince the banker that he had found a surrogate son who was destined to become Occidental's next chief executive and chairman. Then he offered Baird the presidency, and on November 5, 1973, Baird replaced the Hammer-Caverly-Watson troika and became Occidental's third chief operating officer in five years.

Unlike two of his predecessors, Tom Willers and Bill Bellano, who had successfully headed large industrial firms before they joined Occidental, Baird had no experience running a vast industrial complex. On his first day, he turned up dressed in a conservative, well-tailored English business suit. His behavior was as stiff and formal as his manner of dress. Rigid, headstrong, and easily agitated, he was not a likely candidate to achieve a working relationship with Hammer. But Armand needed Baird's financial acumen and decided to allow the banker to have his way.

As soon as the new president learned that Lehman Brothers had refused to handle a public offering because it did not trust Occidental's financial reports, he instituted a system of financial controls. Thus, Occidental was able to begin publishing accurate reports about its liquidity, asset management, debt management, and profitability. Faced with a $1 billion debt, Baird pacified the numerous banks to which Occidental owed money, stretched credit lines, floated preferred stock issues, and instituted lending and bond paydowns. As the debt-to-equity ratio began to improve, he was able to establish new lines of credit.

In order to improve overall effectiveness and reduce risk potential, Baird also initiated monthly management meetings and insisted that Armand hire professional management men. His most sensitive demand was to convert the annual report from what was an expensively produced, glossy tribute to Hammer's achievements to a document that contained a healthy dose of statistical information and reliable financial data about the company. Armand hated revealing anything to anybody, but again he acquiesced.

Ironically, as Occidental began to take on the semblance of a professionally managed corporation during the seventh year of Hammer's regime, Armand's personal finances had become a subject of public controversy. After a long and contentious IRS audit, he had been handed a bill for $800,000 in back taxes for 1965 and 1966, resulting from overvaluation, "mathematical errors," and a violation of the "charitable contributions" rule. Armand had been allowed a maximum deduction of $974,000, and had claimed $6.6 million.

One key issue was the deduction claimed by Armand when he donated his "second" art collection to USC in 1965. IRS agents had removed the paintings from the walls of Fisher Gallery and delivered them to a panel of art experts for appraisal. Armand had deducted $321,500 for six works in the group; the panel reduced that amount to $109,500. One of the jewels of the collection, *Venus Wounded by a Thorn,* had been attributed to Rubens. The panel clipped $30,000 from Hammer's $75,000 claim because it believed the painting was probably actually a product of Ruben's enormous workshop, and after the IRS examined Hammer's other art donations during the two years in question, it concluded that he had overstated the value of almost all of his gifts.

In response to the local front-page news stories about possible tax fraud, Armand ordered me to announce that he had "sent along a provenance from a renowned Rubens scholar, who said the Rubens was genuine." Subsequently, the press discovered that the appraisal had been based solely on a photograph supplied by Hammer and proceeded to print this suspect piece of information. "Our experts never see the paintings," joked Victor. "We pay them huge amounts of under-the-table money to make sure they don't."

Focusing on USC policy, the *Los Angeles Times* demanded to know why the university had failed to investigate the authenticity or market value of the art donations it received. As university officials began to look into these questions, their own staff members began to doubt the authenticity of other paintings in Hammer's collection and ordered that the paintings be placed in storage and exhibited only once a year.

Incensed, Armand insisted that he was going to fight the IRS, but whenever I brought up the subject, he brushed me off. His lawyers had advised him that challenging a decision about art overvaluation would get him nowhere because the IRS chose art experts with impeccable credentials. He eventually paid $267,000, which made him angry. He also never received the honorary doctorate that he had expected from USC, which made him even angrier, and he vowed revenge. "USC cheated me," he fumed. "I don't care how long it takes. I'm going to pay them back for this one. When they least expect it, I'm going to screw them a lot harder than they've screwed me."

. . .

At the beginning of March 1974, the Senate Finance Committee began to debate the Trade Reform Act of 1973. When Secretary of State Kissinger announced that he would recommend that President Nixon veto his own bill if Congress approved it with the Jackson amendment, Armand took Kissinger's ultimatum as a cue to set out for Washington to lobby the Finance Committee members. He had a harder time than usual because the Soviets' refusal to accept the conditions set forth by Jackson had triggered a barrage of other criticisms, especially the fear that after the Soviets formed major joint ventures with U.S. companies and financed them with multibillion-dollar long-term credits from the United States, there would be no reason for them to respect U.S. interests.

The most vitriolic criticism was leveled at the Export-Import Bank, which had used a 1972 blanket presidential order to grant $260 million in loans to the USSR over a two-year period, with $250 million more pending. It was argued that while the market interest rate was 10 percent, the Export-Import Bank charged 6 percent interest, which made the U.S. taxpayer the underwriter of a Soviet foreign aid program and a part guarantor against Soviet defaults. To quell its critics, the Export-Import Bank ordered the Soviets to follow the same procedure as other borrowing nations and make a full disclosure of their gold and monetary reserves. The Soviets stonewalled, which provoked further criticism.

On March 8, Congress's investigative arm, the General Accounting Office, demanded that each loan granted to the USSR in the future be subjected to an individual presidential review to decide if it was in the national interest. In response, the Export-Import Bank suspended all loans, pending clarification of the legal issue. Then, on March 23, the Export-Import Bank announced that it was operating within its legal rights and granted a $36 million loan for the design, engineering, and construction by Occidental of the international trade center in Moscow.

It was a victory for Armand, and he claimed full credit. Two days earlier the press had reported that one of the tapes submitted by President Nixon to the House Judiciary Committee was not "ambiguous," as Nixon had insisted. The next day Senator James Buckley had called for Nixon's resignation, and talk of impeachment was everywhere. In that context, Armand again insisted that the loan had been granted because "Nixon's got his hands full with Watergate and he's counting on me to hold détente together."

Another of Armand's friends in high places was having his own problems with the government. When David Karr testified before the SEC on a matter that had nothing to do with Occidental, he had managed to say for the record that Victor Hammer had confided to him that Armand had given Soviet Minister of Culture Yekaterina Furtseva a $100,000 bribe. In situations like these, Armand usually asked his lawyers to draft rebuttal letters and designated someone other than himself to sign them. Subsequently, *The New York Times* published a letter to the editor from Joe Baird, who discounted the charges and stated that they had been made by a "disgruntled former employee." It was a standard legal defense, but almost every employee who left Occidental was disgruntled and, in my experience, usually told the truth.

As a result of the publicity surrounding Karr's allegation, the Kremlin made Furtseva a token scapegoat to prove that it would not tolerate corruption. She was accused of daring to build a *third* dacha for herself at a cost of $160,000, demanding cut-rate construction prices at an $80,000 savings, and giving the dacha to her daughter as a gift in violation of party rules about the ownership of private property. Furtseva received an official reprimand and was ordered to reimburse $80,000 to the state. When she produced the money on short notice, it was taken as proof that she had found an illegal way to accumulate enormous wealth under the Communist system.

Furtseva was a well-known cultural figure, and the scandal was reported at length in the international press. It seemed inevitable that she was going to lose her ministry and her seat in the Supreme Soviet, but she didn't. "Brezhnev wanted to spare his government further embarrassment and he didn't want any more newspaper articles, so he let it drop," Armand explained with relief.

A short time later the Soviet government announced that Furtseva had died of a heart attack. Armand was so shocked he could barely talk. Victor was also taken aback, but his cynicism remained intact. "Armand knows they executed her to set an example," he told me. "He's convinced himself that he's upset about her death. But what he's really upset about is whether or not he's in trouble. She's far from the only minister he's bribed."

Scandal was also about to erupt around another of Armand's deals with the Soviets. According to the identical letters of endorsement signed by the Soviets and Commerce in June 1973, the Soviets had been guaranteed a $180 million Export-Import Bank loan to underwrite the Occidental-Soviet fertilizer pact, by far the largest loan yet made to the Soviets. Although this information had been leaked at the time, it had never been confirmed or denied officially, either by the Export-Import Bank or Occidental. Early in April, based on what appeared to be information obtained from sources close to Occidental's vast north-central Florida phosphate rock mines and chemicals complex, Florida Secretary of State Richard Stone concluded that the Occidental-Soviet fertilizer pact had become operational, a clear indication that the Export-Import Bank had made a secret loan guarantee to the Soviets.

Stone, who was planning to run for the Senate, sensed he was on the verge of uncovering a potent campaign issue. He contacted the Export-Import Bank and demanded that it make a full disclosure about the loan. Export-Import Bank President William Casey replied that he was more than willing to make public detailed information but Stone never heard another word about whether the bank had used the mutual letters of endorsement as the basis for approving the loan.

On April 26, the Senate Banking Committee held a hearing on its proposal to suspend further credits to the Soviets until after the congressional review of Export-Import Bank activities scheduled for June 30. Stone and Hammer were among those who testified, and Stone voiced a number of concerns, including his belief that the phosphatic material that Occidental was going to ship to the USSR was critical raw material that would be used by the Soviets to manufacture steel and explosives for military purposes. Armand's lawyers had drafted an eloquent response, and Armand used his appearance to deliver an urgent plea for world peace and the use of trade and credits to eliminate world hunger.

After the hearing Stone continued to hound the Export-Import Bank, but he got nowhere. Then Armand received a tip that the Florida official was about to hold a press conference and describe how the bank was stonewalling him. On May 21, Stone summoned reporters and told them that even though William Casey had promised to supply the facts about the loan, he subsequently said that the data could be made available only to the parties involved. Stone pointed out that the parties involved already knew the facts and demanded to know why a government-owned bank refused to reveal its transactions and insisted on conducting business with the USSR in secret.

The next day the Export-Import Bank announced that it had *just* granted the loan "to finance USSR purchases of goods," stating that the determining factor had been a recommendation in writing from President Nixon that it had received the day before. This maneuver, which reflected one of Hammer's favorite ploys, shifted the controversy away from the year-old secret approval of the loan to the loan itself, and the fact that it was a fait accompli and there was not much anyone could to about it.

A study of the information released by the Export-Import Bank confirmed the rumor that Occidental was supplying no financing except for necessary capital expenditures for the required fertilizer facilities in the United States, and the Soviets were supplying only 10 percent of the capital. Therefore, Occidental would suffer very small losses if the deal failed. Financial writer Elliot Janeway summed it up when he commented that Occidental had become "the U.S. government's chosen instrument . . . for doing business with Russia by giving Russia the money to do business with the U.S."

Nixon had written to the Export-Import Bank on the same day that Judge John Sirica had ordered him to turn over sixty-four tapes subpoenaed by Watergate Special Prosecutor Leon Jaworski. "With all of that amazing pressure on Nixon I don't know how Armand got him to do it," I commented to Victor.

He posed a rhetorical question: "Did you know that Maurice Stans asked Armand for another $250,000 right after the election?"

"Did he get it?" I asked.

"Despite Nixon's troubles," Victor replied, "isn't he giving Armand everything he's asked for?"

Just after Armand celebrated his seventy-sixth birthday on May 21, he arranged an exhibition of Soviet-owned paintings at the County Museum and funded a trustees' dinner in honor of himself. The museum provided a guide, Martha Kaufman, an attractive woman with radiant eyes and high cheekbones, and when I visited the exhibition, I was impressed by her knowledgeable presentation. I introduced myself, and Martha told me that she wrote for an airline flight magazine and asked if she could interview Armand about his art collection for a forthcoming article. Armand was always so hungry for attention, I was delighted. She did the interview, and when it appeared in print, Armand told me that he liked it. I assumed that was that, and I turned my attention to defending Occidental against a new barrage of criticism concerning its fertilizer pact with the Soviets.

William Stowasser, the most knowledgeable phosphate commodity specialist in the U.S. Bureau of Mines, had released a report that challenged Occidental's contention that it owned enough recoverable phosphate to fulfill its twenty-year commitment to the

Soviets. Stowasser pointed out that the Florida phosphate reserves had been mined heavily for years and would be depleted in the year 2000, which would force domestic farmers to turn to imported phosphates and produce a sharp increase in food prices. The GAO confirmed Stowasser's assertion and other respected mining engineers agreed that it was not in the national interest to trade phosphate rock in short supply for ammonia, potash, and urea that could be produced easily in the United States. Fearing the competition that would result when large amounts of cheap Soviet fertilizers were dumped on the United States market, domestic producers launched their own campaign against the barter agreement.

Armand used the new controversy as a platform to preach the benefits of détente. His slogan was "The U.S. must trade with the Soviets if we are to have peace" and he said it again and again. Simultaneously, the Kremlin did its own sloganeering and insisted that détente was "irreversible," had been forced on the United States by Soviet strength, and actually created "more favorable conditions" for Communism.

On June 19, after innumerable delays caused by Hammer's inability to deliver a final fertilizer agreement with the Soviets, NBC finally broadcast *The Russian Connection*. Hammer and his activities within the Kremlin remained the focus of Lucy Jarvis's documentary, but the scene that seemed to have the most resonance for viewers and TV critics had nothing to do with Moscow. It consisted of a meeting between Armand and J. Paul Getty, and Armand had begun his conversation by remarking, "Do you know what they're paying now for Nigerian oil? Fifteen dollars a barrel!"

Getty, eighty-two years old, became so excited that he wasn't able to talk and had wheezed with delight. John O'Conner of *The New York Times* commented that it was "worthy of a scene from Dickens."

Armand was annoyed because Edwin Newman's narration had alluded to the peculiarity of the Hammer family's business dealings with the USSR, the shadier aspects of some of his business activities, and his dictatorial rule of Occidental. It then dawned on him that he could hire his own film crew, which would enable him to maintain complete control over the finished product. He asked me to hire a free-lance film crew to travel to Moscow with him and film the long-awaited signing of the final fertilizer contracts on June 28. "NBC didn't have the patience, so they lost out on filming this historic moment," he told me. "But I never lose out on anything."

On his return he related that the signing ceremony had been "a very big moment in my life. From the time I was a young man, I've been deeply concerned about the crop shortage in the Soviet Union. Closing these deals will help the Soviets solve their food problems and will make a lot of money for us. This pact is going to go down as the greatest achievement of my career."

Unlike the signing of the protocol and the preliminary agreement, which had been spectacularly publicized, Armand did not want to exacerbate already inflamed public opinion and told me not to announce that Occidental had, after five years of hard work, achieved a done deal. I was also to downplay the fact that Occidental was gearing up to construct a huge ammonia plant at Togliatti, 550 miles southeast of Moscow; port terminals at Odessa and at Ventspils, Latvia; and pipelines and other essential facilities. Shortly thereafter, Armand received word from the Department of Defense that it was concerned that the deep-water ports Occidental planned to construct in the Soviet Union had the capability to dock Soviet nuclear submarines.

He was nonplussed. "I can't read blueprints. And even if I could, why would I build nuclear submarine ports? for Russia? And why would Mr. Brezhnev ask me to? I know him, and I know he's a man of peace. I can't believe anyone would think that he'd use Oxy to find a way to aim nuclear submarine missiles at the West."

A few days later, Armand asked me to set up a screening of the unedited footage shot during his Moscow journey. We sat together and watched as he and Frances were preparing to disembark at the end of the trip. A look crossed Hammer's face that I knew well. He wanted to be photographed getting off the plane alone. "Get out of my way," he yelled at Frances as he tried to push past his wife. Frances was so busy gathering up her possessions that she didn't seem to hear him, and he began to pantomime shoving motions in an attempt to get her moving. His anger seemed to make her nervous and actually slowed her down. His face contorted in rage, Armand bent close to her, screamed, "Get off the plane! Go! Go!" and began to hurl profanities at her.

Armand was angry at what he had just seen and heard, angry that it embarrassed him and angry that his embarrassment showed. He jumped up and yelled, "Take that damn scene out of the film and destroy it!"

On August 8, Nixon resigned the office of the presidency, and Vice President Gerald Ford became president. When reporters called Armand for his comments, Nixon was already out of his mind. "I'm hoping to meet with President Ford soon," he said, "so that I can encourage him to use the power of his office to eliminate tariff restrictions between the Soviets and the U.S. We should be bighearted enough to grant them MFN status. America can afford to make these moves. America is rich enough to pay the freight."

When the FBI interviewed Tim Babcock about his Nixon campaign "contribution," he told them that he had borrowed $54,000 from John Tigrett.

Subsequently, the Watergate Prosecution Task Force investigated Babcock's finances and raised questions about the methods he had used to obtain a loan from the Small Business Administration for his motel and convention center in Montana. Babcock was also aware that his Montanan friends had told the truth about the campaign contribution to the federal grand jury, and he decided that he would cooperate.

Babcock entered into a plea bargain, agreeing to tell the truth and to plead guilty in return for the charges being limited to the single misdemeanor of making a federal political contribution in the name of another person or persons. Babcock was under the assumption that he was going to be fined but would not receive a jail sentence.

On the witness stand Babcock admitted that he had concealed the identity of Hammer as the source of the illegal $54,000 contribution and that he had helped Hammer break the campaign contribution law. Because there was no paper trail and, therefore, no evidence, Armand's decision was to stonewall. In the belief that it boiled down to a question of whether he or Babcock had the greater credibility, his first move was to vilify Babcock to everyone within earshot. He called him a "jerk," a "horse's ass," and a "no-good lying bum." "Don't ever say that bastard's name to me again. I don't want to hear it."

As Armand had attempted in 1971 to provide the SEC with evidence that would discredit Walter Davis and paint him as a "disgruntled former employee," he now set out to discredit Babcock to the Watergate investigators. Unaware that Babcock's finances were already under examination after Babcock "resigned" from Occidental and returned to Montana, Armand hired a private investigator, Herbert Itkin, who had been supplied with a new identity by the Federal Witness Protection Program after testifying in a number of racketeering cases that resulted in the conviction of eighteen Mafia members. Itkin was dispatched to Montana, where he approached Babcock and pretended to be a potential buyer for his motel and convention center. Babcock later told me, "He went through my financial records and was able to find out a lot of things about my finances. He even had one of my 'puppet' companies audited." Eventually, the Watergate Special Prosecution Task Force would attempt to determine whether Hammer's actions had constituted an obstruction of justice.

The Watergate investigators had also received reports that some of the cash that had been contributed to CREEP might have been laundered through Switzerland and that the arrangement had been made by Marvin Watson and John Tigrett.

After John Tigrett invoked the Fifth Amendment and declared that he did not have to testify on the grounds of possible self-incrimination, Special Prosecutor Leon Jaworski asked for grants of immunity for Tigrett and James Patten, Occidental International's legal counsel.

Subsequently, the investigators approached Hammer's lawyers to discuss the possibility that he would have to stand trial.

On September 5, Washington newspapers reported that an inspection of Senate Watergate Committee files revealed "some uncertainty" about whether the actual cash involved in the donation by Babcock's friends had ever "touched the hands of the listed donors." The press seized upon this speculation and set out to locate Armand. Finally, a reporter got him on the phone and asked if he had become the subject of a probe.

"There's no truth to it," he replied, pretending utter ignorance. "You've really got me floored."

In mid-September, to my surprise, Armand hired Martha Kaufman and assigned her to my department. "I'll be her boss," he told me, "but you'll oversee her activities to make sure she does things right."

Martha was going to be in charge of the office art and work for the Armand Hammer Foundation. I chose not to remind Armand that there was no art in Occidental's offices. On September 23, Martha officially became a member of my PR department. My budget was going to provide $12,000 of her $18,000 yearly salary; the remainder would come from the foundation's budget. Two weeks later Armand granted Martha a $6,000 raise. Shortly thereafter, he raised her salary again, and then again. No one received a single raise, especially in such a short period of time, unless Armand believed the person had something essential to offer Occidental—or to him.

When I mentioned this to Victor, he asked, "What makes you think that Armand and Martha just met? Who do you think got Martha to volunteer to work for the County Museum in the first place?" I was genuinely surprised. Their "initial" meeting in Armand's office had seemed so spontaneous it was hard for me to accept that it might have been an acting job.

During the seventeen years that I had known Frances and Armand, his determination that the world perceive them as the perfect couple had never wavered. In public Frances remained a compulsively loyal caretaker and Armand was always sweet and chivalrous to her. When the world wasn't watching, however, he paid no attention to her. Often when I called him at home over a weekend, Frances told me that he was at the office. I never told her that I was calling from the office and that he wasn't there. Now the attention that Armand refused to give Frances seemed focused entirely on Martha. "Armand has never respected Frances because she's so nice," Victor explained, "but Martha's another story. Armand respects her because she's tough. She's the toughest woman he's met since he got involved with that Soviet bitch."

In short order Martha became Occidental's "director of corporate art," and began to curate and book tours for the Armand Hammer Collection. She also wrote articles about its many exhibitions for Occidental's corporate publication, *Oxy Today,* and produced a series of filmstrips about Hammer's other art activities. Armand found it necessary to send for her on a regular basis, and their conferences stretched on for hours behind his closed office door.

One day Martha confided that Armand "doesn't look important enough for such a legendary man. I hate his rumpled suits. I'm going to take him to the best tailor in L.A. and have him fitted for some smashing custom-made suits. Then I'm going to make him buy himself some wonderful new shirts, ties, and shoes. And I'm going to replace those awful glasses he wears with some elegant new frames."

Armand hated spending money, but he was determined to please Martha and plunged into his makeover with relish. After Martha insisted that he go on the Atkins diet, he lost thirty-five pounds. The next time he set out for Moscow, he took copies of *Dr. Atkins' Diet Revolution* with him and attempted to persuade the Soviet leadership to undertake the weight-reduction program Martha had established for him.

One day I found Martha removing a large painting from my

office wall. "The color scheme is wrong," she said. "I'm going to repaint it."

I insisted that the painting was fine the way it was and told her to put it back. She stared at me in disbelief. Determined to have her way, she ordered me to stand aside. We began to argue, and when she saw that I was going to stand firm, she began to yell. Then she burst into tears. When that didn't work, she launched into a full-blown tantrum. The painting remained unrepainted.

A few weeks later Martha raised her voice again. This time Armand was the object of her wrath. His office door was open, and not only I but also other executives listened as she dressed him down. Nobody ever dared shout at Armand, but Martha roared her disapproval at his decision-making process and administrative abilities. Everything about his "color scheme" was wrong, and she was determined to "repaint" it, too. Armand listened obediently, and when Martha was through, he giggled nervously like a guilty little boy.

Around the time that Martha came to work for Occidental, Julian was arrested after he took out a gun in a restaurant, dropped it, and whipped out another gun after a patron at the next table picked up the first gun and attempted to hand it to him. He was charged with displaying a gun in a threatening manner and subsequently was fined $200 and placed on two years' probation. The story was front-page news in Los Angeles, but Armand ignored it. I had not seen Julian since Armand had terminated him in 1967, and Armand never mentioned him. When I asked, Armand told me that he had been hospitalized, but that it had not done much good, if any. "He's forty-five years old," he said. "What can you do for a forty-five-year-old man? But it's not his fault. It's a case of bad genes on his mother's side."

At the end of fiscal 1974 Occidental was going to declare a record-breaking operating profit of $280 million on gross sales of $5.5 billion. Two-thirds of these earnings were derived from nonoil domestic operations, including the Hooker Chemicals Division, whose profit growth exceeded that of any other U.S. chemical company; the Island Creek Coal Division, which had become the most profitable U.S. coal company; and the exceptionally profitable Permian domestic oil marketing and transportation division.

Armand continued to believe that Occidental's entry into synthetic fuels was going to make its oil interests as profitable as its nonoil interests. Therefore, he couldn't resist announcing the construction of a full-scale commercial shale-oil production facility on a four-thousand-acre tract in the Colorado Rocky Mountains. When he saw how much positive publicity his announcement generated, he also announced that the research launched by Occidental in 1971 to convert garbage into synthetic fuel oil was on the verge of completion and that Occidental was about to build a demonstration plant that would convert two hundred tons of municipal garbage a day in San Diego, to be followed by the construction of other plants in Bridgeport, Connecticut, and Tokyo.

This startling news provoked an avalanche of phone calls. But I discovered the announcement was the usual Hammer hyperbole when executives at Occidental's Garrett Research and Development subsidiary confided that the garbage conversion project was "a small experiment then and it hasn't gotten much bigger."

A "very strange phone call" from the chairman of Standard Oil Company (Indiana), John Swearingen, came on the heels of these "news breaks." "Swearingen's coming to visit me tomorrow," Armand said. "He didn't tell me what he wanted, but he's not flying all the way from Chicago to pay a courtesy call."

Ever since the tanker lease debacle in 1972, there had been persistent rumors on Wall Street that Occidental was about to become the target of a takeover and Hammer spent the next few hours polling executives and concluding that a takeover was not the thing that was on Indiana's mind. Prompted by the energy crisis and the oil price explosion, Indiana and Gulf had jointly acquired a 5,000-acre tract containing an estimated 1.3 billion barrels of recoverable high-grade shale oil.

That, Armand decided, was the purpose of the surprise visit. "Swearingen either wants to discuss Oxy's highly publicized activities in the Soviet Union, propose a joint venture for Standard of Indiana's shale-oil tract, or make an offer to license our shale-oil extraction process. I'm going to fly our shale-oil guy in from Colorado so he can answer questions."

Swearingen was a distinguished-looking, graying, southern gentleman in his mid-fifties. Accompanying him was another man whom everyone assumed was his assistant. After Swearingen entered Armand's office, he patiently viewed a PR film about Occidental's shale-oil process. Then he asked Armand to excuse his shale-oil expert. According to Armand, Swearingen then explained that Indiana was already in the shale-oil business but wasn't in the coal business, and that Occidental owned one of the largest coal companies in the United States.

"Swearingen's smug and arrogant," Armand told me, "and he reminds me of Ken Jamieson. He said, 'I'd like to swap some Standard of Indiana shares for *all* of Occidental Petroleum's shares,' and proceeded to propose the terms of an acquisition that, if successful, would be the largest takeover in business history."

Indiana had offered to buy Occidental with Standard of Indiana stock at $17 per share—$3 more per share than the trading price on the New York Stock Exchange that day. Swearingen had also told Armand that Indiana would take responsibility for all of Occidental's preferred shares and that it planned to retain Occidental's key executives, including him.

"I was stunned," Armand said. "I knew the deal would allow me to make a personal profit of $21 million on my shares, but that wasn't the point. I leaned forward, pointed a finger at Swearingen, and said. 'I'll tell you what, John. I'd like to swap some Occidental shares for all of Standard of Indiana's shares!' Nobody's going to take over this company as long as I'm running it. This is war and I'm going to beat the pants off that bastard!"

Two hours after the meeting, Swearingen called Armand and said that SEC regulations required Indiana to issue a press release revealing that the two men had met and discussed a possible merger. The last thing Armand wanted was to have the Occidental shareholders learn about the offer and speculate that it might be profitable for them, and he did his best to convince the Indiana chairman that it was better for both parties if they simply forgot about the meeting. He got nowhere. "Swearingen said that because I had said that I was at least interested in discussing the merger, his company was obligated to obey the rules of disclosure. What bullshit! He just wants to get at our shareholders."

That same day Armand, the directors, and the lawyers decided to fight Indiana's plan by contending that a merger between the sixth-largest and the eleventh-largest U.S. oil companies could be considered a violation of antitrust laws because it would tend substantially to lessen competition. The position that Occidental was an underdog fighting for its life against a corporate giant would be used as the launching pad for an attack on all fronts, and Armand notified his Occidental International staff in Washington to start lobbying for an appearance before a Senate subcommittee that was investigating the business operations of domestic integrated oil companies.

Then he discovered that Swearingen's companion at the meeting had been not an assistant, but Robert Greenhill, an important executive with the large investment firm Morgan Stanley. "Morgan

Stanley is working on some real estate deals with us, and we have them under contract," he told me. "They have all this confidential information about us." In short order, Armand instructed his lawyers to sue Morgan Stanley.

On December 3, Occidental announced that it had filed suit against Indiana in U.S. District Court to prevent the proposed merger and was seeking an injunction based on the potential violation of antitrust laws to prevent Indiana from going ahead. Occidental also persuaded the FTC to investigate eight different potential antitrust violations that it had located in Indiana's merger plan.

That same day Swearingen and Hammer appeared before the Senate subcommittee. Swearingen was astonished by Occidental's lobbying efforts. Not only did the committee seem like an Occidental cheering section but it also asked questions that had been drafted by Occidental's staff. Armand's lawyers had provided him with an especially dramatic statement. He warned that if Occidental were to fall into the hands of Standard of Indiana, the American public would lose the largest independent oil company in the world and that Indiana's takeover attempt was nothing less than "an unprecedented challenge to the antitrust policies of the United States."

After the subcommittee referred the matter to the FTC, Swearingen, taken aback by the no-holds-barred ferocity of Hammer's attack, announced that Indiana would hold off while the antitrust agency studied the proposed merger.

In order to conduct discovery, Occidental subpoenaed Indiana's records but was bound by oath not to reveal anything that would be considered an unwarranted intrusion into its opponent's files. A battery of lawyers combed through Indiana's records around the clock, and they believed they had struck pay dirt when they located a report that outlined a plan to drive Chicago's independently owned gas stations out of business by building new gas stations next to them and selling Standard gas at ridiculously low prices.

Armand was thrilled. "This stuff is dynamite. It will bolster our claim to the Federal Trade Commission that Standard of Indiana has an established pattern of attempting to violate federal antitrust statutes. We're legally bound to keep this information a secret. But there's got to be a way to let it out."

A short time later FTC investigators began to search through the records of Occidental and Indiana. "I'll keep my fingers crossed," Armand said. "If they find that report about the gas stations, it will sink Swearingen!"

When the investigators arrived at Occidental, Armand sat with the investigators behind closed doors for about an hour, and before the day was over they had somehow located the document. In the future Armand would "explain" this occurrence by saying he had merely suggested that the investigators perform a careful search of Indiana's files that dealt with competition from independents but no one believed him.

In the six weeks since Swearingen had met with Hammer, Indiana had become the object of litigation by Occidental and the FTC and faced a potential Justice Department antitrust action regarding its plan to put independent gas retailers out of business. Therefore, it was understandable when Indiana announced that it had decided to abandon the merger proposal.

"I gave Swearingen exactly what he deserves," Armand rejoiced. Then he hired Joseph Flom of Skadden Arps to devise a plan to protect Occidental from any takeover attempts in the future. "Joe's the world's best lawyer when it comes to takeovers," he explained. "I've run down all of Oxy's vulnerabilities for him, and he's promised to find a way to cover our bases on each and every one. Trust me when I tell you that Joe is going to protect us. No one is ever going to try to take us over again!"

On January 31, 1975, after Tim Babcock had pleaded guilty to the single misdeameanor charge of making a federal political contribution in the name of another person or persons in federal district court in Washington, D.C., he returned for sentencing. U.S. District Judge George Hart Jr. began the proceedings by attacking Hammer from the bench and labeling him the principal villain in the scheme. Turning to Babcock, he said, "In your case it was not some untutored underling who had to dance to the tune of a boss. You are independently wealthy. You were decorated for bravery at Remagen bridgehead. You could have told Mr. Hammer that you had no intention of assisting him in breaking the law."

Judge Hart sentenced Babcock to a maximum one-year jail term, suspended eight months of the sentence, and ordered him to begin his four-month imprisonment at Lompoc, a penal institution in California, on March 3. He also fined Babcock $1,000.

Armand did his best to pretend that he was unconcerned, but his hands trembled when he told me, "I have better lawyers than Tim had. They've always kept me out of trouble before. There's no reason they can't do it again."

He didn't sound convinced.

20.

BREZHNEV DISAPPEARS FROM VIEW

On December 29, 1974, the Trade Reform Act of 1973 was voted into law. It retained the Jackson amendment but included additional language that would allow President Ford to grant nondiscriminatory tariffs and Export-Import Bank loans of not more than $300 million over a four-year period to the USSR. These qualifications were based on assurances Secretary of State Kissinger said he had received from Soviet Foreign Minister Andrei Gromkyo, guaranteeing that Soviet citizens who applied for exit visas would receive them without harassment.

Gromkyo denied agreeing to the linkage and other Soviet officials accused the United States of reneging on its two-year-old pledge to grant unconditional trade credits. At the same time Kremlin hard-liners attacked the principle of détente itself and insisted that it could never be allowed to impinge on the basic ideological contest between capitalism and Soviet socialism or weaken the resolve of Communist revolutionaries in the West and the Third World. On January 10, 1975, the Soviets nullified the agreement, leaving Ford with no option but to nullify the accord also.

The ceiling placed on the Export-Import Bank lending program meant that U.S. corporations had no choice but to beat a hasty retreat from the Soviet Union. But the Soviets knew that Armand would remain and would continue to be their staunch defender. They reinforced his allegiance by turning on the state-controlled publicity apparatus and launched a program to create a cult of personality around him. Eventually so many articles would appear in the Soviet press portraying Armand as a great man, a trusted American friend, a man of peace, a champion of U.S.-Soviet trade, and a leader in the war against reactionary forces that he would become even more famous in the USSR than he was in the United States.

As Lenin had allowed him to live in the Brown House in the 1920s, the Politburo gave him the rent-free use of a two-bedroom apartment on Kutuzovsky Prospect in a fashionable district that was close to the Kremlin and policed by KGB patrols, another sign that the Soviets valued the "Hammer connection." "It's plush by Soviet standards, but the apartment building is rather run-down," Frances told me. "The halls are lit by hanging light bulbs. And the rooms are rather small."

Armand never had any interest in his surroundings, but he knew the Soviets were fascinated by opulent displays of wealth. So he hired a team of high-priced West German interior decorators and craftspeople to turn the apartment into a showplace and decorated its walls with masterpieces from his art holdings. Every Occidental executive who visited it agreed that the results were stunning. Because it was bugged, Armand had to turn up the radio and the TV full blast during meetings. Some of the same executives who attended these meetings accompanied him to a meeting with Soviet Ambassador to the United States Anatoly Dobrynin in a Paris hotel room, where Dobrynin himself had turned up the radio and the TV before starting the conversation. Armand later admitted that he had originally learned the technique from the Soviets, who eavesdropped on each other with the same frequency that they eavesdropped on foreigners.

After more than two years of negotiation, Occidental, El Paso Natural Gas, and Tokyo Gas had signed a final agreement with the USSR to develop the natural-gas fields in Siberia. The financing had originally been going to include loans of $100 million each from the Export-Import Bank, the Export-Import Bank of Japan, and a consortium of private banks, but the ceiling placed on the Export-Import Bank lending program to the Soviets had scuttled the plan and Armand set out for Moscow to convince the Soviets that he would be able to locate alternative financing.

On his return he described a banquet that had been held in his honor in Leningrad. "The most important Soviet officials and Communist Party members were there," he boasted. "When I proposed a toast to the ideals that brought us together, everyone cheered. They jumped from their seats and ran to my table so they could clink my glass with theirs. The response was so emotional, I'll never forget it."

Yekaterina Furtseva's death did not deter Armand from persuading the Soviet Ministry of Culture to allow him to stage a new commercial for détente before U.S.–USSR relations soured completely. Permission was granted for Armand to sponsor a six-month American tour of forty-seven paintings, including distinguished works by Caravaggio, Cézanne, Fragonard, Gauguin, Gainsborough, Hals, Matisse, Picasso, Rembrandt, Rubens, Tiepolo, van Dyck, and Veronese that had never been seen in the West. Committed to an exchange of art as a symbol of détente, he arranged to have fifty-four paintings by American artists exhibited in the USSR at the same time, including fifteen paintings of American frontier life.

After President Ford declined Armand's request to write an introductory statement that would be included in the catalog for the forthcoming exhibitions alongside a statement from Leonid Brezhnev, Hammer demanded a meeting. He argued at length that Richard Nixon had supplied catalog copy for the prior tour, but the president refused to be budged. Subsequently the Occidental International staff told him that the Ford administration believed that détente had become a way for the Soviets to improve their economic position while attempting to erode the military effectiveness of the NATO countries. Ford was especially appalled when the Soviets dispatched twelve thousand Cuban troops to Angola and established a Marxist regime. From the president's point of view Hammer's art exchange boiled down to a pro-Soviet propaganda exercise designed to distract Americans from the determination of the Soviets to establish pro-Soviet Marxist dictatorships in the Third World.

Armand remained undeterred. Resolving to become the "number one" businessman in the East Bloc nations as well as in the Soviet Union, he began flying contingents of senior staffers to and from Poland, Hungary, Bulgaria, and especially Romania, where Occidental and the Romanian Ministry of Foreign Trade began to negotiate a coal sales agreement. There, Armand also made another new "best friend," Romanian President Nicolae Ceauşescu, whom he described as "a great leader, a fine, warmhearted man, and a humanitarian who loves his people and has compassion for them. That's why he's so easy to do business with."

Occidental executives kept to themselves their belief that going into business with these nations was not economically viable. For starters, before any deal could be completed, Occidental would have to secure a loan for the country in order to put it into business. Joe Baird was assigned the task of working out the financial arrangements. Thus, the president of Occidental Petroleum Corporation became a part-time loan officer for the East Bloc nations.

Armand could never have approached the East Bloc nations without obtaining the permission of Leonid Brezhnev. But the Soviet leader had disappeared from view on January 7 and had remained in seclusion for fifty-one days. During his absence reporters from all over the world called me to ask Hammer if he knew whether Brezhnev was seriously ill.

Armand was unusually frank when I broached the subject. "Brezhnev loves vodka, and he loves getting drunk," he told me. "He's a chain-smoker, and he needs to go on a diet. I've done my best to get him to curb these abuses, but he's got an addictive nature and it's very hard to get anywhere with him. Thankfully, his bad habits don't affect his intelligence, warmth, leadership abilities, and humanitarianism. Sober or drunk, he's a great man. If I close my eyes when I'm with him, it would be easy for me to believe that I was in the presence of Lenin."

"Is he sick?" I asked.

"Brezhnev is a major womanizer," Armand replied, and he has one or two beautiful mistresses in every Russian city. But his addictions have taken their toll, and he's been having a problem getting an erection, which has made him very upset. He's been in Romania at Dr. Ana Aslan's clinic undergoing rejuvenation therapy. Dr. Aslan has a wonder drug called Gerovital which she injects into you. It restores youth and vitality."

"Does it work?"

"I've just come from Romania," he replied. "I was there when Brezhnev was there. I know for a fact that it's helped him. If it's good enough for him, it's good enough for me."

Whether or not Armand had undertaken Dr. Aslan's treatment, he still maintained his appreciation for beautiful women and even though he was seventy-seven, an occasional frisky moment continued to crop up. A venerable show business legend, also in his mid-seventies, had recently accepted a dinner invitation from Armand, and Armand couldn't stop bragging about it. But for some reason the evening hadn't gone well, and when Armand wouldn't explain why, I asked Victor. He told me that after their dinner, Armand had taken the star to a tawdry Hollywood night spot to watch naked female mud wrestling.

"Armand really gets turned on by things like that," Victor said, "but his guest was embarrassed and wanted to leave. Then Armand dragged him to the house in Benedict Canyon, where several stunning hookers were waiting for them. One of the girls put her arms around the star, pressed close to him, and said, 'I'm yours, honey.' But he turned to Armand and said, 'Please take me home.' "

Victor began to laugh. "Armand told him not to worry because it was tax deductible and explained this was how he always entertained visiting Soviet ministers."

Around this same time, Armand ordered me to fire my mail clerk, and I demanded to know why. "You don't need to know the reason," he replied. "I know the reason. That's good enough."

A few days later he asked if the man was gone. I argued that the mail clerk was an excellent employee and had a wife and family to support and urged Armand to change his mind. "Not a chance," he said. "I *ordered* you to fire him. Now do it. He had better be gone by Friday."

I sat down with the employee and explained what I had to do and how bad it made me feel. He said he knew it was coming and told me why. After having made an arrangement with me to come in after lunch one day and make up the time by staying late, after everyone had left for the day, he had heard strange noises coming from Armand's office. Concerned, he had opened the door, and to his surprise had found Armand entertaining an attractive woman.

"Dr. Hammer began to yell real loud," the man said. "He accused me of being a Peeping Tom and said that if I told anybody about what was going on, he'd have me killed. He sounded like he meant it."

After California Secretary of State Jerry Brown swept the 1974 Democratic primary for governor with 46 percent of the vote Armand instantly became a supporter. He had originally met Brown through David Karr, who was serving as a key member of Brown's campaign team. But Armand and Karr had parted on acrimonious terms, and fearing that Karr would use his influence to turn Brown against him if Brown won the statehouse, Armand bombarded the candidate with a series of elaborate promises. "Jerry knows he's a shoo-in for governor, but what he wants more than anything is to be president," Armand told me. "I let him know that I'm going to use my resources to help him get the presidential nomination. Brown's also concerned about less polluting energy sources. So am I. That's another reason why we're going to be good friends."

During Brown's campaign, the State Court of California ordered Sam Yorty to testify under oath about his ownership of Occidental stock. Yorty's story that he had never owned any shares had undergone revision, and he had already admitted that he had purchased stock worth $10,000. Yorty testified that he had bought 3,000 shares of Occidental stock shortly after the proposal was made to swap city land for land owned by Occidental and that from 1966 to 1974 he had purchased stock valued, at times, at as much as $75,000. His subpoenaed stock records revealed seventy-three stock transactions involving Occidental stock purchased in the name of his deceased stockbroker, Sam Ungerleider. The first had been made in November 1965, around the time of the land swap. Over the former mayor's strong disclaimers, the committee declared that the cumulative transactions amounted to $500,000.

Reporters barraged me with calls to find out if Armand had provided inside information to Yorty, allowing the former mayor to trade on the basis of such information. Hammer waved aside the questions. "Sam was a great mayor. Why shouldn't he have had the chance to make a few bucks like everybody else?"

In March 1974, after Carlos Andrés Pérez's landslide victory in the Venezuelan presidential election, he demanded "emergency economic powers" and issued 211 economic decrees one after the other. Armand responded by firing John Ryan, vice president and general manager of Occidental's Venezuelan subsidiary. No reason for his termination was given to the public. Subsequently, Pérez established a Nationalization Commission to formulate the policy for the takeover of Venezuela's oil industry. Armand refused to discuss this development, but he did devise a strategy to get to Pérez. Just as Leonid Brezhnev had received two Lenin letters, he paved the way for a meeting with Pérez by sending him a statue of Venezuela's liberator, Simón Bolívar. An invitation to come to Miraflores, the presidential palace, arrived a short time later. "President Pérez was hospitable, warm, and friendly," Armand announced, predictably, on his return. "He not only understands South American matters but has a good grasp of world affairs. He even invited me to exhibit the Armand Hammer Collection in Caracas. Oxy has nothing to worry about in Venezuela, thanks to me."

The Venezuelan government inducted those who made signifi-

cant contributions to the country's cultural life into the Order of
Andrés Bello and Armand set out to convince the Pérez administration that the forthcoming exhibition of the Armand Hammer
Collection would help establish Caracas as an international cultural
capital, especially if Pérez personally decorated him with the state
honor at a major media event during the exhibition. But just before the Armand Hammer Collection left for Caracas at the beginning of March 1975, the Nationalization Commission presented its
findings to Pérez. Although a takeover was now imminent, Armand continued to pretend that everything was fine, and I was
reminded that he had also ignored the information passed to him
from his Libyan operatives that King Idris was going to be deposed. Not too long after Pérez pinned the Order of Andrés Bello
on him, a final version of a nationalization bill was sent to the
Venezuelan National Congress. The reality of what was about to
happen could be ignored no longer. "Those lousy bastards are
really going to do it!" Armand exclaimed. "The lug nuts in President Pérez's brain must have come loose!"

From the outset of his administration, Pérez had made it clear
that the oil companies were going to be compensated for the loss
of their holdings, but these reparations were not to exceed net
book value and would be paid in public debt bonds. At the beginning of May a government team began to negotiate the size of these
payments, and after rejecting Occidental's $42 million claim, the
negotiators offered $27.5 million.

Armand wouldn't hear of it. "Talk about a swindle. They're
trying to ream us. Our $72 million 'commercial' reimbursements
claim hasn't been paid yet, and we deserve $42 million in compen-
sation and not a penny less. They owe us a total of $114 million,
and they damn well better pay up, or we'll sue the hell out of
them."

But a new development was so explosive that it held the potential
of providing Pérez with the perfect opportunity to cancel all payments to Occidental. Former Occidental Venezuelan general manager John Ryan, who now was practicing law in Houston, filed a
$1.5 million employment suit in the Texas State Court against
Occidental, Hammer, Occidental's Latin American operations
manager, David Martin, Hammer's Venezuelan consultant, John
Askew, and Askew's drilling firm, Perforaciones Altamar. Ryan
claimed that the defendants had formed a dummy company in the
Bahamas, Noark Ltd., paid $3 million into Noark's Panamanian
bank account, and allowed Askew to use the money for bribes,

campaign contributions, and payoffs so that Occidental could obtain its Venezuelan service contracts. Ryan also charged that after the contracts had been awarded, the defendants had received kickbacks from drilling contractors, oil service operators, and suppliers and had participated in a conspiracy to hide their illegalities, and that after the reform-minded Pérez had become president, Ryan had attempted to halt these practices and was fired. Another former executive in Occidental's Venezuela office, J.A. Kauffman, also filed bribery and kickback charges similar to Ryan's.

Armand was determined to bring a quick end to the financial deliberations with the Venezuelans in order to collect as much money as possible before the charges became public knowledge. To gain time, Occidental's lawyers claimed that the Texas State Court had no jurisdiction over Hammer. It was a weak shot, and Armand knew it.

The allegations in the Ryan suit did not escape the SEC, and Armand was notified that the federal investigators were beginning a preliminary investigation into Occidental's overseas financial practices in order to determine if it really had placed $3 million into a Bahamian dummy corporation and violated the rules of disclosure by keeping the deposit a secret. Hammer was instructed to fill out a questionnaire and hand over Occidental's payment records to foreign countries beginning on January 1, 1969. Armand feared the investigation of Ryan's charges would inevitably halt Occidental's attempt to salvage a portion of its Venezuelan investment. His reaction was vehement, if predictable. "Ryan is a disgruntled former employee out for vengeance," he said to me. "The fact that the SEC is taking him seriously proves they're still out to get me. I've signed two consent decrees, and it's gotten me nowhere. This time I'm not giving them a thing. I'm going to have the lawyers file for an extension."

The impending Venezuelan nationalization, Ryan's lawsuit, and the reappearance of the SEC all made Armand angry; the next thing that happened filled him with dread. On May 14, Maurice Stans pleaded guilty to five misdemeanor violations of the federal election finance laws, which included the late reporting of contributions made through Tim Babcock. In his defense, Stans stated that the late reporting had occurred after he had solicited Hammer for a contribution on March 30, 1972, which directly contradicted Armand's written response on the Watergate Special Prosecution Task Force questionnaire that Stans had never solicited him for a campaign contribution.

Born in 1898, Armand Hammer was five years old by the time his family had moved from a tenement on the Lower East Side to a large house in the Bronx. Armand's father, Julius, launched a medical practice from his new home and buried his assets before declaring bankruptcy for a chain of drugstores he owned.

1

Despite this demonstration of Mama Rose's maternal affection for Armand (right) and his older half-brother Harry (left), all three Hammer sons were dispatched from home to live with other families when they were growing up.

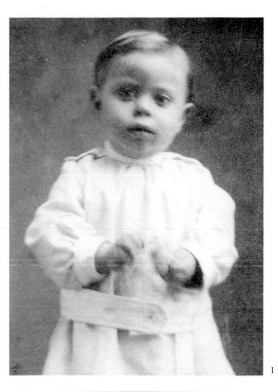

2

To comrade Armand Hammer
from N. Oulianoff (Lenin)
10. XI. 1921.
В. Ленин

Lenin never signed autographs for "capitalist imperialists" but he honored Armand's request because he viewed him as a "comrade," and rewarded him with potentially lucrative business concessions to induce other foreign capitalists to invest in the USSR.

▼ **At 23, a graduate of** Columbia University College of Physicians and Surgeons and already a rich man from a business in drugs, Armand (center) claimed he didn't know a soul when he arrived in Moscow in 1921. In reality, he was surrounded by family friends, employees, and important Bolshevik officials who eagerly welcomed the young entrepreneur.

5

▲ **Armand disembarking in New** York on June 13, 1922, after his second trip to the USSR. Living in Moscow in grand style during the 1920s, he would make another fortune doing business with the Soviets. It was revealed seventy years later that he was also acting as a courier for the Comintern.

◄ **Armand wanted to divorce** his vivacious Russian wife, Olga, before he left Moscow permanently in 1930. But the Soviets demanded that he bring her to America where she could serve, ostensibly, as an OGPU intelligence agent. Armand virtually abandoned Olga and their young son, Julian, and they eventually divorced.

► **Victor, Armand's younger** brother and loyal business associate, with his Russian wife, Vavara. Their seven-year marriage ended abruptly in 1929 when Victor learned of Vavara's infidelity.

6

7

Mama Rose and Julius during a return visit to Moscow in 1932. By this time, Julius, a doctor, an entrepreneur, and one of the founders of the American Communist Party, had served a two-and-a-half-year jail sentence in Sing Sing for first-degree manslaughter after performing a fatal illegal abortion, and had also been jailed in Germany for fraud.

9

▲ **Viewing marriage as a business** proposition, Armand used funds he acquired from his mercurial second wife, Angela Zevely (second from left with Armand, Mama Rose, and Julius), to build a multimillion-dollar cattle breeding business. Their marriage ended in a widely publicized and very messy divorce.

▶ **Victor's second wife, Ireene** Wicker, radio's fabled "Singing Lady," who was blacklisted because she had married into "the aristocracy of the Communist leadership." Her career was destroyed when Armand ordered her not to respond to the accusations. He did not want the House Un-American Activities Committee to learn that he still had secret business ties to the Soviets.

10

11

Armand (left) with his third wife, millionairess Frances Tolman (sec- ond from left), at a family reunion with (from right to left) Victor, Harry, Ireene, and Mama Rose. They all smiled for the camera, but family relationships were tense and often hostile.

12

Armand made it his business to court politicians—and anyone else— who could do him favors. Senator Albert Gore, Sr., (left, with his wife, Pauline, and their children, Nancy and Albert Jr.) became a close friend and business associate, and was rewarded when he left office with a highly paid executive position at Occidental.

◀ **Armand assumed the** presidency in 1957 after he invested (partly with his wife's money) in the nearly bankrupt Occidental Petroleum Corporation as a tax shelter. With tireless energy, ingenuity, determination—and not a little guile—he would build Oxy into the sixteenth largest industrial company in America.

13

▶ **Soviet General Secretary** Nikita Khrushchev autographed this photograph: "To Mr. A. Hammer, the first concessionaire who conferred with V. I. Lenin." After Stalin's death, Armand was welcomed back into the inner circles of Soviet power as a useful contact with the West.

14

15

Armand and Frances stationed on the balcony of the New York Stock Exchange on March 2, 1964, the day Oxy was listed on the Big Board for the first time. Armand still had to prove that his company was a good investment, and that he was a capable manager.

◀ **Armand wanted his only** son Julian (36 years old when this photograph was taken), to follow in his footsteps. It didn't work out. Nor did any of Armand's other plans for a rudderless, moody, and unpredictable young man who often carried a gun and more than once used it, or threatened to.

16

▶ **Armand was just** as eager to ingratiate himself with American presidents as with Soviet premiers. But Lyndon Johnson refused to hold this meeting until he became a lame duck president and saw no political danger from the encounter.

To Dr. Armand Hammer
With best wishes,

17

Little Oxy made the big time when it struck oil in Libya. Armand spent $1 million to celebrate the triumph, rolling out the red carpet for King Idris I and walking proudly by his side.

It took an international publicity stunt and a $100,000 campaign contri-bution before President Richard Nixon consented to meet with Armand. The contribution would later embroil Armand in the Watergate scandal.

20

Armand adored "tough mommies," especially Soviet Minister of Cul-ture Yekaterina Furtseva who together with Armand arranged a number of art exhibitions as cultural exchanges between America and the Soviet Union. She suffered "a fatal heart attack" when Victor (left) revealed that Armand had slipped her a $100,000 bribe.

Terrified of going to jail, Ar-mand spent six weeks hiding in a hospital "on the verge of death" before pleading guilty to violations of the federal campaign contributions law during the Nixon re-election campaign. When he did not receive a jail sentence and was sure no one was looking, he hopped out of his wheelchair and danced a jig.

21

The two "Comrade Chairmen" of the USSR, Armand and Leonid Brezhnev. Armand held more meetings with the Soviet general secretary than any other foreigner, and Brezhnev confided to him that he was suffering from impotence.

22

23

Oxy's next big oil strike occurred in Venezuela, and Armand was pho-tographed with his "good friend" President Carlos Andrés Pérez. When the country's oil industry was nationalized, Pérez accused Hammer of bribery to obtain oil concessions, and Oxy became the only foreign oil company in Venezuela to go uncompensated.

24

Carl Blumay (second from left) was always at Armand's side when something important happened, including the arrival of Rembrandt's *Juno* at Los Angeles International Airport. Martha Wade Kaufman (left) was employed as Occidental's Curator of Art and also served Armand in a number of other ways.

23

Armand viewed Jimmy Carter as his most successful presidential con-
quest and liked to boast that it had taken him only eleven months to put
Carter in his pocket.

26

As part of his business dealings with the Communist countries of the Eastern bloc, Armand supported Romanian president Nicolae Ceauşescu declaring that he was a "gentle man who cares only for his people." In 1989, Ceauşescu and his wife, Elena, found guilty of genocide and gross abuse of power, were shot to death by a firing squad.

27

In his latest brush with the law, Julian Hammer (foreground) was ar-rested on suspicion of assault with a deadly weapon. He pleaded no contest to a lesser charge, and subsequently his long police record mysteriously vanished.

28

Armand took the Armand Hammer Collection around America and the
world year after year in order to drum up publicity for himself and make
new business and social contacts. Here Armand and *Juno* are on the road
in Cincinnati in 1981.

The dramatic unveiling of Columbia University's Health Sciences Cen-
ter, toward which Armand contributed $5 million (ABOVE). In return, he
demanded that the building bear his and his father's names. He also
insisted that he receive an honorary law degree, and he did (BELOW).

◀ **Armand and another** "good friend," Vice-Party Chairman Deng Xiaoping, met in China's Great Hall of the People in 1982. Armand's multimillion-dollar deals with the Communist countries were money losers and his activities in China played havoc with Deng's economy.

▼ **Palm Beach was aghast** when it learned that Armand's black-tie gala for the Prince and Princess of Wales was, in fact, in honor of himself and a fund-raiser for his United World College, a cause Armand had promised to support entirely by himself.

33

Never shy when publicity was favorable, Armand kept an unusually low profile during two of Occidental's most horrendous disasters: Love Canal (ABOVE) and the explosion of a North Sea oil platform that caused the deaths of 167 workers (BELOW).

34

◀ **Armand buttonholed Mikhail** Gorbachev at a State Department luncheon during the December 1987 summit. In his relentless pursuit of the new Soviet leader, Armand turned up unannounced with Barbara Walters during Raisa Gorbachev's tour of the National Gallery of Art.

▼ **Armand never received** more than grudging recognition from President Ronald Reagan, who discredited his efforts on behalf of the Soviet government as propaganda and refused to grant Armand a presidential pardon for his 1976 conviction. The pardon was finally granted by President George Bush.

35

36

37

Armand, Ireene, Frances, and Victor standing in front of *Oxy One*,
Armand's private jet. Armand kept a file on Victor's finances and would
claim his estate after his brother died. Legal challenges to Armand's
handling of his wife's estate are still unresolved.

38

Armand appointed a new and improved Hilary Gibson (a.k.a. Martha
Wade Kaufman) as a director and spokesperson for the Armand Hammer Museum of Art and Cultural Center. Occidental shareholders were
outraged at the cost of the museum, and critics called it a monument to
Armand's vanity.

Armand and Frances with Armand's grandchildren, Casey and Mi-
chael Armand. Armand was grooming Michael to take his place, but
thirteen months after his death, Occidental's board gave Michael $1.5
million in severance pay and he resigned his post as the company's
corporate secretary. The board also embarked on a lengthy campaign
to restore the company's fiscal stability and remove the last traces of
Armand Hammer.

40

Millionaire businessman, art patron, philanthropist, friend of the rich and famous, confidant of world leaders, and international peacemaker. "There has never been anyone like me," Armand Hammer declared. "And my likes will never be seen again."

Armand was filled with foreboding. "They fined Maurice five thousand dollars, but he could have gotten five years," he said. "If they can sentence an innocent guy like Maurice, they can stick it to me, too. At least he got off easier than Tim Babcock. Tim's going to Lompoc. That prison is even worse than Sing Sing, where they sent my father."

The annual meeting, scheduled for May 21, Armand's seventy-seventh birthday, was only a week away, but he was too nervous and unfocused to discuss it. Fearing that he might be unable to chair it successfully, I installed a button at the lectern that signaled the sound engineer to cut off the shareholders' floor microphones. In this way Armand could silence any shareholder who confused or upset him and call on someone else. In the middle of the week, Armand sent me to New York on an assignment. After I arrived, he called me at one in the morning to ask what I was doing there. On my return Frances confided that Armand had made her go with him to Lompoc so that he could see his "new home."

Just before the annual meeting, Armand received advance copies of Bob Considine's *The Remarkable Life of Dr. Armand Hammer*, and his depression lifted. He piled huge stacks of the book in his office, and word spread that he wanted every employee to request a signed copy. Office guests were also handed one automatically, signed with a flourish by Armand, whether they wanted it or not.

Flattering endorsements from Armand's influential friends, including Louis Nizer, Walter Cronkite, and Senator Mike Mansfield, formed part of the extensive advertising campaign created to promote and sell the book. And for the most part the reviews were positive. A review in *The New York Times* described Hammer as "a twentieth century phenomenon . . . a character so versatile and unbelievable most writers would be embarrassed to put him in a novel." Armand insisted that the book was absolutely true in every way. But one critic wrote that he had neither given President Roosevelt the idea for Lend-Lease nor received an appointment from President Kennedy to be a roving economic emissary. In response, Armand called Jimmy Roosevelt and got him to write a letter saying that, based on his firsthand experiences with his father and Kennedy, he was able to confirm that every word in *The Remarkable Life of Dr. Armand Hammer* was completely accurate.

Armand urged me to use the book to generate even more publicity for him and his life story. After the favorable *Times* review, it seemed probable that civic and business organizations would be eager to hear from the "twentieth century phenomenon," and I used the book to launch Armand as a public speaker. While I was busy booking engagements, Armand made his own list and traded financial donations for other "invitations." Each appearance became a carefully planned publicity event with a healthy dose of advance promotion and full press coverage of his talk. The fact that he was holding off the Watergate Special Prosecution Task Force and the SEC and attempting to close the Venezuelan negotiations and suppress the news of the lawsuit in Houston did not deter Armand from setting off to lecture about his most beloved topic: himself.

Around this time "The One-Man Flying Multi-International," a two-part profile of Hammer by journalist and author Daniel Yergin, appeared in *Atlantic Monthly*. Unlike Considine, Yergin was not on the payroll and he maintained his objectivity. Acknowledging that Hammer's grandfatherly charm was overwhelming, Yergin was more impressed by his dazzling, daring entrepreneurship and the fact that after reaching the age of retirement he had transformed Occidental from a tax shelter into a multibillion-dollar multinational corporation.

Yergin described Hammer accurately and a little sadly as "the last of a line, a privateer from the past, an anachronism, a patriarchal grain merchant from nineteenth century Odessa who has learned to sell everything. . . . Forty years ago, he might have succeeded in establishing a great Hammer empire, Carnegie or Rockefeller style, but today, in an age of multinational corporations, that is no longer possible and when he is gone from Occidental, Occidental will change, or even disappear, for it certainly will be bureaucratized, and perhaps another company will take it over."

The metaphor of Hammer as twentieth-century Yankee trader had appeared once before, in an article in *The New York Times*. Armand did share a lot in common with Cornelius Vanderbilt, the first Yankee trader to amass a vast industrial fortune. Both operated entirely off their hunches, possessed enormous energy and crafty minds, lacked a conscience, had no respect for the law, ran their business operations without regard to controls and systems, and were just as aggressive and competitive in their seventies as they had been fifty years before.

If Vanderbilt was the first in a line, Yergin was right: Armand was the last.

At the end of August, after three months of getting nowhere, the SEC announced the beginning of a formal investigation of Occidental. "I don't care. I'm not giving them a thing," Armand repeated.

He was all set to travel to Moscow to attend the international trade center ground-breaking ceremony on September 1, when he caught the flu. "This is one of my biggest disappointments," he complained. "I got the Soviets to allow me—not one of them—to lay the cornerstone." Incapable of allowing himself to be ignored, he reached for straws and insisted that I make an official announcement that he had "disclosed" the news that the trade center facilities would include an eighteen-hole championship golf course. But I did not announce that the trade center construction costs had escalated from $110 million to $180 million over the past two years and that he was desperately searching for a way to obtain an additional $28 million loan from the Export-Import Bank to pay for the overrides.

As Armand was recuperating in bed and U.S. Ambassador to the Soviet Union Walter Stoessel was laying the cornerstone in his place, two years of relative calm evaporated in Libya when the Libyans arbitrarily reduced Occidental's daily production levels from 513,000 barrels to 210,000 and demanded another tax increase. Simultaneously, in an obvious act of contrariness and spite, Libya raised the production levels of two other companies.

Claiming damages of $1 billion, Occidental filed for international arbitration in the International Court of Justice and suspended oil royalty and tax payments to Libya. "They've singled us out," Armand grumbled. "It's an illegal and disgusting act of malice. All of Qaddafi's talk about freeing the oppressed masses and obeying the Moslem Koran—it's bullshit! No matter what Qaddafi says, the only thing he cares about is money, and the only way to bring him to his knees is by not paying him."

A few days later Armand marched into my office and tossed a book onto my desk. *Making Democracy Safe for Oil* by Christopher Rand was an insider's account of the international oil business containing two chapters about Occidental's activities in Libya. In *The Remarkable Life of Dr. Armand Hammer,* Bob Considine had portrayed the Libyan adventure as a "colossal coup"; Rand contended that Occidental had obtained its concessions through bribery, reneged on promises to the Libyans, overproduced its oil fields, and underwritten its vaunted Kufra Oasis project with Libyan funds.

The last thing Armand wanted to see in print was accusations of bribery at a time when similar information about Occidental's Venezuelan activities was undergoing discovery in Texas and the SEC was investigating Occidental's overseas financial practices. Rand's accusation that Bechtel supervisor John McGuire's life had been threatened after he became a whistle-blower made him even more upset. "Deny everything he says, especially the death threat crap," he told me. "Do everything you can to discredit him. I'm going to call the lawyers. If there's a way to drown this bastard in litigation, I'll find it."

After the Libyans shut down company production and shipment facilities, ignored the arbitration notices arriving from the International Court of Justice, and pumped the oil from Occidental's huge storage tanks and sold it directly, they were served with court orders to bar illegal confiscation. They responded with a declaration that none of Occidental's non-Libyan employees, their wives, or their children would be allowed to leave the country. Armand immediately wrote to President Ford and Secretary of State Kissinger, advising them that the Libyan government had taken 520 hostages. The travel ban was lifted after the Libyans received a firm warning from the State Department.

After Occidental witheld payment for four months, the Libyans caved in. "Oxy owes them $440 million, but the entire book value of our Libyan assets is $272 million. They couldn't live with the fact that they'd accidentally given us full compensation *and* a $168 million profit," Armand explained. "I told them that Oxy would pay them the $168 million but that we were going to take the remaining $272 million and deposit it in banks outside of Libya to protect Oxy against further nationalization or any more illegal seizures. They're not ready to nationalize our forty-nine percent share, and they couldn't wait to get their hands on the $168 million, so they agreed. For once, we beat them at their own game."

Armand's ability to reverse course never failed to astonish me. "Carl, I've got something to tell you," he announced. "I did give Tim Babcock another $54,000 to contribute to the Nixon reelection campaign. He was hurting financially, so I bet he used the money and then replaced it later. I never knew that he turned it in months after the deadline. Then he tried to put the blame on me by claiming that he helped me make an illegal contribution. That miserable knucklehead has no conscience. I trusted him, and that sneaky jerk did me in."

The senior executives of the company listened blank-faced as Armand repeated this story. Finally one said, "You follow through on the smallest detail and check up on everybody and everything.

Why didn't you check up on whether or not Babcock made the delivery?"

"You know how much I've got on my mind these days," Armand replied. "I can't think of everything. Haven't *you* got any work to do?"

The reason why Armand had admitted the "truth" became clear when he made a second admission. His ten-month secret negotiation with the Watergate investigators was nearing a conclusion, a trial was imminent, and he was planning to plead guilty to violating the campaign contribution disclosure law and face possible criminal prosecution. "Those lousy bastards have given me two choices," he complained bitterly, "plead guilty now or await further indictments by the federal grand jury. Both stink to high heaven. I've hired Edward Bennett Williams, the best trial lawyer in the United States. He pointed out that the new grand jury indictments are going to be felonies, not misdemeanors, and will carry a much stiffer sentence. So I've made a pretrial agreement to go to court on October first and plead guilty. In return, the charges are being limited to misdemeanors."

Despite the pretrial agreement, the idea of making a court appearance was so terrifying for Armand that he ordered Edward Bennett Williams to petition Watergate Special Prosecutor Thomas McBride to claim that he had a serious heart condition and should not undergo the rigors of standing trial. This claim astonished the staff; Armand seemed to be in terrific shape. The special prosecutor shared our astonishment and wondered out loud where such a fragile man found the stamina to fly all over the world and maintain such a hectic schedule. After Williams continued to insist that Hammer was too ill to appear, the prosecutor's office assigned a physician to examine him and Armand was given a clean bill of health.

On September 26, the Venezuelan Ministry of Mines and Hydrocarbons unexpectedly overruled the national oil company, declaring that Occidental's Block E was producing a "commercial" amount of oil and granting a reimbursement of $27.6 million. Armand was so upset by the fact that he had to stand trial in five days that he barely responded to the news of this victory.

On October 1, as he reluctantly approached the federal district courthouse in Washington, D.C., accompanied by Edward Bennett Williams and Louis Nizer, TV news reporters surrounded him. One asked if he was Armand Hammer.

"No," he replied.

Inside the courtoom, Hammer stood erect before U.S. District Judge William Jones and listened intently as the charges were read: three misdemeanor counts of having violated federal campaign laws by making campaign donations in the names of other persons and illegally disguising the fact that he was the actual donor. His voice quavered as he admitted that he had given false answers on the Senate Watergate Committee questionnaire. Then he pleaded guilty to each count.

Judge Jones explained that the maximum penalty for each count was one year in prison, a $1,000 fine, or both. He asked if Hammer understood clearly that the consequences of his plea included the possibility of receiving the maximum sentence, three years' confinement and a $3,000 fine.

It was a routine question, and everyone expected a routine reply. But Armand said, "I am advised by my counsel that while the statute so says, the maximum will be a fine." This burst of legalese took Judge Jones by surprise. He repeated his request. "You have got to tell me you understand that this court could sentence you to a maximum of three years in prison and assess a three-thousand-dollar fine."

"I am advised by my counsel that while the statute so says, the maximum will be a fine," Armand repeated.

Judge Jones asked the question a third time, and Armand made the same response. The judge tried again, and after another round or two, Jones, pounding his fist on the bench for emphasis, shouted, "If I can't get an affirmative answer, I cannot accept his guilty plea!" and threatened to throw the case out of court.

The judge called a thirty-minute recess, suggested that Hammer and Williams use the time to confer, and left the courtroom. The one thing Williams did not want was to leave Hammer vulnerable to new indictments by the federal grand jury, and he took the position that Armand's surprise response had failed and that he had no choice but to abide by his pretrial agreement and go through the formality of entering a guilty plea without reservation. Armand was adamant about not admitting publicly that he understood that he could be imprisoned. As they argued back and forth, their voices grew so loud the sergeant at arms ordered them to quiet down. Finally, Williams threatened to withdraw from the case then and there and leave Hammer without counsel.

As soon as the court session resumed, Judge Jones repeated the question and Armand mumbled a meek, almost inaudible, "Yes, sir."

The judge accepted his plea, released Armand without bond, and explained that he was not going to impose sentence until after he had studied the probation department's presentence report. He instructed Armand to report to the probation department so that a probation officer could be assigned, and adjourned the court.

The first thing Armand did when he returned to Los Angeles was to order the board of directors to announce that it had complete confidence in his integrity and leadership. The purpose of this was twofold: to counter the HAMMER PLEADS GUILTY headlines that were breaking out across the nation and to discourage the shareholders from demanding his resignation because they believed that he might be going to jail, which would leave the company without a chief executive.

Over the years Armand had remained convinced that Eleanor Roosevelt's testimony on his behalf during one of his disputes with the IRS had proved a valuable aid, and now he contacted every famous person he knew and urged them all to write to Judge Jones. "So far he's heard from Bob Hope, Henry Ford II, Lowell Thomas, Rabbi Edgar Magnin, William Simon, Dr. Norman Vincent Peale, Arthur Ochs Sulzberger, Lady Bird Johnson, Mayor Bradley, and Cardinal McIntyre," he said proudly as he went over his checklist. One hundred letters eventually would arrive at the courthouse, each praising Hammer and recommending leniency.

From the moment Armand pleaded guilty I had been deluged with requests from the press to talk to him. My policy was to keep him under wraps. When I got a call from a *New York Times* reporter toward the end of the week, I assumed that he wanted to speak to Hammer for the same reason every other reporter did, but I was wrong. Somehow the *Times* had gotten hold of the discovery documents that were emerging from the John Ryan suit in Houston and learned about the second whistle-blower and his accusations that he knew of two bribes of $5,000 each that had been paid to Venezuelan legislators in July 1970, that the money had been described as "down payments," and that an important Occidental official had stated that from twelve to eighteen Venezuelan legislators had received payoffs. The *Times* was about to print the story and wanted Armand's reaction. We prepared a statement that called the charges "groundless, preposterous, and absurd" and classified Ryan as a "disgruntled former employee." Then Armand himself got on the phone and read the statement to the *Times*.

On October 9, exactly a week after he pleaded guilty to making illegal campaign contributions, the *Times* broke the story of Ryan's lawsuit under the headline HAMMER ACCUSED OF FOREIGN BRIBES. Coming so close on the heels of the news stories about his guilty plea, this account of Ryan's charges that Hammer had laundered $3 million through the Bahamas and Panama in order to bribe Venezuelan officials created another furor.

As Hammer suspected, President Pérez used these accusations to demonstrate how much corruption had existed under the prior regime and how quickly he could deal with it. The same day the story appeared, he called an emergency meeting of his cabinet. When it was over, he announced a halt to negotiations with Occidental, ordered a congressional investigation, and directed his Justice Department to take whatever actions were necessary to determine whether criminal charges should be pressed.

Armand huddled with his lawyers and then wired Pérez the personal message that "neither Occidental Petroleum Corporation nor I have ever tried to make illegal payments, either to Venezuelan officials or [to] legislators." He also volunteered to fly to Caracas and make himself available to help in the investigation. Two days later the Pérez administration announced that it was going to pay the nationalized companies $1.1 billion in compensation, but that Occidental would be the one company to be excluded from the plan. This painful and embarrassing blow was compounded by the fact that Occidental was also not going to be allowed to obtain any of the lucrative technical assistance and oil supply contracts that the Venezuelans planned to negotiate with the other companies in order to provide an uninterrupted flow of crude to market.

Armand had his own interpretation of these events. "Many of the Venezuelan officials come from poor backgrounds," he told me. "It's affected the way they think, and they're perpetually confused. That's why they're able to call themselves a democracy and then nationalize the oil companies just like some banana republic. When they saw how much money they owed us, they decided to accuse Oxy of bribery and keep the money for themselves. Underneath it all they're a dishonest, greedy bunch of crooks who are not above violating their own constitution and breaking their own laws. We'll take this thing to court down there, if necessary, and I know we'll be cleared of these dumb charges."

I pointed out that reporters were going to ask why Occidental was the only victim of trumped-up charges.

Armand always had an answer. "Some of the politicians and government officials dislike us more than they dislike the others. that's why."

A few days later, the SEC responded to the *Times* article by subpoenaing Occidental's financial records and demanding an interview with Hammer. More determined than ever to convince President Pérez that the bribery charges were unfounded and that Occidental deserved to collect its compensation and "commercial" payments, Armand was equally determined not to give the SEC information that could be used to confirm Ryan's allegations. Requesting another postponement, Occidental argued that before it turned over any documents it required a written agreement from the regulators that the information would be kept confidential. Otherwise, any disclosures might prejudice the Venezuelan government during its investigation. The SEC turned down the petition, explaining that the terms suggested by Occidental would violate either agency rules or the Freedom of Information Act. In turn, Occidental filed an appeal.

Occidental's problems in Venezuela were compounded by the resignation of CVP chief Carlos Carnevali Rangel. Even though Rangel denied that he was resigning in protest over the decision of the Ministry of Mines and Hydrocarbons to overrule the national oil company and award Occidental a $27.6 million "commercial" reimbursement, his denial succeeded in provoking embarrassing questions about the ministry's decision. The day after Rangel resigned, the Pérez administration ordered Armand to fulfill his promise to travel to Caracas and testify. After Armand's lawyers warned him that there was the possibility that he might be arrested once he got there, word was sent to the Venezuelans that Hammer's "severe angina" prohibited him from traveling. The claim was supported with a physician's affidavit. The Venezuelans announced that they had no alternative but to send a group of congressional investigators to Los Angeles and question Hammer there. Armand's lawyers responded that he was too sick to testify anywhere, and the Venezuelans finally agreed to have him supply written answers under oath.

Of the many problems Armand faced at this time, the one that concerned him the most remained his admission to Judge Jones that he understood he could be imprisoned and the distinct possibility that he could be jailed. Again, his belief that he knew better than anybody what was best led him to take matters into his own hands.

On October 27, while his probation officer, James Walker, was in the midst of preparing his report for Judge Jones, Armand wrote a twenty-page letter to Walker declaring that he was "the victim, not the principal. . . . [Tim Babcock] was not my agent. I was not his principal in these acts." Babcock had testified that Hammer had delivered the $54,000 to him on September 6, 1972; in his letter Armand contended that he had gone to his bank vault on April 3, 1972, four days before the legal cutoff, removed the money, and turned it over for delivery that day. "My bank records, which have been examined by the special prosecutor, show that I visited my safe deposit box on April 3, 1972."

Babcock maintained that he was not in Los Angeles but in Helena, Montana, on April 3, and had witnesses. Hammer wrote; "Since Babcock is a pilot, it is conceivable that he could have flown into L.A. and back without using a commercial airline. . . . What motive could I have had not to give my entire contribution before April 7, 1972? No one suggests that I didn't have the funds to make the payment. My net worth is substantially in excess of $20 million. . . . It is difficult to think of any reason why I should want to hold on to $54,000 in cash for five additional months at the risk of breaking the law."

After explaining that he had been advised by counsel that the special prosecutor had intended to indict him if he did not enter a plea of guilty, he added that he had decided to follow this instruction because of "the possibility of a failure of memory . . . my age, the serious disease from which I suffer and the danger that the strain of a criminal trial might result in my death. . . . I am convinced that the ordeal of a trial or the pronouncement of serving a jail sentence could provoke a massive, crippling heart attack or be fatal to me."

Edward Bennett Williams urged Armand not to send the letter, but Williams had advised him to make the public acknowledgment that he could go to jail, which Armand considered a near-fatal mistake. Therefore, he replied that he *was* going to send it. Williams concluded that he could not continue to represent Armand and was replaced by Armand's two most trusted legal advisers, Louis Nizer and Arthur Groman. Armand mailed the letter, and a probation-report hearing was scheduled for December 12.

The letter was not the only tactic Armand employed to prove his innocence. After Occidental's legal counsel Bob Rose had "resigned" in 1966, he had run into Armand in Tripoli, and Armand had gone out of his way to ignore him. That had been their last encounter. Suddenly, from out of nowhere, Rose received a call from Hammer. "I understand John King of King Resources has been on your yacht," Armand said. "Do you remember the date?"

Rose replied that the visit had occurred sometime in 1970.

"Did Tim Babcock come aboard that day?"

Babcock had never been on Rose's boat.

"That's not the way I heard it," Armand said. "You, John King, and Tim were on the boat together in *1972*. Tim handed you a paper bag with money in it. It was the money that eventually was delivered to the Nixon reelection campaign."

Rose denied the story, but Armand was not going to be dissuaded. He repeated the story. "Babcock either gave the money to John King to give to you or gave it directly to you to deliver to the Nixon people."

Finally, Armand convinced Rose to meet with a private investigator he had hired to look into the campaign contribution matter. About a half hour later the investigator called and set up a meeting. And as Rose sat there, the stranger tried repeatedly to get him to admit that he had accepted the money from Babcock.

"Why don't you do me a favor and do one for yourself at the same time?" he said suggestively. "Look carefully through your records again and see if you can't refresh your memory about what actually did happen." The investigator stared at Rose. "And keep this in mind: Dr. Hammer can be *very* generous, especially to those who are willing to search their memories on his behalf."

"Honesty and truth demanded that I not avail myself of Hammer's 'generosity,' " Rose later told me. "And even if I was the kind of person who was inclined to accept it, what could he have given me that would be worth a ruined career, a ruined reputation, and a ruined life?"

Whatever slings and arrows were aimed at me at Occidental, I could always count on Virginia, my wife of thirty years, and our three children, five grandchildren, and happy home. Or so I thought.

One night Virginia told me gently that she had decided to leave me and was also planning to ask for a divorce. "You never stop working," she said. "You're on call all day, every day, around the clock. I have to get all these dramas out of my life. The only way you're going to be able to see if it's possible for you to live without Armand and all of the drama that goes with him, and whether you want to, is by my leaving."

Just a few nights before, Armand had called at 2:30 A.M., kept me on the phone for forty minutes, then called back an hour later for another long conversation. The next night I had received five separate calls from him between midnight and 6 A.M. Naturally, after Virginia left, Armand kept calling. In the past I'd been able to hash these calls over with her. Now, there was no one to talk to.

21.

THE PERIL OF DEATH

On December 11, the SEC filed a motion in federal district court asking that Occidental be required to comply with its investigation. Its application stated that "the testimony sought from Hammer and the documents called for by the subpoena relate to information which Hammer and Occidental may have regarding falsification of Occidental's corporate records and the disbursement of millions of dollars to foreign government officials in connection with the acquisition of foreign business. . . . It is the belief of the staff that Hammer is the only person to have knowledge of Occidental's operations. . . . He and he alone has the first hand knowledge of what, if anything, was paid to government officials to obtain business for Occidental."

The next morning Armand was in Washington for his probation-report hearing. Judge Jones began by telling him that his letter to his probation officer raised serious questions about "the validity" of his "earlier admission of guilt." He explained that Armand's assertion of innocence and his claim that the sole reason he had agreed to plead guilty was poor health implied that had he been in good health, he would have pleaded not guilty. Therefore, the only conclusion that could be reached was that he had lied when he entered the guilty plea. The judge looked piercingly at Hammer. "I withdraw the defendant's guilty pleas, and I enter a plea of not guilty for him on all of the misdeameanor counts in the original charge."

Now Armand was vulnerable to new federal grand jury indictments, the last thing Arthur Groman and Louis Nizer wanted to see happen. Groman approached the bench and explained that the letter was merely "the outpouring of the heart of a troubled man" and urged the judge to let the guilty plea stand. Otherwise, the continuing strain of the proceedings "could very easily lead to a catastrophic effect—a major heart attack or fatality. This is no capital offense," Groman pleaded. "Dr. Hammer should not be exposed to the peril of death!"

Jones remained expressionless, so the attorney tried even harder. "The mere pronouncement of sentence could produce a fatal result!" And to reinforce the point that Armand was seriously ill, he asked permission to have him examined by a renowned Los Angeles cardiologist, H. J. C. Swan, M.D.

"If this court wants a cardiologist," Judge Jones said, "it will call its own."

Nizer attempted to take up the cause, but Jones stopped him dead in his tracks. "I only hear one counsel at a time."

Groman's next move was to request that Hammer be sentenced immediately. The judge refused, explaining that his withdrawal of Armand's plea had left him and the new Watergate special prosecutor, Charles Ruff, unprepared to go to trial. He instructed Armand's lawyers to let him know over the next five days when they would be ready, adding that he hoped to hold the trial in three weeks' time.

Armand was fuming. "Who does that damn judge think he is? He implied that I was a liar. I thought my letter presented my case logically and convincingly. It should have impressed him, not made him mad. Actually, I think he's showing off. He's merely using me to get publicity for himself."

A day or two later newly filed court documents revealed that Ruff was planning to seek a new federal grand jury indictment against Hammer and that he was going to be charged with two felonies, which carried the threat of a substantially longer prison term. Groman and Nizer made a direct appeal to Ruff to help them get Judge Jones to reverse his ruling so that Armand could reenter his guilty plea, arguing that Armand should not be treated like an ordinary criminal because he was a famous man with failing health.

Ruff replied that Hammer's fame was "irrelevant. Any citizen who is the subject of an indictment suffers embarrassment, tensions, and anxiety. Criminal justice must be evenhanded. It cannot treat the famous in one way and the unknown in another."

On December 16, Groman and Nizer faced Federal District Judge John Pratt at a hearing in Washington, D.C., about Occidental's noncompliance with the SEC subpoena, while Hammer and another team of lawyers were in Los Angeles responding to the set of questions that had just been delivered to them by three visiting Venezuelan congressmen.

Judge Pratt, noting that the regulators had spent seven months attempting to obtain the pertinent documents and to take Hammer's testimony, accused Occidental of stonewalling. Even though Hammer had appeared before Judge Jones in Washington four days earlier, Groman described him as a frail old man who lived only a few blocks from his office, arrived for work late in the morning, went home for lunch, and napped in the afternoon. He argued that Hammer was so sick that he should not be forced to submit to questioning by the SEC. A series of medical affidavits confirmed that Hammer had a serious heart condition and could suffer congestive heart failure, a heart attack, or cardiac arrest at any time.

Pratt replied that Armand was a highly publicized industrialist who made continual trips overseas and ran a multibillion-dollar multinational corporation. "Hammer can't be as sick as the doctors say he is and maintain this hectic schedule. It's just contrary to fact."

Groman continued to argue the point, but the judge dismissed his arguments with a wave of his hand. "Okay, let's assume that Hammer has a serious heart disease as you say. Like all of us, he is going to die someday. Every breath he takes is one breath less. It may happen to him a little sooner."

Groman noted that the Venezuelan committee that was currently investigating Occidental was accepting written answers from Hammer that very day and requested that the SEC also submit questions in writing. "I can't believe that the Securities and Exchange Commission is less humane than the Venezuelan committee."

"It's very difficult to frame interrogatories to cover the waterfront. There are too many follow-up questions," Judge Pratt replied, going on to note that if Hammer was permitted to respond to written questions, "he will have the advice of his legal counsel standing by him with respect to every word he writes."

The judge ordered Occidental to turn over the requested documents to the SEC by December 31, 1975, and Hammer to submit to an oral interrogation before the end of January 1976. Meanwhile, in Los Angeles, under oath, Armand denied in writing having any personal knowledge of any wrongdoing by Occidental or himself in Venezuela. In response to questions about John Askew, the purported briber, he explained that Askew had been paid $3 million as a consultant's fee.

The Venezuelan congressmen were accompanied by a press officer who told me he was working out of the Venezuelan consulate in San Francisco. The next day I issued a news release with the headline OCCIDENTAL CHAIRMAN DENIES BRIBERY CHARGES BY OCCIDENTAL IN VENEZUELA UNDER OATH. My Venezuelan colleague announced that the committee had conducted a vigorous examination of Hammer. Later that day we spoke on the phone, joked about the self-serving nature of so many of our PR efforts, and began a dialogue that would stretch on for years.

My announcement prompted a number of reporters to call for a set of Hammer's answers. I replied that they were the property of the government of Venezuela and could be obtained only from Venezuelan officials. It was my hunch that the reporters weren't going to take that additional step, and I was glad when they didn't.

The Venezuelan interrogation behind them, Armand and his lawyers turned to the problem of how to deal with the SEC and began submitting the requested financial documents. They also told the regulators that the main thrust of Occidental's response was going to be the creation of "an internal audit committee" consisting of three outside directors. After this committee conducted a thorough investigation of Occidental's overseas payment practices, its findings would be reported to the federal agency. Nowhere was it mentioned that each of the three outside directors who were going to serve on the committee was a close friend of Hammer's.

On December 18 the Watergate special prosecutor's office sent word to Judge Jones that it was ready to prosecute Hammer. Groman and Nizer responded by filing an appeal in the U.S. District Court of Appeals, asking for a reversal of Jones's decision to withdraw Hammer's guilty pleas. A hearing before the three appeals judges was scheduled for January 20, 1976.

On December 31, while Venezuelan air force jet fighters flew overhead, army cannons fired a military salute, and a military band struck up the Venezuelan national anthem, President Pérez hoisted the Venezuelan flag on the site of the nation's first commercial oil well in Zulia state. The ceremony marked the complete government takeover of the most sophisticated petroleum complex in Latin and South America. The same day Occidental wrote off its total $73.4 million Venezuelan investment and its $33.3 million Nigerian investment. The justification for the Venezuelan write-off was that Occidental's interests in its service contracts terminated on December 31, 1975; the Nigerian losses were attributed to a failure to produce a commercial amount of oil. Whenever a reporter asked if the bribery charges were the reason for the Venezuelan write-off, I replied, "No. Our lease expired."

Armand was philosophical. "We got fleeced in Venezuela, but that's the way it goes in the oil business. You've just got to keep forging ahead to bigger and bigger things. If you stop, you die."

A few days after the nationalization ceremony, Pérez announced that the congressional investigating committee had discovered that Occidental had bribed Alberto Flores Ortega, Venezuela's governor to OPEC and director of the petroleum economics department of the Ministry of Mines and Hydrocarbons. In return, Ortega had used his influence to overrule CVP and obtain a commercial reimbursement for Occidental. The evidence consisted of a canceled check in the amount of $106,400 that had been drawn on a Nassau bank and paid to Ortega's father, which Pérez displayed on national TV. Ortega was recalled from Iran and forced to resign in disgrace.

The Venezuelan congressional committee turned next to Armand's relationship with John Askew and when the Venezuelan press began to print leaks about Askew's relationship to Occidental, I had to field calls asking for more information. Armand wanted to reveal nothing, but something had to be said. So Occidental released a statement on January 15 that refuted the bribery charges for a second time. If anything, reporters became even more determined to learn more about Askew. Four days later, under increasing pressure from the news media, I suggested that Occidental announce that Armand had hired a "consultant" and paid him an "override royalty."

Armand agreed but was so determined to maintain Occidental's innocence that he refused to allow me to include Askew's name even though it had appeared in newspapers all over the world. Nor would he authorize the release of the amounts that Occidental had paid to its "consultant." "If worse comes to worst," he said, "we can always say later that the consultant sold a portion of his override back to Occidental for $3 million."

I cautioned him that the release of this information would encourage reporters to ask if any of the $3 million could have been used for bribes. Armand bristled. "But we *didn't* authorize anybody to pay bribes. We've *never* authorized anybody to pay bribes. As long as I'm alive, deny any charge of bribery whenever you hear it, and never stop denying it."

I don't know whether Armand repeated these assertions when

he satisfied Judge Pratt's order to submit to an interview by the SEC before the end of January. He refused to discuss the session. Nor did he want anyone to know that during this appearance he was attached to heart-monitoring equipment and that the SEC had been warned that if he suffered a heart attack during the proceedings, the U.S. government was going to be held responsible.

On January 20, the day that Groman and Nizer were scheduled to present their arguments before the U.S. District Court of Appeals, Watergate Special Prosecutor Ruff intensified the pressure by announcing that he was ready to ask the federal grand jury to indict Hammer on two felony charges in addition to the two misdemeanor charges. Groman and Nizer met with Ruff and came to an agreement that if Armand withdrew the letter to his probation officer and reentered his guilty pleas, the special prosecutor would be willing to drop the felony counts and abide by the original plea-bargain arrangement.

At the appeals hearing Nizer insisted that Hammer's volatile letter had never been intended to be a repudiation of his guilty plea and he and Groman assured the court that Hammer would disavow and withdraw his letter to his probation officer and comply with his pretrial agreement. In return Ruff confirmed the arrangement that he had worked out with Hammer's lawyers. Relieved, Nizer commented that Armand would be willing to fly to Washington "within the next three days" to reaffirm his guilty plea under oath "if it could be set up."

Noting that "this is the longest, most drawn out plea of guilty I have ever seen," Appeals Judge Roger Robb remanded the case to Judge Jones and instructed him to reconsider the sincerity of Hammer's plea. Nizer was wary, expressing his concern about whether Jones would be likely to treat Armand fairly as a result of the many problems that had occurred in his courtroom. But the appeals court refused to alter its decision.

Later that day Armand called from home with an astonishing piece of news. "Everyone thought the big problem was going to be Judge Jones," he said. "But he's decided to recuse himself. They didn't even use a revolving wheel to pick the new judge. Jones really wanted to get me, so he turned the case over to Judge Hart, the guy who sent Tim Babcock to jail. Hart has already condemned me from the bench as a villain, a schemer, and a manipulator. He *really* has it in for me!"

The next day Judge Jones announced officially that Armand's case had been "protracted" and that a backlog of cases and various other duties had forced him to recuse himself and assign the case to Judge George L. Hart, Jr. Hart immediately announced that he had decided to take Nizer at his word when he told the appeals court that Armand would be willing to come to Washington "within three days" and ordered Hammer to appear in two days' time, on January 23.

On January 23, Nizer and Groman appeared before Judge Hart, but Armand wasn't there. The lawyers told Hart that on the afternoon of the 20th, Hammer had begun to experience shortness of breath and chest pains, had gone to see his family doctor, Rexford Kennamer, and that Kennamer had decided to admit Hammer to Cedars of Lebanon Hospital after his condition worsened. According to Kennamer's affidavit, Hammer was diagnosed as suffering from "congestive heart failure, preinfarction angina, and disturbance of the cardiac rhythm." Groman submitted his own affidavit, which confirmed the events and told the judge that Hammer was going to remain in the hospital for at least two weeks, making it impossible to say when he would be well enough to make the trip to Washington.

Judge Hart observed that it was a situation that could repeat itself and therefore it was essential to obtain expert information about Hammer's medical condition. He ordered Hammer's lawyers and Ruff to choose two of the best cardiologists in Washington to go to L.A. to examine Hammer.

Then Nizer turned to the issue that Hammer and his lawyers considered the most crucial: the fact that Hart had demonstrated bias against Hammer by castigating him from the bench. Convinced that Hart could not be impartial, Nizer demanded that the jurist remove himself from the case. He further stated that Hart had been improperly assigned because judicial replacements were supposed to be chosen at random from a revolving wheel and not handpicked by a chief judge. "I have a duty to see that judge shopping is not permitted," Hart replied, "and I will therefore not disqualify myself from the case."

At first Nizer hinted that he might appeal Hart's decision not to remove himself, then he tried another tack. He proposed that the case be moved to Los Angeles so that Hammer could be "spared the necessity of having to travel." This would remove the case from Hart's jurisdiction. The request was also rejected, and the only thing left for Nizer to do was to work with Ruff to choose the doctors who would examine Hammer.

The minute the story of Hammer's illness became public knowledge, a number of reporters called and expressed their disbelief. To make sure the press did not have an opportunity to make its own observations, I kept the name of the hospital secret. And to discourage eyewitness accounts, Hammer was allowed no visitors.

During the next week Armand ran Occidental from his hospital bed. Executives memoed him continually and received speedy replies. Whenever he called me, he sounded fine and on top of everything. Usually, when I called him, I got a busy signal and I left a message with the floor nurse. One day she remarked that Armand "was the busiest patient they'd ever had." Frances concurred. "He's running me ragged. The only thing he wants to eat are corned beef sandwiches. I'm always on the run to the deli."

"That's some diet for a man with a serious heart condition," I remarked.

Frances laughed, and so did I. It seemed nobody believed that Armand was seriously ill, but no one was going to voice that opinion out loud.

In 1974 Armand had assigned free-lance PR man Curley Harris the task of getting him onto the cover of *Time*. After attempting to convince *Time*'s editorial board that Armand deserved to be on the cover, I had gotten nowhere and Harris didn't have any luck either. "The doctor's tried so hard for so long, he's annoyed the hell out of the editors," Harris told me. "They're never going to give it to him."

The January 1976 cover of *Time* saluted the 1975 Man of the Year: "Women of the Year," twelve prominent American women. Armand was stricken. "Curley promised that he could get me on the cover of *Time*, and he hasn't. And now, *Time* has started to choose *women* to be man of the year. That makes my odds even worse. Why didn't Curley stop them?" Harris "resigned" after Armand terminated him from his hospital bed.

On January 29, Ross Fletcher and George Kesler, the two court-appointed physicians, filed their report with Judge Hart. After reading it the judge disclosed that Hammer was "under close medical surveillance" to prevent a heart attack, that the court-appointed doctors had determined he would be incapacitated for at least another six to eight weeks, and that a decision would be made within the week as to whether Hammer would have to undergo heart surgery. The doctors had also recommended that the case be transferred to Los Angeles and Kesler had submitted his own plea that Hart move quickly to resolve the matter because the stress was proving so injurious to Hammer.

Victor confided that Armand really had had symptoms of heart trouble over the years but had insisted on defying them and keeping them secret. "Armand's natural sense of drama allows him to seem a great deal sicker than he really is," he told me. "If he can put himself to sleep at will and wake up exactly when he wants to, you can imagine how good he is at making himself look like he's at death's door.

"He was betting on the fact that no doctor was going to put a seventy-seven-year-old man with chest pains and shortness of breath into an even more stressful situation. Suppose the doctors said he was medically fit and then Armand went to court and dropped dead while he was there? Think of the malpractice suits that would be slapped on those doctors. They were never going to take that kind of a chance."

On February 5, 1976, fifteen days after Armand was admitted to Cedars of Lebanon Hospital, Judge Hart followed in Judge Jones's footsteps and washed his hands of the case by agreeing to its transfer to Los Angeles. But Armand was not going to climb out of that hospital bed until a Los Angeles judge ruled that he did not have to go to jail.

Unlike the procedure that had been used in Washington to pick Hammer's judge, a revolving wheel was used in Los Angeles, and Lawrence Lydick, a jurist known for his stern approach and insistence on upholding the letter of the law, was the "winner." Explaining that Hammer's already threatened life would be placed in even greater danger if he were forced to make a court appearance, Nizer and Groman filed a petition requesting that Judge Lydick try the case at Hammer's bedside.

Judge Lydick scheduled a hearing on February 23 so that the attorneys could present their arguments. Groman's two witnesses, Armand's personal cardiologists, H. J. C. Swan and Ross Kennamer, testified that Armand was so sick he had only just begun to sit up and become strong enough to walk to the bathroom, adding that Hammer's concern about the trial was so stressful that he was taking phenobarbital in addition to his heart medication and that this stress was so injurious to his health, it was essential that the case be disposed of quickly. Finally, Lydick was asked to hold a special court session in the hospital at Hammer's bedside. The judge refused. Their testimony took more than an hour, and when it was over, Groman added that Hammer's condition was "irreversible and progressive." He, too, urged Lydick to move quickly.

If the purpose of the testimony was to place the judge into the position of having to decide whether to impose a jail sentence on someone who was confined to a hospital sickbed and could suffer a heart attack at any moment, it backfired. Judge Lydick maintained that the validity of a plea depended on the ability of the defendant to enter the plea "knowledgeably, voluntarily, and with full awareness of the consequences." Therefore, if Hammer's condition was as grave as had been stated, he had strong reservations about the legal validity of accepting a plea. The judge emphasized his point by declaring that the description of Hammer's enormous anxiety constituted sufficient grounds to declare that he was suffering from duress, and, therefore, incapable of making rational judgments. But psychiatrists, not cardiologists, the judge continued, were the only medical practitioners qualified to render medical opinions about the mental health of a patient. For that reason, before the decision could be made about whether to allow Hammer to reenter his plea, he had decided to order a new medical evaluation to determine Hammer's physical, mental, and emotional competency. Until he received that evaluation, he had no choice but to postpone the proceedings "indefinitely."

Groman replied that a competency hearing had to be scheduled *immediately*. But Lydick wasn't so sure; it might be better to wait until Hammer improved—or didn't. Even though the doctors had spent an hour attempting to convince the judge to try Armand in the hospital because he was too sick to be moved, they changed their minds on the spot and chimed in that if Armand was attached to portable heart-monitoring equipment, he could be taken to the courthouse in a wheelchair immediately. Lydick ignored them, ordered a new probation report and said that sentencing would follow shortly after he received it.

After the hearing, reporters bombarded me with questions about the doctors' testimony. They pointed out that the standard procedure for heart conditions, even the most severe, involved medication and a modified, supervised exercise program so that the heart muscles wouldn't atrophy. Therefore, they didn't understand why Armand had been kept in bed for thirty-three days and wanted to know if he was even sicker than had been reported or if the court was being fed a cock-and-bull story. I ducked the issue by replying that Armand was receiving excellent medical care and every effort was being made to get him well enough to make a court appearance.

A few days later the court was informed that Hammer's doctors believed he had improved sufficiently to appear in court. If that was the case, Judge Lydick responded, he saw no reason for a medical evaluation. Instead he would question Hammer from the bench and make his own determination about whether he was capable of entering a plea voluntarily. The court appearance was set for March 6, twelve days after Armand's two doctors and two lawyers had pleaded that he might die on the spot if he had to leave his hospital bed. What the press had to see was a man with a heart condition so severe that he had been hospitalized and bedridden for six weeks. And Lydick had to see a man who, even though he could die at any second, possessed the competence and self-control to be able believably to admit to breaking the law.

On March 6, Armand, flanked by two bodyguards, was wheeled from Cedars of Lebanon Hospital to a station wagon parked at the curb. He was dressed in one of his old, baggy pre—Atkins-diet gray suits. Because he had lost thirty-five pounds, he looked like a shriveled gnome. While he was lifted into the vehicle, guards surrounded him so that no photographs could be taken. Security guards again secured his way as he was wheeled into the courthouse. In the courtroom a team of cardiologists hovered over him as they attached him to portable heart monitors operated by radio telemetry. The equipment would be monitored in a small witness chamber off the courtroom.

Judge Lydick was unfazed by all of the activity and drama. His tone was severe as he asked Armand if he understood that by entering a plea of guilty he was giving up his constitutional rights to a trial. Armand replied affirmatively in a firm voice. The judge asked him if he agreed to withdraw the letter he had written to his first probation officer.

"Yes, sir."

He was asked if he comprehended the gravity of his plea and its consequences—a maximum of three years in prison, a $3,000 fine, or both.

"Yes, sir."

Judge Lydick allowed the first misdemeanor charge to be read, and Hammer pleaded guilty. After the reading of the second charge, he entered another plea of guilty. After the third, he entered his last guilty plea.

When the judge asked him to explain why he had chosen to enter these pleas, Armand replied that although he was concerned about the situation, he was "pleading guilty because I am guilty and not to avoid a trial."

While it was assumed that Armand would have to make two

court appearances, one to reenter his guilty pleas and the other to receive sentencing, there was hope that Lydick would sentence him directly after he entered his pleas. That hope was dashed when the judge announced that he would set a date for sentencing after he received and reviewed the new probation report, which had not yet arrived.

Twenty minutes after Armand's arrival in the courtroom, he was wheeled back onto the street, lifted from the wheelchair, helped into the station wagon, and taken back to the hospital, where there was nothing for him to do but wait. Two weeks later Judge Lydick announced that he had read the probation report and that sentencing was scheduled for March 24. By then Armand had been hospitalized for three months.

Armand's appearance at his sentencing duplicated his appearance to reenter his pleas. Wired up and sitting limply in his wheelchair, his medical staff in attendance, he looked sicker than ever. Speaking on behalf of his client, Groman began a methodical summary of the case, concentrating on Armand's medical problems and providing a blow-by-blow outline of his physical deterioration over the six months since he had made his first appearance in Judge Jones's courtroom. Repeatedly he reminded the bench that Hammer was suffering from a serious heart ailment that could easily lead to a fatal heart attack—if he were sentenced to prison.

While the attorney droned on, Judge Lydick began to fidget, and he ordered Groman to bring his argument to a conclusion. But this was Groman's last chance, and he refused to stop. Finally, Judge Lydick said sharply, "Look. I do not intend to impose a prison sentence on a man who is seventy-seven years old, and all you can do if you keep this up is talk me into it."

Armand suddenly sat up straight in his wheelchair, and his eyes lit up. Groman, also surprised, rapidly ended his arguments by telling the court that Hammer's actions had not been motivated by evil intent and that his fine record of public service demanded that he receive a monetary fine and no more.

The judge asked Hammer to speak. "This is the first time that I have been charged with a criminal offense, and I greatly regret my actions," Hammer said. "I have tried to lead a useful life. I trust the time that would be allowed for me to live, Your Honor, will give me the opportunity to be a useful member of society."

Lydick fined Hammer $3,000 and sentenced him to one year's probation.

As Armand was wheeled from the courtroom he was talkative,

alert, and friendly. When he returned to the hospital, unaware that reporters were watching, he waved away the wheelchair and strode into the building. A reporter called later and told me that he had sneaked into the hospital and had seen Hammer literally dance a little victory jig once he thought he was out of view.

A week went by, and no one heard a word. Suddenly, Armand was back at work. There was no wheelchair and no heart-monitoring equipment. But there was an unending succession of curt notes, memos, queries, instructions, and telephone calls. Before the day was out everyone was feeling the strain all over again. I was so busy I didn't have a chance to chat with him about anything other than business until a day or two after his return. Again he confided that the thought of going to jail had terrified him. "I was incredibly sick," he said. "I was on the verge of dying. But I never lost faith. I knew I would triumph, and I have. I've had a miraculous recovery and I've proved that I'm invincible!"

Even though Armand had pleaded guilty to a federal crime, had pretended he was on the verge of death in order to avoid a harsh penalty, had received a minimal sentence, and had been involved in a series of confrontations with the IRS and the SEC over the years, the next thing he did was to ask his lawyers to research the requirements for a presidential pardon. "Pop lost his medical license unjustly in 1920," he commented. "It took me more than twenty years to get it reinstated, but I never gave up because I was determined to turn a wrong into a right."

Armand's lawyers told him that he was going to have to live an exemplary life for at least the next five years and make a public declaration of remorse. But he insisted that his life was already an exemplary one and that he was innocent and had been framed. Obviously, there was no reason for him to issue a statement of remorse and a presidential pardon was not what the situation called for. The only option that made any sense to him was to have the president issue a declaration of innocence. "I'm not going to stop until I get the president of the United States to intervene personally," he declared.

22.

MIRACULOUS
RECOVERY

Occidental had promised the SEC that it would submit an inter-
nal audit committee report detailing its questionable or illegal foreign payments from 1969 to 1975. During Armand's absence the
committee submitted a twenty-eight-page "preliminary report" declaring that its "one-month" investigation had uncovered illegal or
questionable payments of $181,500. Back in the office, Armand
fastened the preliminary report to the current Form 10-K, which
detailed the financial status of the company, and sent both to the
SEC. The senior staff was speechless. It was public knowledge that
Occidental had been accused of spending $3 million on bribes in
just *one* nation, Venezuela, and it seemed impossible to believe that
the SEC would accept this modest confession.

Reporters inevitably were going to rib me about Armand's "miraculous recovery," and Occidental's latest financial disclosures
would certainly reinforce the impression of Hammer's deceitful-
ness. When the legal department advised me not to issue a news
release about the report, even though it automatically became public information when it was filed, I was relieved. If asked, I was to
say that it "was in the process of revision."

A few days later the Venezuelan press printed the conclusions
of another preliminary report. Unlike the humble conclusions
reached by Occidental's internal audit committee, the Venezuelan
congressional committee declared that it had "sufficiently proven"
that Occidental had engaged in "irregular and fraudulent" activities and that Hammer's Venezuelan operative, John Askew, had
used the $3 million paid to him by Occidental to make high-level
government payoffs. It was the committee's unanimous recom-

mendation that Askew be prosecuted and that the Venezuelan government disallow Occidental's compensation payments.

This time I issued a news release categorically denying that Occidental had any knowledge of the alleged payoffs and stating that Askew had not been authorized to deal with Venezuelan officials on Occidental's behalf. Subsequently the Caracas daily *El Nacional* reported that because of his involvement in the bribery scandal, the Council of Andrés Bello was planning to strip Hammer of his Venezuelan state honor. This news story was picked up by UPI and reported worldwide.

Armand was infuriated. "According to Venezuelan law, the Order of Andrés Bello *can't* be rescinded unless the recipient has been convicted and sentenced for a crime. Get me a retraction." UPI responded to my three-page letter with a one-sentence correction.

Armand became even angrier when Venezuelan press reports appeared stating that of the $3 million that had been laundered into the account of Askew's drilling company, Perforaciones Altamar, only $534,000 had been paid to Venezuelan officials. "How dare they suggest that anyone could get away with cheating me?" he asked out loud. "It just goes to prove they have no idea about the kind of man I am."

At the end of April, Occidental's 10-K was officially released and also published in the proxy notice for the forthcoming annual meeting on May 22. The next day news stories under headlines reading OCCIDENTAL PETROLEUM ADMITS MAKING ILLEGAL PAYMENTS appeared across the country. The fact that Occidental had not named the individuals who had received the payoffs or their countries of origin produced a flurry of calls from reporters. When I refused to provide this additional information, they searched through the proxy notice looking for clues and in the process came upon a one-sentence footnote in small type announcing Marvin Watson's "resignation." Watson had testified before the federal grand jury that he had participated in the Nixon campaign-contribution coverup at Hammer's request and had been commended by the Watergate prosecutor for providing "important documentary information not available to others." His testimony had eventually enabled the government to obtain a disposition against "the principal offender."

In order to quash further questions, Armand had chosen the resignation tactic as a way of fulfilling the public disclosure requirement.

But Watson's departure provoked so many new questions that Armand finally allowed me to release a statement that the resignation had "been in the works for several months" and that Occidental had asked Watson "to be available for consultation." He was never seen again.

A few days before the annual meeting, Armand reported that he had received a mysterious cable from Iranian Prime Minister Amir Abbas Hoveyda. "The shah is sending Cyrus Ansary to meet with me," he told me. "But Hoveyda didn't say why."

Ansary was the brother of the Iranian minister of finance, and Armand speculated that "the shah must want to make a deal about something." His guess was confirmed when Ansary told him that the shah wanted to purchase 10 percent of Occidental's company shares, obtain an option to purchase an additional 10 percent, and place an Iranian on the board of directors. The senior staff had grave objections to having the shah become Occidental's largest shareholder, but Armand was enthralled.

"The shah is a majestic leader even if he is a pompous ass," he said. "We lost hundreds of millions of dollars when he invaded Sharjah. But he's willing to pay us $125 million in cash to make this deal and it's a great opportunity to earn back some of our losses! Oxy will also have a chance to develop fertilizer and chemical businesses in Iran and become involved with Iranian oil. The possibilities are tremendous. Even though the shah is sneaky and deceitful, we'll anticipate his every move. This time I'm determined to beat this bastard at his own game."

Armand ordered his army of top-notch lawyers to negotiate an airtight deal with the shah that could never be turned against Occidental. But after negotiations got under way, the Ford administration expressed its "grave objections" to Occidental International's senior staff. Ford and his advisers were especially concerned about the fact that the high-level Iranian who would sit on Occidental's board of directors would have access to sensitive information about U.S. energy policy that the administration did not want to share with the shah.

Occidental International's staff lobbied the White House and got nowhere. Finally, Armand simply brushed off the problem. "Jerry Ford has every reason to be afraid of the shah," he said. "He's never tangled with him. But I have, and I know how to beat him!"

Armand's plan was to present the shah with an agreement that contained clauses granting Occidental the right of first refusal in the event that Iran decided to sell its stock and prohibiting the

Iranians from purchasing additional stock unless the offering came directly from Occidental. "These terms," he explained, "prevent the shah from selling his block of stock to someone at slightly above market price and initiating a tender offer that could result in a takeover. If he agrees to them, he'll never be able to hurt us. If he doesn't, he can shove it."

The shah did not raise a single objection.

It had been a trying year for Armand, and most of the two thousand shareholders who attended the annual meeting were concerned and curious about their chief executive's health and well-being. But a small but vocal group led by Clarinda Phillips, the owner of 300 shares of preferred stock, was hell-bent on reform. These activist shareholders objected to Occidental's admission of bribery in its 10-K, the cancellation of compensation payments by the Venezuelan government, and the fact that the board of directors had acceded to Hammer's demand to have Occidental pay for his $1 million Nixon campaign contribution legal defense. According to California law, an executive can be indemnified by his corporation for legal expenses when he commits a criminal action as an agent for his corporation, but Armand had admitted that he had made his contribution as a private citizen. Therefore, the dissident shareholders insisted that it was illegal to use company funds to pay his legal bill.

Armand stepped forward and accepted congratulations on his seventy-eighth birthday. Then he pulled a "legal opinion" from his breast pocket and read it to the shareholders with the conviction reserved for a Supreme Court decision. Unsurprisingly, the opinion confirmed that Occidental was acting within legal bounds by paying the legal fees. By the time he was done, the dissident shareholders knew they didn't stand a chance.

Another small group—they held three shares among them—were members of the Jewish Defense League. Led by Irv Rubin, this contingent was determined to confront Armand because of his lack of support for Soviet Jews and other Soviet dissidents. Just before the question-and-answer period came to an end, Rubin began to castigate Hammer. The shareholders began to boo, Rubin shouted over them, and they booed louder. Suddenly Rubin began to scream at the top of his voice, and the audience responded with a roar of disapproval. It was an ugly moment that held the potential of turning violent at any second.

Armand had his own way of creating order. He announced that

he had "just received" inside information that the final edition of the Venezuelan congressional committee report was going to exonerate Occidental from all charges of bribery, paving the way for Occidental to receive its compensation payment. No one realized that he had invented this stunning surprise on the spot, and the "news" brought cheers.

The next day the *Los Angeles Times* printed a vivid description of Armand's tangle with Irv Rubin, noting that Hammer had "displayed his characteristic forceful personality . . . in sharp contrast to [his] physical state in the U.S. District Court." Armand believed that the reports of the Rubin incident could trigger other demonstrations. Therefore, when Rubin demanded to see him, he dismissed the objections that he was placing himself in danger and agreed to hold a meeting. Flanked by security guards, Armand let the activist have his say. Then he turned on the charm. Oozing concern, he delivered an endless monologue about his grand strategy for a future filled with peace and harmony. After Rubin was thoroughly worn down, Armand confided to him that he was holding secret negotiations with the Soviet leadership but could not discuss them because he did not want to endanger the progress he was making or jeopardize the lives of important Jewish dissidents. At the end of his marathon performance, Armand issued an invitation to Rubin to join him in his secret mission on behalf of Soviet Jewry.

Rubin staggered from the room.

"That's the end of protesting," Armand remarked.

On June 3, two weeks after Hammer told the shareholders at the annual meeting that the Venezuelans were going to exonerate Occidental, the Pérez administration released its final report, which declared that Occidental's $3 million payment to John Askew had been used for an "irregular purpose" and Occidental was guilty of "illicit conduct." According to the report, the contents of an official document revealed the names of five Venezuelan officials and a schedule of payments that would be made to them in return for their efforts on behalf of Occidental. The payments ranged from $25,000 to $319,000. The SEC had also confirmed that Hammer had initiated the banking transactions that eventually led to the transfer of $3 million into Askew's corporate account. The Venezuelan committee recommended for a second time that compensation not be paid.

Occidental issued a statement declaring the report "inconclusive" because it lacked "supportive evidence." It did not, however, deter reform shareholder Clarinda Phillips from filing a class-action suit against Occidental, Hammer, and ten other Occidental directors and officers, accusing them of fraudulent and illegal business practices and demanding unspecified damages and restitution to the plaintiffs of the corporate money used in all illegal practices, with interest. When this class-action suit was settled in 1979, all the plaintiffs received was their legal fees.

The reform element became even more incensed when it learned that Occidental had not only paid for Hammer's Nixon campaign contribution defense but had also paid Marvin Watson's legal expenses. Armand ignored their rage and continued to maintain that Tim Babcock had framed him and that Babcock was really to blame for the shareholders' wrath. The more he said it, the more he believed it and the more determined he became to find a new way to try to prove that Babcock was a liar.

On June 4, after the U.S. District Court of Appeals had rejected Babcock's appeal, Judge Hart declared that because Hammer, the architect of the scheme, had merely received probation, "it would be a terrible miscarriage of justice to send his agent, his legman, to jail." The judge canceled Babcock's four-month jail sentence and reduced his fine to $1,000. Subsequently Marvin Watson appeared before Judge Hart for sentencing. Watson told the court, "I allowed loyalty to cloud my judgment. I was wrong. I do believe that the Lord will help me be strong in the future." He then pleaded guilty to being an accessory before the fact. Judge Hart fined Watson $500.

Years later, when I discussed this episode with Babcock, he commented, "Whenever I work for someone, I'm as loyal as I can be. Unfortunately, in this case I was too loyal." Watson offered his own opinion of Armand's behavior. He recalled a security man who had once told him that "there are some people who know something but say the opposite, and then convince themselves that the lie is the truth. If they were hooked up to a lie detector machine, their lies couldn't be detected because they've done such a good sell job on themselves. That's the way it was with Armand."

On June 6, J. Paul Getty, a member of the North Sea oil consortium led by Occidental, died at the age of eighty-four. Armand was fascinated by the provisions of Getty's will, which left his entire $2.2 billion estate to the Getty Trust. "The trust endows a private foundation," he told me, "which is mandated to disperse yearly 4.25 percent of the assets of the estate to avoid taxation and to use the money solely to pay for the Getty Museum in Malibu and its art projects. It comes to ninety million dollars a year, and it's being spent to keep Getty's name alive forever." That kind of immortality, I thought, would certainly appeal to Armand.

On the day of Getty's funeral, Armand's office door opened and his secretary, Dorothy Prell, peeked in. "Doctor, it's time for you to leave for the service."

He ignored her.

A few minutes later she reappeared. "You must go right now, or you'll be late."

Armand did not respond.

When Prell opened the door for a third time, before she had a chance to say a word, he said sharply, "Dorothy, I'm *Armand Hammer*. They *can't* start without me!"

Armand secretly supported Governor Jerry Brown's campaign to secure the 1976 Democratic presidential nomination. But his real concern was his Soviet partner David Karr's involvement in Sargent Shriver's campaign for the nomination. Resentful of Karr's seemingly unlimited use of Kennedy family funds on behalf of Shriver, he feared that if Shriver became president he would be shut out of the White House. When Jimmy Carter won the first Democratic presidential primary in Iowa on January 19, 1976, and Shriver placed fifth with 3 percent of the vote, he breathed a sigh of relief.

By early June, it was clear that Carter was going to sweep the Democratic convention. Eager to climb onto the Carter bandwagon, Armand secretly sent word to the Carter campaign that he was throwing his allegiance to Carter, while he continued to pledge his loyalty publicly to Brown. Finally, Brown left the race on June 26 and Armand was able to go public. He made arrangements to travel to New York City to attend the convention in Madison Square Garden on July 15 to see "his" candidate receive the nomination.

Just as he was getting ready to leave, Armand received word that the Venezuelan government had filed conspiracy charges against John Askew, former Occidental subsidiary manager Charles Hatfield, and the five Venezuelan officials named on Askew's list of bribe recipients and that a court order had been issued for their arrest. One of the Venezuelans escaped arrest by fleeing the country. While I was busy issuing Occidental's fifth denial of the bribery charges, Armand summoned a team of lawyers to draw up an appeal on behalf of Askew and Hatfield, which they planned to file in the Venezuelan superior court.

The next day Armand prowled around Madison Square Garden in search of an "opportunity" to meet the Democratic presidential candidate. He learned that Carter had decided that if he became president he was going to accede to Panamanian demands and allow Panama to take control of the Canal Zone, including the canal. Armand quickly saw a way to ingratiate himself with the candidate. "I sent word to him that I was thrilled that our next president was going to do the right thing about our Latin American neighbor," he told me. "I let him know that I'm going to do everything I can to help him achieve this important goal."

In short order Armand transformed his office into a pro–Panama Canal treaty information and lobbying center. While he was on the phone pleading Carter's case for "fairness" in Latin America, assistants addressed and mailed endless stacks of protreaty literature. Public opinion was running heavily against the "give-away," and most senior executives were also opposed to the proposal as well as to the expenditure of company funds and the use of company personnel on behalf of a partisan campaign issue. But, as usual, the merest hint of opposition provoked an overpowering tirade from Armand. "Do you want all of the Latin American countries to turn against us? Do you want the Panamanians to blow up the canal? Or declare war on us?" he thundered.

The following month Gerald Ford became the Republican presidential candidate. A week later Lew Wasserman, chief executive of Music Corporation of America, kicked off Carter's postprimary fund-raising drive with an exclusive dinner party in his Beverly Hills mansion. When the guest list was announced, the press noted the presence of two "controversial" figures: attorney Sydney Korshak, who reportedly had ties to key underworld figures, and Hammer, a convicted felon who had made illegal contributions to the Nixon campaign and was not the likeliest guest at a fund-raiser for a man who was running on a ticket that repudiated Watergate and everything it stood for.

The night of the party, undeterred, Armand worked the room until he buttonholed Carter. According to Armand, the candidate told him that he was pro-détente and eager to increase U.S.-USSR trade, but he was a Washington outsider with no experience with the Soviets. Armand instantly spotted a new opportunity to become Carter's unofficial emissary to the Kremlin.

Armand was scheduled to attend another fund-raiser in Plains,

Georgia, at the home of Jimmy Carter's mother, Miss Lillian. Before going to Plains, he stopped in New York and met with Soviet Foreign Minister Andrei Gromyko. The SALT negotiations had been deadlocked for seven months, and Gromyko supplied Armand with the information he believed Carter had to know if he became president and was serious about achieving an arms agreement with the Soviets. In Plains, Hammer briefed Carter. The candidate appreciated Armand's efforts, but Carter's staff concluded that Armand was operating as a propaganda tool for the Soviets.

The deal with the shah was still in the works, and weeks of intense negotiation had finally produced a satisfactory agreement. Armand set off for Paris and the signing ceremony, and everything was going along smoothly until, literally, the moment arrived for him to sign his name. Iranian Minister of Finance Hushang Ansary beckoned to him and whispered that the shah had changed his mind and wanted Armand to delete the clause granting Occidental the right of first refusal if the Iranians chose to sell their block of stock. Armand instantly realized that the shah had been angling from the very beginning to place himself in a position to launch a takeover of Occidental and had used Armand's own technique of stringing his opponent along until the very last minute in order to get what he wanted.

He looked Ansary in the eye and replied, "You can tell the shah I'm never going to give him the opportunity to screw me again. The deal is off." A half hour later he was in the air and headed back to Los Angeles with the news that an Iranian was not going to sit on the board of directors. This relieved the senior staff, but they viewed the negotiations with Iran as another demonstration that Armand's judgments were becoming increasingly irrational.

On November 2, Jimmy Carter was elected president. Armand's euphoria was amplified by the news that the Venezuelan superior court had dismissed the charges against everyone who was arrested in connection with the bribery scandal, clearing the way for Occidental to file a compensation claim with the Ministry of Mines and Hydrocarbons. President Pérez promptly ordered his attorney general to appeal the ruling in the Venezuelan Supreme Court, but Armand remained convinced that Pérez didn't have a chance.

The next time I saw my friend, the Venezuelan press attaché, I mentioned this unexpected turn of events. He explained discreetly that "some of our judges are unpredictable. They swing and sway, if you know what I mean." The fact that several Occidental executives had recently traveled back and forth to Venezuela confirmed my suspicions about the corruption in the Venezuelan federal court system and the susceptibility of its judges to bribes.

After the higher court upheld the ruling, Armand declared confidently that President Pérez would never disobey a Supreme Court decision and that Occidental was going to get paid. But after Pérez remained defiant, Occidental was left with one option: to sue the Venezuelan government in the Venezuelan Supreme Court. After a number of postponements, the legal department concluded that Pérez was intervening personally to block the court from ruling on the case.

Hammer dug in his heels. "When someone tries to cheat me, I hang in until they give up. No matter how long it takes, I'm going to stay on the case until the Venezuelans pay us." This holy mission joined an ever-lengthening list that already included Occidental's dream of drilling for oil in Pacific Palisades, its attempt to create a financially viable shale-oil operation, the Occidental-Soviet-Japanese Siberian natural-gas project, and Armand's determination to prove that Tim Babcock had framed him.

And last but not least, there was Armand's determination to cozy up to Jimmy Carter. When he and the president-elect lunched together in early December, Armand suggested that he arrange a Carter-Brezhnev summit meeting. Carter was friendly but noncommittal. Armand, who was never discouraged by even a flat no, was thrilled by this nonrefusal. He declared that Carter was the best president the country ever had and it was pointless to remind him that Carter had three weeks to go before he assumed office.

At the same time that Armand was wooing the president-elect, he became flabbergasted when Los Angeles County Museum director Ken Donahue told him that the Armand Hammer Collection "lacked unity" and was "a mixed batch." "That fool wants to break my collection up after I die and spread it around the museum so that each painting can be displayed with other paintings of a similar kind," he fumed. "I put my foot down, but he accused me of lacking 'a sensible approach' and putting my name and interests before the welfare of the museum. I've been a saint to that museum, and now they're trying to screw me. Don't be surprised if I screw them first."

He repeated his conversation with Donahue to everyone within earshot, growing angrier each time. Then he called Donahue and shouted over the phone, "I paid for the Frances and Armand

Hammer Wing, and that's the only place I want the Armand Hammer Collection exhibited after I die! And that's that!"

A spectacular art-buying spree followed, stimulated in part by Armand's desire to show Donahue what the County Museum could lose if it did not accede to his wishes. Occidental's "director of corporate art, Martha Kaufman, hunted down purchasing opportunities for Armand, conducted initial meetings with dealers and collectors on his behalf, and drew up fact sheets that enabled Armand to appear knowledgeable about the paintings he was attempting to acquire. In return he spent even more time with her, granted her a substantial $10,000 raise, and allowed her to have a secretary.

On behalf of Knoedler Galleries, he paid $5,125,000 for the eighty-eight painting collection of the late actor Edward G. Robinson, which included paintings by Monet, Renoir, and Rouault. *Hospital at Saint-Remy* by van Gogh was acquired for $1.2 million, and another $2 million was paid for *Portrait of a Man Holding a Black Hat* by Rembrandt. Armand's trusteeship at the County Museum enabled him to learn that a collector, George Longstreet, had decided to sell the museum six thousand lithographs by the nineteenth-century French political cartoonist and lithographer Honoré Daumier. The price was $250,000. To make sure he got them, Armand made a more generous offer—he refused to reveal the figure—which enabled him to purchase the collection out from under the museum in violation of a trustees' rule that in the case of a conflict between a trustee and the museum, the museum would always prevail.

Fearing that Armand would cancel his promise to donate his art collection to the museum, the other trustees decided not to invoke the bylaw. Instead, they extracted a promise from Armand to donate the lithographs to the museum from six months to a year after the date of purchase. But after Armand took possession of the collection, he told the trustees that the museum would receive the lithographs upon his death. Then he and Martha began to plan a heavily publicized tour of the newly named Armand Hammer Daumier Collection that would substantially inflate its value. Armand also compiled a list of other owners of Daumier lithographs, among them the Hungarian-born actress Ilona Massey, whom Armand knew casually. He began to lunch with Massey once or twice a year and went out of his way to be charming to her, even calling Leonid Brezhnev so that her son, Curtis Roberts, could present a production of *Show Boat* in Moscow. Then he made an offer to buy her Daumiers. When Massey turned him down, he waited awhile and then resumed his courtship with even more intensity.

Armand next acquired Rembrandt's large, magisterial portrait of the queen of the gods, *Juno*, and announced that he would bequeath it to the County Museum. The prior owner, J. William Middendorf II, former Secretary of the Navy during the Ford administration had given the painting to the Knoedler Gallery on consignment. The asking price was set at $5 million, and Armand retained the right of first refusal if it remained unsold. When there were no takers, Middendorf offered the painting to the Getty Museum, asking a price of $3.25 million. The record purchase price for a Rembrandt had been set by the Metropolitan Museum of Art when it paid $2.3 million to acquire *Aristotle Contemplating the Bust of Homer*. Realizing that the purchase of *Juno* for $3.25 million was going to set a new record and become front-page news, Armand invoked his right of first refusal, bought the painting, and reaped another round of international publicity.

The Daumier and Rembrandt acquisitions led art critics to pose questions about the potential conflicts of interest that surround someone who is simultaneously a dealer, a private collector, and a museum trustee. Was it ethical for Hammer to use the information he received in his capacity as a trustee to enrich his own collection? And was it ethical for him to purchase a work of art for his private collection at a price below the price he had promised to obtain for it in his role as a dealer, especially after the work had been pledged to a reputable museum?

Ignoring the criticisms, Armand concentrated on publicizing his acquisition of *Juno*. When the painting was flown from Washington to Los Angeles, I used the same technique I had used when I went to work for him almost twenty years before. Guards armed with rifles waited on the airstrip, and an armored truck was poised to transport the painting to the County Museum. Again the publicity was enormous. Armand told the press that $3.25 million was a "bargain" because Middendorf had originally asked $5 million. He did not say, however, that he had been the one who had made the promise to obtain that sum for Middendorf in the first place. He also announced that he had "beat out" the Getty Museum in a competition for the painting. Getty Museum director Norris Bramlett countered that the Getty Museum had made an offer of only $1.5 million and would never have paid the sum spent by Hammer. Nevertheless, in his autobiography, *Hammer*, published in 1987, Armand took his boast one step further and wrote, "Paul Getty

raised hell with me ever afterward. He could never see me without chiding, 'You do know that you stole that Rembrandt from me?'"
In fact, Getty had been dead three months when Armand made the acquisition.

It was Armand's plan to tour the world with *Juno* in tow, gathering publicity everywhere he touched down. Despite admonitions from art authorities that he was subjecting the painting to drastic changes in atmospheric pressure and temperature and exposing it to unnecessary humidity, he insisted that the Rembrandt always travel by his side. On board the Gulfstream, it was wrapped in a pink flannel blanket and sandwiched between mattresses in the aircraft's master bedroom. Martha Kaufman hovered in the background as Armand told the press that, apart from his wife Frances, Juno was the only woman he allowed to sleep beside him. Soon clippings began to arrive accusing him of using circuslike methods to inflate the price of a work that should have been hanging safely in a museum. "They're jealous of me," he commented as he threw them in the trash.

Despite the "fame" accruing to the Armand Hammer Collection as a result of its constant touring, Armand's overture to exhibit it in the Louvre was politely rebuffed. Undeterred in his determination to make a big splash in the Paris art world, he began to search for another venue. The journey led him to art historian René Huyghe, a member of the French Academy and the French Institute. Huyghe was the director of the Musée Jacquemart-André, which occupied a delapidated mansion on Boulevard Haussmann owned by the French Institute.

Armand and Huyghe evolved a plan. Armand would utilize a $1 million Armand Hammer Foundation grant to restore the mansion to its former glory. Then, as the restoration neared completion, he would approach officials of the Louvre and tell them that he wanted to make a donation of *The Weaver* by van Gogh and "suggest" that he receive an "invitation" to exhibit his paintings at the Louvre. This exhibition would take place at the same time as an exhibition of Hammer's graphic works at the newly refurbished Musée Jacquemart-André. In that way Armand would receive simultaneous publicity for his spectacular restoration, his generous donation of the van Gogh, and two exhibitions of his art holdings.

After putting this plan into action, Armand believed he deserved an even grander payoff: the Legion of Honor, the highest award of the French government. The Legion of Honor is granted only to those who have given eminent service to France over at least a twenty-year period and foreign nominees must receive the sponsorship of the French Ministry of Foreign Affairs. Therefore, discreet requests were made to the important academicians, government officials, arts leaders, and society figures in Huyghe's circle of friends to position Armand with the ministry as a man who had rendered a lifetime of service to the world and was truly deserving of this distinguished reward.

Toward the end of 1976, the Malibu sheriff's department received a tip that Armand's son Julian was harboring stolen property in his home. A request for a search warrant met with the reply that the matter was "too hot to handle." When the police refused to be put off, a special meeting was held between the sheriff's department and the chief deputy district attorney, and a warrant was issued.

On December 21, the police raided Julian's home and discovered an antique dagger and an expensive ring that had been reported stolen and amounts of LSD and Quaaludes. Julian was arrested and booked on suspicion of receiving stolen property. A thirty-seven-year-old woman, described as his "housekeeper," was also booked on suspicion of possessing dangerous drugs. Armand called his lawyers, and nothing more was heard about the incident.

In April 1977, Julian and another "housekeeper" were in a bar and began to argue. Julian struck the woman across the face and knocked her down. She got up, fled from the bar, and decided to hitchhike. A nineteen-year-old man picked her up and drove her to Julian's house. Later, when Julian arrived home and found his companion with the young man, he grabbed a shotgun, pointed it at the stranger, and threatened to kill him. Then he struck the woman a few more times and ordered her to move out. Eventually the police were summoned. They surrounded the house and ordered Julian to surrender. When he stepped outside, the police confiscated the shotgun, charged him with attempted assault with a deadly weapon, and arrested him. At the end of the week this charge was dropped because the young man "refused to cooperate" and Julian was freed.

The media picked up the story, and ABC-TV *Eyewitness News* posed the question of whether there was a different standard of justice for the rich and the poor. Reporter Leo McElroy commented that "Armand Hammer is best known for Occidental Petroleum. To law enforcement, though, he is best known as the father of a regular customer," a son who seems to possess a "charmed life," a "seeming immunity from prosecution," and a long string of arrests, "but nothing seems to stick." It was pointed out that five months had elapsed since Julian's arrest on suspicion of receiving stolen property, and a court date had still not been set. McElroy also told his viewers that Julian's prior arrest records had disappeared from police files.

When reporters called to discover if Armand was responsible for the missing files, he replied, "There's a lot of dumb clerical help these days. Maybe some clerk pulled them and forgot to put them back. They're all civil service, and they know it's almost impossible to fire them."

The next month, Julian finally went to court. The charges were reduced to three misdemeanors, and he was sentenced to three years' probation and fined $319.

On August 21, a man named Vincent West arrived at Julian's house to collect a $1,000 gambling debt. Julian threw open the door, shouted, "I don't want to talk to you," and fired a shot at West, barely missing him. When the police arrived, they arrested Julian, handcuffed the two young women and the man who were also in the house, confiscated Julian's .357 magnum revolver, and charged him with assault, carrying a dangerous weapon, and firing a gun in an inhabited area.

The following day a three-column photo of Julian and his guests lying prone and handcuffed on the ground as four uniformed and armed police officers hovered over them appeared in the *Los Angeles Times*. "I'll take care of it," Armand said brusquely. Eventually the new charges were also substantially reduced, and Julian did not receive a jail sentence.

New troubles were brewing for Occidental that could not so easily be brushed under the rug. After an executive returned from a meeting at a Hooker Chemicals Division plant in Montague, Michigan, he came into my office and confided his distress. "I just told the doctor that their dump site has got to be cleaned up or this company is going to find itself in a lot of trouble. He yessed me and brushed it off. Would you talk to him?"

When I approached Armand, he gave me the same treatment. "All chemical plants, not just ours, have to dump their wastes somewhere," he declared. "It's a fact of life. Anyone who complains about it is purposely making a big thing out of nothing so he can look like a hero and get a raise."

The next complaint came from a resident of Montague, who told the Michigan Environmental Enforcement Agency that the drinking water in his new home had a foul taste and smell. When investigators began to look into the environmental practices of Hooker's plant, they learned that for twenty-two years it had been disposing of its chemical wastes by placing them in fifty-five-gallon drums and dropping the drums into a field on the plant grounds. As the drums rotted, a large variety of toxic chemicals was being absorbed into the soil and contaminating the groundwater beneath the plant. The groundwater was traveling to nearby White Lake, the source of Montague's drinking water, which led the Michigan Water Resources Commission to demand that Hooker reduce the amount of waste chemicals deposited in its dump site. Eventually the Michigan attorney general would order Hooker to pay $176,000 in damages to the State of Michigan because the waste chemicals that had leached into White Lake had poisoned aquatic life.

Hooker had known about the contamination ever since 1968, the year it was being acquired by Occidental, but had kept the information secret. By 1975 Occidental had learned that toxic wastes dumped by Hooker had also leached into groundwater in North Tonawanda and Hicksville, New York; Columbus, Missouri; Columbia, Tennessee; and Tacoma, Washington. I knew, furthermore, that Hooker's plant in Houston was pouring five tons of pesticide wastes a year into an unlined lagoon from which the residues were filtering into the underground water supply and thus into neighboring wells, and that its operations in Niagara Falls, New York, had buried four thousand tons of toxic wastes containing dioxin at various dump sites around that city.

Subsequently New York State environmental authorities discovered concentrations of dioxin in Bloody Run Creek and Lake Ontario, both sources of local drinking water. Traces of Mirex, a chlorinated hydrocarbon pesticide used to fight fire ants and manufactured exclusively by Hooker, were also discovered in Lake Ontario and in the eggs of herring gulls and fish, which forced the environmental officials to initiate a ban on fishing, cancel a salmon-stocking program, and delay plans for a $10 million fish hatchery. At Occidental Chemical's (formerly Best Fertilizers') plant in Lathrop, California, a plant manager observed a dog accidentally step into water that was percolating from the waste pond and then lick itself clean. By the end of the day the dog was dead. In a confidential memorandum to his supervisor, the manager wrote, "Our laboratory records indicate that we are slowly contaminating all wells in our area and two of our own wells are contaminated to the point of being toxic to animals or humans. *This is a time bomb we must defuse."*

Another employee at the Lathrop plant disclosed in a confidential memorandum to his supervisor that "We have been discharging more than ten thousand tons of waste water containing about five tons of pesticides per year into the ground. This discharge point is less than five hundred feet from our neighbor's drinking well water. I believe that we have fooled around long enough and have already overpressed our luck."

A confidential memorandum written by a third employee revealed the decision-making process of Lathrop's senior staff: "I don't believe the Water Quality Control Board is even aware that we process pesticides. Since this report isn't exactly accurate even though the inaccuracy is due to omission rather than outright falsehood, I don't really feel comfortable in signing it. However, I don't think it would be wise to explain the discrepancy to the state at this time."

Lathrop's environmental engineers periodically demanded that the senior management authorize a cleanup action because the plant was contaminating wells in a three-mile radius. But the cost was estimated at $2.58 million and management did not want to spend the money. Nor did it want to call attention to the contamination for fear that bad publicity could trigger a rash of lawsuits. There was also the concern that the initiation of a cleanup program would be an admission of liability. Therefore, a decision was made to do nothing for the moment.

After workers at the Life Science Products plant in Hopeville, Virginia, lodged complaints of sterility, memory loss, uncontrollable trembling, and brain and liver damage, the Virginia Department of Health discovered that the ailments were being caused by the handling of another toxic chlorinated hydrocarbon, Kepone, an insecticide that resembles DDT and was being manufactured from chemical formulations purchased from Hooker. Life Science Products disposed of Kepone residues by dumping them into the James River, and the Department of Health discovered that the fish in the river contained higher-than-acceptable levels of the insecticide. A hundred-mile stretch of the river was ordered closed to fishing, and the plant was ordered shut down.

On April 19, 1976, a group of former Life Science Products workers named Hooker as a codefendant and sued for $62.9 million in damages, claiming that they had not been warned about the dangers of working with Kepone. The same day Hooker was named as a codefendant in a $26.5 million class-action suit by local Virginia fishermen who charged that the alleged contamination of the seafood and oyster beds in the James River had deprived them of their income. A third suit, this one for $5 million, was based on the alleged pollution of the Chesapeake Bay as a result of water flowing into the bay from the James River.

Every attempt would be made to settle these suits quietly with no announcement of the settlement or the dollar amount involved. Additional internal information generated by Occidental and Hooker about their environmental problems was also to be kept secret. Nor would Occidental disclose the potential costs it faced for constructing pollution-control facilities and for cleaning up old waste sites.

On January 2, 1977, three civil suits filed by the Life Science Products workers were settled out of court. The Hooker PR staff was told not to announce the sizes of the settlements and, if asked, to say that although Hooker didn't believe that it would have to be held liable in court, the company nevertheless had agreed to the settlements to avoid protracted litigation. It was the standard operating procedure in matters like this.

Not too long after that, male workers in the Lathrop pesticide unit reported that they were suffering from sterility. They underwent fertility tests; all those who had worked in the unit for more than four years had zero sperm counts. Armand reacted to this news with simple irritation. "I don't give a damn about environmental problems and I'm sick of these workers making our plant their scapegoat," he said. "Millions of men who don't work in pesticide plants are sterile. These fellows ought to be men and stop trying to save their pride by blaming others for their potency problems. They ought to appreciate the fact that our Lathrop plant provides them with good jobs."

Further studies revealed that the sterility had been caused by handling DBCP, a pesticide used to kill nematodes, microscopic worms that attack the roots of plants. During the manufacturing process, the workers had not worn gloves, and their work clothes had often gotten soaked through with the formulation. Occidental and Hooker had never been warned about the toxicity of DBCP but somehow had also avoided learning about how harmful it is to humans.

Subsequently, the agricultural chemical division of the Lathrop plant suspended operations so that new safety factors could be instituted. Armand was not pleased by this interruption in Lathrop's operations and vowed to find a solution to the problem. "I'm even discussing the idea of hiring only men who have had vasectomies or are already sterile. We might even find a way to turn DBCP into a male contraceptive," he told me. "As long as I'm alive, nothing or nobody shuts me down."

23.

UNOFFICIAL
REPRESENTATIVE

A week after President Carter took office on January 20, 1977,
the State Department issued a statement that the USSR would
violate "accepted standards of human rights" if it attempted to
silence its best-known dissident, Nobel Peace Prize recipient Andrei Sakharov. Carter added that he planned to send Sakharov a
personal letter of support and meet with another Soviet dissident,
Vladimir Bukovsky.

It was the first time the United States had declared public support for Soviet dissidents, and the Kremlin perceived Carter's actions as subversion. Although angry, the Soviet bureaucracy
believed that only a naïve man could have that much concern about
the rights of an individual when the fate of nations was at stake
and that Carter could be easily manipulated in a one-to-one summit encounter. "The Soviets had urged me to press for a summit
meeting," Armand informed me. "It seems I'm the only one who
can put things right between our two countries."

On March 21, Brezhnev spoke out against Carter's human rights
stand, accusing the United States of blatant interference in Soviet
internal affairs and pronouncing it "unthinkable" that a relationship between the two countries could develop normally in this context. Meanwhile, it was business as usual at Occidental. To prepare
for the arrival of the first shipment of ammonia from the Soviets
and to gear up to ship large amounts of phosphate fertilizers to
the USSR under the terms of the Occidental-Soviet fertilizer deal,
Armand had ordered the board of directors to authorize $237
million to construct an ammonia storage and handling terminal in
Savannah, Georgia, and to expand Occidental's phosphate mine

and port facilities in Florida. In private the senior executives wondered whether U.S. firms were going to buy large amounts of Soviet ammonia when détente was falling apart.

Armand continued to radiate optimism, but he paid strict attention to the encounter between Secretary of State Cyrus Vance and the Soviets during Vance's visit to Moscow the week after Brezhnev's remarks. Carter had run on a much stronger arms control policy than Ford, and Vance suggested that the two nations shelve the arms accords reached in 1974 and turn directly to the negotiation of major reductions in nuclear weapons. Armand greeted the proposal with disbelief. "Vance doesn't understand that it takes the Soviets forever and a day to take a single step. They're not ready to deal with a new group of politicians, much less entertain his dramatic offer."

He was right. Five days later the talks fell apart.

The next week Brezhnev sent a two-page letter to Armand, who informed me of its contents. "He wanted me to tell America that the U.S. refuses to treat Russia as an equal and that the Soviets are never going to permit this country to achieve military superiority. He also told me to tell our government that global politics isn't child's play! And he's right. Brezhnev is a great man and an outstanding leader who wants peace. I'm proud he's chosen me to be his unofficial representative in the United States."

During his next speaking engagements, Armand fervently pleaded Brezhnev's cause, urging his listeners to believe that the Soviet leader was trustworthy and demanding that the United States treat the USSR with fairness and respect. In response to the comments of Defense Secretary Harold Brown that the latest Soviet missile development program would allow the Soviets to pose a significant threat to the United States, Armand made it a special point to call for the rejection of demands for a new military buildup. Couching his disarmament message in business terms, he insisted that arms spending was bankrupting the nation and that it was insane to build weapons that were never going to be used.

His audiences were conservative businesspeople who knew that U.S. sales to the USSR had dropped 25 percent and that Soviet hard-liners were pressing for still greater Soviet military adventures in Africa, and they were convinced that military superiority was the best deterrent. But they listened politely to Armand because the man doing the talking was venerable, successful, and exceptionally wealthy.

As Brezhnev's "representative," Armand authorized Occidental to throw a lavish welcoming lunch for Vladimir Alkhimov after he became the head of the Soviet Bank of Foreign Trade. Other Soviet visitors and delegations also received the royal treatment, and a junior executive was given the job of preparing recreational and sight-seeing itineraries for these groups. When one delegation learned that it was being taken to the symphony and the ballet, a spokesman confided that he and his colleagues weren't interested in culture, which they could get at home. What they really wanted to see was an X-rated film they had heard about from other Soviet officials who had visited the United States: *Deep Throat.* They were taken to the theater that was showing the film.

Emboldened by the success of their colleagues, the next group called ahead to say that they wished to visit Sunset Strip nightspots featuring nude dancing girls, and they also got their wish. All these visitors either had KGB agents in their entourages or were tailed by the KGB. A night security guard also said that men could be found sitting in a car near Occidental's headquarters, waiting for Armand to leave the building, and that after he pulled out of the garage they followed him at a discreet distance. It duplicated the pattern observed by the staffers who had traveled with Armand to Russia and elsewhere.

After the Occidental group discovered oil in the North Sea, it had set out to construct a fixed drilling platform—literally, a man-made island that would drill and pump oil from the sea floor. Over a two-year period, a 511-foot platform jacket, nicknamed "the monster," was built bolt by bolt and weld by weld on the shoreline. On completion, it weighted 14,000 tons. In June 1975, "the monster" was moved onto barges and towed toward its anchorage in 425 feet of water 120 miles offshore.

The North Sea is known as "the fiercest of seas" because of its many violent storms. Occidental's drilling and production chief, Charley Horace, was deeply concerned that the platform jacket could be lost if an unexpected storm erupted while it was being towed, and weather conditions had been checked with the British Admiralty. But as soon as the jacket had reached its destination, ninety-mile-per-hour gale-force winds and sixty-foot waves swept over it. It was the beginning of a titanic storm that would rage for two days. To save the jacket, it was temporarily ballasted down and set upright on the sea floor until the weather abated, and then refloated. Finally, in a miraculous effort, the workers got the jacket ballasted in a vertical position and set it down at its proper location on the bottom of the sea. But then it started to slip and, in the nick of time, pilings were hurriedly pounded down to secure it. The fact that the crew not only accomplished this feat, but also survived to tell about it paid triumph to its bravery, ingenuity, and technological skills.

A superstructure for the platform was built, a 130-mile undersea pipeline was constructed, and oil had begun to flow from Occidental's Piper field to its marine terminal and storage facilities at Flotta in the Orkney Islands on December 27, 1976. This achievement was celebrated in *Billion Dollar Bonanza,* a promotional film produced by my department, which received hundreds of airplays on U.S. and European TV.

Armand always used any success to beat the drum for himself and Occidental's British office worked overtime to herald the Piper field achievement. Now Armand decided he had a calling card to meet the Royal Family and to celebrate Queen Elizabeth II's silver jubilee, and he ordered the London branch of the Knoedler Gallery to stage an exhibition of Winston Churchill's paintings. The sole purpose of the event was to entice Prince Charles into attending. The plan worked, and Armand and the prince met for the first time at the exhibition on May 4, 1977. Thereafter, Armand ordered Occidental's English office to bombard Buckingham Palace with invitations for the prince to visit its North Sea operation and began to research a list of charities favored by Prince Charles. "I not only want to win the Nobel Peace Prize," he told me. "I also want Prince Charles to persuade the queen to knight me."

As the annual meeting approached on May 21, Armand's seventy-ninth birthday, he had good news to report and bad news to keep secret. The good news concerned the fact that, after two years of negotiation, Occidental had concluded its first East Bloc deal and Romania was going to purchase 14 million tons of coal from Occidental over a thirty-five-year period beginning in 1980. This agreement would be underwritten with a $53 million U.S. bank loan to Romania that had been arranged by Occidental. Even though Romanian dissidents were subjected to arrest and would-be emigrants denounced as traitors, the Carter administration was urging Congress to extend Romania's MFN trade status in order to encourage its growing independence from the Kremlin. Armand wasted no time sending word to the White House that he had made the deal to demonstrate his support of Carter's foreign policy.

Occidental's bad news concerned a report that Hooker and Island Creek Coal were already or eventually would be the targets of ninety pending or contemplated pollution proceedings begun by state, federal, and local governments and individuals. The estimated amount of the claims came to $1 billion. Armand authorized a very discreet disclosure of almost all of these suits somewhere in the middle of the twelve pages of notes in the annual report. Relying on standard legal procedure, the following comment was provided: "[T]here are various other lawsuits pending against Occidental and its subsidiaries, some of which involve substantial amounts." To offer further reassurance, the shareholders were also informed that "it is impossible to determine the ultimate legal liabilities" but whatever payments were ultimately made, the company would remain unaffected by them. Put to the test, these statements were probably not going to satisfy the SEC demand for adequate disclosure, either for the number or the existence and nature of the ninety pending suits or the potential costs Occidental faced for constructing pollution control facilities and for cleaning up its toxic waste sites.

Just when Armand believed he had found a way to gloss over Occidental's environmental problems, the SEC was ready to go public with the results of its fifteen-month investigation. Hammer and Occidental were going to be charged with the failure to disclose illegal or questionable foreign payments between 1969 and 1975 of $650,000, almost $500,000 more than the amount reported to the SEC by Occidental's internal audit committee. The federal investigators claimed that $220,000 of the $650,000 had been generated by two off-the-books European-based companies, and that $165,000 of the $650,000 had been placed into two numbered Swiss bank accounts, and $59,500 had been placed in a safe-deposit box in a City National Bank branch office on the ground floor of Occidental's corporate headquarters. Yet another $48,000 had been located in a safe-deposit box controlled by an officer of a domestic Occidental subsidiary.

The fact that the investigators had been able to uncover misapplied funds of only $650,000 after such a long investigation was greeted with relief and taken as a tribute to Hammer's ability to hide almost all of the sources of his secret payroll. It seemed merely to demonstrate that a multinational corporation was not to be confused with the Boy Scouts of America. Nonetheless, the allegation that Occidental maintained clandestine companies in Europe fascinated the senior staff. No one seemed to know anything about them or whether others were in existence. Those who did know had undoubtedly been sworn to secrecy and pretended ignorance. Finally, I asked Armand about them. He ignored the question.

For the third time in six years Armand was given the opportunity to sign a consent decree. He went into his familiar routine of defiance and insisted that he was never going to sign. But he and everyone else knew his objections were pure show. Finally, he gave in and Occidental announced that it had consented to the SEC's allegations without admitting or denying guilt. The terms of the consent decree permanently barred Occidental from issuing any more false statements about illegal payments or the existence of improperly accounted for corporate funds and from making any other false entries on its books or any other illegal payments. The company would also be required to make a full public report of *all* of its "sensitive" payments within sixty days and initiate procedures to uncover and disclose other such activities.

In response to his promise to make a full disclosure of Occidental's "sensitive" payments, Armand had the audacity to notify the SEC that he was going to order the internal audit committee to complete its "preliminary" report and that after the report was reviewed by the board of directors, the board would take "such implementing action as it deems proper." Then, all innocence, he assembled the internal audit committee, which was expanded to include a group of friendly outside accountants and lawyers, and ordered it to complete its task. The office joke was that it was going to take years to complete an accounting that had listed illegal payments of only $181,500 in the first place.

It was Armand's "suggestion" that the committee send questionnaires to staff members, asking them to supply information and documents about bribes, kickbacks, and other financial illegalities. The "responses" would provide the raw data for its report. At the same time the committee also asked Occidental's outside accountants, Arthur Andersen & Co., to conduct an internal audit of the books over the six years in question.

As far as I knew, not a single senior staff member got a questionnaire, but that didn't stop the executives from having a laugh about Armand's ingeniousness. After all, only those who were in the market to "resign" were going to tell the truth. When Armand got his questionnaire, he wrote his name across the top, looked over the five questions, and, because he didn't know a single thing about any illegal activities that might have occurred, left the form blank. He even had the nerve to apply to the SEC for an extension, claiming that the distribution, collection, and tabulation of these forms required an enormous amount of time.

Inevitably, financial reporters called to needle me about Occidental's secret companies, Swiss bank accounts, and slush funds. Their comments suggested that they had begun to perceive Occidental as an outlaw company and a bastion of white-collar crime. This skepticism was echoed on Wall Street, but Armand brushed aside the criticisms. "None of it will harm us in the least. The public forgets quickly and is always swayed by the positive things that happen. We can't allow anything to upset us or slow us down."

In another corporation, problems like these might provoke the board of directors to order a change in management or encourage the shareholders to revolt. Neither was possible at a company whose chief executive had transformed the board into a clubhouse and whose shareholders were both star-struck and contented with their inflated dividends. Meanwhile, Armand once again took the signing of a consent decree as a challenge to try even harder to circumvent the regulators. And at the annual meeting not one word was said about Occidental's most recent problems with the SEC or the fact that the company was doing nothing to acknowledge, much less dismantle, its environmental time bomb.

On June 10, Armand traveled to Bucharest to sign the coal contract with the Romanian Ministry of Foreign Trade. Then he set off for Moscow for Leonid Brezhnev's seventieth birthday celebration on June 16, when he was to deliver a tribute to the Soviet leader on Radio Moscow, an adjunct of the Soviet International Information Department's propaganda apparatus. This event marked the apogee of Brezhnev's "cult of personality" campaign and he was made a Hero of the Soviet Union for a second time and received his fifth Order of Lenin. Both medals were made of the purest gold. On his return Armand described one of Brezhnev's many "wonderful" birthday presents. "He was unanimously elected chairman of the Supreme Soviet *and* president of the Presidium. That makes him the official head of the government *and* the Communist Party. Now everyone calls him 'Comrade Chairman'! There's only one other person in all of Russia who's addressed the same way: me!"

It had taken him more than forty years, but Armand believed he had finally achieved his goal. "I'm the only man in the world," he gloated, "who can truthfully say that I'm the unofficial representative of the president of the United States and a comrade chairman of the USSR."

Carter's radical energy policy stressed conservation, penalized energy overuse, and called for the lifting of price controls so that domestic oil and natural gas would rise to the prices of foreign oil. Infuriated by the proposals to limit oil use and raise prices at the same time, the domestic energy industry set out to demolish the program. As Congress watered down the legislation, Carter stepped up his attacks on Big Oil and its highly organized, well-funded petroleum lobby.

It was only natural that Armand would use the squabble as another way to ingratiate himself with the president. Occidental and Ashland Oil had formed a joint venture to develop a 5,090-acre federal oil-shale lease tract in Colorado. After Occidental produced 3,500 barrels of shale oil, Armand declared that he was determined to build a $440 million plant on the site and produce 57,000 barrels a day. Then he sent word to the White House that he was not going to take the side of the oil industry against Carter or speak out on Carter's behalf. What he was going to do was support the administration's commitment to conservation by demonstrating the viability of Occidental's shale-oil process. His environment-minded concerns—and his silence—were quietly rewarded with a $6 million grant.

Armand then set out to generate some favorable publicity for the shale-oil project—and himself. Occidental's research and development chief, Don Baeder, was awakened by a call from Armand at 4:30 A.M. "I think I can nail down an *enormous* federal grant, and I want you to prepare a new promotional film to show the Department of Energy," he said. "We're leaving for Colorado to take a look at the shale-oil project and decide what should be filmed. Call me back at 6:30 and I'll tell you when to meet me at my plane."

Armand and Baeder flew to Colorado, and after filming was completed, Armand expressed dissatisfaction with the rough cut, but didn't say why. Baeder asked me to take a look at it. The problem was obvious. "Armand isn't *central* enough," I commented. "Make him the hero of the film, and I assure you he'll like it."

Baeder followed my suggestion, and the new edit featured Hammer in almost every other scene. "Now the movie really shows Oxy at its best!" Armand declared after viewing and approving it. Meanwhile, as the feud between Carter and the oil companies raged on, Occidental received a $20-million-a-year grant extending over ten years to develop its shale-oil project.

Just after Labor Day, President Carter and the Panamian chief of state, General Omar Torrijos Herrera, signed the Panama Canal treaty agreement. The administration faced an uphill battle when the treaties were sent to the Senate for ratification, and Armand, ever eager to serve a new president, worked his way down a list of senators and subjected each to a monologue on behalf of the treaties. Armand also inserted a series of full-page protreaty ads in major newspapers across the country. When a protreaty organization, Americans for the Canal Treaties, selected forty prominent Americans, Armand among them, to donate $15,000 apiece to fund a media blitz, Armand was thrilled. He told me the contributors were being invited to a reception at the apartment of Carter's special trade representative, Robert Strauss, followed by a White House dinner hosted by the president. "This is terrific!" he exclaimed.

Not everyone thought so. Some of the other invitees complained to reporters that the office of the president was being used to sponsor a partisan fund-raising event, and as a result the reception and dinner were canceled. It was one of those little things that drove Armand into a frenzy. "Oxy is still going to make the donation," he announced, "but those dunderheads gypped me out of having dinner with Jimmy! I know their names and no matter how long it takes, I'm going to get even with each and every one of them!"

Mexico had enormous proven oil reserves, and its new president, José López Portillo, was looking for financing and technology to develop his nation's oil industry. Bearing that in mind, Armand decided that the time had come for him to better relations between the United States and Mexico with his money and art collection serving as useful diplomatic tools. He began by ordering the senior staff at Hooker's Mexican subsidiary, Hooker Mexicana, to set up a meeting with López Portillo. Presenting himself as a patron of the arts whose dream was to mount a definitive exhibition of the best examples of Mexico's Pre-Columbian art and tour it across the United States, he persuaded the Mexican president to sanction the tour. Then he sent word that he planned to donate *The Young Boy and the Coquette* by Fragonard to the Mexican government and received an "invitation" to exhibit the Armand Hammer Collection in the Palacio de Bellas Artes in Mexico City. López Portillo's sister, Doña Margarita, had a pet project, the restoration of a seventeenth-century nunnery, the Cloister of Sor Juana Ines, and its subsequent conversion into a cultural center. Armand donated 1 million pesos on the spot and accepted an "invitation" to exhibit the Armand Hammer Daumier Collection in the nunnery after the restoration was completed.

The senior staff saw these activities as more proof that Hammer was increasingly indulging himself in impractical fantasies. Mexico's national oil company, Pemex, was too fiercely nationalistic to enter into a joint venture with Occidental. What López Portillo was hoping to do, they told Armand, was encourage him to use his self-proclaimed influence with Carter to obtain loans to Mexico so that it could develop its own oil resources. Armand didn't listen and launched into a campaign to demonstrate his largesse to the entire Carter family.

President Carter's son Chip worked for the Institutional Development Corporation, which provided funds and services to inner-city schools. Armand initiated discussions with Chip about becoming a donor and eventually gave $100,000, making sure to hand his check personally to the Carter son and have his photograph taken as he did so. And when Armand learned that the High Museum in Atlanta was a Carter family favorite, he arranged to exhibit the Armand Hammer Collection there, accompanied by a donation of N. C. Wyeth's *The Petitioner* and a $25,000 contribution to a special museum fund. From the time he had attempted to entice Lady Bird Johnson to the Hammer Galleries in 1965, Armand had dreamed of having a First Lady on his arm at one of his art events, and he extended an invitation to Rosalynn Carter to attend the opening night festivities. When she accepted, his dream at last came true and he posed with the First Lady in front of Rembrandt's *Juno*, his most cherished—and expensive—painting. "Jimmy's in my hip pocket, and he's been in office less than a year," he later remarked to me. "The time has come to have a talk with him about Mexico."

Taking his standard position of global altruist, Armand told the president that U.S. investment in Mexico would revitalize the Mexican economy, which, in turn, would generate more sales of American goods to Mexico. The utilization of Mexican oil would also help the United States wean itself from its dependence on Arab oil. This pitch was accompanied by a detailed report prepared by Occidental's Latin American experts.

Occidental International's senior staffers reported that although Carter was favorably disposed, Carter's national security adviser, Zbigniew Brzezinski, viewed the plan as opportunistic and an attempt to have the U.S. government become the ultimate underwriter of a potential coventure between Occidental and Pemex, much the way the Export-Import Bank had underwritten Occidental's Soviet ventures. Brzezinski, a hard-line anti-Communist, had already infuriated Armand by announcing for publication that détente was over and that a new cold war was in progress. Before joining the Carter administration, he had been in charge of Columbia University's Research Institute on Communist Affairs. "Brzezinski was the dean of the School of Soviet Hatred. I hate him, and so do the Soviets," Armand scoffed.

Utilizing a $750,000 Armand Hammer Foundation grant, Armand went ahead with his diplomatic campaign and mounted "Treasures of Mexico," a definitive exhibition of pre-Columbian art objects. The formal reception gala at the Smithsonian Institution was designed to place senior members of the Carter administration in the same room with their counterparts in the López Portillo administration, with Armand shuttling back and forth between the two groups. A few days later he escorted Rosalynn Carter on a private tour. And subsequently the Mexican American Opportunity Foundation awarded Armand the Mexican Order of the Aztec Eagle, which López Portillo personally pinned to his chest at a ceremony in the presidential palace. A new round of correspondence with Brzezinski concerning the need for U.S. investment in Mexico got Armand nowhere. But he remained convinced that he would find a way to get the countries to make a deal and that he would emerge the big winner.

The 1980 Summer Olympic Games were going to be held in Moscow. This would entitle the Soviets to mint and sell commemorative Olympic coins, and they anticipated earning profits of $300 million in hard currency from this venture. During 1976 they began to negotiate selling agreements with the other participating nations and accept bids from companies seeking the right to merchandise and distribute the Soviet-made coins around the world.

One bidder was Leo Henzel, an American doing business in the USSR and the head of a company called United Eram. Henzel made fifteen trips to Moscow, often traveling with his partner Dudley Cates, a vice president of Loeb Rhoades, an investment firm. Like other Westerners, Henzel and Cates found themselves trapped in the incredibly slow, suspicion-filled process that characterized Soviet negotiations. Hoping that Armand's expertise with the Soviets would enable him to close the deal, Henzel invited him to become a partner. Subsequently a consortium was formed that gave Occidental 70 percent of the profits, Loeb Rhoades, 22.5 percent, and United Eram, 7.5 percent.

Occidental was now in the coin-selling business, but after the arrangement was finalized, Armand decided to get rid of Henzel.

"I don't care if he did ask me to join," he told me. "It doesn't matter how much legwork he did. The only reason the Soviets would think of making a deal with him is because of me. So who needs him? He's a blockhead and if I don't oust him, he'll gum up the works."

Henzel's profits were estimated at $12.7 million, so when Armand offered to buy him out for $250,000, he dismissed the offer. Then Hammer learned that David Karr was also attempting to obtain the distribution rights and that Karr's good friend, Dzherman Gvishiani, deputy chairman of the Soviet State Committee for Science and Technology, had thrown his weight behind Karr, even going so far as to enlist the support of his father-in-law, Premier Kosygin. To Armand, Karr's involvement was a declaration of war. "I'm the number one businessman in the Soviet Union, not David!" he exploded. "He's doing this because he's greedy and because he's trying to show me up. I'm going to beat him into the ground."

One foreign correspondent told me by phone that the subsequent competition between Hammer and Karr was "open warfare between the two greediest fellow travelers on earth." Another observed that Hammer and Karr were spending so much on bribes, the ministers were beginning to realize that the sale of the distribution rights could be the most profitable part of the deal." Finally, Armand made a direct appeal to Leonid Brezhnev. At that point, the Soviets "solved" the problem by demanding that Hammer and Karr become partners. Armand was appalled. "The Soviets know us, and they don't know the other bidders," he said. "They trust me, and I guess they trust David, too, although I can't understand why."

Aware that Occidental's share of the profits was about to undergo a large reduction, Armand told Henzel, the originator of the deal, that cutting Karr and Gvishiani into the package meant that he had to go. But Henzel replied that he had sufficient grounds to sue; his percentage could be construed as a perfectly legal finder's fee, and he had other contingencies. Armand bluntly stated that he'd rather spend a fortune litigating against Henzel than keep him around, adding that if Henzel resorted to legal remedies, he was not going to stop until he drowned him in expensive litigation.

After Henzel appeared to back off, Hammer and Karr formed a new syndicate, Numinter, Ltd. In this arrangement, a Karr company, Financial Engineers, was given 40 percent, with half going to Karr personally, and Occidental's share was reduced from 70 percent to 33 percent. The other partners were Paramount Coin

Company, 10 percent, Loeb Rhoades, 7 percent, and two banks, Banque Nationale de Paris and Lazard Frères, 5 percent each. Lazard Frères became involved because it had a working relationship with Karr.

American Express was Numinter's leading competitor. The Soviet champion in its corner was Vladimir Alkhimov, head of the Soviet Bank of Foreign Trade. Most impartial observers felt that American Express, with its international credit card operation, huge list of members, and worldwide network of offices, seemed the more intelligent choice, and Alkhimov's support indicated that his bank felt the same way. The award of the franchise to Numinter led observers to conclude that Hammer and Karr must have supplied large payoffs to the Soviet Bank of Foreign Trade. Occidental and Lazard Frères were required to pay a $150 million advance, and once the check was turned over to the bank, Soviet mints began to churn out the silver, gold, and platinum commemorative rubles.

Numinter racked up advance sales of $59 million, which didn't stop Armand from insisting that Karr was cheating him. "He's keeping double books, just like he does when he sells Soviet arms to Libya and Uganda. David's Jewish, but that doesn't stop him from selling weapons to the PLO. And he takes commissions from both sides. The Soviets are suspicious of all capitalists. If they find out that he's cheating them, something terrible could happen to him! I wouldn't want to guess where that dishonorable bastard's going to end up!"

Armand was afraid of anyone he believed could pose a challenge to his preeminence in the Soviet Union. For eight years independent film producer Allan Sandler had created industrial promotional films for Occidental that had given the Soviets numerous opportunities to get to know him and see his work. In 1977 they asked him to come to Moscow to discuss the possibility of coproducing a feature film with them.

During his absence Armand stormed into my office. "What the hell is Sandler doing in Moscow? Trying to undercut me?"

I explained that the Soviets had made the approach to him and not the other way around.

"Bullshit! He's using my name and bragging that he knows me so that he can be a big shot over there. I won't have it! I'm the number one American businessman in the Soviet Union and the number one spokesman for the Kremlin in this country. And there's no need for a number two. The next time you see Sandler, tell him to stay away from Russia or I'll run him out of Oxy on a rail!"

I sat and listened to Armand complain about Sandler's "betrayal" time and time again until he finally got around to terminating him, claiming that Sandler "was gouging us and taking us to the cleaners." At the next annual meeting Armand told the shareholders that Sandler was being replaced by Fireline Productions, an in-house film production unit under his direct control. He described the change as "an economy move."

To my knowledge, Armand was the only chief executive to have his own private film crew, and he began taking it with him on public appearances. Now his entrances were truly dramatic. Lights were turned on, cameras rolled, and a sound man thrust a boom mike in front of him and recorded his every utterance. It appeared that he was so important that a TV news crew followed after him wherever he went. Hardly anyone realized that Armand was spending $1 million a year of company money to make around-the-clock home movies of his life, far more than Sandler had ever charged.

I was kept at arm's length from these activities because Armand did not want me to know that he was spending hours of his time in screening rooms watching footage of himself going about his business. Cassettes were often made of the soundtracks, and behind his closed office door, he played these tapes of his spontaneous conversations over and over again, enjoying them every time.

One event that Armand ordered Occidental's film crew to photodocument scrupulously was his charitable contribution to Columbia University. After he had received a solicitation letter directed to all former graduates, he replied that he was "in no position" to make a donation. Experienced in dealing with multimillionaire donors, the campus fund-raisers understood immediately that Armand was not the type to respond to a form letter by writing a check and simply dropping it into the mail. They began suggesting university projects that he might like to support, among them a $35 million fund-raising drive to reimburse the costs of building a twenty-story medical center.

Armand told me that he and his father were both graduates of the Columbia College of Physicians and Surgeons and that it made perfect sense for him to make a $5 million donation. It was one of the largest private donations in the 223-year history of the institution, and it came with one condition. The building would have to bear Armand's name as well as his father's.

The fund-raisers explained that they had already agreed to name the medical center after Augustus Long, chief executive of Texaco and an old and good friend of the university. When Armand refused to budge, university officials reluctantly approached Long. A real gentleman, Long agreed to have his name taken off the medical building and placed on an off-campus health sciences library. Then Armand made the demand that he also receive an honorary law degree.

Obsessed about the typeface that would be used to chisel his name on the lintel of the building, Armand feared that small, unimpressive letters were going to be employed. "For the money I'm giving them, I expect prominently displayed, easy-to-see big lettering that a film crew will have no difficulty shooting," he declared. My graphics assistants were called on to design appropriate typefaces, and after studying these designs for hours and hours over a number of days, Armand sent off his favorites to the office of the president.

The announcement of Hammer's donation stimulated protests from Columbia University alumni, who were incensed that the building was going to be named after "a Communist father" and "his fellow-traveler son." Armand remained unperturbed. "After they get it out of their systems, they'll forget about it," he said airily. "They always have in the past, and they will continue to do so in the future. Before I'm through, the only thing I'm going to allow people to remember about me is the fact that I've lived a life devoted to helping mankind on a scale previously unheard of. After I'm gone, people are going to look back at my life and pronounce it a miracle."

24.

MAN OF CONSCIENCE

Armand never wavered in his determination to obtain compen-sation for the nationalization of Occidental's holdings in Venezuela. As soon as he learned that he was going to receive the Officer's Cross of the Legion of Honor on January 27, 1978, during a ceremony and formal dinner at the French embassy in Washington, he extended an invitation to Venezuelan ambassador Ignacio Iribarren. The Christian Democratic Party planned to charge the Pérez administration with overspending, corruption, and inefficiency during the forthcoming presidential campaign. It was Armand's intention, he told me, to inform Iribarren that he was "willing to do whatever it takes to help keep Pérez's party in power, on the condition that Venezuela pays up. And if that doesn't work," Armand added, "the only thing that's going to make them pay up is getting Jimmy Carter—or whoever comes after him —to pressure them into doing it. When the time comes, I'll be there to apply the pressure."

The pressure came, as usual, in the form of a gift. Rosalynn Carter had told a reporter that *Cincinnati Enquirer, 1888* by William Harnett was one of the president's two favorite paintings. Even though the canvas was in the White House collection, it was actually owned by J. William Middendorf II. Seizing an opportunity, Armand bought the painting from Middendorf for $360,000 and donated it to the White House on the condition that he could come to the White House and make a formal presentation, followed by a tea in his honor.

Armand wanted full press coverage, but a couple of reporters said that the presentation ceremony for a painting that was already

on permanent loan was not exactly newsworthy. But Armand
firmly believed that whatever he did was news and during the tea
he grabbed *Washington Post* reporter Henry Allen by the arm, and
gave him a complete rundown of his activities. He said he was
"feeling fine. Friends tell me that I look younger than I did several
years ago" and went on to say that he had just arrived from Bolivia,
where he had met the new president, that he had spent the prior
weekend in Warsaw with Polish Communist Party chief Edward
Gierek, and that he had recently met with President López Portillo
and had spoken by telephone with Leonid Brezhnev. He also made
sure that Allen knew that he was receiving an honorary degree
from Columbia University and that he had contributed $5 million
to the institution. Finally, he bragged that Middendorf had wanted
$500,000 for *Cincinnati Enquirer, 1888,* but that he had talked him
down to $360,000. Allen dutifully reported the encounter and
wrote, "Hammer keeps his eyes moving like those of a delighted
chess player who can't wait for you to stop struggling so he can put
you in check again."

Armand had arranged for the Appeal of Conscience Foundation, an organization devoted to promoting understanding among
religious faiths, to present him with its annual Man of Conscience
Award in recognition of his contribution to international understanding. "After I bought Jimmy's favorite painting for him," he
told me, "I didn't think Rosalynn was going to turn me down when
I asked her to serve as honorary chairwoman. And she didn't."

Armand truly believed that the more awards he collected, the
easier it would be for him to convince the Nobel committee to
award him the Peace Prize. After he donated the funds to launch
Pepperdine Associates, an on-campus fund-raising organization,
Pepperdine University awarded him an honorary doctor of laws
degree. Southeastern University, another recipient of his largesse,
also presented him with an honorary degree.

To gather even more glory, Armand was supervising the preparations of "Daumier in Retrospect, 1808–1879: The Armand
Hammer Collection," a celebration of the centenary of Honoré
Daumier's death. This traveling exhibition of five hundred lithographs, the most extensive Daumier collection ever to be seen in
the United States, was going to be launched at the County Museum
in spring 1979. After Armand contributed $250,000 to the Royal
Academy of Fine Arts in London, he received an invitation to take
the Armand Hammer Daumier Collection to London, where he
funded a reception gala that brought out a slew of British notables.

When the Smithsonian Institution presented him with its highest honor, a lifetime membership in the James Smithson Society, he staged another gala that produced even more publicity.

Armand had clinched an appointment to the board of trustees of the Corcoran Gallery of Art in Washington by volunteering to donate $1.15 million to renovate the gallery's auditorium and to establish a free-admission policy. Then he arranged to have the Daumier collection exhibited at the Corcoran Gallery in early fall 1979, accompanied by an elegant trustees' dinner that he would fund. He described this event to me as "an opportunity to cultivate some of the richest and most powerful members of Washington society." When the American Academy of Achievement chose him to receive its Golden Plate Award, he demanded that I turn out the TV news crews. "I won't rest until I see myself on all three networks being handed the golden plate."

After Buckingham Palace notified Armand that Prince Charles was planning to visit Occidental's North Sea operation, he decided to give the prince a personal tour of the facility and to call out the media. It worked splendidly, and he set into motion a plan to exhibit the Armand Hammer Collection at the Edinburgh Festival in August and to have the prince attend the opening.

Everything seemed to be going Armand's way. On March 16, 1978, the Senate ratified the first Panama Canal treaty by a 68-to-32 margin, a single vote more than the required two-thirds majority. The second treaty was ratified by the same slim margin on April 18. Armand was exultant. "What did I tell you! Jimmy and I won!"

But his mood soured a few days later when the administration announced that the pending trial in Moscow of Soviet Jewish dissident Anatoly Shcharansky was a "test" of Soviet-American relations. Newspapers across the United States printed condemnatory articles about the Soviets, and Armand asked me to book him on a round of TV talk shows so that he could speak out on behalf of the Soviets.

When he was scheduled to appear on Tom Snyder's late-night *Tomorrow* show, the interview was going to be a half hour long. Fearing a large dose of pro-Soviet propaganda, I suggested that Armand spend a portion of the time displaying some of the most impressive works in his art collection. He jumped at the chance to appear on TV accompanied by *Juno,* but he also called USC and received permission to borrow Rubens's *Venus Wounded by a Thorn* and two other paintings he had donated in 1965.

On camera, after Armand heaped his obligatory praise onto Lenin, Snyder turned to the subject of Stalin. "Was he the bad guy?"

"Yes," Armand replied. "Stalin was the bad guy. Stalin was the man who thought the Russians could do everything themselves and that he could bring about Communism without the help of the West." Snyder ignored Armand's careless mouthing of Leninist theory and his refusal to acknowledge Stalin's butchery.

Finally, the discussion turned to Hammer's paintings, and he looked fondly at one of the borrowed canvases. "That's Brueghel's *Maytime and the Presence of Dancing*. It's a little gem, and I'm proud to have it."

The painting, actually Brueghel's *Dancing Peasants,* really was a little gem, and Armand's comment reinforced my hunch that he wasn't planning to return it. A few days later, back in Los Angeles, he asked Martha Kaufman to hang Rubens's *Venus Wounded by a Thorn* in his office. "USC should have given me an honorary degree fourteen years ago, and they didn't," he said by way of explanation. "They screwed me. Now it's my turn to screw them! They'll never get that painting away from me."

Then Armand turned to one of the activities that always pleased him: a demonstration of his clout with the Soviet leadership. Occidental President Joe Baird shared a mutual friend with Christina Onassis, and Baird had learned that Onassis wanted Armand's help to gain permission from the Soviet authorities to marry Sergei Kausov, who was rumored to be a KGB agent. The couple had met in Paris, but when their affair became public knowledge, Kausov was quickly hustled back to the Soviet Union. Christina was finally allowed to join Kausov in Moscow, and Armand took full credit.

"Armand convinced the Soviets that the marriage would be of help to them," Victor told me. "He explained that it would give Kausov the opportunity to gather lots of information on the international shipping industry while he's lying beside Christina."

This potential source of information, if that's what it was, soon dried up. The marriage lasted only a few short months.

On April 17, eight months after the original deadline set by the SEC for Occidental to deliver a complete accounting of its sensitive payments between 1969 and 1975 had come and gone, Armand received the internal audit committee's "source memorandum," a fifty-four-page addendum to the twenty-eight-page "preliminary report" that Occidental had submitted to the SEC in March 1976.

Accompanying the report was the audit that Arthur Andersen & Co. had conducted at the request of the internal audit committee as a part of its investigation. Permeated with a spirit of atonement, the source memorandum revealed that Occidental had dispensed $1.2 million under illegal or questionable circumstances during the years in question. In an elegant turn of phrase, the committee went on to explain that this sum had been drawn from a pair of "off balance sheet funds" that had been established by "a currently employed executive of an Occidental subsidiary" and used by "certain former senior executives of Occidental and a European subsidiary."

The report turned next to a breakdown of the illegal payments. Bribes in various amounts were listed and explained with the kind of precision that could best be described as touching. Included among the American recipients of Occidental's largesse were former Tennessee senator and current Republican National Chairman William Brock, whose $5,000 payment was marked "unverified"; Louisiana Governor John McKeithen, $1,500; former Texas governor Preston Smith, $1,500; Texas Governor Dolph Briscoe, $500; and former California congressman Richard Hanna, $250.

The overseas recipients included John Franco, a government official with the Argentinian national steel company, $211,807; Harry Wongkaren, agent-manager of the Indonesian national purchasing agency, $180,694 (with a portion of these payments going directly into numbered Swiss bank accounts); and Maurice Sobajian, a consular secretary for commercial affairs at the Libyan embassy in Washington, $53,361, including a $40,000 personal "retainer." Unidentified Mexican national railway employees who had lowered Occidental freight charges had received $93,000, while unidentified Italian tax collectors who had deducted $100,000 from a tax claim against an Occidental subsidiary had received $14,000. (Arthur Andersen & Co. admitted being directly involved in the last transaction.)

Occidental also paid a $15,357 "commission" to South Korean government official and businessman Tong Sun Park, a key figure in the House "Koreagate" investigation of alleged illegal payments by Korean businessmen to U.S. legislators. Occidental offered the explanation that it had not known that Park was a government official when he was hired to represent Occidental in its dealings with the Korean national oil company.

The day after Armand received the source memorandum and

the audit, behind the closed doors of the boardroom he and six other directors voted to exonerate themselves and other management officials from legal responsibility for all illegal payments. Then the source memorandum was submitted to the SEC and the audit was filed away at Occidental headquarters. While the internal audit committee had relied primarily on questionnaires to produce the source memorandum, the outside accountants had been given access to Occidental's books and other financial records, and it was understood that their audit was by far the more revealing. Therefore, no director would comment on its contents or, for that matter, even acknowledge its existence.

The following day I released the source memorandum to the press, accompanied by an announcement that "no present member of the board of directors or of senior headquarters management appears to have any knowledge of the apparently illegal payments" and that the internal audit committee recommended that no legal action be taken against any of the individuals or entities involved. Around corporate headquarters the memorandum came to be known as "the daub," a mere daub of whipped cream on top of a very big cake.

One item in particular provoked gales of laughter. It concerned Occidental's slush-fund safe-deposit box in the bank on the first floor of corporate headquarters. According to the report, Armand's secretary, Dorothy Prell, had rented the box under the name Oil Trading A.G. (OTAG) in 1968 at the request of two former senior executives. Prell told the audit committee that she had been informed that the safe-deposit box had nothing to do with Occidental business; therefore, she had not mentioned it to Armand until January 1975, when he was in the midst of preparing a response to a subpoena in connection with his Nixon campaign contribution difficulties. What caused the laughter was not the outrageousness of the story, but the idea that any Occidental executive would dare ask Prell to do something for him and that she would not only do it, but also keep it a secret from Armand. She took orders *only* from Hammer, and she told him *everything*.

The release of the source memorandum triggered a series of news stories carrying headlines like "Questionable Payments Admitted by Occidental." But it was nothing compared to what happened next. Between 1942 and 1953, Occidental's subsidiary, Hooker Chemical Corporation, had dumped twenty thousand tons of hazardous materials into an excavation that had been started at the turn of the century but left uncompleted in Love Canal, a neighborhood in Niagara Falls, New York. Subsequently, the dump site was sealed with a supposedly impervious clay cap, homes and a school had been built on top of and near it. Twenty years later additional building and street construction had punctured the clay cap. Now the residents reported that toxic wastes were leaching into their backyards and basements and that children and pets were suffering burns if their skin came into contact with the oozing chemical wastes.

Environmental investigators reported that almost all of the trees, lawns, and gardens in Love Canal were either dying or dead, the air was riddled with poisonous fumes, and rainwater left chemicalized beige and blue stains on the ground. One investigator said that when he accidentally stepped into a puddle, the water ate through the soles of his shoes. Air and water samples taken in the community showed levels of certain toxic chemicals as much as five thousand times higher than those permitted by law. Medical records revealed that the residents suffered from abnormally high rates of hearing loss, hair fallout, cardiac disease, respiratory ailments, and rectal, breast, and blood cancer, as well as a miscarriage rate of 29.4 percent and that four of the twenty-four children born in one part of Love Canal suffered from birth defects and were mentally retarded. Occidental had suddenly found itself in the center of the most serious health hazard in the country and the worst example of chemical pollution in U.S. history.

From the beginning I chose to develop a defensive posture and to stick to it. The media was bombarded with the facts that Hooker's toxic-waste disposal methods had been the accepted practices in the late 1940s and early 1950s; that Hooker had made it clear when it sold Love Canal for one dollar to the Niagara Falls Board of Education in 1953 that hazardous wastes were buried there and that it would assume no risk or liability for anything that might happen in the future and had included this information in the deed to the property; that Hooker had intervened after the board of education had sold some of the dump-site property to private real estate developers without telling them that it had once been a toxic-waste dump and had warned that subsoil construction work would probably disturb the thick clay cap that sealed in the buried wastes. Finally, the media were reminded that Occidental had acquired Hooker in 1968, fifteen years after Hooker had stopped using Love Canal as a dump site.

EPA officials responded that manufacturers of hazardous wastes are responsible for the effects of those wastes for a lifetime even if they no longer own the ground under which those wastes are buried and have warned the new owners. On the heels of this public declaration, the Department of Justice and the House Commerce Oversight and Investigations Subcommittee announced individual investigations. And the press ran with the sensational story and ignored Occidental's rebuttals.

Armand had other matters on his mind. As May 21, his eightieth birthday, approached, he made arrangements to hold elaborate parties in Los Angeles, New York, and Washington and to travel to Moscow for a special birthday present: he was going to receive the Order of Friendship among Peoples at an elaborate ceremony in the Kremlin. This Soviet state honor was usually reserved for Communist leaders and had never been—and has never again been—awarded to an American businessman.

Over the course of the year the Moscow foreign press corps had reported periodically that Leonid Brezhnev was ill and had disappeared from view. The correspondents believed the Soviet leader was suffering from a heart condition that had required the installation of a pacemaker. He also seemed to have some sort of painful jaw disease that could be cancer. According to their eyewitness accounts, during his rare public appearances, he seemed to be heavily medicated and somewhat incoherent.

When the stories of Brezhnev's illness began to appear in print, Armand handed me a batch of photos of him and Brezhnev that had been taken "just a few weeks ago" and asked me to get them into print. Moscow correspondents confided that they believed that KGB head Yuri Andropov and party regular Konstantin Chernenko had asked Armand to help prop up Brezhnev's image in the United States in an attempt to distract the West from thinking that the USSR might be on the verge of a leadership crisis. They also pointed out that as Brezhnev grew weaker, governmental corruption and mismanagement were escalating.

When I asked Armand if Brezhnev really did have cancer, he was in a rare gossipy mood. "No," he said. "Against his doctor's orders, he has been taking massive hormone treatments to correct his impotence. What you're seeing are the disastrous side effects of this treatment. But he'd rather risk his life than give up being a ladies' man."

First Deputy Chairman Vasily Kuznetsov and not Brezhnev pinned the star-shaped silver-and-gold Order of Friendship among Peoples medal to Armand's jacket. Accepting the award, Armand said, "I love what I do for the Soviet people." When reporters asked him whether Brezhnev's decision only to send a written message indicated that he was ill, he replied that the Soviet leader was well and had been busy monitoring a Carter press conference. Carter had called for the removal of any congressional restrictions if it became necessary for him to move quickly in response to Soviet aggression, and Armand was asked about Brezhnev's reaction to the request. He replied diplomatically that both leaders had indicated to him that détente had never been in healthier shape and hinted that a meeting between them was definitely in the works.

From Moscow Armand traveled to Warsaw, where Occidental had been involved in an endless negotiation to achieve a comprehensive agreement involving the trade of Occidental-made phosphate fertilizers for Polish molten sulfur. When the last details were ironed out, Armand called me, bursting with excitement. "I did it again!" he exclaimed. "Oxy just closed a billion-dollar trade deal with the Polish government! Nobody has better entrée to the Communist nations and their leaders than I do. I want Oxy to be known as the leading trade partner of the Soviet Union *and* the Communist countries, and I want you to keep reminding the public of that. Let them know that I am as close to the leaders of the other Communist countries as I am to the Soviet leaders."

A few days later a director spoke to me confidentially on behalf of a majority of the board. Besides the potential costs of Love Canal, a three-month strike against Island Creek Coal, the closing of a refinery in Antwerp, and the postponement of the building of another on Canvey Island near London dictated a write-off of $122.1 million. "That amounts to around three-quarters of last year's net income," the director said. "At the rate we're going, we may not even be able to show any profits at all at the end of the fiscal year. This just isn't the moment to carry on about a far-fetched billion-dollar deal with *Poland* that Wall Street knows will never make a profit. Things are crazy enough without this company looking even crazier."

I agreed. As it turned out, Occidental did report a net income of only $6.7 million in 1978, compared to $153.7 million the year before. Moreover, the fact that Armand was proposing to use another 10 million metric tons of phosphate rock from the shrinking domestic reserves in order to manufacture superphosphoric acid (SPA) to trade with a Communist nation was bound to provoke a round of criticism in the press, and the less said about it, the better.

. . .

Thirteen years had passed since Occidental had discovered oil in Pacific Palisades, and the company was still filing, revising, and resubmitting plans in its attempt to obtain a drilling permit from the City of Los Angeles. Just a few days after Armand returned from Warsaw, the Los Angeles City Planning Commission endorsed the latest drilling plan. Approval from the City Council followed by a vote of 9 to 6.

One step was left, the endorsement of Mayor Tom Bradley. The mayor had opposed the plan when he was a councilman, and although six years had gone by, he had not changed his mind and he vetoed the application the minute it arrived on his desk. That left the City Council with the task of raising the ten votes necessary to override Bradley's veto. Suddenly the six holdouts came under siege from other local politicians, prominent citizens, campaign contributors, and state officials, all urging them to change their votes. "I'm softening them up," Armand explained.

When the time came for the kill, Armand announced that "things only get done around here when I do them." He climbed into his Cadillac limousine, was chauffeured to City Hall, breezed into the building and held individual meetings with the antidrilling council members. The senior staff believed that he had demeaned himself by engaging in this brazenly open lobbying and that subtle behind-the-scenes maneuvering would have been more effective. This opinion was confirmed by the deputy of one council member who complained that Hammer had "leaned heavy" and "didn't even take us to lunch."

The mayor's veto was sustained by a single vote, and the fact that Occidental had worked so hard and long and had come this close only to lose by one vote filled the senior staff with bitterness and anger. But Armand was surprisingly cheerful. "Tom Bradley is just another opportunist," he told me. "He opposed Sam Yorty, so he had to oppose everything Yorty stood for. If he voted for us, he knew he would have looked like a hypocrite. Now that he's had his veto, he's gotten himself off the hook."

Armand passed me his yellow pad on which he had listed items designed to encourage Bradley to revise his mind-set about the drilling proposal:

1. Back Bradley strongly for reelection financially and otherwise.
2. Support Bradley's pet civic projects.
3. Back Bradley's attempt to have L.A. host the Olympic Games.
4. Back Bradley to the hilt when he runs for governor.

"The time has come," said Armand, leaning back in his chair, "to put the mayor in my hip pocket!"

Armand also had another angle. Los Angeles's large and prosperous Jewish business community favored domestic oil activities as a way of diminishing the oil income of the Arab nations, and it supported Occidental's drilling proposal. Aware that Bradley received a great deal of financial backing from the Jewish business community, it suddenly dawned on him that *he* was Jewish and he began to search for a way to woo his fellow Los Angeles Jews in order to get them to apply pressure on Bradley. One of Armand's lawyers, Harry Simon Levi, and Israeli Prime Minister Menachem Begin had both been members of the Israeli resistance, and Levi and Armand began to take secret trips to Israel. After Armand met Begin, he began a campaign to make the Israeli leader his new "best friend" in the belief that nothing would be more impressive to Los Angeles's Jewish business community.

Victor confirmed that Armand's return to his Judaic roots was pure show. He told me that when he, Ireene, and Ireene's daughter, Nancy, had joined Armand and Frances in Armand's carriage house in New York for Christmas dinner, Nancy had brought Armand some art books as gifts. "He stared at the books," Victor said, "and became livid." When I asked why, he explained that Armand always found it impossible to accept a present that came without a motive attached.

But there appeared to be an underlying reason for Armand's rage. Nancy had recently married former Israeli ambassador Arieh Eilan. "Nancy's decided to convert to Judaism," Victor said, "and she's asked me to adopt her legally so she can have a Jewish father. But Armand insists that the Hammers aren't Jewish, and the last thing he wants is to have a former member of the Foreign Office of Israel as a relative."

A few days after Mayor Bradley's veto, I found Armand in a foul mood. He had asked Hooker's president, Don Baeder, to go to Florida with him to inspect an Occidental plant, but Baeder had turned him down because he had made a promise to attend his son's high school graduation ceremony.

After he mulled it over, Armand called Baeder. "Ask your boy if he'd like thirty-five shares of Oxy stock from me as a graduation present in return for releasing you from your promise."

Baeder thanked him for the offer but continued to insist that he had to attend the graduation.

"Let your son decide," Armand ordered. "Call him. Then call me back."

Baeder reported that his son had listened to the offer and said, "Wow, that's a lot of stock! It would be nice to have you see me graduate, Dad, but—"

Armand smiled. "It never fails. There's *nobody* money can't buy!"

When Armand wasn't ducking questions from reporters about Love Canal, he was responding to questions about Francis Jay Crawford. In retaliation for the arrest in New Jersey of two Soviet spies posing as U.N. diplomats, Crawford, the Moscow-based representative of International Harvester Corporation, had been arrested and charged with selling foreign currency illegally to Soviet citizens and having "illicit" relations with Soviet women. Ordinarily, Crawford would have been deported, but the Soviets confined him to Lefortovo Prison, subjected him to unrelenting interrogation, threatened him with a possible eight-year jail sentence, and assigned him a Soviet lawyer whose last client had received the death penalty.

Fearing to antagonize the Soviet leadership, the American business community in Moscow ignored the arrest. But businessmen at home were enraged because Crawford's detention indicated that any American working abroad could be subjected to false arrest and held hostage by a foreign government. When they demanded White House intervention, Treasury Secretary W. Michael Blumenthal approached Soviet premier Kosygin, but Kosygin insisted that nothing was going to dissuade the Soviet government from placing the businessman on trial.

Enter Armand Hammer. At the beginning of August, after a two-month stalemate, he approached the State Department, volunteered his services as a mediator, and began telling everyone that both International Harvester and the State Department had urged him to intercede personally with Leonid Brezhnev. Then he ordered a thorough check on International Harvester to see if it was ripe for a takeover. Finally, he dictated a letter to Brezhnev and told reporters that he planned to take the matter up with the Soviet leader when he traveled to the USSR at the end of the month. When the Soviets set August 29 as Crawford's trial date, Armand remarked to me, "I'm going to see Brezhnev on the twenty-sixth and Crawford will be out of jail by the thirtieth."

At the end of August, Armand set out for the USSR to attend opening-day ceremonies at Occidental's fertilizer facilities in Odessa. After the ceremony, he boarded Leonid Brezhnev's jet and flew to Brezhnev's dacha on the Black Sea. The Moscow foreign correspondents noted that Brezhnev had never before sent his personal plane for an American and that Hammer was only the second American to visit the Soviet leader's vacation home.

The next day Armand summoned the press and told them that Brezhnev felt that Francis Jay Crawford had to be tried because there was "sufficient evidence." He also predicted "that the sentence would be a light one and that, most likely, Crawford would be allowed to leave the country." Asked if he and Brezhnev had discussed the fate of the Soviet spies captured in the United States, he ignored the implication that a deal was in the works to trade the pair for Crawford—a deal that he did not arrange.

Two days later as Armand had predicted, Crawford was tried, given a suspended five-year sentence, and deported. Armand immediately announced that his behind-the-scenes negotiations were responsible for the American's freedom. When reporters questioned U.S. Ambassador to the Soviet Union Malcolm Toon about Hammer's role in the matter, he responded with a terse "He's lying through his teeth."

The Moscow foreign correspondents believed that the Carter administration had, in fact, been working on a deal to trade the two Soviet spies for a group of Soviet dissidents and that the Soviets knew that, whatever they decided to do about Crawford, their agents were going to be able to leave the United States. It appeared that Armand and his Soviet friends had cooked up another international PR stunt that they hoped would help Armand overcome the resistance of the Carter administration to use him as a back channel—and would reinforce his image as a great humanitarian.

25.

IN PURSUIT OF THE NOBEL PRIZE

During 1978, constant rumors circulated that Armand was ill, about to retire, or on the verge of being forced out. These rumors fueled Occidental president Joe Baird's belief that he was destined to be the next chairman and chief executive. Baird organized his own "central staff," a nucleus of senior staffers and other executives who believed that their self-preservation depended on being loyal exclusively to him. After the staff had divided itself into two camps, Baird sought out the assistance of those who remained in the Hammer camp and began treating them as if they were senior executives. Thus, he created the illusion that they would have rosy futures when he took over. This further isolated the Hammer loyalists and led a growing number of them to begin courting Baird. An executive vice president said to me in jest, "I'm having a hard time concentrating on my work these days because of all the puckering sounds coming from Joe's office."

Occidental had announced a $1.5 billion capital-spending program and a $1 billion capital-improvements program for Hooker. An additional $11.5 million was about to be allocated to correct environmental problems at Hooker's plant in Montague, Michigan; the class-action litigation against Occidental resulting from the signing of the first consent decree in 1971 had been settled for $11 million; a $9.9 million write-off was scheduled for Occidental's unprofitable interest in a Libyan methanol plant; and the Occidental-Soviet fertilizer deal had produced first-year losses of $10 million with an additional $5.8 million about to be written off against future losses.

According to the financial department, the company was looking forward to a cash deficiency of over $500 million in 1979, and as much as $100 to $200 million a year would have to be borrowed over the next five years to maintain the company's programs and enable it to pay its inflated dividend. Armand confided to me that he was completely aware of what Baird was up to. The mere thought that anyone would attempt to take his job away made him angry and vengeful, but Armand knew that as long as he kept Baird in place, the bank credit and loans would continue to flow freely. But he was angry, and he used his acid tongue to belittle Baird in public at every opportunity. "Joe," he said, "you're a pencil-sharp, bottom-line obsessive, but you don't have the showmanship to run a big company. You're too staid, you lack entrepreneurial skills, and you're not a risk taker. You're great with numbers, but you stink when it comes to achieving growth."

Stung by these criticisms, Baird started his own propaganda campaign. Having observed Armand's gift of disinformation, the constant repetition of a statement until people accepted it as truth, he began to circumvent me and use press contacts that he had developed himself to get in the newspapers. When a *Wall Street Journal* story appeared under the headline ARMAND HAMMER IS GRADUALLY LOOSENING CONTROLS AT OCCIDENTAL, I was convinced that Baird had been its source.

Many members of the Baird and Hammer contingents joked that Martha Kaufman might very well be the real heir apparent. In her outspoken, emotional way Martha continued to criticize Armand loudly in front of others, which always provoked the same response from him, an attack of the giggles. She also chatted freely with me about their relationship. Describing "a lovely weekend date," she told me that "Armand stopped by on Saturday afternoon and we went for a ride. He even had the driver stop so we could get some ice cream. We sat in the back of the limousine having the best time, laughing and licking each other's ice cream cones."

One Monday morning, Martha showed me some Polaroid snapshots she had taken over the weekend. She had gone to Florida, and Armand had followed her in his jet. He hated vacations, and this was the first time in twenty-three years that I had seen him doing nothing. But he looked as if he was enjoying it. As I thumbed through the photos, Martha confided, "I'm glad I wasn't involved with him when he was young. He's so strong and powerful now, he must have really been something then, and I wouldn't have been able to handle him. Take my word for it, Carl. Being with Armand is like being with a *bull*!"

Around this same time, Armand wrote me a memo ordering me to terminate the services of a certain printing company. Then he ordered me to fire our outside typesetting firm. Other memos in a similar vein continued to appear at regular intervals, and it became clear that Martha was instructing him to fire those suppliers she disliked.

One day Martha disappeared, and no one had the slightest clue about what had happened to her. When I asked Armand, he changed the subject. Finally, Victor explained that Frances had discovered the relationship and had delivered an ultimatum to Armand: get rid of Martha or she'd file for divorce.

"I suppose Armand didn't want the scandal," I remarked.

"It's not that," Victor replied. "Frances is shrewd when it comes to money. After twenty-two years of marriage, she still hasn't given Armand complete control of all of her funds. He didn't divorce Angela until he had everything. He *can't* divorce Frances for the same reason."

A few days after the next annual meeting, one of my employees showed me a photograph of the shareholders. Sitting among them was a woman disguised in an odd wig, a large hat, and big dark-rimmed sunglasses. We studied the image under a magnifying glass and came to the same conclusion: the woman was Martha Kaufman.

Victor confirmed our suspicion. "Martha is not gone and she's not forgotten," he remarked.

Martha's neighbor, a columnist for the *Hollywood Reporter*, worked at home and observed over the next several years Armand's limousine dropping him off at Martha's house three or four afternoons a week. During these lengthy visits his driver stood guard and was usually armed. In the evening hours, after Armand had returned to the office, a younger group would arrive, including a number of handsome men, and the sounds of partying flooded the neighborhood.

During a visit to Bohemian Grove, the exclusive executive retreat in northern California, Joe Baird met James McSwiney, the chairman of Mead Corporation, a successful forestry and paper-products company based in Dayton, Ohio. McSwiney told Baird that

Mead was eager to enter the chemical business. Baird knew that Occidental possessed more than $100 million in unused domestic tax credits. But Occidental did not generate enough domestic income to utilize these credits fully, and they would expire by default between 1981 and the end of 1982 unless the company found a stronger domestic earnings base to offset its large overseas income.

Baird went to Armand, explained that a major domestic acquisition would provide substantial assets and a place to invest the tax credits, and proposed a merger between Occidental and Mead. There was a persistent rumor that Mead was vulnerable and that a number of companies, especially Kennecott Corporation, were considering a takeover. So he urged Armand to allow him to move quickly and secretly to beat Kennecott to the punch.

Armand was noncommittal. "Joe's convinced his rapport with James McSwiney will enable him to position Oxy to initiate a friendly takeover," he remarked to me. "But his real concern is to take over my job. He can't stand it when I tell him he has no entrepreneurial zing and thinks that if he bags a big acquisition he'll be able to show me and the world he's got what it takes. What he's really trying to do is get me to shut up."

Occidental's investment bankers, Kidder Peabody and Dean Witter Reynolds, also had mixed feelings about a merger with Mead. Even if the takeover was friendly, it would be exceptionally costly; if it proved unfriendly, it could provoke a long, expensive, potentially embarrassing public battle that Occidental would stand a real chance of losing. The point was also made that the age of large mergers was winding down, and the analysts urged Armand to target smaller companies, which would probably prove more amenable.

Armand always dismissed this kind of advice out of hand as "negative thinking." But Occidental had just attempted to play the white knight to Husky Oil, a Canadian company, and had lost out because of Canadian regulations designed to discourage U.S. companies from acquiring Canadian businesses. While the drama of launching a large takeover appealed to Armand, he remained ambivalent. Finally, under continuing pressure from Baird, he decided to go ahead. "Whether I do or don't think the takeover is a good idea isn't the point," he told me. "Joe and I defeated Standard of Indiana when it tried to take us over. And we're going to be smart enough and tough enough to be able to scoop up Mead without too many problems."

The last week in July, Hammer and Baird summoned Kidder Peabody Vice President Raymond Raff and asked him to work out the details of the tender offer. Raff proposed a "bear hug," a bid that is so attractive to target company shareholders that an otherwise resistant management is forced to accept it. Newly issued Occidental preferred stock, valued at $35 per share, 51 percent more than the market value of Mead's stock, would be exchanged for all of the outstanding common shares and the voting shares of Mead. Thus, the total cost of the stock-for-stock transaction would come to $997.5 million.

Despite the fact that Occidental was financially troubled and heavily leveraged, Armand decided to spend an additional $1 billion to acquire Mead.

He ordered Raff to draw up the prospectus for a tender offer to Mead shareholders and the legal department to draft a letter from the board of directors to him spelling out the terms of the tender offer and authorizing him to initiate a hostile takeover of Mead. It was Armand and Baird's plan to go to Dayton to undertake a friendly takeover. If McSwiney turned them down, Armand would hand him the letter, and the hostile takeover would be under way.

On August 3, Baird phoned McSwiney, told him that Occidental was interested in acquiring one of Mead's coal companies, and made a date to go to Dayton on August 10 to discuss the deal. After the call Armand directed the executive committee to sign the letter. Then Baird placed another call to McSwiney and asked if he could bring Hammer with him. McSwiney replied that if a takeover was on their minds, he and Hammer would be better off staying home.

On August 9, after Mead's stock jumped from $23.25 to $27 per share, McSwiney phoned Baird and asked if Occidental had done anything to encourage the price change. When Baird professed ignorance, the Mead chairman issued a statement saying that his company did not know the reasons for the burst of trading activity. The next morning a member of Mead's board of directors happened to see a wire from a brokerage firm stating that a takeover rumor had caused the 3¾-point increase, and that if the rumor proved true, the takeover offer would be priced at between $33 and $35 per share.

Later that day, Hammer and Baird arrived at Mead headquarters and offered McSwiney and Mead President Warren Batts $35 per share. Hearing this figure convinced McSwiney that Occidental really was the mysterious "third party," and he dismissed the offer out of hand. When Baird tried to discuss a higher offer, he declared he wasn't interested "at any price."

Turning on the salesmanship, Armand described his habit of

giving generous stock options to new executives, which inevitably turned them into millionaires. He explained that in addition to their salaries, McSwiney would earn $350,000 in annual dividends and Batts, $275,000, and both would take seats on the Occidental board as the current directors retired. "This combined company wouldn't be big enough for both of us," McSwiney said sharply.

His options exhausted, Armand handed over the letter and he and Baird left. It was the beginning of a hostile takeover that one financial writer eventually would call "one of the most bitter, expensive and intensive corporate battles ever waged over a proposed merger" and another would label "the largest contested takeover bid in history." It was also a battle that would bring the invincible Armand Hammer to his knees.

As soon as Hammer and Baird were out the door, McSwiney hired three law firms to represent Mead: Smith & Schnake in Dayton; Troy, Malin & Pottinger in Washington; and Skadden, Arps, Slate, Meagher & Flom in New York. Armand didn't like it a bit. "McSwiney hired Skadden Arps because Joe Flom worked out a plan to help us defeat takeovers and he knows Oxy inside and out. Obviously, it's going to be a dirty fight."

On August 11, Occidental announced that its board of directors had officially approved the takeover plan. McSwiney and Batts used the business pages to reply that Occidental's bid was substantially lower than the average premium paid for companies in the paper-products industry. They also pointed out that Mead was going to earn $100 million in 1978 while the preferred Occidental dividend would come to only $95 million, an indication that Occidental was attempting to acquire a $2 billion company without spending a penny in cash and might even wind up with an enhanced cash flow.

Armand brushed aside the criticisms. "I'm betting that most of Mead's shareholders jump at the chance to make a profit on their stock." Then he sped off to Scotland for the exhibition of the Armand Hammer Collection at the Edinburgh Festival and ordered Baird to take full charge of the takeover attack. "It was his idea, so he can go for it," he told me.

Confident that nothing was to stand in Occidental's way, Baird told Wall Street that Occidental was going to offer investment bankers twenty cents for every share of Mead stock they delivered, a total of $5 million in commissions. At the same time Armand was also being extremely generous. The next day, at a luncheon attended by Prince Charles, he announced three donations, each in the amount of $50,000, to causes favored by the prince, including United World Colleges, an international network of progressive schools of which Prince Charles was president. It was the beginning of a donations program to woo the Royal Family that would find Armand spending a total of $14 million on the prince's various charities.

During Armand's absence Mead's board of directors voted unanimously to reject Occidental's takeover bid and to raise Mead's quarterly dividend twelve cents per share. The same day Mead's lawyers appeared before Judge Samuel Rubin of the U.S. District Court in Dayton and asked him to issue a temporary restraining order against the takeover plan. It was their contention that Occidental had attempted to deceive Mead and then intimidate it into endorsing an inadequate and illegal offer. They also contended that Occidental had manipulated Mead's stock price and trading volume in order to precondition Mead shareholders and the marketplace to facilitate the takeover. Occidental filed a countersuit claiming that Mead had made "misleading" statements in its complaint. On the same day as this filing, Occidental also filed a securities registration statement with the SEC. Following standard procedure, it contained an explanation of the purpose and financial details of the proposed tender offer to Mead's shareholders, a history of Occidental's operations and management, and other relevant facts.

Duplicating the method Occidental had used to defeat Standard of Indiana's takeover attempt, Mead's legal team set out to attack on all fronts. If the lawyers proved that the information on Occidental's registration certificate was incomplete or incorrect, the offering would automatically be delayed, and their first move was to launch a search for evidence that would demonstrate that Occidental had not provided full disclosure.

The newspapers were filled with stories about New York State's evacuation of Love Canal families and President Carter's declaration that Love Canal was a federal disaster area, and Mead's lawyers assumed that Occidental had not fully disclosed the probable costs of its environmental problems. So they utilized the Freedom of Information Act and hired environmental consultants, paired them with lawyers, and dispatched the teams to ten environmental agencies near Hooker plants to obtain accurate financial estimates.

Another of their goals was to check the accuracy of Occidental's internal audit committee "source memorandum," which had been filed with the SEC only four months before the launch of the takeover attempt. A list of rumors about Occidental's business practices was compiled, and interviews were scheduled with former Occidental employees, government sources in the United States and abroad, and investment bankers who might be able to substantiate these rumors.

Stanley Pottinger of Troy, Malin & Pottinger pursued another line of attack. He had heard that Hammer required new members of the Occidental board to sign undated letters of resignation, and, on a long shot, he called former Occidental board member and Vice President of Finance Dorman Commons. Commons confirmed the story, admitted that he was among those who had signed such a letter, and agreed to testify under oath. This discovery carried the implication that Occidental was, by definition, incapable of full disclosure because every piece of information it released was automatically "approved" by a board that merely rubber-stamped Hammer's decisions. "It was like bells going off," Pottinger later told reporters. "We thought it was a major break because it was such a bizarre practice that it would ignite the SEC."

Mead quietly supplied the SEC with this information and hoped it would inspire the federal regulators to file a securities complaint against Occidental. Then the lawyers began to compare Occidental's product lines with those of Mead and discovered that Occidental and Mead competed in ten product lines. Subsequently they petitioned the Department of Justice to file an antitrust action against Occidental.

In order to file suits against Occidental on the state level, the lawyers also searched for violations of the rules of the Ohio Division of Securities, which is charged with the review of takeover cases under state statutes. Then Mead sent a seven-page letter to its shareholders, which was also reproduced in two-page advertisements in major financial and consumer newspapers nationwide. The letter stated that Occidental's offer was "inadequate" and "that the actual value of the Occidental paper is subject to conjecture." Mead cited several reasons for this conclusion: Occidental had experienced a net loss of $35.9 million for the six months ending July 30, 1978; it was subject to a number of lawsuits that could have a material effect on the value of its securities; 20 percent of its revenues were derived from "unstable" Libya and were "questionable"; and its North Sea earnings were going to be significantly reduced after the British government raised its oil profits taxes from 45 percent to 60 percent on January 1, 1979.

It was Mead's contention that the combined companies would be too heavily leveraged to be able to achieve growth, that Occidental's performance under its present management was "unimpressive," and that Hammer was a convicted felon and at eighty years old was considerably past retirement age but continued to insist publicly that he still made "the important decisions."

Armand's visibility was not going to be an asset in this battle, not only because of his age and his criminal conviction but also because Occidental was perceived as a shady company because of his management. Therefore, all PR decisions were left to Baird. Convinced that nothing could stop the takeover, he declared, "We're going to have Mead in our hip pocket by Christmas" and ignored Mead's attacks. Baird also seemed to have no objections to seeing Mead pillory Armand in print, which it was doing with a vengeance. When I told him that we had better counterattack, he replied that as far as PR was concerned all Occidental had to do was "sit tight and do absolutely nothing." Baird maintained that stance throughout the Oxy-Mead fracas.

While Mead was battering Armand and Occidental in the media, the media were battering Occidental about Love Canal, and hardly a day went by without Occidental and Hooker being painted as criminals and villains. The enormous amount of negative coverage generated by Love Canal panicked some senior staffers, and they complained about my low-key approach. But I resisted their demand for a more aggressive tack, which led them to go to Armand with their ideas about how to enhance Hooker's image. Among other things, they wanted Occidental to initiate a Hooker "good deeds" program, including funding and building a recreational park in Niagara Falls.

Armand loved the idea, but I was dead set against it because Hooker was involved in three other dump sites in Niagara Falls that were about to explode into the news, and it had environmental problems in other parts of the country as well. "Until Hooker cleans up its act, nothing is going to help," I insisted.

My "negative thinking" made Armand so angry he didn't talk to me for days. I would have liked nothing better than to take on Mead, but Baird had insisted that I hold off; everyone at Occidental wanted me to fight the battle of Love Canal, which I remained convinced was exactly the wrong thing to do. So Occidental continued to be savaged by Mead's PR onslaughts *and* the criticisms generated by Love Canal.

. . .

An underwriter of a new offering is allowed to conduct a due diligence meeting so that brokers can question representatives of the issuer about its background and financial reliability. On September 8, Mead's lawyers informed Judge Rubin that Mead had a responsibility to its shareholders to act as their broker and subject Occidental to a due diligence investigation in order to determine the integrity of Occidental's management, its financial stability, and the true value of the securities it proposed to offer Mead's shareholders. If Rubin ruled in Mead's favor, it would be the first time that the conduct of a corporate management and the history of the illegal payments made by that management had been considered in a takeover suit.

The basis of Mead's request was its observation that Occidental had achieved sales of $6 billion by a "single-minded emphasis on growth and an over-dependence on high-risk ventures at the expense of a sound financial base" and the fact that Occidental had signed three consent decrees with the SEC in six years. Mead also accused Occidental of practicing improper accounting procedures, making "sensitive" payments and illegal political contributions that caused Hammer and former Occidental employees to be convicted of federal crimes that "may be jeopardizing sources of Occidental's revenues," and "a variety of other distasteful and questionable business practices" that had generated costly litigation. A raft of supporting documentation accompanied the request. The lawyers added that it was essential that they be granted permission to inspect all of the internal memos and documents that had been used by Occidental's internal audit committee to compile its source memorandum.

Occidental replied that Mead was incorporated in Ohio and that Ohio's takeover code did not require a separate securities registration statement for a proposed offering. Therefore, Mead had no obligation to undertake this kind of investigation on behalf of its shareholders. Mead's lawyers immediately prevailed on the Ohio Division of Securities, which sprang into action and announced that a two-week hearing would begin in Columbus the following day to determine whether or not Occidental had correctly interpreted the state takeover code and was providing sufficient information about its financial integrity and reliability.

The next morning Armand testified before Hearing Officer Nodine Miller. Baird appeared the next day, followed by Finance Vice President Jack Dorgan. After reading the transcripts of five days of testimony, Judge Rubin declared from the bench that "it's apparent even at this early stage of the litigation that the conduct of the management of Occidental Petroleum Corporation may be a matter pertinent to decisions by shareholders on the exchange offer" and ordered Occidental to turn over to Mead every document that had been used by its internal audit committee to prepare the source memorandum. The same day, Mead filed antitrust complaints in the Dayton courthouse and the Columbus hearing room, alleging that the acquisition would lessen competition in ten product lines.

The confidentiality agreement Occidental negotiated with Mead allowed Mead to use only seven lawyers and one accountant to examine the almost one million Occidental documents in the short period of time granted by Judge Rubin. At the same time Occidental filed a motion contending that the documents were subject to attorney-client privilege because they reflected communication between a "client" and a committee composed of outside employees and independently contracted lawyers and accountants. For that reason Occidental had almost all of the documents, including many inconsequential ones, stamped CONFIDENTIAL—FOR ATTORNEY'S EYES ONLY.

In the middle of all this, Armand had to fly to New York to attend the unveiling of the granite plaque bearing his and his father's names at the Columbia University medical center he had helped to fund. University president Howard McGill took the occasion to hail Armand as FDR's "adviser," a member of Harry S Truman's National Food Committee and Dwight Eisenhower's Council for the Study of Peace in the World, and JFK's "roving economic minister" and presented him with an honorary doctor of laws degree.

Meanwhile the battle with Mead was heating up. On his return Armand learned that during discovery Mead had located a memorandum drafted to Joe Baird on August 1, 1976, from an Occidental employee named E. J. Birch, concerning "improper activities on Occidental's behalf in Libya." Birch had quoted another Occidental employee, Jim Henry, as saying that "there is substance to the alleged payoffs and other irregularities on the part of expatriate Occidental employees."

Mead intended to introduce this memo in federal court to establish that Occidental's source memorandum might be incomplete and to encourage the SEC to open a new investigation and it dispatched a lawyer to Libya in an attempt to gather depositions from those who might have been directly involved in the alleged bribery charges.

In the Dayton courthouse, Occidental insisted that the memo

was not really about foreign payoffs but dealt with possible domestic payoffs. At first Baird "didn't recall" the correspondence, but eventually he confirmed Occidental's position when he "remembered" that the kickbacks had emanated not from Libya but from Occidental's Houston office, that the employees who were involved had been fired, and that Occidental had lost $750,000 as a result of their activities.

"Did you send this information to the SEC?" I asked him.

"It didn't qualify as a material fact and was of no significance to the shareholders," he replied.

The war over the admissibility of this memo and other Occidental documents was so fiercely contested that Judge Rubin appointed a special master, J. W. Brown. The job of this judicial officer was to hear testimony and make reports, which Judge Rubin would approve and would then become the decision of the court. In the interim, Occidental set out to dissuade Justice from filing an antitrust suit based on concerns that the merger might produce unfair competition in the production of coking coal and the manufacture of sodium chlorate and especially carbonless carbon paper. In an exchange of confidential letters, Occidental offered to sign a consent decree agreeing that, if the merger took place, it would sell one of Hooker's sodium chlorate plants, divest itself of two of Mead's coal properties and not sell coal to Mead for five years, and terminate an exclusive resin-sales agreement and agree not to sell resins for copy paper to Mead for five years. Justice replied that each antitrust problem had to be solved immediately or it would sue.

"What are you going to do now?" I asked Armand.

He replied, "I'll let you know when I get back from Moscow."

The Moscow foreign press corps had reported at length about Boris and Natalia Kats who claimed that their baby daughter Jessica, who was suffering from a malabsorption syndrome that prevented her digesting solids and milk, was being refused proper medical treatment because she was Jewish. The Katses also insisted that the Soviets had refused to grant them an exit visa even though Harvard University Medical School Professor Dr. Richard Feinbloom, an authority on malabsorption syndrome, had volunteered to treat the infant in Boston. Subsequently, scores of prominent Americans had launched unsuccessful personal appeals to Leonid Brezhnev to allow the Kats family to leave before Jessica died.

In Moscow Armand came to little Jessica's rescue—or so it appeared. Presumably at the request of the Soviets, who wanted to counter all the bad publicity, he told reporters that friends had alerted him to Jessica's illness, that he had met with a respected UCLA pediatrician, Dr. Marvin Ament, and that Ament had explained that the Soviets lacked the state-of-the-art medical equipment necessary to make a precise diagnosis and prescribe the proper course of treatment for the baby. Armand announced that he had flown this equipment to Moscow and donated it to Moscow Children's Hospital, where Jessica was now being treated by seven prominent Soviet physicians.

A reporter asked to see the equipment, but his request was denied with the excuse that it was already in use. Another reporter commented that the issue wasn't really the baby's medical treatment in the USSR but the ability of the Kats family to receive an exit visa in order to exercise their right to have Jessica treated in the United States. Had Hammer raised that issue with Brezhnev? Armand replied that it hadn't been necessary and repeated the official Soviet position that "the doctors felt that the treatment could be given right here in Russia." When he was asked if he had visited Jessica, he said that he hadn't had the time.

Despite their reservations about the way Hammer had interjected himself into the Kats matter, most correspondents printed the "facts" as they heard them, and hailed Armand's humanitarian gesture. But then *Los Angeles Times* Moscow correspondent Dan Fisher called to tell me that he knew for a fact that the Soviets were doing nothing for the baby, and that Armand's press conference had been a classic red herring on behalf of the Kremlin. The truth came out several months later, when unrelenting pressure from all over the world forced the Soviets to allow the Katses to emigrate. After the family arrived in Boston, Jessica showed rapid improvement. But the Kremlin issued a statement claiming that her illness had been used as a ruse to mobilize public opinion in order to compel the government to allow the Katses to emigrate. That pulled the rug of credibility out from under Armand, and the press was now aware that the real ruse had been Armand's "gift" of medical equipment. One reporter called to tell me that it must be an extraordinary privilege to work for a man who was suffering from a severe heart condition but willing to risk his life flying back and forth to Moscow to save an innocent baby. Each word dripped with sarcasm.

October 10 had been set as the date of record, the deadline for Occidental's shareholders to qualify for eligibility to vote on Occidental's tender offer for Mead. It was also the date that Ohio Division of Securities Hearing Officer Nodine Miller chose to deliver an eighty-one-page preliminary ruling on whether Occidental had made full disclosure.

Miller observed that if one were to accept Joe Baird's testimony that Occidental was acquiring Mead in order to apply a portion of its $100 million in offsetting tax credits, the urgency of the acquisition made no sense because the credits were not going to start expiring until 1982. Nor could she comprehend how it took a company fewer than ten days to make a decision to incur a $1 billion obligation. She also wondered whether Occidental had the financial capacity to pay for the acquisition and still maintain spending programs for both companies.

Baird had testified in response to questions about Occidental's probable $500 million cash deficiency in 1979 that the senior management had enormous flexibility and that a decision could always be made to "simply stop" any proposed project. Miller responded that "without continuing its substantial capital-expenditures program, Occidental will suffer irreparable financial harm. Yet senior management is ready to cut, snip, revise and amend that capital-expenditures program to fit in the Mead acquisition . . . [and is] hiding its arbitrary handling of this corporation under a cloak of flexibility. The record is fraught with examples of senior management making plans and disregarding them, recognizing risks but failing to plan for them, or spotlighting a project but abandoning it." She added that Occidental would have to raise $1 billion in outside financing over the next five years, while Mead, on its own, had the financial resources for substantial capital spending. Why, therefore, would Mead's shareholders find the merger advantageous? she asked out loud.

Miller further declared that Occidental's prospectus for its tender offer ignored a number of serious financial risks, including Hooker's obligation to spend $321 million on the Occidental-Soviet fertilizer deal at a time when it was facing "unknown toxological and environmental liabilities, high costs of production, shrinking markets, faded technology and obsolete markets"; political instability in Libya which could, at any moment, hurt earnings; a renegotiation of Island Creek Coal's leases with the Tennessee Valley Authority which could cost an additional $25 million; and the possibility of a foreign-exchange crisis in Peru, where Occidental had a $250 million investment. Moreover, Miller noted, as a favor to the Peruvians, Occidental had deposited $25 million in Peruvian banks, where it was not earning interest, and had failed to disclose this on any filings. Finally, Occidental had also failed to disclose that its shale-oil process had the potential to contaminate groundwater through leaching and that other processes "may prove superior."

It was Miller's recommendation that the tender offer be postponed until it was amended to provide adequate disclosures in the fourteen areas she felt were especially underrepresented. Commentators reported on this ruling at length, noting that it was the first time a state securities division had rendered such a long and detailed condemnation of a corporation. Occidental's only option was to postpone the date of record and cancel the shareholders' vote on the tender offer.

Armand was enraged, not because Miller had revealed so much that was true, but because she was a woman and "prejudiced." "That bitch must be having her period!" he ranted. "She's hysterical, and she's carrying her emotional feelings for Mead on her sleeve. She's just a local girl supporting local interests and doesn't deserve to have an important job."

Over the next eleven days Occidental suffered three more judicial setbacks: Justice asked the Dayton court to issue a temporary restraining order prohibiting Occidental from proceeding with the tender offer because Occidental and Mead had "overlapping interests" in three product lines; the Ohio commissioner of securities issued a final decision that confirmed Miller's preliminary ruling; and the Dayton court ruled that attorney-client privilege did not apply to Occidental's financial documents and granted Mead the right to introduce into evidence anything suspicious in Occidental's 1 million financial documents.

Armand had never seemed passionate about making the Mead acquisition in the first place, and the time had come to call it quits. But he insisted that he was going to tough it out because Occidental's substantial decrease in earnings demanded that something be done to "crawl out of the hole" and it was his belief that the acquisition would be profitable. It was impossible to determine if he had harbored this fantasy from the beginning or was just using it as an excuse because he hated to give up.

About this same time, another volley of criticism was aimed at Occidental. Secret negotiations between Armand and the Carter administration had produced an agreement from the Maritime Administration to pick up 50 percent of the costs of three special vessels that had been commissioned by Occidental to transport superphosphoric acid to the Soviets based on Occidental's pledge to use a domestic shipyard. When the government's plan to spend $78 million of the taxpayers' money on this project became public, critics blasted the "large government subsidy" for a corporation run by "Lenin's businessman." Armand's response was to ignore the brouhaha and concentrate on finding appropriate names for the ships, which he eventually decided to christen *Armand Hammer, Frances Hammer,* and *Julius Hammer.*

He was also busy putting into motion a plan that he believed would silence his critics forever. During the activities surrounding the restoration of the Musée Jacquemart-André in Paris and his campaign to win the French Legion of Honor, Armand had gotten to know former French premier Edgar Faure, who now headed the International Institute of Human Rights. Armand was so impressed by Faure's efforts he volunteered to fund an international Armand Hammer Conference on Peace and Human Rights under the sponsorship of Faure's institute. He chose Oslo for the site and set December 22 as the conference date, the exact time when the Nobel nominating committee would begin the process of reviewing written nominations for the 1979 Peace Prize. Armand then decided to stage the conference within walking distance of Nobel committee headquarters. And to make sure he had the opportunity to meet all of the key players, he scheduled an exhibition of the Armand Hammer Collection in Oslo and arranged to throw an enormous reception gala to which all committee members would be invited. "I've got even bigger plans," he confided to me. "This is merely the first step toward getting Jimmy Carter to place my name in nomination with the Nobel committee."

On October 22, Occidental responded in the Dayton courthouse to Mead's antitrust complaints by making public the plan for eliminating its antitrust problems that it had previously presented to Justice on a confidential basis. But the antitrust regulators filed an amended complaint, stating that unfair competition in the carbonless carbon paper market would continue to exist if the merger occurred and that it was their intention to seek a preliminary injunction, pending a full trial. "That would really kill us," Armand confessed. "The injunction will remain in effect while the court tries the antitrust charges and during any appeals, which could tie us up for several years. That would make it really difficult for us to continue our fight and we wouldn't be allowed to make any other acquisitions while we were tied up in court."

In an attempt to pacify Justice, Occidental quickly worked out a tentative deal to sell Hooker's sodium chlorate plant on the condition that it spend $1 million to upgrade the facilities. And to comply with the ruling of the state securities division, Occidental added fourteen disclosures to the prospectus for the tender offer. This information was also included on an amended registration statement that Occidental was required to file with the SEC.

After reviewing the drastic set of revisions, the SEC informed Armand that it was about to take the unprecedented action of launching its fourth investigation of Occidental in seven years. This investigation was going to focus on "Occidental's failure to disclose material facts in public statements made after January 1, 1975 in connection with company plans to issue securities."

Ironically, Armand was scheduled to receive the Man of Conscience Award in New York City on October 31. "Make sure you let the press know that I'm joining a select circle of great humanitarians that includes Coretta Scott King and Nelson Rockefeller," he urged. As he was preparing to leave for New York, attorneys in New York State were rushing to meet the October 30 deadline for the filing of claims against state and municipal governments and agencies in the Love Canal matter. The minute Armand disembarked from the Gulfstream in New York City, reporters told him that 350 claims had been filed and that their total amount exceeded $11 billion.

After Armand accepted his award, he announced that he had inside information that a Carter-Brezhnev summit meeting was going to take place in the next few months. A handful of reporters called to voice suspicions that he had made this statement to deflect questions about the stupendous size of the Love Canal litigation, which could only work in Mead's favor.

So many things had gone wrong during the attempt to take over Mead that the senior staff was genuinely amazed when the state securities division ruled on November 11 that Occidental had fulfilled its demand for full disclosure. Armand explained that a judge had recently declared Idaho's takeover law unconstitutional and that Idaho's law was not very different from Ohio's.

"The State of Ohio and its corporations know that their law is weak," he elaborated, "but it's still a good initial defense against takeovers and Ohio had no desire to be drawn into an extended court case. So our lawyers made a smart move. They used the Idaho decision as a precedent and filed in the federal court in Columbus to have Ohio's takeover law declared unconstitutional.

As they expected, the state and its big corporations pressured the securities division to back down in return for us withdrawing the suit and sparing everyone a meaningless court battle."

On the same day, Mead appealed this decision in the Franklin County Common Pleas Court in Columbus, arguing that the ruling had been decided on a record that did not include all of the material information that Mead shareholders would find significant and that Occidental's prospectus still failed to supply full disclosure. To support this contention Mead submitted two lengthy dossiers, each sixty pages in length. The first contained everything Mead had learned about Occidental's environmental problems. The second contained everything that had been learned from a review of Occidental's financial documents and from the sworn depositions Mead's lawyers had obtained over the past three months. Included among these documents were a copy of the audit Arthur Andersen & Co. had conducted concurrently with the internal audit committee investigation and a Department of Energy audit of pricing violations by Occidental's Permian Corporation.

Arthur Andersen & Co.'s audit revealed that Occidental had spent an additional $28 million on illegal and other questionable payments. At the same time the Department of Energy audit revealed that Permian had raised more than $28 million in overbillings, apparently the source of the funds for the "sensitive" payments" listed in the Arthur Andersen audit. Other information submitted by Mead to the court indicated that Occidental's subsidiary INTERORE had raised $9.8 million in overbillings and had also paid "commissions" of $20.6 million that could not be fully substantiated. If all of the figures were correct, Armand had in actuality dispensed more than $59 million from his private slush fund over the six years from 1969 to 1975.

By filing this information in the common pleas court, Mead forced Occidental to amend its registration statement with the SEC for a third time and to include this new information. Now the information would be a part of the public record, and three days after it filed in the common pleas court, Mead withdrew its appeal, explaining that it planned to pursue the alleged deficiencies in Occidental's merger offer as part of the federal court action that was still pending in Dayton. The real damage had been accomplished.

There was more bad news to come. Toward the end of November, New York State announced that after purchasing 237 abandoned Love Canal homes, it had begun to raze them and construct a ditch system in order to drain the contaminated water at a cost of between $8 and $10 million. Hooker announced simultaneously that it was building a drainage site around a much larger landfill on the northern side of Niagara Falls. This landfill had been used as a dump site until 1975 and contained eighty thousand tons of toxic wastes, which were leaching into the groundwater and fouling a nearby creek that was part of the city's drinking-water supply. Reports that cats playing near the creek had lost their fur and teeth and that goats had died after grazing on its banks had already begun to appear in print.

Armand and I did not discuss the results of surveys conducted by the Hooker environmental engineering staff, which stated that the company's three dump sites in Niagara Falls posed a potentially more dangerous problem than Love Canal, but we both knew that they confirmed my observation that Hooker's environmental problems could not be camouflaged by PR. In order to publicize something good for a change, I began to beat the drum for the opening ceremonies of the $20 million Armand Hammer Technical Center in Irvine, California, on December 1. This facility was going to house a research division devoted to investigating alternative energy sources and inventing a low-cost process for the manufacture of SPA. "Make sure you let them know that Jerry Brown is going to stand next to me during the dedication," Armand demanded. At the ceremonies, he noticed my expression of surprise when the governor did make an appearance, and he held up his hand so that I could see it and then slipped it into his pocket.

When Occidental filed its amended registration statement with the SEC, it became part of the public record, and it was no surprise that Mead tipped the press to its availability. The resulting coverage revealed that the amendment included the information that the SEC was investigating to determine whether Occidental had lied or failed to disclose to shareholders material facts about its domestic and international oil operations, contracts with foreign agents and governments, possible violations of environmental laws and accounting and auditing procedures, and whether it had entered into secret contracts with its officers and directors that should have been revealed to shareholders.

On December 6, Mead presented final arguments on its request for a restraining order to block the takeover. At the same time the press somehow obtained summaries of the information about Occidental's unpublished audit, which Mead had filed in common pleas court. Over the next few days the nation's business pages devoted generous amounts of space to the fact that Occidental had responded to a consent decree ordering it to make public all of its illegal and questionable payments by listing payments of only $1.2 million at the same time that it had available an audit placing these payments at $30 million. Included in these articles was the observation that Judge Joseph Waddy, who had originally signed the consent decree, had been too sick to review Occidental's submission, which had been accepted without question. Finally, *The New York Times* reported that it appeared that Occidental had continued to make questionable payments after 1975 and issue misleading financial statements in violation of the consent decree that it had signed and that "any new complaint from the S.E.C. might lead to criminal sanctions against the company and a jail term for the eighty-year-old Dr. Hammer."

On December 11, to no one's surprise, Mead won its temporary restraining order. Judge Rubin noted that it could be extended until year-end 1978 while he considered a request from Mead and Justice for a preliminary injunction. One week later, after five months of warfare and an expenditure of $6 million on legal fees, Occidental decided to bring the battle to an end, and the board of directors voted to withdraw the tender offer. When I asked Armand if he or Baird had made the recommendation to the board to pull out, he replied, "You don't need to know that. But there's one thing I'll tell you for sure. This is the last time I'll try an unfriendly takeover!"

After speaking individually to the directors, I learned that Armand had made the recommendation and that Baird had challenged it. Only three votes had been cast in favor of continuing. Baird had been stunned to learn that he had so little support, and Armand had been stunned because three directors had dared to vote against him.

Armand's motives for approving the attempted takeover remained a mystery. The senior staff speculated that either he had believed the merger was a sound venture, he was addicted to the excitement of a good fight, he had been convinced that he could get away with anything, or he was setting Baird up to make a colossal fool of himself which would make it easier to get rid of him at the appropriate moment. Whatever Armand's motives, Occidental had been badly beaten, but Armand confided to me that the real reason behind his decision to back down was the fact that the SEC had begun to investigate his private art businesses. I remembered Victor telling me that Armand had used the profits from the business of his second wife, Angela Zevely, to buy art for the Hammer Galleries. Now I began to wonder whether he had been using company funds to buy art for his private holdings and whether Occidental shareholders were in fact the owners of the most prized paintings in the Armand Hammer Collection.

Showing no signs of defeat, Armand left for Oslo to host the first Armand Hammer Conference on Peace and Human Rights. It was no mere coincidence that the Nobel Peace Prize Committee happened to be headquartered in Oslo. Just before he stepped out the door, he told me, "From now on, start referring to me in news releases and other communications as 'the future Nobel laureate.' By the time I get back, I'm going to have the Nobel Peace Prize in my hip pocket." On his return Armand declared the conference "a major success. But," he confessed, "it may take as many as three or four before my reputation as an international peacemaker is secured. There's nothing to worry about. I've got all the time in the world!"

One of the bribes included in Occidental's source memorandum was a $20,000 payment to two unidentified Guatemalan congressmen who had helped pass a petroleum law in a form that Occidental believed would prove helpful. This charge surfaced in print as a result of the activities of another Occidental whistle-blower, John Shaver Nava, a lawyer who had worked for Occidental in Bolivia and Guatemala, and who said he had been fired after protesting Occidental's bribery tactics in Guatemala. Shaver Nava came to be known as "the most disgruntled" of the many "disgruntled former employees" when he began bombarding South American government officials and the press with letters about Occidental's corrupt business practices, among them the bribing of the Guatemalan congressmen.

On January 11, 1979, Shaver Nava sued Occidental for $25 million in damages, charging that he had been named incorrectly in the source memorandum as the bribe payer and that the document had been used "to shift the blame . . . to employees." He also claimed that Occidental's report was incomplete and that additional improper payments had been made. On January 30, Dan Dorfman's "Full Disclosure" column in *Esquire* was entitled "Inside Oxy: That Old Man Hammer Just Ain't What He Used to Be." Quoting an investment manager "with a big position in Oxy shares" as his source, Dorfman wrote that Joe Baird had suggested that Hammer "had outlived his usefulness to the company and ought to make way for a younger man." And quoting an oil analyst, he wrote that Baird had remarked that he agreed with estimates that Occidental's stock price would jump two to three points "if Hammer got out . . . and he should."

Armand responded to these comments by telling Dorfman that he had no plans to retire. "I work seven days a week, fourteen hours a day, and I carry my weight."

On February 13, a lengthy analysis of the Mead takeover attempt appeared in *The New York Times* under the headline "How Is Occidental Run?" and it reiterated at length the charges that had been leveled against Occidental. But Armand was most concerned about two items in the *Times'* story: that a "former employee"—David Karr—had told the SEC that he had bribed Yekaterina Furtseva and that he had dropped the takeover after federal investigators had begun to look into his personal art businesses. The following day this allegation was featured on the business page of every major newspaper in the United States. Now there was something new to be concerned about. Was Armand or were the shareholders the real owners of works that were included in the Armand Hammer Collection?

26.

DR. HAMMER'S DOG AND PONY SHOW

Armand next focused his attention on the impending Brezhnev-Carter summit conference in Washington scheduled for the end of January 1979. But Brezhnev decided suddenly to postpone his trip. "Deng Xiaoping is scheduled to arrive in the United States directly afterward. The Russians are paranoid, and they're afraid that China, Japan, and the U.S. are attempting to form an alliance against them," Armand explained. "And Brezhnev was afraid that Deng was going to upstage him."

The itinerary for Deng's visit included a barbecue in Houston, hosted by President Carter, on February 2. Armand hadn't been invited and was convinced that Zbigniew Brzezinski was keeping him off the guest list because Brzezinski feared that his relationship with Brezhnev would alienate the Chinese Vice Premier and Communist Party Vice Chairman. Armand started making calls, and he did not get off the phone until his name had been placed on the guest list.

When I asked if his encounter with Deng might jeopardize his relationship with the Soviets, he replied that he didn't see a problem. "China and Russia may have their differences, but they're both Communist nations. And they both need me."

During the days that followed Armand gave a number of private interviews with members of the Soviet press. Victor explained that the reporters were really KGB agents, a fact that Armand also freely admitted to me. "In return for Brezhnev's permission to launch business discussions with Deng," Victor told me, "Armand's being briefed about the things the Russians want him to tell them about the Chinese leadership once Deng and he become friends."

This new mission was almost subverted when Armand and Frances arrived at the barbecue and Armand discovered that despite prior assurances, his name was not on the guest list. He later told me how he had solved that problem. "I spotted the name Robert McGee [a Robert McGee worked for Occidental International] and said that he was my employee and that his name must have been accidentally substituted for mine. After I talked my way in, I headed straight for the receiving line and introduced myself to Deng. He was thrilled to meet me. As he extended his hand he said, 'You're the man who was Lenin's friend. Why don't you come to China and help us the way you're helping the Russians?' "

I knew what was coming next, a hymn of praise for Deng—and for himself. "Deng is an impressive figure," Armand continued. "He's just like me. I'm eighty-one. He's seventy-six. I'm the engine behind this multibillion-dollar corporation. He's the driving force behind an unprecedented modernization program in his backward country. And we're both pragmatists. That's why Deng downplayed ideology. He knew that's what he had to do to get economic support. I'm looking forward to getting to know him better and making Oxy the number one Chinese business partner." As an afterthought Armand added, "I also met the real Robert McGee. He's a nice man, too."

Democratic Party officials later insisted that Armand's name had been left off the list by accident and that they had introduced him to Deng. Meanwhile, Armand ordered Occidental International's staff to send word to the Chinese that if he became the first American allowed to land a private jet on a Chinese airfield, he would fly to China and begin discussions about initiating a number of co-ventures between Occidental and the Chinese government. "It's a status symbol that will make them acknowledge how important I am," Armand said. "It's the first step toward getting the upper hand."

Permission was granted without a hitch. And aware that the Chinese had already invited a number of U.S. coal companies to become involved in Chinese mining ventures, Armand decided "to beat them to the punch" and achieve "the biggest U.S.-Chinese coal deal in history."

After preparations for the Chinese trip were under way, Armand traveled to Leonid Brezhnev's dacha for a second time. In

1963 France had reaped reams of favorable publicity when the Louvre had sent Leonardo's *Mona Lisa* on a U.S. tour. The Soviets owned a sole Leonardo, *Madonna with a Flower,* also known as *Benois Madonna,* and in an attempt to duplicate the attention that had previously been accorded France, Armand and Brezhnev arranged to make the Leonardo the centerpiece of a thirty-painting exhibition of artworks from the Hermitage Museum that would visit the National Gallery of Art in Washington on the first leg of a tour that would also include the obligatory stops at the Knoedler Gallery in New York City and the Los Angeles County Museum. This spectacular goodwill gesture was going to be timed to take place after Brezhnev and Carter signed the new bilateral strategic arms limitation treaty (SALT II) and the treaty was sent to the Senate for ratification. It was hoped that the exhibition and the favorable press accompanying it would encourage the Senate to take positive action.

In order to get the paintings out of the country, Armand confided that he was going to have to "help" the Soviets financially, although he didn't reveal the amount of his "help" or what the payment covered. After these arrangements were concluded, he left for China. The trip produced preliminary agreements involving geophysical surveys for offshore oil exploration, coal mining, and agricultural development, which included an exchange of Chinese hybrid rice seeds for domestic hybrid cotton seeds developed by Occidental.

It was not clear whether the Soviets were punishing Hammer or the United States or just being contrary, but not too long after Armand's visit to China, they decided to reduce the number of paintings that were going to be included in the forthcoming exhibition from thirty to eleven. Because it was a cultural exchange, Armand arranged to have eleven American-owned Italian Renaissance paintings lent to the USSR.

Thirty years to the day after he started working for Dow Chemical, Dow chairman Zoltan Merszei submitted his resignation. Detailed news stories on the financial pages characterized Merszei as "the nation's fourth highest paid industrialist" and described how he had built Dow's European division from scratch until it had become one of the company's most profitable assets.

Impressed by what he had read, Armand wrote to Merszei. When there was no response, he began to call him. When his calls weren't returned, he escalated his campaign with a dramatic gesture. Merszei went to Switzerland, and so did Armand. And after Armand sent word that he was "sending his plane" for him, Merszei, flattered by this level of attention, decided to have the meeting.

Armand wanted Merszei to run Occidental's international divisions and duplicate the success he had achieved with Dow. Merszei's advisers had warned him that Armand was not to be trusted, but had also made the point that he was not going to live forever and that Occidental would be a fine company for Merszei to run. Therefore, Merszei told Armand that what really interested him was taking over Occidental after he departed. Armand breathed an enormous sigh of relief. He confided that he was planning to step down in two years and was convinced Merszei had the capability to replace him. Armand made it clear that meeting Merszei was just like finding a long-lost son.

Merszei negotiated an ironclad employment agreement that included an annual starting salary of $350,000, an $800,000 bonus for agreeing to join Occidental, an additional first-year bonus of $112,000, and 50,000 shares of stock. Thus his entire first-year compensation was $1.2 million, considerably more than the $361,000 earned by Occidental president Joe Baird and more than double Hammer's $560,000. On April 16, he joined Occidental as chairman and chief executive of Hooker and vice chairman of Occidental's board of directors, the first person to hold this title in eight years. I announced that Merszei had been hired "to establish and implement international planning and development."

"We Hungarians are arrogant but lovable," he told me when we met. "I have great ambition, I'm a real good manager. I've always believed firmly that I'm the top man." At the same time Armand raved, "Zoltan is the best acquisition I've ever made! He reminds me a lot of myself when I was his age."

Inveterate name-droppers and glad-handers, both men thrived on risk taking, wheeling and dealing, and long hours. But Merszei had two things Armand didn't have, a terrific recipe for Hungarian goulash and sharply honed managerial skills. Merszei caught on almost immediately that Occidental was not a corporation but a mismanaged empire run by an emperor who operated on whim. One executive told him that he had once received a call from Hammer, who had said, "I'm flying over the North Pole and I'll only have you in phone range for five or ten minutes. So we've got to be quick. Tell me everything that's going on in your division." Another reported that he had been on his way to Catalina Island in his sailboat when an Occidental helicopter flew overhead and a voice boomed through a bullhorn, "Call Dr. Hammer immediately! He wants you to answer a question." Armand had asked about the whereabouts of another executive, who was relocating from New York. Told that the man was driving his family across the country to Los Angeles, he had roared, "That's the trouble with that guy! He thinks more about his family than he does of the company!"

Despite the reforms instituted by Joe Baird over his six-year presidency, it seemed to Merszei that unlike the superbly organized Dow Chemical, Occidental lacked a single functional operating system. Nothing was done efficiently, there was no coordination among divisions, and there was plenty of "Mickey Mouse with the numbers." Among the things that Merszei found the most puzzling were Hammer's involvement with the USSR and his craving for recognition from heads of state. He told me that Armand's Soviet activities were "lousy business" but "an emotional issue for Hammer, a love test. Making you accompany him to the Soviet Union is his way of making you demonstrate your affection for him."

Just before Merszei came to Occidental, President Carter had decontrolled domestic oil prices and called for a windfall profits tax on the billions of dollars that were about to be earned by the energy industry. These funds would be used to help poor families meet rising fuel bills, finance public transportation projects, and underwrite research for alternative sources of energy. Armand was the only domestic oil executive who supported the windfall profits tax, and he had transformed his office into a lobbying organization for the proposal. In response, infuriated energy industry leaders had labeled him "a Marxist capitalist" who "makes his profits by manipulating the government, with little regard for a free market or free exchange."

It wasn't long before Armand's motive surfaced. The second Armand Hammer Conference on Peace and Human Rights was going to be held on August 25 at Roosevelt Campobello International Park, and he was angling to have Carter as the keynote speaker. "I'm going to present two gold medals at the conference," he told me. "One is for Jimmy, the other is for me. The only way Jimmy's going to be able to get his medal is by showing up to claim it."

It was the first time in Merszei's long corporate career that he had seen a company lobby for a tax that would hurt its own profits so that its chief executive could persuade the president of the

United States to nominate him for the Nobel Peace Prize. Ultimately Carter declined the invitation to Campobello, but he did send a message to be read at the conference. Subsequently Zbigniew Brzezinski said of Armand's shameless campaign to win the prize, "If it can be bought, his chances of winning are quite high."

Merszei never disguised his expectation that he would replace Armand. But local newspapers continued to print stories about Joe Baird's increased authority under headlines such as "Armand Hammer Loosens Tight Grip," which I continued to believe Baird was behind. These new stories implied that Armand was either sick or close to death. "Old exploiters like Armand never die. They just steal away," company director Neil Jacoby scoffed after he read them.

Armand, too, dismissed the thought that he was "loosening his tight grip." By way of illustration, he said, "Rabbi Edgar Magnin [the Beverly Hills 'celebrity' rabbi] is in his nineties and still serves his congregation on a daily basis. He told me, 'I tell people what to do, and they do it. Being the boss is what keeps me young.' I knew exactly what he was talking about."

Armand's physician, Jack Magit, was a director of the Wisdom Society, a nonprofit organization devoted to the advancement of knowledge, learning, and research. Therefore, it was no surprise when Hammer bragged that he was going to receive the Wisdom Award of Honor. "The prior recipients include Winston Churchill, Albert Einstein, Dwight Eisenhower, Carl Jung, Eleanor Roosevelt, Jonas Salk, and Albert Schweitzer," he informed me. "Don't leave any of their names out when you write your release."

"In all my years at Dow, I never saw the PR department make such crazy announcements," Zoltan Merszei remarked when this release landed on his desk. Another thing that surprised Merszei was Armand's peculiar relationship with the Jewish Defense League. At the annual meeting on May 21, Hammer's eighty-first birthday, JDL member Barry Kruegel arrived with his brother Earl and Irv Rubin and got into a prolonged shouting match with Armand. But Rubin sat silently. The senior staff explained to Merszei that Rubin had remained quiet because Armand had put him under a "spell" three years before when they had met after the 1976 meeting.

Much of Kruegel's anger was motivated by Hammer's activities on behalf of a delegation of Libyan officials and businessmen. Sensing "a great opportunity to ingratiate ourselves with the Libyan leadership," Armand had called Mayor Bradley and had asked him to welcome the Libyans to City Hall personally for the benefit of the press and TV cameras. A spokesperson had replied that the mayor "didn't have time." Armand later learned that Bradley's advisers had warned him that the gesture would infuriate his large Jewish constituency. When he substituted a luncheon at a plush restaurant in Sacramento, JDL members, Jewish leaders, and a group of legislators who had received invitations but were opposed to Libya's policies toward Israel blocked the entranceway.

On June 15, Jimmy Carter and Leonid Brezhnev met for the first time in Vienna to sign the SALT II treaty. Brezhnev was too weak to fly long distances, and Konstantin Chernenko had become his constant traveling companion, leading observers to believe that he was Brezhnev's chosen successor. When Brezhnev accidentally marched into a crowd of onlookers, Chernenko did his job by turning the Soviet leader in the right direction. This was the summit that Armand had spent three years insisting he was going to arrange. He covered his tracks by telling reporters that he had engaged in innumerable consultations with both men before their meeting.

Soon after the summit conference, Armand was tipped that the SEC, which was in the seventh month of its latest investigation, had subpoenaed David Karr to testify about Occidental's failure to disclose material facts about its Soviet deals. Even worse, in an interview Karr admitted publicly for the first time that he had been the one to tell the SEC that Victor Hammer had confided to him that Armand had bribed Yekaterina Furtseva. "I can't imagine the lies he's going to tell the SEC this time," Armand brooded.

On July 7, Karr returned home to Paris after attending a dedication ceremony in Moscow for the 1,800-room American-style Cosmos Hotel, which he had financed. Twelve hours later, he was found dead in his bed. The French police classified the death as "an apparent heart attack," but Karr's widow, Evia, insisted that her husband had been murdered. Otherwise why would his glasses have been broken and why would there have been bloodstains on his pillowcase? Evia added that every time Karr returned from Moscow he felt ill, and it appeared likely that someone had been trying to poison him. The implication was that the "someone" was the KGB.

Armand ignored Karr's death, but it had to be a relief. It reinstated him as "the number one businessman in the Soviet Union" and removed his fears that Occidental was being cheated in the Soviet Olympic coins consortium and that Karr was once again going to betray him to the SEC.

After numerous protests from Evia Karr, the French govern-

ment reclassified the death a "homicide against persons unknown."
This news whetted the curiosity of the press, and *The New York Times,* among others, set out to do an in-depth profile. *Times* re-searchers soon discovered that Karr had become one of Hammer's business associates in 1971, had left the partnership under un-pleasant circumstances, had given damaging testimony about Hammer's relationship with Yekaterina Furtseva to the SEC, and had been forced by the Soviets to resume his partnership with Hammer over Armand's strong objections. Despite Armand's warnings, Leo Henzel, whom he had forced out of the coin consor-tium, had filed suit for breach of contract. Henzel's description of Hammer implied that he could have behaved just as ruthlessly with Karr.

Armand advised me to respond to questions about Karr's death by telling reporters that "they're supposed to deal in facts, and the fact is that David died of a heart attack. They're trying to make something sensational out of his death because they want to sell papers." When a reporter asked him directly if Karr had been his biggest competitor in the USSR, he bristled. "*I* got David into Rus-sia for the first time. *I* taught him everything he knew. *I* was re-sponsible for his success. There was no way he could have ever been my competitor."

Subsequently reporters learned that Karr had 100 percent own-ership of holding companies in three different tax havens and controlled corporations in Asia, France, and New York. These companies had billions of dollars of contracts with major corpora-tions all over the world, including Mitsubishi and Peugeot-Citroën. Karr was also in the process of raising $750 million in bank loans for the Soviets. And additional information surfaced that in his dealings with the Soviets Karr had inflated expenses, concealed profits, and collected double commissions, confirming what Ar-mand had already told me about Karr's business practices.

A rumor was circulating in Moscow that it had taken all of Ar-mand's clout to convince the KGB to assassinate Karr because the agency ordinarily did not kill someone who was in the process of obtaining a huge loan for its government. Armand also heard the rumor. "David had a heart attack," he repeated. "Everyone's at-tempting to pacify Evia by saying otherwise. Did you know she was David's fourth wife? They'd only been married a year and were already having marital problems. Just before he died, David had promised her a million dollars, but his estate was valued at ten million, and he was worth more to her dead than alive. Maybe she's making such a big fuss because she's trying to cover her own tracks. Why doesn't someone ask her if *she* paid the KGB to get rid of David?" It was the last thing he ever said on the subject.

Armand turned next to convincing Zoltan Merszei to replace Joe Baird, obviously the thing that had been in his mind when he had hired Merszei three months before. Some speculated that it was Armand's revenge for the Mead fiasco, but Merszei believed his decision had not been precipitated by anything Baird had done. Armand simply got bored after people had been around for a while.

Merszei's arrival had not, however, seemed to faze Baird. He had even taken credit for hiring the flashy newcomer and told reporters that *he* had approached Merszei as soon as he learned that he had left Dow Chemical. Armand laughed out loud when he read this comment in the newspapers. Surprisingly, Baird did not view Merszei as a threat and remained convinced that he was going to continue at Occidental for many years to come.

Working by Armand's side for several years, Baird had seen plenty, and Armand listed on his legal-sized yellow pad those items he did not want Baird to discuss when he left the company. It was quite a lengthy list and Armand wrote across the bottom of the page: "Have Baird sign privileged information document in return for seven years of salary, all corporate benefits, travel costs, and an expense account."

On July 23, I had a meeting with Baird about other matters. Not for one second had he wavered in his belief that he would be Occidental's next chairman. But he was in for a shocking surprise. The next day Armand told me to prepare an announcement stating that Baird had "resigned" but would continue to serve as a "consultant." I was also to announce that Zoltan Merszei was replacing him and was about to become Occidental's fourth president and chief operating officer in twelve years. "Joe was foolish," Armand commented. "He became so impatient to replace me that he couldn't wait to let nature take its normal course. But he was great at reducing our debt and improving our relations with the banks."

At the beginning of 1979, negotiations between the State of Michigan and Hooker concerning environmental violations at Hooker's plant in Montague had collapsed. Subsequently, Michigan announced that Hooker had leaked half a ton of chemical wastes per day into White Lake and sued to have the company ordered to clean up the toxic-waste site. At the same time the State of California and the National Institute for Occupational Health had launched separate investigations of Occidental Chemical Company's plant in Lathrop. Eventually California sued Occidental for knowingly endangering public health by polluting groundwater with radioactive and cancer-causing wastes, and California Attorney General George Deukmejian asked the court to order Occidental to clean up nearly fifteen years of pollution in the Lathrop vicinity.

These actions prompted the Department of Justice, acting on behalf of the EPA, to accuse Occidental of violating the Federal Resources Conservation and Recovery Act, the Safe Water Drinking Law, and other California state laws and to join California in pressing the action. Simultaneously the House Commerce Oversight and Investigations Subcommittee released a series of Occidental Chemical Company memoranda that the SEC had received from Mead. Among them were documents revealing that a dog had died after drinking water contaminated by the Lathrop plant and that Lathrop officials seemed to have misled the state. The news that Occidental was a "dog killer" made headlines all over the country. After the California Water Quality Control Board voted unanimously to authorize a criminal investigation, Hooker was ordered to stop discharging pollutants from the plant and to present a decontamination plan.

Additional documents released by the House commerce subcommittee described an exchange about Love Canal between Hooker and the Niagara Falls Pollution Control Department in 1957. After Hooker officials were told that several children had been burned by chemical wastes oozing to the surface of the canal and that the waste-filled drums were breaking through the protective clay seal on top of the canal, they had passed the information on to the developers but hadn't publicized it, warned the residents, or even covered the area with soil.

The implication was that Hooker had not wanted to do anything that would encourage Love Canal residents to sue the owner of the site, which might lead to suits against Hooker. The fact that Hooker had maintained silence about this toxic time bomb for twenty-two years led a subcommittee member to comment, "The tragic events could have been avoided if the first warnings, when the children were burned, had been heeded."

The day after this information was released, Justice officials told the Senate Judiciary Committee that they were considering prosecuting Hooker because its year-long investigation had been hampered by the company's refusal to supply a 1968 study of the contamination of groundwater near its dump in Montague. Committee members assumed that Hooker's defiance reflected the fact that it had known about the contamination since 1968 yet had done nothing. A subsequent congressional study confirmed this suspicion.

Traces of chemicals in groundwater near a Niagara Falls municipal water-treatment plant located close to an inactive Hooker landfill site and in the water itself led to concerns that the Niagara Falls drinking-water supply could be contaminated. This belief was reinforced by *The New York Times* when it printed a 1975 Hooker engineering report that mercury, chlorine, phosphorus-based gases, and carcinogenic pesticides were being discharged into the air and sewers of Niagara Falls and that faulty plant equipment was being pushed beyond capacity and operated by undertrained workers who were unaware of the dangers to themselves and the community of the toxic chemicals they were handling. Justice and the EPA subsequently announced that they had gathered sufficient evidence and were ready to file a major civil suit against Hooker.

On August 5, the House commerce subcommittee released unpublished documents from the files of the Florida Department of Environmental Regulation revealing that managers at Occidental's phosphates plant in White Springs were aware that more violations existed than had been reported. Occidental was fined $10,000 by the EPA and $1.5 million by the Florida DER for ignoring pollution laws and falsifying reports in 1977 to numerous federal agencies, the EPA, and the Senate and House investigative subcommittees. Subsequently the New York State Environmental Conservation Department accused Hooker of dumping 1.6 million pounds a year of toxic wastes, four hundred times more than the amount allowed by state law, in a dump site in Bethpage, and released a Hooker memo marked "confidential" stating that the company knew that the wastes contained suspected carcinogens.

In response to each of these actions Armand ordered me to "take care of it." At the same time that I was addressing these matters, a folder on my desk grew thick with caustic reactions to Joe Baird's departure and Occidental's "revolving-door presidency." Typical were the comments of one business reporter who wrote that "the offices in the executive suite at Occidental's headquarters are redecorated almost as often as department store windows" and another who wrote that "Occidental's corporate boardroom has the fastest revolving door west of the Italian cabinet room." These clippings produced a drop in Occidental's already undervalued stock price and reinforced the view held by the financial community that Armand was unstable and that Occidental stock was a dangerous investment.

When a business reporter wrote that Occidental's stock price was not going to improve until Hammer either retired or died and that his departure, one way or the other, was going to be the biggest financial contribution he could make to his shareholders, Armand was driven to the point of frenzy. "They're all stupid!" he shouted. "They don't know what they're talking about! No one can tell *me* how to run *my* company! *I* am Oxy! I can hire and fire anybody I please, anytime I please!"

He then proceeded to lecture me about his great accomplishments. "This company had experienced forty years of failure and was nothing but a corporate shell when I became its president on July 1, 1957. All Oxy had to its name was a forty-five percent interest in eight largely depleted oil wells. There was a loss of $43,000 on the books, and it looked like the game was over. Twenty-two years later, Oxy has net sales of $12.5 billion. I single-handedly turned a tiny shell into an oil giant and made it a leader in chemicals, fertilizers, agricultural products, and plastics. I've made Oxy one of the great multinational corporations. And that's not the half of it.

"I'm not only a great industrialist, I'm a distinguished philanthropist and art collector, and a champion of peace and human rights. During the sixteen years that Leonid Brezhnev has been in power, I've chalked up more private meetings with the general secretary than any other non-Soviet in the entire world. I'm America's unofficial ambassador to the Soviet Union."

When he stopped to take a breath, I scooted out the door. "I may be eighty-one, but I'm indestructible!" he thundered after me. "There will never be another Armand Hammer! And who knows? Maybe, this one is going to live forever!"

Later that day Armand told me that Frances wasn't feeling well and asked me to go with him to a reception at the County Museum that night. As soon as he entered the reception area, Occidental's film crew turned on its lights and began to photograph the scene. Important people stepped forward to shake hands and extend their greetings, and photographers snapped candid news photos.

A museum official standing in a small group turned to greet Armand. "It's nice to see you, too, Mr. Blumay," he added. Addressing the group, the official explained, "Mr. Blumay is Dr. Hammer's public relations director."

Armand's disarming, grandfatherly public persona snapped into place. "Carl, I want you to tell all of these people how many years you've been with me." The articles about Occidental's revolving-door presidency must have been eating into his soul.

"Twenty-five years," I replied.

He chuckled and looked pleased. "Yes, Carl has been with me a very long time." The sight of the eighty-one-year-old paterfamilias of one of the world's great multinational corporations standing side by side with his devoted sixty-eight-year-old retainer of a quarter of a century provoked smiles from everyone in the group.

A day or two later Armand and I attended a luncheon given by the mayor of Los Angeles. As dessert was being served he suddenly piped up, "Carl, tell these people how many years you've been with me."

"Twenty-five years."

Again he chuckled and crowed the response he had previously delivered at the reception. "Yes, Carl has been with me a very long time." But this was a harder-bitten group than the one at the museum; their smiles were polite but uncomfortable.

The following week the ritual was repeated at a Soviet-U.S. cultural exchange meeting. "Yes, Carl has been with me for a very long time," Armand said proudly as the Soviets nodded stiffly.

For the next few weeks every time he and I were with a group of strangers he repeated this little act. I had become the costar of "Dr. Armand Hammer's Dog and Pony Show." No matter how much I loved Occidental, I realized the time had finally come for my departure and I decided then and there to become the first executive ever to resign before he was fired.

Armand had been invited to a private session at the *Los Angeles Times* designed to give the publisher, editor in chief, and members of the editorial board a chance to interview Los Angeles' most distinguished and powerful citizens in an informal setting. He knew the rules of the game and was willing to answer their questions. But he also wanted to use the occasion to generate publicity for Occidental's Colorado Rockies oil-shale development. My department had produced a film that featured him, hard hat perched on his head, taking a chauffeur-driven jeep tour of the facilities, and he liked my idea of showing the film at the meeting. As soon as it was over and before anyone had a chance to speak, he announced that it had been produced under my supervision. "Carl, tell these men how long you've been my public relations director."

"Twenty-five years," I replied through clenched teeth.

He smiled, chuckled and said, "Yes, Carl has been with me a long time."

Everybody nodded politely. No matter what they may have heard or known about how difficult it was to work for him, he was convinced that he had demonstrated that he was Mr. Nice Guy.

During the limousine ride back to headquarters, I remarked quietly that I was thinking about retiring.

"How can you retire?" Armand asked incredulously. "You'll lose a large portion of your life. *I'm* a large portion of your life. You're almost seventy. What will you do with yourself? Feed pigeons? You're too old to start a new life. If I retired, I know I could find something new to do. I was retired when I took over little Oxy, and look at what I've done. I know I could do it all over again with something new. But you don't have my gifts. Nobody has. There has never been anyone like me. There is no one like me now. There will never again be anyone like me. I'm the greatest industrial genius who ever lived."

It was just like Armand to try to talk me out of retiring not by telling me how valuable I was, but how important he was. I repeated this remark to a former colleague at Occidental. Reminding me of Armand's spitefulness and meanness to anyone who crossed him, he told me that Armand had phoned key members of the banking and business community to make sure that Baird was blackballed, and he had no way of fighting back because he had signed the privileged-information document. Another top-level corporate executive said that Baird hadn't had a single happy day at Occidental and was suffering from ulcers, high blood pressure, and a heart condition. Baird had put his head on the block for Hammer and Hammer had chopped it off without an ounce of appreciation. When he died Baird was going to go to the cemetery and spit on his grave.

As Occidental's new president, Zoltan Merszei soon began to bombard Armand with suggestions about improving the company. "Who does Zoltan think he is? I'm the big idea man around here," Armand complained.

After reading Merszei's comments in *Fortune* magazine that Occidental lacked management and that he would be the one to "put on the roof, the walls and build the edifice," Armand said to me, "We've already got a roof and walls. *I'm* the one who put them up. Zoltan's too outspoken, too confident, too egotistical, too convinced he's going to be the next boss. Don't be surprised if I yank the carpet right out from under him."

Merszei's days were numbered.

27.

PIMP OF THE POLITBURO

On October 4 Jane Fonda and Tom Hayden went to Love Canal and called a press conference. Vietnam veterans carrying signs reading JANE FONDA GAVE AID AND COMFORT TO THE ENEMY and TRAITOR paraded back and forth across the street while Fonda, tears spilling from her eyes, stood in front of the vacated homes and gave solace to the hapless residents. That evening film of Fonda weeping over the Love Canal victims was featured on a number of local and national newscasts.

Armand was enraged. "I know for a fact that Jane and Tom were paid five thousand dollars apiece to go to Niagara Falls to make speeches," he told me. "Then they scooted over to Love Canal to get some publicity for themselves. I'm always touting Russia and its leaders, but Americans don't hate me the way they hate Jane. They think of me as a hero and view her as an unpatriotic radical. A phony and a hypocrite is what she really is and I'm not going to forget that she exploited Oxy's problems for her own benefit. I'm going to get even with that publicity-hungry bitch."

Armand's latest U.S.–Soviet art exchange, "From Leonardo to Titian: Italian Renaissance Paintings from the Hermitage" was scheduled to open at the National Gallery of Art in Washington on October 28. After Armand insured the Leonardo for $15 million and the other ten paintings for almost as much, he scheduled a press conference and announced that he had negotiated for two years before it had dawned on him to make a direct appeal to Brezhnev to allow him to export the paintings. Not a single reporter asked if the Soviets had really lent the Leonardo to create a favorable impression on the Senate before it took up the SALT II treaty.

After Armand's announcement, photographers began to snap pictures of the paintings, which were lined up around the edge of the room. Failing to see the priceless twelve-by-nineteen-inch Leonardo, which was tilted casually against a wall, one photographer stepped back and was about to bring his foot down on it, but a Soviet curator rushed forward and pushed him away. Armand paled when he told me of the incident. "A great American industrialist, a Russian curator, and the head of an international insurance company almost dropped dead all at the same time. That clumsy son of a bitch almost started World War Three."

The next thing to upset Armand was the release of a U.S. International Trade Commission report stating that U.S. imports of Soviet ammonia, mainly under the auspices of Occidental, had been responsible for eighteen permanent and fourteen temporary domestic ammonia plant shutdowns. The report, which appeared just as Occidental's Soviet ammonia pipeline was about to be completed and its Odessa port facility was approaching start up, recommended the imposition of a three-year quota limiting the imports to no more than 1.3 million tons. "Brzezinski is to blame for this!" Armand stormed. "He's jealous of my relationships with the Soviet leaders and he's determined to hurt me, that's why he had the quota set at 1.3 million tons. He knows that Oxy is contracted to import 1.5 million tons from the Soviets during 1980."

Armand began applying pressure to his army of friendly legislators in order to produce a congressional groundswell against the quota. A few days later he "learned" that, after he had funded the Dr. Armand Hammer Research Fellowship at the City of Hope National Medical Center, the City of Hope had elected to award him its most prestigious honor, the Spirit of Life. When he asked me to set up a series of interviews so that he could have a forum to fight the ITC and tout his new award, I received a call from Dana Rohrabacher of Orange County, California's most conservative newspaper, The Register. I didn't like the idea of Armand talking to Rohrabacher, who would be elected to the House of Representatives from the State of California in 1989, but Armand insisted that he was up to tackling the conservative journalist. During the interview, Armand even had the audacity to tell Rohrabacher that "the Russians have everything going for them. They have no unemployment, and everybody is guaranteed a job for life. They have no poverty. Nobody is hungry in Russia, nobody is without clothing. Everybody has a place to live, and they enjoy the theater. They enjoy life. There is a lot to be said for their system."

The interview in its entirety appeared in print accompanied by a scathing editorial contending that Hammer "seems almost unable to elaborate on the dictatorial nature of the [Soviet] government. . . . Hammer's account of its alleged accomplishments is frighteningly like those which gave Adolph Hitler credit for stopping German inflation." The editorial concluded that when a chairman of a major oil company proves willing to support a windfall profits tax, it follows that he would also be willing to make a profit from a country that denied its citizens "any of the basic labor freedoms. . . . Is freedom no longer considered by men like Armand Hammer?"

Fuming, Armand rushed off to Bulgaria and returned with a ten-year cooperation agreement in a number of areas. "Make sure you send a copy of your release to *The Register*," he told me. "I want them to see for themselves that I can't be stopped."

Turning right around, he flew to Stockholm so that he could be received by Queen Silvia at the Royal Palace and accept the Royal Order of the Polar Star in recognition of his efforts "to promote international understanding and peace" and because he was a "connoisseur and lover of fine art." Armand had engineered the presentation so that he could also attend the Nobel Prize ceremony in Stockholm and make his presence felt as a distinguished international peacemaker.

The day he returned from Sweden, Justice filed a $124.5 million lawsuit against Occidental and Hooker for their involvement in Love Canal and other contaminated Niagara area dumpsites. Armand was determined to discuss his latest international honor with the press, but the lawsuit was the only subject the reporters wanted to talk about.

On December 27, thousands of Soviet troops invaded Afghanistan, accompanied by airlifts of Soviet military personnel and supplies. Their purpose was threefold: to end the Moslem rebellion against the Marxist regime of Hafizullah Amin, to eliminate the fear of a U.S.-backed anti-Soviet regime coming to power, and to avoid the possibility that the USSR's Moslem population would join forces with Afghan Moslems in an Islamic revolution against the Soviet-backed Afghan leadership. When President Carter warned the Soviets of the "severe political consequences of their actions," Leonid Brezhnev responded by calling Carter "malicious and wicked." On December 31, Carter imposed a ban on all grain sales to the Soviet Union and Zbigniew Brzezinski proposed a ban on phosphate exports and a one-year quota on ammonia imports.

"That bastard has decided to give Oxy and me another slap in the face," Armand declared.

Later that week Armand and Frances left for Europe. A high point on their itinerary was a visit to the Vatican. Armand told me he had engineered an audience with Pope John Paul II in order "to impress the pontiff with my efforts to bring about world peace. I want him on my side when the time comes to sell the Nobel committee on my nomination."

During his absence, Jim Drinkhall of *The Wall Street Journal* called. Drinkhall explained that he had received a tip that the FBI was conducting an investigation to determine if Herbert Itkin, the private detective Armand had previously dispatched to Helena, Montana, to obtain confidential information about Tim Babcock, had attempted to bribe a member of the city council in 1978 in order to win votes to override Mayor Bradley's veto of the Pacific Palisades drilling plan, and asked for my reaction.

I called Armand in Rome. He insisted that there was no truth to the rumor, and we worked up a six-word comment for *The Journal*: "We know absolutely nothing about it." The lawyers drafted their own statement, but Armand and I agreed to stick with our original reply. It was shorter, and "the less we say, the better."

Two days later Drinkhall called to tell me that the FBI's Political Corruption Squad was definitely conducting an investigation and was attempting to determine if Hammer had provided Itkin with $120,000 to pay off councilwoman Pat Russell in order to achieve the majority to override Bradley's veto. The next day he reported in *The Journal* that the FBI had received a tip that Occidental had paid $60,000 directly to Itkin and another $60,000 to a company that allegedly had converted Occidental's checks into cash and passed the cash to Itkin, and that the investigators were trying to determine exactly what Itkin had done with these funds.

From out of nowhere, reporters confronted White House Press Secretary Jody Powell with the information that Armand had made a contribution to Carter's preconvention campaign fund through a political action committee and asked why the president was accepting money from a convicted felon. From Rome Armand told me to ignore the questions about his Carter contribution and concentrate on pacifying the problems stemming from the alleged Itkin bribe while he hurried back to Los Angeles to deal with them in person. But the first thing Armand asked me to do when he did return was to publicize a group of photographs taken during his audience with the pope. Somehow, he had managed to have Frances, who was Catholic, excluded from all of them.

It took Armand no time at all to discover that a former Itkin associate had supplied the FBI with records of payments Occidental had made to Itkin and that the FBI had turned up five memos he had written to Itkin authorizing payments totaling $120,000. By the end of the week Itkin and his wife had left for Europe and could not be located by federal authorities. It seemed as if every reporter in Los Angeles called to ask if Armand was responsible for their departure, but Armand instructed me not to comment. After I refused to answer questions from KNBC-TV news reporter Furnell Chatman, he reported that "authorities have reason to believe that money may have been given to one or more members of the Los Angeles City Council to influence how they voted last summer on a controversial oil-drilling proposal."

The legal department decided to send a letter signed by me to the vice president and general manager of KNBC, Tom Straszewski, accusing the station of slander and asking it to make a correction. That night, on camera, a fellow reporter asked Chatman if there was any indication that Hammer knew of Itkin's alleged "Mafia connections." He replied, "It would seem most unusual that he would not know of the man's past. . . ."

Subsequently Councilwoman Russell admitted that she had agreed to discuss her vote with Armand, but that he hadn't kept the appointment. She also told FBI agents that she had not been approached by Itkin, had not received an offer or a bribe, and had voted against Occidental's drilling application and against overriding the mayor's veto.

Without the availability of the key witness, Herbert Itkin, no one could prove why Armand had paid him $120,000 or determine what had happened to the money, and the investigation came to a dead end. As it was winding down, Councilman Joel Wachs told reporters, "This type of talk has been going on for a long time. . . . They [Occidental and Hammer] want that oil pretty badly."

"I'm always innocent," Armand remarked when the furor subsided. "I was innocent in the Nixon campaign mess, but Tim Babcock framed me. That's the one black mark on my spotless record, and I won't stop until I have it erased."

On January 30, 1980, I scheduled Armand to address the Industry and Manufacturers' Council in the City of Industry. During the helicopter ride we went over his address, and I wrote down his last-minute changes so that I could distribute accurate copies to reporters. In response to the Afghan invasion Carter had called for a boycott of the Summer Olympic Games in Moscow, and the U.S. Olympic Committee had voted unanimously to ask the International Olympic Committee to postpone, transfer, or cancel the event. Knowing Armand's penchant to ad lib and make spectacular announcements off the cuff and his determination to subvert the president's call for a boycott, I demanded to know if he was planning to add anything to the speech.

His reply was blunt. "No."

I still expected a surprise, and I wasn't disappointed. Armand delivered his prepared text precisely as written, paused, and then launched into a description of his most recent meeting with his "old friend" Soviet Ambassador to the United States Anatoly Dobrynin. He said Dobrynin had explained that the Soviets had invaded Afghanistan because it was "a hostile country, a real enemy. I think he is being truthful when he tells me that the Russians intend to withdraw their troops from Afghanistan."

Armand's image as the one American in whom the Soviets confided enabled him to make front-page news with his inside information on the Soviet withdrawal. Even though reporters suspected that by minimizing, excusing, and predicting the end of the Afghan invasion Armand and the Soviets were hoping they had found a way to make sure the United States stayed in the Olympic Games, they printed verbatim what he said.

At the beginning of February, dockworkers refused to load Occidental phosphates onto ships bound for the USSR. A presidential embargo on shipments of phosphate fertilizers followed on February 25. Armand issued a public condemnation, but he really was delighted. Occidental was contractually obligated to deliver 20 million tons of superphosphoric acid to the Soviets but did not have the capacity to fulfill its end of the bargain and, for the moment, it was off the hook.

Armand's new concern was his fear that the Soviets were going to respond to the ban by curtailing shipments of the 1.4 million tons of ammonia, urea, and potash they were pledged to deliver. So he rushed to Moscow and "persuaded" the Soviets to remain in the deal by volunteering to pay cash—$2.1 million—which would allow Occidental to sell the Soviet-made ammonia for a profit without having simultaneously to fulfill its phosphates commitment.

Armand relayed this news to the Moscow foreign press corps at the same time that he told them that Leonid Brezhnev had confided to him that troops would be withdrawn from Afghanistan once the Soviets had a guarantee from the United States and the countries bordering Afghanistan that they would not support the Afghan rebels. Then he filed a report of his meeting with Brezhnev with the State Department and also announced the filing to the press. This "news" carried the suggestion that he was acting unofficially as a member of the U.S. diplomatic corps.

Accounts of the meeting by TASS contradicted Hammer's report and showed no softening of the Soviet position. One Moscow foreign press correspondent told me that Armand had always been "America's leading cheerleader and apologist for Moscow" and the most prominent American to support the Soviets, but that he had outdone himself this time. He added that the Moscow foreign press had nicknamed Hammer "the Pimp of the Politburo" because of his endless lies and blatant propaganda on behalf of the Soviet leadership. The correspondent went on to point out that Armand's rosy picture of the Brezhnev administration was pure fabrication, and that the 1979 Soviet harvest had fallen 235 million tons short of the projected target, meat was becoming unavailable, and corruption was rampant. Furthermore, he and the other correspondents shared the belief that because Armand was such a heavy Carter contributor he was being allowed to serve as a Soviet propagandist without fear of reprisal from his own government.

Nonetheless, Armand's attempts to pass himself off as a quasi diplomat led the State Department to dismiss his remarks as a "propaganda exercise." But Armand continued to travel across the United States, repeating that Brezhnev had told him that the USSR was planning to withdraw from Afghanistan and urging that the United States stay in the Olympic Games and maintain trade with the Soviet Union. He also commented that Brezhnev had told him that Afghanistan was part of the Soviets' "sphere of influence," an implication that the world had no right to question the Soviet invasion.

"What happens if Brezhnev doesn't pull out? You're going to look like a fool," I cautioned.

"He told *Pravda* the same thing he told me," Armand replied. "When he says something to sixteen million members of the Communist Party, I have to believe he's telling the truth."

Everywhere there were complaints that Armand was spreading Soviet propaganda and using his media clout to lie to the public and discourage U.S. military support of the Afghan freedom fighters. Editorials wondered if he could be punished legally for interfering in U.S. foreign policy. But Armand remained unstoppable and kept insisting that the Soviet invasion was merely an "overreaction" precipitated by fears of encirclement by China and the NATO countries.

Over an eleven-month period international political and economic uncertainties had driven the price of gold on the precious-metals commodity markets from $226 an ounce to $524 an ounce. The Soviets, despite Armand's friendship with them, demanded that Numinter, the Olympic coins consortium of which Occidental was a member, pay for the gold coins at current prices. When Armand refused to renegotiate, the Soviets curtailed shipments. During the ensuing three-month stalemate, Numinter shipped all of the coins it had in reserve and began to cancel orders, which produced threats of lawsuits. Fearing that his recalcitrance would jeopardize his other Soviet deals, Armand finally capitulated, and on February 10, 1980, Occidental announced that Numinter had agreed to the price increase demanded by the USSR and that the company was not going to pass the increase on to its customers.

Speculation that the invasion of Afghanistan would inevitably result in a major war continued to fuel the epidemic of gold fever. The price climbed until it reached almost $800 an ounce, while silver began to sell at over $400 an ounce, a 700 percent increase over 1979. In response, the billionaire Hunt brothers of Dallas, Texas, began to buy so much silver they threatened to corner the market.

Occidental owned a 60 percent interest in a silver mine and a half interest in a gold mine, both in Nevada. Even though the Hunts and other smart financial people were buying precious metals, Armand reported that he had "sat up all night reviewing the risk" and had decided that "there wasn't going to be a war," which meant that the prices of precious metals were going to crest. His assumption led him to undertake a risky maneuver, and he entered into a number of contracts to "sell forward" the equivalent of two years' worth of silver and gold from Occidental's mines. A continued escalation of prices would obligate Occidental to make up the difference between Hammer's agreed-upon selling price and the significantly higher actual figure.

In March, prices began to plummet. Armand called his commodities broker at Merrill Lynch and gave the order to sell. The result was a pretax profit of $119.6 million. Armand didn't bat an eye. "I bet against a war, and I guessed right. It was the easiest $119 million I ever made," he said. "It's always easier to make big money than little money." Then he asked me to schedule a press conference so that he could announce his latest financial triumph to the world.

Subsequently, Occidental's 40 percent limited partner in the silver mine, Congden and Carey, demanded its $48 million share of the profits. When Occidental refused to pay, Congden and Carey sued, charging that Occidental had deceitfully pledged the mine's output against its future sales and that the company had been manipulated by Occidental into waiving its interest in any gains or losses from future trading.

An arbitration panel decided in Occidental's favor after it inspected an agreement obtained by Hammer before he had pledged the mine's silver production as collateral against his short position. Armand was gleeful. "It stated that Congden and Carey had no claim against any forward sales. I've always known what to get them to sign and when to have them sign it," he boasted. "Actually, I enjoy getting sued and going to court. I always win, and it gives me a chance to show the judge how smart I am when it comes to using the law to beat my opponents."

These profits were included in the fiscal 1979 balance sheet, which posted record operating profits of $561.6 million against record sales of $9.6 billion. Things were so good, even Occidental's tanker fleet was operating in the black.

During 1979 the Carter administration had announced a five-year, $19 billion program to develop synfuels, liquid fuels extracted from coal and oil shale, and set a goal of 2.5 million barrels a day. After Occidental's shale-oil process produced fifty thousand barrels, Occidental formed a partnership with Tenneco Inc. to develop a new federal oil-shale tract. Early in 1980, Armand suddenly announced in the middle of a press conference that Occidental was going to build "a three-to-four-billion-dollar plant" to convert coal into "fifty thousand barrels per day" of gasoline.

The news of this new multibillion-dollar coal conversion plant produced an avalanche of business stories and follow-up phone calls requesting more information. I called Island Creek Coal and learned that its senior staff had recently returned from South Africa, where they had conducted a study of that nation's successful coal-to-gasoline industry. Subsequently Island Creek Coal launched a small preliminary feasibility study, but there were no plans to build a conversion plant. Armand had told a bold-faced lie to set up the Carter administration so that he could obtain a substantial piece of the $19 billion earmarked for the production of synfuels, probably for Occidental's new federal oil-shale tract.

I had a tough time tap dancing around reporters' inquiries as I did my best to protect Armand. When I confronted him about it, he seemed amazed that after all these years I would bother to complain.

"It was getting a little dull around here, and I decided to do something about it," he said. "I've just learned that the USC School of Business has named me Entrepreneur of the Year. I'm only the third guy to get this important award. The other two are Ray Kroc of McDonald's and Sir Freddie Laker. When I get up on stage to pick up my prize, I'm going to tell them the story of how I do it. First I have a dream. Then I tell everybody that my dream is the truth. Then I do whatever has to be done to make that dream real. I guess that makes me America's most incurable optimist. Carl, what does it matter if I'm eighty-one? I've simply made up my mind not to die until I see Oxy hard at work converting coal into fifty thousand barrels of gasoline a day!"

I wondered as I left Armand's office if believing his own lies made him an incurable optimist, an incurable liar, or both. The next day he removed a department head for no reason and reorganized the department in an illogical way. He was again keeping things from getting dull—and becoming increasingly irrational.

28.

THE REAGAN REPUBLICAN

The phone rang just after midnight on a Sunday night toward the end of March. Of course, it was Armand. "Be in my office tomorrow at 9 A.M. to meet the fellow I told you about, Jerry Schecter."

"Who?"

"Jerry's going to be working with you on a number of projects. I'll tell you about it tomorrow."

The following morning, after introductions were made, Armand repeated the lie of the night before, insisting that he had already told me about Schecter and what he was going to be doing for Occidental. "I trust you fellows will be able to work together," he added.

I knew instantly that I had been demoted. "Will Jerry be working for *me*?" I asked sharply.

Armand looked nervous. "Not exactly. Of course, he's going to be the new vice president of public affairs. But you'll continue to do what you've done all along. Why don't you fellows have lunch together?"

I was shocked and upset, but every other day seemed to bring another senseless decision from Armand, and finally, I had been caught up in the maelstrom. I went back to my office and wrote Armand a memo reminding him that we had an "agreement of twenty-five years' standing that I reported only to him." Making it clear that I was not going to accept either a demotion or the loss of my title, I added that if I was being ordered to report to someone else, he was to consider the memo a letter of resignation.

At the end of the week Armand asked me to come to his home on Sunday morning.

After making me cool my heels in the library for quite some time, he stormed into the room.

"Who the hell do you think you are, writing me such an insulting letter? No employee ever had the gall to write me a letter like that!" he began.

An hour-long monologue followed. Its theme was "Oxy in a changing world." "The company has to change with the times. The staff has to focus on the improvement of Oxy's international political and economic relationships. That's where the action is, and that's why I hired Schecter. He was *Time* bureau chief in Moscow and Washington and a member of President Carter's White House team. He can help me here and abroad."

Instantly everything became clear. "You think that Schecter can use his connections at *Time* to get you on the cover," I said. "That's why you hired him."

Turning the tables on me, Armand wrapped himself in moral indignation and accused me of disloyalty. Only a disloyal employee would dare accuse him of such treachery, he insisted. Fearing that I would have to listen to him for another hour, I agreed to stay long enough to help Schecter get started.

I had no way of knowing then that Armand was in the midst of secret negotiations with the chairman and chief executive officer of First Chicago Corporation, A. Robert Abboud, who was to become Occidental's next corporate president. I was being strung along in the hope that I would be so caught up in the events that were to follow that I wouldn't be able to leave.

On Tuesday, Armand ignored the fact that I was on the verge of resigning and subjected me to a dissertation about his Afghan peace plan. "The answer to the dilemma is to hold an international peace conference. The only reasonable result would be an agreement to neutralize Afghanistan by placing a peacekeeping force in the country without forcing the withdrawal of Soviet troops."

Armand had tried repeatedly to present these ideas personally to Carter, but according to an Occidental International executive, Zbigniew Brzezinski sensed that the peace plan had really been concocted in Moscow and that Armand was allowing himself to be used to set into motion a plan that would compromise the U.S. demand for the withdrawal of all Soviet troops from Afghanistan. Therefore, Brzezinski had become even more determined to keep Hammer away from the president.

On April 12, the U.S. Olympic Committee voted to boycott the Moscow games. Armand spoke out against the boycott *and* continued to pressure the White House for an appointment, using the specious argument that "Occidental is losing $500,000 a day" because Carter's embargo against shipments of phosphate fertilizers to the Soviets meant that Occidental could not honor its contractual commitment to sell superphosphoric acid to the USSR. He emphasized that despite these losses, he continued to support the president wholeheartedly.

After he was tipped that France was probably not going to participate in the Olympic Games boycott, Armand saw another opening and decided to persuade French president Valéry Giscard d'Estaing to present "his" plan for resolving the Afghan situation to Brezhnev. It was a diplomatic approach that he believed would carry with it the suggestion that other Western nations favored the idea of an international peace conference. Then, if Brezhnev "approved" the plan, the United States would find it even more difficult to reject it. Armand chose Polish Communist leader Edward Gierek as a go-between to Giscard and began to shuttle back and forth among Paris, Warsaw, and Moscow.

On April 28, in the midst of these international maneuvers, the State of New York announced that it was suing Occidental and Hooker for $635 million because they were responsible for polluting Love Canal. It was the largest suit ever filed by a state against a corporation and was designed to establish new legal precedents for liability in the area of toxic wastes. Armand was too distracted by his unofficial international diplomatic mission to pay much attention. "Giscard *is* going to see Mr. Brezhnev—because of me!" he exclaimed happily. "I'm bound to win the Nobel Peace Prize for this one!"

Giscard went to Moscow on May 18. The results of his meeting were inconclusive, but the French leader stated that some progress had been made toward proposing a conference about Afghanistan with the principals. Meanwhile, Armand told reporters that he had encouraged Giscard and Gierek to attempt to break the deadlock. As Armand had predicted, rather than strain U.S.-French relations, the State Department took a neutral position in public, which inspired Armand to launch a new campaign to meet with Carter. His attempts to resolve the crisis were among the many topics he discussed in a speech to the Los Angeles World Affairs Council. Afterward, when he took questions, an audience member unexpectedly asked, "Isn't it true that your fantastic schedule and your unbelievable success are in some part due to your wife?"

Armand never shared credit with anyone, least of all Frances.

"Well," he replied, "Mrs. Hammer travels with me, and she looks after me to make sure I'm well taken care of while I'm on these journeys."

Later that day a female reporter called. "Was Dr. Hammer talking about his wife, or was he confusing her with his maid?" It was bad enough that Armand's international shenanigans were riling the conservative press. The last thing I needed was the liberals accusing him of sexism. So I invited the reporter to one of Armand's eighty-second birthday celebrations to see for herself "the superb partnership Dr. and Mrs. Hammer have achieved."

Once again spectacular celebrations in Los Angeles, Washington, and New York accompanied Armand's birthday, and a huge cake with eighty-two lighted candles was wheeled onstage at the annual meeting. Huffing and puffing, Armand blew out all of them and received a round of cheers. But activist shareholders later told me that they were determined to have the date of next year's meeting changed because "more time was spent presenting the cake than discussing the vital issue of how to assure a quick selection of successors if our chairman passes away."

I didn't have time to deal with these complaints. The EPA had just revealed that eleven of thirty-six people tested at Love Canal exhibited rare chromosomal damage and Carter had once again invoked the Federal Emergency Act in order to obtain federal funds to help pay for the evacuation of another 710 families. Hooker immediately denied responsibility for the health hazard and declared its opposition to any attempt to make it financially liable for the damages. My concern remained the impossible defense of Hooker's position.

After Armand delivered the ultimatum that he was not going to make more donations to Carter's reelection fund, an appointment for him to meet with the president was set for the end of May. He reported, "I apologized to Jimmy for taking up so much of his time, and the president told me that it was the most stimulating conversation he'd ever had." After Carter left office, Zbigniew Brzezinski would comment, "I always considered Hammer to be a pretentious self-promoter. I did what was necessary to keep him out of the White House."

A few days later the SEC told Armand that it had concluded its six-month investigation. Occidental was going to be charged with the failure to disclose adequately prior to May 1977 the existence or nature of ninety pending or contemplated pollution proceedings begun by state, federal, and local governments against Occidental's subsidiaries, as well as the costs of constructing anti-pollution facilities and the potential liability for the contamination of Love Canal. From 1976 to 1979, Occidental had indicated that pollution correction measures would cost $100 million, but the SEC stated that it planned to charge Occidental with continuing to fail to report the hundreds of millions more it was going to cost to clean up old waste sites, including Love Canal.

The SEC also accused Occidental of failing to disclose various material facts concerning disputes with the government of Libya about oil operations in that country, the financial risks of its attempt to erect a huge petroleum refinery at Canvey Island, England, and losses accompanying the Occidental-Soviet fertilizer deal. Nor had the company announced that it had made a payment to a Soviet official and that members of the board of directors had signed undated letters of resignation.

While Occidental's legal department was negotiating yet another settlement with the SEC, Armand set out to "save Poland." A Polish military tribunal had barred U.N. observers from a hearing during which a U.N. secretary, Alicija Weslowska, had "confessed" to spying for the intelligence service of a member of NATO. Weslowska had received a seven-year jail sentence. Subsequently, the Polish government had staged a crackdown on dissidents all over the country and Edward Zadroysynski, who worked for one of Poland's most widely circulated underground newspapers, was arrested, tried, and given a long jail sentence.

The negative reaction of the international community to these repressive policies had made it virtually impossible for Edward Gierek to conclude negotiations for a $550 million loan from Canadian, European, and American banks. To create a smokescreen that would enable Western banks to justify loans to Poland, Armand decided to stage his third annual Conference on Peace and Human Rights in Warsaw. But he had to find a way to ensure that no Polish activists or dissidents would disrupt the proceedings. "They're not important," he told me. "They make up only a small margin of the population and they haven't anything to kick about. No matter what they say, they're not treated badly."

After preparations were completed, Occidental waited until June 30 to announce that the conference would take place in Warsaw on July 4. This gave the press only four days to ask embarrassing questions about why a peace and human rights conference was being held in a repressive Communist country. But my phone rang off the hook with reporters calling to question the choice of location and to ask why Polish dissidents and human rights activists had been denied credentials.

The next day the SEC announced its charges against Occidental, and Occidental announced that it had signed another consent decree without an admission of guilt. Occidental was going to be required to disclose all of the potential liabilities it faced as a result of its environmental problems and to designate a director, approved by the SEC, who would calculate the costs of complying with environmental regulations over the next three years and the maximum civil penalties faced by Occidental. The director was also required to supply the details of private suits against the company, and recommend procedures to guarantee accurate reporting. It was the most inclusive requirement the SEC had thus far imposed on a company with environmental problems and was designed to warn other companies about what might happen to them if they failed to disclose the accurate costs of their environmental problems to their shareholders.

Just before Armand left for Poland, he received a package accompanied by a card signed "Your shareholders." It contained a needlepoint pillow that bore the message OCCIDENTAL PETROLEUM COMPANY—THE ONLY FORTUNE 500 COMPANY INVESTIGATED BY THE SEC FOUR TIMES IN TEN YEARS. He tossed the anonymous gift into the wastebasket but retrieved it a few minutes later. "One of my Mexican maids will think it's pretty."

While the Armand Hammer Conference on Peace and Human Rights was under way, wildcat strikes broke out all over Poland in response to a rise in meat prices. There were also fears that the Soviet Union was going to invade in order to restore order. Inside the conference hall Armand ignored the tumult going on outside and nodded in agreement as Samuel Zivs, vice president of the Soviet Lawyers Association, stood at the lectern and denounced the leading Soviet dissident, Andrei Sakharov. Then the delegates voted unanimously to call for total détente.

On Armand's return, he learned that reform shareholders Clarinda Phillips and Carl Olson had seized on the new SEC charges as the basis for another set of class-action suits against Occidental for unspecified damages. These suits charged that Occidental had "not acted in good faith" when it required members of the board of directors to sign undated letters of resignation, which made the directors incapable of refusing Hammer's demand to use Occidental's money to pay his $1 million Nixon campaign contribution legal defense. It would take seven years to settle the suits, and these settlements, too, would cost millions.

On July 17, Ronald Reagan became the Republican presidential candidate. Armand had supported Reagan while he was governor of California. Now he declared, "Reagan doesn't have the intelligence, background, ability, or experience to be president. He's a nothing. The only reason that jerk wants to be president is because he can't wait to get his finger on the nuclear trigger. Carter's going to beat him and send him back to the movies."

After Carter's renomination in August, Armand took every opportunity to belittle Reagan in public. But the forthcoming presidential election took second place to his newfound preoccupation with the government of Pakistan. Fearing that the recently elected prime minister of India, Indira Gandhi, would use her close ties to the Soviets to encourage them to further destabilize his country, Pakistan's president, Mohammed Zia ul-Haq, declared that his country felt threatened by the Soviet military presence in neighboring Afghanistan and demanded that the United States agree to send troops if the Soviets crossed the Pakistani border. The Carter administration had suspended military aid to Pakistan because Zia was an erratic Islamic fundamentalist and Pakistan was a nation beset with ethnic rivalries that also refused to promise not to build nuclear weapons. But U.S. military analysts believed that the Soviets were going to invade Pakistan in order to gain control of the Indian Ocean, leading the State Department to conclude that it was essential to rearm Pakistan, and the administration authorized a $400 million military aid package.

Armand suddenly developed a keen interest in Pakistan. Even though other oil companies believed that Pakistan possessed insufficient oil reserves to initiate a major drilling program, he headed to Pakistan, met with President Zia, and agreed to have Occidental invest $17 million in a joint-venture drilling operation with the Oil and Gas Development Corporation of Pakistan. This investment would rise to $170 million when full drilling operations went into effect. But Armand provided himself with the clever out that a *full* drilling program was mandatory and that the other participants had to provide their *full* share of the investment before Occidental fulfilled its financial commitment.

On his return he made a public declaration that Zia had told him that he could "live with a pro-Soviet government in Afghanistan if the superpowers will let me handle it. I can also control the rebels and prevent the insurgents from crossing the border and trying to set up a new government in Afghanistan."

The Soviets feared that any U.S. military aid to Pakistan would inevitably result in the weapons finding their way into the hands of

Afghan freedom fighters, and it appeared that Armand set himself the goal of doing whatever he could to stop the military aid package before it was delivered. But Zia had spent seven months trying to obtain U.S. military aid, and the State Department was appalled by Hammer's preposterous and dangerous lies. State fought back by supplying the press with a number of leaks, including the stunning piece of disinformation that the meeting had not even taken place and that Hammer had made it up just to contradict and therefore weaken the U.S. position. State also leaked its belief that Hammer was attempting to use Occidental's economic power as the pretext to convince Zia that he did not need U.S. military aid in order to make Pakistan a likelier target for Soviet aggression.

In the middle of July, Armand confided that he was replacing Zoltan Merszei with A. Robert Abboud, whom he had known for fifteen years, and explained why. "During Bob's tenure with First Chicago Corporation, he engineered large long-term loans for Oxy from First and pulled groups of banks together so that Oxy could make even more giant-sized loans. He knows how to get the foreign banks to cooperate with us. Because of him Oxy has had access to many, many millions. Bob also made the bold move of holding a First Chicago board of directors meeting in Beijing, which enabled First National Bank of Chicago to become the first Western bank to open an office in the Chinese capital."

On August 4, thirteen months after Zoltan Merszei replaced Joe Baird as president of Occidental, Abboud replaced Merszei. Backed by an airtight employment contract, Merszei remained as vice chairman of the board and chief executive of Hooker. A Wall Street insider told *Forbes* that Merszei had been demoted to "executive vice president in charge of Love Canal." Merszei, whom I really liked and respected, never told me his reaction to his demotion. He did remark that Hammer was a man who never played the game he agreed to play and thought nothing of ruining someone's life in a minute.

I was spared Armand's reaction to the wave of bad publicity surrounding this latest example of "Occidental's revolving-door presidency" because he was in London attending the eightieth birthday celebration for the Queen Mother. On the day of Armand's return I ran into his personal physician, Jack Magit, as he was leaving Hammer's office. Magit looked worried and confused. "Armand is an eighty-two-year-old man with hardening of the arteries, high blood pressure, stomach problems, chronic insomnia, and symptoms of senility. But none of it has stopped him from traveling to Moscow, Paris, Warsaw, New York, Boston, Mexico

City, and London in just three weeks' time. He doesn't listen to anything I tell him because he's convinced himself that he's going to live forever. Armand's always been strange and his body is just as strange."

When I relayed Magit's concern to Armand, he brushed it off. "Doctors are a bunch of worrywarts," he said. "I should know. I'm one of them."

The financial press had portrayed Bob Abboud as a tough guy, but he was warm and friendly when he introduced himself to me a few days later. I noted his shrewdness when he told reporters, "I have never been promised the title of chief executive at Occidental. Armand Hammer will be with us for a long time. He is as youthful and brilliant as ever." Asked about Zoltan Merszei, he remarked that he had "great respect" for the prior president.

Merszei commented that "Bob Abboud and I have known each other for a number of years, but we have never worked together. We'll see." It did not take long before Abboud and Merszei stopped speaking to each other.

On September 5, after two months of labor turmoil, Polish Communist Party leader Edward Gierek was replaced by Stanislaw Kania, the Politburo member in charge of security affairs. Armand immediately left for Poland so that he could be the first American to hold a private meeting with Kania. Subsequently he told *Good Morning, America*'s David Hartman that the whole situation in Poland had "been exaggerated and blown out of proportion. I had a long interview with Mr. Stanislaw Kania. He's been pictured as a sinister individual. I found him warmhearted. He's a typical Polish hero, a nationalist, and a great friend of the Catholic church. I notice that the Catholic church has for the first time come out and supported the Communist government." A few days later the Catholic bishop of Gdansk charged that the Kania administration had intensified its attacks against the church and the papacy.

Armand was determined to use the media to create a smoke-screen around the new Polish government. While he was busy praising Kania and being criticized every time he opened his mouth, I launched yet another counteroffensive on his behalf and issued a series of releases saluting his latest charitable contributions, including a $1 million donation to UCLA to establish the Armand Hammer Center for Leonardo Studies and Research, an additional five-year, $2.5 million grant to the Musée Jacquemart-André, and the funding of an annual Century City Cultural Organization Armand Hammer Award.

To add to his enormous collection of honors, Armand also became the recipient of the Wisdom Hall of Fame Winston Churchill Medal of Wisdom for Distinguished Humanitarian Achievement and the Jewish Federation Council of Los Angeles Maimonides Award. "If there is a Jew in this country who is less deserving of recognition and honor from the Jewish community, I am not aware of his existence," commented a reporter in the local Jewish press.

British Prime Minister Margaret Thatcher was scheduled to tour Occidental's North Sea operation on September 8, and Armand was looking forward to meeting her. "Her election meant the end to England's restrictive taxes on the oil industry, the elimination of the threat of nationalization, and a guarantee that Oxy will be able to increase its North Sea oil production. I plan to wow her."

It was an important meeting for Thatcher, too. Occidental's Piper field in the North Sea was the world's most prolific producer from a single offshore platform, and was delivering 284,000 barrels per day. Armand retained a lifelong fascination with strong women in the tradition of his mother, Mama Rose, and his encounter with Thatcher was no exception. "Maggie's a grand gal, majestic, enthusiastic, and smart as a whip," he said. "She's showing the world in a big way that not every woman's place is in the home. But she's no feminist or leader of the women's movement. She's her own person, and she stands on her own two feet. She's a maverick just like I am. And that's with two strikes against her: she looks dowdy and projects a dull image. But she's hired a smart PR guy, Gordon Reece. He's begun to do wonders."

A few weeks later Armand announced that he was transferring my replacement, Jerrold Schecter, to Washington "to do special assignments" and that Schecter was going to be replaced by Reece. By establishing a working relationship with Reece, Armand believed he would have greater access to Thatcher and the Royal Family, which would help Occidental's business interests in Britain and eventually help him secure an honorary knighthood.

On November 3, two days before the presidential election, Armand woke me at five in the morning. "I want to place full-page advertisements in tomorrow's *New York Times* and *Los Angeles Times*."

"What do you want the ad to say?" I asked.

"Just secure the space!" He slammed down the phone.

I called him back and told him that I was going to be asked questions and therefore I had to know the content of the ads. "You're supposed to be calling the papers, not talking to me," he roared.

"Is it a political ad?"

"Yes." He hung up again.

That morning, I went to his office and said I had obtained the space.

"What did you tell them?" he asked.

"I said it was a pro-Carter ad."

"It isn't. I'm supporting Reagan!"

My phone was ringing when I returned to my office, and I knew it was Armand. "I'm concerned about Schecter," he said. "He's always on the phone with his friends in the White House. I don't want him to find out about the ad and spill the beans to them that I've switched to Reagan. Black him out. Lock the door to the communications room so he can't see the copy for the ad coming over the telecopier from New York. When you get the copy, hide it in a drawer or someplace."

At the end of the day, Armand was ready to explain. A key Carter aide had tipped him that Carter's poll taker, Patrick Cadell, had informed the White House that Reagan definitely was going to be the next president. In order to repair the damage he believed he had done to himself by campaigning vigorously against Reagan for months, and because he would be eligible for a presidential pardon in 1981 to erase his Nixon campaign contribution conviction and would have to apply to Reagan, he had decided to pay for the anonymous ads and use them to convince Reagan that underneath it all he really was a supporter. After Reagan's landslide victory, the first thing Armand ordered was for his assistants to buy stacks of newspapers, clip the ads, and mail them to Reagan, his campaign staff, key Republican party officials, and everyone else of importance connected to the new administration so they would know he had paid for the ads.

The Reagan White House did not respond.

On November 21, I sent Armand another letter of resignation. It went ignored. Later that week we were at NBC's television studios in Burbank and he spotted a vending machine that dispensed apples.

"They sure look good," he said. "Have you got fifty cents?"

Twenty-five years had passed since he and I had started working together, and he was still borrowing small change from me and relishing the fact that he could occasionally get away with it.

A few days later we attended a meeting in Bakersfield. Armand had just replaced the Gulfstream with *Oxy One*, a much larger Boeing 727, at a cost of $8 million. He was like a child with a new toy. "No one has a better corporate jet," he said. "There's a drawing room, paneled bedrooms with full-length beds, an office, a galley for meals, a theater area, and a state-of-the-art air-to-ground communications system. The extra fuel tanks will let me fly non-stop for five thousand miles."

He asked me to fly back to Los Angeles with him so that I could check out *Oxy One* for myself, but I had driven to Bakersfield, so I had to refuse. It would prove to be my only opportunity to fly in the plane. When I got back to the office, I sent a third letter of resignation, advising Armand that December 31 was my last day.

A day or two later he sent for me. "Well," he said, "if it isn't the man who dares to give me deadlines. But you made a big mistake. You said you were resigning. You're not going to resign, you're going to *retire*."

"I'm *resigning*."

"Why don't you extend your deadline until May?"

"You just want to make sure that there's someone around to supervise the annual report."

"How can you leave at a moment like this? I'm about to get the last laugh on all those jerks who bellyache about the way I run this company. I've been told Oxy is going to post a record-breaking operating income of over seven hundred million dollars on sales of more than twelve billion at the end of the fiscal year. That's about a twenty-seven percent increase over last year. Once again, my genius is paying off. You've chosen to leave at precisely the moment I'm about to prove that I'm the world's greatest industrialist."

"Suppose the figures are down next year," I remarked.

"They won't be. They'll set another record. And then there will be another. And another. You're going to miss seeing Oxy drill in the Palisades and in Siberia and launch a multimillion-dollar commercial shale-oil operation. I'm one of the richest, best-known and most powerful men in America. I'm the envy of many men. All America is talking about me. You'd be a fool to leave. There's no time to lose, Carl. I'm in my twilight years, I'm running out of time, and I need your help. If you walk out, you don't even know the meaning of friendship. Rescind your resignation, and I'll give you a promotion. I'll make you an officer. I'll give you a big raise, a new stock option, and a gold-edged guarantee that as long as I'm here you'll always have your job."

Back in my office, I wrote Armand another note saying that I was definitely leaving on December 31 unless I regained full authority over my department, reported only to him, and received his permission to eliminate the chaos that had overtaken Occidental's PR activities, thanks largely to his irrational decisions. One of his aides reported that after Armand read the note, he shouted, "Who does Carl think he is, giving me—Armand Hammer—an ultimatum!" He wrote back, "In view of your uncompromising position, I regretfully accept your resignation, effective December 31, 1980."

Later that day Gordon Reece said, "I understand you're retiring." It was the beginning of Armand's campaign to make people believe that I was "retiring," which really meant that I had been "fired." When staff members dropped in to say "Sorry to hear you were fired" and "Good luck on your retirement," I handed them Armand's memorandum accepting my resignation. I also issued a press release announcing my resignation. It was the one thing Armand didn't want to see in print, and from that moment on, it was as if I had never spent a day at Occidental. He cut off all communication, and I was ostracized by those closest to him.

As December 31 approached I started to call people to say goodbye. When I phoned Frances, she said softly, "We're all having problems with Armand these days. When I talk to him, he looks directly at me but doesn't seem to see me. He nods his head as though he's listening, but he's not paying the slightest bit of attention. It's as though I don't exist."

Victor Hammer was also in poor health. Ever since his first small stroke, he had grown progressively more fragile, and a failing heart had led to the installation of a pacemaker, which was followed by two more strokes. Armand never discussed his brother's health, but he had begun to keep an active file on Victor's finances, and it appeared that he was on a deathwatch and was keeping track of the size of Victor's estate. Across the top sheet in Victor's file, he wrote, "Wait until Ireene non compos." I did not understand the meaning of this notation until after Ireene Hammer's death in 1985.

Later that day, I called Victor to say good-bye, and when I told him that many of the stories about Armand that he had told me over the years seemed too incredible to be true, he replied, "Where my brother is concerned, everything you've heard always turns out to be true."

I kept that in mind when an oil and gas boy had an unusual parting thought for me. He told me that two witnesses in the Venezuelan congressional investigation of Armand in 1975 had mysteriously disappeared before they had testified, and that there were more reasons for Venezuela's feud with Armand than Armand cared to admit.

Less than a week after Armand accepted my resignation, he purchased "Of the Nature, Weight and Movement of Water," a thirty-six-page notebook of scientific writings and drawings by Leonardo. The manuscript had been auctioned at Christie's in London, and the bids had opened at $1.4 million. One minute and twenty-five seconds later Armand was the winner—for $5.28 million plus a 10 percent commission to Christie's, the highest price ever paid for a manuscript. The sale made international front-page news. "I got a terrific bargain," Armand told reporters. "I've been trying to buy it for two years, but the owners and I didn't see eye to eye on a price. So I went the auction route and I won."

Experts agreed that none of the drawings that adorned the margins of the manuscript had any aesthetic interest; nevertheless, they appraised its value at anywhere between $7 and $20 million. "Of the Nature, Weight and Movement of Water" had been owned by the Leicester family, descendants of Thomas Coke, England's first Earl of Leicester. Coke had christened it the Codex Leicester in 1717. Two hundred and sixty-three years later, Armand changed the name to the Codex Hammer and his plan was to use the delicate manuscript the same way he had used *Juno,* flying it around the world to generate publicity for himself.

Meanwhile, Occidental International executives told Armand that President-elect Reagan's immediate concerns were the economy and a tax cut and that he had no interest in trade with the Soviets. Furthermore, they reported, the Reagan senior staff considered Hammer a meddler on the world stage, a pro-Communist spokesman with a suspect family background, and an antibusiness oilman who supported the windfall profits tax. Therefore, they planned to ignore him.

Armand's response was a decision to stage a formal party at the Corcoran Gallery preceding the inaugural balls and place the Codex Hammer on exhibition. Invitations would be extended to the most influential people in Washington, along with the Reagans and their associates, and the party would be promoted as such a spectacular event, the Reagans would have no choice but to attend at Armand's side. But to his dismay, Mrs. Reagan showed up alone, stayed just a few minutes to pose for pictures, and left as quickly as she had arrived. Later my friends told me that Armand had looked as if he had been mortally wounded and had then left the party. If

Nancy Reagan's name was mentioned in the office during the days that followed, Armand responded with a burst of profanity. Subsequently, President Reagan would complain that whenever he went to his favorite Beverly Hills hair-cutting salon, he would find Armand sitting in the chair next to him.

I wrote my final news release for Occidental on December 30 under the headline LEONARDO MANUSCRIPT TO BE EXHIBITED DURING PRESIDENTIAL INAUGURAL. It stated that the exhibition would be "the first event of the inaugural festivities honoring President-elect Ronald Reagan." This was the last time I would have to convince the world that Armand Hammer was intimately involved in every great moment in history. The same day Armand threw a "retirement" party for me in the Occidental boardroom. I did not attend.

Four weeks after I left the company, I ran into an Occidental executive and his wife at a golf tournament in the Ojai Valley in southern California. We had always been friendly, but he was uncomfortable when he saw me and explained that Hammer had issued a "Blumay ban," ordering staff members not to contact me, speak to me, or discuss me with each other or members of the news media. Many staff members obeyed the dictum, but a few strategically placed executives continued to tell me covertly about what was going on.

According to the standard termination policy, I was entitled to life insurance and medical benefits. The company also owed me many thousands of dollars for unused accumulated vacation time. The procedure was to send an explanation of the benefits to the former employee, but the letter never came. Whenever I called, my messages were ignored or I was given the runaround. I knew that Armand's spitefulness had driven him to refuse to authorize the payment.

On July 27, 1981, more than six months after my departure, I wrote him that I found it "pitiful" that Occidental would treat me so shabbily, and I put the company on notice that I planned to file a formal complaint with the State Labor Commission.

I knew exactly what was going to happen. He would discuss the letter with the legal department. When he learned that the commission would probably rule in my favor, and that if it did, he might receive adverse publicity, he would mull it over and finally pay me. Occidental's check arrived at the end of August.

Two days later, company attorney Sam Wolfson called to ask if the check had arrived. Then he invited me to have lunch with him. After an hour's pleasant conversation, he said, "Nobody can understand why you resigned after the doctor made you such an attractive offer. I think you two should talk it over. He'd be delighted to see you, and it would be very rewarding for you."

I replied that I wasn't interested.

"Don't you understand? The doctor always finds people outside the company more alluring than those who are already in it. As an outsider you could write a fantastic employment contract for yourself."

"Did Armand put you up to this?" I asked.

He became flustered. "No. I can see that the doctor misses you, and I'm sure you miss him, too. I'm ready to make an appointment for you to come in and see him. When would you like to make that appointment?"

He was so desperate, I said I'd think it over.

"If I don't hear from you in a couple of days," he said. "I'll call you."

Armand's vanity demanded that I ask to see him, and Wolfson was never going to call. Nor was I. Had Armand called me directly, I would have met with him. But it was one thing he could never do, and the final curtain rang down.

Virginia and I had maintained a very friendly relationship after our divorce. Now there was one piece of unfinished business for me to take care of, and we were remarried at the First Presbyterian Church of Hollywood. Surrounded by our three children and five grandchildren at the reception, we inevitably wound up talking about Armand and what made him tick. I related that soon after I met Armand, Victor had told me that as a young man his brother had learned that money gave him the power to control other people and could give him the recognition he craved. Twenty-five years by Armand's side had confirmed Victor's observation that his brother's entire life had been a sacred mission to gain power and fame by accumulating vast sums of money and then giving it away, but only if he got something in return. Armand had an army of "friends," but all of them were people he had wooed with gifts, money, and favors, and his life lacked a single loving relationship, with the exception of his wife Frances, whose generous nature allowed her to put up with him. Unless Armand bought love and devotion, he did not want them, and I repeated one of Dr. Hammer's favorite "prescriptions": "Friends are worthless unless they can be used. When they are no longer useful, they are not worth having."

One of my friends asked me, "How could you have been so loyal to a man like Armand Hammer for so many years?" My glib reply was that I was a very loyal person by nature. But the roots of our relationship had gone much deeper than that. Armand and I were poles apart politically and morally, but from the very first I had been attracted to him like a moth to a flame because, with all his faults, he was the most stimulating and exciting man I had ever met, and I was fascinated by his creativity, energy, business genius, intense concentration, and determination to overcome any obstacle that stood in his way. I have never forgotten his advice when I first started with him: "People usually aim for the ground. Aim for the stars, Carl. You may never hit one, but you'll get used to aiming high."

Working with Armand had been a continuous challenge, and, despite the bumps along the way, our business relationship had been harmonious. I prided myself that, on occasion at least, I had been able to check some of his most self-serving antics, and if I wasn't always proud of Armand, I was proud to be part of the growth and expansion of Occidental. I did not regret my loyalty to the company, but if I had, in fact, been too loyal to Armand, as my friend's question implied, I was being repaid in a way that was entirely typical. I was no longer useful to Armand and had become a friend who was not worth having.

29.

"THE DOCTOR ISN'T GIVING UP"

My former colleagues told me that shortly after my departure, Armand invited free-lance writer Edward J. Epstein to travel by his side. The invitation occurred after *The New York Times* had commissioned Epstein to profile Armand for the Sunday magazine section and Armand had become obsessed with the notion of using his friendship with *Times* publisher Arthur Sulzberger to obtain a favorable cover story. During my tenure I hadn't allowed journalists to interview Armand unless I was sure they were favorably disposed, and had I remained at Occidental, Epstein would have never gotten to him.

Meanwhile, Armand was busy cultivating a relationship with another prominent Los Angeles businessman and investor David Murdock, whose office was directly above Occidental's corporate suite. Senior staffers reported that Armand seemed genuinely impressed with Murdock for a number of reasons. The fifty-eight-year-old entrepreneur, a high school dropout and, therefore, the "ultimate self-made man," was planning to charge an annual $5,000 fee to the CEOs who became members of his exclusive club in the penthouse of Murdock Plaza, the eighteen-story office tower he was constructing diagonally across the street from Occidental. Murdock had three times as much money as Armand, lived in a sixty-four-room mansion in Bel-Air, and owned a lavish ranch in Ventura. When Armand visited the ranch, he took along his film crew and, dressed as a cowboy, was photographed attempting to mount one of Murdock's prize Arabian stallions. But there was another reason why Armand wanted to ingratiate himself with Murdock. Armand's new "best friend" was the fund-raising chairman of the Republican National Committee and a close friend of the Reagans.

Murdock told Armand that the Soviets bred one of the finest lines of Arabian horses in the world, and that one in particular, Pesniar, was worth $5 million and could earn far more in stud fees. When the Occidental International executives tipped Armand that Reagan was going to lift the Carter administration's embargo on selling phosphate fertilizers to the Soviets on April 24, 1981, he hurried to Moscow to work out the details of the resumption of the "biggest deal in history." While he was there, he paved the way for Murdock to buy Pesniar.

On June 20, Armand flew Murdock to the Soviet Union to visit the Tersk Breeding Farm and inspect Pesniar. Murdock, one of his partners, and Armand decided to acquire the horse jointly and offered the Soviets $1 million, which they eagerly accepted because of their desperate need for hard currency. Stud fees amounting to $3 million were booked within days of the purchase. Smelling a winner, Armand formed a new corporate division, Oxy Arabians, and set out for Hungary to shop for other horses.

It did not take long for another of the underlying reasons for Armand's courtship of Murdock to surface. Murdock owned 19 percent of Iowa Beef Processors (IBP), the nation's largest beef packager, and Armand wanted Occidental to acquire the company. When IBP accepted Armand's offer of $800 million worth of newly issued Occidental common stock and nonconvertible preferred stock, priced at $100 per share, Murdock became Occidental's largest shareholder with a 3.7 percent ownership valued at $135 million.

The acquisition fascinated Wall Street. Bob Abboud attempted to make sense of his company's sudden decision to depend on meat packing for 25 percent of its future sales by telling reporters that the merger reflected Armand's long-term strategy to keep Occidental profitable. He went on to say that "we're going to be running into a food scarcity situation in the 1990s in the same way that we have an energy shortage in the 1980s." To my knowledge, it was the first time any senior executive had ever told the press that Occidental had a long-term strategy. Armand took the loftier position that the unlikely merger of the nation's thirteenth-largest energy company and its largest beef packer reflected his desire "to feed the world."

After the acquisition Armand rushed to Moscow to hold a cookout for the Soviet leadership and pass out samples of IBP meat products. A meat shortage had already caused nationwide strikes in Poland, and I strongly suspected that the Soviets had allowed Murdock to buy Pesniar so that Armand could gain control of IBP and then help them combat their own meat shortage and the poor quality of their beef.

My suspicions were confirmed when Armand announced a "Beef for Brezhnev" program that would make Occidental the world's largest shipper of beef to the USSR. Rather than shipping cattle to the Chicago stockyards, IBP had revolutionized the meat-packing industry by butchering cattle on the spot, packaging the beef, and shipping it across the country in refrigerated trucks. In his enthusiasm Armand had failed to take into account the primitive nature of Soviet refrigeration. "Beef for Brezhnev" was doomed to be another of his impossible dreams.

By all reports David Murdock was a practical man. He was the sole owner of Pacific Holding Corporation, a building-materials conglomerate valued at $286 million, which he had acquired after a brutal proxy fight. Under the umbrella of Pacific Holding, Murdock made shrewd toehold purchases in undervalued target companies, then took them over and sold them for large profits. He also owned 9 percent of a large Houston-based offshore oil-drilling contracting firm, Zapata Corporation, and was Zapata's largest single stockholder. Murdock urged Armand to acquire Zapata, but Armand's $760 million bid was so low even Murdock voted against it. Eventually, Murdock sold his shares back to Zapata for a $40 million profit.

Murdock's considerable investment in Occidental demanded that he place himself in a position to influence company policy, and there was nothing surprising about his decision to become a director. The senior executives told me that Murdock, whom Armand would later describe as "a business barracuda" and "a street fighter," was as smart as Armand was, if not smarter, and that Armand knew it. After consulting with Joe Flom, one of the lawyers who had trounced Occidental during its attempt to take over Mead, Armand told Murdock that even though he had not purchased enough shares to vote himself in as a director, he could become one if he signed a standstill agreement, an accord that prevents a raider from buying shares of a company for a specified period. Armand also let Murdock know that he and Flom would "put up a furious fight against anyone who tries to take over the company." Murdock agreed not to accumulate more than 5 percent of Occidental's outstanding voting stock until 1992 or become involved in any other attempt to gain control of the company.

When Occidental announced that Murdock and Louis Nizer had become outside directors and members of the executive committee, its press release highlighted Nizer's appointment and minimized Murdock's. But the media weren't fooled, and the resulting stories emphasized Murdock over Nizer, leading Wall Street and the shareholders to jump to the conclusion that Armand had promised Murdock that he would be the next chairman and chief executive. As a result the stock price soared.

Shortly after Nancy Reagan moved into the White House, she was heavily criticized for spending $209,000 on new china and declaring that it was going to cost $3 million to redecorate. The commotion led her to turn down a $50,000 congressional allocation and make an appeal for private donations. Armand immediately announced a $20,000 contribution. At the same time he began offering executive positions to people who were close to the Reagans, including the president's brother, retired advertising executive J. Neil Reagan, and former presidents Ford and Nixon. After White House press secretary James Brady was shot on March 30 during John Hinckley's assassination attempt on the president, he also received a job offer.

Armand's determination to obtain an entree to the White House led him to donate $50,000 to the debt-ridden National Symphony Orchestra during the spring, and its conductor, Mstislav Rostropovich, thanked him publicly for "saving" one of Washington's cherished cultural institutions. It was a shrewd PR move that landed Armand on the front pages of the Washington newspapers. A few weeks later, after Armand had volunteered with a vengeance and had bombarded the White House with a slew of letters, Reagan put an end to his unrelenting campaign by appointing him to the voluntary position of chairman of the President's Cancer Panel. Although the panel consisted of a chairman and two researchers whose job was to monitor the activities of the National Cancer Program, with the nuts-and-bolts work performed by the National Cancer Institute, Armand immediately began to tell everyone that he had become a personal adviser to "Ronnie."

Declaring that he planned "to devote as much time as possible to assisting in finding a cure for cancer" and that he believed that "in this decade cures will be found," Armand announced a $1 million Armand Hammer Foundation award to any scientist who discovered a cure and an annual $100,000 Hammer Cancer Prize to the scientist who conducted the most significant research. "The publicity was enormous," a senior executive told me, "but all the doctor did was bitch about not getting an invitation to the White House."

After hosting the fourth annual Armand Hammer Conference on Peace and Human Rights in Aix-en-Provence, France, Armand headed for St. Paul's Cathedral in London and the wedding of Prince Charles and Lady Diana Spencer on July 29. I was told that he worked overtime to make sure his seat in the cathedral was close to Mrs. Reagan's and that he later boasted he had joined the First Lady and Princess Grace of Monaco that evening at a party given by the royals at Claridge's.

When Reagan appointed Sandra Day O'Connor to the Supreme Court in September, Armand attempted to throw a huge party in Washington for O'Connor, which he was sure the Reagans would be unable to ignore, but Justice O'Connor declined. Armand also chose (and, I was told, paid) Bob Hope, a good friend of the Reagans, to introduce him to one thousand leading businessmen and politicians at the Century Plaza Hotel before he presented the Armand Hammer Businessman of the Year Award.

Armand had cultivated a relationship with Israeli Prime Minister Menachem Begin and even went so far as to offer to fly Begin's ailing wife, Alisa, to the United States for medical treatment. Subsequently, Begin defended Hammer to Reagan, who then showed him an internal memo stating that Armand "consistently supported Soviet interests" and had been reported by a deceased former Soviet intelligence officer to be "an agent of Soviet intelligence in the 1920s." When it became clear to Armand that the Reagan administration perceived him as a Soviet agent of influence, he concluded that the president had used the appointment to the cancer panel to get him out of the way.

"The doctor isn't giving up," a senior executive told me, who went on to describe Armand's efforts to cultivate the Mervyn Le Roys. Le Roy had directed Mrs. Reagan in her second MGM film, *East Side, West Side,* in 1949 and had arranged her first meeting with Ronald Reagan. According to the executive, after Armand learned that Le Roy was having an eighty-third-birthday dinner, he jumped to the conclusion that the Reagans were going to attend and made Frances call Mrs. Le Roy and ask to be invited. Mrs. Le Roy replied that the party was strictly for family members, close personal friends, and former colleagues and that they would receive an invitation on another occasion. But Armand insisted that

Frances call back to say that if they were invited he would buy the Le Roys "an elaborate gift." Mrs. Le Roy demurred for a second time.

Armand also enlisted Gordon Reece to arrange an elaborate reception for Margaret Thatcher in Washington. A group of prominent people from Los Angeles was scheduled to fly to Washington on *Oxy One* to attend the reception, and Armand ordered everyone he knew who was friendly with the Le Roys to do whatever was necessary to get them onto the plane. I was told they never went and that the Reagans also stayed away.

Much of this feverish activity was observed by Edward J. Epstein. He later reported that Armand put on his best public face for him and was amiable and unpretentious, a model of patience and politeness, and someone who always behaved generously with his staff. At the same time, he ignored any questions he didn't like, delivered monologues that seemed rehearsed, and became upset if Epstein challenged him. He also tried to impress the reporter by letting him know that Punch Sulzberger was his good friend and suggesting that Epstein could earn an enormous fee by writing Hammer's autobiography. Over the years I had seen Armand use the same tactics on every journalist he considered important.

Another interview request that Armand decided to honor came from Joseph Finder, a graduate student at Harvard University's Russian Research Center. Finder was researching *Red Carpet,* a study of Cyrus Eaton, W. Averell Harriman, Donald Kendall, David Rockefeller, and Hammer, the five leading American proponents of U.S.-Soviet trade. Armand granted Finder an hour at Occidental's New York headquarters, and when Finder arrived, he found Armand deep in conversation with Epstein. Armand turned on the charm, but when he took a call, Finder heard him whisper into the phone, "I want you to cut his balls off."

Ever since he had achieved fame at the age of seventy, Armand's perception of himself had never wavered: he was an unofficial head of state who traveled the world conferring with other heads of state for the benefit of humanity. That his father had been a Communist and had served as an agent of influence for the Bolshevik government in return for economic favors was to be kept out of print at any cost because it could lead to the perception that he, too, functioned as a tool of the Soviets.

Twenty minutes into their conversation, Finder began asking questions about Julius Hammer and his role in the founding of the American Communist Party.

"I've got no more time to talk," Armand barked.

The interview was over.

Finder repeatedly attempted to make contact again. Finally he was told that before another meeting could be arranged, he had to interview ten people who would provide him with the "proper" background materials about Armand's life. Meanwhile, Finder interviewed a number of people who weren't on Armand's list, including Cyrus Eaton Jr., Sargent Shriver, Maurice Stans, and former ambassador Malcolm Toon. He even traveled to Moscow and tracked down Armasha Hammer and Mikhail Bruk. Current and former Occidental executives expressed their fear to Finder that they would lose their benefits if they spoke to him, but many spoke off the record anyway. Others warned Finder that he was putting himself into danger physically if he forged on, which led him to suspect that they had been ordered by Hammer to attempt to scare him off.

Armand even went so far as to contact Marshall Goldman, Finder's mentor at Harvard, and hint that he would donate his Soviet papers to the Harvard University Russian Research Center with the quid pro quo that Goldman convince Finder to abandon his project. It didn't work.

Edward J. Epstein's article "The Riddle of Armand Hammer" appeared in *The New York Times* on November 30. Using declassified State Department documents and Army Intelligence reports, Epstein had pieced together the first accurate version of Hammer's family background. Challenging Armand's lifelong myth about his encounter with Lenin, Epstein pointed out that Lenin "needed a capitalist who would accept a Soviet concession and advertise it in the United States. Hammer seemed a likely candidate."

This assumption led Epstein to ask the one question Armand never wanted to see in print: "Does Hammer merely take advantage of his contacts with the Russians to advance his own interests or does Hammer take advantage of his business contacts to serve Moscow's interests?" Epstein quoted an unnamed member of the Reagan inner circle, suspected of being National Security Adviser Richard Allen, as saying, "We simply don't know which side of the fence Hammer is on." Malcolm Toon told Epstein, "I'm not suggesting any sinister KGB connection—Hammer's probably far too valuable to the Soviets as an organizer of Soviet trade for him to be used by the Soviets for any other purpose."

It was the first time in Armand's life that observations of this nature had appeared in a national publication. He immediately fired off a twenty-five-page, seven-thousand-word rebuttal to the *Times*, which printed a long section. But Armand had been unable to locate a single factual error in Epstein's profile.

I sympathized with any reporter's attempts to penetrate the Hammer myth. The first obstacle was Armand himself; the second, the enforced reticence of the people who worked for him. Dorothy Prell had been Armand's secretary for twenty-six years, working around the clock, seven days a week, to satisfy his every whim. Almost every employee who worked for Hammer for more than five years developed medical problems, and Prell had developed chronic colitis. In 1981 she had gone to the hospital for major surgery. Subsequently, she had "retired."

Later, Virginia and I were having dinner with her, and she told us that even though Armand had a mortal fear of hospitals and illness, he had paid a surprise visit when she was in postsurgical recovery and still feeling weak. Leaning over her bed, he explained that he had decided to reward her for her many years of excellent service and give her a piece of good news that would add ten years to her life. Then he terminated her. "Standing there, looking down at me," Prell recalled, "he was the devil incarnate."

It was the only unkind word she ever spoke about Armand. Rumor had it that he had bought her silence with a $500,000 settlement and a permanent office station at Occidental, with access to the phones, supplies, and office equipment. Other staffers believed she had been paid far more and that Armand had made her "a millionaire." After his death I called her, but even then she refused to reveal anything about what she had seen and heard during her long tenure.

Occidental and China had spent three years negotiating a deal to develop the world's largest open-pit coal mine in northern China, and when the Chinese finally agreed to build railroads and roads to transport the coal and to build housing for seventeen thousand mine workers, Occidental agreed to invest $240 million, with matching funds supplied by the Chinese government. After permission was granted to conduct a feasibility study, Armand chose March 26, 1982, to stage a gigantic celebration in Beijing, which was highlighted by an exhibition of the Armand Hammer Collection.

Aware that the Pacific Palisades drilling proposal was scheduled to come up for another vote before the Los Angeles City Council in early fall, not too long after the Summer Olympics were held in

Los Angeles, during the gala in Beijing, Armand had asked Deng for permission to fly Chinese pandas to Los Angeles at the same time that the games were taking place. "It will be really hard for the Council and Bradley to vote against someone who's providing Los Angeles with such a spectacular tourist attraction," one senior executive told me.

On his return, Armand gave an exclusive interview to *The New York Times* about how to do business in China, which was designed to cement his image as "America's number one businessman in China," establish Occidental as "China's number one U.S. trading partner," and reinforce the fact that he enjoyed a special relationship with Deng. But coal analysts remained skeptical and pointed out that even though the Chinese mine had reserves of 1.4 billion tons and Hammer planned to produce 14 million tons of coal a year, it was impossible to construct and operate such a gigantic mine profitably in a country ill equipped for a massive industrial undertaking.

Another year-long round of negotiations produced an interim agreement, accompanied by more predictions that the coal mine was going to prove unprofitable and that the mine production would glut the market and destabilize the international pricing system. Responding to a severe drop in coal prices, Armand initiated a third round of negotiations to induce the Chinese to make further financial concessions and guarantee the entire $640 million investment through the Bank of China. Meanwhile, the favorable publicity about his Chinese activities never let up. When he obtained a letter from Chinese Communist Party leader Hu Yaobang to Richard Nixon, "the man who opened China to U.S. trade," he ordered Occidental to call the press. Then he traveled to San Clemente, California, to brief the former president and to be photographed by his side.

Armand was furious when *60 Minutes* used an Occidental film division clip and credited it to Occidental's in-house film unit, Fireline Productions. Apoplectic that his name had not appeared on screen, he renamed the division Armand Hammer Productions. The in-house film operation was run by a talented young filmmaker, Kenneth Locker, who had previously done film work for Malcolm Forbes. When Forbes told Locker that he was having trouble obtaining permission to lead a balloon-and-motorcycle trip across China, Locker suggested that he call Armand.

The Chinese couldn't believe that American capitalists were so rich and decadent they would find it a lark to joyride in hot-air balloons across an infrequently visited Communist country. But like the Soviets, they appeared to value Armand's attempts to industrialize their country, and they acceded to his request. Armand headed for Beijing with Locker and an Armand Hammer Productions crew to document the ultimate in capitalist holidays. In Beijing, Forbes presented Chinese officials with his trademark scarf, which bore the motto CAPITALIST TOOL. And after Armand introduced him to President Zia of Pakistan, Forbes received permission to balloon over the Khyber Pass. An executive told me he was convinced that from that moment on it was tacitly understood that *Forbes* magazine would treat Hammer and Occidental gently.

Locker also arranged a lunch between Armand and Linda Ronstadt's manager, Jerry Weintraub, after the State Department refused to grant a visa for Ronstadt to give a concert at the Great Wall. Weintraub, a prominent Hollywood figure, had at one time or another managed or promoted the careers of Elvis Presley, Frank Sinatra, John Denver, and Wayne Newton. He was also an important campaign fund-raiser and a friend of George Bush.

Armand's desire to be surrounded by famous people was piqued by this encounter. During my tenure at Occidental he had cultivated relationships with Bob Hope, Cary Grant, Gregory Peck, and Merv Griffin, who had invited him to be a guest on his TV talk show. Craving even greater entrée into Hollywood, Armand formed a production company with Jerry Weintraub to promote and film entertainment exchanges between the United States and both China and the USSR, and he and Weintraub set out to both countries to sign up acts. After they demanded that the Soviet Ministry of Sports give Weintraub-Hammer Productions exclusive worldwide film and TV rights to *every* Soviet sports figure, an Occidental executive who was accompanying them reported that the minister with whom they were conferring had replied, "I've heard of colonialism, but this is ridiculous."

Subsequently, Weintraub-Hammer Productions announced that it had signed agreements with several Soviet state companies covering joint ventures, and that the first would be the filming of a John Denver concert with a major Soviet orchestra. It didn't happen, nor did any other Weintraub-Hammer production.

Meanwhile, another cloud dimmed Armand's reputation as a brilliant businessman. On April 22, Earth Day, Occidental was named along with Weyerhaeuser Company, Dow Chemical, Republic Steel, and Standard of Indiana as one of the Filthy Five, the five worst corporate polluters. Hooker Chemicals Division was the worst offender, and to erase the stigma of its name, Armand changed it to Occidental Chemical Corporation.

The wife of Armand's longtime lawyer, Arthur Groman, had been the college roommate of advice columnist Abigail van Buren. On May 17, van Buren used her "Dear Abby" column to discuss nuclear war and to ask her readers to mail the column to the White House. President Reagan suggested that the column be sent to Leonid Brezhnev, and van Buren replied in her column that she had "asked our mutual friend, Dr. Armand Hammer, chairman of Occidental Petroleum" to see that the column "is delivered to President Brezhnev, his close personal friend."

This exchange was conveyed to the news media by Occidental's PR department. But seventeen months had elapsed since Reagan's election, and Armand still lacked entry to the White House. As his eighty-fourth birthday approached on May 21, he donated another $250,000 to the National Symphony Orchestra and was given a heavily publicized "surprise" birthday concert featuring Isaac Stern and Robert Merrill, who sang "Happy Birthday." When Armand was invited onstage to conduct "The Stars and Stripes Forever," he announced an additional $500,000 donation and a gift of $250,000 to the Carnegie Hall Renovation Fund, a cause that was especially important to Isaac Stern.

These gestures were apparently meant to offer ongoing proof to Reagan that Armand was on "the right side." Although he had always fought attempts to open the annual meeting with the pledge of allegiance, as another gesture he agreed to start the 1982 meeting with the recitation of the pledge. Still he couldn't resist boasting about his Communist connections, and he told the shareholders that because the Soviets had given him a free apartment, Deng had decided to give him the use of a free villa, which was so big, "the whole Oxy oil division could live there comfortably." He also said he had received a "long" birthday message from Brezhnev.

On June 22, after Hammer agreed to meet his hefty salary demands, Dr. Ray Irani resigned as president and chief operating officer of Olin Corporation and replaced Zoltan Merszei as president of Occidental Chemical. Irani, a forty-seven-year-old Beirut-born chemist, had earned his doctorate in physical chemistry at the age of twenty-two and was acknowledged as a first-rate researcher and executive. Irani inherited Love Canal, but soon after his arrival Occidental tentatively settled 95 percent of the outstanding personal injury claims for $6 million. Subsequently the federal government sued for an additional $45 million for cleaning up the chemical pollution and relocating Love Canal residents.

Meanwhile, Colonel Muammar Qaddafi continued to be another persistent irritation. The Reagan administration had closed the Libyan embassy in Washington and ordered Libyan diplomats to leave the country because of Libyan misconduct and "support of international terrorism," and the State Department had advised U.S. oil companies to begin withdrawing from Libya. It was not an order the oil companies were inclined to accept because they owned the rights to millions of barrels of Libyan oil under production-sharing agreements. Armand knew he had to do something to protect Occidental, and he pursued an ingenious solution to the problem.

On July 11, Armand hosted the fifth annual Armand Hammer Conference on Peace and Human Rights in Hyde Park, participated in ceremonies at the graves of Eleanor and Franklin Roosevelt, and conducted a press conference in front of the replica of FDR's Oval Office in the Roosevelt Museum. Austrian Foreign Minister Willibald Pahn served as conference chairman. It seemed an unlikely choice but it reflected the fact that Austria had just become the first Western nation to entertain a state visit from Qaddafi. It was Armand's hope that the Libyan leader would not be antagonized if he chose to sell Austria a portion of Occidental's Libyan oil interests, and Occidental eventually did sell half of its Libyan assets to the Austrian national oil company in July 1985.

Next, Armand geared up for another go-round with the City Council over the Pacific Palisades drilling initiative by hiring Manatt, Phelps, Rothenberg, and Tunney. The law firm was packed with Democratic heavyweights with proven fund-raising abilities, including Charles Manatt, former chairman of the Democratic National Committee; John Tunney, former senator from California; and Mickey Kantor, Walter Mondale's California campaign manager. Occidental executives assumed that the lawyers were going to attempt to influence Mayor Bradley's vote by volunteering Hammer's financial support to the mayor's campaign for the California statehouse. Former City of Los Angeles administrative officer C. Erwin Piper also received an appointment to Occidental's board, and he attended City Hall meetings on the drilling application, where he could use his clout on Occidental's behalf and report back on what had to be done to get the drilling initiative passed.

On the alert for new ways to impress Los Angeles with his civic-mindedness, Armand contacted the Department of Parks and Recreation and volunteered to maintain in perpetuity an eighteen-hole pitch-and-putt links in a public park a block away from his home if its name was changed to the Armand Hammer Golf Course. The announcement of his gift made the local front pages.

That summer Armand also continued to generate publicity from his association with Prince Charles. He had contributed to a slew of causes involving the prince, including the arduous three-year Transglobe Expedition conducted by Sir Ranulph Fiennes and Charles Burton. Not only had Armand donated the fuel for the journey, but Armand Hammer Productions also photographed the adventure. The result was a feature-length film, *To the Ends of the Earth,* with a narration by Richard Burton and cameo appearances by Hammer and Prince Charles.

In 1978 Armand had volunteered to lend his support to one of Prince Charles's favorite charities, the United World College system, and had purchased a New Mexico landmark known as Montezuma Castle, formerly a resort hotel, Baptist college, and monasterial retreat. The 110-acre site was in extreme disrepair, and Armand had refurbished the delapidated buildings at a cost of $6 million. He had told me on many occasions that he wanted to have a college named after him, and he had made another of his dreams come true. Almost four years later, on September 14, the Armand Hammer United World College of the American West, or more simply Armand Hammer College, opened its doors to two hundred students from forty-one nations.

Armand had also contributed generously to the Mary Rose Trust, formed by Prince Charles to raise Henry VIII's sunken flagship. On October 11, the remains of the *Mary Rose* were hoisted from English waters. Two weeks later, correspondents from seven hundred newspapers arrived in New Mexico to watch Armand and Prince Charles preside over the dedication ceremony of Armand Hammer College. Then, at the next United World College fundraiser in London, when the call for pledges was made, Armand bolted to his feet and announced a donation of $500,000. The audience stirred uneasily. Potential donors later commented that the huge pledge had made them embarrassed to donate lesser amounts, so they hadn't donated anything at all. Others wondered out loud why such a shrewd businessman would be so overwhelmed by his desire to impress Prince Charles that he was incapable of withholding his pledge until the end. After all the excitement died down, I heard that Armand was appalled by the costs of keeping his promise to Prince Charles to maintain a life-long financial commitment to support Armand Hammer College, which he called a "rathole," and had begun to search for someone else to foot the bill.

Doing favors for the Soviets was never far from Armand's mind and he traveled next to Moscow, accompanied by two senior executives of Bechtel Corporation. Armand and Stephen Bechtel had known each other for seventeen years, and former Bechtel executives George Shultz, Caspar Weinberger, Kenneth Davis, and Philip Habib were either members of or close to the Reagan administration. Bechtel's clout with the administration led Armand to announce from Moscow that he was going to ask for permission to use American high technology to build a coal-slurry pipeline stretching from Siberia to Moscow.

Later it was revealed that prior to Occidental's involvement, the Soviets had approached a Dallas firm, Methacoal Corporation, to develop the pipeline, and that Methacoal officials had forwarded the request to the Department of Commerce and received a negative response. Apparently the Soviets were counting on Armand to work his usual magic, and Armand was counting on Bechtel to overcome the administration's view that détente was a one-way street favoring only the Soviets.

After a Methacoal spokesman responded to questions about Occidental's involvement, saying that "it was our patriotic duty not to pass on the technology," a White House spokesman added that it was unlikely that Commerce would grant Occidental an export license, because "the project has obvious military and strategic ramifications." It appeared that the project had reached a dead end.

On November 17, Leonid Brezhnev died in his sleep of a heart attack at the age of seventy-five. Armand set out for the state funeral, accompanied by his film crew and John Bryson, a former *Life* magazine photographer whose impressive body of work included a series of stunning portraits of Marilyn Monroe. For Armand, the funeral was another publicity bonanza and he intended to have Bryson photograph him mourning at Brezhnev's bier and with every other important person he encountered and to publish the photographs in an elaborate coffee-table book.

After standing elbow to elbow with the most powerful Soviet officials at the funeral, Armand read a eulogy at Brezhnev's graveside. News stories all over the world saluted his long relationship with the Soviet leader, but an Occidental official who had accompanied Armand confided to me that Hammer really was not saddened by Brezhnev's death. "He was too busy rushing around trying to shake the hand of the next guy."

The new Soviet leader was former KGB chief Yuri Andropov. Only the sixth man to lead the Soviet Union since the Bolshevik Revolution, Andropov at sixty-eight was the oldest man ever to become a party leader. A rumor circulated that he was suffering from brucellosis, an undulant fever usually communicated by domestic animals, which explained why he looked so tired and haggard.

When Andropov received visiting dignitaries in the Kremlin, Vice President George Bush began by joking that it was nice to see that two former intelligence chiefs had risen to such high and mighty positions. Andropov just smiled enigmatically; it was not clear where he stood on anything. Outside the Kremlin Armand told reporters that Andropov was "a fine man—a man who wants world peace more than anything else!"

Armand was determined to meet with Andropov. But although Andropov invited Hammer to attend the 130th anniversary of the birth of Lenin, he refused to schedule a one-on-one session. Tipped that Andropov had disappeared from view because his kidneys had failed, Armand volunteered to send the world's best kidney specialist to Moscow but was turned down because the Soviets did not want to acknowledge the seriousness of their leader's illness. Thirteen months of effort would be devoted to arranging a meeting, but Armand would be turned away at the last moment because Andropov was too sick to see him.

One thing Armand did get from the Andropov government was permission to film an international Tchaikovsky competition and *Backstage at the Kirov,* a documentary about the distinguished Soviet ballet company. Armand's generosity to Ford's Theatre in Washington enabled him to use the theater to hold a screening for influential Washingtonians. Even though he was invited, President Reagan did not attend, but Jimmy Carter did. Apart from its distrust of Armand, the Reagan administration believed the film was designed to present a positive view of the Soviet Union at a time when the Soviet refusal to acknowledge Andropov's illness and incapacity to lead the country had made it impossible to know what the chain of command was there and with whom to communicate in a time of emergency.

Although Armand still appeared to be indestructible, illness and age were catching up with other members of his family. Ireene Hammer suffered from Korsakoff's disease, a loss of short- and long-term memory caused by the prolonged use of alcohol. Victor told me that Armand had ordered him to take Ireene to Dr. Ana Aslan's Rejuvenation Institute in Romania to receive injections of Aslan's formula, but Ireene's daughter, Nancy, objected to the plan and it was her suspicion that Armand really wanted to have her fragile and confused mother taken to a faraway place and abandoned there. So before Ireene went to Romania, she told a number of people about the trip. With the spotlight focused on Ireene, Nancy felt that Armand would have a much harder time instigating such a dangerous plan.

In 1982, while Victor and Ireene were staying in their Florida condominium, Ireene fell and broke her shoulder. After Victor and some family friends administered an accidental overdose of painkillers, she was rushed to the hospital on the verge of death. She recovered but had to be sent to a nursing home in Palm Beach. Victor related that Armand had agreed to have the nursing home's annual $85,000 fee paid and charged off as a medical expense for a tax deduction of 85 percent.

After undergoing three operations because of a lesion in his intestine, Victor, who was eighty years old, was forced to undergo another long hospitalization after his pacemaker failed. Subsequently Armand flew Victor to California and moved him into a hotel.

During his Los Angeles stay I was told that Armand had bawled out Victor, who was now showing signs of senility, for saying that he was in love with his housekeeper and almost buying a $600,000 apartment for the girlfriend of a former business associate who had turned up at his door dressed in a negligée. Armand also ordered Victor to revise his will. Originally, Nancy had been named executor. The new executors were Armand and James Nemec, Victor's lawyer in Palm Beach.

Not so easily manipulated was Occidental board member David Murdock. After Gulf Oil withdrew an offer to purchase the twelfth-largest domestic oil company, Cities Service, Murdock insisted that even though it would be enormously expensive, he could engineer a merger between Occidental and Cities Service, which would give Occidental large enough domestic oil and gas reserves to reduce its dependence on foreign supplies and would at the same time transform it into the eighth-largest domestic oil company.

It took twelve days and three offers for the Cities Service board to accept Occidental's sweetened merger proposal. The final tender offer came to $55 a share for 45 percent of Cities Service's shares. Occidental then acquired the remaining outstanding common shares to assume 100 percent ownership, making the cost of the merger to Occidental $4.05 billion. I learned that after the deal was approved, Murdock told Armand that he wanted to see a copy of the news release before it was issued and that Armand had ignored his request.

Occidental's sales were heading toward a record $18.2 billion, but drastic reductions in oil, coal, and chemical earnings and the cost of acquiring Cities Service had sent net income plunging downward from $722 million to $155.6 million, while the corporate debt soared from $889 million to $4.1 billion. The senior staff reported that during a stormy board meeting Murdock told Armand that the answer to the financial squeeze was prudent management: Occidental had to stop wasting its money on unprofitable deals with the USSR, China, and the East Bloc nations, stop pouring untold millions into its hopeless shale-oil venture, and stop financing Hammer's constant joyrides around the world in his corporate jet. It was also reported that Bob Abboud maintained a neutral expression and didn't come to Armand's defense, leading to the assumption that he agreed with Murdock. Armand defended himself by saying that the high debt guaranteed the unlikelihood of anyone attempting to take over the company, a position that suggested he believed the debt was helping him stay in power.

I was told that from that moment on, Armand insisted on keeping Murdock in the dark about every decision and challenged him whenever he made a suggestion. Whenever word leaked that they were feuding, the stock price rose, indicating that the investors and shareholders approved of a takeover by Murdock and Hammer's removal. "There's no problem here, no disagreement. We're good friends," Armand repeatedly told financial reporters. When similar questions were proposed to Murdock, he refused comment.

In order to reduce its debt, Occidental sold off the gas unit of Cities Service for $530 million and restructured its employee pension plan for another $100 million in savings. Occidental would eventually sell off so many divisions of Cities Service that the subsidiary's work force shrank from five thousand to two thousand. But Armand could find publicity in anything. When he was ready to repay a bank loan Occidental had taken to acquire the company, he did something unheard of in the world of banking: he called the press. ABC-TV news reported "a glimpse at a financial transaction rarely seen. Today Armand Hammer . . . sat down and wrote out a check for one billion dollars."

30.

DESCENDED FROM THE MACCABEES

Despite Armand's attempts to derail Joseph Finder's *Red Carpet,*
the book was published in October 1983. Finder had concluded
that Hammer was a man who seemed to care only about money,
which had led him to attempt to discover why Hammer was so
obsessed about having his company make deals with the USSR that
were doomed to financial failure. He had searched for the answer
by scouring the National Archives and the State Department General
Records and using the Freedom of Information Act to obtain
declassified FBI files. The result was the most detailed picture to
date of Armand's early years in the Soviet Union and an equally
detailed section about his activities in the 1960s and 1970s, but
Finder could find no answer to the question of whether Armand
was working for the Soviet government, other than his quest for
"diplomatic prestige." He wrote, "If there is any other reason, it
will probably not be found out until Hammer has passed away, and
maybe not even then."

Just as *Red Carpet* was beginning to appear in bookstores, Louis
Nizer published an Op-Ed article in *The New York Times* entitled
"Understanding Libel." Nizer vigorously defended victims of libel
and wrote that "he hoped to contribute something" that would
help them seek redress. The article seemed to Finder to be directed
specifically at him and his publisher, and it terrified him. But Armand
and Nizer took no action against the author, perhaps fearing
that publicity would increase sales.

On February 3, 1984, President Mika Spiljak of Yugoslavia became the first leader of a European Communist nation to meet with President Reagan. The Yugoslav leader next flew to Los Angeles to meet with Armand and discuss Armand's sudden desire to explore for oil in Yugoslavia. The meeting produced an $800-million-a-year trade barter agreement of ten years' duration involving the exchange of oil, coal, and phosphates for Yugoslav chemicals, lumber, and finished goods and was accompanied by permission to develop Yugoslavia's oil resources.

Six days later Yuri Andropov died after fewer than fifteen months in office. My friends at Occidental confided that Armand had obtained the exclusive film rights for Andropov's funeral for Occidental board member and Metromedia television station owner John Kluge, and Armand was going to be the eyewitness TV commentator with no competition from any other reporters.

The Politburo chose as the new secretary general Leonid Brezhnev's most faithful retainer, Konstantin Chernenko. He was over seventy, as addicted to American filter-tip cigarettes and vodka as Brezhnev had been, and suffered from emphysema. Andropov's choice, fifty-three-year-old Mikhail Gorbachev, had been passed over because the Politburo feared that Gorbachev would purge the government of Brezhnev's contemporaries and replace them with younger men. Broadcasting from Moscow, Armand reported to his international radio and TV audience that he had "received a warm welcome" from Chernenko. "I think he is a warmhearted man, and I think he is a reasonable man—a middle-of-the-roader, not a hard-liner. He's a man of great integrity."

In follow-up interviews, Armand, once again assumed his role as a self-appointed diplomat, and commented that the Soviets wanted some "concrete evidence" that President Reagan was serious about wishing to establish better relations. He defined that "concrete evidence" as the "modification" of the terms for a new defense agreement and suggested a procedure for the modification process, which would be climaxed by a Reagan-Chernenko summit. His "modifications" were a direct reflection of Soviet fears that Reagan's Strategic Defense Initiative (SDI)—"Star Wars"—could drastically alter to the advantage of the United States the strategic parity that had been achieved after an unprecedented Soviet military buildup and leave the USSR far behind in a vastly expensive, uncontrollable competition for high-tech space-based weaponry. The Reagan administration responded by leaking opinions that Hammer's "modifications" were pro-Soviet propaganda.

· · ·

Over the eighteen months since Armand and David Murdock had become involved, Murdock's skills as a raider had enabled him to increase the value of his Pacific Holding Corporation from $286 million to $750 million. When he told Armand that he wanted his standstill agreement amended so that he could exceed the 5 percent limit placed on his Occidental stock purchases, it looked as if he was planning another raid.

To forestall a takeover attempt, in the largest transaction in stock exchange history, on March 2, 1984, Occidental quickly spent $334.5 million to repurchase 3 million shares of its preferred stock. At the same time Murdock bought up enough shares to reach the 5 percent limit. The fact that he had become the owner of 5 million common shares and 1 million shares of preferred voting stock, an investment of $200 million, fanned speculations that Murdock was going to resign from the board so that he could acquire even more stock and then launch a takeover and produced a substantial rise in Occidental's stock price. A source close to Murdock told a financial reporter, "I can tell you something will be happening in the future."

If a shareholder acquires 5 percent or more of a company's stock, he is required to report his purchases to the SEC and state whether he is planning to stage a raid by purchasing a controlling interest. Murdock delivered an enigmatic response to the federal regulators, saying that he was interested in Occidental for investment purposes but also planned to take an active role in the company to achieve "further enhancement in stockholder values."

It was a cat-and-mouse game with two options: either Murdock was going to strike, or Armand was going to have to buy him out. My friends at Occidental believed a takeover attempt was imminent, and they were betting on Murdock. One explained that if Murdock "was a rat that got caught in a trap he would chew his feet off to escape—and that's a compliment."

Murdock failed to show up at several board of directors meetings, but did put in an appearance at the annual shareholders' meeting on May 22, a celebration of Hammer's eighty-sixth birthday. The shareholders expected fireworks, but Murdock sat quietly through the proceedings. The next day Wall Street speculated that Murdock's absence would have started rumors that he had lost interest in taking over the company, which would have hurt the stock price, something a man who was receiving a $12.5 million yearly dividend from his 5 million common shares and millions more from his 734,000 preferred shares was not inclined to do.

Just a month later, Armand could offer his shareholders further proof of his genius as an oilman. Occidental's experience in Colombia had looked like another of "Hammer's follies." From 1977 until 1984, Occidental had spent $50 million drilling thirty wells. All were dry holes, but despite the consternation of his staff, once again Armand refused to give up.

Then in June, Occidental finally struck oil and brought in a discovery well, followed by a number of other successful development wells indicating that it had discovered a field with reserves of 1 billion barrels. Out of nowhere, the debt-ridden company had made a strike that rivaled its prior successes in Libya and the North Sea.

From then on it was business as usual, and Armand commissioned the Bechtel Corporation to construct a pipeline that could transport 250,000 barrels a day. Colombia was gripped by guerrilla fighting, so Armand paid off the guerrillas, gave them jobs, and ignored criticisms that the guerrillas were using Occidental's money to buy weapons. When members of the Colombian leftist Popular Liberation Army (EPL), known for its indiscriminate killing, kidnapped two employees of Occidental and Bechtel Corporation and demanded a ransom of $6 million, Armand secretly settled. Charges were leveled that he didn't care who got paid or how much as long as he got his way, and they were also ignored.

Occidental's enormous oil strike made it an even more desirable takeover target, and I was told that Murdock and Armand were both digging in their heels over the battle that was about to ensue. Armand's solution to Murdock's takeover threat was a generous greenmail payment. On July 19, Occidental's stock closed at $28.25. That day, Occidental offered Murdock $40.10 per share, 42 percent above market price, for his common shares. Murdock had paid $137 million for his stock, and by accepting Occidental's $194 million offer, his twenty-two-month experience with Armand earned him a profit of $56 million.

Murdock retained ownership of his preferred shares, which he agreed always to vote with management, and Occidental retained the right of first refusal if Murdock chose to sell them. A year later Murdock sold these shares back to the company for an additional $9 million profit. He also agreed not to buy Occidental securities for ten years, which meant that he was going to have to wait until Armand was ninety-six before he could threaten him again.

As a result of the Mead takeover attempt, Armand was acutely sensitive to allegations that he was using company money for his personal donations and benefit, including the purchase of art. It appeared to me that Armand's greenmail proposal was another of his attempts to head off an in-depth investigation of the company's books.

Occidental shareholders were not happy with the whole affair. They filed nineteen suits against Occidental, Hammer, and Murdock. Claiming that Armand and the other directors had engaged in "grossly unfair, unjust and inequitable transactions" solely to entrench themselves in office, they petitioned the Los Angeles County Superior Court to issue an injunction to stop the agreement, which they were determined to prove was illegal.

In 1992, the Los Angeles Superior Court ruled that the directors had acted in good faith in approving the stock buyback, and approved a nominal settlement for the plaintiffs.

During 1984 U.S.-Soviet relations hit another snag after the Soviets accused the United States of using the Los Angeles Summer Olympic Games as an occasion to encourage anti-Soviet hysteria. They withdrew from the competition, and it was inevitable that Mayor Bradley would ask Armand to intervene. Armand knew he wasn't going to get anywhere. But he did tell Bradley that he had received permission from Chairman Deng to bring the Chinese pandas to Los Angeles in time for the games and was going to allocate $150,000 to fly the animals and their keepers to the United States and pay for their maintenance for ninety days. As a reward he was given a place of honor close to President Reagan at the opening-day festivities. After four years of trying to meet the president, he had at least landed in his vicinity.

Armand's largesse in this matter had a more tangible payoff. At the beginning of January 1985, the City Council voted 10 to 6 in favor of Occidental's Pacific Palisades drilling applications, which then received Mayor Bradley's endorsement. Citing Bradley's stunning reversal of his 1978 veto, the *Los Angeles Times* commented that Armand "had outspent, outmaneuvered and outlasted his opponents." At the same time Bradley's mayoral opponent, council member John Ferraro, accused the mayor of selling out "to be governor."

No Oil Incorporated filed suit to invalidate the decision, based on a claim that an Occidental environmental impact report was incomplete. If the court ruled in favor of the environmental group, Occidental was going to be forced to resubmit its plan during an election year, when environmental issues would be on the front pages, and it would be especially hard to assure its passage. After the California state court ruled in No Oil's favor, a senior staffer told me that Armand was more determined than ever to continue the twenty-year-old battle.

On January 10, Armand celebrated Ronald Reagan's second inauguration with an exhibition of American paintings at the National Gallery of Art. Cold weather had forced the swearing-in ceremony to be moved inside the Capitol, and Armand was one of a small group of civilians who obtained tickets inside the Rotunda. I don't know whether or not he actually met Reagan, but that didn't stop Armand. He told *Good Morning, America,* "Now I know President Reagan. He's given me great honors. He's appointed me twice as his adviser." He also bragged to AP that he had been a guest of the Reagans at their ranch, and later he bragged to senior staffers that David Murdock, of all people, had invited him to a dinner party at his home and that the other guests had been two prominent television producers and *Nancy Reagan.*

If Armand himself was still not welcome at the White House, his money certainly was. My friends at Occidental confided that Reagan had delegated Vice President George Bush, who enjoyed a more liberal reputation than the president, the task of cultivating Armand and that Armand had eagerly responded to each and every Republican Party "soft-money" solicitation during and after the reelection campaign.

Armand disinherited another heir apparent when Occidental announced that A. Robert Abboud had "resigned" on August 23, and would be succeeded by Ray Irani. The financial press categorized Abboud's resignation as part of "Hammer's purge of dissenters on the board and among company executives" who had favored a takeover by David Murdock. The *Los Angeles Times* quoted Murdock as saying that Abboud's "desire to pare down debt, stay out of new adventures and bring more conservative operating methods to the company was in the best interest of all shareholders. But, unfortunately, this was in conflict with Armand Hammer's more flamboyant method of operation. . . . No one had ever stood up against Hammer's autocratic rule." Abboud had earned $700,000 in 1984, owned $3 million worth of Occidental stock, and received severance pay of $500,000 a year for five years, whether or not he took another job. It was not hard to understand why he refused to comment about his resignation and never again said a word in public about Armand.

Some staffers reported that Ray Irani's executive skills had enabled him to leapfrog over fourteen other executive vice presidents and become Armand's sixth heir apparent in sixteen years after only a year at Occidental. Others thought he had been chosen for his unobtrusiveness. Still others believed it was a combination of both. After his appointment Irani wisely commented for publication that his goal was "to help Dr. Hammer define the objectives toward which this corporation is to strive. I have found Dr. Hammer very easy to communicate with. I've found him to be a good listener. If you do your homework, he will listen."

In his understated way and without ruffling Armand's feathers, Irani began to take over day-to-day operations, while Armand devoted almost all of his energies to his public activities, including, belatedly, a public avowal of his Jewish background.

During September he took the Armand Hammer Collection to the Israel Museum and addressed the National Unity cabinet. Victor had told me that his grandfather, Jacob Hammer, had chosen Hammer as the family name because it sounded Swedish and not at all Jewish. But the English translation of Maccabee was "hammer," and with tears running down his cheeks, Armand told the Israeli ministers that he recalled his grandfather telling him that he and his family were direct descendants of the Maccabees, the legendary family of Jewish patriots who headed a successful religious revolt from 174 to 164 B.C.

This performance did not prevent the Israeli press from attacking his lack of support for Soviet Jewry. Guilford Glazer, the multimillionaire owner of Del Amo Fashion Mall, the largest shopping mall in the world, sat on the board of Armand Hammer College and was a great friend of Israel. Speaking on Armand's behalf, he replied that Armand had contributed generously to the United Jewish Appeal and had donated $600,000 to the Tel Aviv Museum. This news was greeted with skepticism because Armand's donations were never kept a secret unless they had been made to political candidates.

During his Israeli trip, Armand also initiated secret discussions with government officials about the possibility of Occidental becoming involved in oil exploration in Israel. It was not clear whether he was attempting to bribe the Israelis the way he had previously enticed the Egyptians, Pakistanis, and Yugoslavs, or whether he felt he could afford to become involved in Israel because Occidental's involvement in Libya was doomed.

Whatever his motives, it soon became apparent that the Israeli government valued Armand for both his money and his Soviet connections. Back in Los Angeles, Armand received the Golda Meir Man of the Year Award at a Bonds for Israel banquet at the Century Plaza Hotel (and also picked up all of the expenses). Israeli Foreign Minister Yitzhak Shamir explained his presence to reporters by indicating that Armand had bought millions of dollars' worth of Israeli bonds and was a good friend of Israel in a number of other ways. This provoked even more questions. Finally, Israeli Prime Minister Shimon Peres revealed that Armand was acting as an intermediary between Israel and the USSR but did not explain the nature of his activities. A senior staffer confided that Peres had asked Armand to approach Konstantin Chernenko about reestablishing diplomatic relations between the two countries.

Closer ties to the White House were never far from Armand's mind, if not with the president, then with the First Lady. Not too long after the banquet at the Century Plaza Hotel, Nancy Reagan came to Los Angeles to receive the Variety Club of Southern California's International Lifeline Award. Armand arrived late, took a seat in the back of the room, and scribbled a note to Joseph Sinay, president of Variety International, asking the cost of the event. The answer came back—$50,000. Just before the evening drew to a close, he sent another note, offering to pay all the expenses personally. Sinay read the note to the audience, and there was thunderous applause. A spotlight was turned on Armand, and he was asked to come to the platform. When he stepped onstage, he received another ovation. Armand announced that he was making the donation in honor of "the greatest living American lady who is married to the greatest living man." Referring to Mrs. Reagan as a dear friend, he remarked that he had great admiration for her husband. As the photographers clicked away, Mrs. Reagan graciously stepped forward and gave her "dear friend" a hug.

A month later Nancy Reagan was the guest of honor at a USO Distinguished American Awards dinner. At a predinner reception, the press reported that she had been joined by a small group of her special friends, who included conservative multimillionaire automobile dealer and Reagan supporter Holmes Tuttle and Mrs. Tuttle, Ginger Rogers, Mr. and Mrs. Bob Hope, Loretta Young— and Armand and Frances Hammer.

On December 4, 1984, after pressuring Soviet ambassador Anatoly Dobrynin for ten months, Armand received an appointment to meet with Konstantin Chernenko. Ever eager to inflate his importance as a diplomat, he announced the meeting at a press conference and added that he planned to discuss "high-level policy matters," including "greater communication between the superpowers" and increased "trade and cultural and scientific exchanges," which would serve as "the bridge that would lead to renewed disarmament talks."

Armand's critics pointed out that Soviet Foreign Minister Gromkyo's visit to the United States and the United Nations in September had signaled that the Soviet Union was already preparing to accept the conditions set by the United States and resume arms talks. Why, they wondered, had Armand inferred that renewed arms talks depended on him? But Armand was unstoppable. Before going to Moscow, he made appointments at the White House and the State Department and then told the press that State had been the one to ask him to make an appearance. Subsequently, National Security Adviser Robert McFarlane denied that the briefings had occurred.

Armand took to his meeting with Chernenko a gift of a letter written by Karl Marx; a three-part plan to improve U.S.-Soviet relations, which included agreements between the two countries not to be the first to use either nuclear or conventional weapons against the other, to hold an annual summit, and to initiate new cultural exchanges; and an export license for the technology necessary to construct a coal-slurry pipeline. He also traveled with a leading lung specialist because he had been tipped that Chernenko was dying of emphysema. During the meeting Chernenko, who had not fully recovered from a recent heart attack, appeared fragile.

Arrangements had been made for Armand to report on the meeting to the world live by satellite. He stated that Chernenko "looked to be in fine health" and was "going to be around for a great many years. I think we're fortunate that he is in charge because he's a kind man. He's a warm man. He's an emotional man. He's very much like Brezhnev." Armand added that he had proposed a summit meeting and Chernenko had replied that he wanted "something more than words from the U.S. He wants deeds!" and had stated that a summit meeting should be predicated on a pledge by the United States not to be the first to use nuclear weapons. When questioned about the issue of the emigration of Soviet Jews, Armand replied that it would be "taken care of."

The day after the meeting Armand left for Madrid and the sixth —and what would be the last—Armand Hammer Conference on Peace and Human Rights. Two weeks later Israeli officials announced that the harassment of Soviet Jews had become intolerable and called for the intervention of the international community. Furthermore, Armand's comments from Moscow infuriated many Reagan staffers, who saw his use of the international media to announce Chernenko's demand for a U.S. "no-first-use" pledge as blatant Soviet propaganda. To insiders at Occidental, it appeared that Armand's ongoing eagerness to allow the Soviet leadership to use him to pursue their own political agendas produced nothing but ill will. As for Armand's personal agenda—the Nobel Peace Prize—that now seemed a most elusive goal.

31.

FAMILY
LOYALTY

On March 11, 1985, when Armand learned that Konstantin Cher-
nenko was dead and Mikhail Gorbachev had been named Soviet
general secretary, he set out immediately for Moscow. In recognition of his special relationship with the Soviet government, he was
given permission to stand alone in front of Chernenko's open casket before the funeral began. Later, at the postfuneral reception,
the visiting dignitaries waited on a receiving line to pay their respects to Gorbachev. Armand was in his element. Reporters commented that his familiarity with so many heads of state belied the
fact that he was a private citizen, and that he had raced up and
down the line chatting with Vice President Bush, Secretary of State
Shultz, Prime Minister Thatcher, Chinese Vice Premier Li Peng,
and President Zia.

This was Bush's first meeting with Gorbachev, and he did not
discuss the encounter with the press. But Armand told reporters
that Bush had teased him because he was at the back of the line,
that Zia had reminded him of a dinner invitation at the end of the
month, and that he had conferred "at length" with Gorbachev and
had found him "full of desire to make a change. I sense a whole
new era beginning."

Armand and Gorbachev had their first meeting three months
later on June 11, and Armand declared that the Soviet leader had
"impressed" him and was "very forthright, very intelligent, with a
good sense of humor, very pragmatic." He added that he had told
Gorbachev that he was willing to do anything to help initiate a
summit, and that Gorbachev had replied that negotiations were
already under way, but Star Wars remained a stumbling block

because it allowed the United States to preserve a first-strike capability. Armand's comments automatically received international attention, but once again the Reagan administration pointedly ignored them.

Armand maintained publicly that he had established a close relationship with Gorbachev on the spot, but the executives who traveled to Moscow with him told me that Gorbachev, although cordial and polite, hadn't given him much time and had delegated older ministers to deal with him. They believed that Armand's close ties to Brezhnev's corrupt, paralytic administration made Gorbachev wary of becoming too friendly. At the same time Gorbachev was eager to establish a new détente so that he could devote his energies to putting revised party programs into motion, and he knew Armand could help him do it, especially by repeating his anti–Star Wars remarks and other comments to the international press.

Four days after the meeting Armand published an Op-Ed article in *The New York Times* saying that the long impasse between the USSR and the United States could be resolved, and that President Reagan had demonstrated his desire to cooperate and could go down in history as a peacemaker. On June 23, he scheduled two Washington meetings, the first with Anatoly Dobrynin, the second with Reagan himself, to "brief" him about his encounter with Gorbachev. This was Armand's first meeting with Reagan, and I was told that he viewed the invitation to the Oval Office as a great personal triumph. Reagan bluntly told Armand that he was insisting that the Soviets play by established rules and that it was the Soviets' turn to come to Washington for a summit, but Gorbachev had refused to travel to the United States. Armand reported that he had done his best to convince Reagan to go to Moscow in the spirit of peace, but administration officials leaked their belief that he was merely repeating what he had been told by Anatoly Dobrynin earlier that day.

On *Good Morning, America* Armand continued his campaign, quoting Gorbachev as saying that "we will never allow the Americans to be superior to us." He called for a U.S. "no-first-strike" declaration because, Armand said, "the Soviets think we Americans are trying to . . . be superior," and he confessed that he was disturbed about Reagan's attitude about the location of the summit. "He ought to be magnanimous and generous and go to Moscow."

That same week Armand traveled to Beijing to attend the signing ceremony for the final Occidental-China coal-mining contract.

I could only speculate about all the disinformation about Chinese, Soviet, and U.S. foreign policies that had to have been tossed around when Armand told Deng and Li Peng about his meetings with Gorbachev and Reagan. As Armand was flying back to the United States, Washington announced that Gorbachev and Reagan would meet in Geneva in November.

Gorbachev immediately launched a skillful anti–Star Wars campaign, utilizing every friend he had in the West to join forces against the U.S. position. On September 22, just before the opening of the U.N. General Assembly, Armand published another *New York Times* Op-Ed article suggesting that the United States and the USSR develop the Star Wars technology cooperatively. The article was distributed to everyone at the United Nations and to the members of Congress. Again Armand portrayed himself as an international peacemaker, but his actions made the Reagan administration's policy of dealing with the Soviets only from a position of strength a subject of controversy in the United States and around the world, just two months before the summit. Criticized again for being the Soviets' mouthpiece, Armand insisted that *he*—and not Gorbachev—had been the one to suggest the compromise.

Armand's self-promotion reached a new high with the publication of John Bryson's *The World of Armand Hammer* in 1985. During their three-year association, Bryson had photographed Armand with four American presidents and four Soviet general secretaries, as well as Deng Xiaoping, Margaret Thatcher, the presidents of Colombia, Ecuador, France, Italy, and Peru, Jacqueline Onassis, Frank Sinatra, Barbara Walters, and Cary Grant. *The World of Armand Hammer* also included photographs of Armand talking on the telephone, inspecting a North Sea drilling platform, blowing out the candles on a birthday cake, attending the 1984 Summer Olympics opening-day ceremonies, walking down a flight of stairs, signing an autograph, reading a newspaper, watching an old Charlie Chaplin film, swimming in his indoor pool, and making a date to have tea with the deputy prime minister of Bulgaria. Michael Kinsley of *The New Republic* labeled the volume "executive porn" and described Armand as "a sad man, measuring his self-worth by the size of his airplane, attracted to people solely because they are rich or powerful or famous, and unaware or indifferent that his so-called friends are attracted to him for the same reason."

This reaction did not stop Armand from ordering the Occidental board to pay the cost of developing the book, which he claimed was a promotional tool for the company and to allocate $1 million so that he could begin work on another promotional tool, his autobiography. His first choice to write this book was Robert Kaiser, former Moscow correspondent for *The Washington Post,* but a closer look at Kaiser's columns led him to move on. Next he chose military historians Clay and Joan Blair. They were plunked down in front of a VCR and shown *Occidental: Visions for the Future,* a collage of footage of Armand and eight world leaders and videotapes of all of Occidental's promotional films. Subsequently he rejected the Blairs' outline, which attempted to give some idea of the truth. Explaining that they were not "PR people," they departed from the project. The job finally fell to English journalist Neil Lyndon, whom Occidental reportedly was going to pay $200,000 plus royalties to tell the "official" story of Armand's life.

As a memorial to that life, Armand had built a large white marble crypt on the grounds of Westwood Cemetery in Los Angeles. This is the celebrity cemetery where Marilyn Monroe was buried. After "The Armand Hammer Family" was carved across the lintel and each letter was flecked with gold leaf, Armand had the bodies of Mama Rose, Julius, and Armand's half-brother, Harry, exumed from their burial places in the Jewish cemetery in New Jersey and installed in the crypt. Left behind was the body of Harry's wife, Bette, whom Armand did not consider a legitimate member of "the family." Victor's turn arrived when he suffered heart failure for the third time and was rushed to a hospital in Palm Beach, Florida, and placed on a life support system. He died on July 21.

Armand was in the hospital recovering from prostate surgery, but he sent word that he wanted the funeral held at Westwood Cemetery and Victor buried in the crypt. Victor's eulogy was delivered by his cousin, a rabbi who lived in California. He spoke of Victor's devotion, respect, and love for Armand, Armand's importance to Victor, and Armand's importance in general. Neither Victor's wife, Ireene, Victor's adopted daughter, Nancy, nor his son, Armasha, were mentioned.

Victor left his entire estate in trust to Ireene with Armand as coexecutor with Jim Nemec. Whatever remained after her death would be split equally between Nancy and Armasha. The estate consisted of $660,000 in cash, 10,000 shares of Occidental stock, Victor's house in Stamford, Connecticut, where Nancy and her husband, Arieh Eilan, made their home, and the condominium coowned by Ireene and Victor in Palm Beach. The house was valued at $400,000 and the condominium at $170,000.

Four days after the funeral, a member of Armand's legal staff called Nancy and told her that the payments for her mother's nursing home were in arrears, but that Armand would continue to pay the bills until the estate was settled—if she would sign some documents. Nancy had no way of knowing that the bills had been paid all along and Hammer was just attempting to weaken her resistance.

The next day she learned that Armand was planning to sue Victor's estate for $660,000—all of the cash—plus 12 percent interest. The claim was based on a series of IOUs dating from the end of 1983 that Victor had signed. Victor had assured Nancy that his estate would maintain Ireene's care, so she wrote to Armand and Frances asking them not to take any action that could deplete the estate of those necessary funds. Armand wrote back that he would discuss the matter at a conference in his New York office the day after the memorial service that was to be held for Victor in New York. He also reminded Nancy that her mother's illness—not he—was the reason why Victor had been forced to borrow money from him.

Armand attended the meeting accompanied by his lawyer, Arthur Groman, and Jim Nemec. Nancy took her lawyer, Donald Goldsmith. Armand began by saying that he was willing to offer "a substantial reduction in the debt," the waiving of his rights to the one month's interest on the IOUs. Donald Goldsmith replied that he had never seen the IOUs. It turned out that they were four-page loan documents with the amounts filled in after Victor's death. Victor had initialed every page and signed on the dotted line, but two memos were unsigned. (Armand had sent them to Victor's housekeeper in Florida, who had sent them back with no explanation.) Aware that it was Victor's lifelong habit to sign everything Armand thrust in front of him, Goldsmith asked if Victor had had legal counsel with him when he signed the documents. Jim Nemec replied that he had not been consulted.

When Nancy asked Armand to explain his motives, he delivered his familiar monologue about his devotion to world peace and finding a cure for cancer and reeled off a list of his charities and donations. He merely wanted the debt repaid, he said. And, besides, it was nobody's business how he spent $660,000 of his own money. It was his suggestion that Nancy remove her mother from the expensive nursing home, place her in a rental apartment, find a housekeeper who would work for $400 to $500 a month, and have Ireene draw up a new will that would give Nancy the house in Stamford and cut out Armasha, who was not even Ireene's legitimate son. Those actions would entitle Nancy to receive whatever was left in the estate after her mother's death.

Goldsmith replied that Ireene had been declared legally incompetent and could not make a new will; furthermore, the house was part of Victor's estate and could not simply be handed over to Nancy by the executors. Nancy added that the house should not even have been included in the estate because Victor had promised to turn over the title to the house to Ireene in partial settlement of the $1.5 million dollars that he had borrowed from her.

As Ireene's guardian, Nancy collected Ireene's Occidental stock dividends which came to approximately $6,400 yearly. Armand now suggested that Ireene start collecting dividends again and that he send Nancy $10,000 a year until Ireene's death. But there were two conditions: that he collect his debt and that Ireene move out of the expensive nursing home. When Nemec read out loud from a confidential medical report stating that Ireene was hovering near death, it became clear that Armand, already a millionaire many times over, was attempting to make a relatively small series of $10,000 payments in order to collect $660,000. Finally, he announced to his lawyers that Nancy was not a blood relative and meant absolutely nothing to him. Then he left. A few days later Nancy received a letter informing her of the deadline to either accept or reject Armand's offer, and she turned it down.

Nancy was the second cardholder on Victor's American Express account, and the Hammer Galleries had been paying her modest monthly bill. Subsequently, the galleries refused to pay the next bill. Because the Connecticut house was used to entertain clients, the Hammer Galleries had paid the fuel, electricity, and water bills as a business expense. These payments were also canceled, as were the payments on the utility bills for Victor and Ireene's condominium. Nancy sold twelve Windsor chairs that belonged to her parents and that had been part of the furnishings of Armand's office in the Empire State Building in the mid-1940s in order to have the cash to meet the expenses.

Armand fought only to win, but Nancy came to the conclusion that her only choice was to fight to keep her stepfather's estate intact and to save her home, and to prove that Victor was Armand's partner in the Hammer Galleries. The brothers had acknowledged this fact publicly many times over the years, even though Armand had insisted on paying Victor a straight salary of $75,000 a year and had always refused to pay him commissions.

Prince Charles and Princess Diana were scheduled to arrive in Washington on November 9 to attend the National Gallery of Art's "Treasure Houses of Britain," an exhibition of 750 objects from 220 British castles and stately homes. Here, too, Armand thought he could save some money, and the impending visit of the royal couple led him to devise an ingenious solution to his annoyance at having to pay the perpetual costs of maintaining Armand Hammer College. He would stage a charity ball on November 12, honoring himself with the royals as special guests. Palm Beach was selected as the location for the event because Armand assumed that the local social set would be willing to spend $10,000 apiece to be in the same room with royalty, even more to be seated near them, and an additional $50,000 to have their pictures taken with them.

When the local press reminded the conservative Palm Beach community of Armand's lifelong association with the USSR, the city refused to issue a party permit. Armand attempted to solve this problem by donating $75,000 to the city in return for the granting of the permit and the scheduling of an "Armand Hammer Day." But the donation brought forth another outcry that "even Palm Beach can be bought."

The chairwomen of the event were Patricia Kluge, the wife of media mogul John Kluge, who was a member of the Occidental board and reported to be one of the richest men in America, and the doyenne of Palm Beach society, Mary Sanford. After the British scandal sheets revealed that Patricia Kluge had been a nude model in the 1970s and that nude photographs of her had appeared in the raunchy English magazine *Knave,* she resigned. Sanford quit as soon as she discovered that Armand was really throwing the charity ball for himself and that he and not the royal couple was the real guest of honor. Business was so bad that Armand was forced to start advertising the fact that Bob Hope, Merv Griffin, Joan Collins, Ted Turner, Donald Trump, and Gregory Peck would be among those attending.

On November 7, Armand sued Victor's estate in the Palm Beach County Probate Court, claiming that it owed him $666,714.74. Nancy Eilan believed there was only one way she stood a chance of winning. On November 12, she called the press and told them about her uncle's attempts to bankrupt her stepfather's estate.

That night, in the Venetian Ballroom of the Breakers Hotel, reporters descended on Armand during his charity ball, and asked about his friendship with Prince Charles, the Reagan-Gorbachev summit, which was a week away, and why he was suing the estate of his late brother. The next day all coverage of the gala included embarrassing discussions of Armand's claim.

It seemed not to faze Armand in the least. In order to avoid a conflict of interest, he appointed a retired judge, James Knott, to replace him as coexecutor of Victor's estate and serve as executor pro tem. Then he ordered the Hammer Galleries to stop paying Ireene's nursing home bill, and sued in Connecticut to gain control of Nancy's house. He also dispatched a lawyer to Moscow to obtain an affidavit from Armasha Hammer demanding the removal of Nancy as Ireene's guardian because Armasha was going to inherit half of Ireene's assets and Nancy was using those assets to fight a claim against Armand that Armasha considered unjust. A senior Occidental executive made a second trip to Moscow just so Armasha could add to the affidavit in his own handwriting a statement that his father had told him on numerous occasions that he was not a co-owner of the Hammer Galleries.

Nancy countersued, charging that Victor had been at the mercy of his brother and under his domination. As her lawyers prepared their case, it appeared that Armand had secretly stashed a number of paintings that Victor owned into a warehouse as collateral against the "loans" and that he was planning to keep them *and* collect the debt.

In his deposition Armand stated that he didn't know any of the financial details of Victor's estate and that even though he had met with coexecutor James Nemec the night before, he couldn't remember anything about the meeting. In his deposition Nemec described Armand as "a terrible business executive." After the Palm Beach County Probate Court ruled against Nancy, one of Armand's attorneys tried to camouflage the ramifications of the decision by releasing a statement expressing Armand's concern that Ireene "remain happy and comfortable for the remainder of her life." Nancy promptly appealed the decision in the Florida Supreme Court.

And there the battle remained for two years, until Ireene Hammer died on November 17, 1987, with no knowledge that her daughter was trapped in litigation with her brother-in-law. Shortly before Nancy's appeal was going to be heard, Judge Knott announced that he was giving up the post of executor pro tem of Victor's estate. After serving for two years, he had discovered that his law firm was handling two Occidental accounts, which presented a potential conflict of interest. Armand responded to the news by suddenly offering Nancy title to the house in Connecticut if she waived all other claims.

With her mother dead and facing legal fees of $200,000, she agreed. Nancy had planned eventually to write a biography of her mother and repackage her mother's old radio broadcasts. But Armand's propensity to lay claim to things that did not belong to him led her to fear that he might insist that her mother's life and work belonged to Victor's estate and fell under his jurisdiction as co-executor. Therefore, she demanded written acknowledgment from him that she unequivocally owned the rights to her mother's life and creative output.

Armand agreed, but only if Nancy would agree in writing that any biography she wrote about her mother would not mention him or the lawsuit in a derogatory manner. This demand echoed the notation "Wait until Ireene non compos," which Armand had written across the top sheet of the file he kept on Victor's finances. It was as if Ireene was harboring a secret Armand did not want revealed about his relationship with her. Nancy perceived her mother as unsophisticated and Armand as someone who was compelled to use any means to gain control over those around him. She could not help wondering how her uncle had been able to exploit Ireene's innocence and whether he was afraid that Ireene had described those actions to her. Nancy was also ordered to hand over seventeen framed photographs of Victor that were in the Connecticut house, another indication that as far as Armand was concerned, she was not a legitimate member of the Hammer family.

Nancy and Armasha were the only family members capable of telling the truth about Armand from the perspective of the Hammer family. Armand believed he had subdued Nancy by having her sign a gag order. In a separate secret agreement, he bought Armasha's silence by establishing a $200,000 trust fund for him and paying him an estimated $100,000 in cash. Victor had made Nancy promise that when Ireene's estate was settled she would meet Armasha in Sweden and slip him his inheritance. It is not known how Armand passed Armasha's money to him.

This payment and Armand's legal fees reduced the amount of money he was going to receive from Victor's estate to less than half of his original $660,000 claim. When he learned that Nancy was receiving $6,000 a year from an insurance policy Victor had taken out for Ireene in 1950 that was not part of the estate, his lawyers demanded that she turn the money over to him. She refused.

The Geneva summit on November 18–21, 1985, the first meeting of a U.S. and a Soviet leader in six years, produced no substantive results. Reagan and Gorbachev did, however, conclude that they could deal with each other, and they agreed to expand educational and cultural exchanges. Determined to be the sponsor of the first cultural exchange under the new détente, Armand set out to obtain permission from the Ministry of Culture to present a collection of masterpieces from the Pushkin and Hermitage museums to coincide with Gorbachev's proposed visit to the United States in 1986. Lacking his former clout, he spent five days negotiating and finally had to camp out in the ministry before permission was granted. Since it was going to be a cultural exchange, Armand decided to send the Armand Hammer Collection on another Soviet tour and entitle the exhibition "Five Centuries of Masterpieces."

Then he began his familiar routine to win the favor of the new Soviet leader, telling Pravda that he was "convinced socialism has much to offer people . . . you have built a mighty power under socialism, and we should acknowledge that. It was very sensible for your leadership to concentrate on developing socialism in the USSR under new lines." Senior executives at Occidental told me that Armand had decided to give Gorbachev a piece of correspondence from Lenin or Marx for Christmas. Manuscript dealer Ken Randell was among those he contacted. "I was amazed that he would argue for half an hour trying to save a thousand dollars," Randell recalled.

If others were perplexed by Armand's penuriousness, I was not. It was all part of the same pattern. He spent money, sometimes in huge amounts, to curry favor with people in power. He pinched pennies to demonstrate his own power over people who were of little or no importance to him.

Oil companies invariably shy away from mergers with natural-gas pipeline firms because of the numerous legal restrictions faced by pipeline companies. Nonetheless, on January 1, 1986, Armand leaped at the chance to make Occidental the first leading oil company to merge with a major pipeline concern, and Occidental, as white knight, rescued Midcon Corporation from a hostile takeover by purchasing it for $3 billion in cash and stock. Wall Street was confused, but financial analysts assumed that the merger reflected Armand's appetite for unlimited growth at any cost and that Occidental would start selling off pieces of Midcon the minute the papers were signed. Indeed, Occidental promptly sold off Midcon's unneeded oil and gas exploration and production subsidiaries for $500 million.

This acquisition nearly tripled Occidental's debt, which climbed to $5.6 billion. Simultaneously, massive overproduction caused the most dramatic decline in crude-oil prices in fifty years, and Occidental's net income fell by $515 million. Occidental was not only forced to slash its capital budget twice, but also initiated a cost-cutting program involving the consolidation of operations and the elimination of two thousand jobs, and sold half its Colombian interests to Royal Dutch/Shell for $1 billion. The perennial optimist, Armand declared that the sale would put the company "in the best financial shape it has ever been in" and that the cash would be used to repurchase preferred stock. But the Colombian government accused Occidental of violating its production agreements by making the sale, and sued for $800 million. Armand fought hard and after a two-year battle, the Colombians were forced to settle for $22 million.

If Armand's business deals were sometimes shrewd, they could also be whimsical. Because of his name, many people thought he was Mr. Arm and Hammer, the baking soda king. Apparently that impelled him to attempt to acquire for Occidental a substantial portion of Church & Dwight, manufacturers of Arm & Hammer baking soda. Over the years the firm had fought him off and made public declarations that it had nothing to do with him, especially because of his involvement with the Soviet Union and his criminal activities in conjunction with the Nixon reelection campaign fund. Before the end of 1985, however, Occidental exchanged a half interest in an Occidental potassium carbonate plant for 1.1 million shares of Church & Dwight stock and $5.3 million in cash. Occidental's 5.4 percent interest enabled Armand to be named to Church & Dwight's board of directors, which, in turn, permitted him to boast that, yes indeed, he did make Arm & Hammer baking soda.

Yet even as he expanded Occidental's scope, another of its vastly more important operations was in jeopardy. After the terrorist bombings of Rome and Vienna airports at the end of December 1985, which left nineteen people dead, including five Americans, Reagan terminated all trade and economic activities with Libya. But Armand didn't want Occidental to leave, and nine days after the announcement, the administration disclosed that Occidental was one of a handful of companies that had been granted a special license to continue Libyan operations. Finally President Reagan ordered that no U.S. company do business with Libya, which left Occidental with no option but to withdraw. But Occidental retained its property rights in Libya, and my friends at the company told me that Armand's new impossible dream was that someday Occidental would make a triumphant return.

After ignoring a dozen phone calls from a man named Steve Weinberg asking for an interview, Armand received a letter from him on January 12, 1986. Weinberg was the executive director of Investigative Reporters and Editors, a professional organization for journalists, and an associate professor of journalism at the University of Missouri. After four years of preliminary research, he had received a contract from Little, Brown and Company to write an unauthorized biography of Armand for an advance of $160,000. Weinberg explained that he was anxious to have Armand speak for himself, but his letter was ignored.

Subsequently, Weinberg wrote in *Regardie's* magazine that "Hammer has created a persona that sometimes seems to conflict with the facts. Without the facts it is hard to know where myth ends and reality begins." The last thing Armand wanted was to see the facts in print, and when Weinberg wrote to him again, the letter again went unanswered. Weinberg went on to conduct seven hundred interviews and gather thousands of pages of documents, which included court records, government files, FBI memoranda, historical archives, and Armand Hammer Foundation reports. After he employed the Freedom of Information Act to gain access to the minutes of the SEC hearings concerning Armand's questionable business practices, Occidental lawyers attempted to stop him by claiming that this information would compromise "national security issues."

They also wrote to his publisher and accused Weinberg of attempting to portray Armand as "unscrupulous and willing to attain personal goals and ambitions through criminal acts, breaches of fiduciary duty or other unconscionable behavior." Declaring Weinberg's book "beyond redemption by corrections," they urged the cancellation of Weinberg's contract.

The threats were meaningless because the book hadn't been published and no evidence existed that Weinberg had libeled Armand. But the author decided that in fairness, when his manuscript was near completion, he would again offer Armand a chance to tell his side of the story. Determined never to set the record straight, Armand refused this invitation, too.

About the same time Mayor Bradley, who was campaigning for the California statehouse, returned $6,000 in campaign contributions to Occidental. A commentator remarked that Bradley was trying to avoid "the Occidental taint." In light of what Weinberg's book might reveal, I'm sure Armand considered Bradley's action a mere slap on the wrist.

On April 28, the Soviets announced that two days earlier an explosion in a reactor at the Chernobyl nuclear power station near Kiev had emitted more long-term radiation into the atmosphere, water, and soil than all previous nuclear explosions combined. The next day, UCLA bone marrow transplant specialist Robert Gale called Armand in Washington, where he was overseeing preparations for the May 1 opening of his latest U.S.-Soviet art exchange at the National Gallery of Art, and explained that he wanted to use the International Bone Marrow Transplant Registry to perform transplant operations on persons seriously contaminated by the accident. Armand immediately cabled the news to Gorbachev.

One week later, Occidental announced that Armand was paying to fly Gale and a team of doctors to the Soviet Union and had used his special relationship with Gorbachev to allow them entry to the contamination zone. His spectacular humanitarian gesture demanded an equally spectacular dose of PR, and the international press was summoned to Armand's private hangar at Los Angeles International Airport to watch the crates of medical supplies being loaded onto *Oxy One*.

Despite his doctrine of *glasnost,* it took Mikhail Gorbachev eighteen days to make a public statement about the disaster. He thanked Gale and his colleagues for their help and lambasted the Western media for its lurid coverage, failing to note that the Kremlin's secrecy had been the reason for so many of the speculations in the press. The next day Armand and Gale held their own press conference in Moscow and told reporters that thirty-five Soviets had suffered serious radiation poisoning and that nineteen bone marrow transplant operations had been performed. Armand added that even though the Soviet government had volunteered to reimburse the costs of the medical expedition, estimated at $600,000, he was donating them to the Soviet people. While he was speaking, he was handed a note saying that Gorbachev would like to see him.

Like Soviet leaders before him, Gorbachev found Armand a useful means of expressing his views to the West, and Armand dutifully reported that Gorbachev maintained that the Chernobyl disaster had sent a signal that Star Wars, which Gorbachev contended held the potential to be a Chernobyl in space, could never be allowed to happen and that a nuclear test ban, ratification of the SALT II defense treaty, and a 50 percent nuclear arms reduction agreement were the prerequisites for another summit with Reagan. Armand added that he had urged Gorbachev not to quarrel about the location of a summit meeting but to schedule one immediately on Thanksgiving, a traditional day of peace.

Armand's efforts on behalf of the Soviets were not limited to medical assistance. Aware that Raisa Gorbachev sat on the board of directors of the Soviet Cultural Fund, he donated eighteen paintings and $100,000 to the organization. Thereafter, Armand and Gale returned to Los Angeles and a blizzard of favorable publicity. Back in Washington, Armand held a private meeting with Secretary of State George Shultz, but Reagan, displeased that Gorbachev was trying to dictate the terms of a summit meeting through Hammer, refused to meet with him.

On July 23, Alexander Goldfarb, a professor of microbiology at Columbia University's Julius and Armand Hammer Medical Center, wrote to Armand, describing the plight of his father, sixty-seven-year-old Soviet Jewish dissident David Goldfarb. The senior Goldfarb was a distinguished microbiologist in his own right and a diabetic, but the Soviets had refused for eight years to grant him an exit visa even though he was now blind, had lost one leg, and was in danger of losing the other. Armand had previously been criticized publicly for not coming to the aid of the elder Goldfarb, but he still ignored Alexander Goldfarb's letter, and would say later that he hadn't received it. On July 28, *The Wall Street Journal* printed the letter on its front page under the headline TO RUSSIA WITH HOPE: A PLEA FOR ARMAND HAMMER'S HELP, placing Armand in the position of having to respond without discrediting the Soviet leadership.

Toward the end of the summer, the FBI arrested Gennadi Zakharov, a Soviet employee attached to the United Nations, as he purchased three classified documents dealing with military aircraft engines. Gorbachev was on vacation, and in his absence the KBG responded to Zakharov's arrest with a vengeance. Minutes after *U.S. News & World Report* Moscow correspondent Nicholas Daniloff received a gift from a Soviet "friend" that turned out to contain two maps marked "Secret," he was arrested, charged with espionage, and confined to Lefortovo Prison.

Led by the American Society of Newspaper Editors, the U.S.

press was in an uproar about Daniloff's framing and the fact that he would have to stand trial and face the death penalty. Their outrage was compounded the day after Daniloff's arrest when Alexander Goldfarb revealed that his father had been approached by the KGB in 1984 and told that he would receive an exit visa if he implicated Daniloff in a phony smuggling scheme. The likely solution was to trade Daniloff for Zakharov, but the State Department made it clear that the trade was unacceptable because Daniloff was innocent and Zakharov wasn't. Therefore, Zakharov could not be released unless Daniloff was released first.

Gorbachev was planning to invite Reagan to a minisummit in a neutral country to work out the agenda for a full summit. Before the goodwill engendered at the Geneva meeting evaporated, the Soviet leader realized, there had to be a quick resolution to the Daniloff matter.

Enter Armand. On September 4, his latest Soviet exhibition moved from the National Gallery of Art in Washington to the Metropolitan Museum in New York. The next day he did two things: he got *The New York Times* to agree to print an addendum to its review of the exhibition, which would mention that Occidental had underwritten the exhibition and name him as coordinator, and he launched a diplomatic initiative that he hoped would lead the Reagan administration to trade Zakharov for Daniloff by approaching Israeli prime minister Shimon Peres and collecting a list of Soviet Jewish dissidents who could be included in the trade. In this way he hoped to motivate Israel to apply pressure to the Reagan administration and get it to alter its position about the exchange.

The State Department continued to fear that a trade would lead the public to accuse the administration of capitulating to the Soviets, and Armand was told to back off. But suddenly word "leaked" that he was involved in back-channel negotiations to free Daniloff, which made his activities front-page news and blocked State from issuing any more direct challenges to him that might prove potentially embarrassing. Finally, the two governments worked out a deal. Daniloff would be released. Then Zakharov would plead *nolo contendere* and be expelled from the United States the next day. On September 23, after the Soviets balked because they did not understand the concept of *nolo contendere*, Armand sped to the Soviet Union to offer a personal explanation. Daniloff was released on September 29. Zakharov was let go the next day. Simultaneously, the United States made the surprising announcement that Reagan and Gorbachev would participate in a minisummit in Reykjavík, Iceland, on October 10 and 11.

Armand, upset that he hadn't received enough credit for his involvement in the freeing of Daniloff, allowed *Life* magazine to construct a "journal" of his rescue efforts. He reported that his activities had received the official blessing of Reagan (which wasn't true), and that he had met with Ambassador Anatoly Dobrynin and spelled out a solution in a letter that Dobrynin had delivered to Gorbachev. Therefore, he was the uncredited architect of the trade. A trade had taken place, but not the trade Armand claimed to have initiated. Zakharov had not been swapped for Daniloff, he had been exchanged for Soviet dissident Yuri Orlov, the former chairman of Helsinki Watch, whom the Soviets had exiled to Siberia. Critics promptly accused Armand of taking undeserved credit for Daniloff's release, and later, in his memoir, *Two Lives, One Russia*, Daniloff spent only one paragraph on Armand's contribution.

The Reykjavík minisummit fell apart over the Star Wars issue, and the plight of David Goldfarb was apparently forgotten. But five days after the failure at Reykjavík, Gorbachev, determined to find ways to reach agreement with Reagan, granted Armand permission to fly Goldfarb and his wife, Cecila, to the United States. From *Oxy One* Armand placed calls to the media, and by the time the plane touched down at Newark Airport, the press was out in full force. Armand even received a handwritten letter of gratitude from the president, signed "Ron." It did not matter that the gesture had been designed to convince the American people that Gorbachev was a genuine humanitarian. Nor did Armand reveal that he had convinced Goldfarb to assign the rights of his life story to him and that he planned to approach the William Morris Talent Agency to package a feature film about the heroic rescue, in which he would star.

These heavily publicized rescue efforts led Israel's Bar-Ilan University to award Armand an honorary doctorate at a $500-a-plate dinner in Los Angeles. Not long afterward, a hit list was introduced into evidence during the trial of the former members of the neo-Nazi organization the Order, who were accused of killing Denver talk show host Alan Berg in 1984. It contained the names of several prominent Jews marked for execution, and Armand, who had spent his whole life ignoring his Jewish heritage, was at the top of it.

32.

DEFIANCE OF

DEATH

On February 14, 1987, Armand joined Claudia Cardinale, John Kenneth Galbraith, Graham Greene, Kris Kristofferson, Norman Mailer, Gregory Peck, Pierre Trudeau, Peter Ustinov, Gore Vidal, and seven hundred other delegates in Moscow to participate in the Soviet-backed international Forum for a Nuclear-Free World and the Survival of Mankind. Attention was focused on one delegate, Soviet dissident Andrei Sakharov, who was making his first public appearance since Gorbachev had ended his six-year exile in Gorky. At the final banquet, Armand asked to be introduced to Sakharov and enumerated for him all the things he was trying to do to bring about a lasting peace. But when Sakharov supplied Armand with the names of nineteen political prisoners to give to Gorbachev, Armand didn't seem at all interested. Armand and Sakharov subsequently joined the board of directors of the International Foundation for the Survival and Development of Humanity. This new U.S.-Soviet organization had been created to address problems concerning human rights, the arms race, the environment, and world hunger. Armand also announced a $200,000 contribution, and I read into this new round of well-publicized activities his continuing quest for the Nobel Peace Prize.

On March 11, Armand and Frances returned to the USSR to attend the opening of "An American Vision: Three Generations of Wyeth Art" at the Soviet Academy of the Arts in Leningrad. This collection of paintings by N. C. Wyeth, his son, Andrew, and Andrew's son, Jamie, was the first American art exhibition to travel to the Soviet Union in eight years. PepsiCo was the official sponsor of the exhibition, but Armand had pestered PepsiCo's chairman,

Donald Kendall, until he received permission to authorize a small contribution from Occidental that would allow him to take part in the festivities.

At the reception that opened the exhibition, as Frances and Armand descended a staircase and headed toward the receiving line to greet Mikhail and Raisa Gorbachev, Frances tripped and fell. Armand was so eager to be photographed with the Gorbachevs he ignored her and kept on going. After that incident Frances stopped traveling with Armand. She was eighty-three, and age and health were given as the reasons, but the senior executives were convinced that she had discovered eight years after the fact that Martha Kaufman was continuing to work for the Armand Hammer Foundation.

Frances was replaced by Armand's "doctor," a Mexican-born anesthesiologist. Explaining that he was suffering from "chronic pain," He eventually moved the anesthesiologist into his house. It appeared that he was being maintained with injections of stimulants to make him appear bright and alert on public occasions as well as injections of the Romanian rejuvenation compound Gerovital, which he was having smuggled into the country from Mexico because it was cheaper than having it smuggled in from Romania.

Over the years Armand had repeatedly promised to donate the superb Old Master drawings in his collection to the National Gallery of Art. As the publication of his autobiography, *Hammer*, neared, he decided to have the drawings installed in the National Gallery and to stage a publication party that would also celebrate the generous donation. During an endless round of negotiations with director J. Carter Brown, Armand insisted on withholding a prized Leonardo. Brown and Armand had known each other for sixteen years, and Brown knew exactly how to break the deadlock. He gave Armand a deadline and explained that if Armand let it pass he would lose the opportunity of staging a major promotion for his book and seeing his name engraved beside the names of other major donors. Armand listened and then relented.

Hammer had been sold to the Putnam Publishing Group for $1 million. Armand adorned the jacket with a stunning array of celebrity endorsements, including blurbs from Menachem Begin, George Bush, Jimmy Carter, Malcolm Forbes, Gerald Ford, Edward Kennedy, Dan Rather, and Arthur Sulzberger. He also compiled a pamphlet of additional quotes for reviewers and organized celebrity-filled publication parties at both the National Gallery of Art and the Los Angeles County Museum's Frances and Armand

Hammer Wing. The Metropolitan Museum of Art had announced that it needed $4 million to renovate the galleries of its arms and armor collection and Armand had pledged $1 million with the condition that the refurbished galleries bear his name. The newly restored Armand Hammer Equestrian Court was selected as the site for a third party.

Permeated with the aura of a fairy tale, *Hammer* told the entertaining story of a saintly but shrewd man whose life consisted of one triumph after another. Along the way almost every head of state expressed his gratitude for Armand's generosity, counsel, and wisdom. Reviewing *Hammer* in *The New York Times*, Ted Morgan commented that its subject "can be forgiven his bursts of self-aggrandizement and his sometimes jejune political views, in light of his ability to do what other men only ponder." The myth of Armand Hammer was so persuasive that other critics were almost as flattering.

Hammer quickly climbed to the top of the best-seller lists and remained there for four months. Later, Armand's writer, Neil Lyndon, remarked that "a lot of sanitizing went on." But that was all he said at the time. Lyndon had signed an agreement not to speak publicly about Armand without his permission for the next ten years. In February 1992, by which time Armand was dead, Lyndon wrote in British *Esquire*, "I was Armand Hammer's alter ego. I had spent two years inventing him in print. I had composed his thoughts, figured out his motives, guessed what he might have said in the scenes I was describing. . . . His character was my creation in a fictional enterprise." Lyndon also wrote that he had earned $500,000 and around $72,000 in expenses for having "flogged every atom of my soul."

Around the publication date of *Hammer*, the *Los Angeles Times* reported the rumor that Armand had sent Ann Landers a jade necklace accompanied by a note asking her to write a letter of recommendation on his behalf to the Nobel Peace Prize nominating committee. Armand denied the story but did say that Gregory Peck and Menachem Begin had voluntarily written letters on his behalf. "I've done nothing actually to get it," he remarked disingenuously. "If it happened, I'd be greatly honored. But I don't think about it."

When the *Times* printed a front-page story indicating that he was "seeking a museum to bear his name," he fired off a letter reaffirming his commitment to donate his art collection to the Los Angeles County Museum. But my friends at Occidental told me that Armand was convinced that Norton Simon was going forward with his plan to establish a museum for his vastly superior art collection on the UCLA campus just six blocks from Armand's office and that Armand was determined to build his own museum and beat Simon to the punch.

Subsequently, Armand sent the County Museum a thirty-nine-page legal document containing his requirements for finalizing the donation of the Armand Hammer Collection. Included in the long list were demands to house the entire collection in the Frances and Armand Hammer Wing, remodel the wing to his specifications, remove the names of any other donors from the plaques on its walls, hire a special curator who would report only to him or his foundation, and hang a life-size portrait of him at the entranceway. The trustees wrote back that they were willing to keep the collection intact, but they refused to hire a curator, remove the names of other donors, or hang a portrait of him in the lobby. Armand did not reply, but the trustees were not disturbed. After all, he had been publicly repeating his bequest for seventeen years, and they assumed that he would eventually fulfill his promise.

In September Armand appointed his thirty-one-year-old grandson, Michael Armand Hammer, assistant corporate secretary. The senior executives took the appointment to mean that Armand was grooming Michael to replace Corporate Secretary Paul Hebner, who had worked side by side with Armand for thirty-three years, ever since the beginning of his presidency, and had always displayed exceptional loyalty to him. Eventually, Armand did replace Hebner with Michael, who also took Hebner's place on the board of directors.

I had met Michael and his sister, Casey, on a number of occasions when they were children. During Michael's adolescence, Armand had told me that his grandson had been "having some problems" and that he was sending him to a boarding school on the East Coast. I sensed that Armand feared that Michael might turn out to be like his father, Julian, who by then had been hospitalized for chronic paranoid schizophrenia. Eventually Julian's wife, Sue, divorced Julian, and he went through another series of disturbing episodes involving firearms. I also heard that he was never able to work and that Armand continued to support him but that, as Julian had grown older, he had finally begun to settle down.

Uncharacteristically, Armand began to shower favors on Michael. When he entered the University of San Diego, Armand supplied him with a tutor, and he graduated with a B.B.A. degree. Then Michael enrolled in Columbia University's Graduate School of Business, where he earned his M.B.A. degree in 1982, joining Occidental soon after. He married Dru Ann Mobley in 1985, and Armand helped the couple buy a home in Los Angeles. I heard that Armand was especially thrilled when Dru Ann became pregnant and he was about to become a great-grandfather. He was even more excited when he discovered that the baby was going to be a boy. Armand's great-grandson was named Armand Douglas Hammer.

Armand was on the front pages again in October, when he performed another dramatic rescue mission by flying Ida Nudel, the so-called "guardian angel of the Soviet refuseniks," to Israel on *Oxy One*. Nudel had spent seventeen years warring publicly against Soviet authorities in order to obtain an exit visa, but I never heard that Armand had ever expressed the slightest bit of interest in her plight. Clearly, her release had been permitted by Gorbachev as another goodwill gesture. Nevertheless, Armand claimed credit for obtaining her freedom and told the Moscow foreign press corps that he had spoken up on her behalf after Gorbachev asked him to help extricate the Soviet Union from Afghanistan. While no independent source could confirm his involvement, Nudel, grateful nonetheless, granted Armand the rights to her life story. An insider at Occidental told me that, ironically, this time he had almost succeeded in putting together a motion picture because Jane Fonda, whom Armand disliked intensely, had expressed an interest in starring.

Armand was tireless in his search for even more publicity. On December 8, Raisa and Mikhail Gorbachev arrived in Washington for the next summit meeting. Mrs. Gorbachev's schedule included a tour of the National Gallery of Art. Accompanied by Barbara Walters and trailed by the press, Armand suddenly turned up and posed happily between Mrs. Gorbachev and Walters. Later in the month he endowed the Armand Hammer Fund for Economic Cooperation in the Middle East to promote cooperation between Israel and her neighbors and raised $1.6 million to launch the construction of the Armand Hammer–Guilford Glazer Arab-Jewish Community Center in Tel Aviv.

After donating four annual $100,000 Armand Hammer Cancer Prizes and another $500,000 to enlarge Stanford University's cancer research laboratory (subsequently renamed the Armand Hammer Cancer Laboratory), Armand gave gifts of $100,000 each to National Cancer Institute immune system researcher Dr. Steven Rosenberg and research teams at UCLA and the Sloan-Kettering Institute for Cancer Research that were performing similar work. He also announced plans to raise "billions" for this area of research and enlisted Bill Cosby to help him raise the money. Following Mrs. Reagan's lead when she had made a guest appearance on *Diff'rent Strokes* to promote her antidrug campaign, Armand appeared on *The Cosby Show* on January 21, 1988, in the role of a philanthropist urging Congress to allocate more money for medical research. A consummate actor in life and a star in his own films, he was equally effective in a sitcom.

Basking in the afterglow of his TV appearance the next day, Armand summoned the press and announced that he was going to build his own museum to house his art collection and open it in time for his ninety-second birthday on May 21, 1990. The Armand Hammer Museum of Art and Cultural Center was going to occupy three floors of the Occidental building and a new two-story structure that would be physically connected to it. Edward Larrabee Barnes had been chosen as the architect, $30 million had been earmarked for construction, and operating costs would be maintained by a $36 million endowment annuity purchased by Occidental.

Shaken by the news, current and former County Museum trustees told reporters that Hammer had a moral obligation to keep his promise to donate his collection to their museum, and that the renunciation of his promise was a violation of the public trust. They added that Hammer had exploited the County museum by using the promise of his bequest to stage seventeen years' worth of self-promotional events at the museum, and that the museum was incalculably damaged by his decision because it had acquired paintings solely because they would complement paintings in the Armand Hammer Collection and had passed up opportunities to acquire other paintings because it expected to receive representative samples from Hammer.

County Museum trustee Franklin Murphy also sat on the board of directors of the *Los Angeles Times*. I was not surprised when the *Times* printed a copy of Armand's demands to the museum trustees. The fact that the museum had refused to remove the names of other donors from the walls of the Frances and Armand Hammer Wing confirmed suspicions that Armand's decision to build his own museum ultimately reflected his desire to leave behind a monument to his own colossal ego. Subsequently, County Museum director Earl Powell expressed his belief that Armand had approached Edward Larrabee Barnes before he presented his demands to the museum, which indicated that they were a setup to establish grounds that would enable him to withdraw his collection.

Armand placed all the blame on the trustees. "They were treating me . . . as somebody that frankly they could push around. . . . They thought I had no place to go," he declared to reporters. That complaint did not assuage the rage of Los Angeles's art and philanthropic communities, the local press, and local museum-goers, and Armand would soon discover that his twenty-year reign as a beloved Los Angeles media celebrity and cultural icon had abruptly come to an end.

Typically, the barrage of criticism did not stop him from escorting a Soviet cultural minister on a tour of the County Museum. Spotting Earl Powell, he asked the director if the County Museum owned any Daumiers. Powell stiffened and replied that, after Armand's press conference, it didn't. Armand grinned, patted Powell on the back, and said teasingly, "I'll send you some."

Armand chose as his method of damage control the launching of a national campaign designed to prove that his altruism was genuine. He and Bill Cosby moderated a U.S.-Soviet satellite TV panel discussion of American and Soviet cancer researchers that was telecast to hospitals all over the United States. His association with Cosby generated enormous positive publicity and provided him the platform to announce Stop Cancer, a fund-raising drive designed to add $1 billion a year to the budget of the National Cancer Institute.

Armand made a public donation of $100,000 to the campaign, raised another $900,000 at a luncheon where he was the guest of honor, and promoted a $2,500-a-plate dinner that raised an additional $2 million. In August, five months into the campaign, he announced that he had raised $5 million. A fund-raiser to coincide with the opening of the World Financial Center in New York City produced another $4 million in contributions. But here, too, his activities generated criticism. Health officials, lawmakers, and political leaders joined together to complain that Hammer was channeling too much money into one form of cancer research, diverting funds from other cancer-fighting organizations, and overemphasizing the need for cancer research at the expense of other life-threatening diseases. Armand responded to the criticisms by publishing an Op-Ed article in *The New York Times* calling for even more funding of his programs.

At the same time the local press reported that Norton Simon

had canceled his plans to build a museum on the UCLA campus, accompanied by speculations that the decision had been prompted by the news that Armand was building his own museum nearby.

In 1986 *Forbes* magazine's list of the 400 richest Americans had placed Hammer's wealth at $180 million. Edward J. Epstein subsequently wrote in *Manhattan, Inc.,* that Armand's 1.5 million shares of Occidental stock (representing the ownership of only 0.8 percent of the company) were worth no more than $35 million, that all of his art holdings were earmarked as donations, and that his "wealth" essentially consisted of shareholder money that he spent at whim. Hammer's name was omitted from the next *"Forbes* Four Hundred" listing.

The will that Frances Hammer wrote in 1971 left her half share of community property to Armand and provided that if he died first, her estate would be placed in a trust for her sisters, brother, niece, and nephew. For tax reasons the will was amended to include the Armand Hammer Foundation as a beneficiary. The legal firm that represented Frances also represented the Armand Hammer Foundation.

On May 12, 1988, Frances hired a lawyer with no involvement with Armand or his foundation to draw up a new will. She disinherited Armand and left all of her own property and her half share of community property to her sister's daughter, Joan Weiss, with whom she had remained close over the years. Frances also left their house, which she owned, to Weiss immediately on Armand's death, and appointed Weiss's husband, Robert, the executor of the new will.

According to the community-property laws of California, Frances was half owner of the Armand Hammer Collection, which Armand was donating to the Hammer Museum. In February 1983, Frances had cosigned without benefit of legal counsel a one-page typewritten letter from Hammer to her, giving him all of the art. The new will, which gave Joan Weiss the legal right to claim possession of half of the paintings after Frances's death, presented a direct challenge to the validity of that letter.

At the time that Frances drafted her new will, rumors were circulating through Occidental that she had become increasingly distressed by Armand's ongoing relationship with Martha Kaufman and his plan to make Martha a director of the Hammer Museum. Nor had Frances recovered from the shock of Armand's attempt to take away Nancy Eilan's home, and she feared that if she died first, he would treat her family with the same viciousness. There was also a belief that she wanted a divorce but feared what Armand might do even to an eighty-five-year-old woman whose usefulness had come to an end.

Armand himself was ninety. He had already traveled to Beijing, where Occidental staged an elaborate reception for him at the Great Wall Hotel. China's president General Yang Shangkun was the host, and the six hundred guests were given copies of *Hammer*, which had been translated into Chinese. In Armand's honor thirty-three young Chinese ballet dancers performed the Christmas sections in Tchaikovsky's *Nutcracker*, and not a word was said about the fact that Occidental's Chinese mine had been shut down because of technical difficulties. Other Chinese mines were having to fill Occidental's coal orders, causing Deng's economy to suffer staggering losses.

Next Armand staged an elaborate birthday gala for himself at the Kennedy Center for the Performing Arts, and tributes to his humanitarianism poured in from all over the world. Eight days later, Reagan went to Moscow for his fourth summit meeting with Gorbachev and Armand followed to sing the praises of U.S.-Soviet cooperation. He told the Moscow foreign press corps that the renewed spirit of détente indicated that the time had finally come to construct a golf course in Moscow, and he ordered Occidental to break ground. He then received an uncomfortable reminder that he was not really at the center of either American or Soviet power. Armand had endowed an American College of Surgeons scholarship and had it named after Nancy Reagan's stepfather, Dr. Loyal Davis. But when he pleaded with the First Lady to invite him to the state dinner at the U.S. embassy during the summit, she bluntly turned him down. Of course, Armand had no difficulty securing an invitation for Gorbachev's dinner for Reagan.

On July 6, a series of devastating explosions rocked Occidental's Piper Alpha platform in the North Sea, shooting flames four hundred feet into the air, destroying the platform, killing 167 workers, and putting the operation out of commission for an entire year. Legendary oil well fighter Red Adair spent twenty-three days putting out the blaze. Armand took exactly the correct PR stance and did not soft-pedal the disaster. He went to Scotland immediately to make his presence felt. Many of the residents of Aberdeen refused to comment on the disaster because they worked for Occidental and were in awe of Armand. An eleven-month investigation produced a report criticizing Occidental for "unsafe practices" and government inspectors for failing to discover safety defects on the rig. It was later revealed that the blast had been caused by a leak in a pump and that safety devices had failed to respond. Occidental and its North Sea partners made offers totaling $187 million to the families of the 167 workers who died in the explosion. An out-of-court settlement was reached just three months after the disaster. With most of the settlement and reconstruction costs covered by insurance, Occidental's losses were minimal.

After a consortium of Soviet museums joined forces with Amsterdam's Stedelijk Museum to mount a touring retrospective of paintings by Kasimir Malevich, it set an asking price of $1.5 million in hard currency. Armand decided that the exhibition would be the perfect opening event for the Hammer Museum, whose construction was well under way. But the new freedoms under Gorbachev challenged Armand's acknowledged methods of doing business in the Soviet Union. Not only had he lost his competitive edge but the possibility that the ruble might be stabilized and become a legitimate hard currency also threatened to make his awkward but ingenious barter deals an anachronism. Nor were the regional ministries treating him with the respect that he had been accorded by the Soviet Ministry of Culture during the Brezhnev years. Thus, he resorted to another familiar weapon in his arsenal. When, on December 7, Armenia was struck by a massive earthquake that killed 25,000 people, injured thousands more, and left 500,000 homeless, he announced a $1 million emergency aid donation. I was told that after he made this gesture he pulled every string at his disposal to obtain permission to import the Malevich exhibition to Los Angeles. Still he had to come up with the $1.5 million fee, and he announced that he was paying the entire amount. In fact, it would be shared equally with IBM and Philip Morris.

Election Day was approaching and Occidental had supplied $7.1 million to the Los Angeles Public and Coastal Protection Committee, which was essentially a front organization that had placed a pro-Pacific Palisades drilling proposition on the ballot. An antidrilling proposition, backed with funds of $2.8 million, was on the same ballot and the ugliest of campaigns was under way.

The pro-Occidental group took the position that the drilling opponents represented only the West Side of Los Angeles. It was a euphemism for wealthy Jews, and carried with it the implication that they were so rich they could afford to oppose growth and had little or no concern for the economic needs of blacks and other minorities. After Occidental was defeated and the slow-growth initiative won, Armand was subjected to another round of severe criticism and accused of using the funds he had raised from prominent local Jewish businessmen to turn his desire to drill in Pacific Palisades into a racial issue that exploited anti-Semitism and pitted rich against poor, whites against blacks, and the West Side of the city against the poverty-striken South Side.

At the same time Reagan was nearing the end of his second term and was also approaching the end of his usefulness to Armand. Still, there was one piece of unfinished business. Armand contributed $1 million to the Reagan Library construction fund and donated Charles Russell's *Fording the Horse Herd,* valued at $750,000, to the White House. Then he ordered his lawyers to apply for the presidential pardon that he had craved for so many years. The Justice Department indicated that he could be pardoned, but I was told that Armand had insisted he was innocent and had been framed and demanded that the government issue a declaration of innocence. Reagan issued thirty-two pardons before his term ended; Armand's pardon was not included. On the day Reagan left office, he modified trade sanctions against Libya so that five U.S. companies, including Occidental, could resume operations. The decision was designed to counter Qaddafi's threat to nationalize the assets of these companies.

It was something, but not enough, and Armand turned his attention to President-elect Bush. He had promised his personal papers to the Library of Congress, and in January 1989, that promise was finally kept. Then he received permission to mount an exhibition of the most impressive correspondence in his papers three days before Bush's inauguration. During the reception, which was packed with ambassadors and legislators, he announced a donation of an additional $100,000 to the Library of Congress. In acknowledgement of his gifts to the library, his contributions to the Bush campaign, and his financial support of the inaugural committee, Armand was seated in a place of honor next to the Reagans and Quayles on the Capitol steps during the swearing-in ceremony.

Once again I knew that Armand had greased his way into a position of prominence, and it was entirely fitting that directly after the inauguration Peruvian president Alan Garcia Pérez announced that Occidental had made a major oil discovery estimated at 600 million barrels, one and a half times Peru's existing reserves. From the Capitol steps, Armand hailed the discovery as comparable to

Occidental's achievements in Libya and Colombia. Subsequently, *The Wall Street Journal* reported that the announcement had "baffled" analysts and that Occidental was "noncommital" in its response to questions about it.

The following October, the Republican National Committee revealed the names of "Team 100," a list of wealthy individuals who had made so-called "soft money" donations of $100,000 or more to Republicans outside Federal campaign contribution limits and were, therefore, required by law to donate this money only at the state or local level. Wedged among the corporate big wigs, the wealthy, and the famous was the name of a former Occidental senior executive. Had Armand been up to his old tricks? I wondered.

In May 1989, investment adviser Alan Kahn filed a class-action suit in the Chancery Court of Delaware, where Occidental was incorporated, on behalf of an Occidental shareholder. Calling Occidental's $30 million charitable contribution to build the Hammer Museum and its purchase of a $36 million endowment annuity to run it "a gift to Hammer's ego" and "a waste of corporate assets," Kahn asked Vice Chancellor of the Court Maurice Harnett to enjoin the company from spending $66 million on a project that would not benefit the shareholders.

Many corporations incorporate in Delaware because of the leniency of the state's business-judgment rule, which gives management and boards of directors considerable free rein. By raising the questions of what limits could be set on corporate contributions and whether a chief executive could make the shareholders pay twice for the same thing—Occidental's shareholders had already paid for the County Museum's Frances and Armand Hammer Wing and were about to pay for the Hammer Museum—Kahn's suit presented a direct challenge to corporate accountability under the rule. The challenge was reinforced by Occidental's sixth-largest outside investor, the California Public Employees Retirement Association (CalPERS), when it joined Kahn's suit and claimed that Occidental was making an "extraordinarily large and unusual donation to a charity, but the charity is Armand Hammer. . . . a clear conflict of interest." Nine days after the Kahn filing another group of shareholders, in an action that came to be known as the Levitan suit, filed a similar class-action suit in the chancery court.

While these legal activities were underway, Martha Kaufman, who would one day, I suspected, find employment in Armand's new museum, underwent a legal change of name and became Hilary Gibson. She had taken voice lessons and changed her hair color, and appeared to be a different person. Later she would explain that her former husband had remarried and her children were grown, so "it seemed like a good time to establish my own identity." The explanation did nothing to eliminate the speculation that the transformation was designed to deceive Frances Hammer.

During June, Armand, Hilary Gibson, and other Occidental executives gave depositions in the Delaware court about the decision to build the museum. But Occidental refused to release their testimony or other significant documents, and the *Los Angeles Times* and *The Wall Street Journal* filed petitions under the Freedom of Information Act to gain access to the court record. Thus, Occidental was left with no option but to begin complying.

Armand's transcript contained a bombshell. The $5.8 million spent to purchase the Codex Hammer had been paid not by Hammer, as he had repeatedly trumpeted to the news media for more than eight years, but through "an unpublicized special appropriations fund" authorized by Occidental's board of directors. Therefore, the shareholders were the real owners of the Leonardo manuscript that Occidental was donating to the Hammer Museum as a charitable contribution. It was Armand's fear of this and similar revelations that had led him to give up Occidental's attempt to take over Mead and to pay off David Murdock to thwart his attempt to take over Occidental.

Other depositions revealed that some board members had objected to building the museum and that the decision to go ahead and allocate the $66 million had been reached after a single two-hour meeting held by a "special committee." The "special committee" had also granted Armand the right to authorize enormous amounts of overtime so that construction would be completed by his ninety-second birthday and to spend $1.3 million yearly for a security force consisting of off-duty and retired police officers to protect him and his collection. When the *Los Angeles Times* located a copy of Martha Kaufman's business plan, it was illegible, but Occidental refused to provide a readable copy.

The settlement of one class-action suit would automatically terminate all the other class-action suits against Occidental and protect it against similar suits in the future. Therefore, Occidental proposed a speedy settlement of the Levitan suit. Over sixteen months, estimated construction costs for the hastily planned museum had risen from $30 million to nearly $78.4 million, and Occidental agreed to hold the building costs to $60 million, which meant that it would be unable to afford to complete construction of the museum's auditorium and restaurant. It also agreed to limit corporate donations to charities favored by Armand; receive 50 percent of the profits should the Hammer Museum sell the company's headquarters, which were going to be donated to the museum by its owner, Oxy Westwood, an Occidental subsidiary; and place the name Occidental on the museum in addition to Armand's. As a final incentive to settle, Occidental agreed to pay Levitan's $1.4 million legal bill.

Stating that Occidental's charitable contribution fell within the jurisdiction of the Delaware business-judgment rule, Vice Chancellor Harnett rejected Kahn's attempt to stall the Levitan settlement. But the judge did complain that Occidental's offer left "substantial doubts" about "the egocentric nature of Dr. Hammer's objections to donating paintings to the County Museum" and "the lack of any direct substantial benefit to the stockholders." He also pointed out that a settlement of this type was usually unfair "because defendants too often are inclined to pay fat fees to opposing lawyers in return for a deal." Lastly, he criticized the "independent group of directors" that had voted to spend what was now $86 million of the shareholders' money without consulting independent counsel. *The Wall Street Journal* reported that the committee was chaired by former Senator Albert Gore, Sr., and that Gore "appears to have misunderstood the project" and those "facts" that had surfaced during the litigation. Occidental immediately responded by choosing Harnett's colleague, former chancellor Grover Brown, to serve as counsel to its "special directors' committee."

After nine hundred employees were laid off in an economy move designed to provide a $100 million saving, dissident shareholders protested anew Occidental's decision to invest $86 million in a museum they had begun to call "The Armand Hammer Mausoleum." Still construction proceeded, and at the beginning of August, the Hammer Museum officially hired Hilary Gibson as a director and spokesperson. "How many women get to build a museum?" Gibson asked reporters after the appointment.

On August 14, Armand finally fulfilled another dream. After agreeing to scale down his original demand from a declaration of innocence to forgiveness, he received a pardon from President Bush. It would later be revealed that four months before the pardon was granted, Armand had made a "soft-money" contribution of $110,000 to the Republican National State Elections Committee and that five of the other contributors had subsequently received ambassadorships. Critics charged that Armand's presidential pardon and the ambassadorships had been awarded in return for the contributions. Armand's reward, I suspected, was the pardon.

But if Armand believed his reputation was now unsullied, he was in for a disappointment. In October *Armand Hammer: The Untold Story* by Steve Weinberg made its appearance in bookstores. Weinberg's biography revealed, among other things, that Armand had been so determined to obtain a presidential pardon that he had tracked down Tim Babcock's banker in 1987 and gotten him to divulge the location of Babcock's old banking records in the hope that he would discover additional evidence that Babcock was the kind of man who would frame him.

Weinberg's account of Hammer's "quest for respect and respectability" and "high-cost, high-visibility quest for immortality" was fair—even generous—but the author's voluminous research had enabled him to include the unpleasant and controversial facts about many aspects of Armand's long life. On August 14, After *The Untold Story* was published in England, Armand filed the most expensive libel action in British history, suing Weinberg on 157 counts of defamation. Weinberg would be forced to spend the next year retracing his steps as he and his lawyers set out to gather depositions from his interviewees to prove that he had written the truth. By the time the process was over, Weinberg's legal bill would mount to $1.2 million.

On November 11, two weeks after the U.S. publication of *The Untold Story,* Armand entered the hospital to receive a pacemaker, and five days later he was back at work. Unfortunately, Frances was not so resilient. During 1988, she had signed two documents waiving her community-property rights. On November 18, exactly a week after Armand's pacemaker implant, she signed a third waiver and turned over her $18 million pension to her husband. The next week she fell, broke her hip, and was taken to the hospital, where she came down with pneumonia and then slipped into a coma.

While Frances was in the hospital, Armand received a call from Dr. Robert Schuller, founder of Orange County's Crystal Cathedral. In the early 1980s, after watching Schuller's weekly *Hour of Power* Christian TV program, Armand had become impressed with Schuller's fame and his huge number of viewers and had made a concerted effort to meet him. He had donated $250,000 to the Crystal Cathedral, had given Schuller *In the Hands of God,* an oil painting by Russian-born artist Mark Klionsky, and had been delighted when Schuller consented to give invocations at his birthday parties.

Schuller told Armand that he had received a call from a Soviet emigré who offered to make arrangements for him to broadcast a one-hour version of *Hour of Power* over Soviet TV on Christmas Day. Even though Frances was in a coma, Armand jumped at the opportunity to fly Schuller to Moscow to meet the vice chairman of the Soviet state television network, Valentin Lazutkin. The Soviet official turned down the idea of airing *Hour of Power* on a weekly basis but granted permission for Schuller to tape an inspirational message to be aired on Christmas Day. Armand was still able to work his Soviet connections.

On December 16, soon after Armand's return to Los Angeles, Frances died without having regained consciousness. The cause of death was listed as "respiratory distress syndrome" brought on by pneumonia. Subsequently Hilary Gibson told reporters that Frances had slipped getting out of bed at night in the dark. "The poor dear," she said solicitously. "She didn't want to wake Armand. They oversedated her, and she never woke up. In that condition, you're subject to a lot of complications."

The story was contradicted by Frances's relatives, who insisted that she had slipped during the afternoon. I also knew for a fact that Frances and Armand had slept in separate bedrooms. Frances' death, like so much in Armand's life, was clouded in mystery. It was rumored that one of the Hammers' maids had told another maid that Armand had waited an hour and a half after the accident before calling for help. There were also allegations that even though she was suffering from pneumonia, she had been kept lying flat on her back, a position that is normally avoided with pneumonia patients, whose lungs can fill so easily. Other allegations questioned the use of the sedatives prescribed for her.

A few days after Frances's death, Armand announced that after eighty-two years he had decided to reclaim his Jewish heritage and have a bar mitzvah. The idea had originally stemmed from Rabbi Daniel Lapin of the Pacific Jewish Center, an Orthodox Jewish synagogue in the Venice Beach area of Los Angeles, whose congregants at one time or another included Bob Dylan, Elliott Gould, and Barbra Streisand. Lapin had been looking for a way to raise enough money to construct a new building and had suggested the idea of a belated bar mitzvah to Hammer's adminstrative assistant, Rick Jacobs.

Instead of the traditional Saturday morning service, Armand decided to celebrate his bar mitzvah on the first night of Chanukah in December 1991 at a heavily publicized formal $500-a-plate dinner at the Beverly Hilton Hotel and to donate the proceeds to the Pacific Jewish Center and the Jerusalem College of Technology. Among the stipulations, Armand insisted that because he could not read Hebrew, he would not have to read from the Torah.

A few days later CalPERS wrote to Hammer, demanding the creation of a special watchdog advisory committee to monitor the Occidental board on behalf of the shareholders. Occidental immediately wrote to the SEC, requesting permission to omit the proposal on its next proxy statement. Meanwhile, Armand was preparing to spend even more money on his museum. The determination that the Armand Hammer Collection did not include enough paintings to fill the walls of the Hammer Museum led him to approach USC and initiate negotiations to repurchase "at fair market value" the forty-nine paintings he had donated in 1965, including Rubens' *Venus Wounded by a Thorn*, which Armand had borrowed and never returned. No precedent existed for the sale of a donation back to its donor and although university officials estimated that the two paintings by Rubens were worth between $15 million and $30 million, they replied that they would have to submit the collection for appraisal before they set a sale price. The minute this news became public, Alan Kahn filed in Delaware to obtain sworn information from Hilary Gibson about the source of the funds to make the repurchase.

After the California state attorney general's office approved the repurchase plan, Armand and USC each agreed to appoint independent appraisers to determine the value of the collection. But Armand refused to sign a letter from USC's appraiser, Sotheby, agreeing not to sue if he disagreed with its appraisal, and negotiations reached a dead end.

On Christmas Day, as Dr. Schuller's inspirational Christian message was being broadcast from Moscow to 200 million Soviets, Eastern Europeans, and Chinese, one of Armand's many "good friends" over the years, Romanian President Nicolae Ceaușescu, and his wife, Elena, were convicted of genocide and gross abuse of power by a military tribunal and shot to death by a firing squad. It was the beginning of the end of Soviet domination of Eastern Europe, the collapse of Communism, and the disintegration of the Soviet Union, events that I was certain Armand would deplore.

But there was good news from another quarter. Just before 1989 came to an end, Venezuela announced that it was going to make the $42.2 million compensation payment—with oil not cash—to Occidental that it had been refusing to pay since 1975. The decision was particularly surprising because Armand's nemesis, Carlos Andrés Pérez, had just been reelected president after being out of office for ten years. Financial analysts noted that Venezuela was in perilous financial shape, was attempting to negotiate a 50 percent cut in its $20.3 billion foreign debt, and needed the help of the Bush administration to accomplish this goal. It was their assumption that Venezuela's payment to Occidental was part of their quid pro quo with the Bush administration to obtain that cooperation. It had taken Armand fourteen years to collect this debt, but it was not in his nature to give up, and he had finally gotten his way.

33.

"HE'S LIVED TWO YEARS TOO LONG"

On January 2, 1990, Occidental announced that it had reached a settlement in the Levitan suit. After reviewing the settlement Vice Chancellor of the Court Harnett commented that "if the court was a stockholder of Occidental, it might vote for new directors." Harnett gave his approval anyway and scheduled a final hearing on April 4, but Alan Kahn and CalPERS filed appeals to overturn the agreement in the Delaware Supreme Court. It was their contention that an $86 million corporate charitable contribution exceeded the scope of Delaware's business-judgment rule and was "outside the bounds of reason" and that the proposed pact was "a cosmetic gesture" that "does nothing to resolve the claims of waste."

Another large institutional shareholder, Battery March Financial Management, launched its own appeal and demanded that the shareholders be given the opportunity to vote on whether to continue building the museum. But of all the objections that were raised, the most disturbing came from Richard Cleary, the attorney representing Frances Hammer's niece and sole heir, Joan Weiss. Cleary told the court that the Frances Hammer Estate claimed "ownership of a substantial interest" of the Armand Hammer Collection and that the disclaimers Frances had apparently signed before her death, which had already been entered into evidence, were unenforceable because Frances had not had independent legal counsel when she signed them; the signature on the third waiver apparently was not hers; she had never informed Robert

Weiss, the executor of the estate, or Joan Weiss, her closest relative, about their existence; and no copies had been found in her carefully organized personal papers. A story was circulating around Occidental that after Armand had obtained Frances's signature on one of these documents, she appeared to be so heavily sedated she could hardly walk.

When the Los Angeles Times finally located and printed a copy of Hilary Gibson's business plan and a number of other significant documents relating to the musuem, the dissident shareholders became even more incensed. The Hammer Museum had been incorporated as a nonprofit institution, but Gibson's proposal cast it as "an entrepreneurial venture" that was supposed to generate a net profit of $1.5 million during its first year and show additional yearly profits that would exceed 20 percent by 1995. Gibson planned to generate these profits by eliminating the costs typically associated with a cultural or scholarly institution, including a curatorial department and an acquisitions fund. In their place, aggressive marketing was going to be used to sell the museum as a trendy hangout for affluent southern Californians. In addition, the bottom line was going to be pumped up by auditorium rental fees, profits from the Daumier Bistro and the Courtyard Café, "where one might have seen Monet sipping his espresso over an afternoon repast at a similar café of the period," and the rental of the courtyard as the "in" place to throw expensive parties. It was pointed out, however, that because of budget cuts the construction of the auditorium and the Daumier Bistro had been dropped from the plans.

The other documents included details of the museum's extravagant decor. An allocation of $1 million had been made for marble flooring; $258,000 for a VIP lounge known as the Armand Hammer Memorabilia Room and its focal point, the $25,000 Armand Hammer Fireplace; $75,000 to chisel Hammer's name in the marble façade in letters three feet high; and $60,000 to reproduce for the entranceway a metal gate that Hammer had seen at the Moscow airport.

According to the Times, another set of documents revealed that "the budget crisis apparently prompted Occidental to move more than $2 million in costs from bookkeeping accounts reserved for the museum to those of Oxy Westwood Corporation." Occidental refused to answer questions about the alleged transfers. Speculating that such an act would be considered a deception, Alan Kahn stated that he was considering raising the issue at the final hearing on the Occidental-Levitan settlement in Delaware in April.

On February 14, in a move *The New York Times* characterized as "highly unusual," Occidental announced that Ray Irani would replace Hammer as chairman and chief executive if he should die or retire. Wall Street responded favorably to the news that there finally was an "heir apparently" and noted that Irani had successfully organized Occidental's chemicals operations into an integrated company that had become the company's most successful division and accounted for 76 percent of Occidental's income. On the day that Armand had slipped in the bathtub and cracked three ribs, the market value of Occidental stock had increased by $306 million and the announcement would help calm the volatility in the stock price that accompanied any news that Armand was ill. Finally, the announcement served as an indication that once Irani replaced Hammer, Occidental would be able to reduce its monstrous debt by selling off pieces of Armand's bloated and unwieldy corporate empire.

A senior staffer who insisted on remaining anonymous commented that Irani "just made up his mind, come hell or high water, to put up with [Hammer]. Ambition only goes so far, but Irani was willing to do it. I admire the guy's patience; he lets Dr. Hammer take credit for anything." Always the model of discretion, Irani told reporters, "To speculate on what I might do is very strange, particularly since Dr. Hammer and I work together very closely." Former presidents Joe Baird, Zoltan Merszei, and Bob Abboud refused any comment, leading to the assumption that each had signed a gag order in return for a generous financial settlement.

On April 3, the day before the final settlement hearing about the Occidental-Levitan suit in Delaware, Occidental filed its annual 10-K report. It disclosed that art holdings worth an additional $1.4 million and believed to be owned by Hammer were really owned by Occidental, that Occidental had donated these paintings to the Hammer Museum, and that it intended to spend another $2.3 million on construction. This sum was apparently the money the *Times* had suggested Occidental was trying to bury in another corporate account.

Occidental obtained a court order sealing Hilary Gibson's deposition on the grounds that it dealt with confidential business strategies and fund-raising techniques, and the *Los Angeles Times* filed immediately to have the deposition made public. It appeared that Occidental did not want details of Armand's professional and personal relationship with Hilary Gibson to be publicized. Focusing on Gibson, the *Times* revealed that Armand hired Gibson in 1974 to be Occidental's curator of art and that she had drawn yearly consulting fees totaling $256,500 from the foundation from 1979 to 1990.

After the hearing the next day, Institutional Shareholders Services (ISS), a consulting firm that monitors public corporations for large institutional investors, declared that the Hammer Museum was "the twentieth-century equivalent of the pyramids. If a company clerk takes money for something personal, it's embezzlement. If Armand Hammer does it, it's the business-judgment rule." ISS recommended that its two hundred subscribers oppose the settlement.

More bad news for the museum came during April, when Armand discovered that Joan Weiss was planning to sue him for fraud and financial misconduct. A number of major publications had reported that Jay Goldberg, whose clients included Donald Trump, was considered "a lawyer's lawyer" and New York City's "best pure trial lawyer." So Armand hired Goldberg to represent him against the pending lawsuit, which he declared was going to be "the most difficult struggle of his long life."

Armand gave Goldberg and his wife, Rima, the full treatment. He flew to New York especially to have them to dinner at his Greenwich Village carriage house, where the traffic was cordoned off so waiters could rush back and forth from the Italian restaurant across the street to cater the meal. He presented Mrs. Goldberg with a jade ring and told fascinating stories about his early days in Russia and his relationship with Lenin. Even though he was over ninety, his energy seemed boundless and he was still sharp and tough—every inch one of history's greatest industrial living legends in the flesh, and Goldberg decided to do everything possible to defend him.

Questioned by shareholders about the Hammer Museum at the annual meeting on his ninety-second birthday on May 21, Armand pointed out that van Gogh's *Irises* had recently been sold to the J. Paul Getty Museum for an all-time record of $53.9 million. But he owned an even better van Gogh, *Hospital at Saint-Remy*. "I have the whole garden," he boasted. "I don't know what it would bring at auction. Some experts tell me a hundred million dollars. And I am giving it to the people of Los Angeles . . . without any compensation to me." The record sale of the van Gogh had already produced estimates that, in the inflated market of that moment, the value of the Armand Hammer Collection had climbed to somewhere between $300 million and $400 million.

When another shareholder questioned Armand about his

health, he replied that his pacemaker was guaranteed for eight years. "And then I'll get a new battery." Later, at a formal birthday dinner at the Beverly Hills Hotel whose theme was the Gay Nineties, a reporter questioned him about the collapse of the Berlin Wall. Despite his lifelong fervent support of the Communist leadership of the Soviet Union and the East Bloc countries, he declared happily, "We'll have capitalism and socialism working together. Now all I've got to do is get rid of cancer."

The next week Hammer and Dr. Schuller flew to Washington for the Bush-Gorbachev summit. Schuller had previously responded to Soviet requests and had taped a message that was aired directly after a statement by Gorbachev designed to end a nationwide wave of panic buying. At a summit banquet Gorbachev singled out Schuller for his help in restoring order with his TV sermon. Subsequently Schuller and Vice Chairman of the Soviet state television network Valentin Lazutkin held a joint press conference to announce that they had reached an agreement to broadcast a monthly edition of Schuller's *Hour of Power* over Soviet TV.

Armand's ability to help Schuller preach in the Soviet Union had generated far more publicity than anything he had been able to accomplish for himself at the summit, and when Gorbachev left for Minneapolis to address 145 top corporate executives, Armand was just one of many in the audience. But Armand had already negotiated an agreement with the Soviets to build two plastics factories in the Ukraine, had utilized the United States Trade and Economic Council to send four hundred corporate leaders to Moscow to meet with and be wined and dined by the Gorbachev government, and had worked feverishly to organize consortia to invest in Soviet industry under Gorbachev's détente. If it appeared to many observers that Gorbachev's days were numbered and that the Soviet Union was on the verge of collapse, Armand seemed indestructible.

On July 11, Joan Weiss filed an eighteen-count suit in Los Angeles Superior Court against Hammer, Occidental, the Armand Hammer Foundation, the law firm of Lewis, Overbeck & Furman, and two partners in the firm, David Creagan Jr. and John Burdock. Alleging fraud, legal malpractice, and financial misconduct, Weiss claimed damages of $700 million.

Weiss's suit was a bombshell. It contended that Armand's $400 million estate was either directly attributable to Frances's separate assets or was community property that belonged to them both; that he had amassed his fortune and art collection using property Frances had brought into the marriage; that he had exercised complete control over that fortune, holding the couple's Occidental stock, valued at $34 million, solely in his name and treating the art he had purchased using his and Frances's property as solely his own; that he had financed his original investments in Occidental with money he had borrowed from Frances or through bank loans she had helped secure for him, which he had obtained "through the exercise of undue influence"; and that, by March 1958, after three years of marriage, he had owed Frances $442,000 at the "unconscionably low" interest rate of 2 percent and that most of the interest had either gone unpaid or been paid by his earnings. (Under California community property laws, half of these earnings already belonged to Frances.)

The suit also charged that over a thirty-year period Armand had "embarked upon a scheme designed to take from Frances Hammer her interests in their fortune" by inducing her to sign away her rights; that he had been aided by her lawyers, who had simultaneously represented her and the Armand Hammer Foundation in "an incurable conflict of interest"; and that his fraudulent transactions had allowed him to deprive Frances of her ownership interests in thousands of shares of stock and millions of dollars paid to him in salary and as fringe benefits.

Subsequently, Weiss told reporters that Frances would have wanted her fortune used for charities that better reflected her own interests, particularly charities for children, "far more than to see her money spent building a monument to Armand Hammer's ego. There's no way in hell she would have her money go to a museum run by Martha Kaufman."

Expressing suitable shock, Armand called the claim "an affront to the long and loving relationship I had with my wife" and insisted that his museum was not a reflection of his megalomania. "I made big money here in Los Angeles after I came from New York, and I feel that I'd like to do something for the city that made my great success." Jay Goldberg commented that there were documents, waivers, and declarations to a variety of people demonstrating that Frances had ceded her right to the art collection to her husband. Referring to Joan Weiss, Armand's long-term lawyer, Arthur Groman, added that "you'd think someone who'd just been given sixteen million dollars would be content with it, wouldn't you?"

The week after the filing, Armand sat for an interview with *The Wall Street Journal*. Dressed in a blue pin-striped suit with his Legion of Honor ribbon pinned on his lapel, he contradicted the description in *Hammer* that portrayed him and Frances as two lonely, aging multimillionaire lovebirds at the time of their marriage. "I was strapped for cash. I had a lot of debts, and most of my cash went to cover those debts. Mrs. Hammer made loans to me which I was happy to accept."

He also claimed that Frances had intended before her death in December to clarify the apparent contradiction in her will involving community property and his sole ownership of the Armand Hammer Collection. Asked why Frances had written him out of her will in 1988, he explained that she was fond of Joan Weiss's two sons and wanted to provide for them. He added that after Frances had been informed by a family lawyer that her new will presented a conflict because it contained a clause allowing her to retain her rights to her half of their community property, which she had already signed over to him, she "realized that she had made a mistake."

Two days after the interview, first-time visitors to the $21 million Richard Nixon Library and Birthplace in Yorba Linda, California, discovered Armand's name among 180 others chiseled in a marble wall in the library. The names were listed by the size of their contribution; Hammer's was among the top ten.

Jay Goldberg conducted a three-day videotaped deposition of Joan Weiss, and the word all over Occidental was that he had performed brilliantly. It was reported that Armand was relieved but that he seemed to be losing his strength. One of Armand's advisers told me that Armand's weakness seemed to be occurring simultaneously with his imbibing large quantities of herbal tea, which seemed to have had a diuretic effect on him and caused him to urinate frequently. The adviser told this to a long-term friend of Armand's, who replied, "Don't worry about it. Armand's lived two years too long anyway." The implication was that Armand's death would enable Occidental to be placed on an even keel, and that his demise ultimately would become another profit-making venture for the company.

A few days later the *Los Angeles Times* revealed that Occidental was attempting to secure $13 million from an unidentified Japanese corporation in order to complete the Hammer Museum and that start-up and first-year operating costs had increased more than seven times during the past year. The financial problems faced by the Hammer Museum were amplified when a group of museums that owned paintings by Kasimir Malevich decided to remove their holdings from the opening exhibition because of their concern that the canvases were too fragile to be displayed in a building with insufficient heating, air-conditioning, water, and security systems.

On October 19, Armand executed a new will. Using J. Paul Getty's will as a model, he bequeathed his entire estate to the Armand Hammer Living Trust, a device that would enable him to keep the size of his estate and the terms of his will out of probate court and, therefore, away from public scrutiny. The senior staff believed Armand had designated two charity beneficiaries, the Hammer Museum and Armand Hammer College. It was estimated that the estate contained cash and stock holdings of no more than $100 million. Therefore, the 4.25 percent of the assets that were to be dispersed yearly to the college and the museum would amount to only $4.25 million.

Skipping over Julian, Armand named his grandson, Michael Armand, executor of his estate, sole successor trustee of his trust, and administrator of the Hammer Museum. Only Michael and Armand's lawyers would know the beneficiaries and terms of the will. Julian was mentioned, but Armand disinherited Julian's former wife and his adopted daughter and barred them from challenging the will. The will also contained instructions about the way his museum would handle his collection, including orders that no paintings could be sold and that a specified number of paintings had to be on permanent display at all times. The other financial terms were a secret. Therefore, it was impossible to determine what Armand had left Julian or anyone else. But a rumor would later circulate that he had included financial arrangements for two mysterious women.

At the beginning of November, Los Angeles was flooded by a promotional mailing containing a personal letter from Armand announcing the opening of his museum on November 28 and the information that a charter membership was going to cost $40 and that charter members would be given the opportunity to attend a preview and "meet Dr. Hammer and mingle with his other guests." As the opening neared, Hilary Gibson escorted reporters through the building, explaining that "we're after a restrained elegance. It's what the Tate is about, what the Frick is about" and pointing out that the Carrera marble used for the façade came from the same quarry used by Michelangelo. During a photo session for *The Washington Post*, she and Armand held hands.

On November 27, Armand held a formal dinner and preview at the museum for eight hundred guests. Sipping flutes of champagne, they descended the marble staircase to five softly lit galleries, two of which contained the Armand Hammer Collection and another two, the Kasimir Malevich exhibition. Edward Larrabee Barnes was a modernist, and the last gallery, meant to display the Codex Hammer (which was yet to be installed), was conceived as a small, darkened chapel dimly lit by low-level spotlights.

Surrounded by a contingent of executives and security guards, Armand sat at the head table on the main floor between his friend Danielle Mitterrand, the wife of French President François Mitterrand, and Hilary Gibson. His anesthesiologist sat one seat away. Across from him sat Mayor Tom Bradley. The other guests included his sixty-one-year-old son, Julian, and his grandchildren, Michael Armand and Casey. After telling reporters that he was feeling great, Armand said of his museum, "It's a miracle." His conduct that night led art historian John Richardson to report that "there was even a certain heroism to this senile pirate's defiance of death."

If Armand's decision to build the museum created an uproar in the press, the critical outcry about the Armand Hammer Museum of Art and Cultural Center and the Armand Hammer Collection was even more devastating. Critics scoffed at the tiny plaque bearing the name "Occidental" on the front of the building and the huge portrait of Armand in the lobby. They declared the 79,000-square-foot gray-and-white marble building "discreet to the point of anonymity," "banal yet overblown," and a "striped marble lump." Armand's collection was dismissed as "a slew of unspeakable paintings" and "too thin, too frankly mediocre to sustain a museum of its own."

After *Time*'s art critic, Robert Hughes, had criticized Armand for decreasing the value of the Codex Hammer by hustling it around the world for publicity purposes, Armand approached *Time*'s senior management and attempted to have Hughes removed. Then Hughes fired another shot. "Nobody can say for sure which museum is the worst," he wrote. "But now we know which is the vainest. . . . The idea of wasting $98 million on this trivial package seems obscene . . . a monument, in short, to the vanity of vanities."

If Armand was wounded, he soon had another cause for celebration. Six days later, after a thirty-one-month battle, the Chancery Court of Delaware gave its final approval to the Occidental-Levitan settlement. It turned out to be Hammer's last victory.

34.

EMPTY STAGE

Armand died at home just after 7 P.M. on December 10, 1990.
According to a company contingency plan, Occidental's security
force immediately sealed off his office and home. When Joan
Weiss's lawyer, Richard Cleary, heard the news, he drove to the
house and arrived around midnight. Spotting a dozen men carrying boxes and suitcases out of Hammer's house, which now belonged to Weiss, he called his client on his car phone, and she
called the police and reported a robbery. At first the police were
refused entry; finally Michael Armand Hammer opened the door.

Cleary and Michael's lawyer stood on the sidewalk negotiating
and came to an agreement to have the boxes and suitcases returned
to Armand's bedroom. No one was able to ascertain what had been
removed before Cleary arrived on the scene. I heard reports that
an inspection of the house revealed hypodermic needles scattered
around the bedroom, a medicine chest that had been stripped
bare, and the removal of Armand's taping system. Whatever tapes
might have been in his possession at the time of his death were
gone.

The next morning the world awoke to the front-page news that
Hammer had died after a "brief illness." No other cause of death
was stated, but *The Washington Post* attributed the death to cerebral
arteriosclerosis.

Armand was recalled in *The New York Times* as virtually the only
man who had been able to "tell Mikhail Gorbachev firsthand what
Lenin was like," in the *Los Angeles Times* as a man whose "new idea
was to see beyond ideology to what business could accomplish,"
and in *The Wall Street Journal* as "one of the most colorful and
forceful entrepreneurs of the 20th century." Orange County's *Register* recalled him as "living proof that with enough money, charm,
philanthropy, and carefully crafted public relations, a persistent

apologist for communism in its brutal phases can buy his way into conservative and Republican circles."

This reaction and others like it led George Bush to decline comment. Mikhail Gorbachev stated merely that Hammer was "associated with one of the most valuable pages of Soviet history." Occidental's new chairman and chief executive, Ray Irani, declared that Hammer's "creativity, enthusiasm, and unyielding sense of optimism will be sorely missed," and David Murdock commented that Armand "was a man who never let anything stand in his way. And he wasn't above taking credit for something he knew nothing about." Hilary Gibson eventually told reporters that Armand had "an enlightened self-interest, but it's the best kind of self-interest to have." Subsequently, I received a letter from Walter Davis, founder of Permian Corporation and Armand's first unofficial heir apparent. Davis wrote that Armand was "the worst son-of-a-bitch I have known in my life . . . he had no morals of any kind."

On a normal day a little over 600,000 shares of Occidental stock were traded. The day after Hammer's death, 8.1 million shares changed hands and the stock price closed at $22.62, up $1.875. But the predicted explosion in the stock price never materialized and Wall Street insiders commented that Occidental, although a prime takeover target, was an "overleveraged chemical company in a recession" and that no corporation was going to spend billions of dollars to acquire a company with an $8.5 billion long-term debt that paid an inflated 11 percent annual dividend of $2.50 at a cost of $750 million a year. Financial analysts stated that Occidental's only choice was to sell off a number of nonprofitable and profitable subsidiaries and write off $2 billion to recover from the disastrous effects of Hammer's management during the last years of his life.

The same day, Armand's lawyers placed his will into probate, which enabled them to obtain a standstill agreement. This temporary restraining order barred Joan Weiss from removing any more property from the house. Michael Hammer received the sole key to Armand's bedroom, Weiss changed the outside locks, and both sides posted their own security guards. The lawyers representing each estate also agreed to impound the contents of Hammer's Greenwich Village carriage house and Moscow apartment until the Weiss suit was settled. At the same time Arthur Groman notified Jay Goldberg that he was going to take over the Hammer Estate defense against Joan Weiss's claim.

According to the terms of the "golden casket clause" in Hammer's employment agreement, Occidental was required to pay

$18,291,579 to the Armand Hammer Foundation (which contained a reserve of less than $6 million), $4.6 million to the Armand Hammer Living Trust, $1.9 million in unidentified "additional benefits," and $318,000, including contributions, to Hammer's savings plan and supplemental benefits program. Restrictions on a grant of 67,712 shares of stock lapsed automatically, allowing the estate to receive an additional stock award worth $1.23 million. In addition to his salary of $1.14 million, a short time before his death, even though his health was failing and Occidental was being reviled in the press because of its $90 million expenditure on the Hammer Museum, Occidental's board had voted Armand a $923,000 bonus. Therefore, Hammer's total compensation for 1990 came to $28.67 million, and his death had made him the highest-paid executive in the state of California.

Armand's bar mitzvah fund-raiser was scheduled for December 11, the night after his death. The benefit committee converted the $500-a-plate formal dinner into a memorial tribute, which inspired an additional 160 people to purchase tickets. Armand received the Hebrew name of Avraham Ben Yehuda Maccabee posthumously, and the heavily publicized event raised $400,000. After that, the "world" that Armand had created for himself slowly began to crumble.

By the end of the week, under *glasnost*, Soviet ecologists reported that Occidental's fertilizer operations in Odessa were pumping excessive amounts of ammonia and nitrogen dioxide into the already heavily polluted air and that a poisonous ammonia cloud could form over the city. After voicing bitter complaints, the citizens of Odessa voted overwhelmingly to shut down the plants. But when the International Fertilizer Association stepped in and established guidelines that Occidental agreed to honor, the protest faded away. For the moment, at least, Armand's "biggest deal in history" remained intact.

On January 14, 1991, thirty-five days after Armand died, Ray Irani was ready to announce the plan that had been prepared secretly before Hammer's death. He declared 1991 the year of the "new Oxy" and began to clean up the terrible mess he had inherited from Armand. Irani outlined a two-year restructuring program involving the sale of $3 billion worth of assets and a dividend reduction of Occidental's bloated dividend from $2.50 a share to $1. He also ordered a $2 billion write-off against anticipated losses resulting from the sale of Occidental's unprofitable businesses and the allocation of $500 million for potential environmental costs, including Love Canal litigation and $130 million for severance pay for terminated employees. This measure was designed to produce a long-term debt reduction of 40 percent and an increase in yearly profits of $200 million. At the end of fiscal 1990 Occidental had reported net income of $351 million against record sales of $26.7 billion. At the end of fiscal 1991, the last year of Hammer's management, the $2 billion write-off led Occidental to declare a loss of $1.7 billion.

Wall Street was impressed by Irani's desire to make the "new Oxy" a streamlined oil and chemicals operation. One analyst commented that "Occidental is writing off everything but the kitchen sink" as the company dispensed with its shale-oil research program, film production company, Arabian horse-breeding farm, and Black Angus cattle ranch. Negotiations were launched with the government of China to sell it Occidental's share in the coal-mining joint venture. The sale of 51 percent of Iowa Beef Processors was also put into motion in order to raise an additional $600 million to $900 million. Next Occidental sold its 5.4 percent interest in Church & Dwight, makers of Arm & Hammer baking soda, for $19 million; a half interest in an Antwerp natural-gas liquids terminal for $38 million; its industrial phosphate and phosphoric acid business for $100 million; its natural-liquid-gas business for $691 million; and its North Sea oil and natural-gas assets for $1.35 billion.

The Kasimir Malevich exhibition closed at the Hammer Museum on January 13, and nothing was scheduled to take its place. Museum director Stephen Garrett outlined the problems faced by the museum: it had "no acquisition fund and no artistic policy"; the Armand Hammer Living Trust was sealed by litigation and unable to provide revenues and the museum was depending solely on the yearly $3.5 million provided by Occidental's endowment annuity; and if Joan Weiss won her suit, half or more of its critically scorned but valuable collection would have to be surrendered to her under the terms of the California community property law. USC also issued a formal request for the return of the two Rubens paintings that Armand had borrowed from the university's Fisher Gallery and had refused to give back, and indicated that there was the possibility of a lawsuit if Occidental chose not to comply.

On January 16, Joan Weiss filed a new suit against the Hammer estate. She claimed that Frances Hammer's "torment" over what she believed to be Armand's long-standing infidelity with Martha Kaufman had been a substantial factor in her decision to execute a new will in 1988; that it had been Frances's desire to see that none of her community property passed into the "care and control" of Kaufman; that Kaufman had legally changed her name to Hilary Gibson in 1989 in order to disguise the fact that she was going to hold an executive position at the Hammer Museum; that Hammer "had made substantial gifts of money and other things of value" to Kaufman and had arranged to have her hired by Occidental and the Armand Hammer Foundation; and that Frances had agonized about private details of Armand's relationship with Kaufman and written down those details, which included Kaufman's ambition for advancement in organizations controlled by Hammer and descriptions of claimed sexual activity with him. The *Los Angeles Times* reported that other legal documents and people familiar with the situation "indicate that Frances even considered separating from her husband."

Both Julian Hammer and his stepdaughter filed individual challenges to block the appointment of Michael Hammer as sole executor of Armand's estate and to protest the fact that the stepdaughter had been disinherited. The case was resolved and Michael Hammer was confirmed as the "special administrator" (sole executor) of his grandfather's estate. Another claim was filed by a woman who had been mentioned in a prior draft of Armand's will written without Michael Hammer's participation. It was thought that she and her mother might be the two women named in the current will and that Armand had given small amounts of money to them over the years.

On January 23, lawyers for Occidental's dissident shareholders argued their appeal in the Delaware Supreme Court and demanded a $90 million reimbursement claiming that the Hammer Museum was "little more than an egocentric monument to Hammer." A settlement was approved by the Delaware Supreme Court. No cash payment to the shareholders was involved, but Occidental's board of directors was ordered once again to limit the funding for the museum.

A bust of Hammer had faced the elevators on the fifteenth floor of the Occidental building. I was told that the bust had been removed, but nothing had been put in its place. It was as if any reminder of Armand Hammer was graffiti that had to be scrubbed clean. Unlike previous annual reports, the new report was terse and professional and contained no pictures of Armand, no homage to his life, no description of his museum. The only mention consisted of a dedication on the inside front cover: "In memoriam,

Dr. Armand Hammer, 1898–1990." The typeface couldn't have been smaller, and on the same page was a caption for the picture of the drilling rig on the cover. The proxy notice for the annual meeting included the news that the $480,000 allocation earmarked for the sequel to Armand's best-selling autobiography had been canceled.

"The board is afraid of a shareholders' revolt because they've rubber-stamped all of Hammer's decisions," an Occidental executive told me. "The 'new Oxy's' de-Stalinization program was planned a long time time ago, so that the directors can prove that the company can be professionally managed. That's the way they think they're going to be able to save their jobs." Trained by Hammer, his oldest and closest business associates had proved to be the ones to have plotted the erasure of his memory and it was the same group that believed he had "lived two years too long."

A week after the first annual meeting since Armand's death on May 21, Occidental launched discussions with UCLA to assume the programming and curatorial operations of the Hammer Museum. It was hoped that this association would end the controversies surrounding the museum and the quality of its collection and lend a note of academic legitimacy to the enterprise. In order to make the museum viable, Occidental's lawyers were also looking for legal ways to break the restrictions in Hammer's will concerning the Armand Hammer Collection so that it could be moved from the main galleries to the smaller visiting galleries.

Occidental was experiencing an annual loss of $31 million on its Chinese coal-mining joint venture, and during June it announced that it was selling its 25 percent share in the mine to the government of China in return for the assumption of $145 million in loan guarantees by the Chinese government. It also ended its twenty-five-year battle to drill in Pacific Palisades by deeding the disputed property to the city, and it announced that it was returning the two Rubens paintings to USC. Following that, Ray Irani issued a statement that the initial phase of the Occidental restructuring program had generated $1.8 billion in after-tax proceeds.

Scott Dietrick, an old college friend of Michael Hammer's, had gone to work for Occidental as a "records information technician" for two months ending in February 1990. Shortly after Armand's death, Dietrick returned as administrator of the Armand Hammer Foundation and second in command to Michael. He also moved into Michael's guest house. According to court records in Minneapolis, Dietrick flew from London to Minneapolis on October 11,

1991, and was waiting for a connecting flight to Los Angeles when he was stopped and questioned by customs agents about the amount of cash he was carrying. Bringing cash in excess of $10,000 into the United States is a violation of the federal currency law that had been designed to curb international drug trafficking and money laundering.

Dietrick said he wasn't carrying more than $10,000 and signed a customs form stating this fact, but a search revealed that he was carrying $60,000, $40,000 of it in one-hundred-dollar bills stashed in his cowboy boots. The agents put the money in a cabinet, sent for a drug-detector dog, and watched as the dog went immediately to the cabinet. The indication that there were traces of drugs on the money led to Dietrick's arrest. Subsequently his passport revealed he had made at least eleven trips to Europe and Asia over a two-year period, including stops in London, Malaysia, Singapore, South Korea, and Thailand and that many of them had lasted only one or two days.

After he pleaded not guilty to violating the federal currency law, a federal prosecutor said at a bail hearing that the authorities suspected him of being a drug courier. Michael Armand Hammer wired Dietrich's $250,000 cash bond directly from a personal account to the Treasury Department.

A few weeks later, just eleven months after the death of his grandfather, Michael Hammer announced that he was stepping down as vice president and corporate secretary but would remain as a company director and chairman of the board of the Hammer Museum. *The Wall Street Journal* reported that Occidental had agreed to pay severance pay to Hammer in excess of $1.5 million and that the agreement was meant to be kept secret. *The Journal* also stated the opinion that the move would "further consolidate" Ray Irani's control over the company.

On November 16, Scott Dietrick returned to Minneapolis and attempted to make a conditional guilty plea to the charge of failing to report all of the cash he brought into the United States. He explained that he wanted to appeal an earlier ruling that the Customs search at the airport did not violate his constitutional rights and that a successful appeal would enable him to change his plea from guilty to not guilty. But U.S. District Judge James Rosenbaum rejected his plea and demanded that Dietrick stand trial. Assistant U.S. Attorney Mike Ward added that Dietrick had not cooperated with the investigation and that it had still not been determined where the $60,000 had come from and what it was for.

Even though Dietrick had denied that he was carrying more than $10,000 and had supplied the same answer on a customs form, he was being tried only for not filling out an additional form stating he was carrying the extra cash. Therefore, on May 15, 1992, after a seven-hour deliberation, a federal jury found him not guilty.

When reporters asked Hilary Gibson to comment about Michael Hammer and Scott Dietrick, she replied, "We're talking about the highest calibre of human beings." Subsequently, Gibson's daughter, Melinda Wade, turned up in New York City acting in *Hot Keys* on Fridays and Saturdays at midnight in a theater called Naked Angels. Filled with graphic simulated displays of gay sex, *Hot Keys* was the story of a young male hustler who picks up older men and bites them to death, and Wade was cast as one of three "rich over-privileged white girls."

A reporter introduced himself to Wade after one of her performances. Tears streaming down her face, she ordered him not to ask a single question and burst into hysterics. Over and over again she screamed, "Don't you dare open your mouth! Don't you dare!" Her combination of hysteria and imperiousness reminded me of the way her mother had treated Armand and me.

After Kenneth Locker left his position as the head of Armand Hammer Productions, he went on to become executive vice president of RHI Entertainment, a well-known production company. Locker had accompanied Hammer to Chernobyl in 1986 and subsequently had produced a dramatic version of these events for the TNT television network that starred Jason Robards Jr. as Hammer.

In November 1991 Locker went to Moscow to meet with General Alexander Karbanianov, a senior political intelligence officer of the First Chief Directorate of the KGB, and to discuss the acquisition of classified material in the KGB files that could be used as the basis for a series of TV docudramas. When Locker mentioned Hammer's name to General Karbanianov, the KGB official located Hammer's KGB counterintelligence file, showed it to Locker, and pointed out that Hammer was identified in the counterintelligence records as an *agent vliyana,* an agent of influence for the Soviet government. Karbanianov added that Hammer's file was for sale to American TV in return for hard currency.

Victor Hammer once told me that Armand wanted the last laugh on the U.S. government. Locker had no reason to doubt Karbanianov, and it appeared to me that Hammer's "last laugh" was that he had made millions of dollars at the same time that he had worked zealously to help a belligerent and hostile government in every way possible. Now that government had fallen from power in ignominy, and the "last laugh" turned out to be that only a year after his death Armand's deepest secret was for sale.

My replacement at Occidental, Jerrold Schecter, had become the founding editor of *We/Myi*, a weekly Russian-English newspaper published in Moscow by Hearst Publications. In June 1992 Schecter and Yuri Buranov, chief of the Department of Research of the Center for the Preservation and Study of Modern History, the agency in charge of maintaining Communist Party archives, coauthored a front-page news story in *We/Myi* under the headline "Documents Tie Hammer to Communists." Schecter and Buranov based their account on two declassified reports from Communist Party files, a secret police report on the Hammer family and an OGPU report. According to these documents, after the completion of his asbestos deal with Lenin, even though Armand had maintained throughout his entire life that he had never been a member of or a contributor to the Communist Party or any Communist front organization, he had delivered $34,000 in cash to the United States to help fund the American Communist Party. He had carried out this mission at the request of the Comintern. The documents added that Armand's original grain deal had a "political side" that "must not be be overlooked"—it had been designed by the Hammer family and the Bolshevik hierarchy to present a challenge to the U.S. embargo of the USSR. In the secret police report Julius Hammer was described "as having unswerving loyalty to the Comintern. . . . He is morally entitled to one-fifth of the Hammer family assets and is always ready to turn it over to the Communist Party." Before the week was over newspapers across the United States carried reports that official Soviet documents stated that Armand had been a courier for the Communists in the 1920s.

At the age of eighty-one, Cornelius Vanderbilt, then the richest man in America, climbed out of his deathbed and screamed to reporters, "I am not dying!" Andrew Carnegie dealt with his foes by simply threatening to destroy them. Henry Clay Frick was known for his ferocious temper. J. P. Morgan enjoyed announcing that he "owed the public nothing," and John D. Rockefeller was reviled by the press and the public for his cannibalistic business practices. Perhaps as some form of atonement, all of these men left monuments to their wealth and greatness.

Cut from the same cloth, Armand Hammer made many, many

millions late in life by turning a corporate shell into the sixteenth-largest industrial company in America. He was the twentieth-century equivalent of a nineteenth-century robber baron. And he, too, gave away millions to memorialize his name. Pondering his accomplishments, I wondered how he differed from his predecessors. Perhaps, I thought, the difference might lie not in his business practices or his philanthropy, but in his personality. His lust for wealth, fame, and power, his vanity, and his feelings of omnipotence and immortality had colored his every word and deed. He had been a man of many contradictions, capable of great generosity and petty cruelty, of rare moments of concern but mostly callous indifference, because he was always motivated by his own selfish interests.

Armand had spent a lifetime creating himself and he was, indeed, a unique creation. I helped to polish the image he sought for himself, and he perpetrated it. But Armand believed that the image could pass for the man. Had the man been more like the image, he might have achieved the greatness he hungered for. Instead he chose to act the part of a great man. And when his performance came to an end, the only thing he left behind was an empty stage.

ACKNOWLEDGMENTS

While most of the information in this book stems from my twenty-five-year-long close relationship and experience with Armand Hammer, from the many conversations we had, from my vivid remembrances and from the wide array of documentation, notes, and other material accumulated through the years, I am deeply grateful to everyone who contributed generously with additional data of intrinsic value to help make this book possible.

I am especially appreciative of those wonderful people who granted interviews, readily imparting their knowledge about Hammer and the experiences they had with him, and who contributed in other ways—Bruce Angwin, Tim Babcock, Donald L. Baeder, Stonie Barker, Jr., C. James (Jim) Blom, David Bransby, Walter Davis, Nancy Eilan, Joe Houser, Zoltan Merszei, E. F. (Bud) Reid, Robert S. (Bob) Rose, Mark Selko, Richard H. (Dick) Vaughan, W. Marvin Watson, and my former secretary at Occidental Petroleum Corporation, Sandra (Sandy) Wolf.

A special thanks, too, to those who imparted excellent information but for various reasons do not want their names divulged. By the nature of the relationship they had with Hammer, I feel obliged to respect their desire for anonymity.

I wish to thank Renee Golden for having steered me to my literary agent, John D. Diamond, and I am deeply grateful that John and Frederic W. Hills, vice president and senior editor of Simon & Schuster, believed in the concept of this book and successfully guided it through to publication. I also express my heartfelt thanks to Fred Hills's associate, Burton Beals, for his expert and helpful editing of the manuscript.

Carl Blumay
Laguna Niguel, California

My thanks to editor Frederic Hills, and his talented colleagues Burton Beals, Daphne Bien, and Paul Gillow. Their counsel and their unfailing graciousness during the writing of *The Dark Side of Power* provided the underpinning for the entire experience. Additional thanks to John Diamond, who represented the book from the outset, and to my long-term agent and dear friend Ron Bernstein for his counsel and concern. My thanks as well to Renee Sacks, whose love, affection, and telling comments about the manuscript also proved invaluable.

I am also grateful for the generosity of spirit displayed by three other writers, Steve Weinberg, author of *Armand Hammer—The Untold Story,* Joseph Finder, author of *Red Carpet,* and Daniel Yergin, author of *The Prize.* Aware of the rocky road that awaited me, they were kind enough to volunteer their expertise as guides.

Shakespeare wrote that "friendship is a constant in all other things." I will never forget the constancy of my friends during this writing experience. Ariane Canas and Jimmy Windus, Alexandra Morgan and Dr. Eugene E. Landy, Spiros Milonas, Gerald Newman, Joan Rivers, David Rockwell, Paula and Rod Steiger, James Truman, Clark Wolf, and, especially, Myrna Zimmerman: I will never rest until I have the opportunity to perform as faithfully for you.

Henry Edwards
New York City, New York

INDEX

Abboud, A. Robert, 376, 382, 383,
    393, 408, 414, 455
ABC News, 224, 225, 295, 408
Abu Musa, 159, 161, 188, 189
Acción Democrática (Venezuela), 140,
    225–26
Adair, Paul Neal "Red," 443
Afghanistan, Soviet presence in, 367,
    369–71, 372, 376–77, 381–82,
    439
Agnew, Spiro, 140, 142, 190
Ajman, 154
Alamerico, 45–46, 47, 49, 105, 146
Alba Madonna (Raphael), 105
Alkhimov, Vladimir, 148, 215, 216,
    217, 303, 313
Allen, Charles, 93, 129–30
Allen, Henry, 317
Allen, Herbert, 93, 128, 129–30
Allen, Richard, 398
Allen & Co., 93–94, 98, 128–30
Allied American Corporation, 45
Allied Chemical Corporation, 153,
    198
Allied Drug and Chemical
    Corporation, 40
Ament, Marvin, 341
American Aberdeen Angus Breeders'
    Association, 18
American Academy of Achievement,
    318
American Express, 313
Americans for the Canal Treaties,
    309
American Society of Newspaper
    Editors, 432–33
American Stock Exchange, 61, 78
Amin, Hafizullah, 367
Amtorg, 47

Arthur Andersen & Co., 114, 181,
    182, 306, 320, 346
Anderson, Jack, 66
Anderson, Jerome, 207, 221
Anderton, Nina, 224, 225
Andropov, Yuri, 323, 406, 410
Angwin, Bruce, 70, 71
Ansary, Cyrus, 284
Ansary, Hushang, 290
Apollo 2, 156
Appeal of Conscience Foundation,
    317
Arcos Ltd., 49
Aristotle Contemplating the Bust of Homer
    (Rembrandt), 293
Armand Hammer (biography by
    Weinberg), 449
Armand Hammer (tanker), 164, 344
Arm & Hammer baking soda, 26,
    120, 429, 465
Armenia, earthquake in, 444
Armour Agricultural Chemical, 88
Ashland Oil, 308
Askew, John, 112, 255, 271–72, 273,
    282–83, 286, 288–89
Aslan, Ana, 252, 407
Associated Press, 34
Atlantic Monthly, 258
Azias, Prince Abdul Ahmed, 110

Babcock, Tim, 141–44, 147–48, 189,
    190, 203, 368
  illegal campaign contribution and,
    198–99, 206–7, 209, 221–22,
    241–42, 248, 256, 257, 260, 261,
    266, 267, 274, 369, 449
  jail sentence of, 248, 257, 274, 287
Backstage at the Kirov, 406
Baeder, Don, 308, 326–27

Baird, Joseph, 232–33, 236, 252, 319, 354, 355, 455
  Mead takeover effort and, 331–34, 337, 338, 339, 340, 342, 348, 359
  Occidental politics and, 329, 330, 332, 348, 349–50, 356, 359
  replacement of, 359, 361, 364, 382
Balsam, Elmer, 207, 221
Bank of America, 208, 215, 216
Banque Nationale de Paris, 313
Barber family, 169
Bar-Ilan University, 434
Barnes, Edward Larrabee, 440, 441, 461
Barnsdall Park Municipal Gallery, 21
Barnum, P. T., 10
Barran, Sir David, 176, 177
Battery March Financial Management, 453
Batts, Warren, 333, 334
Bechtel, Stephen, 122, 405
Bechtel Corporation, 121–23, 133, 162, 186–87, 260, 405, 412
Begin, Alisa, 396
Begin, Menachem, 326, 396, 436, 437
Bellano, Bill, 156, 164, 192, 194, 233
Berg, Alan, 434
Berry, Lowell, 72–73, 87–88, 113
Best Fertilizers Company, 72, 73, 87, 297
Billion Dollar Bonanza, 304
Birch, E. J., 339
Blair, Clay, 422
Blair, Joan, 422
Blumay, Carl:
  AH's first encounter with, 13–15
  on AH's temper, 26, 79–81
  background of, 33
  on bribery schemes, 32–33, 272
  Julian Hammer and, 125–27
  marriage of, 267–68, 390
  public relations work of, 9, 13–14, 21–22, 23, 26, 30–31, 33, 34, 54–55, 61–62, 68–69, 71, 101–2, 111, 120, 123, 125, 181–82, 195, 199–200, 272, 337, 363–64, 373–74, 384–85, 391, 392; *see also* Hammer, Armand, public relations efforts for; Occidental Petroleum Corporation, public relations for
  resignation of, 362–64, 375–76, 385, 386–88, 389–90
Blumay, John, 25
Blumay, Nancy, 25
Blumay, Steve, 25
Blumay, Virginia, 25, 63, 64, 107, 108, 150, 267–68, 390, 399
Blumenthal, W. Michael, 327
Boggs, Hale, 139, 140
Bolsheviks, 28–29, 40, 41, 91, 92
Bonds for Israel, 416
Bradley, Tom, 263, 325–26, 356–57, 368, 400, 403, 413, 430–31, 461
Brady, James, 395
Bramlett, Norris, 293
Brezhnev, Leonid, 92, 109, 110, 135, 145, 228, 236, 312, 317, 444
  Afghan conflict and, 367, 370–71, 377
  AH's cultivation of, 147, 201, 209–210, 211–12, 227, 229, 231, 236, 240, 252, 291, 302, 307, 327–28, 362, 402, 417, 420
  art exchanges and, 352–53, 365
  Carter and, 291, 345, 351, 353, 357, 367
  death of, 405–6
  health of, 252, 323, 324, 357, 410
  on human rights issues, 208, 230, 301, 340, 341
  on military strength, 302
  Nixon's détente with, 201, 202, 211, 213, 217, 231
  SALT II signed by, 353, 357
  U.S. trade and, 215, 216, 217–18
Brezhnev, Yuri, 212
Bridges, Styles, 16, 17, 32, 42, 51
Bril, Paul, 108
Briscoe, Dolph, 320
British Petroleum, 60, 116, 153, 189
  see also Seven Sisters
Brock, William, 320
Brooks, George, 75, 88
Brown, Edmund G. "Pat," 118
Brown, Edmund G., Jr. "Jerry," 253–254, 288, 347
Brown, Grover, 448
Brown, Harold, 302
Brown, J. Carter, 191, 436
Brown, J. W., 340
Brown House, 91, 102, 104, 250
Brueghel, Pieter, 319
Bruk, Michael, 92–93, 149, 205–6, 398
Bryson, John, 405, 421
Brzezinski, Zbigniew, 310–11, 351, 356, 366, 367–68, 376, 378
Buckley, James, 235
Buckley, John, 136
Bukovsky, Vladimir, 301
Bulgaria, Occidental deals with, 367
Buranov, Yuri, 470

Burdock, John, 457
Burger, Warren, 213
Burton, Charles, 404
Burton, Richard, 404
Bush, George, 436, 452, 457, 463
    AH pardoned by, 448–49
    election campaigns of, 401, 445
    as vice president, 406, 414, 419
Business Development Fund, 137,
    138
Business International, 190
Buttes Gas and Oil, 154, 159

Cadell, Patrick, 385
Caldera, Rafael, 140–41, 185–86
California, 366
    environmental issues in, 359–60,
        414
    1974 gubernatorial campaign in,
        253–54
    Public Utilities Commission, 53–54
    state assembly of, 32, 57
California Public Employees
    Retirement Association
    (CalPERS), 446, 451, 453
California, University of, at Los
    Angeles (UCLA), 383, 431, 438,
    440, 442, 467
Campobello, 32, 63–65, 70–71, 78,
    89
cancer research, 174–75, 395–96,
    439–40, 441
Caracas Resolution, 177
Cardinale, Claudia, 435
Carnegie, Andrew, 470
Carnegie Hall Renovation Fund, 402
Carpenter, Liz, 109–10
Carter, Chip, 310
Carter, Jimmy, 301, 436
    campaigns of, 288, 289–90, 368,
        371, 378, 381, 385
    cultural interests of, 310, 316–17,
        406
    Deng's visit with, 351–52
    energy policy of, 307–8, 355, 373
    on Love Canal, 335, 378
    Nobel nominations and, 344, 355–
        356
    Panama Canal and, 289, 308–9,
        318
    Soviet relations and, 289, 290, 291,
        301, 318, 324, 328, 345, 351,
        353, 357, 367, 369, 376–77, 393
    trade policy of, 289, 304, 310–11,
        343–44, 367, 377, 393
Carter, Lillian, 290
Carter, Rosalynn, 310, 311, 316, 317

Casey, William, 237
Cassini, Oleg, 24
Caterpillar Tractors, 85–86
Cates, Dudley, 311
Caverly, Robert, 193, 233
Ceauşescu, Elena, 451
Ceauşescu, Nicolae, 251, 451
Center for Law in the Public Interest,
    170
Central Intelligence Agency (CIA),
    162
Century City Cultural Organization
    Armand Hammer Award, 383
Chaplin, Charlie, 421
Charles, Prince of Wales, 304, 318,
    334–35, 396, 404–5, 425
Chase Manhattan Bank, 98
Chatman, Furnell, 369
Cheka, 44, 91
Chernenko, Konstantin, 323, 357,
    410, 416, 417, 418, 419
Chernobyl nuclear power station,
    431, 469
China, People's Republic of, 382,
    400–401
    Occidental interests in, 352, 353,
        399, 400, 420–21, 443, 465, 467
    Soviet relations with, 189, 351–52,
        371
    U.S. relations with, 189, 351, 400
Christian Democratic Party (COPEI)
    (Venezuela), 140, 225, 316
Christie's, 388
Church & Dwight, 429, 465
Churchill, Winston, 304, 356
Winston Churchill Medal of Wisdom
    for Distinguished Humanitarian
    Achievement, 384
CIA (Central Intelligence Agency),
    162
Cincinnati Enquirer, 1888 (Harnett),
    316, 317
Cities Service, 407–8
City National Bank, 305
City of Hope National Medical
    Center, 366
Clausen, A. W., 215
Cleary, Richard, 453, 462
Cleyton International, 147
Cloister of Sor Juana Ines, 309
Codex Hammer, 388, 389–90, 447,
    461
Cole, Nat King, 24
Collins, Joan, 425
Colmery, Frances, 169
Colombia, 412, 429
Colt's Manufacturing, 148

Columbia College of Physicians and
    Surgeons, 27, 314
Columbia University, 311, 439
    AH's donation to, 314–15, 317,
    339, 432
Commerce Department, U.S.:
    Foreign Trade Zones Board, 137,
    138, 141
    Soviet trade terms and, 215–16,
    217, 236, 405
Committee for the Re-Election of the
    President (CREEP), 197, 198–99,
    206–7, 209, 216, 220–21, 242
Common Cause, 220
Commons, Dorman, 113, 114, 143,
    164, 181, 183, 336
Communist Party (U.S.), 36–37, 40,
    41, 45, 46, 48, 148, 397, 470
Congden and Carey, 373
Congress, U.S.:
    Carter energy policy and, 308
    Maine refinery project and, 137,
    139
    Soviet trade terms and, 207, 208,
    212, 214–20, 231, 235
    see also House of Representatives,
    U.S.; Senate, U.S.
Connally, John, 197
Conservative Party (Great Britain),
    89, 90
Considine, Bob, 226–27, 257, 258,
    259
COPEI (Christian Democratic Party)
    (Venezuela), 140, 225, 316
Corcoran Gallery of Art, 318, 388
Corey, Walter, 137
Corporación Venezolana del Petróleo
    (CVP), 112, 134, 169, 265, 273
Cosby, Bill, 440, 441
Cosby Show, The, 440
Cosmos Hotel, 357
Crawford, Francis Jay, 327, 328
Creagan, David, Jr., 457
CREEP, see Committee for the Re-
    Election of the President
Cronkite, Walter, 257
cummings, e. e., 48
Curtis, Kenneth, 137, 138–39
CVP (Corporación Venezolana del
    Petróleo), 112, 134, 169, 265,
    273

Daily Worker, 148
Dancing Peasants (Brueghel), 319
Danenberg, Bernard, 192
Daniloff, Nicholas, 432–34
Darwin, Charles, 228

Daumier, Honoré, 292–93, 309, 317,
    318, 441
Davis, Kenneth, 405
Davis, Loyal, 443
Davis, Walter, 113–14, 140, 142,
    149–50, 152, 168, 463
    SEC investigations and, 150, 156,
    168, 241
DBCP, 299–300
Dean, John, 209, 221–22
Dean Witter Reynolds, 332
Deane Brothers, 99
De Bakey, Michael, 168
Deep Throat, 303
Defense Department, U.S., 139, 240
DeGolyer and MacNaughton, 122
Del Amo Fashion Mall, 415
De Leon, Daniel, 39
Democratic National Committee
    (U.S.), 110–11, 124
Democratic Party (U.S.), 137, 352,
    403
    presidential candidates of, 136,
    199, 288, 289
Democrats for Nixon, 197
Deng Xiaoping, 351–52, 400, 402,
    413, 421, 443
Dent, Frederick, 215, 217
Denver, John, 401
de Rovin, Pegulu (François Fortune
    Louis Pegulu), 93, 128–29, 130
Detroit Institute of Art, 227
Deukmejian, George, 360
Dewey, John, 91
Diana, Princess of Wales, 396, 425
Dietrick, Scott, 467–69
Diff'rent Strokes, 440
Dobrynin, Anatoly, 250, 370, 416,
    420, 434
Doering, Gordon, 207, 221
Donahue, Kenneth, 171–72, 291–
    292
Dorfman, Dan, 349–50
Dorgan, Jack, 338
Douglas-Home, Sir Alec, 89, 90
Dow Chemical, 353, 354, 355, 359,
    401–2
Drinkhall, Jim, 368
Dufy, Raoul, 213, 218
Duranty, Walter, 48, 63, 103
Dylan, Bob, 450

East Side, West Side, 396
Eaton, Cyrus, Jr., 147–48, 149, 190,
    206, 398
Eaton, Cyrus, Sr., 145–46, 147, 148,
    190, 199, 206, 208–9, 221, 397

Edinburgh Festival, 318, 334
Edison, Thomas A., 29
Egypt, 121, 158–59, 203
Ehrlichman, John, 221
Eilan, Arieh, 326, 422
Eilan, Nancy Wicker, 50, 66, 326,
    407, 422–27, 442
Eimi (cummings), 48
Einstein, Albert, 356
Eisenhower, Dwight D., 31, 127, 339,
    356
Eldridge, Florence, 50
Elizabeth II, Queen of England, 304
El Paso Natural Gas, 208, 250
Energy Department, U.S., 308, 346
Environmental Protection Agency
    (EPA), 322–23, 360, 361, 378
Epstein, Edward J., 392, 397, 398–99,
    442
Esquire, 349
Esso-Libya, 111, 116, 117–18, 122,
    129, 131, 158, 162, 163, 188
Evans, Jack, 136–37, 138
Export-Import Bank, 81, 208, 215,
    217, 231, 235, 236–38, 249, 250,
    259
Exxon, 60

Fabergé, Peter Carl, 63, 103, 106
Faber Pencil Company, 88
Fairbanks, Douglas, 91
Fairbanks Whitney Corporation, 148
Faisal, King of Saudi Arabia, 110
Family Realty Corporation, 99
Farouk I, King of Egypt, 14, 107
Faure, Edgar, 344
Federal Bureau of Investigation
    (FBI), 42, 190, 221, 222, 241,
    368, 369, 409, 432
Federal Corrupt Practices Act, 197
Federal Emergency Act, 378
Federal Resources Conservation and
    Recovery Act, 360
Federal Trade Commission (FTC),
    247, 248
Feinbloom, Richard, 340
Feldman, Myer, 66, 84, 142
Ferraro, John, 413
Fiennes, Sir Ranulph, 404
Financial Engineers, 312
Finder, Joseph, 397–98, 409
Fireline Productions, 314, 400
First Chicago Corporation, 376, 382
First National Bank of Chicago, 382
Fisher, Dan, 341
Fletcher, Ross, 276
Flom, Joseph, 248, 334, 394

Florida Department of
    Environmental Regulations, 361
Fonda, Jane, 365, 439
Forbes, 382, 401, 442
Forbes, Malcolm, 400, 401, 436
Ford Foundation, 170
Ford, Gerald R., 240–41, 249, 251,
    260, 284, 302, 395, 436
Ford, Henry, 29, 35, 37, 46
Ford, Henry, II, 227, 263
Fording the Horse Herd (Russell), 445
Henry Ford Library, 37
Ford Motor Company, 29, 46–47
Ford's Theatre, 406
Foreign Trade Zones Board, 137,
    138, 141
Fortune, 135, 364, 380
Forum for a Nuclear-Free World and
    the Survival of Mankind, 435
Foster, Sir John, 154, 173
Fragonard, Jean-Honoré, 251, 309
France, Afghan conflict and, 377
Frances Hammer, 164, 344
Franco, John, 320
Franklin, Benjamin, 36
Freedom of Information Act, 265,
    335, 409, 430, 447
Frick, Henry Clay, 470
"From Leonardo to Titian," 365–
    366
FTC (Federal Trade Commission),
    247, 248
Furtseva, Yekaterina, 83–84, 109,
    191–92, 210–11, 213, 218–19,
    236, 251, 350, 357, 358

Galbraith, John Kenneth, 435
Gale, Robert, 431, 432
Galic, Ferdinand, 93, 98, 128, 130
Gandhi, Indira, 381
Garcia Pérez, Alan, 445
Garrett Research and Development
    Company, 135, 230, 245
Garrett, Stephen, 465
Geismar, Claude, 164
General Electric, 26
Gest, Morris, 104, 105
Getty, J. Paul, 153, 198, 227, 239,
    287–88, 293–94, 460
J. Paul Getty Museum, 288, 293, 456
Gibson, Hilary, *see* Kaufman, Martha
Gierek, Edward, 317, 377, 379, 383
Gillette, Noeth, 68
Gimbel, Benjamin, 101
Giscard d'Estaing, Valéry, 377
Gitlow, Benjamin, 48
Glazer, Guilford, 415

Goldberg, Jay, 456, 458, 459, 463
Goldberg, Rima, 456
Gold Coin, 17
Golden Plate Award, 318
Goldfarb, Alexander, 432, 433
Goldfarb, Cecilia, 434
Goldfarb, David, 432, 433, 434
Goldman, Marshall, 398
Goldsmith, Donald, 423, 424
Goldwater, Barry, 84–85
Gomberg, Alexander "Uncle Sasha," 46
Good Morning, America, 383, 414, 420
Gorbachev, Mikhail, 410, 431–32, 435, 436, 439, 444
    AH's death and, 462, 463
    at summit meetings, 419–21, 425, 427–28, 433–34, 439, 443, 457
Gorbachev, Raisa, 432, 436, 439
Gordon, Mitch, 55
Gore, Albert, Sr., 57, 76, 81, 131, 156, 448
Gould, Elliot, 450
Gounduroff, Prince Mikhail, 106
Gowon, Yakubu, 155
Goya, Francisco de, 191–92, 210
Grace, Princess of Monaco, 396
Grant, Cary, 401, 421
Gray, L. Patrick, 221
Great Britain, 43, 49, 89, 90
    North Sea oil and, 153, 185, 186, 198, 232, 303–4, 318, 336, 384, 443–44, 465
    Persian Gulf withdrawal of, 159–160, 178, 188, 189
Greene, Graham, 435
Greenhill, Robert, 246
Griffin, Merv, 401, 425
Groman, Arthur, 16, 18, 170, 266, 269–71, 402, 423, 458, 463
    campaign contributions case and, 269–70, 272, 274, 275, 277–78, 280
Gromyko, Andrei, 92, 208, 249, 290, 417
Group (oil consortium), 153, 198
Guatemala, 349
Guaterma, Alexander, 23
Gulf Oil, 60, 124, 245, 407
    see also Seven Sisters
Gurewitsch, David, 65, 71
Gvishiani, Dzherman, 146, 148, 190, 203, 312

Habib, Philip, 405
Haldeman, H. R., 221

Hammer (Hammer), 293–94, 436–37, 459
Hammer, Angela Zevely (second wife), 17, 18–19, 57, 331, 349
Hammer, Armand:
    alias used by, 98, 105
    as art collector, 10, 13, 14–16, 101, 108, 291–95, 319, 388; *see also* Armand Hammer Collection
    as art dealer, 14, 50, 102–17, 192, 219, 293, 348–49; *see also* Hammer Galleries; Knoedler Gallery
    autobiography of, 293–94, 397, 436–37, 467
    bar mitzvah of, 450–51, 464
    biographies of, 226–27, 257–58, 259, 421–22, 430, 449
    birthday celebrations for, 72, 73, 378, 402, 411, 440, 443, 447, 450, 457
    birth of, 27
    bribery schemes and, 32–33, 57, 128–30, 139–40, 151, 154, 155, 161, 186, 211, 223, 236, 255–56, 259–60, 263–65, 269, 271–72, 273, 286, 306, 312, 319–21
    in cattle-breeding business, 18, 57, 84, 137
    childhood of, 38, 39
    criminal conviction of, 256–57, 260–63, 265–67, 269–70, 272, 274–81, 285, 289, 337, 385, 429, 445, 448–49
    cultural exchanges aided by, 83–84, 210–11, 213, 218–19, 251, 353, 365–66, 401, 428, 431, 435–436, 450, 457
    daily work schedule of, 24–25, 76
    death of, 9, 459, 462–64
    distillery owned by, 14, 17, 31, 42
    documentary film on, 227–29, 239
    education of, 27
    energetic nature of, 55, 144, 199, 227, 382–83, 456
    estate of, 460, 464, 465, 466
    family background of, 27, 397–98, 415
    frugality of, 16, 199, 385, 428
    health of, 55, 112, 176–77, 261, 265, 266, 269–70, 271, 274, 275–281, 285, 382–83, 422, 436, 449, 455, 457, 459
    honors awarded to, 101, 255, 283, 294–95, 311, 315, 316, 317, 318, 323, 339, 344, 345, 355–56, 366, 367, 374, 383–84, 434, 459

Hammer, Armand (*cont.*)
illegal campaign contributions
arranged by, 198–99, 205–9,
221–22, 241–42, 248, 256–57,
260–63, 265–67, 269–70, 272,
274–81, 283, 285, 289, 321, 369,
380, 385, 429
in jade business, 78
jet planes acquired by, 143, 385–
386
Jewish ancestry of, 38, 97, 169, 326,
384, 415, 434, 450–51
Los Angeles home of, 24, 442
marriages of, *see* Hammer, Angela
Zevely; Hammer, Frances
Tolman; Hammer, Olga von
Root
medical training of, 27–28, 30–31,
34
name of, 38, 119, 415
negotiation tactics employed by, 74,
87, 96–98, 118–19, 122–23,
128–29, 164, 165–66, 201, 203–
204, 325–26
Nobel Prize sought by, 195, 304,
317, 344, 349, 356, 367, 368,
377, 418, 435, 437
Occidental purchased by, 11, 20,
21, 458
personnel management by, 68, 69–
70, 76, 79–81, 87–88, 111, 113–
114, 118, 154–55, 184, 192–93,
195, 201, 206, 220, 225, 253,
283–84, 326–27, 330, 336, 353–
354, 359, 363–64, 374–76, 382,
386–87, 389–90, 399, 408, 414–
415, 438
philanthropic efforts of, 64, 66,
70–71, 170–71, 174–75, 190–91,
234, 310, 314–15, 317, 318, 334–
335, 344, 366, 383, 395–96, 402,
403–5, 415, 416, 425, 431, 432,
437–41, 444, 445, 449–50, 459
in photographs, 195–96, 240, 368,
405, 421
physical appearance of, 13, 195–
196, 243, 279
political contacts cultivated by, 16–
17, 31, 32, 57–60, 63–66, 70–71,
75, 77–78, 81, 82, 89, 109–11,
124–25, 134–35, 193, 198, 240–
241, 281, 289–90, 291, 304, 309,
310–11, 316–17, 328, 355–56,
377, 378, 385, 393, 395, 402,
405, 413, 414, 416, 443, 445
presidential politics and, 56–57,
84–85, 136, 140, 199–200, 206,

253–54, 288, 289–90, 368, 381,
385
public image as concern of, 9–10,
11, 22, 27, 30–32, 68, 101, 184,
216, 226–27, 250, 258, 363–64
public relations efforts for, 9–10,
13–14, 21–23, 27, 59, 101–2,
111, 120, 123, 201–3, 328, 365–
366, 434
radio network purchased by, 21,
22, 65, 66
real estate investments of, 99
retirement of, 15, 354, 362, 364
romantic involvements of, 17–18,
25, 84, 94, 172, 191, 210, 242–
244, 252–53, 330–31, 455–56,
460, 465–66
SEC investigators handled by, 167–
168, 180, 207, 348; *see also*
Occidental Petroleum
Corporation, SEC scrutiny of
secrecy employed by, 18, 30, 33, 56,
80, 98, 112, 201, 385
self-promotion of, 14, 54–55, 62,
120, 191, 195, 227–28, 238, 304,
308, 314, 316–17, 349, 362, 378,
405, 421–22, 440, 471
Soviet business dealings of, 28–30,
34, 36, 43–49, 51, 53, 58, 81–83,
85–86, 89–93, 102–7, 116–17,
145–49, 158, 189–90, 197–98,
201–12, 214–20, 226–27, 236–
241, 249–53, 311–14, 355, 444,
457, 470; *see also* Occidental
Petroleum Corporation, Soviet
projects of
Soviet system admired by, 29, 34,
35, 152, 208, 218, 229–30, 251,
366–67, 428
as speaker, 31, 32, 258, 369–70,
377
taping system installed by, 204–5,
462
tax problems of, 19, 31, 71, 105,
233–34, 263
television appearances of, 318–19,
383, 400, 410, 414, 420, 440
as Unitarian, 97
U.S.-Soviet relations promoted by,
35–36, 57–59, 63, 109–10, 213,
239, 289–90, 291, 301, 302, 318–
319, 323–24, 327–28, 340–41,
357, 362, 366–67, 370–71, 397–
398, 402, 406, 409, 410, 416–20,
431–32, 443, 457, 469–70
wealth of, 10, 14–15, 22, 28, 41–
42, 103, 442, 460, 464

Hammer, Armand Douglas (great-
grandson), 439
Hammer, Armand Victorvich
"Armasha" (nephew), 49, 51, 66,
93, 149, 211, 398
Victor Hammer's estate and, 422,
424, 426, 427
Hammer, Bette Barber (sister-in-law),
169, 422
Hammer, Casey (granddaughter), 85,
438, 461
Hammer, Dru Ann Mobley
(grandson's wife), 439
Hammer, Frances Tolman (third
wife), 70, 85, 205, 257, 294, 326,
362, 396–97, 416
on AH's business habits, 16, 79, 213
on AH's health, 276, 387
AH's marriage to, 17–18, 79, 210,
222, 243, 331, 390, 436, 443,
447, 458–59, 466
on business trips, 131–32, 143, 147,
240, 250, 352, 368, 377–78, 435
Catholicism of, 368
death of, 449–50
finances of, 19, 20, 21, 22, 331,
123, 442–43, 449, 453–54, 457–
459
Los Angeles home of, 24, 442
Occidental Petroleum and, 20, 21,
78–79, 458
paintings by, 219
physical appearance of, 15
Hammer, Glenna Sue Ervin
(daughter-in-law), 16, 85, 438
Hammer, Harry (half brother), 17,
54
background of, 27
in business, 14, 38, 65, 105
death of, 168–69, 422
Soviet links with, 49
Hammer, Ireene Wicker (sister-in-
law), 37, 326
AH's dislike of, 66
blacklisting of, 50–51, 64
death of, 387, 426
finances of, 422–24, 426, 427
illness of, 406–7, 423
as radio performer, 50, 64, 427
on Roosevelt family, 63–64
Hammer, Jacob (grandfather), 27,
415
Hammer, Julian (son), 461
AH's estate and, 460, 466
arrest of, 15, 16, 19
birth of, 49
Goldwater backed by, 84–85

guns of, 15, 16, 19, 56, 85, 86–87,
244, 295, 296, 438
at Occidental, 85, 125–27
physical appearance of, 84
psychological treatment for, 244,
438
Hammer, Julius (father), 367, 422
background of, 27, 38
business career of, 27, 28, 39, 48
citizenship of, 47, 50
imprisonment of, 42, 47, 49, 257
marriage of, 27, 37–38
as physician, 27, 39, 281
political involvement of, 36, 38–42,
48, 50, 91, 397, 470
Soviet business interests of, 37, 39,
40–43, 44, 45, 47, 48, 49, 228
Hammer, Michael Armand
(grandson), 85, 438–39, 460–63,
466, 467–68, 469
Hammer, Olga von Root (first wife),
18, 19, 49, 56, 85, 86, 126
Hammer, Rose Lipshitz (mother):
death of, 150, 422
dominant personality of, 84, 384
Julian Hammer raised by, 85, 86
marriages of, 27, 37–38
in Moscow, 47, 49
motherhood of, 38, 39, 42
political involvement of, 37, 50
Hammer, Sue (granddaughter), 85
Hammer, Vavara Sumski (sister-in-
law), 49, 66, 149
Hammer, Victor (brother):
as AH's business associate, 15, 22,
30, 46, 50, 54, 65, 192, 424, 426
on AH's financial success, 17, 41–
42, 390
on AH's health, 277
on AH's political contacts, 16–17,
59, 65–66, 78, 222
on AH's Soviet dealings, 36, 82,
92–93, 104–7, 149, 202–3, 351–
352, 469
on AH with women, 18–19, 56, 84,
191, 192, 211, 236, 243, 252–53,
331, 357
art collections and, 13, 14, 101,
234, 349–50, 426
as art dealer, 102, 104–7, 112, 192
birth of, 27
death of, 422
education of, 46
estate of, 407, 422–27
on family history, 37–51, 84, 91
as father, 49, 51, 211, 422
on FDR estate, 63, 64–65

Hammer, Victor (brother) (*cont.*)
   on Harry Hammer's death, 168–69
   illness of, 199, 387, 407
   on Jewish background, 326
   on Khrushchev, 58, 82
   marriages of, 49, 50, 64, 66
   physical appearance of, 13
   Rose Hammer's death and, 150
Hammer, Victoria (grandmother),
      27
Armand Hammer Businessman of
   the Year Award, 396
Armand Hammer Cancer Prizes, 396,
   439
Armand Hammer Center for Cancer
   Biology, 174
Armand Hammer Collection:
   assessments of, 171–74, 234, 291,
      456
   authenticity of, 173, 234
   contents of, 13, 16–17, 171, 174,
      191–92, 292, 293
   Daumier Collection, 292–93, 309,
      317, 318
   donations from, 101–2, 104, 107,
      171, 234, 318, 319, 374, 436–38,
      440–42, 448, 451, 465, 467
   exhibitions of, 13, 21–22, 171, 172,
      173, 174, 190–91, 192, 210, 243,
      254–55, 294, 309, 310, 318, 334,
      344, 399, 415, 428, 433, 461
   finances of, 349
   Frances Hammer's copies of
      painting in, 219
   Occidental expenditures on, 446,
      447
   ownership of, 349, 442, 453–54,
      455, 458, 459
   publicity on, 13–14, 17, 22, 293–
      294
Armand Hammer College, 404–5,
   415, 425, 460
Armand Hammer Conference on
   Peace and Human Rights, 344,
   349, 355, 379–80, 396, 403, 418
Armand Hammer Foundation, 170–
   171, 242, 294, 311, 395–96, 430,
   442, 458, 464, 466, 467
Armand Hammer Fund for
   Economic Cooperation in the
   Middle East, 439
Hammer Galleries, 14, 17, 38, 310
   artists represented by, 83, 112
   finances of, 18, 348–49, 424, 426
   Russian art sales and, 63–64, 103,
      105, 107, 109
Armand Hammer Golf Course, 404

Armand Hammer-Guilford Glazer
   Arab-Jewish Community Center,
   439
Armand Hammer Living Trust, 460,
   464, 465
Frances and Armand Hammer
   Million Dollar Purchase Fund,
   171
Armand Hammer Museum of Art
   and Cultural Center, 438, 440–
   442, 444, 446–48, 451, 453–56,
   458–61, 464–68
A. Hammer Pencil Company, 29, 48,
   49, 88, 105
Armand Hammer Productions, 400,
   401, 404, 465
Dr. Armand Hammer Research
   Fellowship, 366
Armand Hammer Technical Center,
   347
Hanna, Richard, 320
Harju Bank, 29, 47
Harnett, Maurice, 446, 448, 453
Harnett, William, 316
Harper & Row, 226
Harriman, W. Averell, 91, 397
Harris, Curley, 276
Harris, Dave, 21, 23
Hart, George, Jr., 248, 274–75, 276,
   277, 287
Hartman, David, 383
Harvard University, 397, 398
Hassan II, King of Morocco, 76–77,
   124
Hatfield, Charles, 186, 225, 288–89
Hayden, Tom, 365
Hearst, William Randolph, 103–4
Hebner, Paul, 69, 438
Heller, Abe, 43
Hennock, Frieda, 21
Henry, Jim, 339
Henzel, Leo, 311–12, 358
Hermitage, 104, 105, 210, 353, 365,
   428
Hickel, Walter, 141, 142
High Museum, 310
Hinckley, John, 395
Hodges, Luther, 57
Holiday Inns, 124, 146–47
Hollis, Henry French, 49
Holter, Bill, 207, 221
Hooker Chemical Corporation, 135,
   136, 139, 153, 155, 156, 244
   environmental issues and, 296–300,
   304–5, 321–22, 329, 335, 337,
   347, 359–61, 367, 377, 378, 382,
   402

executives of, 135, 326, 354, 382
Mead takeover attempt and, 340,
342, 345
Hooker Mexicana, 309
Hoover, Herbert, 31
Hoover, J. Edgar, 41
Hope, Bob, 263, 396, 401, 416,
425
Horace, Charley, 52, 303
Hospital at Saint-Remy (van Gogh),
292, 456
Hour of Power, 449, 450, 457
House of Representatives, U.S., 231,
366
environmental oversight by, 323,
360, 361
Un-American Activities Committee,
36, 50, 51
see also Congress, U.S.
Hoveyda, Amir Abbas, 284
Hughes, Howard, 193
Hughes, Robert, 461
Humphrey, Hubert, 136, 140
S. V. Hunsaker Sons, 99
Hunt brothers, 372
Hunt, Bunker, 177
Hurd, John, 140, 142
Husky Oil, 332
Hu Yaobang, 400
Huyghe, René, 294–95

IBM, 444
IBP (Iowa Beef Processors), 393–94,
465
Idris I, King of Libya, 76, 93, 96,
118–19, 131–32, 133, 150–51,
165, 255
Imhoff, Joseph, 78
Imperial Jade, 78
Independent Fuel Oil Marketers of
America, 196
India, fertilizer plant in, 143
Infantile Paralysis Fund, 64
Ingersoll-Rand, 29
"Inside Oxy" (Dorfman), 349–50
Institutional Development
Corporation, 310
Institutional Shareholders Services
(ISS), 456
Internal Revenue Service (IRS), 19,
31, 105, 233–34, 263
International Bone Marrow
Transplant Registry, 431
International Court of Justice, 259,
260
International Fertilizer Association,
464

International Foundation for the
Survival and Development of
Humanity, 435
International Harvester Corporation,
327
International Institute of Human
Rights, 344
International Monetary Fund, 90
International Olympic Committee,
369–70
International Ore and Fertilizer
Corporation (INTERORE), 75,
76, 77, 346
International Trade Commission
(ITC), U.S., 366
In the Hands of God (Klionsky), 449–
450
Investigative Reporters and Editors,
430
Iowa Beef Processors (IBP), 393–94,
465
IPC, 143
Iran, 160–61, 179, 188–89, 284–85,
290
oil industry of, 160–62, 164–65,
176, 178–80, 189
Irani, Ray, 402–3, 414, 415, 455, 463,
464–65, 467, 468
Iraq, 121, 176, 189
Iribarren, Ignacio, 316
IRS (Internal Revenue Service), 19,
31, 105, 233–34, 263
Island Creek Coal Company, 135,
156, 244, 304–5, 324, 342, 373
Israel:
Arab oil industry and, 121, 177,
415
Soviet relations with, 416, 418,
433
Israel Museum, 415
ISS (Institutional Shareholders
Services), 456
ITC (International Trade
Commission), U.S., 366
Itkin, Herbert, 241–42, 368–69
Izvestia, 215

Jackson, Henry "Scoop," 207, 208,
212, 214, 215, 219, 220, 231,
235, 249
Jacobs, Rick, 450
Jacoby, Neil, 356
Jalloud, Abdel Salaam Ahmed, 165–
166, 176
Jamieson, Kenneth, 117–18, 162–63,
167, 176, 246
Janeway, Elliot, 238

Japan, Export-Import Bank of, 250
Jarvis, Lucy, 227, 228, 239
Jaworski, Leon, 226, 238, 242
Jefferson Lake Sulphur Company,
    75
Jerusalem College of Technology,
    451
Jewish Board of Guardians, 47
Jewish Defense League (JDL), 218,
    230, 285, 356, 357
Jewish Federation Council of
    Los Angeles, 384
John Paul II, Pope, 368
Johnson, Lady Bird, 78, 89, 109–10,
    124, 125, 160, 263, 310
Johnson, Luci, 109
Johnson, Lynda, 109
Johnson, Lyndon B., 204
    AH's cultivation of, 77–78, 124–25,
        134–35, 140, 141, 209
    appointments made by, 135, 142
    in elections, 84, 110, 134
    oil industry and, 124, 140, 160
    Soviet trade and, 81, 82, 89, 110
Jones, Robert Trent, Jr., 229
Jones, William, 262–63, 265, 269–70,
    271, 272, 274–75, 277, 280
Josephson, Marvin, 228
Julius Hammer, 344
Jung, Carl, 356
Juno (Rembrandt), 293–94, 310, 318,
    388
Justice Department, U.S., 41
    antitrust concerns of, 248, 336
    environmental regulations enforced
        by, 323, 360–61, 367

Kabazi, Fuad, 93, 98, 123, 128, 129,
    130
Kagan, Lawrence, 168
Kahn, Alan, 446, 448, 451, 453, 454
Kaiser, Robert, 422
Kania, Stanislaw, 383
Kantor, Mickey, 403
Karbanianov, Alexander, 469
Karr, David, 148, 199, 220, 235–36,
    253, 288, 312–13, 350, 357–59
Karr, Evia, 357–59
Kats, Boris, 340, 341
Kats, Jessica, 340–41
Kats, Natalia, 340, 341
Kauffman, J. A., 256
Kaufman, Martha (Hilary Gibson),
    319, 436, 450, 463, 469
    AH's relationship with, 238, 242–
        244, 292, 294, 330–31, 455–56,
        465–66

Armand Hammer Museum and,
    442, 446–47, 448, 451, 454, 455,
    458, 460, 461, 465–66
Kausov, Sergei, 319
Kearns, Henry, 215
Kendall, Donald, 397, 436
Kennamer, Rexford, 275, 277
Kennecott Corporation, 332
Kennedy, Edward M., 436
Kennedy, John F., 75, 115, 205, 257,
    339
    Campobello gift and, 65–66, 70–71
    death of, 77
    Soviet relations and, 57–58, 59–60,
        65–66, 82
Kennedy family, 199, 288
Kepone, 298
Kesler, George, 276
KGB, 48, 83, 192, 210, 303, 323, 406,
    432, 433
    AH's links with, 93, 147–48, 158,
        201, 205–6, 351–52, 358–59,
        469
Khrushchev, Nikita, 35, 57–59, 65–
    66
    Eleanor Roosevelt's meetings with,
        51, 58, 65, 71
    replacement of, 92, 145
    Western trade sought by, 82, 83,
        90
Kidder Peabody, 332
King, Coretta Scott, 345
King, John, 266, 267
Kinsley, Michael, 421
Kirkeby Center Building, 67
Kissinger, Henry, 160, 178, 179, 189,
    203, 216, 260
    on trade bill, 219–20, 235, 249
Kleindienst, Richard, 221
Klionsky, Mark, 450
Kluge, John, 410, 425
Kluge, Patricia, 425
KNBC-TV, 369
M. Knoedler and Company, 192
Knoedler Gallery, 218, 292, 293, 304,
    353
Knott, James, 426
Komarov, Nikolai, 214
Korin, Pavel, 83, 109
Korshak, Sydney, 289
Kosygin, Aleksei, 92, 109, 135, 145,
    146, 147, 190, 205, 228, 312,
    327
Kristofferson, Kris, 435
Kroc, Ray, 374
Kruegel, Barry, 356
Kruegel, Earl, 356

Kufra, irrigation project at, 96, 112,
132, 133, 259
Kuznetsov, Vasily, 323

Labour Party (Great Britain), 89, 90
Laker, Sir Freddie, 374
Landers, Ann, 437
Lapin, Daniel, 450
LaSalle National Bank, 147
Lazard Frères, 313
Lazutkin, Valentin, 450, 457
Lee, Charles, 181
Leffler, Jack, 34
Left Wing, 36, 40
Legion of Honor, 294–95, 344, 458–
459
Lehman Brothers, 233
Leibovitz, Maury, 192
Leicester, Thomas Coke, Earl of, 388
Lend-Lease, 32, 205, 257
Lenin, V. I., 38, 41
AH's relationship with, 29, 34, 35,
37, 44–45, 47–48, 53, 58, 120,
127, 146, 149, 190, 204, 211,
218, 319, 456, 462
death of, 30, 47–48, 104, 228
symbolic importance of, 145, 209–
210, 211, 212, 307, 352, 406
U.S. Communists and, 36, 40, 43,
45
Western trade cultivated by, 29, 30,
44–45, 82, 90, 91, 92, 202, 250,
398, 470
Leonardo da Vinci, 353, 365, 366,
388, 389, 436, 447
Leoni, Raúl, 112
L'Ermitage Art Gallery, 105
Le Roy, Mervyn, 396–97
Le Tourneau Tree Crusher, 187
Levi, Harry Simon, 326
Levitan lawsuit, 146, 447–48, 453,
454, 455, 461
Lewis, Overbeck & Furman, 457
Library of Congress, 445
Libya, 96, 133, 157–58
Arab-Israeli conflicts and, 121, 177,
356–57
Kufra water project in, 96, 112,
132, 133, 259
leadership of, 118–19, 150–52,
157–58, 162
nationalization in, 162, 177, 189,
223–24
Occidental interests in, 60, 76, 77,
93–98, 111–24, 127–34, 151–52,
156–59, 161, 162–67, 176–80,
185, 188, 189, 223–24, 259–60,
329, 336, 339–40, 342, 379, 403,
415, 429–30, 445
Libyan Producers Mutual Protection
Pact, 177–78
Liddy, G. Gordon, 221
Life, 405, 434
Life Science Products, 298, 299
Li Peng, 419, 421
Little, Brown and Company, 430
Locker, Kenneth, 400, 401, 469
Loeb Rhoades, 311, 313
Long, Augustus, 315
Longstreet, George, 292
López Portillo, José, 309, 310, 311,
317
Lord & Taylor, 103
Los Angeles, Calif.:
Jewish business community of, 326,
356–57, 444–45
Occidental interests and, 99–101,
170, 224, 226, 325–26, 368–69,
399, 403–4, 413, 444–45, 467
Los Angeles Beautiful Award, 101
Los Angeles County Museum of Art,
172
collection promised to, 291–92,
293, 437–38, 440–41, 448
exhibitions at, 190, 238, 317, 353
Frances and Armand Hammer
Wing, 171, 218, 436–37, 438,
440, 446
Los Angeles Examiner, 59
Los Angeles Municipal Art
Department, 13
Los Angeles Times, 10, 182, 191, 234,
286, 296, 341, 363, 384, 413,
414, 437, 440, 447, 454, 455,
459, 462, 466
Los Angeles World Affairs Council,
377
Loudenslager, Gladys, 69, 70, 80, 90,
100
Louvre, 294, 353
Love Canal, 321–23, 327, 335, 337,
345–47, 365, 382
financial claims from, 324, 360,
367, 377, 378–79, 402–3, 465
Lovestone, Jay, 48
Lydick, Lawrence, 277–80
Lyndon, Neil, 422, 437
Lyons, Leonard, 58

Mabrouk, Izz al-Din al-, 157–58, 165,
166
McBride, Thomas, 261
McCarthy, Joseph, 30, 107
McCord, James, 221

McDonnell, James, 160
McDonnell Douglas, 160, 161
McElroy, Leo, 295–96
MacFarlane, Robert, 417
McGee, Robert, 352
McGill, Howard, 339
McGovern, George, 199
McGuire, John, 133–34, 260
McIntyre, Cardinal James Francis,
    118, 263
McIntyre, Thomas, 137
McKeithen, John, 320
McSwiney, James, 331–32, 333–34
McWood Corporation, 135
Madonna with a Flower (Leonardo),
    353
Magit, Jack, 55, 356, 382–83
Magnin, Edgar, 263, 356
Mailer, Norman, 435
Maine, oil refinery project in, 136–
    141, 142
Making Democracy Safe for Oil (Rand),
    259–60
Malevich, Kasimir, 219, 444, 460,
    461, 465
Manatt, Charles, 403
Manatt, Phelps, Rothenberg, and
    Tunney, 403
Manhattan, Inc. (Epstein), 442
Man of Conscience Award, 317, 345
Mansfield, Mike, 124, 257
March, Fredric, 50
Martens, Ludwig, 36, 40, 42, 43, 45
Martin, David, 255
Marx, Karl, 417
Mary Rose, 404
Massey, Ilona, 292–93
Mead Corporation, 331–40, 342–48,
    350, 359, 394, 412
Meat for Wild Men (Russell), 124, 125
Mecom, John, 84, 153
Golda Meir Man of the Year Award,
    416
Mellon, Andrew, 105
Merrill, Robert, 402
Merszei, Zoltan, 353–55, 359, 364,
    382, 383, 402, 455
Methacoal Corporation, 405
Metropolitan Museum of Art, 293,
    433, 437
Mexican American Opportunity
    Foundation, 311
Mexico, 309–11
Michelangelo, 213, 460
Midcon Corporation, 428–29
Middendorf, J. William, II, 293, 316,
    317

Midland Bank, 46
Mikoyan, Anastas, 58, 92, 104, 105,
    106
Miller, Nodine, 338, 342–43
Mirex, 297
Mishell, Boris, 43
Mitchell, John, 216, 221
Mitterrand, Danielle, 461
Mobil Oil, 60, 116, 118, 169, 186
    see also Seven Sisters
Modigliani, Amedeo, 171, 219
Mohammad Reza Pahlavi, Shah of
    Iran, 160, 161–62, 164–65, 178,
    179, 188–89, 284–85, 290
Mona Lisa (Leonardo), 353
Monarch Investment Company, 99,
    168
Mondale, Walter F., 403
Moness Chemical Company, 49
Monroe, Marilyn, 405, 422
Montezuma Castle, 404
Moore, Dorothy, 224, 225
Morani, Ray, 224, 225
Morgan, J. P., 470
Morgan, Ted, 437
Morgan Stanley, 246–47
Morocco, 76–77
Morozov, Ivan, 210–11, 213, 218,
    227
Moses, Anna Mary (Grandma Moses),
    83, 92
Mu'alla, Sheikh Sultan al-, 153–54
Murdock, David, 392–95, 407, 408,
    411–13, 414, 447, 463
Murdy, Jim, 181
Murphy, Franklin, 191, 440
Musée Jacquemart-André, 294, 344,
    383
Muskie, Edmund, 137, 138
Mutual Broadcasting System, 21, 22,
    23, 65, 66
Mutual Life Insurance Company,
    69

Nasser, Gamal Abdel, 158–59
National Cancer Institute, 395, 440,
    441
National City Bank, 40
National Gallery of Art, 173, 190–91,
    213, 353, 365, 414, 425, 431,
    433, 436, 439
National Gallery of Dublin, 190
National Hotel, 147, 205
National Institute for Occupational
    Health, 360
National Iranian Oil Company
    (NIOC), 160, 161, 164–65

National Symphony Orchestra, 395, 402
NATO (North Atlantic Treaty Organization), 81, 251, 371, 379
NBC, 227, 228–29, 239
Nemec, James, 407, 422, 423, 424, 426
Newman, Edwin, 228, 239
New Republic, 421
Newton, Wayne, 401
New York Post, 58
New York Society of Security Analysts, 98, 194–95
New York State Environmental Conservation Department, 361
New York Stock Exchange, 78–79, 127, 202
New York Times, 41, 47, 48, 54–55, 59, 90, 103, 139, 145, 214, 216, 236, 239, 257, 258, 263–64, 265, 348, 350, 358, 361, 384, 392, 398–99, 400, 409, 433, 437, 455, 462
AH's Op-Ed pieces in, 420, 421, 441
Nicholas II, Czar of Russia, 40
Nigeria, oil interests in, 154–55, 188, 239, 272, 273
NIOC (National Iranian Oil Company), 160, 161, 164–65
Nixon, Richard M., 141–42, 190, 178–79, 195, 240, 395, 400
in elections, 56–57, 136, 140, 206, 209, 220
financial backing for, 193, 197–99, 205–9, 220–22, 260, 283, 285, 289, 321, 369, 380, 385, 429
oil industry and, 141, 189, 205, 230
Soviet relations and, 190, 201, 202, 203, 204, 205, 208, 211–17, 229, 231, 237–38, 251
Watergate affair and, 216, 220, 221, 231, 235, 238
Richard Nixon Library and Birthplace, 459
Nizer, Louis, 19, 257, 266, 409
campaign contribution case handled by, 261, 269, 270, 272, 274, 275, 277
on Occidental board, 395
Noark Ltd., 255
Nobel Peace Prize, 145, 301
quest for, 195, 304, 317, 344, 349, 356, 367, 368, 377, 418, 435, 437
No Oil Incorporated, 170, 224, 225, 413–14
North Atlantic Treaty Organization (NATO), 81, 251, 371, 379

Northrop Communications, 223
North Sea, oil fields in, 153, 185, 186, 198, 232, 303–4, 318, 336, 384, 443–44, 465
North Star, 197, 198
Novosti, 93
Nudel, Ida, 439
Numinter, Ltd., 312–13, 372

Oasis, 166
Occidental: Visions for the Future, 422
Occidental Chemical Company, 297, 360
Occidental International Corporation, 142–43, 192–93, 197, 204, 205, 214, 284
Occidental Petroleum Corporation:
agrichemical business of, 72–75, 77, 82, 88, 148, 214, 296–300
AH's death and, 9, 459, 462, 463–464, 466–67
AH's prosecution and, 285, 287, 368–69, 380
AH's investment in, 10, 20–21, 458
annual shareholders' meetings of, 72, 73, 120, 150, 199–200, 257, 285–86, 356, 378, 411, 456–57, 467
board of directors at, 70, 72, 115, 152, 263, 324, 334, 336, 348, 354, 379, 380, 394–95, 403, 411, 413, 425, 438, 447, 448, 451, 467
Chinese projects with, 353, 399, 400, 420–21, 443, 465, 467
Colombian interests of, 412, 429
companies acquired by, 52, 67, 72–76, 99, 123, 135, 138, 168, 393–394, 407–8, 428–29
debt accumulated by, 9, 34, 68–69, 122, 216–17, 232–33, 330, 408, 429, 455, 463, 465
in Eastern Bloc countries, 251–52, 304, 307, 324, 367, 409–10
environmental issues and, 170, 224, 225, 296–300, 304–5, 307, 321–323, 329, 335, 337, 343, 345, 346–47, 359–61, 367, 377, 378–379, 380, 401–3, 413–14, 464–465
executives of, 23, 73, 87–88, 113–114, 118, 135–36, 142, 149–50, 154–56, 168, 181, 184, 192–93, 200–201, 206, 225, 233, 283–84, 306, 329–30, 332, 353–56, 359, 361–64, 375–76, 382–83, 389–390, 395, 398, 402, 414–15, 438, 455, 463, 468

Occidental Petroleum Corporation
  (*cont.*)
 food-preservation process
  developed for, 73, 96, 98–99
 growth of, 10, 25, 34, 60, 61, 67,
  68–69, 77, 338, 362
 in hotel joint venture, 146–47
 Iranian negotiations with, 160–62,
  164–65, 284–85, 290
 labor issues at, 87, 370
 lawsuits against, 87–88, 128–30,
  182, 195, 255–56, 263–65, 287,
  298–99, 305, 329, 336, 345, 349,
  367, 377, 380, 413, 429, 446,
  447–48, 453–56, 461, 466
 Libyan operations of, 60, 76, 77,
  93–98, 111–24, 127–34, 151–52,
  156–59, 161–67, 176–80, 185,
  188, 189, 223–24, 259–60, 329,
  336, 339–40, 342, 379, 403, 415,
  429–30, 445
 Los Angeles drilling operation of,
  99–101, 170, 224, 226, 325–26,
  368–69, 399, 403, 413, 444–45,
  467
 management style at, 155–56, 192–
  193, 233, 354–55, 393, 414, 455,
  464–65, 467
 Mead takeover attempted by, 331–
  340, 342–48, 350, 359, 394, 412
 minerals division of, 114, 372–73
 net worth of, 98, 216
 New England refinery for, 136–41,
  142
 Nigerian oil and, 154–55, 188, 272,
  273
 North Sea drilling and, 153, 185,
  186, 198, 232, 303–4, 318, 336,
  384, 443–44, 465
 offices of, 23, 24–25, 67, 466
 Olympic coin sales and, 311–13,
  372
 Pakistani deals with, 381, 382
 in Peruvian oil industry, 143–44,
  186–88, 342–43, 445–46
 philanthropic activities supported
  by, 142–43, 171, 393, 436, 440,
  446–48, 453–56, 459, 461, 465,
  466
 political contributions of, 139, 430–
  431
 profitability of, 34, 62, 67, 69, 168,
  180, 193–94, 232, 244, 324, 329–
  330, 336, 343, 373, 386, 393,
  408, 429, 465
 promotional films for, 123, 195,
  304, 308, 313–14, 363, 400, 422

 public relations for, 9, 22–23, 26–
  27, 53–54, 61–62, 67–68, 77,
  79–81, 100–101, 111, 114, 181–
  182, 193–95, 214, 216–17, 244–
  245, 272, 273, 282, 283, 284, 304,
  322, 337, 347, 361, 362, 375–76,
  384, 387, 401, 402, 421–422
 real estate division of, 99, 113, 180,
  246
 research division of, 347
 SEC scrutiny of, 10, 53, 114, 122,
  139, 150, 156, 167–68, 180–82,
  184, 187, 193, 194, 204, 207,
  230–31, 256, 258–60, 265, 269,
  270–72, 274, 282, 286, 305–7,
  319–21, 335–36, 338, 339, 345,
  346, 347–48, 378–79, 380
 Soviet projects of, 53, 81–83, 89,
  90, 92, 147–49, 189, 190, 197–
  198, 201–12, 214–20, 231, 236–
  241, 250, 301–3, 327, 329–30,
  342, 366, 370, 372, 377, 379,
  393, 405, 443, 464
 staff members at, 69–70, 111, 242–
  244, 321, 389, 399
 Standard Oil negotiations with,
  116–20, 123–24, 162–63, 167
 stock exchange listing of, 61, 78–79
 stock prices for, 69, 88, 114, 127,
  193, 194, 202, 204, 205, 215,
  362, 393, 411, 412, 455, 463
 synthetic-fuel business of, 230,
  244–45, 308, 343, 373, 374, 465
 takeover threats against, 9, 194,
  245–48, 285, 335, 394–95, 411,
  412–13, 463
 transport business of, 163–64, 185,
  193, 194, 195, 231, 343–44, 373
 in Trucial States, 153–54, 159
 Venezuelan oil industry and, 112,
  134, 140–41, 169–70, 185–86,
  223, 225–26, 254, 255–56, 259,
  261, 263–65, 271–73, 282–83,
  286, 288–89, 290–91, 316, 452
Occidental Petroleum Land and
  Development Corporation, 180
Occidental Worldwide Investment
  Corporation, 195
O'Conner, John, 239
O'Connor, Sandra Day, 396
Officer's Cross of the Legion of
  Honor, 316
"Of the Nature, Weight and
  Movement of Water" (Leonardo),
  388
Oganescoff, Marie, 42
Ogbi, Taher, 93, 128, 129

OGPU, 48, 56, 91, 470
Okhrana, 91
Olson, Carl, 380
Olympic Games, 80, 228, 311, 325, 369–70, 371, 372, 376–77, 399–400, 413
Onassis, Christina, 319
Onassis, Jacqueline Kennedy, 421
"One-Man Flying Multi-International, The" (Yergin), 258
Order (neo-Nazi organization), 434
Order of Andrés Bello, 255, 283
Order of Friendship among Peoples, 323–24
Order of the Aztec Eagle, 311
Organization of Petroleum Exporting Countries (OPEC), 176, 177–79
Orlov, Yuri, 434
Ortega, Alberto Flores, 273
Oxy Arabians, 393
OXYLIBYA, 60, 76, 165
    see also Occidental Petroleum Corporation, Libyan operations of
Oxy One, 385–86, 397, 431, 439
Oxy Today, 243
OXYTROL, 73, 96, 98–99, 138
Oxy Westwood Corporation, 448, 454

Pacific Coast Stock Exchange, 61, 78
Pacific Holding Corporation, 394, 411
Pacific Jewish Center, 450, 451
Pahn, Willibald, 403
Pakistan, 381, 382
Palacio de Bellas Artes, 309
Palestine Liberation Organization (PLO), 313
Paley, William, 21
Palmer, A. Mitchell, 41
Panama Canal, 289, 308–9, 318
pan-Arabism, 158
Paramount Coin Company, 312–13
Parker Pen, 29
Patten, James, 242
Peale, Norman Vincent, 263
Pearson, Drew, 66, 142, 148
Pearson, Lester, 70
Peck, Gregory, 401, 425, 435, 437
Pegulu, François Fortune Louis (Pegulu de Rovin), 93, 128–29, 130
Pemex, 310
Pepperdine University, 317
Pepsico, 435–36
Peres, Shimon, 416, 433

Pérez Rodríguez, Carlos Andrés, 225–26, 254–56, 264, 265, 272, 273, 286, 290–91, 316, 452
Perforaciones Altamar, 255, 283
Permian Corporation, 113, 135, 149, 346, 463
Peru, 143–44, 186–88, 342–43, 445–446
Pesniar, 393, 394
Peterson, Peter, 197, 203, 204, 205
Petitioner, The (Wyeth), 310
Petroleum Club of Los Angeles, 229
Petroperu, 186
Philip Morris, 44
Phillips, Clarinda, 285, 287, 380
Pickford, Mary, 91
Pietà (Michelangelo), 213
Piper, C. Erwin, 57, 403
PLO (Palestine Liberation Organization), 313
Poland, 324, 379–80, 383, 394
Portrait of a Man Holding a Black Hat (Rembrandt), 292
Pottinger, Stanley, 336
Powell, Earl, 441
Powell, Jody, 368
Pratt, John, 270–71, 274
Pravda, 214, 371, 428
Prell, Dorothy, 69, 76, 288, 321, 399
Presley, Elvis, 401
Princeton University, 46
Profumo, John, 153
Project Independence, 230
Publicker Alcohol and Chemical, 14
Pushkin Museum, 83, 92, 192, 210, 211, 218, 428
Putnam Publishing Group, 436

Qaddafi, Muammar el-, 162, 165, 403
    oil industry and, 151–52, 157–58, 159, 161, 163, 177, 178, 189, 259, 445
Quayle, J. Danforth, 445
Quayle, Marilyn, 445
Quest of the Romanoff Treasure, The (Hammer), 103

Raff, Raymond, 332–33
Rand, Christopher, 259, 260
Randell, Ken, 428
Rangel, Carlos Carnevali, 265
Raphael, 105
Rather, Dan, 436
RCC (Revolutionary Command Council), 151–52, 166
Reagan, J. Neil, 395

Reagan, Nancy, 388–89, 395, 396,
  414, 416, 440, 443
Reagan, Ronald, 26, 398, 405
  AH's cultivation of, 385, 388–89,
    393, 395–97, 402, 405, 413, 414,
    416, 420, 434, 443, 445
  Gorbachev's meetings with, 425,
    427–28, 433–34
  inaugurations of, 389, 414
  in 1980 campaign, 381, 385
  Soviet relations and, 393, 406, 410,
    418, 420, 421, 432, 443
  trade policy of, 388, 393, 429, 445
Red Army Chorus, 83
Red Carpet (Finder), 397, 409
Red Plot Against America, The
  (Considine), 226
Reece, Gordon, 384, 387, 397
Reedy, George, 78
Regardie's, 430
Register, 366, 367, 462–63
Reid, Bud, 52, 53, 67, 169–70, 187–
  188
Reid, Gene, 52–53, 61, 72, 112, 114–
  115, 134, 166
Gene Reid Drilling, 52–53
Reinstein, Boris, 41, 43–44
Remarkable Life of Dr. Hammer, The
  (Considine), 257–58, 259
Rembrandt van Rijn, 173, 251, 292,
  293–94, 310
Remington, Frederic, 124
Renoir, Pierre-Auguste, 171, 213, 292
Republican Party (U.S.):
  fund-raising for, 393, 414, 446, 448
  presidential candidates of, 56–57,
    84, 136, 289
Republic Steel, 401–2
Reston, James, 214
Rest on the Flight into Egypt
  (Rottenhammer and Bril), 108
Revolutionary Command Council
  (RCC), 151–52, 166
RHI Entertainment, 469
Richard, Paul, 173
Richardson, John, 218–19, 461
"Riddle of Armand Hammer, The"
  (Epstein), 398–99
Hal Roach Studios, 22, 23
Robards, Jason, Jr., 469
Robb, Roger, 274
Roberts, Curtis, 292
Roberts, Paul, 21, 22
Robinson, Edward G., 292
Rockefeller, David, 397
Rockefeller, John D., 470
Rockefeller, Nelson, 345

Rogers, Ginger, 416
Rogers, Will, 91
Rogers, William, 213
Rohrabacher, Dana, 366
Romania, 251, 304, 307
Romanoff family, 105, 106
Ronstadt, Linda, 401
Roosevelt, Eleanor, 15, 356, 403
  Campobello and, 32, 63–65, 71
  Khrushchev's meetings with, 51, 58,
    65
Roosevelt, Elliott, 16–17, 63–65
Roosevelt, Franklin D., 16, 31–32, 49,
  63–64, 205, 257, 339, 403
Roosevelt, Franklin D., Jr., 64
Roosevelt, James, 16–17, 32, 57, 59,
  70, 257
Roosevelt Campobello International
  Park, 89, 355
Eleanor Roosevelt Memorial
  Foundation, 66, 124
Rose, Robert, 68, 77, 87, 97, 118,
  266–67
Rosenbaum, James, 468
Rosenberg, Steven, 440
Ross, Ken, 13
Rostropovich, Mstislav, 395
Rottenhammer, Hans, 108
Royal Academy of Fine Arts, 190, 317
Royal Dutch/Shell, 60, 169, 186, 429
Royal Order of the Polar Star, 367
Rubens, Peter Paul, 173, 234, 251,
  318, 319, 451, 465, 467
Rubin, Irv, 285, 286, 356
Rubin, Samuel, 335, 338–39, 340,
  348
Ruff, Charles, 270, 274, 275
Russell, Charles, 101, 124, 125, 141,
  445
Russell, Pat, 368, 369
Russian Connection, The, 227–29, 239
Ryan, John, 225, 254, 255–56, 263–65

Sadat, Anwar, 203
Safety Net Agreement, 177
Sakharov, Andrei, 301, 380, 435
Sakho, Emery, 102, 104
Salinger, Pierre, 71
Salk, Jonas, 174, 175, 356
Salk Institute for Biological Studies,
  174
SALT (stategic arms limitations
  treaties), 290, 353, 365, 432
Sandler, Allan, 313–14
Sands, Nancy, 25
Sanford, Mary, 425
Sargent, John Singer, 171

Sarkisan, Nicholas, 152
Saudi Arabia, oil industry and, 77,
   121
Schecter, Jerrold, 375, 376, 384, 385,
   470
Schenley's, 14
Schuller, Robert, 449–50, 451, 457
Schweitzer, Albert, 356
Scotland Yard, 36, 43, 49
Scruggs-Vandervoort-Barney, 103
SDI (Strategic Defense Initiative; Star
   Wars), 410, 419–21, 431–32
Securities and Exchange Commission
   (SEC), 236
   AH's business practices reviewed
      by, 348, 430
   Karr's testimony to, 350, 357–58
   Occidental scrutinized by, 10, 53,
      114, 122, 139, 150, 156, 167–68,
      180–82, 184, 187, 193, 194, 204,
      207, 230–31, 256, 258–60, 265,
      269, 270–72, 274, 282, 286, 305–
      307, 319–21, 335–36, 338, 339,
      345, 346, 347–48, 378–79, 380
   takeover attempts and, 335–36,
      338, 339, 346, 347, 360, 411
Seldis, Henry, 191
Sellers, "Duck," 139
Senate, U.S., 247
   and bribery allegations against AH,
      57
   communism and, 30, 148
   environmental violations and, 360–
      361
   Occidental investigated by, 184
   Panama Canal treaty and, 309, 318
   SALT II ratification and, 353, 365
   on trade issues, 137, 235, 237
   Watergate affair and, 216, 221–22,
      226, 242
   see also Congress, U.S.
Seven Sisters, 60, 123
   Iranian agreements with, 161–62,
      165
   Mideast oil prices and, 96, 152,
      165, 167
   Occidental rivalry with, 95, 111,
      116, 134, 165, 167, 177
   Soviet oil industry vs., 157–58
   see also British Petroleum; Gulf Oil;
      Mobil Oil; Royal Dutch/ Shell;
      Socal; Standard Oil Company of
      New Jersey; Texaco
Shah of Iran (Mohammad Reza Pah-
   lavi), 160, 161–62, 164–65, 178,
   179, 188–89, 284–85, 290
Shalhi, Omar, 93, 128, 129

Shamir, Yitzhak, 416
Sharjah, 154, 159, 160, 162, 188, 284
Shaver Nava, John, 349
Shcharansky, Anatoly, 318
Shchukin, Sergei, 210–11, 213, 218,
   227
Shell Oil, 176
Shriver, R. Sargent, 148, 199, 288,
   398
Shultz, George P., 405, 419, 432
Signal Oil and Gas Company, 98,
   123–24
Signet Oil and Gas Company, 67
Silvia, Queen of Sweden, 367
Simon, Norton, 438, 441–42
Simon, William, 230, 263
Sinatra, Frank, 401, 421
Sinay, Joseph, 416
Sirica, John, 238
Six-Day War (1967), 121, 158
60 Minutes, 400
Skadden, Arps, Slate, Mcagher &
   Flom, 248, 334
Sloan-Kettering Institute for Cancer
   Research, 440
Smith, Alfred E., 47
Smith, C. R., 137
Smith, Preston, 320
Smith & Schnake, 334
Smithsonian Institution of Natural
   History, 171, 172, 173, 311, 318
James Smithson Society, 318
Snyder, Tom, 318, 319
Sobajian, Maurice, 320
Socal, 60
   see also Seven Sisters
Socialist Labor Party (U.S.), 37, 38,
   39, 40
South Africa, synfuels in, 373
Southeastern University, 317
Southern California, University of,
   101–2, 104, 107, 171, 234, 318,
   319, 374, 451, 465, 467
Soviet Bank of Foreign Trade, 303,
   313
Soviet Cultural Fund, 432
Soviet Life, 93
Soviet State Committee for Science
   and Technology, 201, 202
Soviet Union:
   in Afghan conflict, 367, 369–71,
      372, 376–77, 381–82, 439
   AH's business relationship with,
      28–30, 34, 36, 43–49, 51, 53, 58,
      81–83, 85–86, 89–93, 102–7,
      116–17, 145–49, 158, 189–90,
      197–98, 201–12, 214–20, 226–

Soviet Union:
AH's business relationship with (*cont.*)
227, 236–41, 249–53, 311–14,
355, 444, 457, 470
archives of, 469–70
art collectibles from, 102–7
Chinese relations with, 189, 351,
371
cultural exchanges with, 83–84,
210–11, 213, 251, 353, 365–66,
401, 428, 431, 435–36, 450, 451,
457
currency of, 45, 105, 106, 444
defense capacity of, 240, 302, 410
disintegration of, 451, 457
espionage arrests in, 327–28, 432–
434
food shortages in, 28, 29, 96, 394
horse breeding in, 393, 394
human rights issues and, 230, 301,
318, 340–41, 367, 432
Israeli relations with, 416, 418, 433
Jewish population in, 207–8, 218,
229–30, 285, 286, 318, 415, 417,
418, 433
leadership changes in, 30, 92, 104,
323, 357, 405–6, 410, 419
Libyan oil development and, 157–
158
Occidental projects in, 53, 81–83,
89, 90, 92, 147–49, 189, 190,
197–98, 201–12, 214–20, 231,
236–41, 250, 301–3, 327, 329–
330, 342, 366, 370, 372, 377,
379, 393, 405, 443, 464
oil industry in, 116–17
Olympic Games of 1980 held in,
228, 311–13, 369–72, 376–77
Polish dissidents and, 380
secret police of, 44, 48, 56, 91; *see
also* KGB
social programs of, 29, 34, 35, 152,
366
U.S. Communists and, 40–41, 45,
46, 48
U.S. relations with, 32, 35–36, 40,
57–60, 63, 64, 65–66, 81, 82, 89,
109–10, 189, 190, 201–5, 208,
211–20, 229, 231, 235, 236–38,
249–51, 289, 290, 291, 301–2,
318, 323–24, 327–28, 340–41,
345, 351, 353, 357, 362, 366,
367, 369–71, 376–77, 393, 397–
398, 402, 406, 409, 410, 413,
417–21, 425, 427–28, 431–34,
443, 457, 469–70
SPA, *see* superphosphoric acid

Spiljak, Mika, 409–10
Spirit of Life award, 366
Stalin, Joseph, 58, 78, 103, 104, 127
Soviet art sales and, 104, 107
Western capitalists and, 30, 48, 49,
85, 319
Standard Oil Company (Indiana),
245–48, 332, 335, 401–2
Standard Oil Company of New
Jersey, 60, 116–20, 123–24, 129,
162–63, 167
see also Esso-Libya; Seven Sisters
standstill agreement, 394
Stanford University, 439–40
Stans, Maurice, 190, 197–99, 209,
216, 221, 238, 256–57, 398
Star Wars (Strategic Defense
Initiative), 410, 419–21, 431–32
State Department, U.S., 401
AH's diplomatic efforts and, 371,
377, 382, 417, 433
Soviet art exchanges and, 83–84
Stedelijk Museum, 444
Stern, Isaac, 402
Stoessel, Walter, 259
Stone, Richard, 237
Stop Cancer, 441
Stowasser, William, 238–39
Straszewski, Tom, 369
strategic arms limitation treaties
(SALT), 290, 353, 365, 421, 432,
433
Strategic Defense Initiative (SDI; Star
Wars), 410, 419–21, 431–32
Strauss, Robert, 309
Streisand, Barbra, 450
Suez Canal, 121
Sulzberger, Arthur Ochs "Punch,"
216, 217, 263, 392, 397, 436
superphosphoric acid (SPA), 75, 77,
88, 214, 324, 347
Suprematist movement, 219
Swan, H. J. C., 270, 277
Swearingen, John, 245–48
synfuels, 373

Tariki, Abdullah, 152
Tchaikovsky competition, 406
Tehran Oil Price Agreement, 179
Teitsworth, Bob, 52, 61, 62, 75
Tel Aviv Museum, 415
Tenneco Inc., 373
Tersk Breeding Farm, 393
Texaco, 60, 61, 315
see also Seven Sisters
Thatcher, Margaret, 384, 397, 419,
421

Thierfelder, Everett, 154–55, 188
Thomas, Lowell, 263
Thomson, Lord Roy, 89, 153, 154, 158, 198, 202
Tierney, Gene, 24
Tigrett, John, 164, 176, 222, 241, 242
Time, 195, 196, 228, 276, 376, 461
Titian, 365
TNT, 469
Tokyo Gas Company, 208, 250
Tolman, Elmer, 17, 19, 24
Tolman, Frances, *see* Hammer, Frances Tolman
Tomorrow, 318–19
Tong Sun Park, 320
Toon, Malcolm, 328, 398
Topping, Norman, 101
Torrijos Herrera, Omar, 308
To the Ends of the Earth, 404
Tower International, 147, 148, 206
Trade Reform Act (1973), 208, 214, 219–20, 231, 249
Transglobe Expedition, 404
Trotsky, Leon, 39–40, 48
Troy, Malin & Pottinger, 334, 336
Trucial States, 153, 154, 159–60, 188
see also Sharjah; Umm al-Qaywayn
Trudeau, Pierre, 435
Trujillo, Rafael, 23
Truman, Harry, 31, 339
Trump, Donald, 425, 456
Tunney, Gene, 91
Tunney, John, 403
Turner, Ted, 425
Tuttle, Holmes, 416
Two Lives, One Russia (Daniloff), 434

UCLA (University of California at Los Angeles), 383, 431, 438, 440, 442, 467
Umm al-Qaywayn, 153–54, 159, 160, 162, 188
Underwood Typewriter, 29
Ungerleider, Sam, 254
Unitarianism, 97
United Arab Emirates, 160, 188
United Eram, 311
United Jewish Appeal, 415
United Nations, 379, 421, 432
United World Colleges, 335, 404–5
Ural-American Refining and Trading Company, 45
USC, *see* Southern California, University of
U.S. Rubber, 29
Ustinov, Peter, 435
Utrillo, Maurice, 15–16

Vahlco Corporation, 138
Vahlsing, Fred, Jr., 137–38
Vahlsing, Fred, Sr., 137
Vahlsing Inc., 138
van Buren, Abigail, 402
Vance, Cyrus, 302
Vanderbilt, Cornelius, 258, 470
van Gogh, Vincent, 213, 292, 294, 456
van Wingen, Nico, 52
Variety Club, 416
Vaughan, Dick, 52, 169–70, 185, 186
Velasco Alvarado, Juan, 143, 144, 152, 187
Venezuela:
cultural award given by, 254–55, 283
nationalization in, 254, 255, 264, 272, 317
oil industry in, 112, 134, 140–41, 169–70, 177, 185–86, 189, 228, 254–56, 261, 263–65, 271–73, 282–83, 286, 288–89, 290–91, 316, 387–88, 452
presidency of, 140, 185–86, 225–226, 254, 256, 316, 452
Venus Wounded by a Thorn (Rubens), 234, 318, 319, 451
Vidal, Gore, 435
Vietnam War, 135, 145, 178, 189, 201, 365
VLCCs (Very Large Crude Carriers), 164

Wachs, Joel, 369
Wachtell, Tom, 97, 183, 187
Waddy, Joseph, 348
Wade, Melinda, 469
Wadley, J. F. G., 20
Walker, James, 265
Walker, John, 173–74, 190–91
Walker River Indian Reservation, 114
Wall Street Journal, 33, 55, 61, 93, 128, 150, 330, 368, 432, 446, 447, 448, 458, 462, 468
Walters, Barbara, 421, 439
Ward, Mike, 468
Washington Post, 71, 139, 173, 317, 422, 460, 462
Wasserman, Lew, 289
Watergate affair, 216, 220–22, 226, 231, 235, 238, 241–42, 289
criminal prosecutions and, 256–57, 261–63, 270, 272, 274–81, 283
Watson, W. Marvin, 110–11, 125, 134–35, 142–44, 193, 204, 233

Watson, W. Marvin (*cont.*)
  Nixon campaign contributions and,
    222, 242, 283, 287
  resignation of, 283–84
Weaver, The (van Gogh), 294
Weinberg, Lawrence, 99
Weinberg, Steve, 430–31, 449
Weinberg, William, 99
Weinberger, Caspar, 405
Weintraub, Jerry, 401
Weiss, Joan, 442, 453, 454, 456, 457–
    459, 462, 463, 465–66
Weiss, Robert, 442, 453–54
Wells, H. G., 91
We/Myi, 470
Weslowska, Alicija, 379
West, Vincent, 296
Western American Bank (Europe)
    Ltd., 233
West Kentucky Coal, 146
Westwood Cemetery, 422
Weyerhaeuser Company, 401–2
White, Tel, 53
Whitlock, Bruce, 15, 16
Wicker, Nancy, 50, 66, 326, 407,
    422–27, 442
Wicker, Walter, Jr., 50
Willers, Tom, 135–36, 154, 155–56,
    184, 194, 233
William Development Corporation,
    99
Williams, Edward Bennett, 261, 262,
    266
Wilson, Harold, 89

Wisdom Society, 356, 384
Wolfson, Sam, 389–90
Woman of the People (Modigliani), 219
Wongkaren, Harry, 320
Woods, Rose Mary, 197
WOR, 21
World of Armand Hammer, The (Bry-
    son), 421–22
Wyeth, Andrew, 435
Wyeth, Jamie, 435
Wyeth, N. C., 310, 435
Wynne, Hugh, 117

Yang Shangkun, 443
Yergin, Daniel, 258
Yorty, Elizabeth Hensel, 224, 225,
    230–31
Yorty, Samuel, 57, 100, 101, 170,
    224, 225, 230–31, 254, 325
Young, Loretta, 416
Young Boy and the Coquette, The
    (Fragonard), 309
Yugoslavia, 409–10
Yusuf, Joseph Tanko, 155

Zadroysynski, Edward, 379
Zakharov, Gennadi, 432, 433, 434
Zapata Corporation, 394
Z-Comm Establishment, 223
Zevely, Angela, *see* Hammer, Angela
    Zevely
Zia ul-Haq, Mohammed, 381–82,
    401, 419
Zivs, Samuel, 380

PHOTO CREDITS

ABOUT THE AUTHORS

Carl Blumay served for a quarter of a century as public relations and advertising consultant, advisor, and director for Dr. Armand Hammer and the company he headed, Occidental Petroleum Corporation. Blumay, formerly a radio announcer and newscaster and a newswriter, is a member of the Western States Advertising Agencies Association, the Advertising Club of Los Angeles, and the Association of Petroleum Writers, and has been a member of the Public Relations Society of America. He lives in Laguna Niguel, California.

Henry Edwards is the author or coauthor of *Harlan Smythe Grossfeld, What Happened to My Mother, Loving John—The Untold Story,* and *Stardust—The David Bowie Story.* He has a wide array of film, television, and theatrical credits, from Dylan Thomas's *A Child's Christmas in Wales* starring Sir Michael Redgrave to *The Joni Mitchell Project,* which received its world premiere at the Los Angeles Theatre Center. His articles and criticism have appeared in *The New York Times, Details, New York, Penthouse* and *Vogue.* Mr. Edwards is the recipient of the Christopher Award and the Aspen Writer's Workshop Rose Scholarship for Distinguished First Novel.